Photographer and mechanic with a 2004 Infiniti G35 sedan

ACKNOWLEDGEMENTS

Technical writers who contributed to this project include John Wegmann, Mike Stubblefield and Joe Hamilton. Wiring diagrams originated exclusively for Haynes North America, Inc. by Solution Builders.

NISSAN

350Z & INFINITI G35
2003-08 REPAIR MANUAL

Deleted

**Covers U.S. and Canadian models of
Nissan 350Z & Infiniti G35**

Does not include Infiniti G37 models

by Jay Storer

CHILTON *Automotive Books*

PUBLISHED BY **HAYNES NORTH AMERICA. Inc.**

Manufactured in USA
©2008 Haynes North America, Inc.
ISBN-13: 978-1-56392-731-7
ISBN-10: 1-56392-731-4
Library of Congress Control Number 2008931936

Haynes Publishing Group
Sparkford Nr Yeovil
Somerset BA22 7JJ England

Haynes North America, Inc
861 Lawrence Drive
Newbury Park
California 91320 USA

ABCDE
FGHIJ
KLMNO
PQRST

Contents

INTRODUCTORY PAGES

1

TUNE-UP AND ROUTINE MAINTENANCE – 1-1

2

3.5L V6 ENGINE – 2A-1
GENERAL ENGINE OVERHAUL PROCEDURES – 2B-1

3

COOLING, HEATING AND AIR CONDITIONING SYSTEMS – 3-1

4

FUEL AND EXHAUST SYSTEMS – 4-1

5

ENGINE ELECTRICAL SYSTEMS – 5-1

6

EMISSIONS AND ENGINE CONTROL SYSTEMS – 6-1

About this manual

ITS PURPOSE

The purpose of this manual is to help you get the best value from your vehicle. It can do so in several ways. It can help you decide what work must be done, even if you choose to have it done by a dealer service department or a repair shop; it provides information and procedures for routine maintenance and servicing; and it offers diagnostic and repair procedures to follow when trouble occurs.

We hope you use the manual to tackle the work yourself. For many simpler jobs, doing it yourself may be quicker than arranging an appointment to get the vehicle into a shop and making the trips to leave it and pick it up. More importantly, a lot of money can be saved by avoiding the expense the shop must pass on to you to cover its labor and overhead costs. An added benefit is the sense of satisfaction and accomplishment that you feel after doing the job yourself.

USING THE MANUAL

The manual is divided into Chapters. Each Chapter is divided into numbered Sections, which are headed in bold type between horizontal lines. Each Section consists of consecutively numbered paragraphs.

At the beginning of each numbered Section you will be referred to any illustrations which apply to the procedures in that Section. The reference numbers used in illustration captions pinpoint the pertinent Section and the Step within that Section. That is, illustration 3.2 means the illustration refers to Section 3 and Step (or paragraph) 2 within that Section.

Procedures, once described in the text, are not normally repeated. When it's necessary to refer to another Chapter, the reference will be given as Chapter and Section number. Cross references given without use of the word "Chapter" apply to Sections and/or paragraphs in the same Chapter. For example, "see Section 8" means in the same Chapter.

References to the left or right side of the vehicle assume you are sitting in the driver's seat, facing forward.

Even though we have prepared this manual with extreme care, neither the publisher nor the author can accept responsibility for any errors in, or omissions from, the information given.

➡NOTE

A *Note* provides information necessary to properly complete a procedure or information which will make the procedure easier to understand.

❋❋ CAUTION

A *Caution* provides a special procedure or special steps which must be taken while completing the procedure where the Caution is found. Not heeding a Caution can result in damage to the assembly being worked on.

❋❋ WARNING

A *Warning* provides a special procedure or special steps which must be taken while completing the procedure where the Warning is found. Not heeding a Warning can result in personal injury.

Introduction

This manual covers the Nissan 350Z and Infiniti G35. Both models feature a 3.5L Dual Overhead Camshaft (DOHC) V6 engine.

The engine drives the rear wheels through either a six-speed manual or a five-speed automatic transmission via a driveshaft, rear differential, and two rear driveaxles. On AWD models, the front wheels are also propelled, via two driveaxles.

Suspension is independent at all four wheels. The front suspension uses upper and lower control arms and shock absorber/coil spring assemblies. The rear suspension system is a multi-link suspension consisting of shock absorbers, coil springs and several specialized links. The steering system consists of a rack-and-pinion steering gear.

All models are equipped with hydraulically operated front and rear disc brake systems.

Vehicle identification numbers

Modifications are a continuing and unpublicized process in vehicle manufacturing. Since spare parts lists and manuals are compiled on a numerical basis, the individual vehicle numbers are necessary to correctly identify the component required.

VEHICLE IDENTIFICATION NUMBER (VIN)

This very important identification number is stamped on a plate attached to the dashboard inside the windshield on the driver's side of the vehicle (see illustration). The VIN also appears on the Vehicle Certificate of Title and Registration. It contains information such as where and when the vehicle was manufactured, the model year and the body style.

VIN MODEL YEAR CODE

Counting from the left, the model year code letter designation is the 10th digit.

On the models covered by this manual the model year codes are:

3	2003
4	2004
5	2005
6	2006
7	2007
8	2008

VEHICLE CERTIFICATION LABEL

The Vehicle Certification Label is attached to the driver's side door pillar (see illustration). Information on this label includes the name of the manufacturer, the month and year of production, as well as information on the options with which it is equipped. This label is especially useful for matching the color and type of paint for repair work.

ENGINE IDENTIFICATION NUMBER

The engine code, engine number and build date can be found stamped onto a machined pad on the external surface of the engine block.

AUTOMATIC TRANSMISSION IDENTIFICATION NUMBER

The automatic transmission ID number is affixed to a label on the right side of the case.

MANUAL TRANSMISSION IDENTIFICATION NUMBER

The manual transmission ID number is stamped on a tag which is bolted to the right side of the bellhousing.

VEHICLE EMISSIONS CONTROL INFORMATION LABEL

This label is found in the engine compartment. See Chapter 6 for more information on this label.

The VIN number is visible through the windshield on the driver's side

The vehicle certification label is affixed the to the driver's side door pillar

The engine serial number can be found at the rear of the engine, on the right side

Recall information

Vehicle recalls are carried out by the manufacturer in the rare event of a possible safety-related defect. The vehicle's registered owner is contacted at the address on file at the Department of Motor Vehicles and given the details of the recall. Remedial work is carried out free of charge at a dealer service department.

If you are the new owner of a used vehicle which was subject to a recall and you want to be sure that the work has been carried out, it's best to contact a dealer service department and ask about your individual vehicle - you'll need to furnish them your Vehicle Identification Number (VIN).

The table below is based on information provided by the National Highway Traffic Safety Administration (NHTSA), the body which oversees vehicle recalls in the United States. The recall database is updated constantly. For the latest information on vehicle recalls, check the NHTSA website at www.nhtsa.gov, or call the NHTSA hotline at 1-888-327-4236.

Recall date	Recall campaign number	Model(s) affected	Concern
Dec 10, 2002	02V331000	2003 G35	Certain sedans fail to comply with the requirements of Federal Motor Vehicle Safety Standard No. 108, Lamps, reflective device, and associated equipment. In the assembly of the headlamps, it is necessary to have the means to adjust the headlamps. Tamperproof caps to prevent the horizontal adjustment of the headlamps are then installed. Some of these vehicles are missing the tamperproof caps. Dealers will install the missing tamperproof caps on the headlamp assemblies.
May 28, 2003	03V200000	2003 G35	On certain sedan and coupe model vehicles, The brake light switch may malfunction. If this occurs, the brake lights may not illuminate when the brake is applied, which could result in a crash without warning.
Nov 04, 2003	03V455000	2003 G35 2003 350Z	On certain passenger vehicles, the circuit board for the crank position sensor or cam position sensor may have an improper solder joint due to solder deformation caused by heat stress accelerated by the existence of flux residue during the soldering process. This could cause the "service engine soon" warning light to come on, create a no start condition, cause reduced engine power, or cause the engine to stop running without warning during vehicle operation, which could result in a crash.
Nov 28, 2005	05V555000	2003, 2004 G35 2003, 2004 350Z	On certain passenger and sport utility vehicles, the fuel filler hose may crack and result in fuel leakage from the hose while refueling. Fuel leakage in the presence of an ignition source could result in fire.

Recall information (continued)

Recall date	Recall campaign number	Model(s) affected	Concern
May 22, 2006	06E049000	2003-2005 350Z	Certain CK motorsports combination headlights, clear corner, bumper, and side marker lights sold as replacement lamp for use on passenger vehicles listed. Some combination lamps that are not equipped with amber side reflectors fail to conform to federal motor vehicle safety standard No. 108, lamps, reflective devices, and associated equipment. Without the amber reflectors, the vehicle will be poorly illuminated, possibly resulting in a vehicle crash without warning.
Jun 20, 2006	06E060000	2003, 2004 G35	Certain AAI motorsports combination lamps sold as replacement lamps for use on these passenger vehicles. Combination lamps not equipped with amber side reflectors fail to conform with the requirements of the Federal Motor Vehicle Safety Standard No. 108, lamps, reflective devices, and associated equipment. Lack of amber side reflectors in the lamps will decrease lighting visibility to other drivers and may possibly result in a vehicle cash
Oct 09, 2006	06V394000	2006, 2007 G35	Certain vehicles fail to comply with the vertical gradient and headlamp photometric values, Requirements of the federal motor vehicle safety standard no. 108, lamps, reflective devices, and associated equipment This standard is to reduce crashes, injuries and deaths by providing adequate illumination of the road way, and by enhancing the conspicuity of motor vehicles on the public roads so that their presence is perceived and their signals understood, both in daylight and in darkness or other conditions of reduced visibility.
Sept 10, 2007	02V245000	2003 G35	On certain passenger vehicles, the fuel hose connection for the outlet of the fuel pump, which is located at the top of the fuel tank, may not have been properly attached when the vehicle was assembled and could come loose while driving or when starting the engine. If connection comes loose while driving, the engine will stop running due to lack of fuel, increasing the risk of a crash. Also, if the connection comes loose while driving or attempting to start or restart the engine, some fuel will discharge from the fuel pump. If this should occur in the presence of an external ignition source, a fire could result.

Buying parts

Replacement parts are available from many sources, which generally fall into one of two categories - authorized dealer parts departments and independent retail auto parts stores. Our advice concerning these parts is as follows:

Retail auto parts stores: Good auto parts stores will stock frequently needed components which wear out relatively fast, such as clutch components, exhaust systems, brake parts, tune-up parts, etc. These stores often supply new or reconditioned parts on an exchange basis, which can save a considerable amount of money. Discount auto parts stores are often very good places to buy materials and parts needed for general vehicle maintenance such as oil, grease, filters, spark plugs, belts, touch-up paint, bulbs, etc. They also usually sell tools and general accessories, have convenient hours, charge lower prices and can often be found not far from home.

Authorized dealer parts department: This is the best source for parts which are unique to the vehicle and not generally available elsewhere (such as major engine parts, transmission parts, trim pieces, etc.).

Warranty information: If the vehicle is still covered under warranty, be sure that any replacement parts purchased - regardless of the source - do not invalidate the warranty!

To be sure of obtaining the correct parts, have engine and chassis numbers available and, if possible, take the old parts along for positive identification.

Maintenance techniques, tools and working facilities

MAINTENANCE TECHNIQUES

There are a number of techniques involved in maintenance and repair that will be referred to throughout this manual. Application of these techniques will enable the home mechanic to be more efficient, better organized and capable of performing the various tasks properly, which will ensure that the repair job is thorough and complete.

Fasteners

Fasteners are nuts, bolts, studs and screws used to hold two or more parts together. There are a few things to keep in mind when working with fasteners. Almost all of them use a locking device of some type, either a lockwasher, locknut, locking tab or thread adhesive. All threaded fasteners should be clean and straight, with undamaged threads and undamaged corners on the hex head where the wrench fits. Develop the habit of replacing all damaged nuts and bolts with new ones. Special locknuts with nylon or fiber inserts can only be used once. If they are removed, they lose their locking ability and must be replaced with new ones.

Rusted nuts and bolts should be treated with a penetrating fluid to ease removal and prevent breakage. Some mechanics use turpentine in a spout-type oil can, which works quite well. After applying the rust penetrant, let it work for a few minutes before trying to loosen the nut or bolt. Badly rusted fasteners may have to be chiseled or sawed off or removed with a special nut breaker, available at tool stores.

If a bolt or stud breaks off in an assembly, it can be drilled and removed with a special tool commonly available for this purpose. Most automotive machine shops can perform this task, as well as other repair procedures, such as the repair of threaded holes that have been stripped out.

Flat washers and lockwashers, when removed from an assembly, should always be replaced exactly as removed. Replace any damaged washers with new ones. Never use a lockwasher on any soft metal surface (such as aluminum), thin sheet metal or plastic.

Fastener sizes

For a number of reasons, automobile manufacturers are making wider and wider use of metric fasteners. Therefore, it is important to be able to tell the difference between standard (sometimes called U.S.

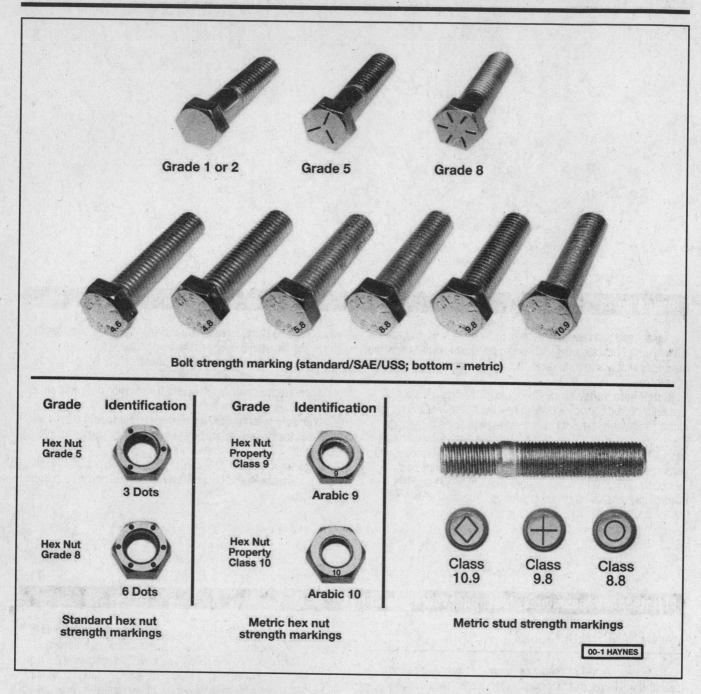

Grade 1 or 2   Grade 5   Grade 8

Bolt strength marking (standard/SAE/USS; bottom - metric)

Grade	Identification
Hex Nut Grade 5	3 Dots
Hex Nut Grade 8	6 Dots

Standard hex nut strength markings

Grade	Identification
Hex Nut Property Class 9	Arabic 9
Hex Nut Property Class 10	Arabic 10

Metric hex nut strength markings

Class 10.9   Class 9.8   Class 8.8

Metric stud strength markings

00-1 HAYNES

or SAE) and metric hardware, since they cannot be interchanged.

All bolts, whether standard or metric, are sized according to diameter, thread pitch and length. For example, a standard 1/2 - 13 x 1 bolt is 1/2 inch in diameter, has 13 threads per inch and is 1 inch long. An M12 - 1.75 x 25 metric bolt is 12 mm in diameter, has a thread pitch of 1.75 mm (the distance between threads) and is 25 mm long. The two bolts are nearly identical, and easily confused, but they are not interchangeable.

In addition to the differences in diameter, thread pitch and length, metric and standard bolts can also be distinguished by examining the bolt heads. To begin with, the distance across the flats on a standard bolt head is measured in inches, while the same dimension on a metric bolt is sized in millimeters (the same is true for nuts). As a result, a standard wrench should not be used on a metric bolt and a metric wrench should not be used on a standard bolt. Also, most standard bolts have slashes radiating out from the center of the head to denote the grade or strength of the bolt, which is an indication of the amount of torque that can be applied to it. The greater the number of slashes, the greater the strength of the bolt. Grades 0 through 5 are commonly used on automobiles. Metric bolts have a property class (grade) number, rather than a slash, molded into their heads to indicate bolt strength. In this case, the higher the number, the stronger the bolt. Property class numbers 8.8, 9.8 and 10.9 are commonly used on automobiles.

Strength markings can also be used to distinguish standard hex nuts from metric hex nuts. Many standard nuts have dots stamped into one side, while metric nuts are marked with a number. The greater the number of dots, or the higher the number, the greater the strength of the nut.

Metric studs are also marked on their ends according to property class (grade). Larger studs are numbered (the same as metric bolts), while smaller studs carry a geometric code to denote grade.

Metric thread sizes	Ft-lbs	Nm
M-6	6 to 9	9 to 12
M-8	14 to 21	19 to 28
M-10	28 to 40	38 to 54
M-12	50 to 71	68 to 96
M-14	80 to 140	109 to 154

Pipe thread sizes		
1/8	5 to 8	7 to 10
1/4	12 to 18	17 to 24
3/8	22 to 33	30 to 44
1/2	25 to 35	34 to 47

U.S. thread sizes		
1/4 - 20	6 to 9	9 to 12
5/16 - 18	12 to 18	17 to 24
5/16 - 24	14 to 20	19 to 27
3/8 - 16	22 to 32	30 to 43
3/8 - 24	27 to 38	37 to 51
7/16 - 14	40 to 55	55 to 74
7/16 - 20	40 to 60	55 to 81
1/2 - 13	55 to 80	75 to 108

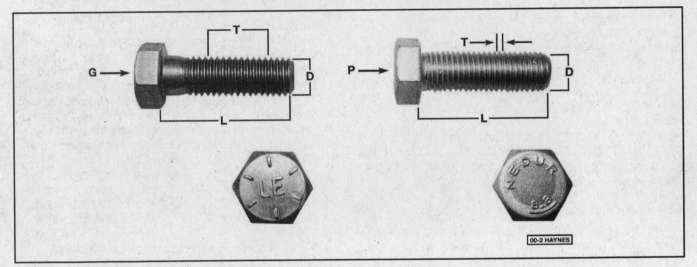

00-2 HAYNES

Standard (SAE and USS) bolt dimensions/grade marks

G   Grade marks (bolt strength)
L   Length (in inches)
T   Thread pitch (number of threads per inch)
D   Nominal diameter (in inches)

Metric bolt dimensions/grade marks

P   Property class (bolt strength)
L   Length (in millimeters)
T   Thread pitch (distance between threads in millimeters)
D   Diameter

It should be noted that many fasteners, especially Grades 0 through 2, have no distinguishing marks on them. When such is the case, the only way to determine whether it is standard or metric is to measure the thread pitch or compare it to a known fastener of the same size.

Standard fasteners are often referred to as SAE, as opposed to metric. However, it should be noted that SAE technically refers to a non-metric fine thread fastener only. Coarse thread non-metric fasteners are referred to as USS sizes.

Since fasteners of the same size (both standard and metric) may have different strength ratings, be sure to reinstall any bolts, studs or nuts removed from your vehicle in their original locations. Also, when replacing a fastener with a new one, make sure that the new one has a strength rating equal to or greater than the original.

Tightening sequences and procedures

Most threaded fasteners should be tightened to a specific torque value (torque is the twisting force applied to a threaded component such as a nut or bolt). Overtightening the fastener can weaken it and cause it to break, while undertightening can cause it to eventually come loose. Bolts, screws and studs, depending on the material they are made of and their thread diameters, have specific torque values, many of which are noted in the Specifications at the end of each Chapter. Be sure to follow the torque recommendations closely. For fasteners not assigned a specific torque, a general torque value chart is presented here as a guide. These torque values are for dry (unlubricated) fasteners threaded into steel or cast iron (not aluminum). As was previously mentioned, the size and grade of a fastener determine the amount of torque that can

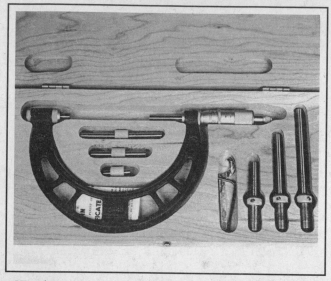

Micrometer set

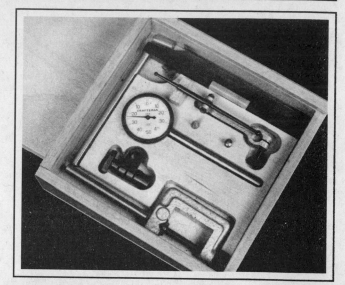

Dial indicator set

safely be applied to it. The figures listed here are approximate for Grade 2 and Grade 3 fasteners. Higher grades can tolerate higher torque values.

Fasteners laid out in a pattern, such as cylinder head bolts, oil pan bolts, differential cover bolts, etc., must be loosened or tightened in sequence to avoid warping the component. This sequence will normally be shown in the appropriate Chapter. If a specific pattern is not given, the following procedures can be used to prevent warping.

Initially, the bolts or nuts should be assembled finger-tight only. Next, they should be tightened one full turn each, in a criss-cross or diagonal pattern. After each one has been tightened one full turn, return to the first one and tighten them all one-half turn, following the same pattern. Finally, tighten each of them one-quarter turn at a time until each fastener has been tightened to the proper torque. To loosen and remove the fasteners, the procedure would be reversed.

Component disassembly

Component disassembly should be done with care and purpose to help ensure that the parts go back together properly. Always keep track of the sequence in which parts are removed. Make note of special characteristics or marks on parts that can be installed more than one way, such as a grooved thrust washer on a shaft. It is a good idea to lay the disassembled parts out on a clean surface in the order that they were removed. It may also be helpful to make sketches or take instant photos of components before removal.

When removing fasteners from a component, keep track of their locations. Sometimes threading a bolt back in a part, or putting the washers and nut back on a stud, can prevent mix-ups later. If nuts and bolts cannot be returned to their original locations, they should be kept in a compartmented box or a series of small boxes. A cupcake or muffin tin is ideal for this purpose, since each cavity can hold the bolts and nuts from a particular area (i.e. oil pan bolts, valve cover bolts, engine mount bolts, etc.). A pan of this type is especially helpful when working on assemblies with very small parts, such as the carburetor, alternator, valve train or interior dash and trim pieces. The cavities can be marked with paint or tape to identify the contents.

Whenever wiring looms, harnesses or connectors are separated, it is a good idea to identify the two halves with numbered pieces of masking tape so they can be easily reconnected.

Gasket sealing surfaces

Throughout any vehicle, gaskets are used to seal the mating surfaces between two parts and keep lubricants, fluids, vacuum or pressure contained in an assembly.

Many times these gaskets are coated with a liquid or paste-type gasket sealing compound before assembly. Age, heat and pressure can sometimes cause the two parts to stick together so tightly that they are very difficult to separate. Often, the assembly can be loosened by striking it with a soft-face hammer near the mating surfaces. A regular hammer can be used if a block of wood is placed between the hammer and the part. Do not hammer on cast parts or parts that could be easily damaged. With any particularly stubborn part, always recheck to make sure that every fastener has been removed.

Avoid using a screwdriver or bar to pry apart an assembly, as they can easily mar the gasket sealing surfaces of the parts, which must remain smooth. If prying is absolutely necessary, use an old broom handle, but keep in mind that extra clean up will be necessary if the wood splinters.

After the parts are separated, the old gasket must be carefully scraped off and the gasket surfaces cleaned. Stubborn gasket material can be soaked with rust penetrant or treated with a special chemical to soften it so it can be easily scraped off.

> **❋❋ CAUTION:**
>
> **Never use gasket removal solutions or caustic chemicals on plastic or other composite components.**

A scraper can be fashioned from a piece of copper tubing by flattening and sharpening one end. Copper is recommended because it is usually softer than the surfaces to be scraped, which reduces the chance of gouging the part. Some gaskets can be removed with a wire brush, but regardless of the method used, the mating surfaces must be left clean and smooth. If for some reason the gasket surface is gouged, then a gasket sealer thick enough to fill scratches will have to be used during reassembly of the components. For most applications, a non-drying (or semi-drying) gasket sealer should be used.

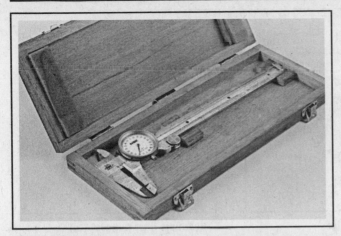

Dial caliper

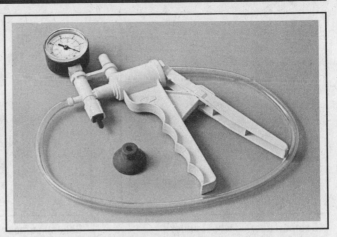

Hand-operated vacuum pump

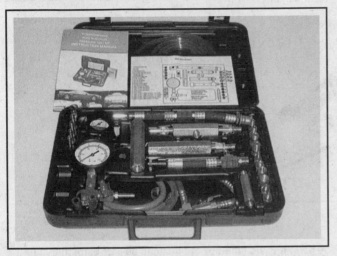

Fuel pressure gauge set

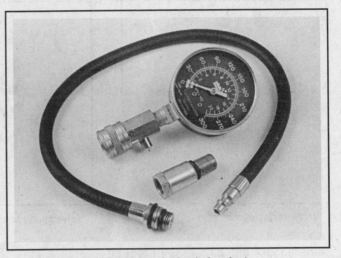

Compression gauge with spark plug hole adapter

Hose removal tips

❊❊❊ WARNING:

If the vehicle is equipped with air conditioning, do not disconnect any of the A/C hoses without first having the system depressurized by a dealer service department or a service station.

Hose removal precautions closely parallel gasket removal precautions. Avoid scratching or gouging the surface that the hose mates against or the connection may leak. This is especially true for radiator hoses. Because of various chemical reactions, the rubber in hoses can bond itself to the metal spigot that the hose fits over. To remove a hose, first loosen the hose clamps that secure it to the spigot. Then, with slip-joint pliers, grab the hose at the clamp and rotate it around the spigot. Work it back and forth until it is completely free, then pull it off. Silicone or other lubricants will ease removal if they can be applied between the hose and the outside of the spigot. Apply the same lubricant to the inside of the hose and the outside of the spigot to simplify installation.

As a last resort (and if the hose is to be replaced with a new one anyway), the rubber can be slit with a knife and the hose peeled from the spigot. If this must be done, be careful that the metal connection is not damaged.

If a hose clamp is broken or damaged, do not reuse it. Wire-type clamps usually weaken with age, so it is a good idea to replace them with screw-type clamps whenever a hose is removed.

TOOLS

A selection of good tools is a basic requirement for anyone who plans to maintain and repair his or her own vehicle. For the owner who has few tools, the initial investment might seem high, but when compared to the spiraling costs of professional auto maintenance and repair, it is a wise one.

To help the owner decide which tools are needed to perform the tasks detailed in this manual, the following tool lists are offered: *Maintenance and minor repair, Repair/overhaul and Special.*

The newcomer to practical mechanics should start off with the *maintenance and minor repair* tool kit, which is adequate for the simpler jobs performed on a vehicle. Then, as confidence and experience grow, the owner can tackle more difficult tasks, buying additional tools as they are needed. Eventually the basic kit will be expanded into the *repair and overhaul* tool set. Over a period of time, the experienced do-it-yourselfer will assemble a tool set complete enough for most repair and overhaul procedures and will add tools from the special category when it is felt that the expense is justified by the frequency of use.

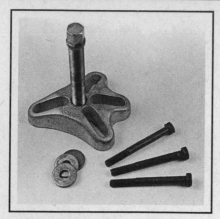

Damper/steering wheel puller

General purpose puller

Hydraulic lifter removal tool

Valve spring compressor

Valve spring compressor

Ridge reamer

Maintenance and minor repair tool kit

The tools in this list should be considered the minimum required for performance of routine maintenance, servicing and minor repair work. We recommend the purchase of combination wrenches (box-end and open-end combined in one wrench). While more expensive than open end wrenches, they offer the advantages of both types of wrench.

> *Combination wrench set (1/4-inch to 1 inch or 6 mm to 19 mm)*
> *Adjustable wrench, 8 inch*
> *Spark plug wrench with rubber insert*
> *Spark plug gap adjusting tool*
> *Feeler gauge set*
> *Brake bleeder wrench*
> *Standard screwdriver (5/16-inch x 6 inch)*
> *Phillips screwdriver (No. 2 x 6 inch)*
> *Combination pliers - 6 inch*
> *Hacksaw and assortment of blades*
> *Tire pressure gauge*
> *Grease gun*
> *Oil can*
> *Fine emery cloth*
> *Wire brush*
> *Battery post and cable cleaning tool*
> *Oil filter wrench*
> *Funnel (medium size)*
> *Safety goggles*
> *Jackstands (2)*
> *Drain pan*

➡**Note: If basic tune-ups are going to be part of routine maintenance, it will be necessary to purchase a good quality stroboscopic timing light and combination tachometer/dwell meter. Although they are included in the list of special tools, it is mentioned here because they are absolutely necessary for tuning most vehicles properly.**

Repair and overhaul tool set

These tools are essential for anyone who plans to perform major repairs and are in addition to those in the maintenance and minor repair tool kit. Included is a comprehensive set of sockets which, though expensive, are invaluable because of their versatility, especially when various extensions and drives are available. We recommend the 1/2-inch drive over the 3/8-inch drive. Although the larger drive is bulky and more expensive, it has the capacity of accepting a very wide range of large sockets. Ideally, however, the mechanic should have a 3/8-inch drive set and a 1/2-inch drive set.

> *Socket set(s)*
> *Reversible ratchet*
> *Extension - 10 inch*
> *Universal joint*
> *Torque wrench (same size drive as sockets)*
> *Ball peen hammer - 8 ounce*
> *Soft-face hammer (plastic/rubber)*
> *Standard screwdriver (1/4-inch x 6 inch)*
> *Standard screwdriver (stubby - 5/16-inch)*
> *Phillips screwdriver (No. 3 x 8 inch)*
> *Phillips screwdriver (stubby - No. 2)*
> *Pliers - vise grip*

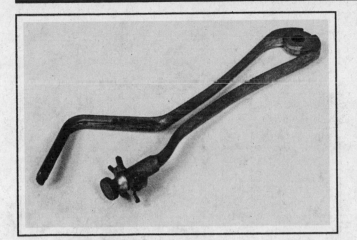

Piston ring groove cleaning tool

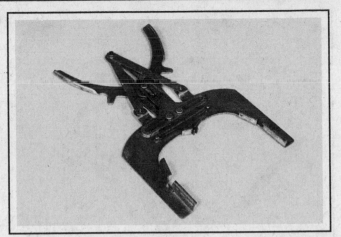

Ring removal/installation tool

Ring compressor

Cylinder hone

Brake hold-down spring tool

Pliers - lineman's
Pliers - needle nose
Pliers - snap-ring (internal and external)
Cold chisel - 1/2-inch
Scribe
Scraper (made from flattened copper tubing)
Centerpunch
Pin punches (1/16, 1/8, 3/16-inch)
Steel rule/straightedge - 12 inch
Allen wrench set (1/8 to 3/8-inch or 4 mm to 10 mm)
A selection of files
Wire brush (large)
Jackstands (second set)
Jack (scissor or hydraulic type)

➡**Note: Another tool which is often useful is an electric drill with a chuck capacity of 3/8-inch and a set of good quality drill bits.**

Special tools

The tools in this list include those which are not used regularly, are expensive to buy, or which need to be used in accordance with their manufacturer's instructions. Unless these tools will be used frequently, it is not very economical to purchase many of them. A consideration would be to split the cost and use between yourself and a friend or friends. In addition, most of these tools can be obtained from a tool rental shop on a temporary basis.

This list primarily contains only those tools and instruments widely available to the public, and not those special tools produced by the vehicle manufacturer for distribution to dealer service depart-

ments. Occasionally, references to the manufacturer's special tools are included in the text of this manual. Generally, an alternative method of doing the job without the special tool is offered. However, sometimes there is no alternative to their use. Where this is the case, and the tool cannot be purchased or borrowed, the work should be turned over to the dealer service department or an automotive repair shop.

Valve spring compressor
Piston ring groove cleaning tool
Piston ring compressor
Piston ring installation tool
Cylinder compression gauge
Cylinder ridge reamer
Cylinder surfacing hone
Cylinder bore gauge
Micrometers and/or dial calipers
Hydraulic lifter removal tool
Balljoint separator
Universal-type puller
Impact screwdriver
Dial indicator set
Stroboscopic timing light (inductive pick-up)
Hand operated vacuum/pressure pump
Tachometer/dwell meter
Universal electrical multimeter
Cable hoist
Brake spring removal and installation tools
Floor jack

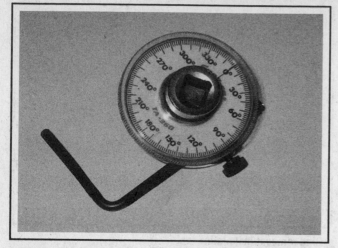

Torque angle gauge

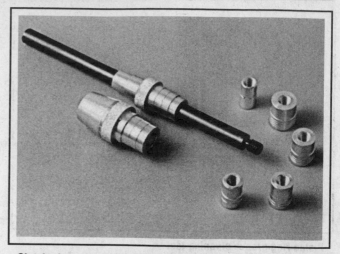

Clutch plate alignment tool

Buying tools

For the do-it-yourselfer who is just starting to get involved in vehicle maintenance and repair, there are a number of options available when purchasing tools. If maintenance and minor repair is the extent of the work to be done, the purchase of individual tools is satisfactory. If, on the other hand, extensive work is planned, it would be a good idea to purchase a modest tool set from one of the large retail chain stores. A set can usually be bought at a substantial savings over the individual tool prices, and they often come with a tool box. As additional tools are needed, add-on sets, individual tools and a larger tool box can be purchased to expand the tool selection. Building a tool set gradually allows the cost of the tools to be spread over a longer period of time and gives the mechanic the freedom to choose only those tools that will actually be used.

Tool stores will often be the only source of some of the special tools that are needed, but regardless of where tools are bought, try to avoid cheap ones, especially when buying screwdrivers and sockets, because they won't last very long. The expense involved in replacing cheap tools will eventually be greater than the initial cost of quality tools.

Care and maintenance of tools

Good tools are expensive, so it makes sense to treat them with respect. Keep them clean and in usable condition and store them properly when not in use. Always wipe off any dirt, grease or metal chips before putting them away. Never leave tools lying around in the work area. Upon completion of a job, always check closely under the hood for tools that may have been left there so they won't get lost during a test drive.

Some tools, such as screwdrivers, pliers, wrenches and sockets, can be hung on a panel mounted on the garage or workshop wall, while others should be kept in a tool box or tray. Measuring instruments, gauges, meters, etc. must be carefully stored where they cannot be damaged by weather or impact from other tools.

When tools are used with care and stored properly, they will last a very long time. Even with the best of care, though, tools will wear out if used frequently. When a tool is damaged or worn out, replace it. Subsequent jobs will be safer and more enjoyable if you do.

HOW TO REPAIR DAMAGED THREADS

Sometimes, the internal threads of a nut or bolt hole can become stripped, usually from overtightening. Stripping threads is an all-too-

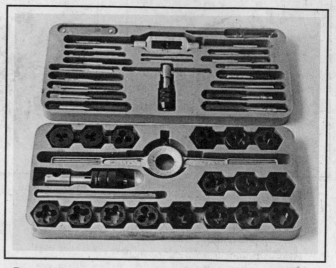

Tap and die set

common occurrence, especially when working with aluminum parts, because aluminum is so soft that it easily strips out.

Usually, external or internal threads are only partially stripped. After they've been cleaned up with a tap or die, they'll still work. Sometimes, however, threads are badly damaged. When this happens, you've got three choices:

1) Drill and tap the hole to the next suitable oversize and install a larger diameter bolt, screw or stud.
2) Drill and tap the hole to accept a threaded plug, then drill and tap the plug to the original screw size. You can also buy a plug already threaded to the original size. Then you simply drill a hole to the specified size, then run the threaded plug into the hole with a bolt and jam nut. Once the plug is fully seated, remove the jam nut and bolt.
3) The third method uses a patented thread repair kit like Heli-Coil or Slimsert. These easy-to-use kits are designed to repair damaged threads in straight-through holes and blind holes. Both are available as kits which can handle a variety of sizes and thread patterns. Drill the hole, then tap it with the special included tap. Install the Heli-Coil and the hole is back to its original diameter and thread pitch.

Regardless of which method you use, be sure to proceed calmly and carefully. A little impatience or carelessness during one of these relatively simple procedures can ruin your whole day's work and cost you a bundle if you wreck an expensive part.

WORKING FACILITIES

Not to be overlooked when discussing tools is the workshop. If anything more than routine maintenance is to be carried out, some sort of suitable work area is essential.

It is understood, and appreciated, that many home mechanics do not have a good workshop or garage available, and end up removing an engine or doing major repairs outside. It is recommended, however, that the overhaul or repair be completed under the cover of a roof.

A clean, flat workbench or table of comfortable working height is an absolute necessity. The workbench should be equipped with a vise that has a jaw opening of at least four inches.

As mentioned previously, some clean, dry storage space is also

required for tools, as well as the lubricants, fluids, cleaning solvents, etc. which soon become necessary.

Sometimes waste oil and fluids, drained from the engine or cooling зуэtcm during normal maintenance or repairs, present a disposal problem. To avoid pouring them on the ground or into a sewage system, pour the used fluids into large containers, seal them with caps and take them to an authorized disposal site or recycling center. Plastic jugs, such as old antifreeze containers, are ideal for this purpose.

Always keep a supply of old newspapers and clean rags available. Old towels are excellent for mopping up spills. Many mechanics use rolls of paper towels for most work because they are readily available and disposable. To help keep the area under the vehicle clean, a large cardboard box can be cut open and flattened to protect the garage or shop floor.

Whenever working over a painted surface, such as when leaning over a fender to service something under the hood, always cover it with an old blanket or bedspread to protect the finish. Vinyl covered pads, made especially for this purpose, are available at auto parts stores.

Booster battery (jump) starting

Observe the following precautions when using a booster battery to start a vehicle:

a) *Before connecting the booster battery, make sure the ignition switch is in the Off position.*

b) *Turn off the lights, heater and other electrical loads.*

c) *Your eyes should be shielded. Safety goggles are a good idea.*

d) *Make sure the booster battery is the same voltage as the dead one in the vehicle.*

e) *The two vehicles MUST NOT TOUCH each other!*

f) *Make sure the transmission is in Neutral (manual) or Park (automatic).*

g) *If the booster battery is not a maintenance-free type, remove the vent caps and lay a cloth over the vent holes.*

Lift up the battery cover, then connect one jumper lead between the positive (+) terminals of the two batteries (see illustrations). Connect the other jumper lead first to the negative (-) terminal of the booster battery, then to a good engine ground on the vehicle to be started. Attach the lead at least 18 inches from the battery, if possible. Make sure the that the jumper leads will not contact the fan, drivebelt or other moving parts of the engine.

Start the engine using the booster battery, then, with the engine running at idle speed, disconnect the jumper cables in the reverse order of connection.

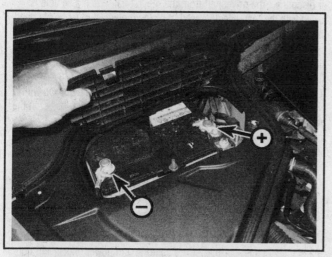

The battery on these models is located in the right rear corner of the engine compartment, under a cover

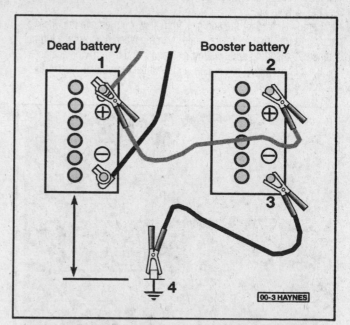

Make the booster battery cable connections in the numerical order shown (note that the negative cable of the booster battery is NOT attached to the negative terminal of the dead battery)

Jacking and towing

JACKING

The jack supplied with the vehicle should only be used for raising the vehicle for changing a tire or placing jackstands under the frame.

✳✳ WARNING:

The jack supplied with the vehicle should only be used for changing a tire or placing jackstands under the frame. Never work under the vehicle or start the engine while this jack is being used as the only means of support.

The vehicle should be on level ground. Place the shift lever in Park, if you have an automatic, or Reverse if you have a manual transmission. Block the wheel diagonally opposite the wheel being changed. Set the parking brake.

Remove the spare tire and jack from stowage. Remove the wheel cover and trim ring (if so equipped) with the tapered end of the lug nut wrench by inserting and twisting the handle and then prying against the back of the wheel cover. Loosen the wheel lug nuts about 1/4-to-1/2 turn each.

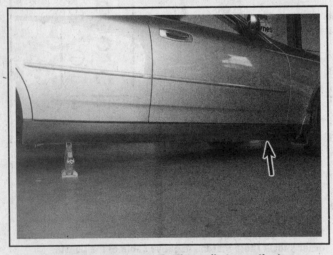

Place the jack so it engages the flange (between the two notches) rocker panel nearest the wheel to be raised

Place the scissors-type jack under the side of the vehicle and adjust the jack height until it fits between the notches in the vertical rocker panel flange nearest the wheel to be changed. There is a front and rear jacking point on each side of the vehicle (see illustration).

Turn the jack handle clockwise until the tire clears the ground. Remove the lug nuts and pull the wheel off. Replace it with the spare.

Install the lug nuts with the beveled edges facing in. Tighten them snugly. Don't attempt to tighten them completely until the vehicle is lowered or it could slip off the jack. Turn the jack handle counterclockwise to lower the vehicle. Remove the jack and tighten the lug nuts in a diagonal pattern.

Install the cover (and trim ring, if used) and be sure it's snapped into place all the way around.

Stow the tire, jack and wrench. Unblock the wheels.

TOWING

As a general rule, the vehicle should be towed with the rear wheels off the ground. If they can't be raised, either place them on a dolly or disconnect the driveshaft from the differential. When a vehicle is towed with the rear wheels raised, the steering wheel must be clamped in the straight ahead position with a special device designed for use during towing. The ignition key must be in the OFF position, since the steering lock mechanism isn't strong enough to hold the front wheels straight while towing.

Vehicles equipped with a manual transmission can be towed with the rear wheels on the ground or from the front with four wheels on the ground, provided that the speeds don't exceed 50 mph (80 km/h) and the distance is not over 500 miles (800 km). Release the parking brake, put the transmission in Neutral and place the ignition key in the OFF position.

Equipment specifically designed for towing should be used. It should be attached to the main structural members of the vehicle, not the bumpers or brackets.

Safety is a major consideration when towing and all applicable state and local laws must be obeyed. A safety chain system must be used at all times. Remember that power steering and power brakes will not work with the engine off.

Automotive chemicals and lubricants

A number of automotive chemicals and lubricants are available for use during vehicle maintenance and repair. They include a wide variety of products ranging from cleaning solvents and degreasers to lubricants and protective sprays for rubber, plastic and vinyl.

CLEANERS

Carburetor cleaner and choke cleaner is a strong solvent for gum, varnish and carbon. Most carburetor cleaners leave a dry-type lubricant film which will not harden or gum up. Because of this film it is not recommended for use on electrical components.

Brake system cleaner is used to remove brake dust, grease and brake fluid from the brake system, where clean surfaces are absolutely necessary. It leaves no residue and often eliminates brake squeal caused by contaminants.

Electrical cleaner removes oxidation, corrosion and carbon deposits from electrical contacts, restoring full current flow. It can also be used to clean spark plugs, carburetor jets, voltage regulators and other parts where an oil-free surface is desired.

Demoisturants remove water and moisture from electrical components such as alternators, voltage regulators, electrical connectors and fuse blocks. They are non-conductive and non-corrosive.

Degreasers are heavy-duty solvents used to remove grease from the outside of the engine and from chassis components. They can be sprayed or brushed on and, depending on the type, are rinsed off either with water or solvent.

LUBRICANTS

Motor oil is the lubricant formulated for use in engines. It normally contains a wide variety of additives to prevent corrosion and reduce foaming and wear. Motor oil comes in various weights (viscosity ratings) from 0 to 50. The recommended weight of the oil depends on the season, temperature and the demands on the engine. Light oil is used in cold climates and under light load conditions. Heavy oil is used in hot climates and where high loads are encountered. Multi-viscosity oils are designed to have characteristics of both light and heavy oils and are available in a number of weights from 5W-20 to 20W-50.

Gear oil is designed to be used in differentials, manual transmissions and other areas where high-temperature lubrication is required.

Chassis and wheel bearing grease is a heavy grease used where increased loads and friction are encountered, such as for wheel bearings, balljoints, tie-rod ends and universal joints.

High-temperature wheel bearing grease is designed to withstand the extreme temperatures encountered by wheel bearings in disc brake equipped vehicles. It usually contains molybdenum disulfide (moly), which is a dry-type lubricant.

White grease is a heavy grease for metal-to-metal applications where water is a problem. White grease stays soft under both low and high temperatures (usually from -100 to +190-degrees F), and will not wash off or dilute in the presence of water.

Assembly lube is a special extreme pressure lubricant, usually containing moly, used to lubricate high-load parts (such as main and rod bearings and cam lobes) for initial start-up of a new engine. The assembly lube lubricates the parts without being squeezed out or washed away until the engine oiling system begins to function.

Silicone lubricants are used to protect rubber, plastic, vinyl and nylon parts.

Graphite lubricants are used where oils cannot be used due to contamination problems, such as in locks. The dry graphite will lubricate metal parts while remaining uncontaminated by dirt, water, oil or acids. It is electrically conductive and will not foul electrical contacts in locks such as the ignition switch.

Moly penetrants loosen and lubricate frozen, rusted and corroded fasteners and prevent future rusting or freezing.

Heat-sink grease is a special electrically non-conductive grease that is used for mounting electronic ignition modules where it is essential that heat is transferred away from the module.

SEALANTS

RTV sealant is one of the most widely used gasket compounds. Made from silicone, RTV is air curing, it seals, bonds, waterproofs, fills surface irregularities, remains flexible, doesn't shrink, is relatively easy to remove, and is used as a supplementary sealer with almost all low and medium temperature gaskets.

Anaerobic sealant is much like RTV in that it can be used either to seal gaskets or to form gaskets by itself. It remains flexible, is solvent resistant and fills surface imperfections. The difference between an anaerobic sealant and an RTV-type sealant is in the curing. RTV cures when exposed to air, while an anaerobic sealant cures only in the absence of air. This means that an anaerobic sealant cures only after the assembly of parts, sealing them together.

Thread and pipe sealant is used for sealing hydraulic and pneumatic fittings and vacuum lines. It is usually made from a Teflon compound, and comes in a spray, a paint-on liquid and as a wrap-around tape.

CHEMICALS

Anti-seize compound prevents seizing, galling, cold welding, rust and corrosion in fasteners. High-temperature anti-seize, usually made with copper and graphite lubricants, is used for exhaust system and exhaust manifold bolts.

Anaerobic locking compounds are used to keep fasteners from vibrating or working loose and cure only after installation, in the absence of air. Medium strength locking compound is used for small nuts, bolts and screws that may be removed later. High-strength locking compound is for large nuts, bolts and studs which aren't removed on a regular basis.

Oil additives range from viscosity index improvers to chemical treatments that claim to reduce internal engine friction. It should be noted that most oil manufacturers caution against using additives with their oils.

Gas additives perform several functions, depending on their chemical makeup. They usually contain solvents that help dissolve gum and varnish that build up on carburetor, fuel injection and intake parts. They also serve to break down carbon deposits that form on the inside surfaces of the combustion chambers. Some additives contain upper cylinder lubricants for valves and piston rings, and others contain chemicals to remove condensation from the gas tank.

MISCELLANEOUS

Brake fluid is specially formulated hydraulic fluid that can withstand the heat and pressure encountered in brake systems. Care must be taken so this fluid does not come in contact with painted surfaces or plastics. An opened container should always be resealed to prevent contamination by water or dirt.

Weatherstrip adhesive is used to bond weatherstripping around doors, windows and trunk lids. It is sometimes used to attach trim pieces.

Undercoating is a petroleum-based, tar-like substance that is designed to protect metal surfaces on the underside of the vehicle from corrosion. It also acts as a sound-deadening agent by insulating the bottom of the vehicle.

Waxes and polishes are used to help protect painted and plated surfaces from the weather. Different types of paint may require the use of different types of wax and polish. Some polishes utilize a chemical or abrasive cleaner to help remove the top layer of oxidized (dull) paint on older vehicles. In recent years many non-wax polishes that contain a wide variety of chemicals such as polymers and silicones have been introduced. These non-wax polishes are usually easier to apply and last longer than conventional waxes and polishes.

CONVERSION FACTORS

LENGTH (distance)

Inches (in)	X 25.4	= Millimeters (mm)	X 0.0394	= Inches (in)	
Feet (ft)	X 0.305	= Meters (m)	X 3.281	= Feet (ft)	
Miles	X 1.609	= Kilometers (km)	X 0.621	= Miles	

VOLUME (capacity)

Cubic inches (cu in; in³)	X 16.387	= Cubic centimeters (cc; cm³)	X 0.061	= Cubic inches (cu in; in³)	
Imperial pints (Imp pt)	X 0.568	= Liters (l)	X 1.76	= Imperial pints (Imp pt)	
Imperial quarts (Imp qt)	X 1.137	= Liters (l)	X 0.88	= Imperial quarts (Imp qt)	
Imperial quarts (Imp qt)	X 1.201	= US quarts (US qt)	X 0.833	= Imperial quarts (Imp qt)	
US quarts (US qt)	X 0.946	= Liters (l)	X 1.057	= US quarts (US qt)	
Imperial gallons (Imp gal)	X 4.546	= Liters (l)	X 0.22	= Imperial gallons (Imp gal)	
Imperial gallons (Imp gal)	X 1.201	= US gallons (US gal)	X 0.833	= Imperial gallons (Imp gal)	
US gallons (US gal)	X 3.785	= Liters (l)	X 0.264	= US gallons (US gal)	

MASS (weight)

Ounces (oz)	X 28.35	= Grams (g)	X 0.035	= Ounces (oz)	
Pounds (lb)	X 0.454	= Kilograms (kg)	X 2.205	= Pounds (lb)	

FORCE

Ounces-force (ozf; oz)	X 0.278	= Newtons (N)	X 3.6	= Ounces-force (ozf; oz)	
Pounds-force (lbf; lb)	X 4.448	= Newtons (N)	X 0.225	= Pounds-force (lbf; lb)	
Newtons (N)	X 0.1	= Kilograms-force (kgf; kg)	X 9.81	= Newtons (N)	

PRESSURE

Pounds-force per square inch (psi; lbf/in²; lb/in²)	X 0.070	= Kilograms-force per square centimeter (kgf/cm²; kg/cm²)	X 14.223	= Pounds-force per square inch (psi; lbf/in²; lb/in²)	
Pounds-force per square inch (psi; lbf/in²; lb/in²)	X 0.068	= Atmospheres (atm)	X 14.696	= Pounds-force per square inch (psi; lbf/in²; lb/in²)	
Pounds-force per square inch (psi; lbf/in²; lb/in²)	X 0.069	= Bars	X 14.5	= Pounds-force per square inch (psi; lbf/in²; lb/in²)	
Pounds-force per square inch (psi; lbf/in²; lb/in²)	X 6.895	= Kilopascals (kPa)	X 0.145	= Pounds-force per square inch (psi; lbf/in²; lb/in²)	
Kilopascals (kPa)	X 0.01	= Kilograms-force per square centimeter (kgf/cm²; kg/cm²)	X 98.1	= Kilopascals (kPa)	

TORQUE (moment of force)

Pounds-force inches (lbf in; lb in)	X 1.152	= Kilograms-force centimeter (kgf cm; kg cm)	X 0.868	= Pounds-force inches (lbf in; lb in)	
Pounds-force inches (lbf in; lb in)	X 0.113	= Newton meters (Nm)	X 8.85	= Pounds-force inches (lbf in; lb in)	
Pounds-force inches (lbf in; lb in)	X 0.083	= Pounds-force feet (lbf ft; lb ft)	X 12	= Pounds-force inches (lbf in; lb in)	
Pounds-force feet (lbf ft; lb ft)	X 0.138	= Kilograms-force meters (kgf m; kg m)	X 7.233	= Pounds-force feet (lbf ft; lb ft)	
Pounds-force feet (lbf ft; lb ft)	X 1.356	= Newton meters (Nm)	X 0.738	= Pounds-force feet (lbf ft; lb ft)	
Newton meters (Nm)	X 0.102	= Kilograms-force meters (kgf m; kg m)	X 9.804	= Newton meters (Nm)	

VACUUM

Inches mercury (in. Hg)	X 3.377	= Kilopascals (kPa)	X 0.2961	= Inches mercury	
Inches mercury (in. Hg)	X 25.4	= Millimeters mercury (mm Hg)	X 0.0394	= Inches mercury	

POWER

Horsepower (hp)	X 745.7	= Watts (W)	X 0.0013	= Horsepower (hp)	

VELOCITY (speed)

Miles per hour (miles/hr; mph)	X 1.609	= Kilometers per hour (km/hr; kph)	X 0.621	= Miles per hour (miles/hr; mph)	

FUEL CONSUMPTION *

Miles per gallon, Imperial (mpg)	X 0.354	= Kilometers per liter (km/l)	X 2.825	= Miles per gallon, Imperial (mpg)	
Miles per gallon, US (mpg)	X 0.425	= Kilometers per liter (km/l)	X 2.352	= Miles per gallon, US (mpg)	

TEMPERATURE

Degrees Fahrenheit = (°C x 1.8) + 32   Degrees Celsius (Degrees Centigrade; °C) = (°F - 32) x 0.56

*It is common practice to convert from miles per gallon (mpg) to liters/100 kilometers (l/100km), where mpg (Imperial) x l/100 km = 282 and mpg (US) x l/100 km = 235

FRACTION/DECIMAL/MILLIMETER EQUIVALENTS

DECIMALS TO MILLIMETERS

Decimal	mm	Decimal	mm
0.001	0.0254	0.500	12.7000
0.002	0.0508	0.510	12.9540
0.003	0.0762	0.520	13.2080
0.004	0.1016	0.530	13.4620
0.005	0.1270	0.540	13.7160
0.006	0.1524	0.550	13.9700
0.007	0.1778	0.560	14.2240
0.008	0.2032	0.570	14.4780
0.009	0.2286	0.580	14.7320
		0.590	14.9860
0.010	0.2540		
0.020	0.5080		
0.030	0.7620		
0.040	1.0160	0.600	15.2400
0.050	1.2700	0.610	15.4940
0.060	1.5240	0.620	15.7480
0.070	1.7780	0.630	16.0020
0.080	2.0320	0.640	16.2560
0.090	2.2860	0.650	16.5100
		0.660	16.7640
0.100	2.5400	0.670	17.0180
0.110	2.7940	0.680	17.2720
0.120	3.0480	0.690	17.5260
0.130	3.3020		
0.140	3.5560		
0.150	3.8100		
0.160	4.0640	0.700	17.7800
0.170	4.3180	0.710	18.0340
0.180	4.5720	0.720	18.2880
0.190	4.8260	0.730	18.5420
		0.740	18.7960
0.200	5.0800	0.750	19.0500
0.210	5.3340	0.760	19.3040
0.220	5.5880	0.770	19.5580
0.230	5.8420	0.780	19.8120
0.240	6.0960	0.790	20.0660
0.250	6.3500		
0.260	6.6040		
0.270	6.8580	0.800	20.3200
0.280	7.1120	0.810	20.5740
0.290	7.3660	0.820	21.8280
		0.830	21.0820
0.300	7.6200	0.840	21.3360
0.310	7.8740	0.850	21.5900
0.320	8.1280	0.860	21.8440
0.330	8.3820	0.870	22.0980
0.340	8.6360	0.880	22.3520
0.350	8.9900	0.890	22.6060
0.360	9.1440		
0.370	9.3980		
0.380	9.6520		
0.390	9.9060	0.900	22.8600
0.400	10.1600	0.910	23.1140
0.410	10.4140	0.920	23.3680
0.420	10.6680	0.930	23.6220
0.430	10.9220	0.940	23.8760
0.440	11.1760	0.950	24.1300
0.450	11.4300	0.960	24.3840
0.460	11.6840	0.970	24.6380
0.470	11.9380	0.980	24.8920
0.480	12.1920	0.990	25.1460
0.490	12.4460	1.000	25.4000

FRACTIONS TO DECIMALS TO MILLIMETERS

Fraction	Decimal	mm	Fraction	Decimal	mm
1/64	0.0156	0.3969	33/64	0.5156	13.0969
1/32	0.0312	0.7938	17/32	0.5312	13.4938
3/64	0.0469	1.1906	35/64	0.5469	13.8906
1/16	0.0625	1.5875	9/16	0.5625	14.2875
5/64	0.0781	1.9844	37/64	0.5781	14.6844
3/32	0.0938	2.3812	19/32	0.5938	15.0812
7/64	0.1094	2.7781	39/64	0.6094	15.4781
1/8	0.1250	3.1750	5/8	0.6250	15.8750
9/64	0.1406	3.5719	41/64	0.6406	16.2719
5/32	0.1562	3.9688	21/32	0.6562	16.6688
11/64	0.1719	4.3656	43/64	0.6719	17.0656
3/16	0.1875	4.7625	11/16	0.6875	17.4625
13/64	0.2031	5.1594	45/64	0.7031	17.8594
7/32	0.2188	5.5562	23/32	0.7188	18.2562
15/64	0.2344	5.9531	47/64	0.7344	18.6531
1/4	0.2500	6.3500	3/4	0.7500	19.0500
17/64	0.2656	6.7469	49/64	0.7656	19.4469
9/32	0.2812	7.1438	25/32	0.7812	19.8438
19/64	0.2969	7.5406	51/64	0.7969	20.2406
5/16	0.3125	7.9375	13/16	0.8125	20.6375
21/64	0.3281	8.3344	53/64	0.8281	21.0344
11/32	0.3438	8.7312	27/32	0.8438	21.4312
23/64	0.3594	9.1281	55/64	0.8594	21.8281
3/8	0.3750	9.5250	7/8	0.8750	22.2250
25/64	0.3906	9.9219	57/64	0.8906	22.6219
13/32	0.4062	10.3188	29/32	0.9062	23.0188
27/64	0.4219	10.7156	59/64	0.9219	23.4156
7/16	0.4375	11.1125	15/16	0.9375	23.8125
29/64	0.4531	11.5094	61/64	0.9531	24.2094
15/32	0.4688	11.9062	31/32	0.9688	24.6062
31/64	0.4844	12.3031	63/64	0.9844	25.0031
1/2	0.5000	12.7000	1	1.0000	25.4000

Safety first!

Regardless of how enthusiastic you may be about getting on with the job at hand, take the time to ensure that your safety is not jeopardized. A moment's lack of attention can result in an accident, as can failure to observe certain simple safety precautions. The possibility of an accident will always exist, and the following points should not be considered a comprehensive list of all dangers. Rather, they are intended to make you aware of the risks and to encourage a safety conscious approach to all work you carry out on your vehicle.

ESSENTIAL DOS AND DON'TS

DON'T rely on a jack when working under the vehicle. Always use approved jackstands to support the weight of the vehicle and place them under the recommended lift or support points.

DON'T attempt to loosen extremely tight fasteners (i.e. wheel lug nuts) while the vehicle is on a jack - it may fall.

DON'T start the engine without first making sure that the transmission is in Neutral (or Park where applicable) and the parking brake is set.

DON'T remove the radiator cap from a hot cooling system - let it cool or cover it with a cloth and release the pressure gradually.

DON'T attempt to drain the engine oil until you are sure it has cooled to the point that it will not burn you.

DON'T touch any part of the engine or exhaust system until it has cooled sufficiently to avoid burns.

DON'T siphon toxic liquids such as gasoline, antifreeze and brake fluid by mouth, or allow them to remain on your skin.

DON'T inhale brake lining dust - it is potentially hazardous (see Asbestos below).

DON'T allow spilled oil or grease to remain on the floor - wipe it up before someone slips on it.

DON'T use loose fitting wrenches or other tools which may slip and cause injury.

DON'T push on wrenches when loosening or tightening nuts or bolts. Always try to pull the wrench toward you. If the situation calls for pushing the wrench away, push with an open hand to avoid scraped knuckles if the wrench should slip.

DON'T attempt to lift a heavy component alone - get someone to help you.

DON'T rush or take unsafe shortcuts to finish a job.

DON'T allow children or animals in or around the vehicle while you are working on it.

DO wear eye protection when using power tools such as a drill, sander, bench grinder, etc. and when working under a vehicle.

DO keep loose clothing and long hair well out of the way of moving parts.

DO make sure that any hoist used has a safe working load rating adequate for the job.

DO get someone to check on you periodically when working alone on a vehicle.

DO carry out work in a logical sequence and make sure that everything is correctly assembled and tightened.

DO keep chemicals and fluids tightly capped and out of the reach of children and pets.

DO remember that your vehicle's safety affects that of yourself and others. If in doubt on any point, get professional advice.

STEERING, SUSPENSION AND BRAKES

These systems are essential to driving safety, so make sure you have a qualified shop or individual check your work. Also, compressed suspension springs can cause injury if released suddenly - be sure to use a spring compressor.

AIRBAGS

Airbags are explosive devices that can CAUSE injury if they deploy while you're working on the vehicle. Follow the manufacturer's instructions to disable the airbag whenever you're working in the vicinity of airbag components.

ASBESTOS

Certain friction, insulating, sealing, and other products - such as brake linings, brake bands, clutch linings, torque converters, gaskets, etc. - may contain asbestos or other hazardous friction material. Extreme care must be taken to avoid inhalation of dust from such products, since it is hazardous to health. If in doubt, assume that they do contain asbestos.

FIRE

Remember at all times that gasoline is highly flammable. Never smoke or have any kind of open flame around when working on a vehicle. But the risk does not end there. A spark caused by an electrical short circuit, by two metal surfaces contacting each other, or even by static electricity built up in your body under certain conditions, can ignite gasoline vapors, which in a confined space are highly explosive. Do not, under any circumstances, use gasoline for cleaning parts. Use an approved safety solvent.

Always disconnect the battery ground (-) cable at the battery before working on any part of the fuel system or electrical system. Never risk spilling fuel on a hot engine or exhaust component. It is strongly recommended that a fire extinguisher suitable for use on fuel and electrical fires be kept handy in the garage or workshop at all times. Never try to extinguish a fuel or electrical fire with water.

FUMES

Certain fumes are highly toxic and can quickly cause unconsciousness and even death if inhaled to any extent. Gasoline vapor falls into this category, as do the vapors from some cleaning solvents. Any draining or pouring of such volatile fluids should be done in a well ventilated area.

When using cleaning fluids and solvents, read the instructions on the container carefully. Never use materials from unmarked containers.

Never run the engine in an enclosed space, such as a garage. Exhaust fumes contain carbon monoxide, which is extremely poisonous. If you need to run the engine, always do so in the open air, or at least have the rear of the vehicle outside the work area.

THE BATTERY

Never create a spark or allow a bare light bulb near a battery. They normally give off a certain amount of hydrogen gas, which is highly explosive.

Always disconnect the battery ground (-) cable at the battery before working on the fuel or electrical systems.

If possible, loosen the filler caps or cover when charging the battery from an external source (this does not apply to sealed or maintenance-free batteries). Do not charge at an excessive rate or the battery may burst.

Take care when adding water to a non maintenance-free battery and when carrying a battery. The electrolyte, even when diluted, is very corrosive and should not be allowed to contact clothing or skin.

Always wear eye protection when cleaning the battery to prevent the caustic deposits from entering your eyes.

HOUSEHOLD CURRENT

When using an electric power tool, inspection light, etc., which operates on household current, always make sure that the tool is correctly connected to its plug and that, where necessary, it is properly grounded. Do not use such items in damp conditions and, again, do not create a spark or apply excessive heat in the vicinity of fuel or fuel vapor.

SECONDARY IGNITION SYSTEM VOLTAGE

A severe electric shock can result from touching certain parts of the ignition system (such as the spark plug wires) when the engine is running or being cranked, particularly if components are damp or the insulation is defective. In the case of an electronic ignition system, the secondary system voltage is much higher and could prove fatal.

HYDROFLUORIC ACID

This extremely corrosive acid is formed when certain types of synthetic rubber, found in some O-rings, oil seals, fuel hoses, etc. are exposed to temperatures above 750-degrees F (400-degrees C). The rubber changes into a charred or sticky substance containing the acid. *Once formed, the acid remains dangerous for years. If it gets onto the skin, it may be necessary to amputate the limb concerned.*

When dealing with a vehicle which has suffered a fire, or with components salvaged from such a vehicle, wear protective gloves and discard them after use.

Troubleshooting

CONTENTS

This Section provides an easy reference guide to the more common problems which may occur during the operation of your vehicle. These problems and their possible causes are grouped under headings denoting various components or systems, such as Engine, Cooling system, etc. They also refer you to the Chapter and/or Section which deals with the problem.

Remember that successful troubleshooting is not a mysterious art practiced only by professional mechanics. It is simply the result of the right knowledge combined with an intelligent, systematic approach to the problem. Always work by a process of elimination, starting with the simplest solution and working through to the most complex - and never overlook the obvious. Anyone can run the gas tank dry or leave the lights on overnight, so don't assume that you are exempt from such oversights.

Finally, always establish a clear idea of why a problem has occurred and take steps to ensure that it doesn't happen again. If the electrical system fails because of a poor connection, check the other connections in the system to make sure that they don't fail as well. If a particular fuse continues to blow, find out why - don't just replace one fuse after another. Remember, failure of a small component can often be indicative of potential failure or incorrect functioning of a more important component or system.

ENGINE

1 Engine will not rotate when attempting to start

1   Battery terminal connections loose or corroded. Check the cable terminals at the battery; tighten cable clamp and/or clean off corrosion as necessary (see Chapter 1).
2   Battery discharged or faulty. If the cable ends are clean and tight on the battery posts, turn the key to the On position and switch on the headlights or windshield wipers. If they won't run, the battery is discharged.
3   Automatic transmission not engaged in park (P) or Neutral (N).
4   Broken, loose or disconnected wires in the starting circuit. Inspect all wires and connectors at the battery, starter solenoid and ignition switch (on steering column).
5   Starter motor pinion jammed in flywheel/driveplate ring gear. Remove the starter (Chapter 5) and inspect the pinion and ring gear (Chapter 2).
6   Starter solenoid faulty (Chapter 5).
7   Starter motor faulty (Chapter 5).
8   Ignition switch faulty (Chapter 12).
9   Engine seized. Try to turn the crankshaft with a large socket and breaker bar on the pulley bolt.
10 Starter relay faulty (Chapter 4).
11 Transmission Range (TR) sensor out of adjustment or defective (Chapter 6).

2 Engine rotates but will not start

1   Fuel tank empty.
2   Battery discharged (engine rotates slowly).
3   Battery terminal connections loose or corroded.
4   Fuel not reaching fuel injectors. Check for clogged fuel filter or lines and defective fuel pump. Also make sure the tank vent lines aren't clogged (Chapter 4).
5   Low cylinder compression. Check as described in Chapter 2.
6   Water in fuel. Drain tank and fill with new fuel.
7   Defective ignition coil(s) (Chapter 5).
8   Dirty or clogged fuel injector(s) (Chapter 4).
9   Wet or damaged ignition components (Chapters 1 and 5).
10 Worn, faulty or incorrectly gapped spark plugs (Chapter 1).
11 Broken, loose or disconnected wires in the starting circuit (see previous Section).
12 Broken, loose or disconnected wires at the ignition coil or faulty coil (Chapter 5).
13 Timing chain failure or wear affecting valve timing (Chapter 2).
14 Fuel injection or engine control systems failure (Chapters 4 and 6).
15 Defective MAF sensor (Chapter 6)

3 Starter motor operates without turning engine

1   Starter pinion sticking. Remove the starter (Chapter 5) and inspect.
2   Starter pinion or flywheel/driveplate teeth worn or broken. Remove the inspection cover and inspect.

4 Engine hard to start when cold

1   Battery discharged or low. Check as described in Chapter 1.
2   Fuel not reaching the fuel injectors. Check the fuel filter, lines and fuel pump (Chapters 1 and 4).
3   Defective spark plugs (Chapter 1).
4   Defective engine coolant temperature sensor (Chapter 6).
5   Fuel injection or engine control systems malfunction (Chapters 4 and 6).

5 Engine hard to start when hot

1   Air filter dirty (Chapter 1).
2   Fuel not reaching the fuel injection (see Section 4). Check for a vapor lock situation, brought about by clogged fuel tank vent lines.
3   Bad engine ground connection.
4   Fuel injection or engine control systems malfunction (Chapters 4 and 6).

6 Starter motor noisy or engages roughly

1   Pinion or driveplate teeth worn or broken. Remove the inspection cover on the left side of the engine and inspect.
2   Starter motor mounting bolts loose or missing.

7 Engine starts but stops immediately

1   Loose or damaged wire harness connections at coil or alternator.
2   Intake manifold vacuum leaks. Make sure all mounting bolts/nuts are tight and all vacuum hoses connected to the manifold are attached properly and in good condition.
3   Insufficient fuel pressure (see Chapter 4).
4   Fuel injection or engine control systems malfunction (Chapters 4 and 6).

8 Engine 'lopes' while idling or idles erratically

1 Vacuum leaks. Check mounting bolts at the intake manifold for tightness. Make sure that all vacuum hoses are connected and in good condition. Use a stethoscope or a length of fuel hose held against your ear to listen for vacuum leaks while the engine is running. A hissing sound will be heard. A soapy water solution will also detect leaks. Check the intake manifold gasket surfaces.
2 Leaking EGR valve or plugged PCV valve (see Chapter 6).
3 Air filter clogged (Chapter 1).
4 Fuel pump not delivering sufficient fuel (Chapter 4).
5 Leaking head gasket. Perform a cylinder compression check (Chapter 2).
6 Timing chain(s) worn (Chapter 2).
7 Camshaft lobes worn (Chapter 2).
8 Valves burned or otherwise leaking (Chapter 2).
9 Ignition system not operating properly (Chapters 1 and 5).
10 Fuel injection or engine control systems malfunction (Chapters 4 and 6).

9 Engine misses at idle speed

1 Spark plugs faulty or not gapped properly (Chapter 1).
2 Faulty spark plug wires (Chapter 1).
3 Short circuits in ignition, coil or spark plug wires.
4 Sticking or faulty emissions systems (see Chapter 6).
5 Clogged fuel filter and/or foreign matter in fuel.
6 Vacuum leaks at intake manifold or hose connections. Check as described in Section 8.
7 Low or uneven cylinder compression. Check as described in Chapter 2.
8 Fuel injection or engine control systems malfunction (Chapters 4 and 6).

10 Excessively high idle speed

1 Sticking throttle linkage (Chapter 4).
2 Vacuum leaks at intake manifold or hose connections. Check as described in Section 8.
3 Fuel injection or engine control systems malfunction (Chapters 4 and 6).

11 Battery will not hold a charge

1 Alternator drivebelt defective or not adjusted properly (Chapter 1).
2 Battery cables loose or corroded (Chapter 1).
3 Alternator not charging properly (Chapter 5).
4 Loose, broken or faulty wires in the charging circuit (Chapter 5).
5 Short circuit causing a continuous drain on the battery.
6 Battery defective internally.

12 Alternator light stays on

1 Fault in alternator or charging circuit (Chapter 5).
2 Alternator drivebelt defective or not properly adjusted (Chapter 1).

13 Alternator light fails to come on when key is turned on

1 Faulty bulb (Chapter 12).
2 Defective alternator (Chapter 5).
3 Fault in the printed circuit, dash wiring or bulb holder (Chapter 12).

14 Engine misses throughout driving speed range

1 Fuel filter clogged and/or impurities in the fuel system.
2 Faulty or incorrectly gapped spark plugs (Chapter 1).
3 Defective spark plug wires (Chapter 1).
4 Emissions system components faulty (Chapter 6).
5 Low or uneven cylinder compression pressures. Check as described in Chapter 2.
6 Weak or faulty ignition coil(s) (Chapter 5).
7 Weak or faulty ignition system (Chapter 5).
8 Vacuum leaks at intake manifold or vacuum hoses (see Section 8).
9 Dirty or clogged fuel injector(s) (Chapter 4).
10 Leaky EGR valve (Chapter 6).
11 Fuel injection or engine control systems malfunction (Chapters 4 and 6).

15 Hesitation or stumble during acceleration

1 Ignition system not operating properly (Chapter 5).
2 Dirty or clogged fuel injector(s) (Chapter 4).
3 Low fuel pressure. Check for proper operation of the fuel pump and for restrictions in the fuel filter and lines (Chapter 4).
4 Fuel injection or engine control systems malfunction (Chapters 4 and 6).

16 Engine stalls

1 Fuel filter clogged and/or water and impurities in the fuel system (Chapter 1).
2 Emissions system components faulty (Chapter 6).
3 Faulty or incorrectly gapped spark plugs (Chapter 1).
4 Vacuum leak at the intake manifold or vacuum hoses. Check as described in Section 8.
5 Fuel injection or engine control systems malfunction (Chapters 4 and 6).

17 Engine lacks power

1 Faulty or incorrectly gapped spark plugs (Chapter 1).
2 Air filter dirty (Chapter 1).
3 Faulty ignition coil(s) (Chapter 5).
4 Brakes binding (Chapters 1 and 9).
5 Automatic transmission fluid level incorrect, causing slippage (Chapter 1).
6 Fuel filter clogged and/or impurities in the fuel system (Chapter 4).
7 EGR system not functioning properly (Chapter 6).
8 Use of sub-standard fuel. Fill tank with proper octane fuel.
9 Low or uneven cylinder compression pressures. Check as described in Chapter 2.

10 Vacuum leak at intake manifold or vacuum hoses (check as described in Section 8).
11 Dirty or clogged fuel injector(s) (Chapters 1 and 4).
12 Fuel injection or engine control systems malfunction (Chapters 4 and 6).
13 Restricted exhaust system (Chapter 4).

18 Engine backfires

1 EGR system not functioning properly (Chapter 6).
2 Vacuum leak (refer to Section 8).
3 Damaged valve springs or sticking valves (Chapter 2).
4 Vacuum leak at the intake manifold or vacuum hoses (see Section 8).

19 Engine surges while holding accelerator steady

1 Vacuum leak at the intake manifold or vacuum hoses (see Section 8).
2 Restricted air filter (Chapter 1).
3 Fuel pump or pressure regulator defective (Chapter 4).
4 Fuel injection or engine control systems malfunction (Chapters 4 and 6).

20 Pinging or knocking engine sounds when engine is under load

1 Incorrect grade of fuel. Fill tank with fuel of the proper octane rating.
2 Carbon build-up in combustion chambers. Remove cylinder head(s) and clean combustion chambers (Chapter 2).
3 Incorrect spark plugs (Chapter 1).
4 Fuel injection or engine control systems malfunction (Chapters 4 and 6).
5 Restricted exhaust system (Chapter 4).

21 Engine diesels (continues to run) after being turned off

1 Incorrect spark plug heat range (Chapter 1).
2 Vacuum leak at the intake manifold or vacuum hoses (see Section 8).
3 Carbon build-up in combustion chambers. Remove the cylinder head(s) and clean the combustion chambers (Chapter 2).
4 Valves sticking (Chapter 2).
5 EGR system not operating properly (Chapter 6).
6 Fuel injection or engine control systems malfunction (Chapters 4 and 6).
7 Check for causes of overheating (Section 27).

22 Low oil pressure

1 Improper grade of oil.
2 Oil pump worn or damaged (Chapter 2).
3 Engine overheating (refer to Section 27).
4 Clogged oil filter (Chapter 1).
5 Clogged oil strainer (Chapter 2).
6 Oil pressure gauge not working properly (Chapter 2)

23 Excessive oil consumption

1 Loose oil drain plug.
2 Loose bolts or damaged oil pan gasket (Chapter 2).
3 Loose bolts or damaged front cover gasket (Chapter 2).
4 Front or rear crankshaft oil seal leaking (Chapter 2).
5 Loose bolts or damaged valve cover gasket (Chapter 2).
6 Loose oil filter (Chapter 1).
7 Loose or damaged oil pressure switch (Chapter 2).
8 Pistons and cylinders excessively worn (Chapter 2).
9 Piston rings not installed correctly on pistons (Chapter 2).
10 Worn or damaged piston rings (Chapter 2).
11 Intake and/or exhaust valve oil seals worn or damaged (Chapter 2).
12 Worn valve stems or guides.
13 Worn or damaged valves/guides (Chapter 2).
14 Faulty or incorrect PCV valve allowing too much crankcase airflow.

24 Excessive fuel consumption

1 Dirty or clogged air filter element (Chapter 1).
2 Low tire pressure or incorrect tire size (Chapter 10).
3 Inspect for binding brakes.
4 Fuel leakage. Check all connections, lines and components in the fuel system (Chapter 4).
5 Dirty or clogged fuel injectors (Chapter 4).
6 Fuel injection or engine control systems malfunction (Chapters 4 and 6).
7 Thermostat stuck open or not installed.
8 Improperly operating transmission.

25 Fuel odor

1 Fuel leakage. Check all connections, lines and components in the fuel system (Chapter 4).
2 Fuel tank overfilled. Fill only to automatic shut-off.
3 Charcoal canister filter in Evaporative Emissions Control system clogged (Chapter 1).
4 Vapor leaks from Evaporative Emissions Control system lines (Chapter 6).

26 Miscellaneous engine noises

1 A strong dull noise that becomes more rapid as the engine accelerates indicates worn or damaged crankshaft bearings or an unevenly worn crankshaft. To pinpoint the trouble spot, disconnect the electrical connector from one coil at a time and crank the engine over. If the noise stops, the cylinder with the removed plug wire or disconnected coil indicates the problem area. Replace the bearing and/or service or replace the crankshaft (Chapter 2).

2 A similar (yet slightly higher pitched) noise to the crankshaft knocking described in the previous paragraph, that becomes more rapid as the engine accelerates, indicates worn or damaged connecting rod bearings (Chapter 2). The procedure for locating the problem cylinder is the same as described in Paragraph 1.

3 An overlapping metallic noise that increases in intensity as the engine speed increases, yet diminishes as the engine warms up indicates abnormal piston and cylinder wear (Chapter 2). To locate the problem cylinder, use the procedure described in Paragraph 1.

4   A rapid clicking noise that becomes faster as the engine accelerates indicates a worn piston pin or piston pin hole. This sound will happen each time the piston hits the highest and lowest points in the stroke (Chapter 2). The procedure for locating the problem piston is described in Paragraph 1.

5   A metallic clicking noise coming from the water pump indicates worn or damaged water pump bearings or pump. Replace the water pump with a new one (Chapter 3).

6   A rapid tapping sound or clicking sound that becomes faster as the engine speed increases indicates "valve tapping." This can be identified by holding one end of a section of hose to your ear and placing the other end at different spots along the valve cover. The point where the sound is loudest indicates the problem valve. If the pushrod and rocker arm components are in good shape, you likely have a collapsed valve lifter. Changing the engine oil and adding a high viscosity oil treatment will sometimes cure a stuck lifter problem. If the problem persists, the lifters, pushrods and rocker arms must be removed for inspection (see Chapter 2).

7   A steady metallic rattling or rapping sound coming from the area of the timing chain cover indicates a worn, damaged or out-of-adjustment timing chain. Service or replace the chain and related components (Chapter 2).

COOLING SYSTEM

27   Overheating

1   Insufficient coolant in system (Chapter 1).
2   Drivebelt defective or not adjusted properly (Chapter 1).
3   Radiator core blocked or dirty and restricted (Chapter 3).
4   Thermostat faulty (Chapter 3).
5   Cooling fan not functioning properly (Chapter 3).
6   Expansion tank cap not maintaining proper pressure. Have cap pressure tested by gas station or repair shop.
7   Defective water pump (Chapter 3).
8   Improper grade of engine oil.
9   Inaccurate temperature gauge (Chapter 12).

28   Overcooling

1   Thermostat faulty (Chapter 3).
2   Inaccurate temperature gauge (Chapter 12).

29   External coolant leakage

1   Deteriorated or damaged hoses. Loose clamps at hose connections (Chapter 1).
2   Water pump seals defective. If this is the case, water will drip from the weep hole in the water pump body (Chapter 3).
3   Leakage from radiator core or header tank. This will require the radiator to be professionally repaired (see Chapter 3 for removal procedures).
4   Leakage from the expansion tank or cap.
5   Engine drain plugs or water jacket freeze plugs leaking (see Chapters 1 and 2).
6   Leak from coolant temperature switch (Chapter 3).
7   Leak from damaged gaskets or small cracks (Chapter 2).

30   Internal coolant leakage

➡**Note: Internal coolant leaks can usually be detected by examining the oil. Check the dipstick and the underside of the engine oil filler cap for water deposits and an oil consistency like that of a milkshake.**

1   Leaking cylinder head gasket. Have the system pressure tested or remove the cylinder head (Chapter 2) and inspect.
2   Cracked cylinder bore or cylinder head. Dismantle engine and inspect (Chapter 2).

31   Abnormal coolant loss

1   Overfilled cooling system (Chapter 1).
2   Coolant boiling away due to overheating (see causes in Section 27).
3   Internal or external leakage (see Sections 29 and 30).
4   Faulty expansion tank cap. Have the cap pressure tested.
5   Cooling system being pressurized by engine compression. This could be due to a cracked head or block or leaking head gasket(s). Have the system tested for the presence of combustion gas in the coolant at a shop. (Combustion leak detectors are also available at some auto parts stores.)

32   Poor coolant circulation

1   Inoperative water pump. A quick test is to pinch the top radiator hose closed with your hand while the engine is idling, then release it. You should feel a surge of coolant if the pump is working properly (Chapter 3).
2   Restriction in cooling system. Drain, flush and refill the system (Chapter 1). If necessary, remove the radiator (Chapter 3) and have it reverse flushed or professionally cleaned.
3   Loose water pump drivebelt (Chapter 1).
4   Thermostat sticking (Chapter 3).
5   Insufficient coolant (Chapter 1).

33   Corrosion

1   Excessive impurities in the water. Soft, clean water is recommended. Distilled or rainwater is satisfactory.
2   Insufficient antifreeze solution (refer to Chapter 1 for the proper ratio of water to antifreeze).
3   Infrequent flushing and draining of system. Regular flushing of the cooling system should be carried out at the specified intervals as described in (Chapter 1).

CLUTCH

➡**Note: All clutch service information is located in Chapter 8, unless otherwise noted.**

34   Fails to release (pedal pressed to the floor - shift lever does not move freely in and out of Reverse)

1   Clutch plate warped, distorted or otherwise damaged.
2   Diaphragm spring fatigued. Remove clutch cover/pressure plate assembly and inspect.

3   Insufficient pedal stroke. Check and adjust as necessary.
4   Lack of grease on pilot bushing.

35   Clutch slips (engine speed increases with no increase in vehicle speed)

1   Worn or oil soaked clutch plate.
2   Clutch plate not broken in. It may take 30 or 40 normal starts for a new clutch to seat.
3   Air in clutch hydraulic release system. Bleed system and check for leaks.
4   Defective clutch master or release cylinder.

36   Grabbing (chattering) as clutch is engaged

1   Oil on clutch plate. Remove and inspect. Repair any leaks.
2   Worn or loose engine or transmission mounts. They may move slightly when clutch is released. Inspect mounts and bolts.
3   Worn splines on transmission input shaft. Remove clutch components and inspect.
4   Warped pressure plate or flywheel. Remove clutch components and inspect.
5   Diaphragm spring fatigued. Remove clutch cover/pressure plate assembly and inspect.
6   Clutch linings hardened or warped.
7   Clutch lining rivets loose.

37   Squeal or rumble with clutch engaged (pedal released)

1   Improper pedal adjustment. Adjust pedal free play.
2   Release bearing binding on transmission shaft. Remove clutch components and check bearing. Remove any burrs or nicks, clean and relubricate before reinstallation.
3   Clutch plate cracked.
4   Fatigued clutch plate torsion springs. Replace clutch plate.

38   Squeal or rumble with clutch disengaged (pedal depressed)

1   Worn or damaged release bearing.
2   Worn or broken pressure plate diaphragm fingers.
3   Defective pilot bearing.

39   Clutch pedal stays on floor when disengaged

Defective release system.

MANUAL TRANSMISSION

➡**Note: All manual transmission service information is located in Chapter 7A, unless otherwise noted.**

40   Noisy in Neutral with engine running

1   Input shaft bearing worn.

2   Damaged main drive gear bearing.
3   Insufficient transmission oil (Chapter 1).
4   Transmission oil in poor condition. Drain and fill with proper grade oil. Check old oil for water and debris (Chapter 1).

41   Noisy in all gears

1   Any of the above causes, and/or:
2   Worn or damaged output gear bearings or shaft.

42   Noisy in one particular gear

1   Worn, damaged or chipped gear teeth.
2   Worn or damaged synchronizer.

43   Slips out of gear

1   Shift linkage binding.
2   Broken or loose input gear bearing retainer.
3   Worn linkage.
4   Damaged or worn check balls, fork rod ball grooves or check springs.
5   Worn mainshaft or countershaft bearings.
6   Excessive gear end play.
7   Worn synchronizers.
8   Chipped or worn gear teeth.

44   Oil leaks

1   Excessive amount of lubricant in transmission (see Chapter 1 for correct checking procedures). Drain lubricant as required.
2   Oil seal damaged.
3   To pinpoint a leak, first remove all built-up dirt and grime from the transmission. Degreasing agents and/or steam cleaning will achieve this. With the underside clean, drive the vehicle at low speeds so the air flow will not blow the leak far from its source. Raise the vehicle and determine where the leak is located.

45   Difficulty engaging gears

1   Clutch not releasing completely.
2   Insufficient transmission oil (Chapter 1).
3   Transmission oil in poor condition. Drain and fill with proper grade oil. Check oil for water and debris (Chapter 1).
4   Damaged shift fork.
5   Worn or damaged synchronizer.

46   Noise occurs while shifting gears

1   Check for proper operation of the clutch (Chapter 8).
2   Faulty synchronizer assemblies.

AUTOMATIC TRANSMISSION

➡**Note: Due to the complexity of the automatic transmission, it's difficult for the home mechanic to properly diagnose and service. For problems other than the following, the vehicle should be taken to a reputable mechanic.**

47   Fluid leakage

1   Automatic transmission fluid is a deep red color, and fluid leaks should not be confused with engine oil which can easily be blown by air flow to the transmission.

2   To pinpoint a leak, first remove all built-up dirt and grime from the transmission. Degreasing agents and/or steam cleaning will achieve this. With the underside clean, drive the vehicle at low speeds so the air flow will not blow the leak far from its source. Raise the vehicle and determine where the leak is located. Common areas of leakage are:

   a) **Fluid pan:** *tighten mounting bolts and/or replace pan gasket as necessary (Chapter 1).*
   b) **Rear extension:** *tighten bolts and/or replace oil seal as necessary.*
   c) **Filler pipe:** *replace the rubber oil seal where pipe enters transmission case.*
   d) **Transmission oil lines:** *tighten fittings where lines enter transmission case and/or replace lines.*
   e) **Vent pipe:** *transmission overfilled and/or water in fluid (see checking procedures, Chapter 1).*
   f) **Vehicle speed sensor:** *replace the O-ring where speed sensor enters transmission case.*

48   General shift mechanism problems

Chapter 7 deals with checking and adjusting the shift linkage on automatic transmissions. Common problems which may be caused by out of adjustment linkage are:

   a) Engine starting in gears other than P (park) or N (Neutral).
   b) Indicator pointing to a gear other than the one actually engaged.
   c) Vehicle moves with transmission in P (Park) position.

49   Transmission will not downshift with the accelerator pedal pressed to the floor

Since these transmissions are electronically controlled, check for any diagnostic trouble codes stored in the PCM. The actual repair will most likely have to be performed by a qualified repair shop with the proper equipment.

50   Engine will start in gears other than Park or Neutral

Chapter 7 deals with adjusting the Neutral start switch installed on automatic transmissions.

51   Transmission slips, shifts rough, is noisy or has no drive in forward or Reverse gears

1   There are many probable causes for the above problems, but the home mechanic should concern himself only with one possibility: fluid level.

2   Before taking the vehicle to a shop, check the fluid level and

condition as described in Chapter 1. Add fluid, if necessary, or change the fluid and filter if needed. If problems persist, have a professional diagnose the transmission.

3   Transmission fluid break down after 30,000 miles.

DRIVESHAFT

➡**Note: Refer to Chapter 8, unless otherwise specified, for service information.**

52   Leaks at front of driveshaft

Defective transmission or transfer case seal. See Chapter 7 for replacement procedure. As this is done, check the splined yoke for burrs or roughness that could damage the new seal. Remove burrs with a fine file or whetstone.

53   Knock or clunk when transmission is under initial load (just after transmission is put into gear)

1   Loose or disconnected rear suspension components. Check all mounting bolts and bushings (Chapters 7 and 10).

2   Loose driveshaft bolts. Inspect all bolts and nuts and tighten them securely.

3   Worn or damaged universal joint bearings (Chapter 8).

4   Worn sleeve yoke and mainshaft spline.

54   Metallic grating sound consistent with vehicle speed

Pronounced wear in the universal joint bearings. Replace U-joints or driveshaft, as necessary.

55   Vibration

➡**Note: Before blaming the driveshaft, make sure the tires are perfectly balanced and perform the following test.**

1   Install a tachometer inside the vehicle to monitor engine speed as the vehicle is driven. Drive the vehicle and note the engine speed at which the vibration (roughness) is most pronounced. Now shift the transmission to a different gear and bring the engine speed to the same point.

2   If the vibration occurs at the same engine speed (rpm) regardless of which gear the transmission is in, the driveshaft is NOT at fault since the driveshaft speed varies.

3   If the vibration decreases or is eliminated when the transmission is in a different gear at the same engine speed, refer to the following probable causes:

   a) Bent or dented driveshaft. Inspect and replace as necessary.
   b) Undercoating or built-up dirt, etc. on the driveshaft. Clean the shaft thoroughly.
   c) Worn universal joint bearings. Replace the U-joints or driveshaft as necessary.
   d) Driveshaft and/or companion flange out of balance. Check for missing weights on the shaft. Remove driveshaft and reinstall 180-degrees from original position, then recheck. Have the driveshaft balanced if problem persists.
   e) Loose driveshaft mounting bolts/nuts.
   f) Worn transmission rear bushing (Chapter 7).

56 Scraping noise

Make sure there is nothing, such as an exhaust heat shield, rubbing on the driveshaft.

Axle(s) and differential

➡Note: For differential servicing information, refer to Chapter 8, unless otherwise specified.

57 Noise - same when in drive as when vehicle is coasting

1 Road noise. No corrective action available.
2 Tire noise. Inspect tires and check tire pressures (Chapter 1).
3 Front wheel bearings loose, worn or damaged (Chapter 1).
4 Insufficient differential oil (Chapter 1).
5 Defective differential.

58 Knocking sound when starting or shifting gears

Defective or incorrectly adjusted differential.

59 Noise when turning

Defective differential.

60 Vibration

See probable causes under *Driveshaft*. Proceed under the guidelines listed for the driveshaft. If the problem persists, check the rear wheel bearings by raising the rear of the vehicle and spinning the wheels by hand. Listen for evidence of rough (noisy) bearings. Remove and inspect (Chapter 8).

61 Oil leaks

1 Pinion oil seal damaged (Chapter 8).
2 Axleshaft oil seals damaged (Chapter 8).
3 Differential cover leaking. Tighten mounting bolts or replace the gasket as required.
4 Loose filler plug on differential (Chapter 1).
5 Clogged or damaged breather on differential.

BRAKES

➡Note: Before assuming a brake problem exists, make sure the tires are in good condition and inflated properly, the front end alignment is correct and the vehicle is not loaded with weight in an unequal manner. All service procedures for the brakes are included in Chapter 9, unless otherwise noted.

62 Vehicle pulls to one side during braking

1 Defective, damaged or contaminated brake pad on one side. Inspect as described in Chapter 1. Refer to Chapter 9 if replacement is required.

2 Excessive wear of brake pad material or disc on one side. Inspect and repair as necessary.
3 Loose or disconnected front suspension components. Inspect and tighten all bolts securely (Chapters 1 and 10).
4 Defective front brake caliper assembly. Remove caliper and inspect for stuck piston or damage.
5 Scored or out of round disc.
6 Loose brake caliper mounting bolts.

63 Noise (high-pitched squeal or scraping sound)

1 Brake pads worn out. Replace pads with new ones immediately!
2 Glazed or contaminated pads.
3 Dirty or scored disc.
4 Bent support plate.

64 Excessive brake pedal travel

1 Partial brake system failure. Inspect entire system (Chapter 1) and correct as required.
2 Insufficient fluid in master cylinder. Check (Chapter 1) and add fluid - bleed system if necessary.
3 Air in system. Bleed system.
4 Defective master cylinder.

65 Brake pedal feels spongy when depressed

1 Air in brake lines. Bleed the brake system.
2 Deteriorated rubber brake hoses. Inspect all system hoses and lines. Replace parts as necessary.
3 Master cylinder mounting nuts loose. Inspect master cylinder bolts (nuts) and tighten them securely.
4 Master cylinder faulty.
5 Incorrect brake pad clearance.
6 Clogged reservoir cap vent hole.
7 Deformed rubber brake lines.
8 Soft or swollen caliper seals.
9 Poor quality brake fluid. Bleed entire system and fill with new approved fluid.

66 Excessive effort required to stop vehicle

1 Power brake booster not operating properly.
2 Excessively worn brake pads. Check and replace if necessary.
3 One or more caliper pistons seized or sticking. Inspect and rebuild as required.
4 Brake pads contaminated with oil or grease. Inspect and replace as required.
5 Worn or damaged master cylinder or caliper assemblies. Check particularly for frozen pistons.

67 Pedal travels to the floor with little resistance

Little or no fluid in the master cylinder reservoir caused by leaking caliper piston(s) or loose, damaged or disconnected brake lines. Inspect entire system and repair as necessary

68 Brake pedal pulsates during brake application

1 Wheel bearings damaged, worn or out of adjustment.
2 Caliper not sliding properly due to improper installation or obstructions. Remove and inspect.
3 Disc not within specifications. Check for excessive lateral runout and parallelism. Have the discs resurfaced or replace them with new ones. Also make sure that all discs are the same thickness.

69 Brakes drag (indicated by sluggish engine performance or wheels being very hot after driving)

1 Pushrod adjustment incorrect at the brake pedal or power booster.
2 Master cylinder piston seized in bore. Replace master cylinder.
3 Caliper piston seized in bore.
4 Parking brake assembly will not release.
5 Clogged or internally split brake lines.
6 Brake pedal height improperly adjusted.

70 Rear brakes lock up under light brake application

1 Tire pressures too high.
2 Tires excessively worn (Chapter 1).
3 Defective proportioning valve.

71 Rear brakes lock up under heavy brake application

1 Tire pressures too high.
2 Tires excessively worn (Chapter 1).
3 Front brake pads contaminated with oil, mud or water. Clean or replace the pads.
4 Front brake pads excessively worn.
5 Defective proportioning valve.

Suspension and steering

➡Note: All service procedures for the suspension and steering systems are included in Chapter 10, unless otherwise noted.

72 Vehicle pulls to one side

1 Tire pressures uneven (Chapter 1).
2 Defective tire (Chapter 1).
3 Excessive wear in suspension or steering components (Chapter 1).
4 Front end alignment incorrect.
5 Front brakes dragging. Inspect as described in Section 71.
6 Wheel bearings improperly adjusted (Chapter 1).
7 Wheel lug nuts loose.

73 Shimmy, shake or vibration

1 Tire or wheel out of balance or out of round.
2 Loose, worn or out of adjustment wheel bearings (Chapter 1).
3 Shock absorbers and/or suspension components worn or damaged (see Chapter 10).

74 Excessive pitching and/or rolling around corners or during braking

1 Defective shock absorbers. Replace as a set.
2 Sagging springs.
3 Worn or damaged stabilizer bar or bushings.

75 Wandering or general instability

1 Improper tire pressures.
2 Incorrect front end alignment.
3 Worn or damaged steering linkage or suspension components.
4 Improperly adjusted steering gear.
5 Out-of-balance wheels.
6 Loose wheel lug nuts.
7 Worn rear shock absorbers.

76 Excessively stiff steering

1 Lack of fluid in the power steering fluid reservoir, where appropriate (Chapter 1).
2 Incorrect tire pressures (Chapter 1).
3 Front end out of alignment.
4 Steering gear out of adjustment or lacking lubrication.
5 Worn or damaged steering gear.
6 Low tire pressures.
7 Worn or damaged balljoints.
8 Worn or damaged tie-rod ends.

77 Excessive play in steering

1 Worn wheel bearings (Chapter 1).
2 Excessive wear in suspension bushings (Chapter 1).
3 Steering gear worn.
4 Incorrect front end alignment.
5 Steering gear mounting bolts loose.
6 Worn or damaged tie-rod ends.

78 Lack of power assistance

1 Steering pump drivebelt faulty or ten-sioner defective (Chapter 1).
2 Fluid level low (Chapter 1).
3 Hoses or pipes restricting the flow. Inspect and replace parts as necessary.
4 Air in power steering system. Bleed system.
5 Defective power steering pump.

79 Steering wheel fails to return to straight-ahead position

1 Incorrect front end alignment.
2 Tire pressures low.
3 Worn or damaged balljoint.
4 Worn or damaged tie-rod end.
5 Lack of fluid in power steering pump.

80 Steering effort not the same in both directions

1 Leaks in steering gear.
2 Clogged fluid passage in steering gear.

81 Noisy power steering pump

1 Insufficient fluid in pump.
2 Clogged hoses or oil filter in pump.
3 Loose pulley.
4 Drivebelt faulty or tensioner defective (Chapter 1).
5 Defective pump.

82 Miscellaneous noises

1 Improper tire pressures.
2 Defective balljoint or tie-rod end.
3 Loose or worn steering gear or suspension components.
4 Defective shock absorber.
5 Defective wheel bearing.
6 Worn or damaged suspension bushings.
7 Loose wheel lug nuts.
8 Worn or damaged shock absorber mounting bushing.
9 Worn stabilizer bar bushings.
10 Incorrect rear axle endplay.
11 See also causes of noises at the rear axle and driveshaft.

83 Excessive tire wear (not specific to one area)

1 Incorrect tire pressures.
2 Tires out of balance.
3 Wheels damaged. Inspect and replace as necessary.
4 Suspension or steering components worn (Chapter 1).
5 Front end alignment incorrect.
6 Lack of proper tire rotation routine. See *Routine Maintenance Schedule*, Chapter 1.

84 Excessive tire wear on outside edge

1 Incorrect tire pressure.
2 Excessive speed in turns.
3 Front end alignment incorrect.

85 Excessive tire wear on inside edge

1 Incorrect tire pressure.
2 Front end alignment incorrect.

86 Tire tread worn in one place

1 Tires out of balance.
2 Damaged or buckled wheel. Inspect and replace if necessary.
3 Defective tire.

Section

1

TUNE-UP AND ROUTINE MAINTENANCE

1 Maintenance schedule

The following maintenance intervals are based on the assumption that the vehicle owner will be doing the maintenance or service work, as opposed to having a dealer service department do the work. These are the minimum maintenance intervals recommended by the factory for vehicles that are driven daily. If you wish to keep your vehicle in peak condition at all times, you may wish to perform some of these procedures even more often. Because frequent maintenance enhances the efficiency, performance and resale value of your car, we encourage you to do so. If you drive in dusty areas, tow a trailer, idle or drive at low speeds for extended periods or drive for short distances (less than four miles) in below freezing temperatures, shorter intervals are also recommended.

When the vehicle is new, follow the maintenance schedule to the letter, record the maintenance performed in your owner's manual and keep all receipts to protect the new vehicle warranty. In many cases the initial maintenance check is done at no cost to the owner (check with your dealer service department for more information).

Every 250 miles (400 km) or weekly, whichever comes first

Check the engine oil level (Section 4)
Check the coolant level (Section 4)
Check the windshield washer fluid level (Section 4)
Check the brake and clutch fluid levels (Section 4)
Check the power steering fluid level (Section 4)
Check the automatic transmission fluid level (Section 4)
Check the battery electrolyte level (Section 4)
Check the tires and tire pressures (Section 5)

Every 3000 miles (4800 km) or 3 months, whichever comes first

All items listed above, plus . . .
Change the engine oil and filter (Section 6)

Every 6000 miles (9600 km) or 6 months, whichever comes first

All items listed above, plus . . .
Check the seat belts (Section 7)
Inspect the windshield wiper blades (Section 8)
Check and service the battery (Section 9)
Check the engine drivebelt (Section 10)
Inspect underhood hoses (Section 11)
Check the cooling system (Section 12)
Rotate the tires (Section 13)
Check the exhaust system (Section 14)

Every 15,000 miles (24,000 km) or 12 months, whichever comes first.

All items listed above, plus . . .
Check the manual transmission lubricant level (Section 4)
Check the differential lubricant level (Section 4)
Check the transfer case lubricant level (Section 4)
Check the fuel system (Section 15)
Check the suspension, steering, and driveaxle boots (Section 16)
Check the brake system (Section 17)*
Replace the cabin air filter (Section 18)

Every 30,000 miles (48,000 km) or 24 months, whichever comes first

All items listed above, plus . . .
Change the brake fluid (Section 19)
Replace the air filter (Section 20)*
Check the evaporative emissions control system (Section 21)
Replace the spark plugs (conventional, non-platinum) (Section 22)
Service the cooling system (drain, flush and refill) (Section 23)
Change the automatic transmission fluid (Section 24)**
If noisy, check and, if necessary, adjust the valve clearances (Chapter 2A).

Every 60,000 miles (96,000 km) or 48 months, whichever comes first

Inspect the ignition coils (Section 25)
Change the manual transmission lubricant (Section 26)
Change the differential and transfer case lubricant (Section 27)**

Every 100,000 miles (160,000 km) or 60 months, whichever comes first

Replace the spark plugs (platinum type) (Section 22)
Replace the timing belt (Chapter 2, Part A)
*   This item is affected by "severe" operating conditions, as described below. If the vehicle is operated under severe conditions, perform all maintenance indicated with an asterisk (*) at half the indicated intervals. Severe conditions exist if you mainly operate the vehicle . . .
in dusty areas
towing a trailer
idling for extended periods
driving at low speeds when outside temperatures remain below freezing and most trips are less than four miles long
** Perform this procedure at half the recommended interval if operated under one or more of the following conditions:
in heavy city traffic where the outside temperature regularly reaches 90-degrees F or higher in hilly or mountainous terrain
frequent trailer towing
if the vehicle has been driven through deep water

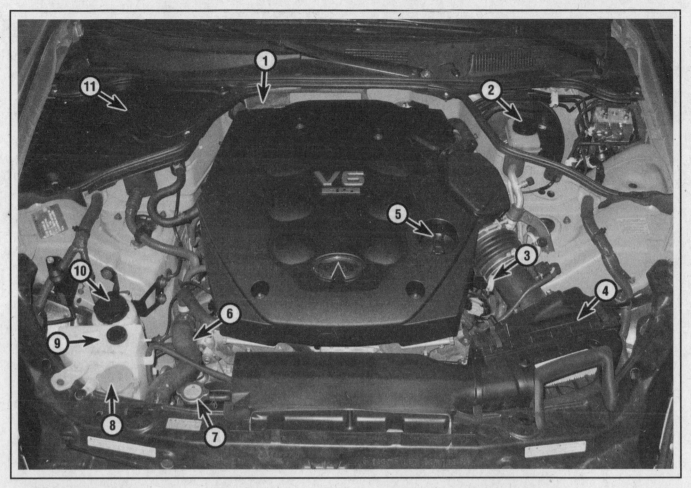

Engine compartment components

1	Automatic transmission fluid dipstick (not visible)	4	Air filter housing
2	Brake fluid reservoir	5	Engine oil filler cap
3	Engine oil dipstick	6	Upper radiator hose
		7	Radiator cap

8	Windshield washer fluid reservoir
9	Coolant reservoir
10	Power steering fluid reservoir
11	Battery compartment

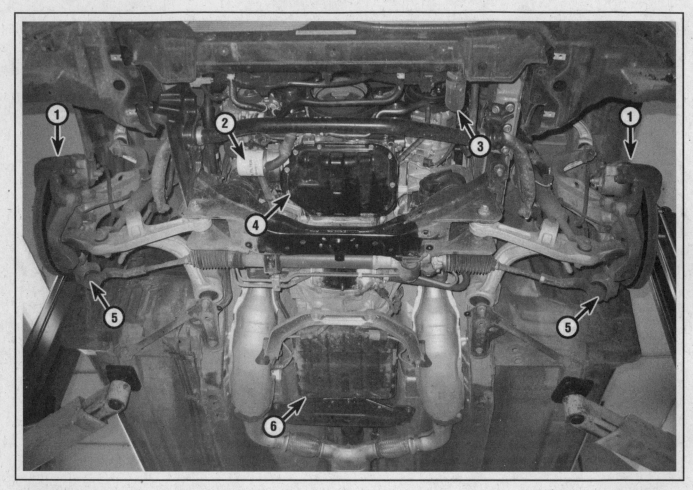

Engine compartment underside components

1	Brake calipers	3	Lower radiator hose	5	Tie-rod end
2	Engine oil filter	4	Engine oil drain plug	6	Automatic transmission drain plug

Rear underside components

1   Muffler

2   Driveaxle boots

3   Differential lubricant
    drain plug

4   Fuel tank

2 Introduction

This Chapter is designed to help the home mechanic maintain the Nissan 350Z and Infiniti G35 with the goals of maximum performance, economy, safety and reliability in mind.

Included is a master maintenance schedule, followed by procedures dealing specifically with each item on the schedule. Visual checks, adjustments, component replacement and other helpful items are included. Refer to the accompanying illustrations of the engine compartment and the underside of the vehicle for the locations of various components.

Servicing your vehicle in accordance with the mileage/time maintenance schedule and the step-by-step procedures will result in a planned maintenance program that should produce a long and reliable service life. Keep in mind that it's a comprehensive plan, so maintaining some items but not others at the specified intervals will not produce the same results.

As you service your vehicle, you will discover that many of the procedures can - and should - be grouped together because of the nature of the particular procedure you're performing or because of the close proximity of two otherwise unrelated components to one another.

For example, if the vehicle is raised for chassis lubrication, you should inspect the exhaust, suspension, steering and fuel systems while you're under the vehicle. When you're rotating the tires, it makes good sense to check the brakes since the wheels are already removed. Finally, let's suppose you have to borrow or rent a torque wrench. Even if you only need it to tighten the spark plugs, you might as well check the torque of as many critical fasteners as time allows.

The first step in this maintenance program is to prepare yourself before the actual work begins. Read through all the procedures you're planning to do, then gather up all the parts and tools needed. If it looks like you might run into problems during a particular job, seek advice from a mechanic or an experienced do-it-yourselfer.

3 Tune-up general information

The term tune-up is used in this manual to represent a combination of individual operations rather than one specific procedure that will maintain a gasoline engine in proper tune.

If, from the time the vehicle is new, the routine maintenance schedule is followed closely and frequent checks are made of fluid levels and high wear items, as suggested throughout this manual, the engine will be kept in relatively good running condition and the need for additional work will be minimized.

More likely than not, however, there may be times when the engine is running poorly due to lack of regular maintenance. This is even more likely if a used vehicle, which has not received regular and frequent maintenance checks, is purchased. In such cases, an engine tune-up will be needed outside of the regular routine maintenance intervals.

The first step in any tune-up or diagnostic procedure to help correct a poor running engine is a cylinder compression check. A compression check (see Chapter 2B) will help determine the condition of internal engine components and should be used as a guide for tune-up and repair procedures. If, for instance, the compression check indicates serious internal engine wear, a conventional tune-up won't improve the performance of the engine and would be a waste of time and money. Because of its importance, the compression check should be done by someone with the right equipment and the knowledge to use it properly.

The following procedures are those most often needed to bring a generally poor running engine back into a proper state of tune.

MINOR TUNE-UP

Check all engine related fluids (Section 4)
Clean, inspect and test the battery (Section 9)
Check the drivebelt (Section 10)
Check all underhood hoses (Section 11)
Check the cooling system (Section 12)
Check the air filter (Section 20)

MAJOR TUNE-UP

All items listed under Minor tune-up, plus . . .
Replace the air filter (Section 20)
Replace the spark plugs (Section 22)
Check the ignition system (Chapter 5)
Check the charging system (Chapter 5)

4 Fluid level checks (every 250 miles [400 km] or weekly)

➡**Note: The following are fluid level checks to be done on a 250 mile or weekly basis. Additional fluid level checks can be found in specific maintenance procedures that follow. Regardless of intervals, be alert to fluid leaks under the vehicle, which would indicate a fault to be corrected immediately.**

1   Fluids are an essential part of the lubrication, cooling, brake, clutch and windshield washer systems. Because the fluids gradually become depleted and/or contaminated during normal operation of the vehicle, they must be periodically replenished. See *Recommended lubricants and fluids* in this Chapter's Specifications before adding fluid to any of the following components.

➡**Note: The vehicle must be on level ground when fluid levels are checked.**

ENGINE OIL

🔸 **Refer to illustrations 4.2, 4.4 and 4.6**

2   The engine oil level is checked with a dipstick that extends through a hole in the left cylinder head, through the engine block and into the oil pan at the bottom of the engine (see illustration).

3   The oil level should be checked before the vehicle has been driven, or about 5 minutes after the engine has been shut off. If the oil is checked immediately after driving the vehicle, some of the oil will remain in the upper engine components, resulting in an inaccurate reading on the dipstick.

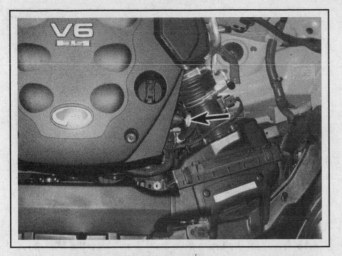

4.2 Location of the engine oil dipstick

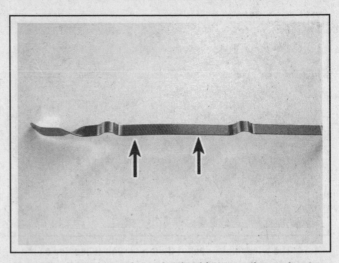

4.4 The oil level must be maintained between the marks at all times - it takes one quart of oil to raise the level from the L to the H mark

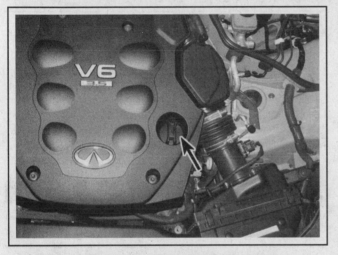

4.6 Oil filler cap location - always make sure the area around the opening is clean before removing the cap to prevent dirt from contaminating the engine

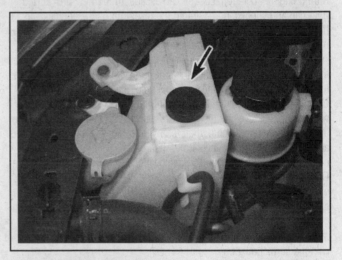

4.8 The coolant reservoir is located at the right side of the engine compartment

4   Pull the dipstick out and wipe all the oil from the end with a clean rag or paper towel. Insert the clean dipstick all the way back into the hole, then pull it out again. Note the oil at the end of the dipstick. Add oil as necessary to keep the level between the L and H marks, or within the cross-hatched zone on the dipstick (see illustration).

5   Do not overfill the engine by adding too much oil, since this may result in oil-fouled spark plugs, oil leaks or oil seal failures.

6   Oil is added to the engine after unscrewing a cap from the valve cover (see illustration). A funnel may help to reduce spills.

7   Checking the oil level is an important preventive maintenance step. A consistently low oil level indicates oil leakage through damaged seals, defective gaskets or past worn rings or valve guides. If the oil looks milky or has water droplets in it, the cylinder head gasket(s) may be blown or the head(s) or block may be cracked. The engine should be checked immediately. The condition of the oil should also be checked. Whenever you check the oil level, slide your thumb and index finger up the dipstick before wiping off the oil. If you see small dirt or metal particles clinging to the dipstick, the oil should be changed (see Section 6).

ENGINE COOLANT

▶ **Refer to illustration 4.8**

※※ **WARNING:**

Do not allow antifreeze to come in contact with your skin or painted surfaces of the vehicle. Flush contaminated areas immediately with plenty of water. Don't store new coolant or leave old coolant lying around where it's accessible to children or pets - they're attracted by its sweet smell. Ingestion of even a small amount of coolant can be fatal! Wipe up garage floor and drip pan spills immediately. Keep antifreeze containers covered and repair cooling system leaks as soon as they're noticed.

8   All models covered by this manual are equipped with a coolant recovery system. The coolant reservoir is connected by a hose to the base of the coolant filler cap (see illustration). If the coolant heats up

4.14 The windshield washer fluid reservoir is located on the right side of the engine compartment

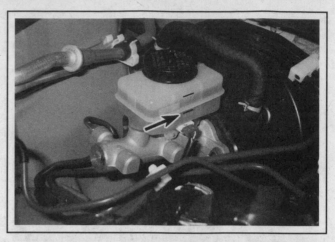

4.16 Never let the brake fluid level drop below the MIN mark

during engine operation, coolant can escape through the pressurized filler cap and connecting hose into the reservoir. As the engine cools, the coolant is automatically drawn back into the cooling system to maintain the correct level.

9 The coolant level should be checked regularly. It must be between the Full and Low lines on the tank. The level will vary with the temperature of the engine. When the engine is cold, the coolant level should be at or slightly above the Low mark on the tank. Once the engine has warmed up, the level should be at or near the Full mark. If it isn't, allow the fluid in the tank to cool, then remove the cap from the reservoir and add coolant to bring the level up to the Full line. Use only the type of coolant listed in this Chapter's Specifications or in your owner's manual. Do not use supplemental inhibitors or additives. If only a small amount of coolant is required to bring the system up to the proper level, water can be used. However, repeated additions of water will dilute the recommended antifreeze and water solution. In order to maintain the proper ratio of antifreeze and water, it is advisable to top up the coolant level with the correct mixture.

10 If the coolant level drops within a short time after replenishment, there may be a leak in the system. Inspect the radiator, hoses, radiator cap, drain plugs, air bleeder plugs and water pump. If no leak is evident, have the radiator cap pressure tested.

❋❋ WARNING:

Never remove the radiator pressure cap when the engine is running or has just been shut down, because the cooling system is hot. Escaping steam and scalding liquid could cause serious injury.

11 If it is necessary to open the radiator cap, wait until the system has cooled completely, then wrap a thick cloth around the cap and turn it to the first stop. If any steam escapes, wait until the system has cooled further, then remove the cap.

12 When checking the coolant level, always note its condition. It should be relatively clear. If it is brown or rust colored, the system should be drained, flushed and refilled. Even if the coolant appears to be normal, the corrosion inhibitors wear out with use, so it must be replaced at the specified intervals.

13 Do not allow antifreeze to come in contact with your skin or painted surfaces of the vehicle. Flush contacted areas immediately with plenty of water.

WINDSHIELD WASHER FLUID

▶ **Refer to illustration 4.14**

14 Fluid for the windshield washer system is located in a plastic reservoir on the right side of the engine compartment (see illustration).

15 In milder climates, plain water can be used in the reservoir, but it should be kept no more than 2/3 full to allow for expansion if the water freezes. In colder climates, use windshield washer system antifreeze, available at any auto parts store, to lower the freezing point of the fluid. Mix the antifreeze with water in accordance with the manufacturer's directions on the container.

❋❋ CAUTION:

Don't use cooling system antifreeze - it will damage the vehicle's paint.

➡Note: **To help prevent icing in cold weather, warm the windshield with the defroster before using the washer.**

BRAKE AND CLUTCH FLUID

▶ **Refer to illustration 4.16**

16 The brake master cylinder is mounted on the front of the power brake booster, on the left (driver's) side of the engine compartment firewall (see illustration). The clutch master cylinder used on manual transmission models is mounted next to the brake master cylinder.

17 The translucent plastic reservoir allows the fluid inside to be checked without removing the cap. Be sure to wipe the area around either reservoir cap with a clean rag to prevent contamination of the brake and/or clutch system before removing the cap. Keep the fluid level at or near the MAX mark.

18 When adding fluid, pour it carefully into the reservoir to avoid spilling it on surrounding painted surfaces. Be sure the specified fluid is used, since mixing different types of brake fluid can cause damage to the system. See *Recommended lubricants and fluids* in this Chapter's Specifications or your owner's manual.

4.27 The power steering fluid reservoir has marks on it so the fluid can be checked hot or cold

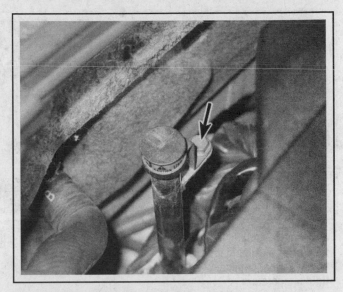

4.32 Remove the bolt securing the automatic transmission dipstick to its bracket, then pull up the dipstick

✳✳ WARNING:

Brake fluid can harm your eyes and damage painted surfaces, so use extreme caution when handling or pouring it. Do not use brake fluid that has been standing open or is more than one year old. Brake fluid absorbs moisture from the air. Moisture in the system can cause a dangerous loss of brake performance.

19 At this time, the fluid and master cylinder can be inspected for contamination. The system should be drained and refilled if deposits, dirt particles or water droplets are seen in the fluid.

20 After filling the reservoir to the proper level, make sure the cap is on tight to prevent fluid leakage.

21 The brake fluid level in the master cylinder will drop slightly as the pads at the front wheels wear down during normal operation. If the master cylinder requires repeated additions to keep it at the proper level, it's an indication of leakage in the brake system, which should be corrected immediately. Check all brake lines and connections (see Section 17 for more information).

22 If, upon checking the master cylinder fluid level, you discover the reservoir empty or nearly empty, the brake system should be bled and thoroughly inspected (see Chapter 9).

POWER STEERING FLUID

▶ **Refer to illustration 4.27**

23 Unlike manual steering, the power steering system relies on fluid which may, over a period of time, require replenishing.

24 All models have remote power steering fluid reservoirs mounted on the right (passenger's) side of the engine compartment. All models have translucent reservoirs which allow the fluid to be checked without removing the cap.

25 For the check, the front wheels should be pointed straight ahead and the engine should be off.

26 Use a clean rag to wipe off the reservoir cap and the area around the cap. This will help prevent any foreign matter from entering the reservoir during the check.

27 Feel the reservoir to check the temperature of the fluid. Check the level of the fluid on the side of the reservoir (see illustration). The level should be at the HOT or MAX mark if the reservoir was hot to the touch. If the reservoir felt cool, the level should be at the COLD mark (but not below the MIN level).

28 If additional fluid is required, pour the specified type directly into the reservoir, using a funnel to prevent spills.

29 If the reservoir requires frequent fluid additions, all power steering hoses, hose connections, steering gear and the power steering pump should be carefully checked for leaks.

AUTOMATIC TRANSMISSION FLUID

▶ **Refer to illustrations 4.32 and 4.35**

30 The automatic transmission fluid level should be carefully maintained. Low fluid level can lead to slipping or loss of drive, while overfilling can cause foaming and loss of fluid.

31 With the parking brake set, start the engine, then move the shift lever through all the gear ranges, ending in Park. The fluid level must be checked with the vehicle level and the engine running at idle.

➥**Note: Incorrect fluid level readings will result if the vehicle has just been driven at high speeds for an extended period, in hot weather in city traffic, or if it has been pulling a trailer. If any of these conditions apply, wait until the fluid has cooled (about 30 minutes).**

32 With the transmission at normal operating temperature, remove the dipstick from the filler tube. The dipstick is located at the rear of the engine on the passenger's side (see illustration).

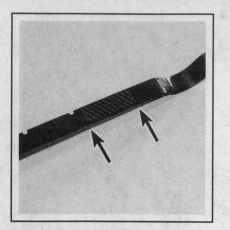

4.35 The automatic transmission fluid must be kept in the cross-hatched area, depending on the fluid temperature

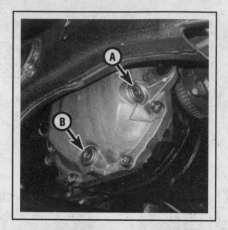

4.42 Differential filler plug (A) and drain plug (B)

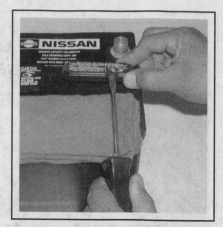

4.49 The electrolyte level can be checked on original equipment batteries; some have individual cell plugs that can be unscrewed, while others have caps which must be pried off

33 Wipe the fluid from the dipstick with a clean rag and push it back into the filler tube until the cap seats.

34 Pull the dipstick out again and note the fluid level.

35 If the fluid is cool to warm, the level should be in the cross-hatched area on the COLD side of the dipstick (see illustration). If it's hot, the level should be in the cross-hatched area on the HOT side of the dipstick. If additional fluid is required, add it directly into the tube using a funnel. It takes about one pint to raise the level from the bottom of the crosshatched area to the top with a hot transmission, so add the fluid a little at a time and keep checking the level until it's correct.

36 The condition of the fluid should also be checked along with the level. If the fluid at the end of the dipstick is a dark reddish-brown color, or if it smells burned, it should be changed. If you are in doubt about the condition of the fluid, purchase some new fluid and compare the two for color and smell.

MANUAL TRANSMISSION LUBRICANT

➡Note: It isn't necessary to check the manual transmission lubricant weekly; every 15,000 miles (24,000 km) or 12 months is sufficient (unless a leak is noticed).

37 The manual transmission has a filler plug which must be removed to check the lubricant level. Raise the vehicle and support it securely on jackstands - DO NOT crawl under a vehicle that is supported only by a jack! Be sure the vehicle is level or the check may be inaccurate.

38 Using the appropriate wrench, unscrew the plug from the transmission.

39 Use your little finger to reach inside the housing to feel the lubricant level. The level should be at or near the bottom of the plug hole. If it isn't, add the recommended lubricant through the plug hole with a syringe or squeeze bottle.

40 Install and tighten the plug. Check for leaks after the first few miles of driving.

DIFFERENTIAL LUBRICANT

▶ Refer to illustration 4.42

➡Note: It isn't necessary to check the differential lubricant weekly; every 15,000 miles (24,000 km) or 12 months is sufficient (unless a leak is noticed).

41 Raise the vehicle and support it securely on jackstands - DO NOT crawl under the vehicle when it's supported only by the jack. Be sure the vehicle is level or the check may not be accurate.

42 Remove the plug from the filler hole in the differential housing or cover (see illustration).

43 The lubricant level should be up to the bottom of the filler hole. If not, use a pump or squeeze bottle to add the recommended lubricant until it just starts to run out of the opening.

44 Install the plug in the filler hole and tighten it to the torque listed in this Chapter's Specifications.

TRANSFER CASE LUBRICANT (AWD MODELS)

➡Note: It isn't necessary to check the transfer case lubricant weekly; every 15,000 miles (24,000 km) or 12 months is sufficient (unless a leak is noticed).

45 Raise the vehicle and support it securely on jackstands - DO NOT crawl under the vehicle when it's supported only by the jack. Be sure the vehicle is level or the check may not be accurate

46 Remove the plug from the filler hole on the rear of the transfer case housing.

47 The lubricant level should be up to the bottom of the filler hole. If not, use a pump or squeeze bottle to add the recommended lubricant until it just starts to run out of the opening.

48 Install the plug in the filler hole and tighten it to the torque listed in this Chapter's Specifications.

BATTERY ELECTROLYTE

Refer to illustration 4.49

49 On models not equipped with a sealed battery, check the electrolyte level of all six battery cells. On models with a translucent battery case, minimum and maximum level marks are present on the side of the case; keep the electrolyte level at the MAX mark. On models with an opaque case, carefully remove the cell caps to check the level or add water. Some batteries have six individual cell plugs that can be unscrewed, but others have two cell caps that must be carefully pried off (see illustration).

50 If the level is low, add distilled water until the level is up to the MAX mark (translucent batteries) or up to the bottom of the split-ring indicators (opaque batteries).

5   Tire and tire pressure checks (every 250 [400 km] miles or weekly)

◆ **Refer to illustrations 5.2, 5.3, 5.4a, 5.4b and 5.8**

1   Periodic inspection of the tires may spare you the inconvenience of being stranded with a flat tire. It can also provide you with vital information regarding possible problems in the steering and suspension systems before major damage occurs.

2   The original tires on this vehicle are equipped with 1/2-inch wide wear bands that will appear when tread depth reaches 1/16-inch, at which point the tires can be considered worn out. Tread wear can be monitored with a simple, inexpensive device known as a tread depth indicator (see illustration).

3   Note any abnormal tread wear (see illustration). Tread pattern irregularities such as cupping, flat spots and more wear on one side than the other are indications of front end alignment and/or balance problems. If any of these conditions are noted, take the vehicle to a tire shop or service station to correct the problem.

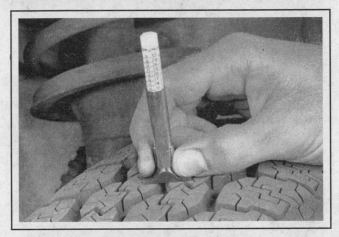

5.2 Use a tire tread depth indicator to monitor tire wear - they are available at auto parts stores and service stations and cost very little

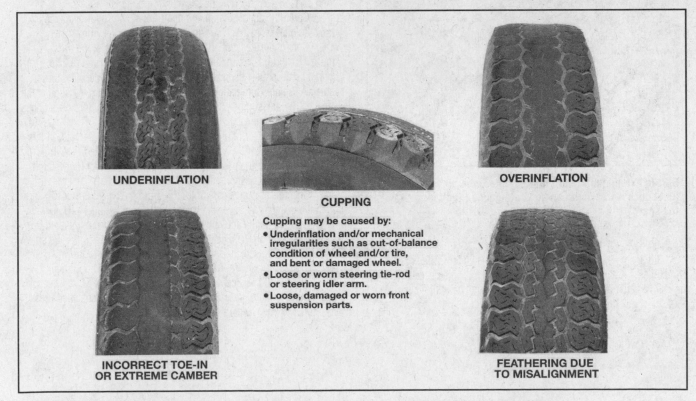

UNDERINFLATION

CUPPING

OVERINFLATION

Cupping may be caused by:
- **Underinflation and/or mechanical irregularities such as out-of-balance condition of wheel and/or tire, and bent or damaged wheel.**
- **Loose or worn steering tie-rod or steering idler arm.**
- **Loose, damaged or worn front suspension parts.**

INCORRECT TOE-IN OR EXTREME CAMBER

FEATHERING DUE TO MISALIGNMENT

5.3 This chart will help you determine the condition of the tires and the probable cause(s) of abnormal wear

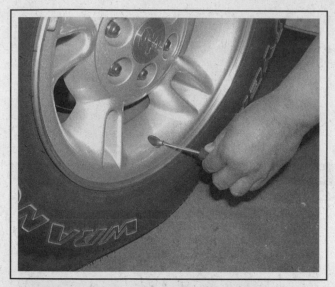

5.4a If a tire loses air on a steady basis, check the valve stem core first to make sure it's snug (special inexpensive wrenches are commonly available at auto parts stores)

5.4b If the valve stem core is tight, raise the corner of the vehicle with the low tire and spray a soapy water solution onto the tread as the tire is turned slowly - leaks will cause small bubbles to appear

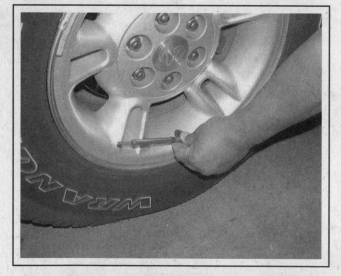

5.8 To extend the life of the tires, check the air pressure at least once a week with an accurate gauge (don't forget the spare!)

4   Look closely for cuts, punctures and embedded nails or tacks. Sometimes a tire will hold air pressure for a short time or leak down very slowly after a nail has embedded itself in the tread. If a slow leak persists, check the valve stem core to make sure it's tight (see illustra-

tion). Examine the tread for an object that may have embedded itself in the tire or for a plug that may have begun to leak (radial tire punctures are repaired with a plug that's installed in a puncture). If a puncture is suspected, it can be easily verified by spraying a solution of soapy water onto the puncture area (see illustration). The soapy solution will bubble if there's a leak. Unless the puncture is unusually large, a tire shop or service station can usually repair the tire.

5   Carefully inspect the inner sidewall of each tire for evidence of brake fluid leakage. If you see any, inspect the brakes immediately.

6   Correct air pressure adds miles to the lifespan of the tires, improves mileage and enhances overall ride quality. Tire pressure cannot be accurately estimated by looking at a tire, especially if it's a radial. A tire pressure gauge is essential. Keep an accurate gauge in the vehicle. The pressure gauges attached to the nozzles of air hoses at gas stations are often inaccurate.

7   Always check tire pressure when the tires are cold. Cold, in this case, means the vehicle has not been driven over a mile in the three hours preceding a tire pressure check. A pressure rise of four to eight pounds is not uncommon once the tires are warm.

8   Unscrew the valve cap protruding from the wheel or hubcap and push the gauge firmly onto the valve stem (see illustration). Note the reading on the gauge and compare the figure to the recommended tire pressure shown on the placard on the driver's side door pillar. Be sure to reinstall the valve cap to keep dirt and moisture out of the valve stem mechanism. Check all four tires and, if necessary, add enough air to bring them up to the recommended pressure.

9   Don't forget to keep the spare tire inflated to the specified pressure (refer to your owner's manual or the tire sidewall).

6   Engine oil and filter change (every 3000 miles [4800 km] or 3 months)

▶ **Refer to illustrations 6.3, 6.9, 6.14 and 6.18**

1   Frequent oil changes are the most important preventive maintenance procedures that can be done by the home mechanic. As engine oil ages, it becomes diluted and contaminated, which leads to premature engine wear.

2   Although some sources recommend oil filter changes every other oil change, we feel that the minimal cost of an oil filter and the relative ease with which it is installed dictate that a new filter be installed every time the oil is changed.

3   Gather together all necessary tools and materials before beginning this procedure (see illustration).

4   You should have plenty of clean rags and newspapers handy to mop up any spills. Access to the under side of the vehicle may be improved if the vehicle can be lifted on a hoist, driven onto ramps or supported by jackstands.

✳✳ WARNING:

Do not work under a vehicle which is supported only by a jack.

5   If this is your first oil change, familiarize yourself with the locations of the oil drain plug and the oil filter.

6   Warm the engine to normal operating temperature. If the new oil or any tools are needed, use this warm-up time to gather everything necessary for the job. The correct type of oil for your application can be found in *Recommended lubricants and fluids* in this Chapter's Specifications.

7   With the engine oil warm (warm engine oil will drain better and more built-up sludge will be removed with it), raise and support the vehicle. Make sure it's safely supported!

8   Move all necessary tools, rags and newspapers under the vehicle. Set the drain pan under the drain plug. Keep in mind that the oil will initially flow from the pan with some force; position the pan accordingly.

9   Being careful not to touch any of the hot exhaust components, use a box-end wrench or a socket to remove the drain plug near the bottom of the oil pan (see illustration). Depending on how hot the oil is, you may want to wear gloves while unscrewing the plug the final few turns.

10 Allow the oil to drain into the pan. It may be necessary to move the pan as the oil flow slows to a trickle.

11 After all the oil has drained, wipe off the drain plug with a clean rag. Small metal particles may cling to the plug and would immediately contaminate the new oil.

12 Clean the area around the drain plug opening and reinstall the plug. Tighten the plug securely with the wrench. If a torque wrench is

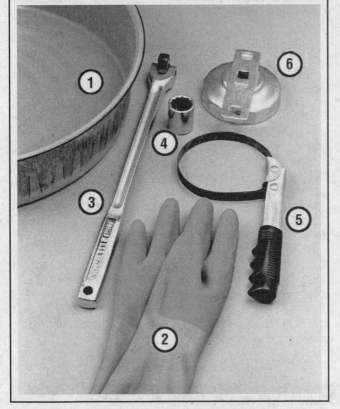

6.3 These tools are required when changing the engine oil and filter

1   *Drain pan* - It should be fairly shallow in depth, but wide to prevent spills
2   *Rubber gloves* - When removing the drain plug and filter, you will get oil on your hands (the gloves will prevent burns)
3   *Breaker bar* - Sometimes the oil drain plug is tight, and a long breaker bar is needed to loosen it
4   *Socket* - To be used with the breaker bar or a ratchet (must be the correct size to fit the drain plug - six-point preferred)
5   *Filter wrench* - This is a metal band-type wrench, which requires clearance around the filter to be effective
6   *Filter wrench* - This type fits on the bottom of the filter and can be turned with a ratchet or breaker bar (different-size wrenches are available for different types of filters)

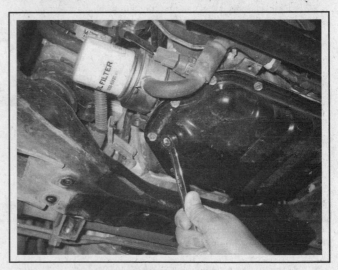

6.9 Use a proper size box-end wrench or socket to remove the oil drain plug and avoid rounding it off

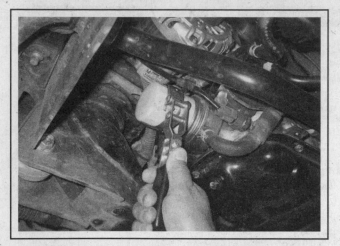

6.14 Use an oil filter wrench to loosen the oil filter

6.18 Lubricate the oil filter gasket with clean engine oil before installing the filter on the engine

available, use it to tighten the plug to the torque listed in this Chapter's Specifications.

13 Move the drain pan into position under the oil filter.

14 Use the oil filter wrench to loosen the oil filter (see illustration).

15 Completely unscrew the old filter. Be careful: it's full of oil. Empty the oil inside the filter into the drain pan, then lower the filter.

16 Compare the old filter with the new one to make sure they're the same type.

17 Use a clean rag to remove all oil, dirt and sludge from the area where the oil filter mounts to the engine. Check the old filter to make sure the rubber gasket isn't stuck to the engine. If the gasket is stuck to the engine (use a flashlight if necessary), remove it.

18 Apply a light coat of clean oil to the rubber gasket on the new oil filter (see illustration).

19 Attach the new filter to the engine, following the tightening directions printed on the filter canister or packing box. Most filter manufacturers recommend against using a filter wrench due to the possibility of overtightening and damage to the seal.

20 Remove all tools, rags, etc. from under the vehicle, being careful not to spill the oil in the drain pan, then lower the vehicle.

21 Move to the engine compartment and locate the oil filler cap.

22 Pour the fresh oil through the filler opening. A funnel may be helpful.

23 Refer to the engine oil capacity in this Chapter's Specifications and add the proper amount of fresh oil into the engine. Wait a few minutes to allow the oil to drain into the pan, then check the level on the oil dipstick (see Section 4, if necessary). If the oil level is above the hatched area, start the engine and allow the new oil to circulate.

24 Run the engine for only about a minute and then shut it off. Immediately look under the vehicle and check for leaks at the oil pan drain plug and around the oil filter.

25 With the new oil circulated and the filter now completely full, recheck the level on the dipstick and add more oil as necessary.

26 During the first few trips after an oil change, make it a point to check frequently for leaks and proper oil level.

27 The old oil drained from the engine cannot be reused in its present state and should be disposed of. Check with your local auto parts store, disposal facility or environmental agency to see if they will accept the oil for recycling. After the oil has cooled it can be drained into a container (capped plastic jugs, topped bottles, milk cartons, etc.) for transport to one of these disposal sites. Don't dispose of the oil by pouring it on the ground or down a drain!

7 Seat belt check (every 6000 miles [9600 km] or 6 months)

1 Check the seat belts, buckles, latch plates and guide loops for obvious damage and signs of wear.

2 Where the seat belt receptacle bolts to the floor of the vehicle, check that the bolts are secure.

3 See if the seat belt reminder light comes on when the key is turned to the Run or Start position. A chime should also sound.

8 Wiper blade inspection and replacement (every 6000 miles [9600 km] or 6 months)

▶ **Refer to illustrations 8.4a and 8.4b**

1 The windshield wiper and blade assembly should be inspected periodically for damage, loose components and cracked or worn blade elements.

2 Road film can build up on the wiper blades and affect their efficiency, so they should be washed regularly with a mild detergent solution.

3 If the wiper blade elements are cracked, worn or warped, or no longer clean adequately, they should be replaced with new ones.

4 Lift the arm assembly away from the glass for clearance, press on the release lever, then slide the wiper blade assembly out of the hook in the end of the arm (see illustrations).

5 Attach the new wiper to the arm. Connection can be confirmed by an audible click.

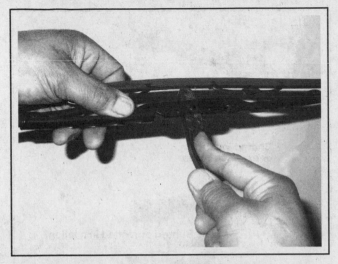

8.4a Depress the release lever (finger is on it here) . . .

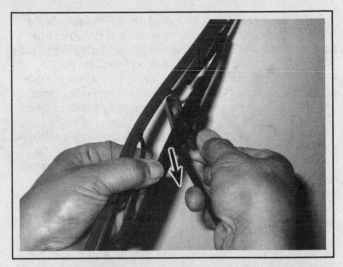

8.4b . . . and slide the wiper assembly down the wiper arm and out of the hook in the end of the arm

9 Battery check, maintenance and charging (every 6000 miles [9600 km] or 6 months)

▶ Refer to illustrations 9.1, 9.5, 9.6a, 9.6b, 9.7a and 9.7b

✲✲ WARNING:

Certain precautions must be followed when checking and servicing the battery. Hydrogen gas, which is highly flammable, is always present in the battery cells, so keep lighted tobacco and all other open flames and sparks away from the battery. The electrolyte inside the battery is actually dilute sulfuric acid, which will cause injury if splashed on your skin or in your eyes. It will also ruin clothes and painted surfaces. When removing the battery cables, always detach the negative cable first and hook it up last!

1   A routine preventive maintenance program for the battery in your vehicle is the only way to ensure quick and reliable starts. But before performing any battery maintenance, make sure that you have the proper equipment necessary to work safely around the battery (see illustration).

2   There are also several precautions that should be taken whenever battery maintenance is performed. Before servicing the battery, always turn the engine and all accessories off and disconnect the cable from the negative terminal of the battery.

3   The battery produces hydrogen gas, which is both flammable and explosive. Never create a spark, smoke or light a match around the battery. Always charge the battery in a ventilated area.

4   Electrolyte contains poisonous and corrosive sulfuric acid. Do not allow it to get in your eyes, on your skin or on your clothes. Never ingest it. Wear protective safety glasses when working near the battery. Keep children away from the battery.

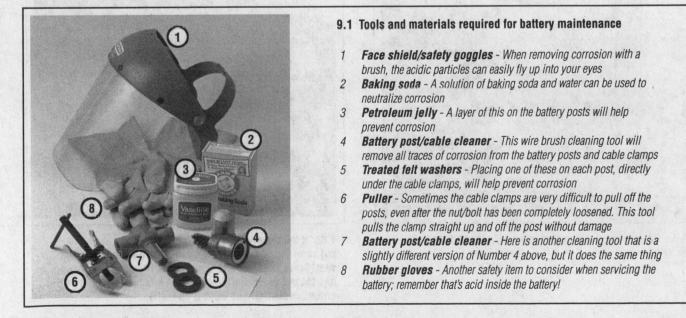

9.1 Tools and materials required for battery maintenance

1   *Face shield/safety goggles* - When removing corrosion with a brush, the acidic particles can easily fly up into your eyes
2   *Baking soda* - A solution of baking soda and water can be used to neutralize corrosion
3   *Petroleum jelly* - A layer of this on the battery posts will help prevent corrosion
4   *Battery post/cable cleaner* - This wire brush cleaning tool will remove all traces of corrosion from the battery posts and cable clamps
5   *Treated felt washers* - Placing one of these on each post, directly under the cable clamps, will help prevent corrosion
6   *Puller* - Sometimes the cable clamps are very difficult to pull off the posts, even after the nut/bolt has been completely loosened. This tool pulls the clamp straight up and off the post without damage
7   *Battery post/cable cleaner* - Here is another cleaning tool that is a slightly different version of Number 4 above, but it does the same thing
8   *Rubber gloves* - Another safety item to consider when servicing the battery; remember that's acid inside the battery!

5   Remove the panel from the cover at the right-rear corner of the engine compartment. Note the external condition of the battery. If the positive terminal and cable clamp on your vehicle's battery is equipped with a rubber protector, make sure that it's not torn or damaged. It should completely cover the terminal. Look for any corroded or loose connections, cracks in the case or cover or loose hold-down clamps. Also check the entire length of each cable for cracks and frayed conductors (see illustration).

6   If corrosion, which looks like white, fluffy deposits is evident, particularly around the terminals, the battery should be removed for cleaning (see illustration). Loosen the cable nuts with a wrench or battery pliers, being careful to remove the ground cable first, and slide them off the terminals (see illustration). Then disconnect the hold-down clamp bolt and nut, remove the clamp and lift the battery from the engine compartment.

7   Clean the cable ends thoroughly with a battery brush or a terminal cleaner and a solution of warm water and baking soda. Wash the terminals and the battery case with the same solution but make sure that the solution doesn't get into the battery. When cleaning the cables, terminals and battery case, wear safety goggles and rubber gloves to prevent any solution from coming in contact with your eyes or hands. Wear old clothes too - even diluted, sulfuric acid splashed onto clothes will burn holes in them. If the terminals have been corroded, clean them up with a terminal cleaner (see illustrations). Thoroughly wash all cleaned areas with plain water.

8   Make sure that the battery tray is in good condition and the hold-down clamp bolts are tight. If the battery is removed from the tray, make sure no parts remain in the bottom of the tray when the battery is reinstalled. When reinstalling the hold-down clamp bolts, do not over-tighten them.

9   Any metal parts of the vehicle damaged by corrosion should be covered with a zinc-based primer, then painted.

10   Information on removing and installing the battery can be found in Chapter 5. Information on jump starting can be found at the front of this manual.

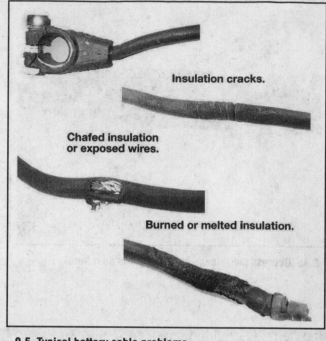

9.5 Typical battery cable problems

Insulation cracks.

Chafed insulation or exposed wires.

Burned or melted insulation.

CHARGING

❊❊ WARNING:

When batteries are being charged, hydrogen gas, which is very explosive and flammable, is produced. Do not smoke or allow open flames near a charging or a recently charged battery. Wear eye protection when near the battery during charging. Also, make sure the charger is unplugged before connecting or disconnecting the battery from the charger.

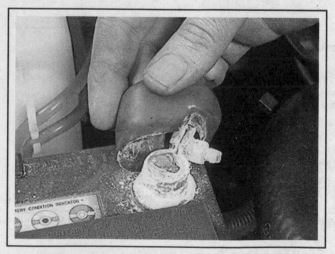

9.6a Battery terminal corrosion usually appears as light, fluffy powder

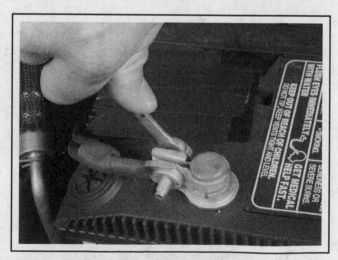

9.6b If the battery cable terminal is in good shape and not corroded, it can usually be loosened with a wrench - sometimes special battery pliers are required if corrosion has caused deterioration of the nut hex (always remove the ground cable first and hook it up last!)

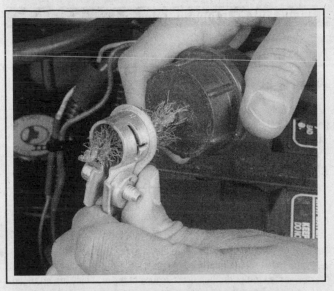

9.7a When cleaning the cable clamps, all corrosion must be removed (the inside of the clamp is tapered to match the taper on the post, so don't remove too much material)

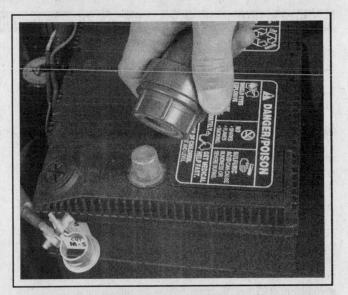

9.7b Regardless of the type of tool used on the battery posts, a clean, shiny surface should be the result

➡Note: It is recommended that the battery be removed from the vehicle for charging because the gas that escapes during this procedure can damage the paint. Fast charging with the battery cables connected can result in damage to the electrical system.

11 Slow-rate charging is the best way to restore a battery that's discharged to the point where it will not start the engine. It's also a good way to maintain the battery charge in a vehicle that's only driven a few miles between starts. Maintaining the battery charge is particularly important in the winter when the battery must work harder to start the engine and electrical accessories that drain the battery are in greater use.

12 It's best to use a one or two-amp battery charger (sometimes called a trickle charger). They are the safest and put the least strain on the battery. They are also the least expensive. For a faster charge, you can use a higher amperage charger, but don't use one rated more than 1/10th the amp/hour rating of the battery. Rapid boost charges that claim to restore the power of the battery in one to two hours are hardest on the battery and can damage batteries not in good condition. This type of charging should only be used in emergency situations.

13 The average time necessary to charge a battery should be listed in the instructions that come with the charger. As a general rule, a trickle charger will charge a battery in 12 to 16 hours.

14 Remove all the cell caps (if equipped - see Section 4) and cover the holes with a clean cloth to prevent spattering electrolyte. Disconnect the negative battery cable and hook the battery charger cable clamps up to the battery posts (positive-to-positive, negative-to-negative), then plug in the charger. Make sure it is set at 12-volts if it has a selector switch.

15 If you're using a charger with a rate higher than two amps, check the battery regularly during charging to make sure it doesn't overheat. If you're using a trickle charger, you can safely let the battery charge overnight after you've checked it regularly for the first couple of hours.

16 If the battery has removable cell caps, measure the specific gravity with a hydrometer every hour during the last few hours of the charging cycle. Hydrometers are available inexpensively from auto parts stores - follow the instructions that come with the hydrometer. Consider the battery charged when there's no change in the specific gravity reading for two hours and the electrolyte in the cells is gassing (bubbling) freely. The specific gravity reading from each cell should be very close to the others. If not, the battery probably has a bad cell(s).

17 Some batteries with sealed tops have built-in hydrometers on the top that indicate the state of charge by the color displayed in the hydrometer window. Normally, a bright-colored hydrometer indicates a full charge and a dark hydrometer indicates the battery still needs charging.

18 If the battery has a sealed top and no built-in hydrometer, you can hook up a digital voltmeter across the battery terminals to check the charge. A fully charged battery should read 12.6 volts or higher.

19 Further information on the battery and jump-starting can be found in Chapter 5 and at the front of this manual.

10 Drivebelt check and replacement (every 6000 miles [9600 km] or 6 months)

CHECK

▶ **Refer to illustration 10.3**

1 The drivebelts are located on the front of the engine. The good condition and proper adjustment of the belts is critical to the operation of the engine. Because of their composition and the high stresses to which they are subjected, drivebelts stretch and deteriorate as they get older. They must therefore be periodically inspected.

2 One belt drives the alternator and power steering. The other transmits power from the crankshaft to the air conditioning compressor.

3 With the engine off, open the hood and locate the drivebelts at the front of the engine compartment. With a flashlight, check each belt for separation of the adhesive rubber on both sides of the core, core separation from the belt side, a severed core, separation of the ribs from the adhesive rubber, cracking or separation of the ribs, and torn or worn ribs or cracks in the inner ridges of the ribs (see illustration). Also check for fraying and glazing, which gives the belt a shiny appearance. Both sides of the belt should be inspected, which means you will have to twist the belt to check the underside. Use your fingers to feel the belt where you can't see it. If any of the above conditions are evident, replace the belt (go to Step 6).

4 The tension of each belt is checked by pushing on the belt at a distance halfway between the pulleys. Push firmly with your thumb and see how much the belt moves (deflects). As rule of thumb, the belt should deflect approximately 1/4-inch.

ADJUSTMENT

▶ **Refer to illustration 10.5**

5 If the belt must be adjusted, loosen the locking nut and turn the adjusting bolt (see illustration). Measure the belt tension in accordance with the above method. Repeat this Step until the drivebelt is adjusted.

REPLACEMENT

6 Raise the vehicle and support it securely on jackstands. Remove the engine splash shield.

7 To replace a belt, follow the procedures for drivebelt adjustment, but slip the belt off the crankshaft pulley and remove it. If you are replacing the air conditioning compressor belt, you will have to remove the power steering pump belt first because of the way they are arranged on the crankshaft pulley. Because of this, and because belts tend to wear out more or less together, it is a good idea to replace both belts at the same time. Mark each belt and its appropriate pulley groove so the replacement belts can be fitted in their proper positions.

8 Take the old belts with you to the parts store to make a direct comparison for length, width and design.

9 After replacing a drivebelt, make sure that it fits properly in the ribbed grooves in the pulleys. It is essential that the belt be properly centered.

10 Adjust the belt(s) in accordance with the procedure outlined earlier in this Section.

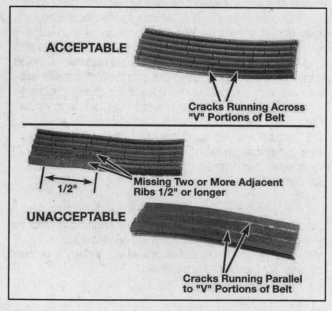

10.3 Check ribbed belts for signs of wear like these

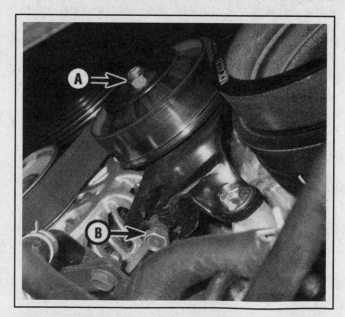

10.5 Loosen the locking nut (A), then turn the adjusting bolt (B)

11 Underhood hose check and replacement (every 6000 miles [9600 km] or 6 months)

GENERAL

> **✳✳ CAUTION:**
>
> **Never remove air conditioning components or hoses until the system has been depressurized by a dealer service department or air conditioning shop that has the equipment to depressurize the system safely and recover the refrigerant.**

1 High temperatures in the engine compartment can cause the deterioration of the rubber and plastic hoses used for engine, accessory and emission systems operation. Periodic inspection should be made for cracks, loose clamps, material hardening and leaks. Information specific to the cooling system hoses can be found in Section 12.

2 Some, but not all, hoses are secured to their fittings with clamps. Where clamps are used, check to be sure they haven't lost their tension, allowing the hose to leak. If clamps aren't used, make sure the hose has not expanded and/or hardened where it slips over the fitting, allowing it to leak.

VACUUM HOSES

3 It's quite common for vacuum hoses, especially those in the emissions system, to be color-coded or identified by colored stripes molded into them. Various systems require hoses with different wall thickness, collapse resistance and temperature resistance. When replacing hoses, be sure the new ones are made of the same material.

4 Often the only effective way to check a hose is to remove it completely from the vehicle. If more than one hose is removed, be sure to label the hoses and fittings to ensure correct installation.

5 When checking vacuum hoses, be sure to include any plastic T-fittings in the check. Inspect the fittings for cracks and the hose where it fits over the fitting for distortion, which could cause leakage.

6 A small piece of vacuum hose (1/4-inch inside diameter) can be used as a stethoscope to detect vacuum leaks. Hold one end of the hose to your ear and probe around vacuum hoses and fittings, listening for the hissing sound characteristic of a vacuum leak

> **✳✳ WARNING:**
>
> **When probing with the vacuum hose stethoscope, be very careful not to come into contact with moving engine components such as the drivebelt, cooling fan, etc.**

FUEL HOSE

> **✳✳ WARNING:**
>
> **Gasoline is extremely flammable, so take extra precautions when you work on any part of the fuel system. Don't smoke or allow open flames or bare light bulbs near the work area, and don't work in a garage where a gas-type appliance (such as a water heater or clothes dryer) is present. Since gasoline is carcinogenic, wear fuel-resistant gloves when there's a possibility of being exposed to fuel, and, if you spill any fuel on your skin, rinse it off immediately with soap and water. Mop up any spills immediately and do not store fuel-soaked rags where they could ignite. When you perform any kind of work on the fuel system, wear safety glasses and have a Class B type fire extinguisher on hand. The fuel system is under pressure, so if any lines must be disconnected, the pressure in the system must be relieved first (see Chapter 4 for more information).**

7 Check all rubber fuel lines for deterioration and chafing. Check especially for cracks in areas where the hose bends and just before fittings, such as where a hose attaches to the fuel filter and fuel injection unit.

8 High quality fuel line, specifically designed for high-pressure fuel injection applications, must be used for fuel line replacement. Never, under any circumstances, use regular fuel line, unreinforced vacuum line, clear plastic tubing or water hose for fuel lines.

9 Spring-type (pinch) clamps are commonly used on fuel lines. These clamps often lose their tension over a period of time, and can be sprung during removal. Replace all spring-type clamps with screw clamps whenever a hose is replaced.

METAL LINES

10 Sections of metal line are routed along the frame, between the fuel tank and the engine. Check carefully to be sure the line has not been bent or crimped and no cracks have started in the line.

11 If a section of metal fuel line must be replaced, only seamless steel tubing should be used, since copper and aluminum tubing don't have the strength necessary to withstand normal engine vibration.

12 Check the metal brake lines where they enter the master cylinder and brake proportioning unit for cracks in the lines or loose fittings. Any sign of brake fluid leakage calls for an immediate and thorough inspection of the brake system.

12 Cooling system check (every 6000 miles [9600 km] or 6 months)

▶ **Refer to illustration 12.4**

❊ WARNING:

The engine must be completely cool before beginning this procedure.

1   Many major engine failures can be attributed to a faulty cooling system. If the vehicle is equipped with an automatic transmission, the cooling system also cools the transmission fluid and thus plays an important role in prolonging transmission life.

2   The cooling system should be checked with the engine cold. Do this before the vehicle is driven for the day or after it has been shut off for at least three hours.

3   Remove the radiator cap and clean the filler neck on the radiator. All traces of corrosion should be removed. The coolant inside the radiator (and coolant reservoir) should be relatively transparent. If it is rust colored, the system should be drained and refilled (see Section 23). If the coolant level is low, add additional antifreeze/coolant mixture (see Section 4).

4   Carefully check the large upper and lower radiator hoses along with any smaller diameter heater hoses that run from the engine to the firewall. Inspect each hose along its entire length, replacing any hose that is cracked, swollen or shows signs of deterioration. Cracks may become more apparent if the hose is squeezed (see illustration).

5   Make sure all hose connections are tight. A leak in the cooling system will usually show up as white or rust-colored deposits on the areas adjoining the leak. If spring-type clamps are used at the ends of the hoses, it may be wise to replace them with more secure, screw-type clamps.

6   Use compressed air or a soft brush to remove bugs, leaves, etc. from the front of the radiator or air conditioning condenser. Be careful not to damage the delicate cooling fins or cut yourself on them.

7   Every other inspection, or at the first indication of cooling system problems, have the cap and system pressure tested. If you don't have a pressure tester, most gas stations and repair shops will do this for a minimal charge.

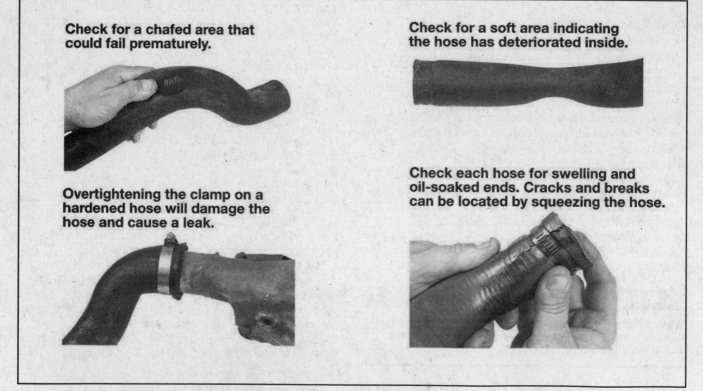

12.4 Hoses, like drivebelts, have a habit of failing at the worst possible time - to prevent the inconvenience of a blown radiator or heater hose, inspect them carefully as shown here

13 Tire rotation (every 6000 miles [9600 km] or 6 months)

➡Note: This procedure only applies to the models specified below; on all other models, the tires cannot be rotated, as the rear tires are a different size than the front tires.

G35 SEDAN (EXCEPT MODELS WITH 18-INCH WHEELS)

▶ **Refer to illustration 13.2**

1   The tires should be rotated at the specified intervals and whenever uneven wear is noticed.

2   Tires must be rotated in the recommended pattern (see illustration).

3   Refer to the information in *Jacking and towing* at the front of this manual for the proper procedures to follow when raising the vehicle and changing a tire. If the brakes are to be checked, don't apply the parking brake as stated. Make sure the tires are blocked to prevent the vehicle from rolling as it's raised. Before raising the vehicle, loosen the wheel lug nuts slightly.

4   Preferably, the entire vehicle should be raised at the same time. This can be done on a hoist or by jacking up each corner and then lowering the vehicle onto jackstands placed under the frame rails. Always use four jackstands and make sure the vehicle is safely supported.

5   After rotation, check and adjust the tire pressures as necessary. Tighten the lug nuts to the torque listed in this Chapter's Specifications.

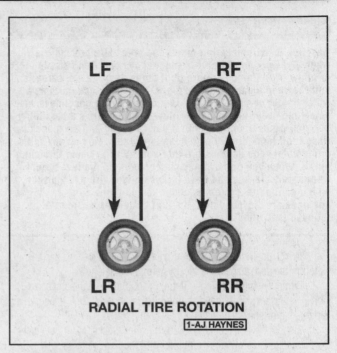

13.2 The recommended tire rotation pattern for G35 Sedan models with 17-inch wheels

14 Exhaust system check (every 6,000 miles [9600 km] or 6 months)

▶ **Refer to illustration 14.2**

1   With the engine cold (at least three hours after the vehicle has been driven), check the complete exhaust system from the manifold to the end of the tailpipe. Be careful around the catalytic converter, which may be hot even after three hours. The inspection should be done with the vehicle on a hoist to permit unrestricted access. If a hoist isn't available, raise the vehicle and support it securely on jackstands.

2   Check the exhaust pipes and connections for signs of leakage and/or corrosion indicating a potential failure. Make sure that all brackets and hangers are in good condition and tight (see illustration).

3   Inspect the underside of the body for holes, corrosion, open seams, etc. which may allow exhaust gasses to enter the passenger compartment. Seal all body openings with silicone sealant or body putty.

4   Rattles and other noises can often be traced to the exhaust system, especially the hangers, mounts and heat shields. Try to move the pipes, mufflers and catalytic converter. If the components can come in contact with the body or suspension parts, secure the exhaust system with new brackets and hangers.

14.2 Inspect the muffler for signs of deterioration, and all hangers

15 Fuel system check (every 15,000 miles [24,000 km] or 12 months)

✳✳ WARNING:

Gasoline is extremely flammable, so take extra precautions when you work on any part of the fuel system. Don't smoke or allow open flames or bare light bulbs near the work area, and don't work in a garage where a gas-type appliance (such as a water heater or clothes dryer) is present. Since gasoline is carcinogenic, wear fuel-resistant gloves when there's a possibility of being exposed to fuel, and, if you spill any fuel on your skin, rinse it off immediately with soap and water. Mop up any spills immediately and do not store fuel-soaked rags where they could ignite. When you perform any kind of work on the fuel system, wear safety glasses and have a Class B type fire extinguisher on hand. The fuel system is under constant pressure, so, before any lines are disconnected, the fuel system pressure must be relieved (see Chapter 4).

1   If you smell gasoline while driving or after the vehicle has been sitting in the sun, inspect the fuel system immediately.

2   Remove the fuel filler cap and inspect it for damage and corrosion. The gasket should have an unbroken sealing imprint. If the gasket is damaged or corroded, install a new cap.

3   Inspect the fuel feed and return lines for cracks. Make sure that the connections between the fuel lines and the fuel injection system are tight.

✳✳ WARNING:

Your vehicle is fuel injected, so you must relieve the fuel system pressure before servicing fuel system components. The fuel system pressure relief procedure is described in Chapter 4.

4   If the fuel injectors are visible, look for signs of fuel leakage (wet spots) around any of the injectors - they may need new O-rings (see Chapter 4).

5   Since some components of the fuel system - the fuel tank and part of the fuel feed line, for example - are underneath the vehicle, they can be inspected more easily with the vehicle raised on a hoist. If that's not possible, raise the vehicle and support it securely on jackstands.

6   With the vehicle raised and safely supported, inspect the fuel tank and filler neck for punctures, cracks and other damage. The connection between the filler neck and the tank is particularly critical. Sometimes a rubber filler neck will leak because of loose clamps or deteriorated rubber. Inspect all fuel tank mounting brackets and straps to be sure that the tank is securely attached to the vehicle.

✳✳ WARNING:

Do not, under any circumstances, try to repair a fuel tank (except rubber components). A welding torch or any open flame can easily cause fuel vapors inside the tank to explode.

7   Carefully check all rubber hoses and metal lines leading away from the fuel tank. Check for loose connections, deteriorated hoses, crimped lines and other damage. Repair or replace damaged sections as necessary (see Chapter 4).

8   The evaporative emissions control system can also be a source of fuel odors. The function of the system is to store fuel vapors from the fuel tank in a charcoal canister until they can be routed to the intake manifold, where they mix with incoming air before being burned in the combustion chambers.

9   The most common symptom of a faulty evaporative emissions system is a strong odor of fuel near the charcoal canister, which is mounted under the rear of the vehicle on all models. If a fuel odor has been detected, and you have already checked the areas described above, check the charcoal canister and the hoses connected to it (see Section 21).

16 Suspension, steering and driveaxle boot check (every 15,000 miles [24,000 km] or 12 months)

➡**Note: The steering linkage and suspension components should be checked periodically. Worn or damaged suspension and steering linkage components can result in excessive and abnormal tire wear, poor ride quality and vehicle handling and reduced fuel economy. For detailed illustrations of the steering and suspension components, refer to Chapter 10.**

SHOCK ABSORBER CHECK

Refer to illustration 16.6

1   Park the vehicle on level ground, turn the engine off and set the parking brake. Check the tire pressures.

2   Push down at one corner of the vehicle, then release it while noting the movement of the body. It should stop moving and come to rest in a level position within one or two bounces.

3   If the vehicle continues to move up-and-down or if it fails to return to its original position, a worn or weak shock absorber is probably the reason.

4   Repeat the above check at each of the three remaining corners of the vehicle.

5   Raise the vehicle and support it securely on jackstands.

6   Check the shock absorbers for evidence of fluid leakage (see illustration). A light film of fluid is no cause for concern. Make sure that any fluid noted is from the shocks and not from some other source. If leakage is noted, replace the shocks as a set (front or rear).

7   Check the shocks to be sure they are securely mounted and undamaged. Check the upper mounts for damage and wear. If damage or wear is noted, replace the shocks as a set (front or rear, or all four).

8   If the shocks must be replaced, refer to Chapter 10 for the procedure.

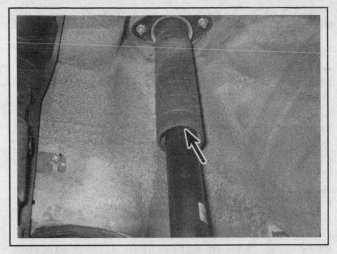

16.6 Check for signs of fluid leakage at this point on shock absorbers

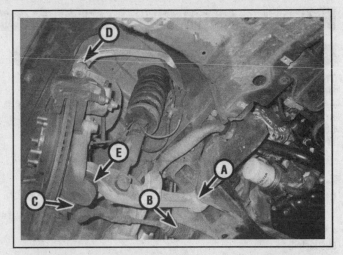

16.9 Front suspension components

A	Control arm inner bushings	D	Upper balljoint
B	Steering gear boot	E	Lower balljoint
C	Tie-rod end		

STEERING AND SUSPENSION CHECK

Refer to illustrations 16.9 and 16.11

9   Visually inspect the steering and suspension components (front and rear) for damage and distortion. Look for damaged seals, boots and bushings and leaks of any kind. Examine the bushings where the control arms meet the chassis (see illustration).

10   Clean the lower end of the steering knuckle. Have an assistant grasp the lower edge of the tire and move the wheel in-and-out while you look for movement at the steering knuckle-to-control arm balljoint. If there is any movement, the suspension balljoint(s) must be replaced.

11   Grasp each front tire at the front and rear edges, push in at the front, pull out at the rear and feel for play in the steering system components (see illustration). If any freeplay is noted, check the idler arm and the tie-rod ends for looseness (see illustration 16.9).

12   Additional steering and suspension system information and illustrations can be found in Chapter 10.

DRIVEAXLE BOOT CHECK

Refer to illustration 16.14

13   The driveaxle boots are very important because they prevent dirt, water and foreign material from entering and damaging the constant velocity (CV) joints. Oil and grease can cause the boot material to deteriorate prematurely, so it's a good idea to wash the boots with soap and water. Because it constantly pivots back and forth following the steering action of the front hub, the outer CV boot wears out sooner and should be inspected regularly.

14   Inspect the boots for tears and cracks as well as loose clamps (see illustration). If there is any evidence of cracks or leaking lubricant, they must be replaced as described in Chapter 8.

16.11 With the steering wheel in the locked position and the vehicle raised, grasp the front tire as shown and try to move it back-and-forth - if any play is noted, check the steering gear mounts and tie-rod ends for looseness

16.14 Inspect the inner and outer driveaxle boots for loose clamps, cracks or signs of leaking lubricant

17 Brake system check (every 15,000 miles [24,000 km] or 12 months)

※ WARNING:

The dust created by the brake system is harmful to your health. Never blow it out with compressed air and don't inhale any of it. An approved filtering mask should be worn when working on the brakes. Do not, under any circumstances, use petroleum-based solvents to clean brake parts. Use brake system cleaner only! Try to use non-asbestos replacement parts whenever possible.

➡Note: For detailed photographs of the brake system, refer to Chapter 9.

1 In addition to the specified intervals, the brakes should be inspected every time the wheels are removed or whenever a defect is suspected.

2 Any of the following symptoms could indicate a potential brake system defect: The vehicle pulls to one side when the brake pedal is depressed; the brakes make squealing or dragging noises when applied; brake pedal travel is excessive; the pedal pulsates; or brake fluid leaks, usually onto the inside of the tire or wheel.

3 Loosen the wheel lug nuts.

4 Raise the vehicle and place it securely on jackstands.

5 Remove the wheels (see *Jacking and towing* at the front of this book, or your owner's manual, if necessary).

DISC BRAKES

▸ **Refer to illustrations 17.7a, 17.7b and 17.9**

6 There are two pads (an outer and an inner) in each caliper. The pads are visible with the wheels removed.

7 Check the pad thickness by looking at each end of the caliper and through the inspection window in the caliper body (see illustrations). If the lining material is less than the thickness listed in this Chapter's Specifications, replace the pads.

➡Note: Keep in mind that the lining material is riveted or bonded to a metal backing plate and the metal portion is not included in this measurement.

8 If it is difficult to determine the exact thickness of the remaining pad material by the above method, or if you are at all concerned about the condition of the pads, remove the pads for further inspection (see Chapter 9).

9 Once the pads are removed from the calipers, clean them with brake cleaner and re-measure them with a ruler or a vernier caliper (see illustration).

10 Measure the disc thickness with a micrometer to make sure that it still has service life remaining. If any disc is thinner than the specified minimum thickness, replace it (see Chapter 9). Even if the disc has service life remaining, check its condition. Look for scoring, gouging and burned spots. If these conditions exist, remove the disc and have it resurfaced (see Chapter 9).

11 Before installing the wheels, check all brake lines and hoses for damage, wear, deformation, cracks, corrosion, leakage, bends and twists, particularly in the vicinity of the rubber hoses at the calipers. Check the clamps for tightness and the connections for leakage. Make sure that all hoses and lines are clear of sharp edges, moving parts and the exhaust system. If any of the above conditions are noted, repair, reroute or replace the lines and/or fittings as necessary (see Chapter 9).

BRAKE BOOSTER CHECK

12 Sit in the driver's seat and perform the following sequence of tests.

13 With the brake fully depressed, start the engine - the pedal should move down a little when the engine starts.

14 With the engine running, depress the brake pedal several times - the travel distance should not change.

17.7a With the wheel off, check the thickness of the inner brake pad through the inspection hole

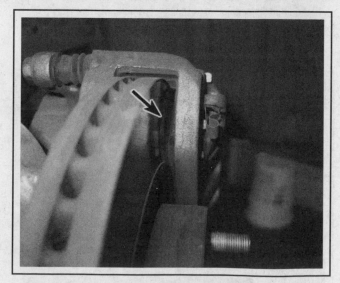

17.7b The outer pad is more easily checked at the edge of the caliper

15 Depress the brake, stop the engine and hold the pedal in for about 30 seconds - the pedal should neither sink nor rise.

16 Restart the engine, run it for about a minute and turn it off. Then firmly depress the brake several times - the pedal travel should decrease with each application.

17 If your brakes do not operate as described, the brake booster has failed. Refer to Chapter 9 for the replacement procedure.

PARKING BRAKE

18 One method of checking the parking brake is to park the vehicle on a steep hill with the parking brake set and the transmission in Neutral (be sure to stay in the vehicle during this check!). If the parking brake cannot prevent the vehicle from rolling, it's in need of adjustment (see Chapter 9).

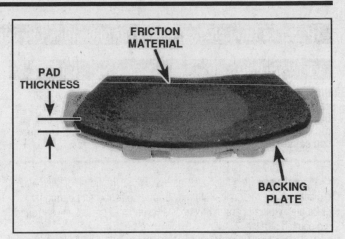

17.9 If a more precise measurement of pad thickness is necessary, remove the pads and measure the remaining friction material

18 Cabin air filter - replacement (every 15,000 miles [24,000 km] or 12 months)

▶ **Refer to illustrations 18.3 and 18.4**

1 The manufacturer recommends replacing the cabin air filters at the specified interval, to maintain the performance of the HVAC system.

2 Remove the lower glove box (see Chapter 11).

3 Remove the cover of the filter drawer in the heating/air conditioning unit (see illustration).

4 Withdraw the filter (see illustration).

5 Install the new filter, which is marked with arrows to indicate which side faces down.

6 The remainder of installation is the reverse of the removal procedure.

18.3 Remove the filter cover . . .

18.4 . . . then withdraw the filter

19 Brake fluid change (every 30,000 miles [48,000 km] or 24 months)

✳✳ WARNING:

Brake fluid can harm your eyes and damage painted surfaces, so use extreme caution when handling or pouring it. Do not use brake fluid that has been standing open or is more than one year old. Brake fluid absorbs moisture from the air. Excess moisture can cause a dangerous loss of braking effectiveness.

1   At the specified intervals, the brake fluid should be drained and replaced. Since the brake fluid may drip or splash when pouring it, place plenty of rags around the master cylinder to protect any surrounding painted surfaces.

2   Before beginning work, purchase the specified brake fluid (see *Recommended lubricants and fluids* in this Chapter's Specifications).

3   Remove the cap from the master cylinder reservoir.

4   Using a hand suction pump or similar device, withdraw the fluid from the master cylinder reservoir.

5   Add new fluid to the master cylinder until it rises to the line indicated on the reservoir.

6   Bleed the brake system as described in Chapter 9 at all four brakes until new and uncontaminated fluid is expelled from the bleeder screw. Be sure to maintain the fluid level in the master cylinder as you perform the bleeding process. If you allow the master cylinder to run dry, air will enter the system.

7   Refill the master cylinder with fluid and check the operation of the brakes. The pedal should feel solid when depressed, with no sponginess.

✳✳ WARNING:

Do not operate the vehicle if you are in doubt about the effectiveness of the brake system.

20 Air filter replacement (every 30,000 miles [48,000 km] or 24 months)

♦ **Refer to illustrations 20.1a, 20.1b, 20.1c, 20.1d and 20.1e**

1   The air filter housing is near the left-front of the engine compartment. On 350Z models, release the two clips securing the filter cartridge into the housing, remove the cartridge and filter (see illustrations). If you're working on a G35 model, remove the inlet air duct, then release the two clips securing the two halves of the air filter housing. Remove the filter (see illustrations).

2   Inspect the outer surface of the filter element. If it is dirty, replace it. If it is only moderately dusty, it can be reused by blowing it clean from the back to the front surface with compressed air. Because it is a pleated paper type filter, it cannot be washed or oiled. If it cannot be cleaned satisfactorily with compressed air, discard and replace it. While the cover is off, be careful not to drop anything down into the housing.

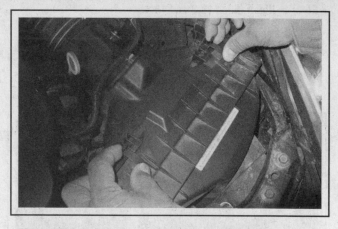

20.1a 350Z: Release the two clips securing the filter cartridge . . .

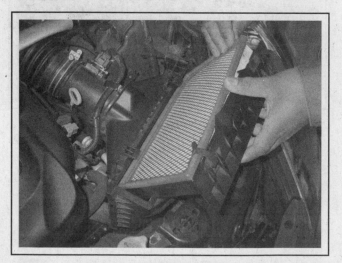

20.1b . . . remove the cartridge and filter

20.1c G35: Remove the fasteners securing the inlet duct . . .

20.1d . . . release the clips securing the two halves . . .

20.1e . . . separate the two halves of the housing, then withdraw the filter

3   Wipe out the inside of the air filter housing.
4   Place the new filter into the air filter housing, making sure it seats properly.
5   Installation of the cover is the reverse of removal.

❊❊ CAUTION:

Never drive the vehicle with the air cleaner removed. Excessive engine wear could result and backfiring could even cause a fire under the hood.

21 Evaporative emissions control system check (every 30,000 miles [48,000 km] or 24 months)

1   The function of the evaporative emissions control system is to draw fuel vapors from the gas tank and fuel system, store them in a charcoal canister and route them to the intake manifold during normal engine operation.
2   The most common symptom of a fault in the evaporative emis-

sions system is a strong fuel odor. If a fuel odor is detected, inspect the charcoal canister, located inboard of the left rear wheel, close to the fuel tank. Check the canister and hoses for damage, leaks or deterioration.
3   The evaporative emissions control system is explained in more detail in Chapter 6.

22 Spark plug replacement (see maintenance schedule for replacement interval)

◗ **Refer to illustrations 22.1, 22.5, 22.7, 22.8 and 22.9**

➡ **Note: The manufacturer recommends against checking the spark plug gap, as the platinum or iridium coating could be scraped off, thereby greatly reducing the life of the spark plugs.**

1   In most cases, the tools necessary for spark plug replacement include a spark plug socket which fits onto a ratchet (spark plug sockets are padded inside to prevent damage to the porcelain insulators on the new plugs), and various extensions (see illustration).

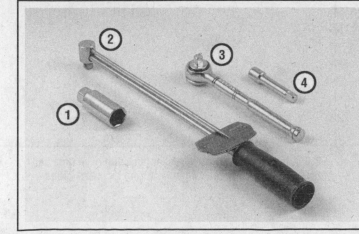

22.1 Tools required for changing spark plugs

1   **Spark plug socket** - This will have special padding inside to protect the spark plug's porcelain insulator
2   **Torque wrench** - Although not mandatory, using this tool is the best way to ensure the plugs are tightened properly
3   **Ratchet** - Standard hand tool to fit the spark plug socket
4   **Extension** - Depending on model and accessories, you may need special extensions and universal joints to reach one or more of the plugs

2   When buying the new spark plugs, be sure to obtain the correct plug type for your particular engine. This information can be found in the vehicle owner's manual and in this Chapter's Specifications.

3   Allow the engine to cool completely before attempting to remove any of the plugs. While you're waiting for the engine to cool, check the new plugs for defects.

4   Remove the air intake duct (see Chapter 4).

5   Disconnect the electrical connector at the ignition coil for one cylinder, then remove the bolt and pull up on the coil/plug boot assembly (see illustration). Replace one plug at a time.

6   If compressed air is available, use it to blow any dirt or foreign material away from the spark plug hole. The idea here is to eliminate the possibility of debris falling into the cylinder as the spark plug is removed.

7   Place the spark plug socket over the plug and remove it from the engine by turning it in a counterclockwise direction (see illustration).

8   Compare the spark plug with the chart on the inside back cover of this manual to get an indication of the general running condition of the engine. Before installing the new plugs, apply a thin coat of anti-seize compound to the threads (see illustration).

9   Thread one of the new plugs into the hole until you can no longer turn it with your fingers, then tighten it with a torque wrench (if available) or the ratchet. It is a good idea to slip a short length of rubber hose over the end of the plug to use as a tool to thread it into place (see illustration). The hose will grip the plug well enough to turn it, but will start to slip if the plug begins to cross-thread in the hole - this will prevent damaged threads and the accompanying repair costs.

10 Attach the ignition coil to the new spark plug, again using a twisting motion on the boot until it's seated on the spark plug.

11 Repeat the procedure for the remaining spark plugs.

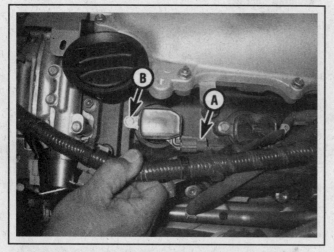

22.5 Disconnect the electrical connector (A) at an ignition coil, then remove the mounting bolt (B) and pull up on the coil/boot assembly to access the spark plug below

22.7 Use a socket and extension to unscrew the spark plugs

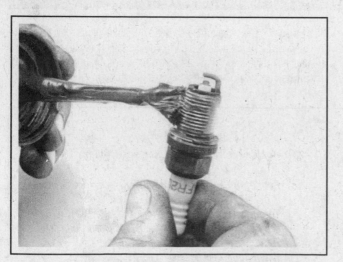

22.8 Apply a thin coat of anti-seize compound to the spark plug threads, being careful not to get any near the lower threads

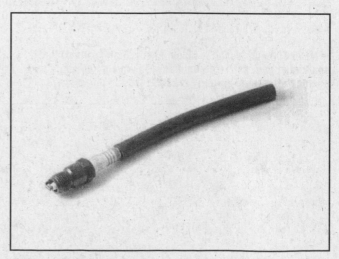

22.9 A length of snug-fitting rubber hose will save time and prevent damaged threads when installing the spark plugs

23 Cooling system servicing (draining, flushing and refilling) (every 30,000 miles [48,000 km] or 24 months)

✳ WARNING:

Do not allow antifreeze to come in contact with your skin or painted surfaces of the vehicle. Flush contacted areas immediately with plenty of water. Do not store new coolant or leave old coolant lying around where it is easily accessible to children and pets, because they are attracted by its sweet smell. Ingestion of even a small amount can be fatal. Wipe up the garage floor and drip pan coolant spills immediately. Keep antifreeze containers covered and repair leaks in your cooling system immediately. Antifreeze is flammable - be sure to read the precautions on the container.

➡Note: Non-toxic coolant is available at local auto parts stores. Although the coolant is non-toxic when fresh, proper disposal is still required.

DRAINING

♦ Refer to illustration 23.3

1 Periodically, the cooling system should be drained, flushed and refilled to replenish the antifreeze mixture and prevent formation of rust and corrosion, which can impair the performance of the cooling system and cause engine damage. When the cooling system is serviced, all hoses and the radiator cap should be checked and replaced if necessary.

2 Apply the parking brake and block the wheels.

✳ WARNING:

If the vehicle has just been driven, wait several hours to allow the engine to cool down before beginning this procedure.

Turn the ignition key to the On position, then set the heater control to the maximum heat position. Wait at least ten seconds, then turn the ignition Off.

3 Move a large container under the radiator drain to catch the coolant. Remove the plastic fasteners from the cover under the radiator (if equipped), then tuck the cover back over the frame for access to the drain plug, which is located in the radiator's lower tank (see illustration). Unscrew the drain fitting with a Phillips screwdriver, then remove the radiator cap.

4 After coolant stops flowing out of the radiator, move the container under the engine block drain plug(s) (there's one on each side of the engine block). Remove the plugs and allow the coolant in the block to drain.

➡Note: Frequently, the coolant will not drain from the block after the plug is removed. This is due to a rust layer that has built up behind the plug. Insert a Phillips screwdriver into the hole to break the rust barrier.

23.3 Loosen the radiator drain plug with a Phillips screwdriver

5 While the coolant is draining, check the condition of the radiator hoses, heater hoses and clamps (refer to Section 12, if necessary). Remove the coolant reservoir (see Chapter 3) and pour the coolant into the drain pan. Rinse out the reservoir with clean water.

6 Once the coolant has drained completely, replace any damaged clamps or hoses. Apply thread sealant to the drain plugs, reinstall them and tighten them securely. Also, temporarily tighten the air relief plug(s).

FLUSHING

♦ Refer to illustration 23.9

➡Note 1: In severe cases of contamination or clogging of the radiator, remove the radiator (see Chapter 3) and have a radiator repair facility clean and repair it if necessary.

➡Note 2: Many deposits can be removed by the chemical action of a cleaner available at auto parts stores. Follow the procedure outlined in the manufacturer's instructions. However, when the coolant is regularly drained and the system refilled with the correct antifreeze/water mixture, there should be no need to use chemical cleaners or descalers.

7 Make sure your heating system controls are still set to Hot, so that the heater core will be flushed at the same time as the rest of the cooling system.

8 Once the system is completely drained, remove the thermostat from the engine (see Chapter 3). Then reinstall the thermostat housing without the thermostat. This will allow the system to be thoroughly flushed.

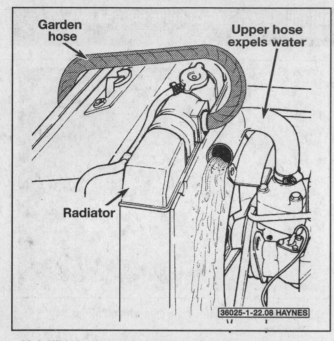

23.9 With the thermostat removed, disconnect the upper radiator hose and flush the radiator and engine block with a garden hose

9 Disconnect the upper radiator hose, then place a garden hose in the upper radiator inlet and flush the system until the water runs clear at the upper radiator hose (see illustration).

REFILLING

▶ **Refer to illustration 23.11**

10 To refill the system, install the thermostat (if removed), reconnect any radiator hoses and install the reservoir and the overflow hose.
11 Place the heater temperature control in the maximum heat position. Open the air relief plug (see illustration).

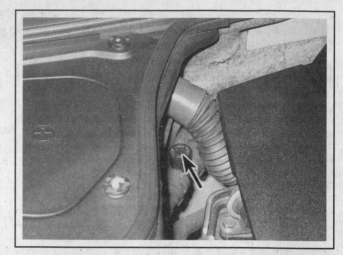

23.11 Open the air relief plug, located near the firewall, inboard of the battery

12 Make sure to use the proper coolant listed in this Chapter's Specifications. Slowly fill the radiator with the recommended mixture of antifreeze and water until coolant reaches the base of the radiator filler neck. Then add coolant to the reservoir until it reaches the FULL COLD mark. When coolant flows from the air relief hole, reinstall the air relief plug. Wait five minutes and recheck the coolant level in the radiator, adding if necessary.
13 Leave the radiator cap off and run the engine in a well-ventilated area until the thermostat opens (coolant will begin flowing through the radiator and the upper radiator hose will become hot).
14 Rev the engine to approximately 2500 rpm for ten seconds then let it idle; do this a few times.
15 Turn the engine off and let it cool. Add more coolant mixture to bring the level back up to the base of the filler neck.
16 Squeeze the upper radiator hose to expel air, then add more coolant mixture if necessary. Reinstall the radiator cap. Add coolant to the reservoir, if necessary.
17 Start the engine, allow it to reach normal operating temperature and check for leaks.

24 Automatic transmission fluid change (every 30,000 miles [48,000 km] or 24 months)

▶ **Refer to illustration 24.5**

1 At the specified intervals, the transmission fluid should be drained and replaced. Since the fluid will remain hot long after driving, perform this procedure only after the engine has cooled down completely.
2 Before beginning work, purchase the specified transmission fluid (see *Recommended lubricants and fluids* in this Chapter's Specifications) and a new filter and pan gasket.
3 Other tools necessary for this job include a floor jack, jackstands to support the vehicle in a raised position, a drain pan capable of holding at least ten quarts, newspapers and clean rags.
4 Raise the vehicle and support it securely on jackstands.
5 Place the drain pan underneath the transmission pan. Remove the drain plug and allow the fluid to drain, then reinsert the plug and tighten it securely (see illustration). Measure the amount of fluid drained (the same amount will be added to the transmission later).

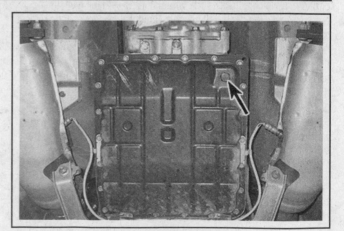

24.5 Transmission pan drain plug

6   Lower the vehicle and add the specified type of automatic transmission fluid (the same amount that was drained in Step 5), through the filler tube (see Section 4).

7   With the transmission in Park and the parking brake set, run the engine at a fast idle, but don't race it.

8   Move the gear selector through each range and back to Park,

then let the engine idle for a few minutes. Check the fluid level. It may be low. Add enough fluid to bring the level to the proper mark on the dipstick. Be careful not to overfill.

9   Check under the vehicle for leaks during the first few trips. Check the fluid level again when the transmission is hot (see Section 4).

25 Ignition coils - cleaning and inspection (every 60,000 miles [96,000 km] or 48 months)

◆ Refer to illustration 25.2

1   All models covered by this manual have an individual ignition coil for each cylinder. These models do not have a traditional distributor or spark plug wires. Each coil has a boot on the bottom that connects directly to the top of its spark plug.

2   Whenever spark plugs are replaced (see Section 22), the coils are removed to access the plugs. Examine the coils for any signs of carbon tracking, cracks or other damage (see illustration). Clean them with a dampened cloth and dry them thoroughly before installation.

25.2 Examine the spark plug boots and the individual ignition coils for signs of damage

26 Manual transmission lubricant change (every 60,000 miles [96,000 km] or 48 months)

1   This procedure should be performed after the vehicle has been driven so the lubricant will be warm and therefore will flow out of the transmission more easily. Raise the vehicle and support it securely on jackstands.

2   Move a drain pan, rags, newspapers and wrenches under the transmission.

3   Remove the fill plug from the side of the transmission case, then remove the transmission drain plug at the bottom of the case and allow the lubricant to drain into the pan.

4   After the lubricant has drained completely, reinstall the drain plug and tighten it to the torque listed in this Chapter's Specifications.

5   Using a hand pump, syringe or squeeze bottle, fill the transmission with the specified lubricant until it just reaches the bottom edge of the hole. Reinstall the fill plug and tighten it to the torque listed in this Chapter's Specifications.

6   Lower the vehicle.

7   Drive the vehicle for a short distance, then check the drain and fill plugs for leakage.

27 Differential and transfer case lubricant change (every 60,000 miles [96,000 km] or 48 months)

1   This procedure should be performed after the vehicle has been driven, so the lubricant will be warm and therefore will flow out of the differential or transfer case more easily.

2   Raise the vehicle and support it securely on jackstands. You'll be draining the lubricant by removing the drain plug, so move a drain pan, rags, newspapers and wrenches under the vehicle.

3   Remove the fill plug, then remove the drain plug (see illustra-

tion 4.42), and allow the lubricant to drain into the pan, then clean and reinstall the drain plug. Tighten the plug to the torque listed in this Chapter's Specifications.

4   Using a hand pump, syringe or squeeze bottle, fill the differential housing or transfer case with the specified lubricant until it's level with the bottom of the fill-plug hole. Install the plug and tighten it to the torque listed in this Chapter's Specifications.

Recommended lubricants and fluids

➡ Note: Listed here are manufacturer recommendations at the time this manual was written. Manufacturers occasionally upgrade their fluid and lubricant specifications, so check with your local auto parts store for current recommendations.

Engine oil	API "certified for gasoline engines"
Viscosity	See accompanying chart
Fuel	91 octane minimum
Automatic transmission fluid	Nissan Matic J automatic transmission fluid
Manual transmission lubricant	75W-85 or 75W-90 GL 4 gear oil
Power steering fluid	
U.S. models	Nissan PSF or equivalent
Canadian models	Nissan PSF, Nissan ATF, DEXRON III or MERCON automatic transmission fluid
Differential lubricant	API GL-5 80W-90 gear oil
Transfer case lubricant	Nissan Matic D automatic transmission fluid
Brake fluid	DOT 3 brake fluid
Clutch fluid	DOT 3 brake fluid
Engine coolant	50/50 mixture of ethylene glycol-based antifreeze and distilled demineralized water
Chassis lubrication grease	NLGI No. 2 moly-based chassis grease

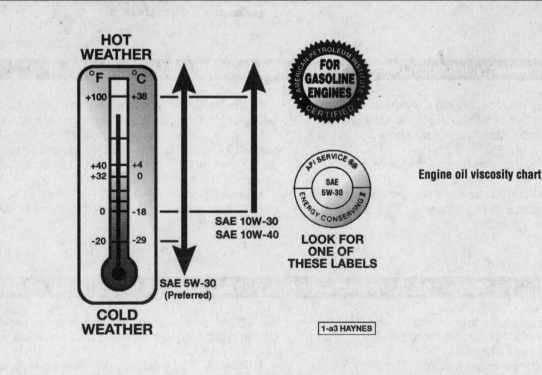

Engine oil viscosity chart

1-a3 HAYNES

Capacities*

Engine oil (including filter)

2007 and earlier G35 models	5 quarts (4.7 liters)
2008 G35 models	5-1/8 quarts (4.9 liters)
2006 and earlier 350Z models	5 quarts (4.7 liters)
2007 and later 350Z models	5-1/8 quarts (4.9 liters)

Manual transmission	3 quarts (2.9 liters)
Automatic transmission (fluid and filter change), all models	Up to 10-7/8 quarts (10.3 liters) (the best way to determine the amount of fluid to add during a routine fluid change is to measure the amount drained. This way you won't overfill the transmission).

Differential

Front (AWD models)	0.7 quart (0.65 liter)
Rear	1.5 quarts (1.4 liters)
Transfer case (AWD models)	1.32 quarts (1.25 liters)
Cooling system	Up to 2.25 gallons (8.5 liters)

All capacities approximate. Add as necessary to bring to the appropriate level.

Brakes

Disc brake pad lining thickness (minimum)	1/8 inch

Ignition system

Spark plug type

G35 models	PLFR5A-11 or equivalent
350Z models	
2006 and earlier models	PLFR5A-11 or equivalent
2007 and later models	FXE22HR-11 or equivalent
Spark plug gap	0.043 inch (1.1 mm)

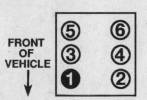

Cylinder numbering diagram

Torque specifications	Ft-lbs (unless otherwise indicated)	Nm

➡**Note: One foot-pound (ft-lb) of torque is equivalent to 12 inch-pounds (in-lbs) of torque. Torque values below approximately 15 ft-lbs are expressed in inch-pounds, since most foot-pound torque wrenches are not accurate at these smaller values.**

	Ft-lbs	Nm
Engine oil drain plug	25	34.5
Automatic transmission drain plug	25	34.5
Manual transmission drain/fill plugs	25	34.5
Differential drain/fill plugs (front and rear)	25	34.5
Transfer case		
Drain plug	22	29.4
Fill plug	26	35
Spark plugs		
G35		
2006 and earlier models	216 inch-lbs	24.5
2007 and later models	168 inch-lbs	19
350Z		
2003 models	180 to 252 inch-lbs	20.3 to 28.4
2004 and later models	216 inch-lbs	24.5
Wheel lug nuts	80	108

Notes

Section

2A
3.5L V6 ENGINE

Reference to other Chapters

1 General information

This Part of Chapter 2 is devoted to in-vehicle repair procedures for the 3.5L Dual Overhead Camshaft (DOHC) V6 engine. Information concerning engine removal, installation and overhaul can be found in Part B of this Chapter.

The following repair procedures are based on the assumption that the engine is installed in the vehicle. If the engine has been removed from the vehicle and mounted on a stand, many of the steps outlined in this Part of Chapter 2 will not apply.

2 Repair operations possible with the engine in the vehicle

Many major repair operations can be accomplished without removing the engine from the vehicle.

Clean the engine compartment and the exterior of the engine with some type of degreaser before any work is done. It will make the job easier and help keep dirt out of the internal areas of the engine.

Depending on the components involved, it may be helpful to remove the hood to improve access to the engine as repairs are performed (refer to Chapter 11 if necessary). Cover the fenders to prevent damage to the paint. Special pads are available, but an old bedspread or blanket will also work.

If vacuum, exhaust, oil or coolant leaks develop, indicating a need for gasket or seal replacement, the repairs can generally be made with the engine in the vehicle. The intake and exhaust manifold gaskets, oil pan gasket, crankshaft oil seals and cylinder head gaskets are all accessible with the engine in place.

Exterior engine components, such as the intake and exhaust manifolds, the oil pan, the oil pump, the water pump (see Chapter 3), the starter motor, the alternator and the fuel system components (see Chapter 4) can be removed for repair with the engine in place.

Since the cylinder heads can be removed without pulling the engine, valve component servicing can also be accomplished with the engine in the vehicle. Replacement of the camshafts, timing chains and sprockets are also possible with the engine in the vehicle.

In extreme cases caused by a lack of necessary equipment, repair or replacement of piston rings, pistons, connecting rods and rod bearings is possible with the engine in the vehicle. However, this practice is not recommended because of the cleaning and preparation work that must be done to the components involved.

3 Top Dead Center (TDC) for number one piston - locating

♦ **Refer to illustration 3.8**

1   Top Dead Center (TDC) is the highest point in the cylinder that each piston reaches as it travels up the cylinder bore. Each piston reaches TDC on the compression stroke and again on the exhaust stroke, but TDC generally refers to piston position on the compression stroke.

2   Positioning the piston(s) at TDC is an essential part of many procedures such as valve timing, camshaft and timing chain/sprocket removal.

3   Before beginning this procedure, be sure to place the transmission in Park (automatic) or Neutral (manual) and apply the parking brake or block the rear wheels. Disable the ignition system by disconnecting the primary electrical connectors at the ignition coil packs, then remove the coil packs and spark plugs (see Chapter 1). Disable the fuel system (see Chapter 4, Section 2).

4   In order to bring any piston to TDC, the crankshaft must be turned using one of the methods outlined below. When looking at the front of the engine, normal crankshaft rotation is clockwise.

a) *The preferred method is to turn the crankshaft with a socket and ratchet attached to the bolt threaded into the front of the crankshaft. Turn the bolt in a clockwise direction.*

b) *A remote starter switch, which may save some time, can also be used. Follow the instructions included with the switch. Once the piston is close to TDC, use a socket and ratchet as described in the previous paragraph.*

c) *If an assistant is available to turn the ignition switch to the Start position in short bursts, you can get the piston close to TDC without a remote starter switch. Make sure your assistant is out of the vehicle, away from the ignition switch, then use a socket and ratchet as described in Paragraph (a) to complete the procedure.*

5   Install a compression pressure gauge in the number one spark plug hole (see Chapter 2B). It should be a gauge with a screw-in fitting and a hose at least six inches long.

6   Rotate the crankshaft using one of the methods described above while observing for pressure on the compression gauge. The moment the gauge shows pressure indicates that the number one cylinder has begun the compression stroke.

7   Once the compression stroke has begun, TDC for the compression stroke is reached by bringing the piston to the top of the cylinder.

8   Continue turning the crankshaft until the TDC notch in the crankshaft damper is aligned with the pointer on the front cover (see illustration). At this point, the number one cylinder is at TDC on the compression stroke. If the marks are aligned but there was no compression, the piston was on the exhaust stroke. Continue rotating the crankshaft 360-degrees (1-turn).

➡**Note: If a compression gauge is not available, you can simply place a blunt object (such as the end of a screwdriver handle) over the spark plug hole and listen for compression as the engine is rotated. Once compression at the No.1 spark plug hole is noted, the remainder of the Step is the same.**

9   After the number one piston has been positioned at TDC on the compression stroke, TDC for any of the remaining cylinders can be located by turning the crankshaft 120 degrees and following the firing order (refer to the Specifications). Rotating the engine 120 degrees past TDC #1 will put the engine at TDC compression for cylinder #2.

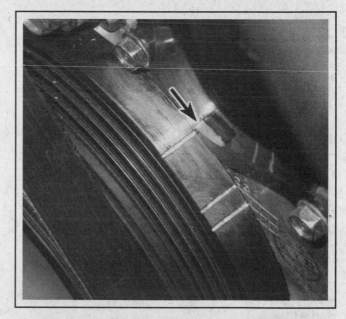

3.8 Align the TDC notch on the crankshaft pulley with the pointer on the timing chain cover (arrow) - the TDC notch is the one farthest to the left when facing the front of the engine, and is typically the line without color

4   Valve covers - removal and installation

REMOVAL

♦ **Refer to illustrations 4.2 and 4.6**

1   Disconnect the cable from the negative terminal of the battery (see Chapter 5, Section 1).

2   Remove the engine cover (see illustration).

3   Remove the intake manifold plenum (see Section 9).

4   Remove the ignition coils from the valve cover (see Chapter 5). If both valve covers are being removed, remove all six of the ignition coils.

5   Remove the breather hose by sliding the hose clamp back and pulling the hose off the fitting on the valve cover.

6   Detach the PCV hose and any wiring which would interfere with valve cover removal (see illustration).

7   Remove the valve cover bolts and washers in the reverse order of the tightening sequence (see illustrations 4.14a and 4.14b).

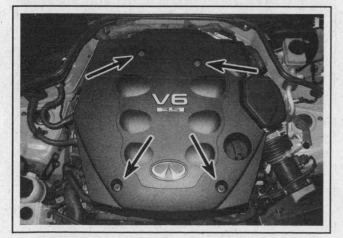

4.2 Remove the fasteners (arrows) and detach the engine cover

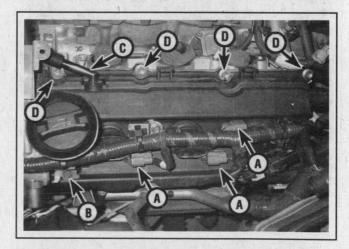

4.6 On the left side valve cover, disconnect the ignition coils (A), unbolt and set aside the electrical harness (B), then disconnect the PCV hose (C) and remove the valve cover bolts (D) (four visible here)

8   Detach the valve cover.

➡**Note: If the cover is stuck to the cylinder head, bump one end with a block of wood and a hammer to jar it loose. If that doesn't work, try to slip a flexible putty knife between the cylinder head and cover to break the gasket seal. Don't pry at the cover-to-cylinder head joint or damage to the sealing surfaces may occur (leading to oil leaks in the future).**

INSTALLATION

▶ **Refer to illustrations 4.11, 4.14a and 4.14b**

9   The mating surfaces of each cylinder head and valve cover must be perfectly clean when the covers are installed. Use a gasket scraper to remove all traces of sealant and old gasket material, then clean the mating surfaces with brake cleaner. If there's sealant or oil on the mating surfaces when the cover is installed, oil leaks may develop.

10   If necessary, clean the mounting bolt threads with a wire wheel to remove any corrosion. Make sure the threaded holes in the cylinder head are clean - run a tap into them to remove corrosion and restore damaged threads.

11   Inspect and replace, if necessary, the spark plug tube sealing washers (see illustration).

12   The valve cover gaskets should be mated to the covers before the covers are installed. Apply a thin coat of RTV sealant to the cover groove and to the corners on the front camshaft journal cap, then position the gasket inside the cover and allow the sealant to set up so the gasket adheres to the cover. If the sealant isn't allowed to set, the gasket may fall out of the cover as it's installed on the engine.

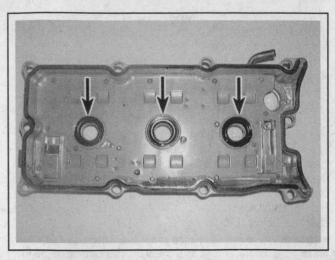

4.11 Make sure to install new spark plug tube seals into the valve cover

13   Carefully position the cover on the cylinder head and install the bolts.

14   Following the recommended tightening sequence, tighten the bolts, in two equal steps, to the torque listed in this Chapter's Specifications (see illustrations).

➡**Note: Models from 2003 to 2006 have 10 mounting bolts, later models have 12 bolts.**

15   The remaining installation steps are the reverse of removal.

16   Start the engine and check carefully for oil leaks.

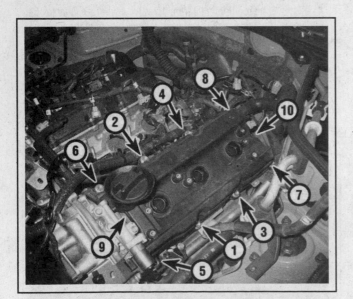

4.14a Valve cover TIGHTENING sequence - 2003 through 2006 models

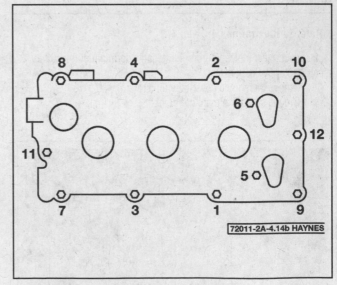

4.14b Valve cover TIGHTENING sequence - 2007 and later models

5   Valve clearance - check and adjustment

◆ **Refer to illustrations 5.6a, 5.6b, 5.7, 5.8 and 5.10**

➡**Note: The manufacturer recommends adjusting the valve clearance at the specified interval only if the valve train is making excessive noise. The following procedure requires the use of special valve lifter tools. The tools are available from specialty tool manufacturers and many auto parts stores. It is impossible to perform this task without them.**

1   Disconnect the cable from the negative terminal of the battery (see Chapter 5, Section 1).

2   Remove the valve cover (see Section 4).

3   On manual transmission vehicles, set the parking brake and place the transmission in the neutral position. On automatic transmission models, place the transmission in Park.

4   Remove the spark plugs (see Chapter 1).

5   Position the number 1 piston at TDC on the compression stroke and align the timing marks (see Section 3).

6   Measure the clearance of the indicated valves with a feeler gauge (see illustrations). Record each measurement and compare your measurements with the desired valve clearance found in this Chapter's Specifications. Note which are out of specification, as this data will be used later to determine the required replacement lifters.

7   Turn the crankshaft 240 degrees clockwise. Measure and record the clearances of the indicated valves (see illustration).

8   Turn the crankshaft an additional 240 degrees clockwise. Measure and record the clearances of the indicated valves (see illustration).

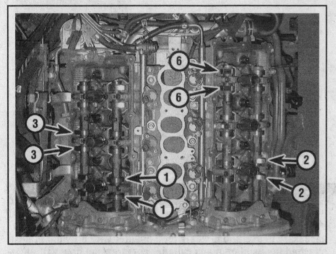

5.6a   When the no. 1 piston is at TDC on the compression stroke, the valve clearance for the no. 1 and no. 6 cylinder intake valves and the no. 2 and no. 3 cylinder exhaust valves can be measured

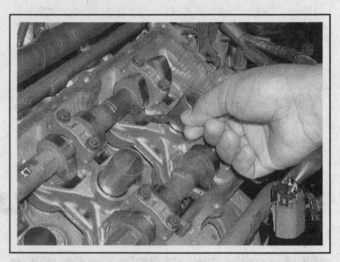

5.6b   Measure the clearance for each valve with a feeler gauge of the specified thickness - if the clearance is correct, you should feel a slight drag on the gauge as you pull it out

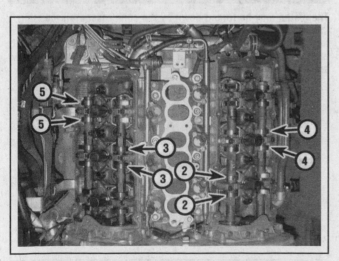

5.7   After checking the valves indicated in illustration 5.6a, turn the crankshaft 240 degrees (1/3-turn) clockwise and check the valve clearances for the no. 2 and no. 3 cylinder intake valves and the no. 4 and no. 5 cylinder exhaust valves

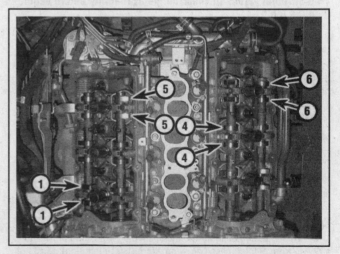

5.8   After checking the valves indicated in illustration 5.7, turn the crankshaft 240 degrees (1/3-turn) clockwise and check the valve clearances for the no. 4 and no. 5 cylinder intake valves and the no. 1 and no. 6 cylinder exhaust valves

9   The V6 engine does not use valve adjusting shims. If a lifter is out of specification for clearance, the lifter must be replaced with a new lifter that has a different thickness head to correct the clearance. Refer to Section 8 and remove the camshafts to access the lifters.

10 Mark the lifters that are to be replaced, and record which valve they came from. Use a micrometer to measure the thickness of the lifter in the center, making sure the measurement is precise and on the center projection on the underside of the lifter (see illustration).

11 To calculate the correct thickness for a replacement lifter that will place the valve clearance within the specified value, use the following formula:

Intake side: $N = R + (M - 0.012$ inch [0.30 mm]$)$
Exhaust side: $N = R + (M - 0.013$ inch [0.33 mm]$)$
R = thickness of old lifter
M = measured valve clearance
N = thickness of new lifter

12 New lifters are available in 27 standard thicknesses, from 0.3102 inch to 0.3291 inch (7.88 to 8.36 mm). Lifters are marked on the underside as to their size.

13 Mark the new lifters as to their destination, lubricate them with engine assembly lube and install them. After replacing the lifters, refer to Section 8 and reinstall the camshafts.

14 The remainder of installation is the reverse of removal.

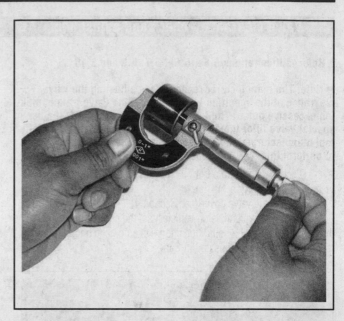

5.10 Measure the lifter thickness with a micrometer

6   Valve springs, retainers and seals - replacement

♦ **Refer to illustrations 6.5, 6.7a, 6.7b, 6.13 and 6.15**

➡**Note: Broken valve springs and defective valve stem seals can be replaced without removing the cylinder heads. Two special tools and a compressed air source are normally required to perform this operation, so read through this Section carefully. The universal shaft-type valve spring compressor required for the tight valve spring pockets of this vehicle may not be available at all tool rental yards, so check on the availability before beginning the job.**

1   Remove the intake plenum (see Section 9) and the valve cover(s) (see Section 4).

2   Refer to Section 7 and remove the timing chain, then refer to Section 8 and remove the camshafts and lifters from the affected cylinder head.

3   Remove the spark plug from the cylinder that has the defective component. If all of the valve stem seals are being replaced, all of the spark plugs should be removed.

4   Turn the crankshaft until the piston in the affected cylinder is at Top Dead Center on the compression stroke (see Section 3). If you're replacing all of the valve stem seals, begin with cylinder number one and work on the valves for one cylinder at a time. Move from cylinder-to-cylinder following the firing order sequence (see this Chapter's Specifications).

5   Thread a long adapter into the spark plug hole and connect an air hose from a compressed air source to it (see illustration). Most auto parts stores can supply the air hose adapter.

➡**Note: Because of the length of the spark plug tubes, it will be necessary to use a long spark plug adapter with a length of hose attached (as used on many cylinder compression gauges), utilizing a quick-disconnect fitting to hook to your air source.**

6   Apply compressed air to the cylinder.

✳✳ WARNING:

The piston may be forced down by the compressed air, causing the crankshaft to turn suddenly. If the wrench used when positioning the number one piston at TDC is still attached to the bolt in the crankshaft nose, it could cause damage or injury when the crankshaft moves.

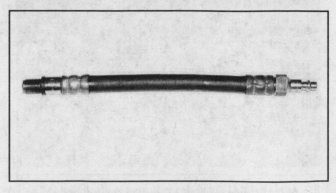

6.5 The air hose adapter threads into the spark plug hole - they're commonly available from auto parts stores

6.7a Compress the valve spring enough to release the valve stem keepers . . .

6.7b . . . and lift them out with a magnet or needle-nose pliers

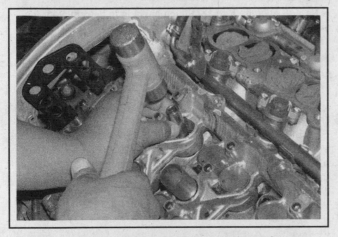

6.13 Using a deep socket and hammer, gently tap the new seals onto the valve guide only until seated

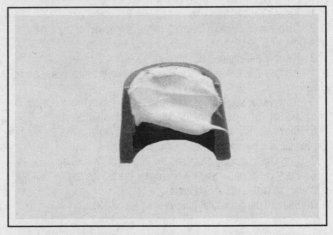

6.15 Apply a small dab of grease to each keeper as shown here before installation - it will hold them in place on the valve stem as the spring is released

7   Stuff shop rags into the cylinder head holes around the valves to prevent parts and tools from falling into the engine, then use a valve spring compressor to compress the spring (see illustrations). Remove the keepers with small needle-nose pliers or a magnet.

➡**Note: The valves should be held in place by the air pressure. If the valve faces or seats are in poor condition, leaks may prevent air pressure from retaining the valves. If the valves cannot hold air, the cylinder head should be removed for a valve job at a machine shop.**

8   Remove the spring retainer and valve spring, then remove the valve stem seal.

9   Wrap a rubber band or tape around the top of the valve stem so the valve won't fall into the combustion chamber, then release the air pressure.

10 Inspect the valve stem for damage. Rotate the valve in the guide and check the end for eccentric movement, which would indicate that the valve is bent.

11 Move the valve up-and-down in the guide and make sure it doesn't bind. If the valve stem binds, either the valve is bent or the guide is damaged. In either case, the cylinder head will have to be removed for repair.

12 Reapply air pressure to the cylinder to retain the valve in the closed position, then remove the tape or rubber band from the valve stem.

13 Lubricate the valve stems with engine oil and install new valve stem seals. Valve stem seals can be installed with a special tool, or a deep socket and hammer - tap the seal only until seated (see illustration).

14 Install the valve spring in position over the valve, with the more closely-wound spring coils and the paint mark toward the cylinder head.

15 Install the valve spring retainer. Compress the valve springs and carefully position the keepers in the groove. Apply a small dab of grease to the inside of each keeper to hold it in place (see illustration).

16 Remove the pressure from the spring tool and make sure the keepers are seated.

17 Disconnect the air hose and remove the adapter from the spark plug hole.

18 Refer to Section 8 and install the camshaft and lifters, then refer to Section 7 and install the timing chain.

19 Refer to Section 4 and install the valve covers.

20 Install the spark plug(s), ignition coils and the upper and lower intake plenum referring to the appropriate Sections as necessary.

21 Start and run the engine, then check for oil leaks and unusual sounds coming from the valve cover area.

7 Timing chains and sprockets - removal, inspection and installation

❋❋ CAUTION:

The engine must be completely cool before beginning this procedure.

➥**Note:** The timing chain procedure for these engines is a difficult procedure for the home mechanic. Great care must be taken to mark the relationship of all parts before disassembly, length of various bolts and their locations must be noted, and instant or digital photos taken for reference as you proceed.

REMOVAL

◆ **Refer to illustrations 7.14, 7.16, 7.19, 7.20, 7.21, 7.22, 7.23a, 7.23b, 7.24 and 7.27**

1 Relieve the system fuel pressure (see Chapter 4).
2 Disconnect the cable from the negative terminal of the battery (see Chapter 5, Section 1).
3 Remove the engine cover (see illustration 4.2).
4 Remove the drivebelts (see Chapter 1) and the idler pulley brackets.
5 Remove the spark plugs (see Chapter 1). Position the number one piston at TDC on the compression stroke (see Section 3).
6 Block the rear wheels and set the parking brake. Raise the front of the vehicle and support it securely on jackstands.
7 Drain the cooling system and the engine oil (see Chapter 1).
8 Remove the upper and lower radiator hoses, the engine cooling fans and the radiator (see Chapter 3).
9 Remove the crankshaft pulley (see Section 12).

➥**Note:** Don't allow the crankshaft to rotate during removal of the pulley. If the crankshaft moves, the number one piston will no longer be at TDC.

10 Remove the air conditioning compressor (see Chapter 3) and position it aside without disconnecting the refrigerant lines. Also remove the air conditioning compressor bracket from the engine.
11 Remove the upper and lower oil pans (see Section 14), then lower the vehicle.

➥**Note:** If the timing chain rear housing is not being removed for another procedure such as cylinder head removal, only the lower oil pan needs to be removed. With the lower pan removed, remove the two front bolts from the upper pan that thread into the timing chain rear cover.

12 Remove the upper and lower halves of the intake manifold plenum (see Section 9).
13 Remove the valve covers (see Section 4).

➥**Note:** If only the primary timing chain is to be removed, the valve covers do not have to be removed.

14 Remove the power steering pump (see Chapter 10) and position it aside without disconnecting the fluid lines. Also remove the fan pulley bracket and the power steering pump bracket (see illustration).
15 Remove the alternator (see Chapter 5).
16 Remove the water by-pass hose from the front of the engine (see illustration).
17 Disconnect the variable valve timing (VVT) sensors from the front timing chain cover (see Chapter 6). Remove the variable valve timing actuator covers. Loosen the bolts in the reverse order of the tightening sequence (see illustration 7.41c) and pull the covers straight out to disengage them from the intake and exhaust camshaft-sprocket actuator assemblies.

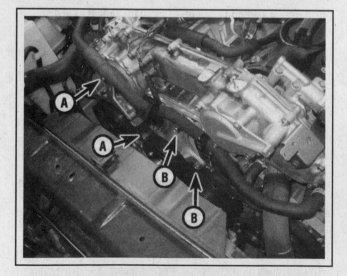

7.14 Remove the power steering pump and its mounting bracket (A), then remove the bolts (2 of 5 seen here) for the fan mounting bracket and idler pulley (B)

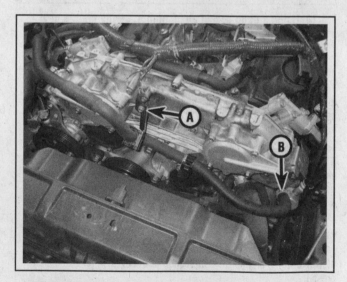

7.16 Remove the fastener securing the water by-pass bracket (A), then disconnect the hose (B)

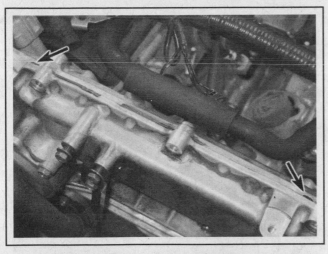

7.19 Insert a square-edged, blunt tool into the notches at the top of the timing chain cover and pull towards the front of the vehicle to pry the front timing cover off the engine

7.20 Verify the engine is at TDC by confirming that the intake and exhaust camshaft lobes on the number one cylinder are pointing upward

✳✳ CAUTION:

On 2005 and later G35 models, 2005 35QZ 35th Anniversary Edition and 2006 and later 350Z models, the VVT assembly differs from previous models in that it has a magnet retarder that operates on the exhaust camshaft. The cover must be pulled straight out from the timing chain front cover and thereafter kept with the engine side facing Up. If the magnet retarder falls out of the cover, the cover and assembly is no longer serviceable and must be replaced.

18 Detach the wiring harness from the brackets at the top of the timing chain cover. Remove the bolts securing the front timing chain cover in the reverse order of the tightening sequence (see illustration 7.40b). Note that various types and sizes of bolts are used. They must be reinstalled in their original locations. Mark each bolt or make a sketch to help remember where they go.

19 Remove the front timing chain cover (see illustration).

➡Note: Use a seal cutter to cut the liquid gasket during this procedure.

20 Confirm that the number one piston is still at TDC on the compression stroke by verifying that the intake and exhaust camshaft lobes on the number one cylinder are pointing upward (see illustration).

21 Relieve tension on the primary timing chain by releasing the spring clip. Depress the primary tensioner inward and lock it into place by inserting a suitable stopper pin into the hole on the front of the tensioner (see illustration).

➡Note: The 3.5L DOHC engine utilizes three timing chains to produce proper valve timing. The primary timing chain runs around the crankshaft sprocket, the water pump and two intake camshaft sprockets. This chain synchronizes the valve timing with the crankshaft and pistons, while two secondary timing chains run around the rear of the intake sprockets and separate exhaust camshaft sprockets to synchronize the intake and exhaust camshaft events.

22 Remove the primary timing chain tensioner, the tensioner pivot arm and the timing chain guides from the primary timing chain (see illustration).

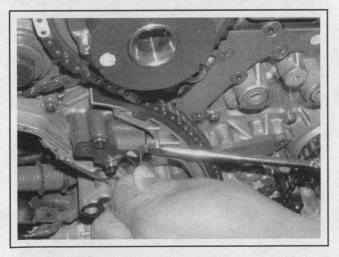

7.21 An ordinary paper clip can be straightened and used to lock the timing chain tensioner(s) in place

7.22 Remove the primary timing chain tensioner mounting bolts (A), the tensioner arm pivot bolt (B) and the chain guides (C) (models without exhaust timing control only)

7.23a Bend two paper clips so that they're long enough to protrude out past the camshaft sprocket once they're installed . . .

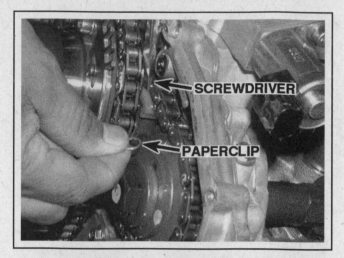

7.23b . . . then depress the secondary tensioners with a screwdriver and lock them in place by inserting a paper clip into the hole on the side of each tensioner - note that the secondary tensioner on the right bank points downward, while the secondary tensioner on the left bank points upward

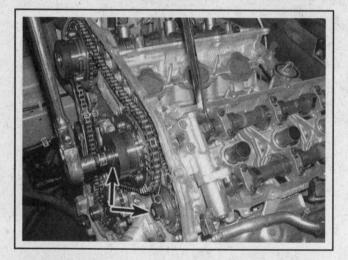

7.24 Hold the hexagonal lug on the camshaft with a wrench to keep it from rotating as the sprocket bolts are loosened

23 Depress the secondary timing chain tensioners and lock the tensioners in place by inserting a suitable stopper pin into the hole on the front of each tensioner (see illustrations).

24 Remove the camshaft sprocket bolts (see illustration).

25 Disengage the primary timing chain from the teeth on the chain sprockets and remove it from the engine.

26 Mark the camshaft sprockets with either an R or L to indicate the right or left side, then remove the camshaft sprockets and the secondary timing chains from the engine. Don't mix the sprockets up. They must be installed on the same camshaft from which they were removed.

⁂⁂ CAUTION:

The intake camshaft sprocket assemblies are identifiable because they have two chain sprockets, while the exhaust connects with only one chain. Do Not disassemble the variable valve timing actuator assembly from the intake camshaft sprocket for any reason. Only the central mounting bolt in any of the sprockets is to be removed, not the peripheral bolts at the front and rear of the sprockets.

27 Remove the crankshaft sprocket (see illustration).

INSPECTION

▶ **Refer to illustrations 7.28a and 7.28b**

28 Inspect the camshaft, water pump and crankshaft sprockets for wear on the teeth and keyways. Inspect the chains for cracks or excessive wear of the rollers. Inspect the facing of the chain guides and the secondary timing chain tensioners for excessive wear (see illustration).

➡**Note: If the secondary timing chain tensioners need to be replaced, the front camshaft bearing cap will have to be removed from the affected cylinder head to allow access to the secondary tensioner bolts (see illustration).**

INSTALLATION

▶ **Refer to illustrations 7.32a, 7.32b, 7.34a, 7.34b, 7.39, 7.40a, 7.40b, 7.41a, 7.41b, 7.41c and 7.41d**

29 Install the crankshaft sprocket with the mark facing up (see illustration 7.27).

7.27 Remove the crankshaft sprocket

7.28a Examine the chain guides for deep grooves and excessive wear - replace them if necessary

7.28b Secondary timing chain tensioner mounting bolts (A) - be sure to replace the O-ring (B) before reinstalling the front camshaft bearing cap

30 Verify that you have the correct timing chains for your vehicle by counting the number of links each chain has and comparing the new chains with the old chains. Also compare the position of the colored links in the new chains with the position of the colored links in the old chains.

31 If the secondary tensioners were removed, reinstall them and make sure the tensioner spring is locked in place.

32 Make sure the camshafts are positioned with the dowels facing up (see illustration 8.11). Install the secondary timing chains and sprocket assemblies on the camshafts with the timing marks aligned as shown (see illustrations). Then install the camshaft sprocket bolts hand tight.

33 Reconfirm that the secondary camshaft sprocket timing marks are aligned correctly with the copper colored links on the secondary timing chains and remove the stopper pins from the secondary chain tensioners (see illustration 7.32b).

34 Install the primary timing chain onto the engine by looping the

chain around the crankshaft sprocket and aligning the yellow or gold colored chain link with the mark on the crankshaft sprocket. Then place the chain around the water pump sprocket and finally around the primary camshaft sprockets making sure the yellow colored links align with their respective marks on the sprockets (see illustrations).

→**Note: It may be necessary to rotate the camshafts slightly in order to align the yellow colored chain links with the marks on the primary timing chain sprockets.**

35 Install the upper timing chain guides.

36 Install the primary tensioner arm/chain guides and the timing chain tensioner assembly (see illustration 7.22). Reconfirm that the number one piston is still at TDC on the compression stroke and that the timing marks on the camshaft and crankshaft sprockets are aligned with the colored links on the chain, then remove the stopper pin from the primary timing chain tensioner.

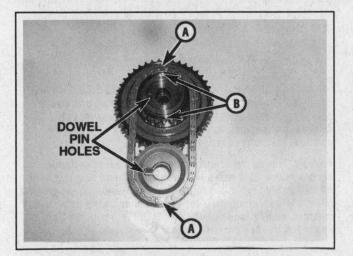

7.32a Align the copper colored links (A) on the secondary chain(s) with the marks on the camshaft sprockets (B) - this secondary timing chain assembly is for the left bank; when aligning the marks for the right bank, the dowel pin holes on the sprockets should point to the right

7.32b Note that the alignment of the exhaust camshaft sprocket mark (B) to the copper colored link (A) of the secondary chain can only be viewed from the front

7.34a The yellow colored or gold link on the timing chain (arrow) aligns with the mark on the crankshaft sprocket

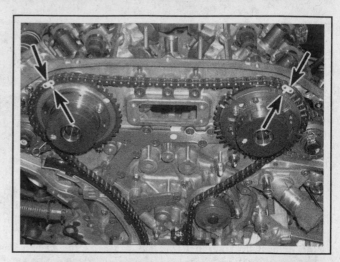

7.34b Make sure the copper colored links (upper arrows) on the primary timing chain align with the marks (lower arrows) on the intake camshaft sprockets

37 Tighten the camshaft sprocket bolts to the torque listed in this Chapter's Specifications.

38 Remove all traces of old sealant from the front timing chain cover, the cover bolts and the rear cover bolt holes.

39 Install new O-rings in the variable valve timing oil control orifice of the rear timing chain cover (see illustration).

40 Apply a 1/8-inch (3 mm) diameter bead of RTV sealant to the timing cover sealing surfaces (see illustration). Place the front timing chain cover in position on the engine and install the bolts in their original locations. Following the recommended tightening sequence, tighten the bolts to the torque listed in this Chapter's Specifications (see illustration).

➡Note: It will also be necessary to install the power steering pump bracket and the fan pulley bracket in order to tighten the bolts in the proper sequence.

41 Install new O-rings in the VVT orifices of the front timing chain cover and on the VVT actuator covers. Then apply a 1/8-inch (3 mm) diameter bead of RTV sealant to the sealing surface of the variable

valve timing actuator covers (see illustrations). Place the VVT covers in position over the dowels on the front timing cover and install the bolts in their original locations. Following the recommended tightening sequence, tighten the bolts to the torque listed in this Chapter's Specifications (see illustrations).

✳✳ CAUTION:

On 2005 and later G35 models, 2005 350Z 35th Anniversary Edition and all 2006 and later 350Z models, the VVT assembly differs from previous models in that it has a magnet retarder that operates on the exhaust camshaft. The cover must be installed straight onto the front timing cover. If the cover is tilted and the magnet retarder falls out, the cover and assembly are no longer serviceable and must be replaced.

42 The remainder of the installation is the reverse of removal. Be sure to follow the sealant manufacturer's recommendations for assembly and sealant curing times. Allow all sealant to fully cure before starting the engine.

43 Install a new oil filter, then refill the crankcase with oil and the cooling system with coolant (see Chapter 1).

44 Start the engine and check for leaks.

➡Note 1: On 2005 and later G35 models, 2005 350Z 35th Anniversary Edition and 2006 and later 350Z models, a computer relearn procedure must be performed if the Exhaust Valve Timing (EVT) components have been disconnected or removed/installed. Follow the Steps below.

➡Note 2: Timing chain noise may be apparent after performing this procedure. This noise is normal and should only last until the air has bled out of the high pressure chamber of the primary timing chain tensioner. If after several minutes the noise is still apparent, simply run the engine at 3,000 rpm with the transmission in Neutral or Park until the noise subsides.

45 Start the procedure with the engine warm and the front wheels in the straight-ahead position.

46 Make sure all electrical accessories are Off, such as the headlights, stereo, or climate-control system.

47 Start the engine and run it for 20 seconds at 1800 to 2000 rpm. Be sure to listen for any unusual noise or vibration.

7.39 Install new O-rings at the indicated area on the right and left side of the rear timing cover case

7.40a Apply RTV sealant to the front timing chain cover at the areas shown - be sure to wipe off any excess sealant

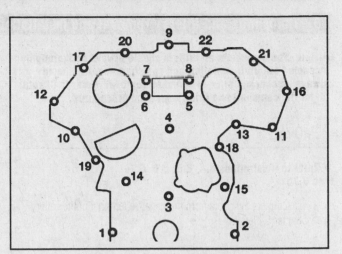

7.40b Front timing chain cover TIGHTENING sequence

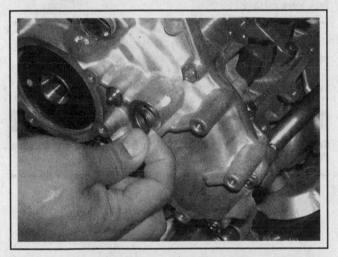

7.41a Install new O-rings in both of the VVT orifices on the front timing chain cover

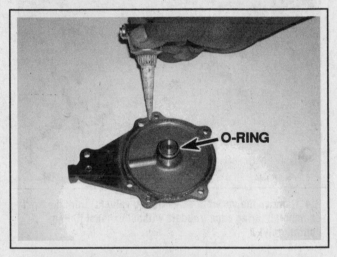

7.41b Apply a light film of engine oil to the new O-rings and install them in the groove on the VVT actuator covers, then apply a 1/8-inch (3 mm) diameter bead of RTV sealant to the indicated areas

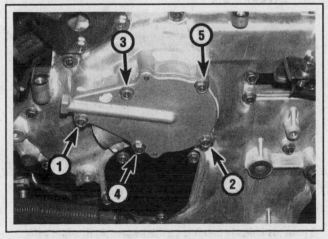

7.41c Variable Valve Timing actuator cover TIGHTENING sequence - models without exhaust timing control

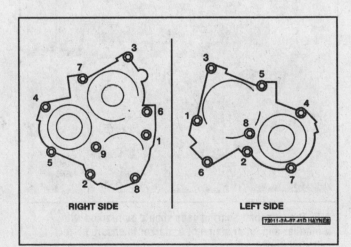

7.41d Variable Valve Timing actuator cover TIGHTENING sequence - all models with exhaust timing control

8 Camshafts and lifters - removal and installation

➡Note: The camshafts and lifters should always be thoroughly inspected before installation and camshaft endplay should always be checked prior to camshaft removal. Refer to Chapter 2B for the camshaft and lifter inspection procedures.

REMOVAL

◆ **Refer to illustrations 8.4, 8.5, 8.6, 8.7a and 8.7b**

1 Disconnect the cable from the negative terminal of the battery (see Chapter 5, Section 1).

8.4 Remove the variable valve timing valve(s) from the No.1 camshaft bearing caps (models without exhaust timing control only)

2 Remove the intake plenum (see Section 9) and the valve covers (see Section 4).

3 Disconnect the electrical connectors at the camshaft position sensors (one for each bank) and remove the sensors (see Chapter 6).

4 Remove the timing chains and the camshaft sprockets (see Section 7). On models without exhaust timing control, remove the variable intake valve timing valve(s) from the top of the number one camshaft journal(s) (see illustration).

5 Mark the camshaft bearing caps from 1 to 4, and with an "I" or an "E," to indicate intake or exhaust. Also mark arrows indicating the front of the engine (see illustration). Loosen the camshaft bearing caps in two or three steps, in the reverse order of the tightening sequence (see illustrations 8.14a and 8.14b).

⁂ CAUTION:

Keep the caps in order. They must go back in the same location they were removed from.

6 Remove the bearing caps and the camshafts. Make a note of the camshaft markings to ensure correct installation (see illustration).

7 Remove the lifters from the cylinder head, keeping track of where they were installed (see illustrations).

⁂ CAUTION:

Keep the lifters in order. They must go back in the same location they were removed from.

8 Inspect the camshaft and lifters as described in Chapter 2B.

8.5 The camshaft bearing caps should be marked with a number and letter stamp or a marker to ensure correct reinstallation

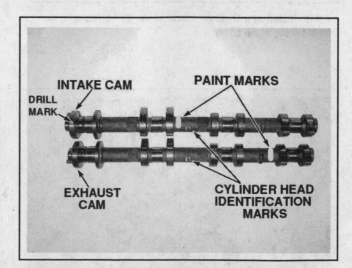

8.6 The ID mark in the center of each camshaft identifies which cylinder head the camshaft belongs to; "L" for left and "R" for right - paint marks between the No. 2 and No. 3 journals indicate that it is an intake camshaft, while paint marks between the No. 3 and No. 4 journals indicate that it is an exhaust camshaft

8.7a Pull straight up to remove each lifter

8.7b The lifters can be stored in individually marked plastic bags or a divided box as shown

INSTALLATION

▶ **Refer to illustrations 8.11, 8.12a, 8.12b, 8.14a and 8.14b**

9   Lubricate the lifters with clean engine oil and install them in their original locations.

10 Apply moly-based engine assembly lubricant to the camshaft lobes and journals.

11 Install the camshafts in their original positions with the dowel pins facing up (180 degrees from the cylinder head mating surface) and inline with the cylinder bank (see illustration).

12 Apply a bead of RTV sealant to the sealing surfaces of the No. 1 bearing cap(s) and the cylinder head. Install new O-rings on the secondary timing chain tensioner(s) and the VVT oil control orifice on the No. 1 bearing cap(s) (see illustrations).

13 Install the bearing caps and bolts and tighten them hand tight.

8.11 Install the camshafts with the dowel pins facing up (180 degrees from the cylinder head mating surface) and inline with the cylinder bank

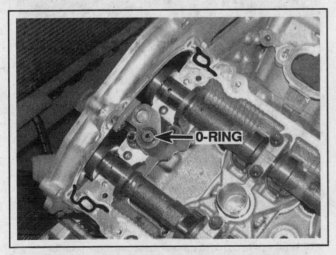

8.12a Apply RTV sealant to the cylinder head at the areas shown and install the secondary tensioner O-ring(s) - be sure to wipe off any excess sealant

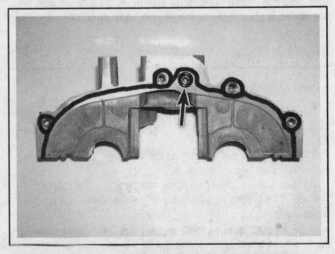

8.12b Apply a small dab of grease to the VVT oil control orifice O-ring (arrow) to hold it in place on the No.1 bearing cap, then apply RTV sealant to the areas shown

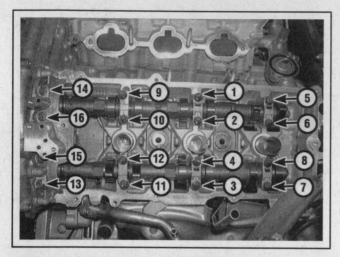

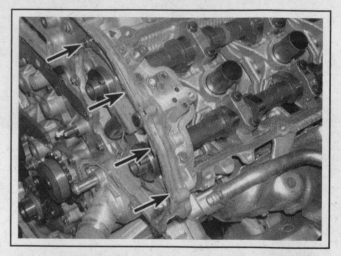

8.14a Camshaft bearing cap TIGHTENING sequence

8.14b After the camshaft bearing caps have been tightened in order, tighten the bolts (arrows) securing the rear timing chain cover to the No.1 bearing cap(s)

14 Tighten the bearing cap bolts in several steps, to the torque listed in this Chapter's Specifications, using the proper tightening sequence (see illustrations).

15 Install the camshaft sprockets and timing chain (see Section 7). Hold the camshafts with a suitable wrench (only on the hex portion) as you tighten the sprocket bolts to the specified torque.

16 The remainder of installation is the reverse of removal. If any part of the valve train was replaced, check and adjust the valve clearance (see Section 5).

➡Note: On 2005 and later G35 models, 2005 350Z 35th Anniversary Edition and all 2006 and later 350Z models, a computer relearn procedure must be performed if the Exhaust Valve Timing (EVT) components have been disconnected or removed/installed. Follow Steps 45 through 47 in Section 7.

9 Intake manifold - removal and installation

➡Note: On the covered models, disconnecting the electrical connector at the throttle body and later reconnecting it will cause the engine management system to require two relearning procedures (see Chapter 5, Section 1). To avoid having to perform this procedure during removal or installation of the plenum, you can unbolt the throttle body from the plenum with the connector in place and set the throttle body aside carefully.

INTAKE PLENUM

▶ **Refer to illustration 9.4**

1 Relieve the fuel pressure (see Chapter 4).

2 Disconnect the cable from the negative terminal of the battery (see Chapter 5, Section 1).

3 Refer to Chapter 4 and remove the air intake duct. Also remove the engine cover (see illustration 4.2).

4 Label and disconnect the hoses and harnesses that may be attached to the plenum (see illustration). See the **Note** at the beginning of this Section.

➡Note: All 2003 through 2006 models and 2007 G35 Coupe models have a two-piece plenum with a single throttle body, while 2007 G35 Sedan, 350Z and all 2008 models have a one-piece plenum with two throttle bodies.

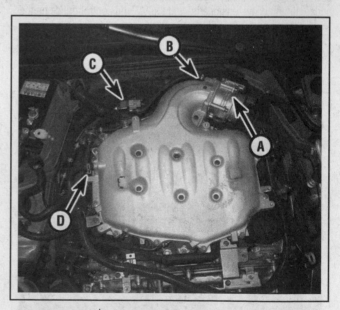

9.4 Plenum mounting details: A, unbolt the throttle body and set it aside; B, pinch off and disconnect the throttle body coolant hoses; C, unbolt and set aside the EVAP control solenoid; D, disconnect the PCV hose

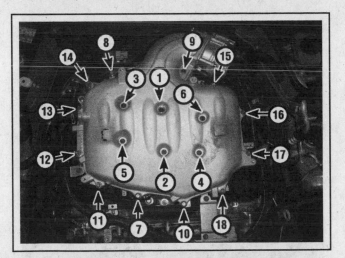

**9.5 Upper intake plenum TIGHTENING sequence
(all 2003 through 2006 models and 2007 G35 coupe models)**

9.6 Lower intake plenum TIGHTENING sequence

All 2003 through 2006 models and 2007 G35 coupe models

▶ **Refer to illustrations 9.5 and 9.6**

5   Loosen the upper intake plenum fasteners in the reverse order of the tightening sequence (see illustration) and remove the upper plenum.

6   Carefully lift the upper plenum off, taking care not to damage the rubber gasket. The lower plenum bolts can now be removed in the reverse order of the tightening sequence (see illustration).

7   To install the lower plenum, clean the mounting surfaces of the intake manifold and the lower and upper plenums with lacquer thinner, removing all traces of the old gasket material or sealant. Install a new gasket on the intake manifold and position the lower plenum on the intake manifold.

8   Align the metal plate over the lower plenum and install the fasteners. Tighten the fasteners, in the proper sequence, to the torque listed in this Chapter's Specifications (see illustration 9.6).

9   Install the new gasket on the lower plenum with the marks (if equipped) facing forward, then install the upper plenum onto the lower plenum and tighten the bolts, in the proper sequence (see illustration 9.5), to the torque listed in this Chapter's Specifications.

10 The remainder of the installation is the reverse of removal.

All other models

▶ **Refer to illustration 9.13**

11 Loosen the intake plenum fasteners in the reverse order of the tightening sequence (see illustration 9.13) and remove the plenum.

12 Clean the underside of the plenum and the intake manifold surface of old gasket material, then install a new gasket on the intake manifold.

13 Tighten the bolts, in the proper sequence, to the torque listed in this Chapter's Specifications (see illustration).

14 The remainder of installation is the reverse of the removal procedure.

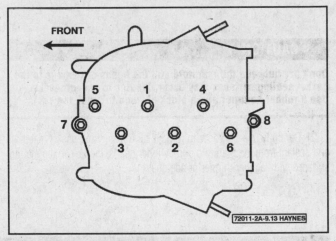

9.13 Intake plenum TIGHTENING sequence (2007 and later G35 Sedan and 350Z models)

INTAKE MANIFOLD

▶ **Refer to illustrations 9.23a and 9.23b**

15 Refer to Steps 1 through 14 above as applicable to the model year and remove the intake plenum(s).

16 Label and detach any remaining hoses which would interfere with the removal of the lower intake manifold.

17 Refer to Chapter 4 and remove the fuel rail and injectors from the lower intake manifold.

18 Make several match marks on the manifold and the cylinder heads to confirm alignment of the ports during assembly.

19 Loosen the manifold mounting bolts/nuts in 1/4-turn increments until they can be removed by hand in the reverse order of the tightening sequence (see illustrations 9.23a and 9.23b).

20 The manifold will probably be stuck to the cylinder heads and force may be required to break the gasket seal.

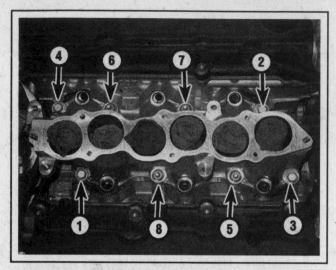

9.23a Intake manifold TIGHTENING sequence (all 2003 through 2006 models and 2007 G35 Coupe models)

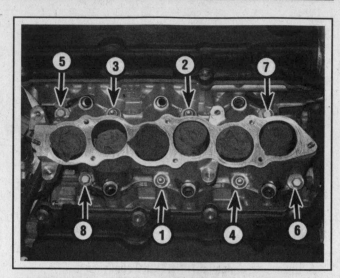

9.23b Intake manifold TIGHTENING sequence (2007 and later G35 Sedan and 350Z models)

⁂ CAUTION:

Don't pry between the manifold and the heads or damage to the gasket sealing surfaces may occur, leading to vacuum leaks. Use a rubber hammer and a block of wood to break the seal.

21 Carefully use a scraper to remove all traces of old gasket material and sealant from the manifold and cylinder heads, then clean the mating surfaces with lacquer thinner or acetone.

22 Install new gaskets, then position the lower manifold on the engine. Make sure the gaskets and manifolds are aligned over the studs in the cylinder heads, then install the nuts. Align the match marks you made during removal.

23 Following the recommended tightening sequence, tighten the nuts/bolts, in several steps, to the torque listed in this Chapter's Specifications (see illustrations).

24 The remainder of the installation is the reverse of the removal procedure. Run the engine and check for fuel, vacuum and coolant leaks.

10 Exhaust manifold - removal and installation

⁂ WARNING:

The engine must be completely cool before beginning this procedure.

REMOVAL

▶ **Refer to illustrations 10.7a and 10.7b**

1 Disconnect the cable from the negative terminal of the battery (see Chapter 5, Section 1).

2 Block the rear wheels and set the parking brake.

3 Raise the front of the vehicle and support it securely on jackstands, then remove the lower splash shield from below the engine

(if equipped). Apply penetrating oil to the fasteners on the exhaust components and allow it to soak in.

4 Refer to Chapter 4 and remove the exhaust Y-pipe (from the two converters to the exhaust pipe) from the vehicle.

5 Disconnect the oxygen sensor connectors.

6 On G35 models, access to the left-side manifold will require that the lower steering joint at the steering gear be disconnected and the lower shaft moved aside (see Chapter 10).

7 Unbolt the exhaust heat shields and remove the catalytic converters from the exhaust manifolds (see illustrations).

8 When removing the left exhaust manifold on G35 models, or either manifold on 350Z models it will be necessary to drain the coolant (see Chapter 1) and remove the coolant tube from the front and sides of the engine (see illustration 11.6).

9 Remove the manifold-to-head nuts/bolts and detach the manifold and gasket.

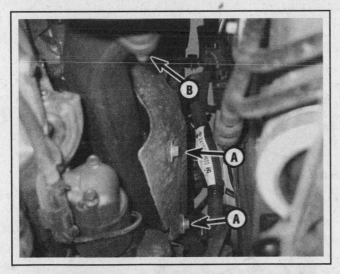

10.7a Remove the heat shield bolts (A) from each exhaust manifold, then soak and remove the bolts (B, one shown) securing the front of the converters

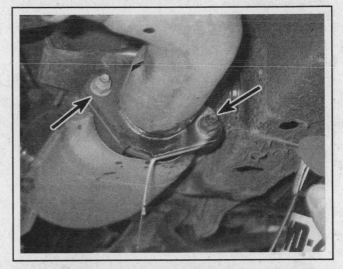

10.7b Spray with penetrant and remove the nuts securing the rear of the converter, then remove the converter

INSTALLATION

10 Use a scraper to remove all traces of old gasket material and carbon deposits from the manifold and cylinder head mating surfaces.

11 Position the new exhaust manifold gaskets over the studs on the cylinder head. The gaskets are marked with an arrow (350Z models) or a large dot (G35 models) which should point Up when installed.

12 Install the manifold and thread the mounting nuts/bolts into place.

13 Working from the center out, tighten the nuts/bolts in several increments, to the torque listed in this Chapter's Specifications.

14 Reinstall the remaining parts in the reverse order of removal.

15 Run the engine and check for exhaust leaks.

11 Cylinder head - removal and installation

❋❋ WARNING:

The engine must be completely cool before beginning this procedure.

➡Note: To remove the rear timing chain cover, the upper oil pan must be removed from the engine. To allow for this, the engine should be raised with a hoist, supported from below with a transmission jack, and the engine mounts disconnected from the frame. Refer to Chapter 10 and remove the front suspension crossmember, then lower the engine down to its original height.

REMOVAL

▶ **Refer to illustrations 11.6 and 11.8**

1 Refer to Section 7, Steps 1 through 27 and remove the timing chain(s) and sprockets.

❋❋ CAUTION:

Be careful not to disturb the crankshaft from TDC on the compression stroke of the No.1 cylinder during the remainder of this procedure.

2 Remove the rear timing chain cover bolts in the reverse order of the tightening sequence (see illustrations 11.22d and 11.22e).

3 Detach the rear timing cover from the engine.

➡Note: If the cover is stuck to the cylinder head or engine block, bump one end with a block of wood and a hammer to jar it loose. If that doesn't work, try to slip a flexible putty knife between the cover and the engine to break the gasket seal. Don't pry at the cover-to-cylinder head joint or damage to the sealing surfaces may occur (leading to oil leaks in the future).

4 Remove the intake manifold (see Section 9) and the exhaust manifold(s) (see Section 10).

5 Remove the camshafts and lifters from the cylinder head (see Section 8).

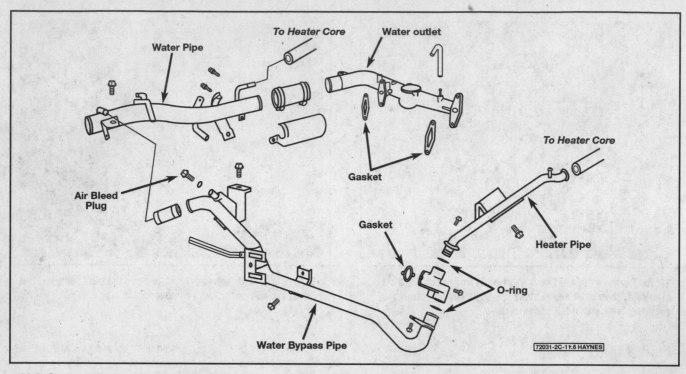

11.6 Coolant tube mounting details - typical

6   Label and remove any remaining items attached to the cylinder head, such as coolant fittings, tubes, cables, hoses, wires or brackets (see illustration).

7   Using a breaker bar and the appropriate sized Allen-head socket, loosen the cylinder head bolts in 1/4-turn increments until they can be removed by hand. Loosen the bolts in the reverse order of the tightening sequence (see illustration 11.20) to avoid warping or cracking the head.

8   Lift the cylinder head off the engine block. If it's stuck, very carefully pry up at a casting protrusion, beyond the gasket surface (see illustration).

9   Remove all external components from the head to allow for thorough cleaning and inspection.

➡**Note: See Chapter 2, Part B, for cylinder head inspection and servicing procedures.**

INSTALLATION

▶ **Refer to illustrations 11.11, 11.14, 11.20, 11.22a, 11.22b, 11.22c, 11.22d and 11.22e**

10   The mating surfaces of the cylinder head and block must be perfectly clean when the head is installed.

11   Use a gasket scraper to remove all traces of carbon and old gasket material from the cylinder head and engine block, then clean the mating surfaces with lacquer thinner or acetone (see illustration). If there's oil on the mating surfaces when the head is installed, the gasket may not seal correctly and leaks could develop. When working on the block, stuff the cylinders with clean shop rags to keep out debris. Use a vacuum cleaner to remove material that falls into the cylinders.

11.8 Pry on a casting protrusion to break the head loose

11.11 Carefully remove all traces of old gasket material from the sealing surfaces

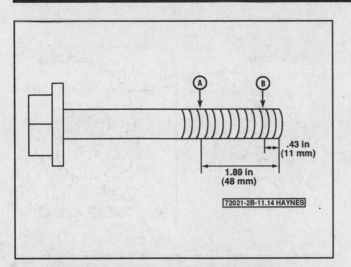

11.14 Measure each cylinder head bolt at point A and point B. If the difference between the two exceeds the specification, the bolt will have to be replaced

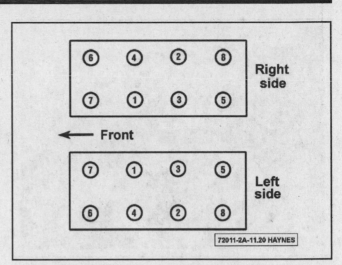

11.20 Cylinder head bolt TIGHTENING sequence

12 Check the block and head mating surfaces for nicks, deep scratches and other damage. If damage is slight, it can be removed with a file; if it's excessive, machining may be the only alternative.

13 Use a tap of the correct size to chase the threads in the head bolt holes, then clean the holes with compressed air - make sure that nothing remains in the holes.

❊❊ WARNING:

Wear eye protection when using compressed air!

---

14 Measure each cylinder head bolt for stretching (see illustration). If the diameter of the bolt threads at point A and the diameter of the bolt threads at point B differ more than 0.0043 inch (0.11 mm), the bolts have exceeded the maximum amount of stretch and will need to be replaced.

15 Check the head gasket surface of the head and the intake and exhaust manifold surfaces for any signs of damage, corrosion, cracks or surface irregularities.

16 Install the components that were removed from the head.

17 Position the new cylinder head gasket over the dowel pins on the block, noting which side of the gasket faces up.

18 Carefully set the head on the block without disturbing the gasket.

19 Before installing the head bolts, apply a small amount of clean engine oil to the threads and the underside of the bolt heads.

20 Install the bolts in their original locations and tighten them finger tight. Then tighten all the bolts in several steps, following the proper sequence (see illustration), to the torque listed in this Chapter's Specifications.

21 Remove all traces of old sealant from the rear timing chain cover and the cover bolts.

22 Apply a bead of RTV sealant to the rear timing chain cover sealing surfaces (see illustration). Install new O-rings in the front of the engine block and in the variable valve timing oil control orifices in the cylinder head (see illustrations). Place the rear timing chain cover in position over the dowels on the engine and install the bolts in their original

locations. Following the recommended tightening sequence, tighten the bolts to the torque listed in this Chapter's Specifications (see illustrations).

23 Install the camshafts as described in Section 8, then install the timing chains and sprockets as described in Section 7. The remaining installation steps are the reverse of removal. If any part of the valve train was replaced, check and adjust the valve clearance (see Section 5).

24 Refill the cooling system, and change the engine oil and filter (see Chapter 1).

25 Start the engine and check for oil and coolant leaks.

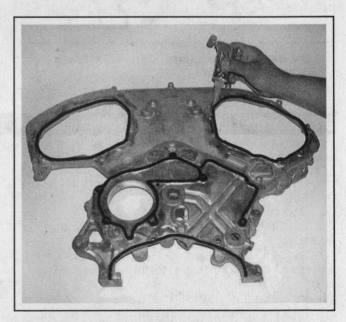

11.22a Apply RTV sealant to the rear timing chain cover at the areas shown - be sure to wipe off any excess sealant

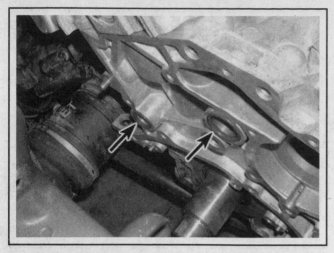

11.22b Install new O-rings in the front of the engine block . . .

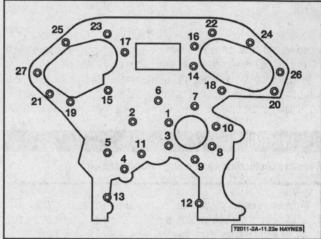

Right Bank   Left Bank
O-ring   O-ring

11.22c . . . and in the variable valve timing oil control orifices in the cylinder head

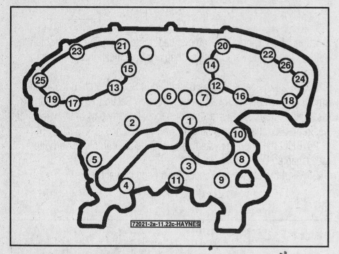

11.22d Rear timing chain cover TIGHTENING sequence - 2003 through 2006 models

11.22e Rear timing chain cover TIGHTENING sequence - 2007 and later models

12 Crankshaft pulley - removal and installation

♦ **Refer to illustrations 12.4 and 12.7**

1   Disconnect the cable from the negative terminal of the battery (see Chapter 5, Section 1).

2   Block the rear wheels and set the parking brake.

3   Raise the front of the vehicle and support it securely on jackstands.

4   Remove the lower splash shield if equipped (see illustration).

5   Remove the engine cooling fan and the fan shroud (see Chapter 3).

6   Remove the drivebelts (see Chapter 1).

7   Use a strap wrench around the crankshaft pulley to keep it from moving while loosening the bolt with a breaker bar and socket. Do not remove the bolt fully - it should stay with the pulley when you remove it (see illustration).

8   Wedge a prybar or two screwdrivers behind the crankshaft pulley and carefully pry it off the crankshaft. If the pulley is difficult to remove, place a two jaw type puller into the openings in the center of the hub

and pull it off. The center rod of the puller should be pushing against the pulley bolt.

❋❋ **CAUTION:**

DO NOT place the puller jaws around the outside of the crankshaft pulley or damage to the pulley will occur.

➡**Note: Depending on the type of puller you have, it may also be necessary to remove the radiator to gain sufficient clearance to use the puller.**

9   To install the crankshaft pulley, align the pulley groove with the key on the crankshaft and slide the pulley onto the crankshaft.

10 Install the crankshaft pulley retaining bolt and tighten it to the torque listed in this Chapter's Specifications.

11 The remainder of installation is the reverse of the removal.

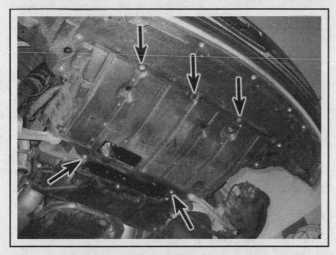

12.4 Lower splash shield mounting details

12.7 Use a strap wrench to hold the crankshaft pulley while removing the center bolt (a chain-type wrench may be used if you wrap a section of old drivebelt around the crankshaft pulley first)

13 Crankshaft front oil seal - replacement

▶ Refer to illustrations 13.2, 13.4 and 13.5

1   Remove the crankshaft pulley from the engine (see Section 12).
2   Carefully pry the seal out of the cover with a seal removal tool or a large screwdriver (see illustration).

✳✳ **CAUTION:**

Be careful not to scratch, gouge or distort the area that the seal fits into or an oil leak will develop.

3   Clean the bore to remove any old seal material and corrosion. Position the new seal in the bore with the seal lip (usually the side with the spring) facing IN (toward the engine). A small amount of oil applied to the outer edge and inner lip of the new seal will make installation easier.
4   Drive the seal into the bore with a seal driver or a large socket and hammer until it's completely seated (see illustration). Select a socket that's the same outside diameter as the seal, and make sure the new seal is pressed into place until it bottoms against the cover flange.

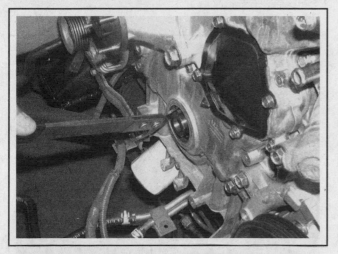

13.2 Pry the seal out very carefully with a seal removal tool or screwdriver, being careful not to nick or gouge the seal bore or the crankshaft

13.4 Use a large socket or seal driver to drive the new seal into the cover

5   Check the surface of the damper that the oil seal rides on. If the surface has been grooved from long-time contact with the seal, a press-on sleeve may be available to renew the sealing surface (see illustration). This sleeve is pressed into place with a hammer and a block of wood and is commonly available from most auto parts stores.

6   Lubricate the seal lips with engine oil and reinstall the crankshaft pulley. Install the crankshaft pulley retaining bolt and tighten it to the torque listed in this Chapter's Specifications.

7   The remainder of installation is the reverse of the removal. Run the engine and check for oil leaks.

13.5 If the sealing surface of the damper hub has a wear groove from contact with the seal, repair sleeves are available at most auto parts stores

14   Oil pan - removal and installation

REMOVAL

▶ **Refer to illustrations 14.6, 14.12 and 14.14**

1   Disconnect the cable from the negative terminal of the battery (see Chapter 5, Section 1).

2   Set the parking brake and block the rear wheels.

3   Raise the front of the vehicle and support it securely on jackstands.

4   Remove the splash shields under the engine (if equipped) (see illustration 12.4).

5   Drain the engine oil and remove the oil filter (see Chapter 1).

6   Remove the mounting bolts for the lower steel pan, and carefully prying between the upper and lower pans with a thin flat-bladed tool, separate and remove the lower pan (see illustration).

7   To remove the upper aluminum pan (also referred to as the lower block plate or block support), refer to Chapter 3 and drain the engine coolant, then disconnect the hoses and remove the oil cooler (see Section 16).

8   On AWD models, remove the driveaxles (see Chapter 8).

➡**Note: The left driveaxle goes through a tube (sealed with O-rings) in the upper oil pan.**

9   Remove the engine oil dipstick and the dipstick tube.

10   Remove the starter (see Chapter 5). Raise the engine slightly with a hoist from above and remove the front mounts. Referring to Chapter 10, remove the suspension front crossmember and steering gear to provide clearance for upper oil pan removal.

11   If equipped with an automatic transmission, unbolt the clamps securing the transmission fluid lines and set the lines aside without disconnecting them.

12   Remove the bolts securing the aluminum oil pan to the transmission (see illustration).

14.6 Remove the lower oil pan mounting bolts

14.12 The upper oil pan is attached to the transmission bellhousing

14.14 Insert a flat-head screwdriver or small pry bar into the notch on the side of the oil pan to break it loose - be careful not to damage the sealing surfaces!

13 Remove the remaining upper aluminum pan mounting bolts in the reverse of the tightening sequence (see illustrations 14.19a and 14.19b).

14 To loosen the upper oil pan from the block, wedge a flat head screwdriver or thin prybar into the notch on the side of the oil pan, being careful not to damage the sealing surfaces of the oil pan or engine block (see illustration).

INSTALLATION

◆ **Refer to illustrations 14.18, 14.19a, 14.19b, 14.22a and 14.22b**

15 Use a scraper to remove all traces of old gasket material and sealant from the upper aluminum section of the oil pan, the lower steel pan and the engine block. Clean the mating surfaces with brake cleaner.

✳✳ CAUTION:

Be careful not to scratch or gouge the gasket surface of the block or oil pan. A leak could develop after the repairs have been completed.

16 Make sure the threaded bolt holes in the block and aluminum section of the oil pan are clean.

17 Apply a bead of RTV sealant to the ends of the timing chain cover gasket and the rear oil seal retainer gasket, then place the gaskets in position on the oil pan. Apply a bead of RTV sealant around the upper aluminum oil pan flange.

➡**Note: The oil pan must be installed within 15 minutes once the sealant has been applied.**

18 Install new O-rings in the engine block and the oil pump body (see illustration).

19 Carefully position the upper aluminum section of the oil pan on the engine block and install the bolts. Following the recommended sequence, tighten the fasteners in three or four steps to the torque listed in this Chapter's Specifications (see illustrations).

20 Install the transmission mounting bolts that go through the upper oil pan (see illustration 14.12).

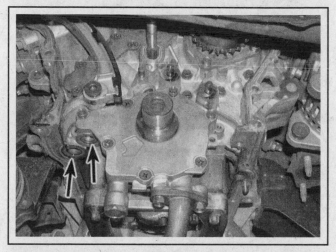

14.18 Install new O-rings in the block and the oil pump housing

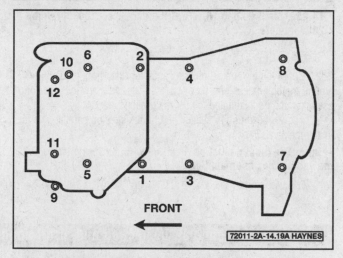

14.19a Aluminum oil pan TIGHTENING sequence - 2003 through 2006 models

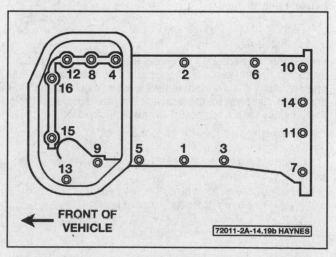

14.19b Aluminum oil pan TIGHTENING sequence - 2007 and 2008 models

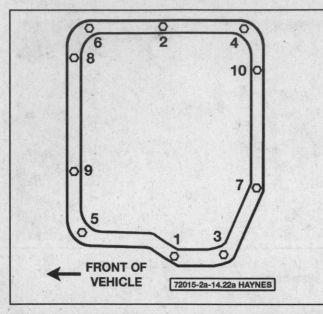

14.22a Steel oil pan TIGHTENING sequence - 2003 through 2006 models

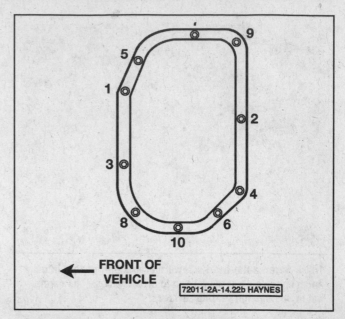

14.22b Steel oil pan TIGHTENING sequence - 2007 and 2008 models

21 Check the lower steel oil pan flange for distortion, particularly around the bolt holes. If necessary, place the pan on a wood block and use a hammer to flatten and restore the gasket surface.

22 Apply a bead of RTV sealant around the steel oil pan flange and install the steel oil pan.

➡Note: The oil pan must be installed within 15 minutes once the sealant has been applied.

Following the recommended sequence, tighten the fasteners in several steps to the torque listed in this Chapter's Specifications (see illustrations).

23 The remainder of installation is the reverse of removal. Be sure to install a new oil filter (see Chapter 1) and wait at least one hour before adding oil.

15 Oil pump - removal, inspection and installation

REMOVAL

▶ **Refer to illustration 15.3**

1 Refer to Section 7 and remove the primary timing chain and the crankshaft sprocket.

➡Note: It is not necessary to remove the camshaft sprockets, the camshaft sprocket bolts, the secondary timing chains or the primary timing chain tensioner pivot arm/chain guide during this procedure. Simply pivot the tensioner arm/chain guide over to the left side to allow removal of the oil pump housing.

2 Remove the steel lower oil pan (see Section 14). Remove the oil pump pick-up tube and screen.

3 Remove the oil pump-to-engine block bolts from the front of the engine (see illustration).

4 Gently pry the oil pump housing outward enough to clear the dowel pins on the engine block and remove it from the engine.

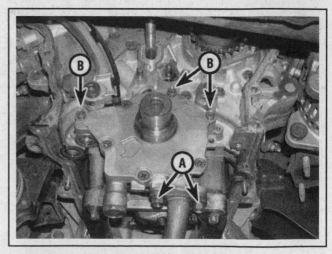

15.3 Remove the mounting bolts (A) and detach the oil pick-up tube from the oil pump, then remove the oil pump housing retaining bolts (B)

15.5 Remove the screws and lift the cover off

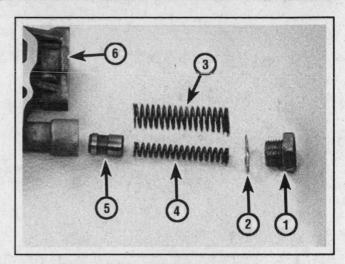

15.7 Oil pressure relief valve components

1	Plug	4	Inner spring (if equipped)
2	Washer	5	Relief valve
3	Outer spring	6	Oil pump housing

INSPECTION

▶ **Refer to illustrations 15.5, 15.7, 15.8a, 15.8b, 15.8c, 15.8d and 15.8e**

5   Use a large Phillips screwdriver to remove the screws holding the front cover on the oil pump housing (see illustration).

6   Clean all components with solvent, then inspect them for wear and damage.

7   Remove the oil pressure regulator cap, washer, spring(s) and valve (see illustration). Check the oil pressure regulator valve sliding surface and valve spring. If either the spring or the valve is damaged, they must be replaced as a set.

8   Check the clearance of the following oil pump components with a feeler gauge (see illustrations) and compare the measurements to the clearance listed in this Chapter's Specifications:

a) Rotor tooth tip clearance
b) Outer rotor-to-body clearance
c) Cover-to-inner rotor clearance
d) Cover-to-outer rotor clearance

If any clearance is excessive, replace the entire oil pump assembly.

9   Pack the pump with petroleum jelly to prime it. Assemble the oil pump and tighten the screws securely. Install the oil pressure regulator valve, spring and washer, then tighten the oil pressure regulator valve cap.

15.8a Use feeler gauges to measure the rotor tooth tip clearance . . .

15.8b . . . and the outer rotor-to-body clearance

15.8c Measure the cover-to-rotor end clearance with a straightedge and feeler gauge - measure (A) above the inner rotor and (B) above the outer rotor

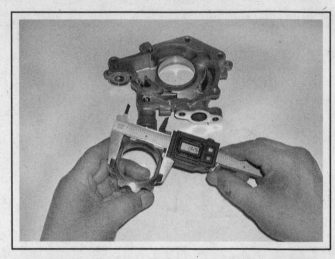

15.8d Use calipers to measure the diameter of the inner rotor ridge (the part of the inner rotor that rides in the pump body) . . .

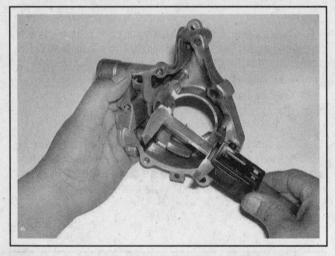

15.8e . . . and subtract the inner rotor ridge diameter from the opening in the pump body where the inner rotor rides to obtain the inner rotor ridge-to-body clearance

15.10 There is a flat surface (arrow) on each side of the crankshaft - align them with the flats on the inner gear

INSTALLATION

♦ Refer to illustration 15.10

10 Use new gaskets (where applicable) on all disassembled parts and reverse the removal procedure for installation. Align the flats on the crankshaft (see illustration) with the flats on the oil pump gear. Tighten all fasteners to the torque listed in this Chapter's Specifications.

➡ Note: Before installing the oil pan, be sure to replace the O-rings on the oil pump housing and engine block (see illustration 14.28).

16 Engine oil cooler and adapter - general information and replacement

GENERAL INFORMATION

1   Engines equipped with automatic transmissions are provided extra engine cooling by an oil cooler (which is mounted to an adapter at the front of the oil pan, next to the oil filter). The oil filter adapter doubles as a housing to which the oil pressure sending unit and the oil cooler are mounted. The oil cooler adapter also incorporates an oil pressure relief valve, which redirects oil flow to bypass the oil cooler when pressures are too high. The oil cooler has two hoses connecting the cooler to the engine, where oil temperature is lowered by the radiator coolant. The hose that connects to the passenger side water pipe is the inlet side of the oil cooler, and the hose that connects to the main thermostat housing (at the front of the engine) is the outlet side of the oil cooler.

REPLACEMENT

▶ **Refer to Illustrations 16.3, 16.5 and 16.8**

❋❋ WARNING:

The engine must be completely cool before beginning this procedure.

2   Drain the engine oil and the cooling system (see Chapter 1).
3   Detach the hose clamps and remove the inlet and outlet hoses from the oil cooler (see illustration).
4   Remove the oil filter from the oil cooler assembly.
5   Loosen the oil cooler retaining nut and remove the oil cooler and O-rings from the adapter (see illustration).
6   If it's necessary to remove the oil cooler adapter, simply remove the three retaining bolts and separate the adapter from the upper aluminum section of the oil pan. Be sure to remove the old gasket and thoroughly clean the mating surfaces of the oil pan and the adapter before

installing the oil cooler adapter and a new gasket back onto the oil pan. Tighten the adapter bolts to the torque listed in this Chapter's Specifications, then install the oil pressure sending unit back onto the adapter using pipe sealant on the threads.

7   Using a small amount of engine oil, lubricate the oil cooler O-rings. Install the large O-ring in the groove on the oil cooler and the small O-ring over the end of the oil cooler retaining bolt until it seats against the bolt head.

8   Position the oil cooler onto the adapter, so that the casting protrusion on the adapter aligns between the two tabs on the oil cooler, and install the retaining nut hand tight (see illustration).

9   Tighten the oil cooler retaining bolt to the torque listed in this Chapter's Specifications. Do not overtighten!

10   Install the oil cooler hoses, then run the engine and check for leaks. Turn off the engine for five minutes and check the oil and coolant levels, adding fluids if necessary.

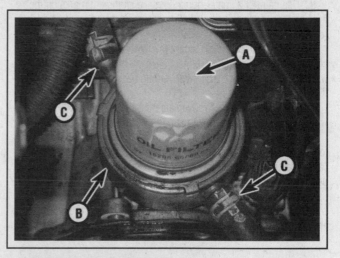

16.3 Oil cooler assembly

A   Oil filter   C   Coolant hoses
B   Oil cooler

16.5 Remove the oil cooler mounting nut

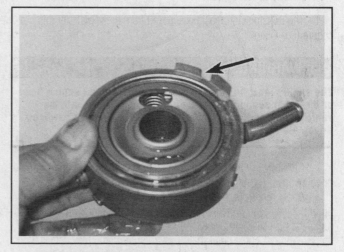

16.8 Align the tabs on the oil cooler with the casting protrusion on the oil cooler adapter

17 Flywheel/driveplate - removal and installation

♦ **Refer to illustration 17.4**

1   Raise the vehicle and support it securely on jackstands, then refer to Chapter 7 and remove the transmission.

✴✴ WARNING:

The engine must be supported from above with an engine hoist or three-bar support fixture before working underneath the vehicle with the transmission removed.

2   If the vehicle is equipped with a manual transmission, remove the pressure plate and clutch disc (see Chapter 8). Now is a good time to check/replace the clutch components and pilot bushing if necessary. If the vehicle is equipped with an automatic transmission, now would be a good time to check and replace the front pump seal/O-ring.

3   Use paint or a center-punch to make alignment marks on the flywheel/driveplate and crankshaft to ensure correct alignment during reinstallation.

4   Remove the bolts that secure the flywheel/driveplate to the crankshaft (see illustration). If the crankshaft turns, hold the flywheel with a pry bar or wedge a screwdriver into the ring gear teeth to jam the flywheel.

5   Remove the flywheel/driveplate from the crankshaft. Since the flywheel is fairly heavy, be sure to support it while removing the last bolt.

6   Clean the flywheel to remove grease and oil. Inspect the surface for cracks, rivet grooves, burned areas and score marks. Light scoring can be removed with emery cloth. Check for cracked and broken ring gear teeth or a loose ring gear. Lay the flywheel on a flat surface and use a straightedge to check for warpage.

7   Clean and inspect the mating surfaces of the flywheel/driveplate and the crankshaft. If the crankshaft rear seal is leaking, replace it before reinstalling the flywheel/driveplate.

8   Position the flywheel/driveplate against the crankshaft. Be sure to align the marks made during removal. Note that some engines have an alignment dowel or staggered bolt holes to ensure correct installation. Before installing the bolts, apply thread locking compound to the threads.

9   Wedge a screwdriver into the ring gear teeth to keep the flywheel/driveplate from turning as you tighten the bolts to the torque listed in this Chapter's Specifications.

10 The remainder of installation is the reverse of the removal.

17.4 Hold a lever against a casting protrusion on the engine block or place a screwdriver through a hole in the driveplate to hold the driveplate while the mounting bolts are removed - note the painted marks made at the crank and driveplate for alignment

18 Rear main oil seal - replacement

♦ **Refer to illustration 18.2**

1   The transmission must be removed from the vehicle for this procedure (see Chapter 7).

✴✴ WARNING:

The engine must be supported from above with an engine hoist or three-bar support fixture before working underneath the vehicle with the transmission removed. Remove the flywheel/driveplate (see Section 17).

2   Carefully pry the old seal out of the block with a seal removal tool or screwdriver (see illustration).

3   Apply multi-purpose grease to the crankshaft seal journal and the lip of the new seal. Preferably, a seal installation tool should be used to press the new seal into place. The lip is stiff, so carefully work it onto the seal journal of the crankshaft. Don't rush it or you may damage the seal.

➡**Note: Install the seal squarely and only until flush with the back of the block, no further.**

4   The remaining steps are the reverse of removal.

18.2 Pry the seal out very carefully with a seal removal tool or screwdriver - if the crankshaft is damaged, the new seal will leak!

19 Engine mounts - check and replacement

1   There are two engine mounts and one transmission mount installed on the vehicles covered by this manual. The two engine mounts are located on the passenger and driver's side of the vehicle attached to the engine block and to each frame rail. The transmission mount is mounted to the rear of the transmission and the transmission crossmember. Refer to Chapter 7B for the transmission mount replacement procedures.

CHECK

2   During the check, the engine must be raised slightly to remove the weight from the mounts.

3   Raise the vehicle and support it securely on jackstands. Support the engine/transmission from above using a hoist or three bar support fixture.

4   Check the mounts to see if the rubber is cracked, hardened or separated from the bushing in the center of the mount.

5   Check for relative movement between the mounts and the engine or frame (use a large screwdriver or prybar to attempt to move the mounts). If movement is noted, lower the engine and tighten the mount fasteners.

6   Rubber preservative should be applied to the mounts to slow deterioration.

REPLACEMENT

▶ **Refer to illustrations 19.9 and 19.10**

7   Disconnect the cable from the negative terminal of the battery

(see Chapter 5, Section 1), set the parking brake and block the rear wheels.

8   Raise the front of the vehicle and support it securely on jackstands. Remove the splash shields from under the vehicle.

9   Remove the engine mount-to-frame nuts. There are two nuts on each side securing the mounts to the frame rails (see illustration).

10 Working in the engine compartment, remove the engine mount-to-engine mount bracket nut(s). There is one nut on each side securing the mounts to the engine mount bracket (see illustration).

➡**Note: The manufacturer advises against removing the engine-mount heat insulator cover retaining bolts, as damper oil will flow out and the insulator will not function.**

11 Attach an engine hoist to the top of the engine for lifting.

✳ CAUTION:

Do not use a jack under the oil pan to support the entire weight of the engine or the oil pump pick-up could be damaged.

12 Raise the engine slightly until the engine mount can be removed from the vehicle.

13 To remove the engine mount brackets, simply unscrew the four retaining bolts securing the mount bracket to each side of the engine.

14 Installation is the reverse of removal. Apply thread locking compound to the mount nuts before installing them, then tighten them to the torque listed in this Chapter's Specifications.

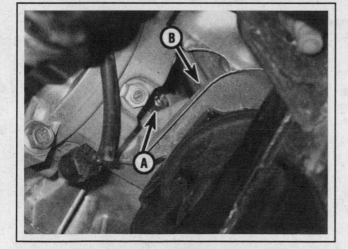

19.9 Engine mount bracket-to-engine bolts (A) (one indicated here) and insulator-to-mount upper nut (B)

19.10 Engine mount insulator-to-frame nut (shown from below)

Specifications

General

Engine type	V6
Displacement	213 cubic inches (3.5 liters)
Bore	3.76 inches (95.5 mm)
Stroke	3.205 inches (81.4 mm)
Cylinder numbers (front to rear)	
Right (passenger side)	1-3-5
Left (driver's side)	2-4-6
Firing order	1-2-3-4-5-6

```
FRONT        ⑤      ⑥
OF
VEHICLE      ③      ④
  ↓
             ❶      ②

72031-1-SPECS HAYNES
```

Cylinder location diagram

Camshaft

Thrust clearance (end play)	0.0045 to 0.0074 inch (0.115 to 0.188 mm)

Valve clearance (cold)

Intake	0.012 inch (0.30 mm)
Exhaust	0.013 inch (0.33 mm)

Oil pump

Body-to-outer rotor clearance	0.0045 to 0.0102 inch (0.114 to 0.260 mm)
Inner rotor-to-outer rotor tip clearance (maximum)	0.0071 inch (0.180 mm)
Inner rotor-to-body clearance	0.0012 to 0.0028 inch (0.030 to 0.070 mm)
Outer rotor-to-body clearance	0.0018 to 0.0035 inch (0.030 to 0.090 mm)

Torque specifications

	Ft-lbs (unless otherwise indicated)	Nm

➡ **Note: One foot-pound (ft-lb) of torque is equivalent to 12 inch-pounds (in-lbs) of torque. Torque values below approximately 15 foot-pounds are expressed in inch-pounds, because most foot-pound torque wrenches are not accurate at these smaller values.**

	Ft-lbs (unless otherwise indicated)	Nm
Camshaft bearing caps		
Step 1 (bolts 7-10)	12 in-lbs	1.96
Step 2 (bolts 1-6)	12 in-lbs	1.96
Step 3 (bolts 7-10)	48 in-lbs	5.5
Camshaft sprocket bolts	76	103
Crankshaft pulley-to-crankshaft bolt		
Step 1	33	44
Step 2	Tighten an additional 90 degrees	
Cylinder head bolts		
Step 1		
All except 2007 and later G35 Sedan and 350Z	72	98
2007 and later G35 Sedan and 350Z	77	105
Step 2	Loosen all bolts in reverse order of tightening	
Step 3	30	40
Step 4	Rotate an additional 90 degrees	
Step 5	Rotate an additional 90 degrees	
Driveplate/flywheel bolts	65	88
Exhaust manifold nuts (new)	22	30
Exhaust manifold heat-shield bolts	51 in-lbs	5.8
Engine mount insulator nuts	68	92

Torque specifications (continued)	Ft-lbs (unless otherwise indicated)	Nm
Engine mount bracket-to-block bolts	36	49
Intake manifold plenum bolts/nuts		
2003 to 2006	114 in-lbs	12.7
2007 and 2008	168 in-lbs	19.6
Intake manifold-to-head bolts/nuts		
Step 1	60 in-lbs	7
Step 2	20	29
Oil filter/cooler adapter housing-to-block		
bolts (AWD)	16	21.6
Oil pressure switch	132 in-lbs	14.7
Oil pump cover bolts	60 in-lbs	7
Oil pump-to-block bolts	60 in-lbs	7
Oil strainer mounting bolts	16	22
Oil pan bolts (steel lower pan)	80 in-lbs	9.0
Oil pan bolts (aluminum upper pan)		
To engine	156 in-lbs	17.6
To transmission	34	46
Oil pan drain plug	25	34
Timing chain tensioner bolts		
Primary chain	72 in-lbs	8.1
Secondary chain	75 in-lbs	8.5
Primary guide pivot bolt	144 in-lbs	15.7
Timing chain cover bolts, front		
2003 to 2006		
M8 bolts	19	25.7
M6 bolts	114 in-lbs	12.7
2007 and 2008		
M10 bolts (1 through 7)	41	55
M6 bolts	108 in-lbs	12
Timing chain cover bolts, rear (all models)	108 in-lbs	12
Valve cover bolts		
Step 1	17 in-lbs	2
Step 2	74 in-lbs	8.3

Notes

Section

Reference to other Chapters

SERVICE ENGINE SOON/MIL light on - See Chapter 6

2B

GENERAL ENGINE OVERHAUL PROCEDURES

1   General information - engine overhaul

▶ **Refer to illustrations 1.1, 1.2, 1.3, 1.4, 1.5 and 1.6**

Included in this portion of Chapter 2 are general information and diagnostic testing procedures for determining the overall mechanical condition of your engine.

The information ranges from advice concerning preparation for an overhaul and the purchase of replacement parts and/or components to detailed, step-by-step procedures covering removal and installation.

The following Sections have been written to help you determine whether your engine needs to be overhauled and how to remove and install it once you've determined it needs to be rebuilt. For information concerning in-vehicle engine repair, see Chapter 2A.

The Specifications included in this Part are general in nature and include only those necessary for testing the oil pressure and engine compression, and bottom-end torque specifications. Refer to Chapter 2A for additional engine Specifications.

It's not always easy to determine when, or if, an engine should be completely overhauled, because a number of factors must be considered.

High mileage is not necessarily an indication that an overhaul is needed, while low mileage doesn't preclude the need for an overhaul. Frequency of servicing is probably the most important consideration. An engine that's had regular and frequent oil and filter changes, as well as other required maintenance, will most likely give many thousands of miles of reliable service. Conversely, a neglected engine may require an overhaul very early in its service life.

Excessive oil consumption is an indication that piston rings, valve seals and/or valve guides are in need of attention. Make sure that oil leaks aren't responsible before deciding that the rings and/or guides are bad. Perform a cylinder compression check to determine the extent of the work required (see Section 3). Also, check the vacuum readings under various conditions (see Section 4).

Check the oil pressure with a gauge installed in place of the oil pressure sending unit and compare it to this Chapter's Specifications (see Section 2). If it's extremely low, the bearings and/or oil pump are probably worn out.

Loss of power, rough running, knocking or metallic engine noises, excessive valve train noise and high fuel consumption rates may also point to the need for an overhaul, especially if they're all present at the same time. If a complete tune-up doesn't remedy the situation, major mechanical work is the only solution.

An engine overhaul involves restoring the internal parts to the specifications of a new engine. During an overhaul, the piston rings are replaced and the cylinder walls are reconditioned (rebored and/or honed) (see illustrations 1.1 and 1.2). If a rebore is done by an automotive machine shop, new oversize pistons will also be installed. The main bearings, connecting rod bearings and camshaft bearings are generally replaced with new ones and, if necessary, the crankshaft may be reground to restore the journals (see illustration 1.3). Generally, the valves are serviced as well, since they're usually in less-than-perfect condition at this point. While the engine is being overhauled, other components, such as the distributor, starter and alternator, can be rebuilt as well. The end result should be similar to a new engine that will give many trouble free miles.

1.1 An engine block being bored. An engine rebuilder will use special machinery to recondition the cylinder bores

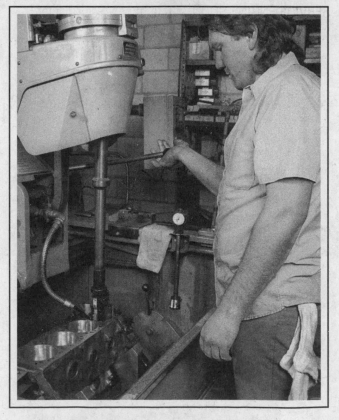

1.2 If the cylinders are bored, the machine shop will normally hone the engine on a machine like this

1.3 A crankshaft having a main bearing journal ground

1.4 A machinist checks for a bent connecting rod, using specialized equipment

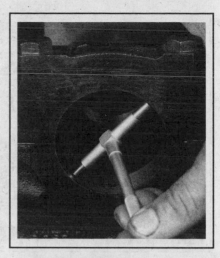

1.5 A bore gauge being used to check the main bearing bore

➡**Note: Critical cooling system components such as the hoses, drivebelts, thermostat and water pump should be replaced with new parts when an engine is overhauled. The radiator should be checked carefully to ensure that it isn't clogged or leaking (see Chapter 3). If you purchase a rebuilt engine or short block, some rebuilders will not warranty their engines unless the radiator has been professionally flushed. Also, we don't recommend overhauling the oil pump - always install a new one when an engine is rebuilt.**

Overhauling the internal components on today's engines is a difficult and time-consuming task which requires a significant amount of specialty tools and is best left to a professional engine rebuilder (see illustrations 1.4, 1.5 and 1.6). A competent engine rebuilder will handle the inspection of your old parts and offer advice concerning the reconditioning or replacement of the original engine, so never purchase parts or have machine work done on other components until the block has been thoroughly inspected by a professional machine shop. As a general rule, time is the primary cost of an overhaul, especially since the vehicle may be tied up for a minimum of two weeks or more. Be aware that some engine builders only have the capability to rebuild the engine you bring them while other rebuilders have a large inventory of rebuilt exchange engines in stock. Also be aware that many machine shops could take as much as two weeks time to completely rebuild your engine depending on shop workload. Sometimes it makes more sense to simply exchange your engine for another engine that's already rebuilt to save time.

1.6 Uneven piston wear like this indicates a bent connecting rod

2   Oil pressure check

▸ **Refer to illustrations 2.2 and 2.3**

1   Low engine oil pressure can be a sign of an engine in need of rebuilding. A "low oil pressure" indicator (often called an "idiot light") is not a test of the oiling system. Such indicators only come on when the oil pressure is dangerously low. Even a factory oil pressure gauge in the instrument panel is only a relative indication, although much better for driver information than a warning light. A better test is with a mechanical (not electrical) oil pressure gauge.

2.2 The oil pressure sending unit is located next to the oil filter

2.3 Install an oil pressure gauge into the block after removing the oil pressure sending unit

2   Locate the oil pressure indicator sending unit - it's located right near the oil filter/cooler assembly. On 2WD models, it is the closest sensor of the two there (see illustration); the one further from the filter is the oil temperature sensor. On AWD models, there are two sensors on the right side of the lower block; the lower of the two is the oil pressure sending unit.

3   Disconnect the electrical connector, unscrew and remove the oil pressure sending unit and then screw in the hose for your oil pressure gauge (see illustration). If necessary, install an adapter fitting. Use Teflon tape or thread sealant on the threads of the adapter and/or the fitting on the end of your gauge's hose.

4   Connect an accurate tachometer to the engine, according to the tachometer manufacturer's instructions.

5   Check the oil pressure with the engine running (normal operating temperature) at the specified engine speed, and compare it to this Chapter's Specifications. If it's extremely low, the bearings and/or oil pump are probably worn out.

6   Installation is the reverse of removal. Clean the threads on the sensor and use new sealant on the threads before installation.

3   Cylinder compression check

♦ **Refer to illustration 3.6**

1   A compression check will tell you what mechanical condition the upper end of your engine (pistons, rings, valves, head gaskets) is in. Specifically, it can tell you if the compression is down due to leakage caused by worn piston rings, defective valves and seats or a blown head gasket.

➡**Note: The engine must be at normal operating temperature and the battery must be fully charged for this check.**

2   Begin by cleaning the area around the spark plugs before you remove them (compressed air should be used, if available). The idea is to prevent dirt from getting into the cylinders as the compression check is being done.

3   Unplug the electrical connectors and remove the ignition coil assemblies (see Chapter 5). Also disable the fuel pump by removing the fuel pump fuse (see Chapter 4, Section 2).

4   Remove all of the spark plugs (see Chapter 1).

5   Detach the air intake duct(s) from the throttle body(ies), then block the throttle(s) wide open.

6   Install a compression gauge in the spark plug hole (see illustration).

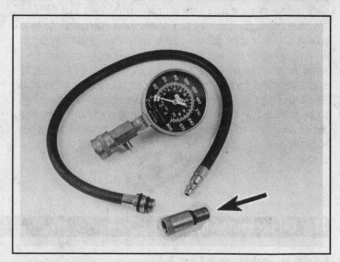

3.6 Use a compression gauge with a threaded fitting for the spark plug hole, not the type that requires hand pressure to maintain the seal

7   Crank the engine over at least seven compression strokes and watch the gauge. The compression should build up quickly in a healthy engine. Low compression on the first stroke, followed by gradually increasing pressure on successive strokes, indicates worn piston rings. A low compression reading on the first stroke, which doesn't build up during successive strokes, indicates leaking valves or a blown head gasket (a cracked head could also be the cause). Deposits on the undersides of the valve heads can also cause low compression. Record the highest gauge reading obtained.

8   Repeat the procedure for the remaining cylinders and compare the results to this Chapter's Specifications.

9   Add some engine oil (about three squirts from a plunger-type oil can) to each cylinder, through the spark plug hole, and repeat the test.

10   If the compression increases after the oil is added, the piston rings are definitely worn. If the compression doesn't increase significantly, the leakage is occurring at the valves or head gasket. Leakage past the valves may be caused by burned valve seats and/or faces or warped, cracked or bent valves.

11   If two adjacent cylinders have equally low compression, there's a strong possibility that the head gasket between them is blown. The appearance of coolant in the combustion chambers or the crankcase would verify this condition.

12   If one cylinder is slightly lower than the others, and the engine has a slightly rough idle, a worn lobe on the camshaft could be the cause.

13   If the compression is unusually high, the combustion chambers are probably coated with carbon deposits. If that's the case, the cylinder head(s) should be removed and decarbonized.

14   If compression is way down or varies greatly between cylinders, it would be a good idea to have a leak-down test performed by an automotive repair shop. This test will pinpoint exactly where the leakage is occurring and how severe it is.

15   After completing the compression check, don't forget to unblock the throttle(s).

4   Vacuum gauge diagnostic checks

♦ **Refer to illustrations 4.4 and 4.6**

A vacuum gauge provides inexpensive but valuable information about what is going on in the engine. You can check for worn rings or cylinder walls, leaking head or intake manifold gaskets, incorrect carburetor adjustments, restricted exhaust, stuck or burned valves, weak valve springs, improper ignition or valve timing and ignition problems.

Unfortunately, vacuum gauge readings are easy to misinterpret, so they should be used in conjunction with other tests to confirm the diagnosis.

Both the absolute readings and the rate of needle movement are important for accurate interpretation. Most gauges measure vacuum in inches of mercury (in-Hg). The following references to vacuum assume the diagnosis is being performed at sea level. As elevation increases (or atmospheric pressure decreases), the reading will decrease. For every 1,000 foot increase in elevation above approximately 2,000 feet, the gauge readings will decrease about one inch of mercury.

Connect the vacuum gauge directly to the intake manifold vacuum, not to ported (throttle body) vacuum (see illustration 4.4). Some models are equipped with a vacuum fitting built into the brake booster vacuum hose grommet at the brake booster. Other models are equipped with a vacuum hose fitting on the intake manifold. Use a T-fitting to access the vacuum signal. Be sure no hoses are left disconnected during the test or false readings will result.

Before you begin the test, allow the engine to warm up completely. Block the wheels and set the parking brake. With the transmission in Park, start the engine and allow it to run at normal idle speed.

✳ WARNING:

Keep your hands and the vacuum gauge clear of the fans.

Read the vacuum gauge; an average, healthy engine should normally produce about 17 to 22 in-Hg with a fairly steady needle (see illustration 4.6). Refer to the following vacuum gauge readings and what they indicate about the engine's condition:

1   A low, steady reading usually indicates a leaking gasket between the intake manifold and cylinder head(s) or throttle body, a leaky vacuum hose, late ignition timing or incorrect camshaft timing. Check ignition timing with a timing light and eliminate all other possible causes, utilizing the tests provided in this Chapter before you remove the timing chain cover to check the timing marks.

2   If the reading is three to eight inches below normal and it fluctuates at that low reading, suspect an intake manifold gasket leak at an intake port or a faulty fuel injector.

3   If the needle has regular drops of about two-to-four inches at a steady rate, the valves are probably leaking. Perform a compression check or leak-down test to confirm this.

4   An irregular drop or down-flick of the needle can be caused by a sticking valve or an ignition misfire. Perform a compression check or leak-down test and read the spark plugs.

4.4 A simple vacuum gauge can be handy in diagnosing engine condition and performance

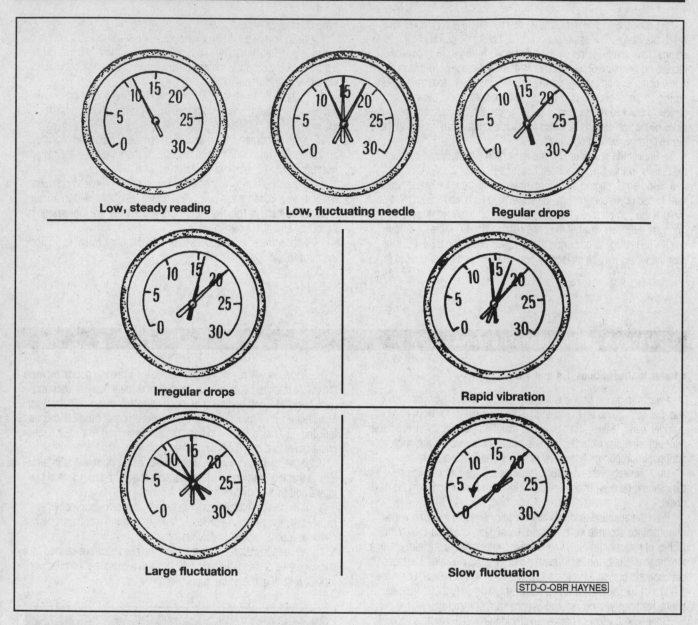

Low, steady reading **Low, fluctuating needle** **Regular drops**

Irregular drops **Rapid vibration**

Large fluctuation **Slow fluctuation**

STD-O-OBR HAYNES

4.6 Typical vacuum gauge readings

5 A rapid vibration of about four in-Hg vibration at idle combined with exhaust smoke indicates worn valve guides. Perform a leak-down test to confirm this. If the rapid vibration occurs with an increase in engine speed, check for a leaking intake manifold gasket or head gasket, weak valve springs, burned valves or ignition misfire.

6 A slight fluctuation, say one inch up and down, may mean ignition problems. Check all the usual tune-up items and, if necessary, run the engine on an ignition analyzer.

7 If there is a large fluctuation, perform a compression or leak-down test to look for a weak or dead cylinder or a blown head gasket.

8 If the needle moves slowly through a wide range, check for a clogged PCV system, incorrect idle fuel mixture, throttle body or intake manifold gasket leaks.

9 Check for a slow return after revving the engine by quickly snapping the throttle open until the engine reaches about 2,500 rpm and let it shut. Normally the reading should drop to near zero, rise above normal idle reading (about 5 in-Hg over) and then return to the previous idle reading. If the vacuum returns slowly and doesn't peak when the throttle is snapped shut, the rings may be worn. If there is a long delay, look for a restricted exhaust system (often the muffler or catalytic converter). An easy way to check this is to temporarily disconnect the exhaust ahead of the suspected part and redo the test.

5 Engine rebuilding alternatives

The do-it-yourselfer is faced with a number of options when purchasing a rebuilt engine. The major considerations are cost, warranty, parts availability and the time required for the rebuilder to complete the project. The decision to replace the engine block, piston/connecting rod assemblies and crankshaft depends on the final inspection results of your engine. Only then can you make a cost effective decision whether to have your engine overhauled or simply purchase an exchange engine for your vehicle.

Some of the rebuilding alternatives include:

Individual parts - If the inspection procedures reveal that the engine block and most engine components are in reusable condition, purchasing individual parts and having a rebuilder rebuild your engine may be the most economical alternative. The block, crankshaft and piston/connecting rod assemblies should all be inspected carefully by a machine shop first.

Short block - A short block consists of an engine block with a crankshaft and piston/connecting rod assemblies already installed. All new bearings are incorporated and all clearances will be correct. The existing camshafts, valve train components, cylinder head and external parts can be bolted to the short block with little or no machine shop work necessary.

Long block - A long block consists of a short block plus an oil pump, oil pan, cylinder head, valve cover, camshaft and valve train components, timing sprockets and chain or gears and timing cover. All components are installed with new bearings, seals and gaskets incorporated throughout. The installation of manifolds and external parts is all that's necessary.

Low mileage used engines - Some companies now offer low mileage used engines which is a very cost effective way to get your vehicle up and running again. These engines often come from vehicles which have been totaled in accidents or come from other countries which have a higher vehicle turn over rate. A low mileage used engine also usually has a warranty similar to the newly remanufactured engines.

Give careful thought to which alternative is best for you and discuss the situation with local automotive machine shops, auto parts dealers and experienced rebuilders before ordering or purchasing replacement parts.

6 Engine removal - methods and precautions

▸ **Refer to illustrations 6.1, 6.2, and 6.3**

If you've decided that an engine must be removed for overhaul or major repair work, several preliminary steps should be taken. Read all removal and installation procedures carefully prior to committing to this job. These engines are removed by lowering the engine to the floor, along with the transmission, and then raising the vehicle sufficiently to slide the assembly out; this will require a vehicle hoist as well as an engine hoist.

Locating a suitable place to work is extremely important. Adequate work space, along with storage space for the vehicle, will be needed. If

a shop or garage isn't available, at the very least a flat, level, clean work surface made of concrete or asphalt is required.

Cleaning the engine compartment and engine before beginning the removal procedure will help keep tools clean and organized (see illustrations 6.1 and 6.2).

A vehicle hoist will be necessary for engine removal, since the engine and transmission are removed as an assembly out the bottom of the vehicle.

An engine hoist will also be necessary and a transmission jack is also very helpful. Make sure the hoist is rated in excess of the

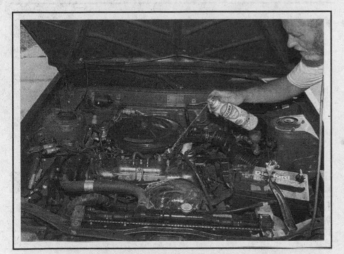

6.1 After tightly wrapping water-vulnerable components, use a spray cleaner on everything, with particular concentration on the greasiest areas, usually around the valve cover and lower edges of the block. If one section dries out, apply more cleaner

6.2 Depending on how dirty the engine is, let the cleaner soak in according to the directions and then hose off the grime and cleaner. Get the rinse water down into every area you can get at; then dry important components with a hair dryer or paper towels

combined weight of the engine and transmission. Safety is of primary importance, considering the potential hazards involved in removing the engine from the vehicle.

If you're a novice at engine removal, get at least one helper. One person cannot easily do all the things you need to do to remove a big heavy engine and transmission assembly from the engine compartment. Also helpful is to seek advice and assistance from someone who's experienced in engine removal.

Plan the operation ahead of time. Arrange for or obtain all of the tools and equipment you'll need prior to beginning the job (see illustration 6.3). Some of the equipment necessary to perform engine removal and installation safely and with relative ease are (in addition to a vehicle hoist and an engine hoist) a heavy duty floor jack (preferably fitted with a transmission jack head adapter), complete sets of wrenches and sockets as described in the front of this manual, wooden blocks, plenty of rags and cleaning solvent for mopping up spilled oil, coolant and gasoline.

Plan for the vehicle to be out of use for quite a while. A machine shop can do the work that is beyond the scope of the home mechanic. Machine shops often have a busy schedule, so before removing the engine, consult the shop for an estimate of how long it will take to rebuild or repair the components that may need work.

6.3 Get an engine stand sturdy enough to firmly support the engine while you're working on it. Stay away from three-wheeled models; they have a tendency to tip over more easily, so get a four-wheeled unit

7 Engine - removal and installation

✸✸ WARNING 1:

Gasoline is extremely flammable, so take extra precautions when you work on any part of the fuel system. Don't smoke or allow open flames or bare light bulbs near the work area, and don't work in a garage where a gas-type appliance (such as a water heater or clothes dryer) is present. Since gasoline is carcinogenic, wear fuel-resistant gloves when there's a possibility of being exposed to fuel, and, if you spill any fuel on your skin, rinse it off immediately with soap and water. Mop up any spills immediately and do not store fuel-soaked rags where they could ignite. The fuel system is under constant pressure, so, if any fuel lines are to be disconnected, the fuel pressure in the system must be relieved first (see Chapter 4 for more information). When you perform any kind of work on the fuel system, wear safety glasses and have a Class B type fire extinguisher on hand.

✸✸ WARNING 2:

The air conditioning system is under high pressure. Do not loosen any hose fittings or remove any components until after the system has been discharged. Air conditioning refrigerant must be properly discharged into an EPA-approved recovery/recycling unit at a dealer service department or an automotive air conditioning repair facility. Always wear eye protection when disconnecting air conditioning system fittings.

✸✸ WARNING 3:

The engine must be completely cool before beginning this procedure.

✸✸ WARNING 4:

The engine is removed from the bottom of the engine compartment; this procedure requires the use of a vehicle hoist. Only begin this procedure if all of the necessary equipment is at hand. With only a floor jack and jackstands, the vehicle can't safely be raised high enough for the engine/transmission to slide out from underneath.

REMOVAL

▶ **Refer to illustration 7.15**

1 Have the air conditioning system discharged by an automotive air conditioning technician.

2 Relieve the fuel system pressure (see Chapter 4), then disconnect the cable from the negative and positive battery terminals (see Chapter 5, Section 1).

3 Park the vehicle squarely on a frame-contact type hoist and adjust the hoist arms to correctly align with the jacking points of the vehicle. Point the wheels straight ahead.

✸✸ WARNING:

Tie the front of the body down to the hoist so the car doesn't tilt back and fall off the hoist when the weight of the engine and transmission is removed.

4 Remove the hood (see Chapter 11).

5 On models with automatic transmission, partially drain the automatic transmission fluid (see Chapter 1).

6 Remove the air filter housing and the intake air duct (see Chapter 4).

7   Drain the cooling system (see Chapter 1).

8   Remove the drivebelt (see Chapter 1).

9   Remove the radiator, shroud and engine cooling fan (see Chapter 3). Also remove the heater hoses and the coolant reservoir.

10   Remove the alternator (see Chapter 5).

11   Remove the power steering reservoir and power steering pump, without disconnecting the hoses, and tie them out of the way (see Chapter 10).

12   Remove the engine cover (see Chapter 2A).

13   Remove the PCV hose (see Chapter 6).

14   Loosen the front wheel lug nuts. If you're working on an all-wheel drive (AWD) model, also loosen the front driveaxle/hub nuts. With the vehicle raised and safely supported, remove the front wheels and the engine undercover.

15   Label and disconnect all wires from the engine (see illustration). Masking tape and/or a touch-up paint applicator work well for marking items. Disconnect the main engine harness connectors at the PCM, and with the passenger-side kick panel and lower instrument panel cover removed, disconnect the engine harness connectors there. Remove the sealing material at the firewall and pull the interior ends of the harness through the firewall to the engine side.

➡Note: Take instant photos or sketch the locations of components and brackets to help with reassembly.

16   Label and remove all vacuum lines between the engine and the firewall (or other components in the engine compartment).

17   If you are working on a model with an automatic transmission, detach the transmission cooler lines from the engine brackets and the transmission (see Chapter 7B).

18   Disconnect the engine block heater, if equipped.

19   Disconnect the oxygen sensors and the crankshaft position sensor connector (see Chapter 6).

20   Remove the automatic transmission dipstick, then pull the dipstick tube from the transmission.

21   Remove the starter (see Chapter 5).

22   Drain the engine oil, and disconnect the coolant hoses from the oil cooler (see Chapter 3).

23   Disconnect the exhaust pipes from the exhaust manifolds and remove the pipes.

24   On automatic transmission models, remove the torque converter-to-driveplate bolts (see Chapter 7B).

25   Remove the transmission-to-oil pan bolts.

26   Remove the driveshaft (see Chapter 8).

27   Refer to Chapter 10 and disconnect the lower end of the steering intermediate shaft from the steering gear. Also remove the lower control arms and the compression rods (350Z and 2006 and earlier G35 Sedans only), and the stabilizer bar links.

28   If you're working on an all-wheel drive (AWD) model, detach the outer ends of the driveaxles from the front hubs.

29   Place jackstands under the subframe and the transmission crossmember, then lower the vehicle slightly to put some weight on the jackstands.

➡Note: The jackstands should be placed on a stout, low-profile wheeled platform. While not absolutely necessary for removal, the wheeled platform will help with the alignment of the engine/transmission assembly to the vehicle during the installation procedure.

30   Unbolt the subframe and transmission crossmember from the vehicle. Verify that there are no harnesses, hoses, etc. that will interfere with raising the vehicle off of the engine/transmission assembly.

31   Slowly raise the vehicle while checking for obstructions. Make

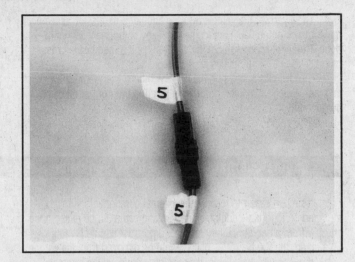

7.15 Label both ends of each wire or vacuum connection before disconnecting them

sure that the engine and transmission are secure.

32   Attach an engine hoist to the engine and raise it just enough to take weight off of the engine mounts.

33   If you're working in an AWD model, remove the fasteners connecting the front driveshaft to the front differential.

34   Securely support the transmission with a jack or blocks of wood, then remove the bolts and separate the transmission from the engine.

35   Remove the engine mount-to-engine nuts, then raise the engine off of the crossmember.

36   Remove the flywheel or driveplate and mount the engine on an engine stand.

INSTALLATION

37   Check the engine mounts. If they're worn or damaged, replace them (see Chapter 2A).

38   On manual transmission models, inspect the clutch components (see Chapter 8). On automatic transmission models, inspect the front transmission fluid seal and bearing.

39   On manual transmission models, apply a dab of grease to the pilot bearing.

40   Attach the hoist to the engine, remove the engine from the engine stand and install the flywheel or driveplate (see Chapter 2A).

41   Use a hoist to lower the engine to the floor and attach the transmission, following the procedures in Chapter 7A or 7B. If you're working on an all-wheel drive model, install the front differential, and front driveshaft, tightening the fasteners to the torque values listed in the Chapter 8 Specifications. On all models, install the crossmember and tighten the engine mount-to-engine nuts to the torque listed in the Chapter 2A Specifications.

42   Use the hoist to position the engine/transmission assembly onto the jackstands/wheeled platform. With an assistant, move the assembly under the vehicle.

➡Note: When positioning the assembly beneath the vehicle, make a plumb-bob from a piece of string and a nut. Hold the string at each subframe bolt hole and transmission crossmember on the body and verify that its corresponding bolt hole is directly below it. This will eliminate (or at least minimize) trying to adjust the assembly as the vehicle is lowered over it.

43 Slowly lower the vehicle over the engine/transmission assembly, making sure no contact is made between any component as this is done. Continue lowering until the subframe and transmission cross-member-to-chassis bolts can be installed.

44 Tighten all the bolts on the crossmembers, then remove the hoist and jack. Refer to Chapter 10 for installation of the front suspension components.

45 Reinstall the remaining components in the reverse order of removal.

46 Add coolant, oil, power steering and transmission fluid as needed (see Chapter 1).

47 Run the engine and check for proper operation and leaks. Shut off the engine and recheck the fluid levels.

8 Engine overhaul - disassembly sequence

1 It's much easier to remove the external components if it's mounted on a portable engine stand. A stand can often be rented quite cheaply from an equipment rental yard. Before the engine is mounted on a stand, the flywheel/driveplate should be removed from the engine.

2 If a stand isn't available, it's possible to remove the external engine components with it blocked up on the floor. Be extra careful not to tip or drop the engine when working without a stand.

3 If you're going to obtain a rebuilt engine, all external components must come off first, to be transferred to the replacement engine. These components include:

Flywheel/driveplate
Ignition system components
Emissions-related components
Engine mounts and mount brackets
Intake/exhaust manifolds
Fuel injection components
Oil filter and oil cooler
Spark plug wires and spark plugs
Thermostat and housing assembly
Water pump

➡**Note: When removing the external components from the engine, pay close attention to details that may be helpful or important during installation. Note the installed position of gaskets, seals, spacers, pins, brackets, washers, bolts and other small items.**

4 If you're going to obtain a short block (assembled engine block, crankshaft, pistons and connecting rods), then remove the timing chain, cylinder heads, oil pan, oil pump pick-up tube, oil pump and water pump from your engine so that you can turn in your old short block to the rebuilder as a core. See *Engine rebuilding alternatives* for additional information regarding the different possibilities to be considered.

9 Pistons and connecting rods - removal and installation

REMOVAL

♦ **Refer to illustrations 9.1, 9.3 and 9.4**

➡**Note: Prior to removing the piston/connecting rod assemblies, remove the cylinder head and oil pan (see Chapter 2A).**

1 Use your fingernail to feel if a ridge has formed at the upper limit of ring travel (about 1/4-inch down from the top of each cylinder). If carbon deposits or cylinder wear have produced ridges, they must be completely removed with a special tool (see illustration). Follow the manufacturer's instructions provided with the tool. Failure to remove the ridges before attempting to remove the piston/connecting rod assemblies may result in piston breakage.

2 After the cylinder ridges have been removed, turn the engine so the crankshaft is facing up.

3 Before the main bearing cap assembly and connecting rods are removed, check the connecting rod endplay with feeler gauges. Slide them between the first connecting rod and the crankshaft throw until the play is removed (see illustration). Repeat this procedure for each connecting rod. The endplay is equal to the thickness of the feeler gauge(s).

9.1 Before you try to remove the pistons, use a ridge reamer to remove the raised material (ridge) from the top of the cylinders

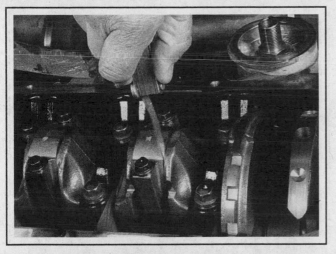

9.3 Checking the connecting rod endplay (side clearance)

9.4 If the connecting rods or caps are not marked, use permanent ink or paint to mark the caps to the rods by cylinder number (for example, this would be number 4 cylinder connecting rod)

Check with an automotive machine shop for the endplay service limit (a typical endplay should measure from 0.005 to 0.015 inch [0.127 to 0.396 mm]). If the play exceeds the service limit, new connecting rods will be required. If new rods (or a new crankshaft) are installed, the endplay may fall under the minimum allowable. If it does, the rods will have to be machined to restore it. If necessary, consult an automotive machine shop for advice.

4   Check the connecting rods and caps for identification marks. If they aren't plainly marked, use paint or marker (see illustration) to clearly identify each rod and cap (1, 2, 3, etc., depending on the cylinder they're associated with). Do not interchange the rod caps. Install the exact same rod cap onto the same connecting rod.

⁜ CAUTION:

Do not use a punch and hammer to mark the connecting rods or they may be damaged.

5   Loosen each of the connecting rod cap bolts or nuts 1/2-turn at a time until they can be removed by hand.

6   Remove the number one connecting rod cap and bearing insert. Don't drop the bearing insert out of the cap.

7   Remove the bearing insert and push the connecting rod/piston assembly out through the top of the engine. Use a wooden or plastic hammer handle to push on the upper bearing surface in the connecting rod. If resistance is felt, double-check to make sure that all of the ridge was removed from the cylinder.

8   Repeat the procedure for the remaining cylinders.

9   After removal, reassemble the connecting rod caps and bearing inserts in their respective connecting rods and install the cap bolts finger tight. Leaving the old bearing inserts in place until reassembly will help prevent the connecting rod bearing surfaces from being accidentally nicked or gouged.

10 The pistons and connecting rods are now ready for inspection and overhaul at an automotive machine shop.

PISTON RING INSTALLATION

▶ **Refer to illustrations 9.13, 9.14, 9.15, 9.19a, 9.19b and 9.22**

11 Before installing the new piston rings, the ring end gaps must be checked. It's assumed that the piston ring side clearance has been checked and verified correct.

12 Lay out the piston/connecting rod assemblies and the new ring sets so the ring sets will be matched with the same piston and cylinder during the end gap measurement and engine assembly.

13 Insert the top (number one) ring into the first cylinder and square it up with the cylinder walls by pushing it in with the top of the piston (see illustration). The ring should be near the bottom of the cylinder, at the lower limit of ring travel.

9.13 Install the piston ring into the cylinder then push it down into position using a piston so the ring will be square in the cylinder

9.14 With the ring square in the cylinder, measure the ring end gap with a feeler gauge

9.15 If the ring end gap is too small, clamp a file in a vise as shown and file the piston ring ends - be sure to remove all raised material

14 To measure the end gap, slip feeler gauges between the ends of the ring until a gauge equal to the gap width is found (see illustration). The feeler gauge should slide between the ring ends with a slight amount of drag. A typical ring gap should fall between 0.010 and 0.020 inch (0.25 to 0.50 mm) for compression rings and up to 0.030 inch (0.76 mm) for the oil ring steel rails. If the gap is larger or smaller than specified, double-check to make sure you have the correct rings before proceeding.

15 If the gap is too small, it must be enlarged or the ring ends may come in contact with each other during engine operation, which can cause serious damage to the engine. If necessary, increase the end gaps by filing the ring ends very carefully with a fine file. Mount the file in a vise equipped with soft jaws, slip the ring over the file with the ends contacting the file face and slowly move the ring to remove material from the ends. When performing this operation, file only by pushing the ring from the outside end of the file towards the vise (see illustration).

16 Excess end gap isn't critical unless it's greater than 0.040 inch

(1.01 mm). Again, double-check to make sure you have the correct ring type.

17 Repeat the procedure for each ring that will be installed in the first cylinder and for each ring in the remaining cylinders. Remember to keep rings, pistons and cylinders matched up.

18 Once the ring end gaps have been checked/corrected, the rings can be installed on the pistons.

19 The oil control ring (lowest one on the piston) is usually installed first. It's composed of three separate components. Slip the spacer/expander into the groove (see illustration). If an anti-rotation tang is used, make sure it's inserted into the drilled hole in the ring groove. Next, install the lower side rail in the same manner (see illustration). Don't use a piston ring installation tool on the oil ring side rails, as they may be damaged. Instead, place one end of the side rail into the groove between the spacer/expander and the ring land, hold it firmly in place and slide a finger around the piston while pushing the rail into the groove. Finally, install the upper side rail.

9.19a Installing the spacer/expander in the oil ring groove

9.19b DO NOT use a piston ring installation tool when installing the oil control side rails

9.22 Use a piston ring installation tool to install the compression rings - on some engines the number two compression ring has a directional mark that must face toward the top of the piston

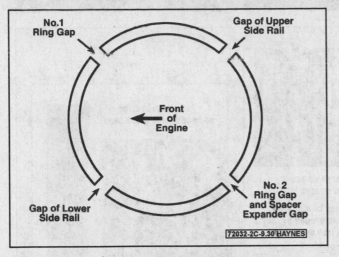

9.30 Position the piston ring end gaps as shown

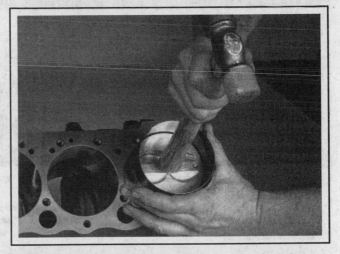

9.35 Use a plastic or wooden hammer handle to push the piston into the cylinder

20 After the three oil ring components have been installed, check to make sure that both the upper and lower side rails can be rotated smoothly inside the ring grooves.

21 The number two (middle) ring is installed next. It's usually stamped with a mark which must face up, toward the top of the piston. Do not mix up the top and middle rings, as they have different cross-sections.

➡Note: Always follow the instructions printed on the ring package or box - different manufacturers may require different approaches.

22 Use a piston ring installation tool and make sure the identification mark is facing the top of the piston, then slip the ring into the middle groove on the piston (see illustration). Don't expand the ring any more than necessary to slide it over the piston.

➡Note: Be careful not to confuse the number one and number two rings.

23 Install the number one (top) ring in the same manner.

24 Repeat the procedure for the remaining pistons and rings.

INSTALLATION

25 Before installing the piston/connecting rod assemblies, the cylinder walls must be perfectly clean, the top edge of each cylinder bore must be chamfered, and the crankshaft must be in place.

26 Remove the cap from the end of the number one connecting rod (refer to the marks made during removal). Remove the original bearing inserts and wipe the bearing surfaces of the connecting rod and cap with a clean, lint-free cloth. They must be kept spotlessly clean.

Connecting rod bearing oil clearance check

◆ Refer to illustrations 9.30, 9.35, 9.37 and 9.41

27 Clean the back side of the new upper bearing insert, then lay it in place in the connecting rod.

28 Make sure the tab on the bearing fits into the recess in the rod.

Don't hammer the bearing insert into place and be very careful not to nick or gouge the bearing face. Don't lubricate the bearing at this time.

29 Clean the back side of the other bearing insert and install it in the rod cap. Again, make sure the tab on the bearing fits into the recess in the cap, and don't apply any lubricant. It's critically important that the mating surfaces of the bearing and connecting rod are perfectly clean and oil free when they're assembled.

30 Position the piston ring gaps at the intervals around the piston as shown (see illustration).

31 Lubricate the piston and rings with clean engine oil and attach a piston ring compressor to the piston. Leave the skirt protruding about 1/4-inch to guide the piston into the cylinder. The rings must be compressed until they're flush with the piston.

32 Rotate the crankshaft until the number one connecting rod journal is at BDC (bottom dead center) and apply a liberal coat of engine oil to the cylinder walls. Refer to the TDC locating procedure in Chapter 2A for additional information.

33 With the "front" mark (letter F or arrow) on the piston facing the front (timing chain end) of the engine, gently insert the piston/connecting rod assembly into the number one cylinder bore and rest the bottom edge of the ring compressor on the engine block.

➡Note: Some engines have a letter "F" marking on the side of the piston near the wrist pin, others have an arrow, an "F" or a dimple or groove on the top of the piston. All of these are marks that indicate the front of the piston.

34 Tap the top edge of the ring compressor to make sure it's contacting the block around its entire circumference.

35 Gently tap on the top of the piston with the end of a wooden or plastic hammer handle (see illustration) while guiding the end of the connecting rod into place on the crankshaft journal. The piston rings may try to pop out of the ring compressor just before entering the cylinder bore, so keep some downward pressure on the ring compressor. Work slowly, and if any resistance is felt as the piston enters the cylinder, stop immediately. Find out what's hanging up and fix it before proceeding. Do not, for any reason, force the piston into the cylinder - you might break a ring and/or the piston.

ENGINE BEARING ANALYSIS

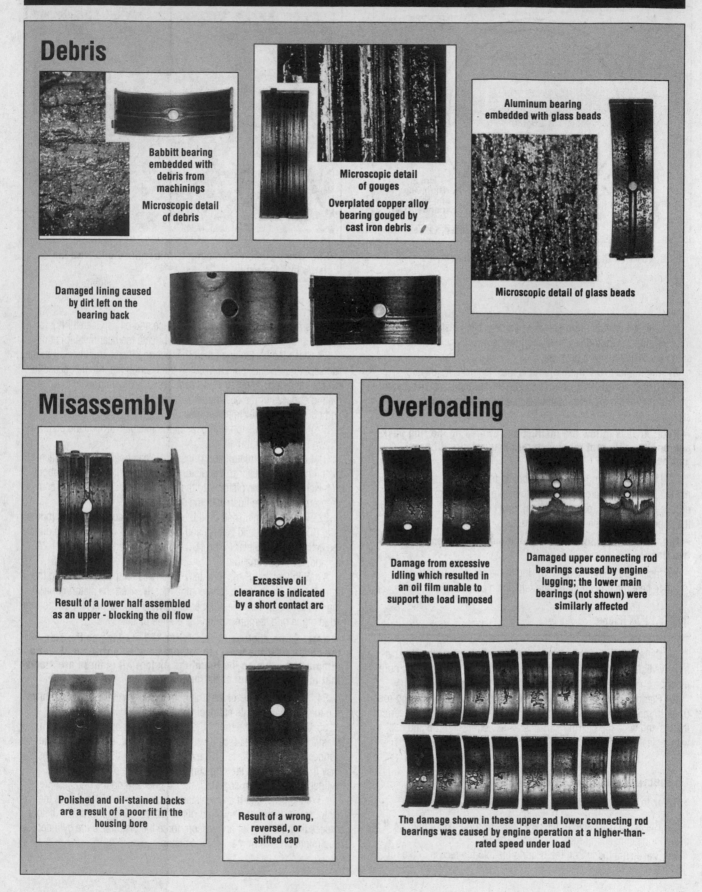

Debris

Babbitt bearing embedded with debris from machinings

Microscopic detail of debris

Microscopic detail of gouges

Overplated copper alloy bearing gouged by cast iron debris

Aluminum bearing embedded with glass beads

Microscopic detail of glass beads

Damaged lining caused by dirt left on the bearing back

Misassembly

Result of a lower half assembled as an upper - blocking the oil flow

Excessive oil clearance is indicated by a short contact arc

Polished and oil-stained backs are a result of a poor fit in the housing bore

Result of a wrong, reversed, or shifted cap

Overloading

Damage from excessive idling which resulted in an oil film unable to support the load imposed

Damaged upper connecting rod bearings caused by engine lugging; the lower main bearings (not shown) were similarly affected

The damage shown in these upper and lower connecting rod bearings was caused by engine operation at a higher-than-rated speed under load

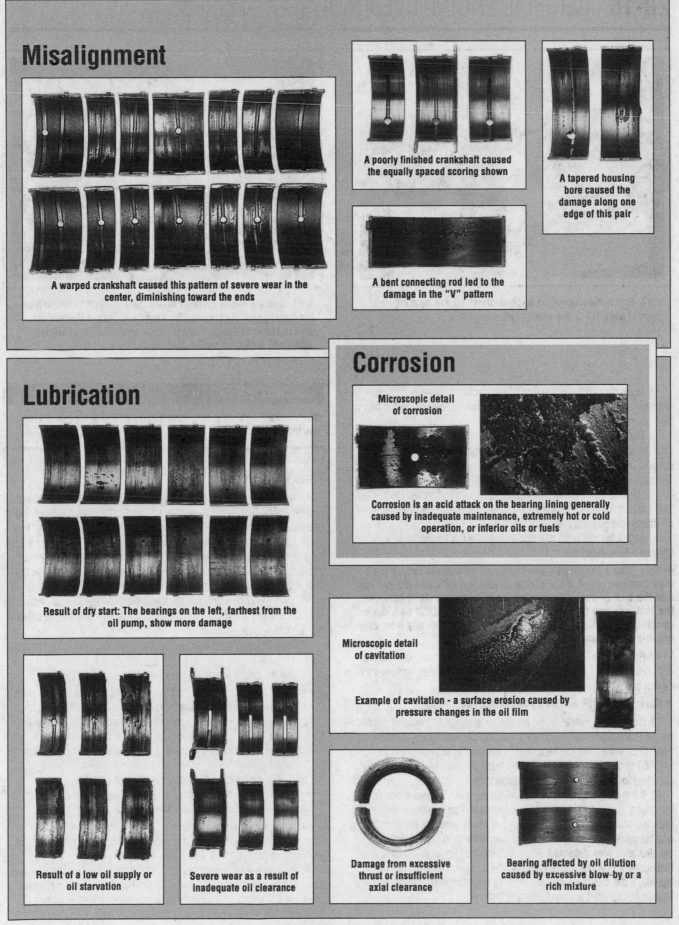

Misalignment

A poorly finished crankshaft caused the equally spaced scoring shown

A tapered housing bore caused the damage along one edge of this pair

A bent connecting rod led to the damage in the "V" pattern

A warped crankshaft caused this pattern of severe wear in the center, diminishing toward the ends

Lubrication

Result of dry start: The bearings on the left, farthest from the oil pump, show more damage

Result of a low oil supply or oil starvation

Severe wear as a result of inadequate oil clearance

Corrosion

Microscopic detail of corrosion

Corrosion is an acid attack on the bearing lining generally caused by inadequate maintenance, extremely hot or cold operation, or inferior oils or fuels

Microscopic detail of cavitation

Example of cavitation - a surface erosion caused by pressure changes in the oil film

Damage from excessive thrust or insufficient axial clearance

Bearing affected by oil dilution caused by excessive blow-by or a rich mixture

9.37 Place Plastigage on each connecting rod bearing journal parallel to the crankshaft centerline

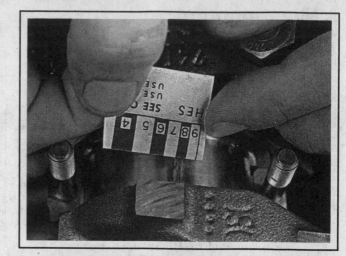

9.41 Use the scale on the Plastigage package to determine the bearing oil clearance - be sure to measure the widest part of the Plastigage and use the correct scale; it comes with both standard and metric scales

36 Once the piston/connecting rod assembly is installed, the connecting rod bearing oil clearance must be checked before the rod cap is permanently installed.

37 Cut a piece of the appropriate size Plastigage slightly shorter than the width of the connecting rod bearing and lay it in place on the number one connecting rod journal, parallel with the journal axis (see illustration).

38 Clean the connecting rod cap bearing face and install the rod cap. Make sure the mating mark on the cap is on the same side as the mark on the connecting rod (see illustration 9.4).

39 Install the rod bolts and tighten them to the torque listed in this Chapter's Specifications.

➡**Note: Use a thin-wall socket to avoid erroneous torque readings that can result if the socket is wedged between the rod cap and the bolt or nut. If the socket tends to wedge itself between the fastener and the cap, lift up on it slightly until it no longer contacts the cap. DO NOT rotate the crankshaft at any time during this operation.**

40 Remove the fasteners and detach the rod cap, being very careful not to disturb the Plastigage. Discard the cap bolts at this time as they cannot be reused.

➡**Note: You MUST use new connecting rod bolts.**

41 Compare the width of the crushed Plastigage to the scale printed on the Plastigage envelope to obtain the oil clearance (see illustration). The connecting rod bearing oil clearance is usually about 0.001 to 0.002 inch. Consult an automotive machine shop for the clearance specified for the rod bearings on your engine.

42 If the clearance is not as specified, the bearing inserts may be the wrong size (which means different ones will be required). Before deciding that different inserts are needed, make sure that no dirt or oil was between the bearing inserts and the connecting rod or cap when the clearance was measured. Also, recheck the journal diameter. If the Plastigage was wider at one end than the other, the journal may be tapered. If the clearance still exceeds the limit specified, the bearing will have to be replaced with an undersize bearing.

⁑ **CAUTION:**

When installing a new crankshaft always use a standard size bearing.

Final installation

43 Carefully scrape all traces of the Plastigage material off the rod journal and/or bearing face. Be very careful not to scratch the bearing - use your fingernail or the edge of a plastic card.

44 Make sure the bearing faces are perfectly clean, then apply a uniform layer of clean moly-base grease or engine assembly lube to both of them. You'll have to push the piston into the cylinder to expose the face of the bearing insert in the connecting rod.

45 Slide the connecting rod back into place on the journal, install the rod cap, install the nuts or bolts and tighten them to the torque listed in this Chapter's Specifications.

46 Repeat the entire procedure for the remaining pistons/connecting rods.

47 The important points to remember are:
a) *Keep the back sides of the bearing inserts and the insides of the connecting rods and caps perfectly clean when assembling them.*
b) *Make sure you have the correct piston/rod assembly for each cylinder.*
c) *The mark on the piston must face the front (timing chain end) of the engine.*
d) *Lubricate the cylinder walls liberally with clean oil.*
e) *Lubricate the bearing faces when installing the rod caps after the oil clearance has been checked.*

48 After all the piston/connecting rod assemblies have been correctly installed, rotate the crankshaft a number of times by hand to check for any obvious binding.

49 As a final step, check the connecting rod endplay again. If it was correct before disassembly and the original crankshaft and rods were reinstalled, it should still be correct. If new rods or a new crankshaft were installed, the endplay may be inadequate. If so, the rods will have to be removed and taken to an automotive machine shop for resizing.

10 Crankshaft - removal and installation

REMOVAL

▶ **Refer to illustrations 10.1 and 10.3**

➡**Note: The crankshaft can be removed only after the engine has been removed from the vehicle. It's assumed that the flywheel or driveplate, crankshaft pulley, timing chain, oil pan, oil pump, oil filter and piston/connecting rod assemblies have already been removed. The rear main oil seal retainer must be unbolted and separated from the block before proceeding with crankshaft removal.**

1 Before the crankshaft is removed, measure the endplay. Mount a dial indicator with the indicator in line with the crankshaft and touching the end of the crankshaft (see illustration).

2 Pry the crankshaft all the way to the rear and zero the dial indicator. Next, pry the crankshaft to the front as far as possible and check the reading on the dial indicator. The distance traveled is the endplay. A typical crankshaft endplay will be from 0.003 to 0.010 inch (0.076 to 0.254 mm). If it is greater than that, check the crankshaft thrust washer/bearing assembly surfaces for wear after it's removed. If no wear is evident, new main bearings should correct the endplay. Refer to Step 14 for the location of the thrust washer/bearing assembly on each engine.

3 If a dial indicator isn't available, feeler gauges can be used. Gently pry the crankshaft all the way to the front of the engine. Slip feeler gauges between the crankshaft and the front face of the thrust bearing or washer to determine the clearance (see illustration).

4 Loosen the main bearing cap/bedplate bolts 1/4-turn at a time each, until they can be removed by hand.

➡**Note: Some models use individual main bearing caps covered by a beam, secured with 16 bolts. Other models use a lower crankcase assembly or "bedplate," with the main bearing caps built in, secured with 26 bolts.**

5 Gently tap the main bearing caps/bedplate assembly with a soft-face hammer around the perimeter of the assembly. Pull the main bearing cap/bedplate assembly straight up and off the cylinder block. Try not to drop the bearing inserts if they come out with the assembly.

✳ CAUTION:

On models with a bedplate (secured with 26 bolts), the bedplate has built-in pry points. If it is stuck, pry ONLY at these points or you might damage the bedplate.

6 Carefully lift the crankshaft out of the engine. It may be a good idea to have an assistant available, since the crankshaft is quite heavy and awkward to handle. With the bearing inserts in place inside the engine block and main bearing caps, reinstall the main bearing cap assembly onto the engine block and tighten the bolts finger tight. Make sure you install the main bearing cap assembly with the arrow facing the front of the engine.

INSTALLATION

7 Crankshaft installation is the first step in engine reassembly. It's assumed at this point that the engine block and crankshaft have been cleaned, inspected and repaired or reconditioned.

8 Position the engine block with the bottom facing up.

9 Remove the mounting bolts and lift off the main bearing cap assembly.

10 If they're still in place, remove the original bearing inserts from the block and from the main bearing cap assembly. Wipe the bearing surfaces of the block and main bearing cap assembly with a clean, lint-free cloth. They must be kept spotlessly clean. This is critical for determining the correct bearing oil clearance.

10.1 Checking crankshaft endplay with a dial indicator

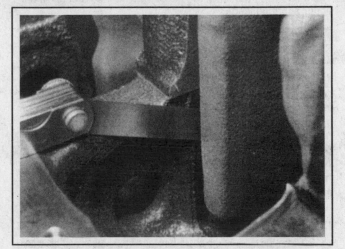

10.3 Checking crankshaft endplay with feeler gauges at the thrust bearing journal

10.14 Insert the thrust washer into the machined surface between the crankshaft and the upper bearing saddle, then rotate it down into the block until it's flush with the parting line on the main bearing saddle - make sure the oil grooves on the thrust washer face the crankshaft

10.17 Place the Plastigage onto the crankshaft bearing journal as shown

MAIN BEARING OIL CLEARANCE CHECK

◆ Refer to illustrations 10.14, 10.17, 10.18a, 10.18b, 10.19a, 19.19b and 10.21

11 Without mixing them up, clean the back sides of the new upper main bearing inserts (with grooves and oil holes) and lay one in each main bearing saddle in the block. Each upper bearing has an oil groove and oil hole in it.

✳✳ CAUTION:

The oil holes in the block must line up with the oil holes in the upper bearing inserts.

Clean the back sides of the lower main bearing inserts and lay them in the corresponding location in the main bearing cap/bedplate. Make sure the tab on the bearing insert fits into the recess in the block or main bearing cap/bedplate. The upper bearings with the oil holes are installed into the engine block while the lower bearings without the oil holes are installed in the caps or bedplate.

✳✳ CAUTION:

Do not hammer the bearing insert into place and don't nick or gouge the bearing faces. DO NOT apply any lubrication at this time.

12 Clean the faces of the bearing inserts in the block and the crankshaft main bearing journals with a clean, lint-free cloth.

13 Check or clean the oil holes in the crankshaft, as any dirt here can go only one way - straight through the new bearings.

14 Once you're certain the crankshaft is clean, carefully lay it in position in the block, which should be oriented on the engine stand to have the bottom side Up. Lube and insert the thrust washers on either side of journal #3 (see illustration). The thrust washers must be installed in the correct journal.

➡Note: Install the thrust washers with the groove in the thrust washer facing the crankshaft with the smooth sides facing the main bearing saddle.

15 Before the crankshaft can be permanently installed, the main bearing oil clearance must be checked.

16 Cut several strips of the appropriate size of Plastigage. They must be slightly shorter than the width of the main bearing journal.

17 Place one piece on each crankshaft main bearing journal, parallel with the journal axis as shown (see illustration).

18 Clean the faces of the bearing inserts in the main bearing caps (see illustrations). Hold the bearing inserts in place and install the caps onto the crankshaft and cylinder block. DO NOT disturb the Plastigage. Make sure you install the main bearing cap bedplate with the arrow facing the front (timing chain end) of the engine.

19 Apply clean engine oil to all bolt threads prior to installation, then install all bolts finger-tight. Tighten main bearing caps/bedplate assembly bolts in the sequence shown (see illustrations) progressing in steps, to the torque listed in this Chapter's Specifications. DO NOT rotate the crankshaft at any time during this operation.

20 Remove the bolts in the reverse order of the tightening sequence and carefully lift the main bearing cap assembly straight up and off the block. Do not disturb the Plastigage or rotate the crankshaft. If the main bearing cap assembly is difficult to remove, tap it gently from side-to-side with a soft-face hammer to loosen it.

21 Compare the width of the crushed Plastigage on each journal to the scale printed on the Plastigage envelope to determine the main bearing oil clearance (see illustration). A typical main bearing oil clearance should fall between 0.0015 and 0.0023-inch. Check with an automotive machine shop for the clearance specified for your engine.

22 If the clearance is not as specified, the bearing inserts may be the wrong size (which means different ones will be required). Before deciding if different inserts are needed, make sure that no dirt or oil was between the bearing inserts and the cap assembly or block when the clearance was measured. If the Plastigage was wider at one end than the other, the crankshaft journal may be tapered. If the clearance still exceeds the limit specified, the bearing insert(s) will have to be replaced with an undersize bearing insert(s).

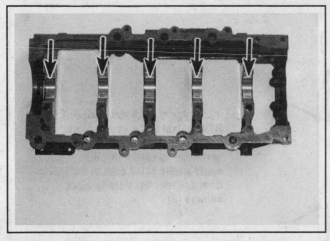

10.18a The bearings are installed into the corresponding saddles in the main caps (typical) . . .

10.18b . . . then the bedplate is set over the crankshaft onto the dowels on the engine block

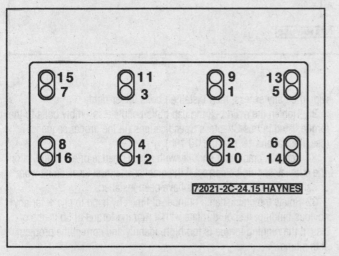

10.19a Main bearing cap bolt tightening sequence - models with individual main bearing caps and beam, secured with 16 bolts

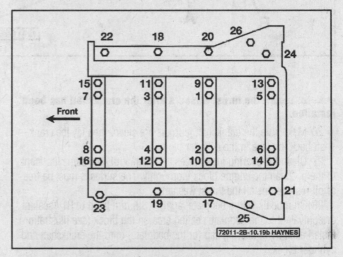

10.19b Main bearing cap bolt tightening sequence - models with a main bearing cap "bedplate," secured with 26 bolts

❋ CAUTION:

When installing a new crankshaft always install a standard bearing insert set.

23 Carefully scrape all traces of the Plastigage material off the main bearing journals and/or the bearing insert faces. Be sure to remove all residue from the oil holes. Use your fingernail or the edge of a plastic card - don't nick or scratch the bearing faces.

FINAL INSTALLATION

◆ **Refer to illustration 10.28**

24 Carefully lift the crankshaft out of the cylinder block.
25 Clean the bearing insert faces in the cylinder block, then apply a thin, uniform layer of moly-base grease or engine assembly lube to each of the bearing surfaces. Be sure to coat the thrust faces as well as the journal face of the thrust washers.

10.21 Use the scale on the Plastigage package to determine the bearing oil clearance - be sure to measure the widest part of the Plastigage and use the correct scale; it comes with both standard and metric scales

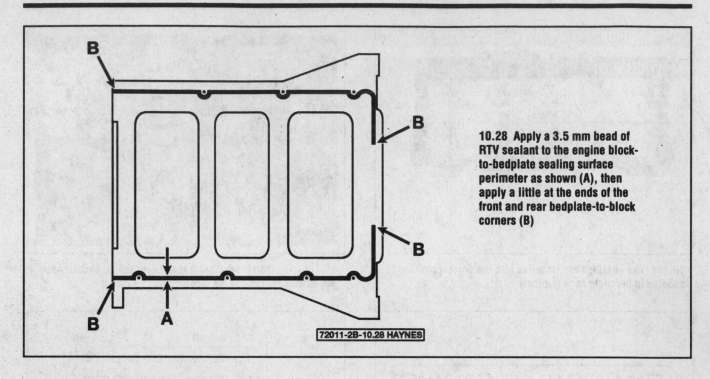

10.28 Apply a 3.5 mm bead of RTV sealant to the engine block-to-bedplate sealing surface perimeter as shown (A), then apply a little at the ends of the front and rear bedplate-to-block corners (B)

➡**Note: Install the thrust washers after the crankshaft has been installed.**

26 Make sure the crankshaft journals are clean, then lay the crankshaft back in place in the cylinder block.

27 Clean the bearing insert faces and then apply the same lubricant to them. Clean the engine block thoroughly. The surfaces must be free of oil residue. Install the thrust washers.

28 On models with a bedplate, apply a 3.5 mm bead of RTV sealant or equivalent to the bedplate sealing area on the block (see illustration). Install each main bearing cap (or the bedplate) onto the crankshaft and cylinder block.

29 Prior to installation, apply clean engine oil to all bolt threads, wiping off any excess, then install all bolts finger-tight.

30 Tighten the main bearing cap bolts/bedplate assembly bolts to the torque listed in this Chapter's Specifications (in the proper sequence) (see illustrations 10.19a and 10.19b).

31 Recheck crankshaft endplay with a feeler gauge or a dial indicator. The endplay should be correct if the crankshaft thrust faces aren't worn or damaged and if new bearings have been installed.

32 Rotate the crankshaft a number of times by hand to check for any obvious binding. It should rotate with a running torque of 50 in-lbs or less. If the running torque is too high, identify and correct the problem at this time.

33 Install the new rear main oil seal (see Chapter 2A).

11 Engine overhaul - reassembly sequence

1   Before beginning engine reassembly, make sure you have all the necessary new parts, gaskets and seals as well as the following items on hand:

   Common hand tools
   A 1/2-inch drive torque wrench
   New engine oil
   Gasket sealant
   Thread locking compound

2   If you obtained a short block, it will be necessary to install the cylinder heads, the oil pump and pick-up tube, the oil pans, the water pump, the timing chain and timing cover, and the valve covers (see Chapter 2A). In order to save time and avoid problems, the external components must be installed in the following general order:

   Thermostat and housing cover
   Water pump
   Intake and exhaust manifolds
   Fuel injection components
   Emission control components
   Spark plugs
   Ignition coils
   Oil filter and oil cooler
   Engine mounts and mount brackets
   Flywheel/driveplate

12 Initial start-up and break-in after overhaul

WARNING:

Have a fire extinguisher handy when starting the engine for the first time.

1   Once the engine has been installed in the vehicle, double-check the engine oil and coolant levels.

2   With the spark plugs out of the engine and the ignition system and fuel pump disabled (see Chapter 4), crank the engine until oil pressure registers on the gauge or the light goes out.

3   Install the spark plugs and ignition coils, and reinstall the fuel pump fuse.

4   Start the engine. It may take a few moments for the fuel system to build up pressure, but the engine should start without a great deal of effort.

5   After the engine starts, it should be allowed to warm up to normal operating temperature. While the engine is warming up, make a thorough check for fuel, oil and coolant leaks.

6   Shut the engine off and recheck the engine oil and coolant levels.

7   Drive the vehicle to an area with minimum traffic, accelerate from 30 to 50 mph, then allow the vehicle to slow to 30 mph with the throttle closed. Repeat the procedure 10 or 12 times. This will load the piston rings and cause them to seat properly against the cylinder walls. Check again for oil and coolant leaks.

8   Drive the vehicle gently for the first 500 miles (no sustained high speeds) and keep a constant check on the oil level. It is not unusual for an engine to use oil during the break-in period.

9   At approximately 500 to 600 miles, change the oil and filter.

10 For the next few hundred miles, drive the vehicle normally. Do not pamper it or abuse it.

11 After 2000 miles, change the oil and filter again and consider the engine broken in.

GLOSSARY

B

Backlash - The amount of play between two parts. Usually refers to how much one gear can be moved back and forth without moving the gear with which it's meshed.

Bearing Caps - The caps held in place by nuts or bolts which, in turn, hold the bearing surface. This space is for lubricating oil to enter.

Bearing clearance - The amount of space left between shaft and bearing surface. This space is for lubricating oil to enter.

Bearing crush - The additional height which is purposely manufactured into each bearing half to ensure complete contact of the bearing back with the housing bore when the engine is assembled.

Bearing knock - The noise created by movement of a part in a loose or worn bearing.

Blueprinting - Dismantling an engine and reassembling it to EXACT specifications.

Bore - An engine cylinder, or any cylindrical hole; also used to describe the process of enlarging or accurately refinishing a hole with a cutting tool, as to bore an engine cylinder. The bore size is the diameter of the hole.

Boring - Renewing the cylinders by cutting them out to a specified size. A boring bar is used to make the cut.

Bottom end - A term which refers collectively to the engine block, crankshaft, main bearings and the big ends of the connecting rods.

Break-in - The period of operation between installation of new or rebuilt parts and time in which parts are worn to the correct fit. Driving at reduced and varying speed for a specified mileage to permit parts to wear to the correct fit.

Bushing - A one-piece sleeve placed in a bore to serve as a bearing surface for shaft, piston pin, etc. Usually replaceable.

C

Camshaft - The shaft in the engine, on which a series of lobes are located for operating the valve mechanisms. The camshaft is driven by gears or sprockets and a timing chain. Usually referred to simply as the cam.

Carbon - Hard, or soft, black deposits found in combustion chamber, on plugs, under rings, on and under valve heads.

Cast iron - An alloy of iron and more than two percent carbon, used for engine blocks and heads because it's relatively inexpensive and easy to mold into complex shapes.

Chamfer - To bevel across (or a bevel on) the sharp edge of an object.

Chase - To repair damaged threads with a tap or die.

Combustion chamber - The space between the piston and the cylinder head, with the piston at top dead center, in which air-fuel mixture is burned.

Compression ratio - The relationship between cylinder volume (clearance volume) when the piston is at top dead center and cylinder volume when the piston is at bottom dead center.

Connecting rod - The rod that connects the crank on the crankshaft with the piston. Sometimes called a con rod.

Connecting rod cap - The part of the connecting rod assembly that attaches the rod to the crankpin.

Core plug - Soft metal plug used to plug the casting holes for the coolant passages in the block.

Crankcase - The lower part of the engine in which the crankshaft rotates; includes the lower section of the cylinder block and the oil pan.

Crank kit - A reground or reconditioned crankshaft and new main and connecting rod bearings.

Crankpin - The part of a crankshaft to which a connecting rod is attached.

Crankshaft - The main rotating member, or shaft, running the length of the crankcase, with offset throws to which the connecting rods are attached; changes the reciprocating motion of the pistons into rotating motion.

Cylinder sleeve - A replaceable sleeve, or liner, pressed into the cylinder block to form the cylinder bore.

D

Deburring - Removing the burrs (rough edges or areas) from a bearing.

Deglazer - A tool, rotated by an electric motor, used to remove glaze from cylinder walls so a new set of rings will seat.

E

Endplay - The amount of lengthwise movement between two parts. As applied to a crankshaft, the distance that the crankshaft can move forward and back in the cylinder block.

F

Face - A machinist's term that refers to removing metal from the end of a shaft or the face of a larger part, such as a flywheel.

Fatigue - A breakdown of material through a large number of loading and unloading cycles. The first signs are cracks followed shortly by breaks.

Feeler gauge - A thin strip of hardened steel, ground to an exact thickness, used to check clearances between parts.

Free height - The unloaded length or height of a spring.

Freeplay - The looseness in a linkage, or an assembly of parts, between the initial application of force and actual movement. Usually perceived as slop or slight delay.

Freeze plug - See Core plug.

G

Gallery - A large passage in the block that forms a reservoir for engine oil pressure.

Glaze - The very smooth, glassy finish that develops on cylinder walls while an engine is in service.

H

Heli-Coil - A rethreading device used when threads are worn or damaged. The device is installed in a retapped hole to reduce the thread size to the original size.

I

Installed height - The spring's measured length or height, as installed on the cylinder head. Installed height is measured from the spring seat to the underside of the spring retainer.

J

Journal - The surface of a rotating shaft which turns in a bearing.

K

Keeper - The split lock that holds the valve spring retainer in position on the valve stem.

Key - A small piece of metal inserted into matching grooves machined into two parts fitted together - such as a gear pressed onto a shaft - which prevents slippage between the two parts.

Knock - The heavy metallic engine sound, produced in the combustion chamber as a result of abnormal combustion - usually detonation. Knock is usually caused by a loose or worn bearing. Also referred to as detonation, pinging and spark knock. Connecting rod or main bearing knocks are created by too much oil clearance or insufficient lubrication.

L

Lands - The portions of metal between the piston ring grooves.

Lapping the valves - Grinding a valve face and its seat together with lapping compound.

Lash - The amount of free motion in a gear train, between gears, or in a mechanical assembly, that occurs before movement can begin. Usually refers to the lash in a valve train.

Lifter - The part that rides against the cam to transfer motion to the rest of the valve train.

M

Machining - The process of using a machine to remove metal from a metal part.

Main bearings - The plain, or babbitt, bearings that support the crankshaft.

Main bearing caps - The cast iron caps, bolted to the bottom of the block, that support the main bearings.

O

O.D. - Outside diameter.

Oil gallery - A pipe or drilled passageway in the engine used to carry engine oil from one area to another.

Oil ring - The lower ring, or rings, of a piston; designed to prevent excessive amounts of oil from working up the cylinder walls and into the combustion chamber. Also called an oil-control ring.

Oil seal - A seal which keeps oil from leaking out of a compartment. Usually refers to a dynamic seal around a rotating shaft or other moving part.

O-ring - A type of sealing ring made of a special rubberlike material; in use, the O-ring is compressed into a groove to provide the sealing action.

Overhaul - To completely disassemble a unit, clean and inspect all parts, reassemble it with the original or new parts and make all adjustments necessary for proper operation.

P

Pilot bearing - A small bearing installed in the center of the flywheel (or the rear end of the crankshaft) to support the front end of the input shaft of the transmission.

Pip mark - A little dot or indentation which indicates the top side of a compression ring.

Piston - The cylindrical part, attached to the connecting rod, that moves up and down in the cylinder as the crankshaft rotates. When the fuel charge is fired, the piston transfers the force of the explosion to the connecting rod, then to the crankshaft.

Piston pin (or wrist pin) - The cylindrical and usually hollow steel pin that passes through the piston. The piston pin fastens the piston to the upper end of the connecting rod.

Piston ring - The split ring fitted to the groove in a piston. The ring contacts the sides of the ring groove and also rubs against the cylinder wall, thus sealing space between piston and wall. There are two types of rings: Compression rings seal the compression pressure in the combustion chamber; oil rings scrape excessive oil off the cylinder wall.

Piston ring groove - The slots or grooves cut in piston heads to hold piston rings in position.

Piston skirt - The portion of the piston below the rings and the piston pin hole.

Plastigage - A thin strip of plastic thread, available in different sizes, used for measuring clearances. For example, a strip of plastigage is laid across a bearing journal and mashed as parts are assembled. Then parts are disassembled and the width of the strip is measured to determine clearance between journal and bearing. Commonly used to measure crankshaft main-bearing and connecting rod bearing clearances.

Press-fit - A tight fit between two parts that requires pressure to force the parts together. Also referred to as drive, or force, fit.

Prussian blue - A blue pigment; in solution, useful in determining the area of contact between two surfaces. Prussian blue is commonly used to determine the width and location of the contact area between the valve face and the valve seat.

R

Race (bearing) - The inner or outer ring that provides a contact surface for balls or rollers in bearing.

Ream - To size, enlarge or smooth a hole by using a round cutting tool with fluted edges.

Ring job - The process of reconditioning the cylinders and installing new rings.

Runout - Wobble. The amount a shaft rotates out-of-true.

S

Saddle - The upper main bearing seat.

Scored - Scratched or grooved, as a cylinder wall may be scored by abrasive particles moved up and down by the piston rings.

Scuffing - A type of wear in which there's a transfer of material between parts moving against each other; shows up as pits or grooves in the mating surfaces.

Seat - The surface upon which another part rests or seats. For example, the valve seat is the matched surface upon which the valve face rests. Also used to refer to wearing into a good fit; for example, piston rings seat after a few miles of driving.

Short block - An engine block complete with crankshaft and piston and, usually, camshaft assemblies.

Static balance - The balance of an object while it's stationary.

Step - The wear on the lower portion of a ring land caused by excessive side and back-clearance. The height of the step indicates the ring's extra side clearance and the length of the step projecting from the back wall of the groove represents the ring's back clearance.

Stroke - The distance the piston moves when traveling from top dead center to bottom dead center, or from bottom dead center to top dead center.

Stud - A metal rod with threads on both ends.

T

Tang - A lip on the end of a plain bearing used to align the bearing during assembly.

Tap - To cut threads in a hole. Also refers to the fluted tool used to cut threads.

Taper - A gradual reduction in the width of a shaft or hole; in an engine cylinder, taper usually takes the form of uneven wear, more pronounced at the top than at the bottom.

Throws - The offset portions of the crankshaft to which the connecting rods are affixed.

Thrust bearing - The main bearing that has thrust faces to prevent excessive endplay, or forward and backward movement of the crankshaft.

Thrust washer - A bronze or hardened steel washer placed between two moving parts. The washer prevents longitudinal movement and provides a bearing surface for thrust surfaces of parts.

Tolerance - The amount of variation permitted from an exact size of measurement. Actual amount from smallest acceptable dimension to largest acceptable dimension.

U

Umbrella - An oil deflector placed near the valve tip to throw oil from the valve stem area.

Undercut - A machined groove below the normal surface.

Undersize bearings - Smaller diameter bearings used with re-ground crankshaft journals.

V

Valve grinding - Refacing a valve in a valve-refacing machine.

Valve train - The valve-operating mechanism of an engine; includes all components from the camshaft to the valve.

Vibration damper - A cylindrical weight attached to the front of the crankshaft to minimize torsional vibration (the twist-untwist actions of the crankshaft caused by the cylinder firing impulses). Also called a harmonic balancer.

W

Water jacket - The spaces around the cylinders, between the inner and outer shells of the cylinder block or head, through which coolant circulates.

Web - A supporting structure across a cavity.

Woodruff key - A key with a radiused backside (viewed from the side).

Specifications

General

Engine type	V6
Displacement	213 cubic inches (3.5 liters)
Bore	3.76 inches (95.5 mm)
Stroke	3.205 inches (81.4 mm)
Cylinder compression pressure	
Minimum	142 psi
Maximum variation between cylinders	15 psi
Oil pressure (minimum, warm engine)	
Idle	14 psi
2000 rpm	43 psi

Torque specifications*	Ft-lbs (unless otherwise indicated)	Nm

→**Note: One foot-pound of torque is equivalent to 12 inch-pounds of torque. Torque values below approximately 15 foot-pounds are expressed in inch-pounds, because most foot-pound torque wrenches are not accurate at these smaller values.**

2003 through 2006 350Z and 2003 through 2007 G35 models (except 2007 G35 Sedan)		
Connecting rod cap bolts		
Step 1	168 to 180 in-lbs	18.6 to 20.6
Step 2	Tighten an additional 90 to 95 degrees	
Main bearing cap bolts		
Step 1, bolts 1-16	24 to 28	32 to 38
Step 2, bolts 1-16	Tighten an additional 90 degrees	
2007 350Z and G35 Sedan models		
Connecting rod cap bolts		
Step 1	21	28.4
Step 2	Loosen	
Step 3	18	25
Main bearing cap/bedplate bolts		
Step 1, bolts 1-16	26	35
Step 2, bolts 1-16	Tighten an additional 90-degrees	
Step 3, bolts 1-16	Loosen	
Step 4, bolts 1-16	26	35
Step 5, bolts 1-16	Tighten an additional 90 degrees	
Step 6, bolts 17-26	16	22

Torque specifications* (continued)	Ft-lbs (unless otherwise indicated)	Nm

➡ **Note: One foot-pound of torque is equivalent to 12 inch-pounds of torque. Torque values below approximately 15 foot-pounds are expressed in inch-pounds, because most foot-pound torque wrenches are not accurate at these smaller values.**

2008 350Z and G35 models		
Connecting rod cap bolts		
Step 1	21	28.4
Step 2	Loosen	
Step 3	18	25
Step 4	Tighten an additional 90 degrees	
Main bearing cap/bedplate bolts		
Step 1, bolts 17-26	18	25
Step 2, bolts 17-26	18	25
Step 3, bolts 1-16	26	35
Step 4, bolts 1-16	Tighten an additional 90 degrees	

*Note: Refer to Part A for additional torque specifications.

Notes

3

COOLING HEATING AND AIR CONDITIONG SYSTEMS

1 General information

ENGINE COOLING SYSTEM

The main components of the cooling system consist of a radiator, a reservoir tank, a pressure cap, a thermostat, cooling fans and a chain-driven water pump.

The radiator cooling fans are mounted in a housing/shroud at the engine side of the radiator. They are designed to come on when the engine reaches a certain temperature, and shut off again when the engine cools down some, thereby keeping the engine in the desired operating-temperature range.

→Note: Some earlier Sedan models are equipped with a belt-driven cooling fan and an electric fan. All other models have two temperature-controlled electric fans.

The coolant reservoir serves as both the point at which fresh coolant is added to the cooling system, to maintain the proper fluid level, and as a holding tank for overheated coolant.

Coolant circulates through the cylinder block and heads around the combustion chambers and valve seats, flows out of the cylinder head into the radiator and heater core.

When the engine is cold, the thermostat restricts the circulation of coolant to the radiator. When the minimum operating temperature is reached, the thermostat begins to open, allowing coolant to flow through the radiator.

All vehicles with an automatic transmission are equipped with a transmission oil cooler that is integrated with the radiator. Hot transmission fluid is directed to the cooler by lines and hoses. Once cooled, the fluid flows back to the transmission.

HEATING SYSTEM

The heating system consists of a blower fan and a heater core located in an air conditioning and heater housing under the dash, with hoses connecting the heater core to the engine cooling system. Hot engine coolant is circulated through the heater core. When the heater is activated, a flap door opens in the housing and directs warm air to the passenger compartment. A fan switch on the heater/air conditioning control activates the blower motor, which creates the flow of warm air into the cab.

AIR CONDITIONING SYSTEM

The air conditioning system consists of a condenser (mounted in front of the radiator), an evaporator (mounted adjacent to the heater core under the dash), a compressor (mounted on the engine), an accumulator (mounted to the condenser) and the plumbing that connects all of these components.

A blower fan forces the warmer air of the passenger compartment through an evaporator core (sort of a radiator-in-reverse), transferring the heat from the air to the refrigerant. The liquid refrigerant boils off into low-pressure vapor, taking the heat with it when it leaves the evaporator.

2 Antifreeze/coolant - general information

♦ Refer to illustration 2.3

※※ WARNING 1:

Do not allow antifreeze to come in contact with your skin or painted surfaces of the vehicle. Rinse off spills immediately with plenty of water. Antifreeze is highly toxic if ingested. Never leave antifreeze lying around in an open container or in puddles on the floor; children and pets are attracted by its sweet smell and may drink it. Check with local authorities about disposing of used antifreeze. Many communities have collection centers which will see that antifreeze is disposed of safely. Never dump used antifreeze on the ground or pour it into drains. Keep antifreeze containers covered and repair leaks in your cooling system as soon as they are noticed.

※ WARNING 2:

Do not remove the radiator cap until the engine has cooled completely.

Never mix different types or colors of coolant; damage to the cooling system can occur. Refer to the Specifications listed in Chapter 1 for the correct type of coolant.

Before adding antifreeze, check all hose connections, because antifreeze tends to leak through very minute openings. Engines don't normally consume coolant, so if the level goes down, find the cause and correct it.

The exact mixture of antifreeze-to-water used depends on the manufacturer's recommendation. Consult the mixture ratio chart on the antifreeze container before adding coolant. Hydrometers are available at most auto parts stores to test the coolant (see illustration).

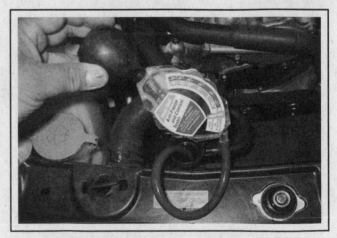

2.3 An inexpensive hydrometer can be used to test the condition of your coolant

3 Thermostat - check and replacement

※※ WARNING:

Do not remove the radiator cap, drain the coolant or replace the thermostat until the engine has cooled completely.

CHECK

1 Before assuming the thermostat is to blame for a cooling system problem, check the coolant level (see Chapter 1) and temperature gauge operation.

2 If the engine seems to be taking a long time to warm up (based on heater output or temperature gauge operation), the thermostat is probably stuck open. Replace the thermostat with a new one.

3 If the engine runs hot, use your hand to check the temperature of the radiator hose that leads from the thermostat to the radiator. If the hose isn't hot, but the engine is, the thermostat is probably stuck closed, preventing the coolant inside the engine from escaping to the radiator. Replace the thermostat.

※※ CAUTION:

Don't drive the vehicle without a thermostat. The vehicle's computer may stay in open-loop (see Chapter 6), possibly resulting in oil sludge, excessive exhaust emissions and higher fuel consumption.

4 If the inlet radiator hose is hot, it means that the coolant is flowing and the thermostat is open. Consult the *Troubleshooting* Section at the front of this manual for cooling system diagnosis.

REPLACEMENT

◆ **Refer to illustrations 3.12 and 3.13**

5 Disconnect the cable from the negative battery terminal (see Chapter 5, Section 1).

6 Raise the vehicle and support it securely on jackstands. Remove the engine lower splash shield (see Chapter 2).

7 Drain the cooling system completely (see Chapter 1). If the coolant is relatively new or in good condition, save it and reuse it (see Section 2).

➡**Note: Be sure to remove the engine drain plug(s).**

8 Remove the engine cover.

9 Remove the air filter housing and intake duct (see Chapter 4).

➡**Note: For vehicles equipped with two air filter housings and related ducts, remove the one on the left (driver's) side.**

10 On all-wheel-drive models (AWD), remove the coolant reservoir and any water pipes that lead to the oil cooler that are in the way.

11 On 2007 and later 350Z or G35 Sedans, remove the left (driver's) side intake valve timing control cover that is mounted to the timing chain cover and in front of the thermostat housing (see Chapter 2).

➡**Note: A new gasket and O-ring will be necessary when installing this component.**

12 Squeeze the tabs on the hose clamp to loosen it, then slide the clamp several inches back up the hose. Detach the hose(s) from the thermostat housing (see illustration).

➡**Note: Special hose clamp pliers are available at most auto parts stores. If the hose is stuck, grasp it near the end with a pair of adjustable pliers and twist it to break the seal, then pull it off. If the hose is old or deteriorated, cut it off and install a new one.**

13 Remove the thermostat housing cover fasteners and remove the housing. The thermostat is mounted to the inside of the housing cover; they are replaced as an assembly (see illustration).

3.12 Remove the hoses from the thermostat housing (2004 G35 Sedan model shown - other models are similar)

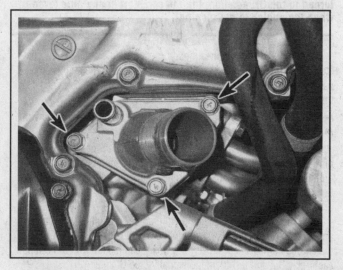

3.13 The thermostat housing cover fasteners (2004 G35 Sedan model shown - other models are similar)

14 Remove the gasket from the engine block and discard it.

15 Clean all mating surfaces before beginning any reassembly.

16 Install a new gasket.

17 The remainder of installation is the reverse of removal. Tighten the thermostat housing cover bolts to the torque listed in this Chapter's Specifications.

18 Reattach the hose(s) to the housing cover and fitting(s), then tighten the hose clamp(s) securely.

19 Refill the cooling system (see Chapter 1).

20 Start the engine and allow it to reach normal operating temperature, then check for leaks and proper operation.

4   Engine cooling fans - check and replacement

※※ WARNING:

To avoid possible injury or damage, DO NOT operate the engine with a damaged fan. Do not attempt to repair fan blades - replace a damaged fan with a new one.

CHECK

1 Most models are equipped with two cooling fans mounted side-by-side behind the radiator. The PCM (the Powertrain Control Module, which is the engine's computer) and three relays are used to operate the fans at Low or High speeds depending on engine needs and other conditions. The fans are protected by fuses inside the engine compartment's fuse/relay box.

2 Some earlier G35 Sedan models are equipped with a belt driven cooling fan behind the radiator and an electric fan in front of the air conditioning condenser. Some 2007 and later models use a fan control module to control the cooling fans instead of using the PCM and relays.

Electric fans

▶ **Refer to illustrations 4.4a, 4.4b and 4.5**

※※ WARNING:

Do not work with your hands near the fan any time the engine is running or with the key in the ON position. When the key is turned to the ON position, the fan can start at any time (even when the engine is not running).

3 If the engine is overheating and neither of the cooling fans operate, check the fuses for the fans. Locate the fuses in the engine compartment fuse/relay box (see Chapter 12). Remove the fuse(s) and check them for continuity (see Chapter 12).

➡**Note: Find the cooling fan fuse locations on the inside cover of the fuse/relay box.**

4 If the fuses test good, check each cooling fan motor by unplugging the fan motor electrical connector and applying battery power directly to the motor terminals with fused jumper wires (see illustrations). When done correctly, the fan should come on. If a fan motor doesn't work, replace the motor.

5 If the fan motors are okay but are still not coming on when the engine gets hot, the fan relays might be defective. Locate the relays in the engine compartment's fuse/relay box (see illustration). You can pull each relay out and test them individually (see Chapter 12).

➡**Note 1: The control circuits that power the fans (through relays or otherwise) are complex. These circuits can only be checked by a dealer service department or qualified repair facility.**

➡**Note 2: On 2007 and later 350Z and G35 Sedans, there are no relays to test.**

6 If the fuses, motors and relays (if equipped) are functional, check all wiring and connections to the fan motors. If no obvious problems are found, have the cooling fan system and circuit diagnosed by a dealer service department or a qualified repair facility.

Belt-driven fan

※※ WARNING 1:

While checking the fan, make sure that the engine is NOT started. If it is, you could be severely injured.

※※ WARNING 2:

Before the fan clutch operation can be checked in Step 7, the engine must be warmed up to its normal operating temperature and then turned off. Even though the engine won't be running during this check, it's HOT! Make sure that you don't touch the engine itself during this check, or you could be burned.

※※ WARNING 3:

Keep hands, tools and clothing away from the fan when the engine is running. To avoid injury or damage DO NOT operate the engine with a damaged fan. Do not attempt to repair fan blades - replace a damaged fan with a new one.

7 Symptoms of fan clutch failure are continuous noisy operation, looseness, vibration and/or silicone fluid leaking from the clutch.

Cold engine checks

8 Rock the fan back and forth by hand to check for excessive bearing play.

9 With the engine cold, turn the blades by hand. The fan should turn freely.

10 Visually inspect for substantial fluid leakage from the fan clutch assembly, a deformed bi-metal spring or grease leakage from the cooling fan bearing. If any of these conditions exist, replace the fan clutch.

Hot engine check

11 Start the engine and allow it to warm up to its normal operating temperature. When the engine is fully warmed up, turn off the ignition switch. Turn the fan by hand. Some resistance should be felt. If the fan turns easily, replace the fan clutch.

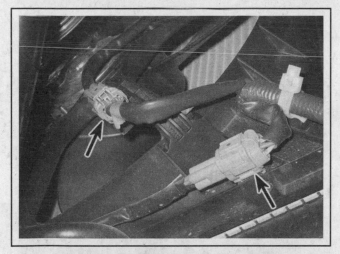

4.4a To test either fan motor, disconnect the electrical connector for the fan you're testing at the harness, or from the very back of the fan motor . . .

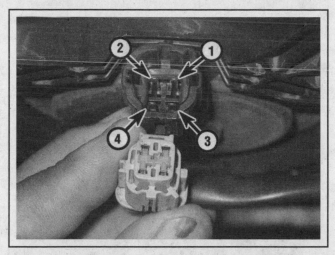

4.4b . . . and use fused jumper wires to apply battery voltage to terminals 1 and 2 and ground to terminals 3 and 4 - if the fan still doesn't work, replace the motor

4.5 The cooling fan relays are located in the fuse/relay box in the engine compartment

4.24 Locations of the fan assembly mounting fasteners

REPLACEMENT

Electric fans

2004 and earlier G35 Sedans (one electric fan)

12 Remove the grille from the bumper cover.

13 Remove the lower engine splash shield (see Chapter 2).

14 Disconnect the cooling fan electrical connector from the back of the fan motor.

15 Remove the cooling fan shroud assembly mounting fasteners (there are three), and remove the assembly.

16 If you are replacing a motor, remove the fan blade mounting nut to separate it from the motor (see illustration 4.26).

➡**Note: The nut for the fan blade could be reverse threaded.**

17 Remove the mounting fasteners for the motor and separate it from the shroud assembly (see illustration 4.27).

18 Installation is the reverse of removal.

2006 and earlier 350Z , G35 Sedans and 2007 and earlier G35 Coupes

▶ Refer to illustrations 4.24, 4.26, 4.27 and 4.28

❋❋ WARNING:

Wail until the engine is completely cool before beginning this procedure.

19 Remove the engine lower splash shield (see Chapter 2).

20 Partially drain the cooling system (see Chapter 1).

21 Remove the upper radiator hose (see Section 6).

22 Remove the air filter housing and intake duct (see Chapter 4).

23 Disconnect the cooling fan electrical connectors from the wiring harness (see illustration 4.4a).

24 Remove the cooling fan shroud assembly mounting fasteners at the top of the assembly (see illustration).

4.26 Fan blade mounting nut

4.27 Fan motor mounting fasteners

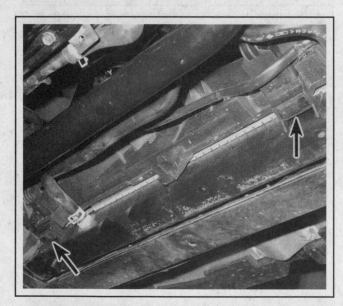

4.28 Fan assembly lower mounts at the radiator

25 Remove the cooling fan assembly by pulling it up and tilting it away from the radiator and disengaging the lower shroud assembly mounting tabs.

26 If you are replacing a motor, remove the fan blade mounting nut to separate it from the motor (see illustration).

27 Remove the mounting fasteners for the motor and separate the motor from the shroud assembly (see illustration).

28 Installation is the reverse of removal. Be sure to engage the bottom of the fan assembly with the plastic mounts that hold it to the bottom of the radiator (see illustration).

29 Fill the cooling system with the proper mixture of antifreeze and water (see Chapter 1).

2007 and later 350Z and G35 Sedans

30 Remove the left (driver's side) air filter housing and duct (see Chapter 4).

31 Remove the coolant reservoir (see Section 5).

32 Disconnect the cooling fan electrical connectors from the fan control module that's mounted on the left top side of the fan shroud:

33 Remove the engine lower splash shield (see Chapter 2A, illustration 12.4).

34 Remove the cooling fan shroud assembly mounting fasteners at the top of the assembly (see illustration 4.24).

35 Remove the cooling fan assembly by disengaging the lower shroud assembly mounting tabs, then guiding the assembly out of the bottom of the engine compartment.

36 If you are replacing a motor, remove the fan blade mounting nut to separate it from the motor (see illustration 4.26).

37 Remove the mounting fasteners for the motor and separate the motor from the shroud assembly (see illustration 4.27).

➡**Note: The motors are designed to fit either the right or left hand side, so label them accordingly.**

38 Installation is the reverse of removal. Be sure to engage the bottom of the fan assembly with the plastic mounts that hold it to the bottom of the radiator (see illustration 4.28).

Belt driven fan

▶ **Refer to illustration 4.45**

39 Remove the air duct between the throttle body and the air filter housing.

40 Remove the lower engine splash shield (see Chapter 2).

41 Disconnect the lower radiator hose and the transmission oil cooler lines from the radiator (see Section 6).

42 Remove the lower radiator shroud.

→**Note: The radiator shroud has a lower part that can be separated from the main part of the shroud.**

43 Remove the drivebelts (see Chapter 1).

44 Remove the fan coupling (clutch) mounting fasteners from the studs on the fan pulley.

45 To remove the fan, remove the fan mounting fasteners from the fan coupling. Note the "F" stamped on the face of where the fan mounts to the coupling. This designates which side faces towards the front of the vehicle (see illustration).

46 Installation is the reverse of the removal procedure. Tighten the fasteners to the torque values listed in this Chapter's Specifications.

47 Fill the cooling system with the proper mixture of antifreeze and water (see Chapter 1).

48 Start the engine and check for leaks. Allow the engine to reach normal operating temperature and recheck the coolant level; add more if required.

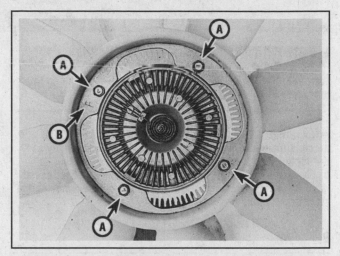

4.45 Fan mounting fasteners (A) and the F (front) stamp (B)

5 Coolant reservoir - removal and installation

▶ **Refer to illustration 5.2**

❋❋ **WARNING:**

Wait until the engine is completely cool before beginning this procedure.

1 Drain the cooling system (see Chapter 1). If the coolant is relatively new and still in good condition, it can be saved and reused.

→**Note: Be careful to clean up any spilled coolant as stated in the Warning at the beginning of Section 2.**

2 Disconnect the hoses from the radiator or the reservoir by sliding the hose clamp away with pliers and removing the hose from the fitting (see illustration). Hoses that are attached to the bottom of the reservoir can be removed when lifting it out in the following steps.

3 Remove the mounting fastener(s) located near the top of the reservoir (see illustration 5.2).

4 Remove the reservoir by pulling it up and away from any mounts on the bottom.

5 Clean out the tank with soapy water and a brush to remove any deposits inside. Inspect the tank carefully for cracks. If you find a crack, replace the tank.

5.2 Disconnect the reservoir hose (A) and remove the mounting fastener (B) (2004 G35 Sedan model shown)

6 Installation is the reverse of removal. Refill the cooling system with the proper concentration of antifreeze (see Chapter 1).

6   Radiator - removal and installation

❋ WARNING:

Wait until the engine is completely cool before beginning this procedure.

➡ Note: On 2007 and later G35 Sedan models, the radiator and air conditioning condenser are built as a single assembly and are removed as a unit. As a result, the A/C system must be discharged of all refrigerant. See the Warning and Cautions at the beginning of Section 13 of this Chapter before removing the radiator assembly on these models.

REMOVAL

◆ **Refer to illustrations 6.6a, 6.6b, 6.9, 6.10, 6.13 and 6.15**

1   On 2007 and later G35 Sedans, have the air conditioning system discharged by a dealer service department or an automotive air conditioning shop before proceeding.

2   Remove the top engine cover and the engine lower splash shield (see Chapter 2A, illustration 12.4).

3   Drain the cooling system (see Chapter 1). If the coolant is relatively new or in good condition, save it and reuse it.

4   Remove the air filter housing and related ducts (see Chapter 4). On 2007 and later G35 Sedans, remove both air filter housings and related ducts.

5   Remove the coolant reservoir and related hoses from the radiator (see Section 5).

6   Detach the upper and lower radiator hoses from the radiator (see illustrations).

7   On 2007 and later G35 Sedans, remove the front grill and the hood latch (see Chapter 11) and the cover over the radiator.

8   On 2007 and later G35 Sedans, remove the refrigerant lines from the air conditioning condenser. They are bolted to fittings on the left-front side of the condenser. Discard the old O-rings.

9   Disconnect the transmission oil cooler hoses from the radiator, if equipped (see illustration). On 2007 and later G35 Sedans, the hose fittings are located on the left side of the radiator and not the bottom.

10   Remove the refrigerant line bracket so that it can be moved aside (see illustration). On 2007 and later G35 Sedans, this step does not apply.

11   On vehicles with two electric cooling fans, remove the cooling fan assembly (see Section 4).

12   On vehicles with a clutch type cooling fan, remove the fan and clutch from its pulley and the related shrouds.

➡ Note: The shroud is comprised of two parts; remove the lower part of the shroud from the bottom first, then remove the large part of the shroud.

13   Remove the upper mounting retainers from the top of the radiator support by turning them 90 degrees counterclockwise (see illustration).

14   Remove the upper mounting fasteners for the air conditioning condenser through the access holes in the radiator support (see illustration 6.13). On 2007 and later G35 Sedans, this step does not apply.

15   Carefully separate the condenser from the radiator by pulling the condenser up slightly to withdraw its mounting tabs from the radiator (see illustration). On 2007 and later G35 Sedans, this step does not apply.

16   Tilt the top of the radiator (or assembly) towards the engine and lift it out of the engine compartment. Be careful not to damage any of the radiator fins, spill coolant or scratch the paint. Note the position of any flexible air deflectors on the sides or top of the radiator.

17   When removing the radiator (or assembly) from the vehicle, check the condition of the lower mounting bushings (see illustration 6.15). If they're cracked, hardened or otherwise deteriorated, replace them.

6.6a Location of the upper radiator hose and clamps (2004 G35 Sedan model shown)

6.6b Location of the lower radiator hose and clamp (2004 G35 Sedan model shown)

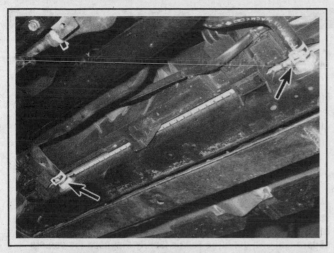

6.9 The location of the transmission oil cooler hoses at the radiator (2004 G35 Sedan model shown)

6.10 Remove the refrigerant line bracket mounting fastener so it can be moved aside

6.13 The radiator retainers (A) and the air conditioning condenser mounting fastener access points (B)

6.15 A mounting tab for the air conditioning condenser (A) and a rubber bushing on the lower radiator mount (B) (right side shown)

INSTALLATION

18 With the radiator removed, it can be inspected for leaks and damage. If it needs repair, have a radiator shop or dealer service department perform the work, as special tools and techniques are required.

19 Bugs and dirt can be removed from the front of the radiator (or assembly) with a garden hose, followed by compressed air and a soft brush. Don't bend the cooling fins as this is done. When blowing out the core, direct the hose or air line from the engine side out only.

20 Inspect the radiator mounts for deterioration and make sure there's nothing in them when the radiator is installed.

21 Installation is the reverse of the removal procedure. On 2007 and later G35 Sedans, install new O-ring seals onto the refrigerant line fittings. Tighten the line fitting bolts to the torque listed in this Chapter's Specifications.

22 Fill the cooling system with the proper mixture of antifreeze and water (see Chapter 1).

23 Start the engine and check for leaks. Allow the engine to reach normal operating temperature and recheck the coolant level; add more if required.

24 On 2007 and later G35 Sedans, have the air conditioning system evacuated, recharged and leak-tested by the shop that discharged it.

7 Water pump - check

1 The water pump on these vehicles is driven by the timing chain and it is located underneath the timing chain cover. On most models, there is an access panel that can be removed, and the impeller shaft can be checked for play while the pump is installed. On 2007 and later G35 and 350Z models, the entire timing cover must be removed to inspect the water pump.

2 A failure in the water pump can cause serious engine damage due to overheating.

3 Checking the water pump is limited because of where it is located. However, some basic checks can be made before deciding to remove the water pump. If the pump is found to be defective, it should be replaced with a new or rebuilt unit.

4 One sign that the water pump may be failing is that the heater (climate control) may not work well. Warm the engine to normal operating temperature, confirm that the coolant level is correct, then run the heater and check for hot air coming from the ducts.

5 Check for noises coming from the water pump area (see illustration 8.11). If the water pump impeller shaft or bearings are failing, there may be a howling sound at the pump while the engine is running.

→**Note: Be careful not to mistake drivebelt noise (squealing) for water pump bearing or shaft failure.**

6 It you suspect water pump failure due to noise, wear can be confirmed by feeling for play at the pump shaft. This can be done by rocking the drive sprocket on the pump shaft up and down. To do this you will need to remove the tension on the timing chain as well as access the water pump (see Section 8).

7 In rare cases or on high-mileage vehicles, another sign of water pump failure may be the presence of coolant in the engine oil. This condition will adversely affect the engine in varying degrees.

→**Note: Finding coolant in the engine oil could indicate other serious issues besides a failed water pump. To determine the cause of this condition, we advise that a dealership service department or a qualified repair facility diagnose the vehicle because of the special tools and expertise required.**

8 Even a pump that exhibits no outward signs of a problem, such as noise or leakage, can still be due for replacement. Removal for close examination is the only sure way to tell. Sometimes the fins on the back of the impellers can corrode to the point that cooling efficiency is diminished significantly.

8 Water pump - removal and installation

✳✳ **WARNING:**

Wait until the engine is completely cool before beginning this procedure.

REMOVAL

♦ **Refer to illustrations 8.7, 8.11a, 8.11b, 8.12 and 8.13**

1 Disconnect the cable from the negative battery terminal (see Chapter 5, Section 1).

8.7 The timing chain tensioner (A) and water pump cover (B) locations

2 Remove the top engine cover and the engine lower splash shield (see Chapter 2A, illustration 12.4).

3 Drain the cooling system (see Chapter 1). If the coolant is relatively new or in good condition, save it and reuse it.

→**Note: Be sure to remove the block drain plugs on the left (driver's) side of the engine block, if equipped.**

4 Remove the air filter housing(s) and related ducts (see Chapter 4).

5 Remove the radiator hoses (see Section 6).

6 Remove the drivebelts (see Chapter 1).

7 If you're working on a 2006 and earlier 350Z, G35 Sedan or 2007 and earlier G35 Coupe model, remove the timing chain tensioner and water pump covers from the timing chain cover (see illustration).

8 If you're working on a 2007 and later 350Z or G35 Sedan model, relieve the fuel pressure (see Chapter 4) and drain the engine oil (see Chapter 1).

9 On 2007 and later 350Z and G35 Sedan models, remove the coolant reservoir (see Section 5).

10 On 2007 and later 350Z and G35 Sedan models, remove the timing chain cover (see Chapter 2A).

11 Retract the timing chain tensioner plunger; press and hold the small lever to release the pawl for the plunger and simultaneously press the timing chain guide to push the plunger into the tensioner body (see illustration). With the small lever in the upper position, place a small tool through the hole in the lever and in the tensioner body to keep the plunger retracted (see illustration).

12 Remove the timing chain tensioner mounting fasteners, then remove the tensioner (see illustration).

✳✳ **CAUTION:**

Be careful not to drop any of the mounting fasteners into the timing chain case.

8.11a Pushing the plunger into the tensioner body

8.11b Using a pin to keep the plunger retracted

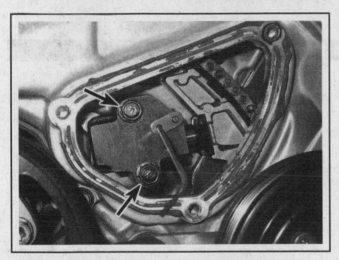

8.12 The timing chain tensioner mounting fasteners

8.13 Remove the water pump mounting fasteners (A) and thread M8 bolts into the upper and lower mounting positions (B) to remove the water pump

13 Remove the water pump mounting bolts (see illustration).

14 Move the crankshaft counterclockwise about 20 degrees so that the timing chain becomes loose around the water pump sprocket

15 Install two M8 bolts, that are 50 mm in length, into the upper and lower water pump mounting holes until they reach the back of the timing case (see illustration 8.13). Alternate tightening each of them a half-turn at a time until the water pump is released from the block.

➡**Note: Be careful not to damage the timing chain or mounting bore when pulling the water pump from the block.**

16 Remove the M8 bolts and O-rings from the water pump.

17 Remove the old sealant from all mating surfaces.

INSTALLATION

18 Compare the new pump to the old one to make sure they're identical. If the old pump is being reused, check the impeller blades on the backside for corrosion and feel for rough bearing operation or play. If there are any concerns, replace the pump with a new one.

19 Remove all traces of the old O-ring seal from the engine and water pump (if the same pump is to be installed).

20 Install new O-ring seals onto the water pump. O-rings that have yellow or white paint marks on them are coated with engine oil and are installed first (facing front of engine). O-rings that are plain (black) or have light blue paint marks on them are coated with clean engine coolant and are installed second (facing the rear of engine).

❋❋❋ CAUTION:

Make sure that the O-rings are seated correctly at the water pump to avoid any leaks.

21 Carefully install the water pump, being careful not to damage the O-rings. Place the timing chain onto the water pump sprocket.

22 Install the mounting bolts finger tight. Proceed to tighten them gradually in a criss-cross pattern; this will draw the water pump into position. Finally, tighten the mounting bolts to the torque listed in this Chapter's Specifications.

※※ **CAUTION:**

Be careful not to drop any of the mounting fasteners into the timing chain case, if applicable.

23 Turn the crankshaft 20 degrees clockwise to bring slack to the timing chain where the timing chain tensioner will be installed.

24 Place the timing chain tensioner into position, install the mounting bolts and tighten them to the torque listed in this Chapter's Specifications.

※※ **CAUTION:**

Be careful not to drop any of the mounting fasteners into the timing chain case.

25 Remove the small pin used to keep the tensioner's plunger retracted. The plunger will extend and contact the timing chain guide.

26 If you're working on a 2007 and later 350Z or G35 Sedan model, install the timing chain tensioner and water pump covers using RTV sealant.

※※ **CAUTION:**

Make sure that the mating surfaces are clean before applying sealant.

27 On 2007 and later 350Z or G35 Sedan models, install the timing chain cover (see Chapter 2).

28 The remainder of installation is the reverse of removal.

29 Wait at least one hour for the sealant to cure. Refill and bleed the cooling system (see Chapter 1). Run the engine and check for leaks and proper operation.

➡**Note: Timing chain noise may occur after the engine starts. This noise is normal and should only be brief. Allow the engine to run at 3,000 rpm with the transmission in Neutral or Park until the noise subsides.**

9 Coolant temperature sending unit - check and replacement

CHECK

1 The coolant temperature indicator system consists of a warning light or a temperature gauge on the dash and a coolant temperature sending unit mounted on the engine. On the models covered by this manual, the Engine Coolant Temperature (ECT) sensor, which is an information sensor for the Powertrain Control Module (PCM), also functions as the coolant temperature sending unit (see Chapter 6).

2 If an overheating indication occurs, check the coolant level in the system, then make sure all connectors in the wiring harness between the sending unit and the indicator light or gauge are tight.

3 When the ignition switch is turned to START and the starter motor is turning, the indicator light (if equipped) should come on. This doesn't mean the engine is overheated; it just means that the bulb is good.

4 If the light doesn't come on when the ignition key is turned to START, the bulb might be burned out, the ignition switch might be faulty or the circuit might be open.

5 As soon as the engine starts, the indicator light should go out and remain off, unless the engine overheats. If the light doesn't go out, refer to Chapter 6 and check for any stored trouble codes in the Powertrain Control Module (PCM).

6 If the engine tends to overheat easily, check the coolant to make sure it's the proper type and concentration (see Chapter 1).

REPLACEMENT

7 See Chapter 6 for the ECT sensor replacement procedure.

10 Blower motor - replacement

▶ **Refer to illustrations 10.1 and 10.2**

※※ **WARNING:**

The models covered by this manual are equipped with a Supplemental Restraint System (SRS), more commonly known as airbags. Always disarm the airbag system before working in the vicinity of any airbag system component to avoid the possibility of accidental deployment of the airbag, which could cause personal injury (see Chapter 12). Do not use a memory saving device to preserve the PCM's memory when working on or near airbag system components.

1 Remove the lower instrument panel insulator below the glove box (see illustration).

2 Disconnect the electrical connector from the blower motor, then remove the mounting screws and lower the blower motor out of the housing (see illustration).

3 If either the fan or motor is damaged, the entire unit must be replaced as an assembly.

4 Installation is the reverse of removal.

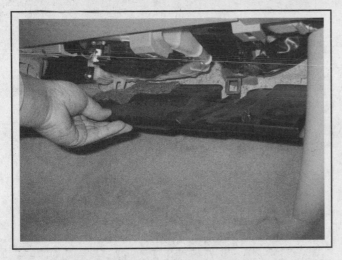

10.1 Remove the insulator panel covering the blower motor

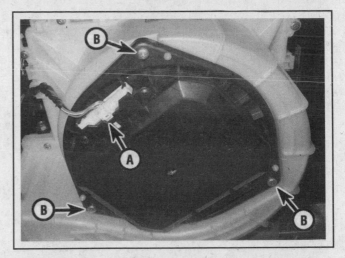

10.2 Remove the electrical connector (A) and the mounting screws (B) for the blower motor

11 Heater/air conditioning control assembly - removal and installation

The air conditioning controls for all models are integrated with the audio controls. Refer to Chapter 12 for the removal and installation of the audio and air conditioning controls.

12 Heater core - removal and installation

❋❋ WARNING 1:

The models covered by this manual are equipped with a Supplemental Restraint System (SRS), more commonly known as airbags. Always disarm the airbag system before working in the vicinity of any airbag system component to avoid the possibility of accidental deployment of the airbag, which could cause personal injury (see Chapter 12). Do not use a memory saving device to preserve the PCM's memory when working on or near airbag system components.

❋❋ WARNING 2:

Wait until the engine is completely cool before beginning this procedure.

❋❋ WARNING 3:

The air conditioning system is under high pressure. Do not loosen any hose fittings or remove any components until after the system has been discharged. Air conditioning refrigerant must be properly discharged into an EPA-approved recovery/recycling unit at a dealer service department or an automotive air conditioning repair facility. Always wear eye protection when disconnecting air conditioning system fittings.

→Note: Replacement of the heater core is a difficult procedure for the home mechanic, involving removal of the entire instrument panel, floor console, and ultimately the heater/air conditioning housing and related wiring connectors. If you attempt this procedure at home, keep track of the assemblies by taking notes and keeping screws and other hardware in small, marked plastic bags for reassembly.

REMOVAL

⬧ Refer to illustrations 12.5, 12.9, 12.10a, 12.10b, 12.11a, 12.11b, 12.11c, 12.12a, 12.12b, 12.12c, 12.15, 12.16 and 12.17

1   Have the air conditioning system discharged by a dealer service department or an automotive air conditioning shop before proceeding (see **Warning 3** above).

2   Disconnect the cable from the negative battery terminal (see Chapter 5, Section 1).

3   Drain the cooling system (see Chapter 1).

4   Working in the engine compartment, remove the cowl cover (see Chapter 11).

5   Working in the engine compartment, disconnect the heater hoses at the firewall (see illustration). Tape or plug all openings.

6   Disconnect the air conditioning refrigerant lines at the firewall (see illustration 12.5). Tape or plug all openings.

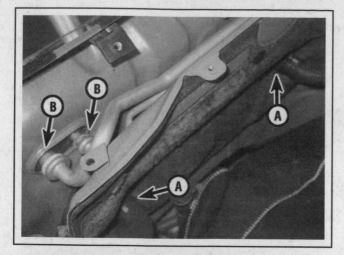

12.5 The location of the heater hoses (A) and air conditioning refrigerant lines (B) at the firewall

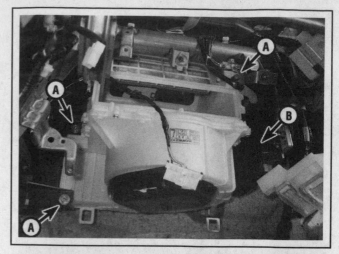

12.9 Remove the blower motor housing mounting fasteners (A) and move the PCM (B) aside if necessary (2004 G35 Sedan shown - other models similar)

➡Note: A special tool is required to separate the lines (see illustrations 16.4b and 16.4c).

7 Remove the instrument panel (see Chapter 11).

8 Remove the steering column (see Chapter 10).

9 Remove the blower motor housing mounting fasteners, move it slightly right, then move it downward and out of the vehicle (see illustration).

➡Note: If necessary, remove the mounting nuts for the Powertrain Control Module (PCM) bracket and move it aside for clearance to move the blower motor rightward.

10 Detach ducts from the top and bottom of the heater/air conditioning housing, detach the evaporator drain hose and remove the mounting fasteners for the housing (see illustrations).

11 Disconnect the electrical connectors from the instrument panel support beam wiring harnesses (see illustrations). Some harnesses will need to be followed and detached from brackets, like the harness that goes through the center floor console (see illustration).

➡Note: The various wiring harnesses that are attached directly to the beam do not need to be removed from it; they just need to be disconnected from other harnesses attached to the body or other brackets so that the beam can be removed.

12 Remove the instrument panel support beam mounting fasteners, then carefully remove the beam, making sure that nothing else is attached to it (see illustrations). It would be helpful to have an assistant during this procedure to help support and guide the beam during removal.

13 Carefully pull the heater/air conditioning housing directly away from the firewall and remove it. The heater core and evaporator pipes will come through the firewall along with the housing.

➡Note: Be prepared for coolant to spill from the heater core pipes by placing towels beneath the housing before removing it.

14 With the heater/air conditioning housing out, remove the rubber seals around both heater core tubes. If they are not reusable, replace them.

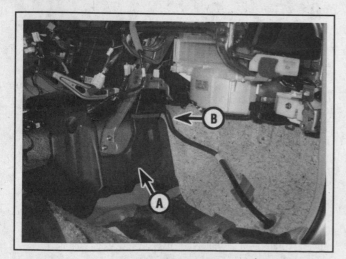

12.10a Detach the floor ducts (A) and the evaporator drain tube (B) from the heater/air conditioning housing (2004 G35 Sedan shown - other models similar)

12.10b Detach the upper ducts (A) and remove the mounting fasteners (B) from the heater/air conditioning housing (2004 G35 Sedan shown - other models similar)

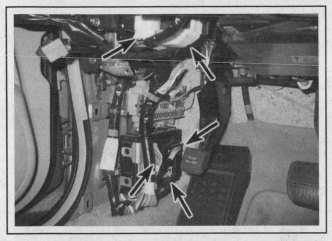

12.11a Harness connectors found at the left (driver's) side of the support beam - not all connectors are visible (2004 G35 Sedan shown - other models similar)

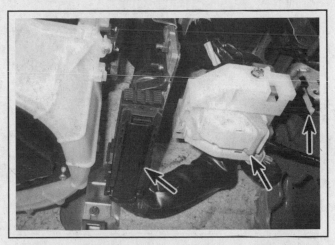

12.11b Harness connectors found at the right (passenger's) side of the support beam - not all connectors are visible (2004 G35 Sedan shown - other models similar)

12.11c Detach the harness from the center console brackets after disconnecting all electrical connectors for the harness - not all connectors are visible (2004 G35 Sedan shown - other models similar)

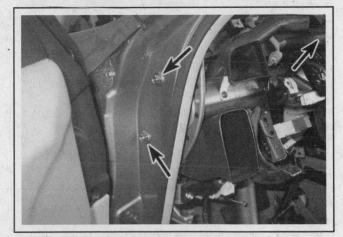

12.12a The left (driver's) side support beam mounting fasteners. Not all fasteners are visible (2004 G35 Sedan shown - other models similar)

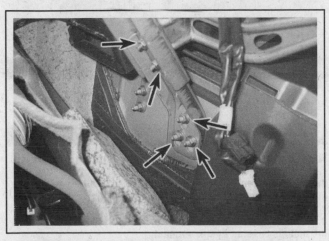

12.12b The left (driver's) support beam center bracket mounting fasteners (2004 G35 Sedan shown - other models similar)

12.12c The right (passenger's) side support beam and center bracket mounting fasteners (2004 G35 Sedan shown - other models similar)

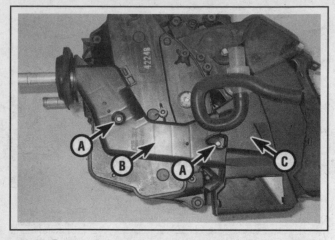

12.15 Remove the mounting fasteners for the heater core pipe cover (A), remove the cover (B), then remove the duct over the pipes (C) (2004 G35 Sedan shown - other models similar)

12.16 Remove the small bracket fitting from the heater/air conditioning housing and the heater core pipe (2004 G35 Sedan shown - other models similar)

➡Note: Also, replace the seal for the air conditioning evaporator pipes, if necessary.

15 Remove the cover over the heater core tubes and the vent ducting over the heater core itself (see illustration).

16 Remove the small bracket fitting for one of the heater core tubes (see illustration).

17 Pull the heater core out of the heater/air conditioning housing while supporting the tubes. Be careful not to damage any seals (see illustration).

INSTALLATION

18 Before installing the heater core, make sure that any foam seals on the core or housing are in place.

19 Carefully slide the heater core into the housing.

20 Reinstall the remaining components in the reverse order of removal.

21 Refill the cooling system (see Chapter 1) and reconnect the battery (see Chapter 5).

22 Start the engine and check for any leaks and for proper heater operation.

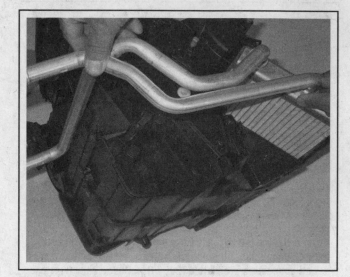

12.17 Pull the heater core out of the heater/air conditioning housing (2004 G35 Sedan shown - other models similar)

13 Air conditioning and heating system - check and maintenance

AIR CONDITIONING SYSTEM

▸ **Refer to illustration 13.1**

❋❋ WARNING:

The air conditioning system is under high pressure. Do not loosen any hose fittings or remove any components until after the system has been discharged. Air conditioning refrigerant must be properly discharged into an EPA-approved recovery/recycling unit at a dealer service department or an automotive air conditioning repair facility. Always wear eye protection when disconnecting air conditioning system fittings.

❋❋ CAUTION 1:

There are two types of refrigerant used in automotive systems; R-12 - which has been widely used on earlier models - and the more environmentally-friendly R-134a used in all models covered by this manual. These two refrigerants (and their appropriate refrigerant oils) are not compatible and must never be mixed or components will be damaged. Use only R-134a refrigerant in the models covered by this manual.

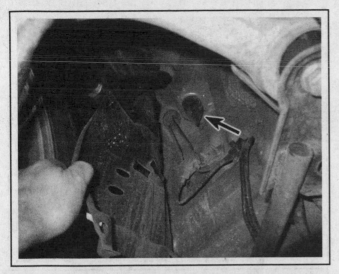

13.1 Check the evaporator housing drain tube for blockage; it's located behind the right (passenger's) inner fender-well splash shield

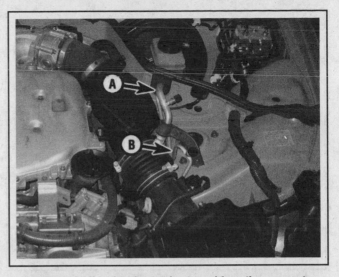

13.9 When feeling the pipes going to and from the evaporator, the larger-diameter pipe (A) should feel much cooler than the smaller-diameter one (B), which may even be hot

✳✳ CAUTION 2:

When replacing entire components, additional refrigerant oil should be added equal to the amount that is removed with the component being replaced. Be sure to read the can before adding any oil to the system, to make sure it is compatible with the R-134a system.

1   The following maintenance checks should be performed on a regular basis to ensure that the air conditioning continues to operate at peak efficiency.

   a) *Inspect the condition of the drivebelt. If it is worn or deteriorated, replace it (see Chapter 1).*

   b) *Inspect the system hoses. Look for cracks, bubbles, hardening and deterioration. Inspect the hoses and all fittings for oil bubbles or seepage. If there is any evidence of wear, damage or leakage, replace the hose(s).*

   c) *Inspect the condenser fins for leaves, bugs and any other foreign material that may have embedded itself in the fins. Use a fin comb or compressed air to remove debris from the condenser.*

   d) *Make sure the system has the correct refrigerant charge.*

   e) *If you hear water sloshing around in the dash area or have water dripping on the carpet, check the evaporator housing drain tube (see illustration) and insert a piece of wire into the opening to check for blockage.*

2   It's a good idea to operate the system for about 10 minutes at least once a month, particularly during the winter. Long-term non-use can cause hardening, and subsequent failure, of the seals.

3   Leaks in the air conditioning system are best spotted when the system is brought up to temperature and pressure, by running the engine with the air conditioning ON for five minutes. Shut the engine off

and inspect the air conditioning hoses and connections. Traces of oil usually indicate refrigerant leaks.

4   Because of the complexity of the air conditioning system and the special equipment necessary to service it, in-depth troubleshooting and repairs are not included in this manual. However, simple checks and component replacement procedures are provided in this Chapter.

5   If the air conditioning system doesn't operate at all, check the fuse panel and the air conditioning relay, located in the relay box in the engine compartment (see Chapter 12).

6   The most common cause of poor cooling is simply a low system refrigerant charge. If a noticeable drop in cool air output occurs, the following quick check will help you determine if the refrigerant level is low.

Checking the refrigerant charge

▶ **Refer to illustration 13.9**

7   Warm the engine up to normal operating temperature.

8   Place the air conditioning temperature selector at the coldest setting and put the blower at the highest setting. Open the doors (to make sure the air conditioning system doesn't cycle off as soon as it cools the passenger compartment).

9   With the compressor engaged, the clutch will make an audible click and the center of the clutch will rotate. Feel the pipes going to and from the evaporator (see illustration); the small diameter pipe should be warm and the large diameter pipe should feel cool.

10   If the larger-diameter pipe isn't considerably cooler, the system charge is probably low. The earliest warning that a system is low on refrigerant is the air temperature coming out of the ducts inside the vehicle. If the air isn't as cold as it used to be, the system probably needs a charge.

11   Further inspection or testing of the system requires special tools and techniques and is beyond the scope of this manual.

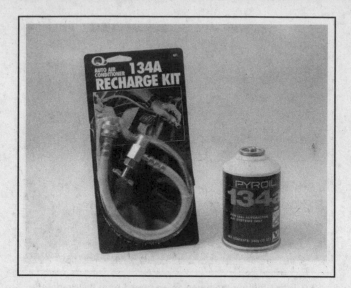

13.12 A basic charging kit for 134a systems is available at most auto parts stores - it must say 134a (not R-12) and so must the can of refrigerant

13.15 Add refrigerant to the system at the low-pressure port

Adding refrigerant

▶ **Refer to illustrations 13.12, 13.15 and 13.18**

12 Buy an automotive charging kit at an auto parts store. A charging kit includes a can of refrigerant, a tap valve and a short section of hose that can be attached between the tap valve and the system low side service valve (see illustration).

☼ CAUTION:

Although the system will hold more than one can of refrigerant, don't add more than one can (you could overfill the system). If more refrigerant than that is required, the system should be evacuated and leak tested.

13 Hook up the charging kit by following the manufacturer's instructions.

☼ WARNING:

DO NOT attempt to hook the charging kit hose to the system high pressure side! The fittings on the charging kit are designed to fit only on the low pressure side of the system.

14 Back off the valve handle on the charging kit and screw the kit onto the refrigerant can, first making sure that the O-ring or rubber seal inside the threaded portion of the kit is in place.

☼ WARNING:

Wear protective eyewear when dealing with pressurized refrigerant cans.

15 Remove the dust cap from the low-side charging port and attach the quick-connect fitting on the kit hose (see illustration).

16 Warm up the engine and turn on the air conditioner. Keep the charging kit hose away from the fan and other moving parts. The charging process requires the compressor to be running.

17 Turn the valve handle on the kit until the stem pierces the can, then back the handle out to release the refrigerant. You should be able to hear the rush of gas. Add refrigerant to the low side of the system until both the accumulator surface and the evaporator inlet pipe feel about the same temperature. Allow stabilization time between each addition.

18 If you have an accurate thermometer, you can place it in the center air conditioning duct inside the vehicle (see illustration) and

13.18 If you have an accurate thermometer, you can place it in the center air conditioning duct and read the temperature

keep track of the outlet air temperature. A charged system that is working properly should cool to approximately 40-degrees F. If the ambient (outside) air temperature is very high, say 110-degrees F, or if the relative humidity is high, the duct air temperature may be as high as 60- to 70-degrees F, but generally the air conditioning is 30 to 50-degrees F cooler than the ambient air.

19 When the can is empty, turn the valve handle to the closed position and release the connection from the low-side port. Replace the dust cap.

20 Remove the charging kit from the can and store the kit for future use with the piercing valve in the UP position to prevent inadvertently piercing the can on the next use.

Eliminating air conditioning odors

◆ Refer to Illustration 13.24

21 Unpleasant odors that often develop in air conditioning systems are caused by the growth of a fungus, usually on the surface of the evaporator core. The warm, humid environment there is a perfect breeding ground for mildew to develop.

22 The evaporator core on most vehicles is difficult to access, and factory dealerships have a lengthy, expensive process for eliminating the fungus by opening up the evaporator case and using a powerful disinfectant and rinse on the core until the fungus is gone. You can service your own system at home, but it takes something much stronger than basic household germ-killers or deodorizers.

23 Aerosol disinfectants for automotive air conditioning systems are available in most auto parts stores, but remember when shopping for them that the most effective treatments are also the most expensive. The basic procedure for using these sprays is to start by running the system in the Recirculating mode for ten minutes with the blower on its highest speed. Use the highest heat mode to dry out the system; keep the compressor from engaging by disconnecting the wiring connector at the compressor (see Section 14).

24 Make sure that the disinfectant can comes with a long spray hose. Work the nozzle through the opening in the heater/air conditioning recirculation housing so that it protrudes just inside the blower motor housing (see illustration), then spray according to the manufacturer's recommendations. Follow the manufacturer's recommendations for the length of spray and waiting time between applications.

25 Once the odor has been eliminated, the best way to prevent the mildew from coming back again is to make sure your evaporator housing drain tube is clear (see illustration 13.1).

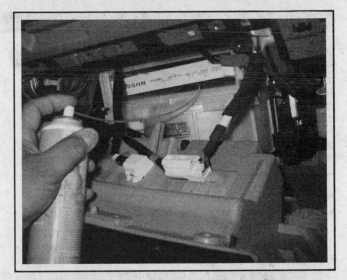

13.24 To disinfect the evaporator housing, insert the nozzle of the disinfectant can through the opening in the recirculation housing and point it toward the evaporator core (which is toward the left of the opening) - glove box removed for access

HEATING SYSTEM

26 If the carpet under the heater core is damp, or if antifreeze vapor or steam is coming through the vents, the heater core is leaking. Remove it (see Section 12) and install a new unit (most radiator shops will not repair a leaking heater core).

27 If the air coming out of the heater vents isn't hot, the problem could stem from any of the following causes:

a) *The thermostat is stuck open, preventing the engine coolant from warming up enough to carry heat to the heater core. Replace the thermostat (see Section 3).*

b) *There is a blockage in the system, preventing the flow of coolant through the heater core. Feel both heater hoses at the firewall. They should be hot. If one of them is cold, there is an obstruction in one of the hoses or in the heater core. Detach the hoses and back flush the heater core with a water hose. If the heater core is clear but circulation is still restricted, remove the two hoses and flush them out with a water hose.*

c) *If flushing fails to remove the blockage from the heater core, the core must be replaced (see Section 12).*

14 Air conditioning compressor - removal and installation

※※ WARNING:

The air conditioning system is under high pressure. Do not loosen any hose fittings or remove any components until after the system has been discharged. Air conditioning refrigerant must be properly discharged into an EPA-approved recovery/recycling unit at a dealer service department or an automotive air conditioning repair facility. Always wear eye protection when disconnecting air conditioning system fittings.

➡ Note: The receiver-drier (see Section 15) should be replaced whenever the compressor is replaced due to an internal failure.

1 Have the air conditioning system discharged by a dealer service department or an automotive air conditioning shop before proceeding (see **Warning** above).

2 Disconnect the cable from the negative battery terminal (see Chapter 5, Section 1).

3 Raise the front of the vehicle and support it securely on jackstands.

4 Remove the top engine cover and the lower engine splash shield (see Chapter 2A, illustration 12.4).

5 Remove the drivebelt (see Chapter 1).

2007 AND LATER 350Z AND G35 SEDANS

6 Drain the engine cooling system (see Chapter 1).

7 Remove the left (driver's) side air filter housing and air duct (see Chapter 4).

8 Remove the cooling fans (see Section 4).

9 Remove the lower radiator hose (see Section 6).

10 Disconnect the compressor clutch and electronic control valve electrical connectors at the compressor (see illustrations 14.15 and 14.17).

11 Disconnect the refrigerant lines from the compressor. Plug the open fittings to prevent the entry of dirt and moisture and discard the O-ring seals (see illustration 14.15).

12 Remove the three mounting bolts, located on the side of the compressor (see illustration 14.17).

13 Carefully remove the compressor out the top of the engine compartment.

2006 AND EARLIER 350Z, G35 SEDANS AND 2007 AND EARLIER G35 COUPES

▸ **Refer to illustrations 14.15 and 14.17**

14 Remove the air filter housing, the intake air duct and the duct leading to the throttle body (see Chapter 4).

15 Disconnect the compressor clutch and electronic control valve electrical connectors (see illustration).

16 Disconnect the refrigerant line fittings from the compressor. Plug the open fittings to prevent the entry of dirt and moisture and discard the O-ring seals (see illustration 4.15).

17 Remove the mounting fasteners and carefully remove the compressor from the bottom of the engine compartment (see illustration).

14.15 Air conditioning compressor details (top view):

1   Compressor clutch electrical connector
2   Refrigerant line fittings

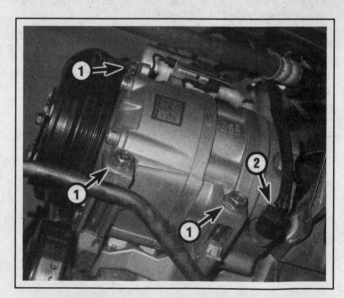

14.17 Air conditioning compressor details (bottom view):

1   Compressor mounting fasteners
2   Electronic control valve electrical connector

ALL MODELS

18 If a new compressor is being installed, follow the directions with the compressor regarding the draining of excess oil prior to installation. Any refrigerant oil added must be compatible with R-134a refrigerant.

19 The clutch may have to be transferred from the original compressor to the new one.

20 Installation is the reverse of removal. Replace all O-rings with new ones specifically made for air conditioning system use and compatible with R-134a refrigerant. Lubricate them with refrigerant oil. Tighten the mounting fasteners and the line fitting nuts to the torque values listed in this Chapter's Specifications.

21 On 2007 and later G35 Sedans and 350Z models, refill the cooling system (see Chapter 1).

22 Have the system evacuated, recharged and leak-tested by the shop that discharged it.

15 Air conditioning receiver-drier - removal and installation

▶ **Refer to illustration 15.4**

※※ WARNING:

The air conditioning system is under high pressure. Do not loosen any hose fittings or remove any components until after the system has been discharged. Air conditioning refrigerant must be properly discharged into an EPA-approved recovery/recycling unit at a dealer service department or an automotive air conditioning repair facility. Always wear eye protection when disconnecting air conditioning system fittings.

1   Have the air conditioning system discharged by a dealer service department or an automotive air conditioning shop before proceeding (see **Warning** above).

2   Remove the front grill (see Chapter 11).

3   On all models except 2007 and later 350Z and G35 Sedans, remove the horn near the receiver-drier (see Chapter 12) and the ambient air sensor bracket (see illustration 16.5).

4   Thoroughly clean the area around the line fittings at the bottom of the receiver-drier and then remove the line fitting retainer bolt (see illustration).

5   Remove the receiver-drier mounting bracket fastener (see illustration 15.4).

6   Pull the receiver-drier directly up from the line fittings at the condenser. Remove the O-ring seals and discard them.

7   Plug all open fittings to prevent entry of dirt and moisture.

8   Using new O-ring seals, install the receiver-drier into the fittings at the condenser. If a new receiver-drier is being installed, add 0.3 oz (10 ml) of new refrigerant oil (a type designated as compatible with R-134a refrigerant) to the new unit.

9   The remainder of installation is the reverse of removal.

10 Take the vehicle back to the shop that discharged it. Have the air conditioning system evacuated, charged and leak tested.

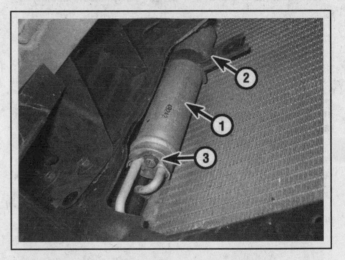

15.4 Air conditioning receiver-drier mounting details:

1 Receiver-drier	*3 Line fitting retainer and bolt*
2 Mounting fastener	

16 Air conditioning condenser - removal and installation

▶ **Refer to illustrations 16.4a, 16.4b, 16.4c and 16.5**

※※ WARNING:

The air conditioning system is under high pressure. Do not loosen any hose fittings or remove any components until after the system has been discharged. Air conditioning refrigerant must be properly discharged into an EPA-approved recovery/recycling unit at a dealer service department or an automotive air conditioning repair facility. Always wear eye protection when disconnecting air conditioning system fittings.

➡ **Note 1: On 2007 and later 350Z and G35 Sedan models, the radiator and air conditioning condenser are built as a single assembly and are removed as a unit. Refer to Section 6 of this Chapter for the removal of the radiator assembly on these models.**

➡ **Note 2: The receiver-drier (see Section 15) should be replaced whenever the condenser is replaced (due to damage, which could allow moisture and contaminants into the system).**

1   Have the air conditioning system discharged by a dealer service department or an automotive air conditioning shop before proceeding (see **Warning** above).

16.4a The location of the refrigerant lines and fittings for the condenser (2004 G35 Sedan shown - other models similar)

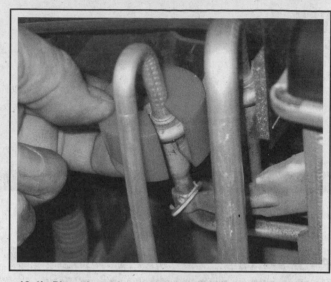

16.4b Place the tool around the fitting and close it

2   Disconnect the cable from the negative battery terminal (see Chapter 5, Section 1).

3   Remove the radiator (see Section 6).

➡**Note: With the exception of those models specified in the above note, the condenser is mounted to the radiator. There are mounting bolts at the top of the condenser and small mounting tabs that fit into brackets on the bottom of the radiator.**

4   Use a special tool to disconnect the refrigerant lines to the condenser. Plug the lines and fittings to prevent the entry of moisture and contaminants. Discard the O-ring seals (see illustrations).

5   Remove the horn (see Chapter 12) and the ambient air sensor bracket (see illustration).

6   Disconnect the air conditioning pressure switch (see Section 17).

7   Carefully remove the condenser from the engine compartment.

8   If the original condenser will be reinstalled, store it in a manner that will help prevent any oil spillage.

9   If a new condenser is being installed, pour 1.2 oz (35 ml) of the appropriate refrigerant oil into it prior to installation.

10   Install new R-134a compatible O-ring seals onto the refrigerant line fittings.

11   Reinstall the components in the reverse order of removal. Tighten the mounting fasteners to the torque listed in this Chapter's Specifications, if applicable.

12   Have the system evacuated, recharged and leak-tested by the shop that discharged it.

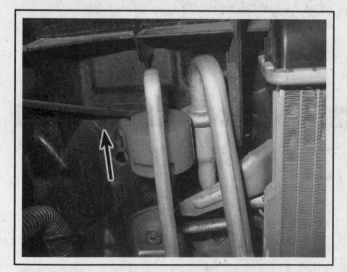

16.4c Pull the tool into the fitting to separate the line

16.5 Ambient air sensor bracket details:

1   *Electrical connector*
2   *Sensor*

3   *Mounting bracket and fastener*

17 Air conditioning pressure switch - replacement

♦ **Refer to illustration 17.3**

※※ WARNING:

The air conditioning system is under high pressure. Do not loosen any hose fittings or remove any components until after the system has been discharged. Air conditioning refrigerant must be properly discharged into an EPA-approved recovery/recycling unit at a dealer service department or an automotive air conditioning repair facility. Always wear eye protection when disconnecting air conditioning system fittings.

1   Have the air conditioning system discharged by a dealer service department or an automotive air conditioning shop before proceeding (see **Warning** above).

2   Remove the radiator grille (from the bumper cover).

➡**Note: It may be easier to get to the line fitting on the bottom of the receiver-drier by removing the engine lower splash shield (see Chapter 2) as well.**

3   Unplug the electrical connector from the air conditioning pressure switch (see illustration).

➡**Note: On 2007 and later G35 Sedan models, the switch is mounted to the top of the receiver-drier.**

4   On 2007 and later G35 Sedan models, unscrew the pressure switch from the top of the receiver-drier. Discard the O-ring seal.

➡**Note: Be careful not to turn the receiver-drier in its mounting bracket when removing the switch.**

5   On all other models, unscrew the pressure switch from the condenser above the receiver-drier. Discard the O-ring seal.

➡**Note: Remove the radiator retainers (see Section 6) and gently push the radiator and condenser away from the radiator support assembly for more clearance around the switch, if necessary.**

6   Lubricate a new R-134a compatible O-ring seal with the appropriate refrigerant oil and place it into position.

7   Install the new switch until hand tight, and then tighten it securely.

8   Have the system evacuated, recharged and leak-tested by the shop that discharged it.

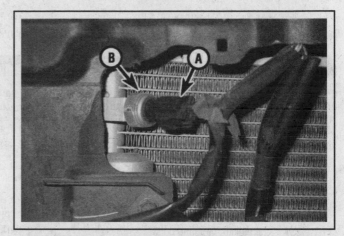

17.3 Unplug the electrical connector (A), then unscrew the switch (B) (2004 G35 Sedan shown - other models similar)

Specifications

General

Coolant capacity	See Chapter 1
Radiator tank cap pressure rating	
350Z	
2006 and earlier models	11 to 14 psi (78 to 98 kPa)
2007 and later models	16 to 18 psi (108 to 127 kPa)
G35	
Coupe	
2007 and earlier models	11 to 14 psi (78 to 98 kPa)
Sedan	
2006 and earlier models	11 to 14 psi (78 to 98 kPa)
2007 and later models	18 to 22 psi (122 to 151 kPa)

Torque specifications

	Ft-lbs (unless otherwise indicated)	Nm

➡ **Note: One foot-pound (ft-lb) of torque is equivalent to 12 inch-pounds (in-lbs) of torque. Torque values below approximately 15 ft-lbs are expressed in inch-pounds, since most foot-pound torque wrenches are not accurate at these smaller values.**

	Ft-lbs (unless otherwise indicated)	Nm
Fan coupling (clutch)-to-pulley mounting bolts	85 in-lbs	9.5
Fan-to-fan coupling (clutch) mounting bolts	54 in-lbs	6
Compressor mounting bolts		
2007 and later G35 Sedan models	23	31
All other models	42	57
Compressor line fitting nuts	120 in-lbs	13.5
Condenser mounting bolts	54 in-lbs	6
Condenser line fitting mounting -		
bolts (2007 and later G35 Sedan models)	50 in-lbs	5.5
Receiver-drier line fitting retainer bolt	50 in-lbs	5.5
Timing chain tensioner mounting bolts	72 in-lbs	8
Thermostat housing bolts	80 in-lbs	9
Water pump mounting bolts	85 in-lbs	9.5

Section

Reference to other Chapters

4

FUEL AND EXHAUST SYSTEMS

1 General information

All models covered by this manual are equipped with a sequential multi-port fuel injection system. This type of fuel injection system uses timed impulses to sequentially inject the fuel directly into the intake ports of each cylinder in the same sequence as the firing order. The Powertrain Control Module (PCM) controls the injectors. The PCM monitors various engine parameters and delivers the exact amount of fuel, in firing order sequence, into the intake ports. For more information about the fuel injection system, see Section 10.

The fuel pump/fuel level sensor/fuel pressure regulator module consists of the fuel inlet strainer, the pump, the fuel pressure regulator, the fuel level sensors and the Fuel Tank Temperature (FTT) sensor. The fuel pump module is located inside the right part of the fuel tank, and can be accessed by removing the rear seat cushion, an access cover in the floor and a retainer on top of the fuel tank. Another fuel level sensor, which is located in the left part of the fuel tank, has its own access cover and retainer, and is accessed in the same manner as the fuel pump module. Neither of these modules is serviceable. You can replace the fuel level sensor separately from the fuel pump module, but if anything else malfunctions on the fuel pump module (inlet strainer, pump or pressure regulator) you must replace the entire unit.

No external (outside the tank) fuel filters are used on any of the vehicles covered by this manual. The inlet strainer is an extended-life part and does not need to be replaced at scheduled maintenance intervals. It should only be replaced if diagnostic testing indicates the need to do so.

The exhaust system consists of the two exhaust manifolds, a pair of catalytic converters, a Y-pipe connecting the two converters to the rest of the exhaust system, a resonator (or pre-muffler) and the muffler/tailpipe assembly. All of these components are replaceable (see Section 14). For information regarding removal/replacement of the catalytic converters, refer to Chapter 6.

2 Fuel pressure relief procedure

▶ **Refer to illustration 2.1**

✳✳ WARNING:

See the Warning in Section 1.

1   The fuel pump fuse and fuel pump relay (see illustration) are both located on the Intelligent Power Distribution Module (IPDM), which is located in the right rear corner of the engine compartment, behind and to the right of the battery.

➡**Note: The accompanying illustration depicts the fuel pump fuse location for 2004 through 2006 G35 Sedans, 2004 through 2007 G35 Coupes and 2004 through 2008 350Z models. The fuel pump fuse is also located on the IPDM on all 2003 models and on 2007 and 2008 G35 Sedans, but its location on the IPDM is slightly different. To locate the fuel pump fuse on one of these models, refer to the fuse guide on the outside of the IPDM cover.**

2   Remove the battery cover.

3   Remove the cover from the IPDM and pull the fuel pump fuse.

4   Turn the ignition key to START and crank over the engine for several seconds. It will either start momentarily and immediately stall, or it won't start at all.

5   Turn the ignition key to the OFF position.

6   Disconnect the cable from the negative battery terminal before beginning work on the fuel system (see Chapter 5, Section 1).

7   Install the fuel pump fuse and the IPDM cover.

8   After all work on the fuel system has been completed, reconnect the battery (see Chapter 5, Section 1).

9   When the engine is started, the CHECK ENGINE light or Malfunction Indicator Light (MIL) might come on because the engine was cranked while the fuel pump fuse was pulled. The light should go out after a period of normal operation. If it does not go out, refer to Chapter 6.

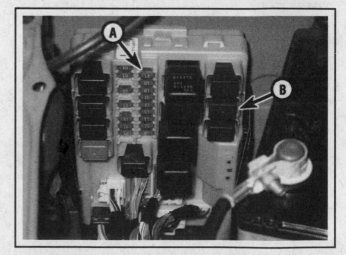

2.1 The fuel pump fuse (A) and the fuel pump relay (B) are both located on the Intelligent Power Distribution Module (IPDM), which is located in the right rear corner of the engine compartment, behind and to the right of the battery

3   Fuel pump/fuel pressure - check

✳✳ WARNING:

See the Warning in Section 1.

PRELIMINARY CHECK

1   The fuel pump is located inside the fuel tank, which muffles its sound when the engine is running. But you can actually hear the fuel pump. Turn the ignition key to ON (not START) and listen carefully for the soft whirring sound made by the fuel pump as it's briefly turned on by the PCM to pressurize the fuel system prior to starting the engine. You will only hear a soft whirring sound for a second or two, but that sound tells you that the pump is working. If you can't hear the pump from inside the vehicle, remove the fuel filler cap and have an assistant turn the ignition switch to ON while you listen for the sound of the pump. If the pump does not come on when the ignition key is turned to ON, check the fuel pump fuse and relay, both of which are located in the right rear corner of the engine compartment, behind and to the right of the battery (see illustration 2.1). If the fuse and relay are okay, check the wiring back to the fuel pump. See Section 5 for the location of the fuel pump electrical connector. If the fuse, relay and wiring are okay, the fuel pump is probably defective. If the pump runs continuously with the ignition key in the ON position, the Powertrain Control Module (PCM) is probably defective. Have the PCM checked by a dealer service department or other qualified repair shop.

PRESSURE CHECK

▶ Refer to illustrations 3.3 and 3.6

➡Note: In order to perform the fuel pressure test, you will need a fuel pressure gauge capable of measuring high fuel pressure.

You'll also need the right fittings or adapters to tee it into the fuel system. Infiniti and Nissan use a special tool (J-44321) that allows you to tee into the fuel system at the remote pulsation damper for the right fuel rail (see illustration 13.9). However, you can also tee into the system at the quick-connect fitting between the fuel pump outlet and the fuel feed line. You'll have to remove the back seat cushion to access the fuel pump, but you won't have to buy an expensive special tool that you will probably use very infrequently.

2   Relieve the fuel system pressure (see Section 2).

3   For this check, you'll need to obtain a fuel pressure gauge with a hose and an adapter suitable for tee-ing it into the quick-connect fitting that connects the fuel pump outlet pipe (on top of the fuel tank) to the fuel feed line (see illustration).

4   Remove the rear seat cushion (see Chapter 11).

5   Remove the fuel pump access cover (see illustrations 5.5a and 5.5b) and disconnect the quick-connect fitting from the fuel pump outlet pipe on top of the fuel pump. If you're unfamiliar with this type of fitting, see Section 4.

6   Tee in your fuel pressure gauge between the fuel pump outlet pipe and the quick connect fitting (see illustration).

7   Start the engine and check the pressure on the gauge, comparing your reading with the pressure listed in this Chapter's Specifications.

8   If the fuel pressure is not within specifications, check the following:

a) If the pressure is lower than specified, check for a restriction in the fuel system. One likely cause is a clogged fuel filter or inlet strainer at the base of the fuel pump/fuel level sensor module in the left fuel tank (see Sections 5 and 6).

➡Note: These components cannot be inspected or replaced separately from the fuel pump.

b) If the fuel pressure is higher than specified, replace the fuel pressure regulator, which is part of the fuel pump/fuel level sensor module (see Sections 5 and 6).

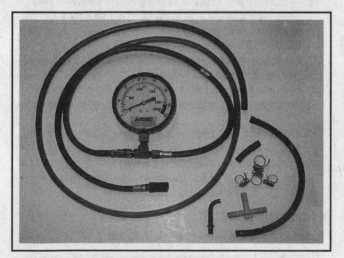

3.3 A typical fuel pressure gauge, with hoses and fittings suitable for tee-ing into the fuel system

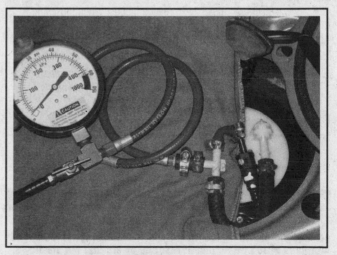

3.6 Fuel gauge connection details

4 Fuel lines and fittings - repair and replacement

❋❋❋ WARNING:

Gasoline is extremely flammable, so take extra precautions when you work on any part of the fuel system. See the Warning in Section 1.

1 Always relieve the fuel pressure before servicing fuel lines or fittings on fuel-injected vehicles (see Section 2).

2 The fuel supply line connects the fuel tank to the fuel rail on the engine. Be sure to inspect the fuel and the Evaporative Emission Control (EVAP) system lines for leaks, kinks and dents whenever you're servicing something underneath the vehicle. All of these lines are secured to the vehicle underbody by plastic clips. To disengage fuel and EVAP lines from these clips, simply pry the clip down and pull out the lines from above.

3 Whenever you're working under the vehicle, be sure to inspect all fuel and EVAP lines for leaks, kinks, dents and other damage. Always replace a damaged fuel line or EVAP line immediately. Leaking fuel and EVAP lines will result in loss of fuel and excessive air pollution (leaking raw fuel emits unburned hydrocarbon vapors into the atmosphere).

4 If you find signs of dirt in the lines during disassembly, disconnect all lines and blow them out with compressed air. If the fuel lines are particularly dirty, you might also have to replace the fuel pump module and the fuel filter module (see Sections 5 and 6). (Neither the inlet strainer at the inlet end of the pump nor the main fuel filter can be inspected for contamination.)

STEEL TUBING

5 Because fuel lines used on fuel-injected vehicles are under fairly high pressure, it is critical that they be replaced with lines of equivalent specification. If you have to replace a steel line, make sure that you use steel tubing that meets the manufacturer's specifications. Don't use copper or aluminum tubing to replace steel tubing. These materials cannot withstand normal vehicle vibration.

6 Some steel fuel lines have threaded fittings. When loosening these fittings to service or replace components:

a) *Use a backup wrench on the stationary portion of the fitting while loosening and tightening the fitting nuts.*

b) *If you're going to replace one of these fittings, use original equipment parts or parts that meet original equipment standards.*

PLASTIC TUBING

7 If you ever have to replace a plastic line, use only the original equipment plastic tubing.

❋❋❋ CAUTION:

When removing or installing plastic fuel line tubing, be careful not to bend or twist it too much, which can damage it. Damaged fuel lines MUST be replaced! Also, be aware that the plastic fuel tubing is NOT heat resistant, so keep it away from excessive heat. Nor is it acid-proof, so don't wipe it off with a shop rag that has been used to wipe off battery electrolyte. If you accidentally spill or wipe electrolyte on plastic fuel or emissions tubing, replace the tubing.

FLEXIBLE HOSES

❋❋❋ WARNING:

Use only original equipment replacement hoses or their equivalent. Unapproved hoses might fail when subjected to the high operating pressures of the fuel system.

8 Don't route fuel hoses within four inches of exhaust system components or within ten inches of a catalytic converter. Make sure that no flexible hoses are installed directly against the vehicle, particularly in places where there is any vibration. If allowed to touch some vibrating part of the vehicle, a hose can easily become chafed and it might start leaking. A good rule of thumb is to maintain a minimum of 1/4-inch clearance around a hose (or metal line) to prevent contact with the vehicle underbody.

FUEL LINE AND EVAP LINE QUICK-CONNECT FITTINGS

❋❋❋ WARNING:

ALWAYS relieve the fuel system pressure (see Section 2) before disconnecting a fuel line fitting.

9 The vehicles covered in this manual use quick-connect fittings for the connection at the fuel pump and the connection between the under-vehicle fuel supply line and the metal line that goes up to the fuel rail.

10 The procedure for releasing quick-connect fittings is simple and straightforward. But a few rules of thumb apply:

a) *ALWAYS relieve the fuel system pressure (see Section 2) before disconnecting a fuel line fitting.*

b) *Inspect the fitting for dirt. If the fitting is dirty, clean it off before disassembling it. The seals in the fitting will stick to the fuel line as they age. Twist the fitting on the line, then push and pull the fitting until it moves freely.*

c) *Always disconnect all fuel line fittings from a fuel system component before removing the component.*

d) *Every time you disconnect a quick-connect fitting, remove and replace the O-ring inside the fitting. Failure to do so could result in leaks (and fires!).*

e) *Always inspect the condition of the retainer before reconnecting the fitting. If the retainer is damaged, replace it.*

f) *In most cases, the fitting itself is a non-removable part of the fuel line, so you might have to replace an entire fuel line if a fitting is damaged or defective.*

Two-tab type fitting

◆ **Refer to illustrations 4.11a, 4.11b, 4.12 and 4.13**

11 This type of fitting is one of the more common quick-connect fittings. It uses a plastic retainer with two release tabs protruding from opposite sides of the fitting. To disconnect it, depress both release tabs with your fingers, then pull the fitting off the fuel line or fuel component (see illustration).

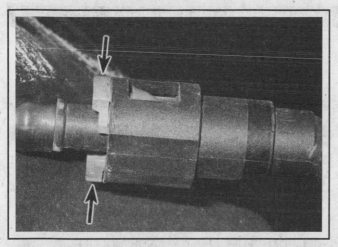

4.11a To disconnect a two-tab type fitting, depress both tabs with your fingers then pull the fuel line and the fitting apart (the plastic retainer comes off with the fuel line)

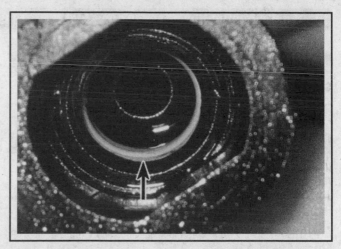

4.11b Inspect the O-ring inside the fitting. If it's cracked, torn, deteriorated or otherwise damaged in any way, replace it

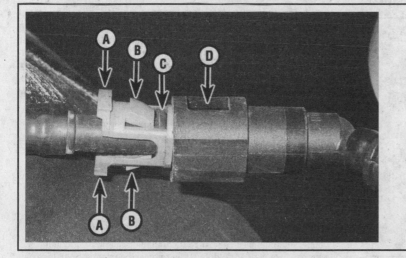

4.12 Before reconnecting a two-tab type fitting, be sure to position the plastic retainer correctly:

A   Plastic retainer release tabs
B   Plastic retainer locking tabs (must be aligned with the window in the fitting)
C   Raised stop (must be visible through the opening in the plastic retainer)
D   Fitting window (must be aligned with the locking tabs on the plastic retainer)

☀☀ CAUTION:

It's okay to use small needle-nose pliers to squeeze the tabs together, but using anything with too much grip (like conventional pliers) might damage the plastic retainer. The retainer will remain on the fuel line or fuel component, and the O-ring (see illustration) will remain inside the fitting. Inspect the condition of the O-ring. If it's cracked, torn, deteriorated or otherwise damaged in any way, replace it.

12 To reconnect a two-tab type fitting, make sure that the retainer is correctly positioned on the fuel line or component, with the locking tabs of the retainer aligned with the windows in the fitting (see illustration). When everything's correctly aligned, push the fitting onto the fuel line or fuel component until the raised stop on the fuel line or fuel component seats against the back of the fitting, then keep pushing until you feel a click. Verify that the fitting is locked into place by firmly pulling the fuel line or component and the fitting in opposite directions.

13 If you're disconnecting or servicing a two-tab fitting located under the vehicle, it might be encased in a removable protective cover (see illustration). To remove this cover, simply pull it off. When installing the cover, make sure that it snaps into place. If the cover doesn't fit tightly after removal, replace it.

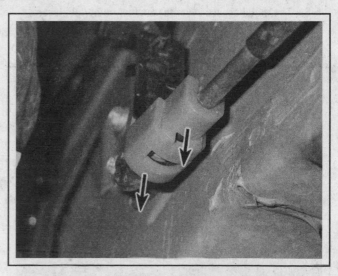

4.13 To remove a protective cover from a two-tab type fitting, simply pull it off. When installing the cover, make sure that it firmly snaps into place. If it doesn't, replace it

5 Fuel pump/fuel level sensor and fuel level sensor modules - removal and installation

※※ **WARNING:**

See the Warning in Section 1.

※※ **CAUTION:**

If you are servicing a G35 Coupe or a 350Z model, be sure to roll down the windows before disconnecting the battery.

1 Relieve the fuel system pressure (see Section 2).
2 Disconnect the cable from the negative battery terminal (see Chapter 5, Section 1).
3 The fuel tank doesn't have to be empty for this procedure, but the fuel level should be about 7/8-full. If the tank is full, drain it to about the 7/8 level with a hose routed through the fuel filler neck hose. Use a hard nylon tube with a 30-degree cut on the end to push open the check

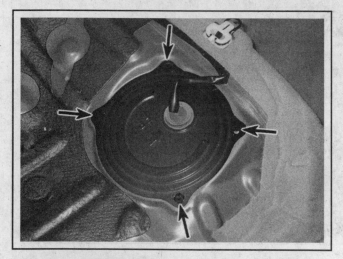

5.5a The metal access cover for the fuel pump/fuel level sensor module is retained by four plastic fasteners . . .

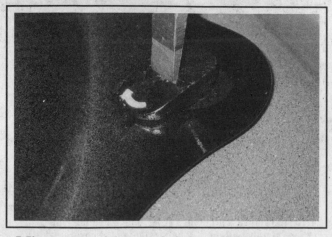

5.5b . . . turn each fastener clockwise and align them with the holes

valve in the fuel filler neck. If you're unable to extract any fuel from the tank because you can't work the siphon hose through the filler neck hose into the tank, then siphon fuel from the tank after you've removed the fuel pump/fuel level sensor module or fuel level sensor module.

※※ **WARNING:**

Do NOT start the siphoning action by mouth! Use a siphoning kit (available at most auto parts stores).

4 Remove the rear seat cushion (see Chapter 11).

FUEL PUMP/FUEL LEVEL SENSOR MODULE

◆ **Refer to illustrations 5.5a, 5.5b, 5.6, 5.7, 5.8, 5.9a, 5.9b, 5.11, 5.13 and 5.15**

➡**Note: The fuel pump/fuel level sensor module is located in the right compartment of the fuel tank. This module includes the fuel pump inlet strainer, the pump, the fuel pressure regulator and the fuel level sensor for the right fuel tank compartment. This Section covers the removal and installation of the complete module, which is removed as a single assembly. On some models, some components on the fuel pump module can be replaced individually (see Section 6).**

5 Remove the metal access cover (see illustrations).
6 Disconnect the electrical connector from the terminal on top of the fuel pump/fuel level sensor module mounting flange (see illustration) and place the harness safely out of the way.
7 Disconnect the fuel supply line quick-connect fitting (see illustration). Plug the end of the fuel supply line to prevent fuel from dripping out.
8 To prevent dirt from entering the fuel tank, clean the area surrounding the retainer that secures the mounting flange for the fuel pump/fuel level sensor module. Then remove the retainer bolts (see illustration) and remove the retainer.

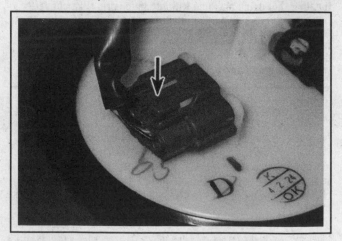

5.6 To disconnect the electrical connector from the fuel pump/fuel level sensor module, depress this release tab

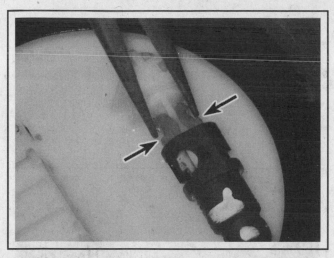

5.7 To disconnect the fuel supply line quick-connect fitting, squeeze the two retainer tabs together and pull the fitting off the fuel supply pipe

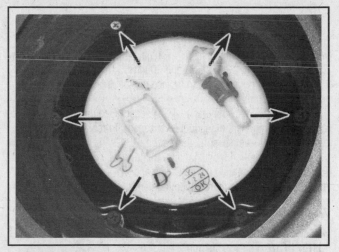

5.8 To detach the fuel pump/fuel level sensor retainer from the fuel tank, remove these bolts

9 Lift the fuel pump/fuel level sensor module up out of the tank far enough to access the fuel crossover tube (see illustration). On 2003 and 2007 and later G35 Sedans, 2003 and 2005 through 2007 G35 Coupes and on all 350Z models, disconnect the crossover tube connector from the fuel pump assembly with a pair of snap-ring pliers. On 2004 through 2006 G35 Sedans and 2004 G35 Coupes, disconnect the crossover tube/jet pump assembly from the fuel pump module (see illustration).

10 Remove the fuel pump/fuel level sensor module from the tank. Tilt the pump/sensor module as necessary to protect the fuel level sensor float arm from damage.

11 Remove and discard the old mounting flange O-ring (see illustration). Always use a new O-ring when installing the fuel pump/fuel level sensor module.

12 If you want to remove or replace any individual components, refer to Section 6.

5.9a Lift the pump/fuel level sensor module up out of the tank far enough to access the fuel crossover tube (2004 G35 Sedan shown) . . .

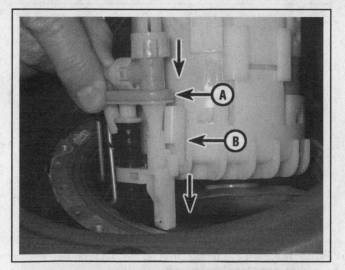

5.9b . . . then disengage the crossover tube/jet pump assembly (A) from its mounting bracket (B) and from the fuel pressure regulator pipe (2004 through 2006 G35 Sedans and 2004 G35 Coupes only; on all other models, disconnect the crossover tube connector with snap-ring pliers)

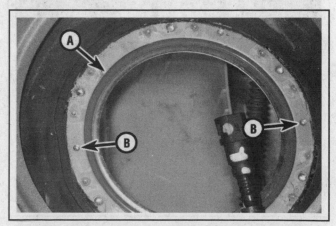

5.11 After removing the fuel pump/fuel level sensor module, remove and discard the old mounting flange O-ring (A) and install a new O-ring. When installing the fuel pump/fuel level sensor module, make sure that the locator pins on the underside of the mounting flange (see illustration 5.15) are aligned with these two holes (B) in the mounting ring

13 Inspect the condition of the fuel inlet strainer (see illustration). If it's dirty, wash it with a soft brush and clean solvent, then blow it off with low-pressure compressed air. You can replace the inlet strainer on 2004 through 2006 G35 Sedans and 2004 G35 Coupes (see Section 6). On all other models you can replace the fuel inlet strainer only by replacing the pump module.

14 The Fuel Tank Temperature (FTT) sensor (see illustration 5.13) is an integral component of the fuel level sensor. To replace it you must replace the fuel level sensor (see Section 6).

15 When installing the fuel pump/fuel level sensor module, be sure to install a new mounting flange O-ring and make sure that the locator pins on the underside of the mounting flange are aligned with their corresponding holes in the mounting ring (see illustration). Installation is otherwise the reverse of removal.

FUEL LEVEL SENSOR MODULE

▶ **Refer to illustrations 5.16, 5.17, 5.18, 5.19 and 5.20**

✳✳ WARNING:

See the Warning in Section 1.

➡**Note: The fuel level sensor module is located in the left compartment of the fuel tank. This Section covers the removal and installation of the complete module, which is replaced as an assembly.**

16 Remove the metal access cover (see illustration).

17 Disconnect the electrical connector from the fuel level sensor module (see illustration).

18 To prevent dirt from entering the fuel tank, clean the area surrounding the retainer that secures the mounting flange for the fuel level sensor module. Then remove the retainer bolts (see illustration) and remove the retainer.

19 Remove the fuel level sensor module (see illustration). Tilt the sensor module as necessary to protect the fuel level sensor float arm from damage.

20 Remove and discard the old sensor mounting flange O-ring (see illustration).

21 Installation is the reverse of removal.

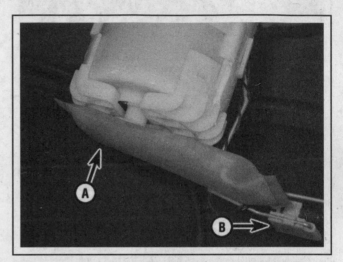

5.13 The fuel inlet strainer (A) is an integral part of the fuel pump (which is itself replaceable), so if it's too dirty to clean, replace the fuel pump (2004 through 2006 G35 Sedans and 2004 G35 Coupes) or the entire fuel pump module (all other models). The Fuel Tank Temperature (FTT) sensor (B) is an integral part of the fuel level sensor assembly and cannot be replaced separately; to replace it you must replace the fuel level sensor

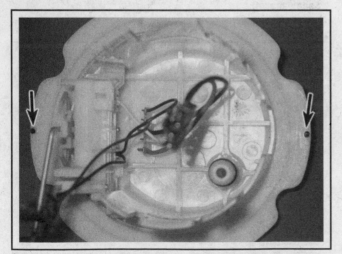

5.15 When installing the fuel pump/fuel level sensor module, make sure these two locator pins are aligned with their corresponding holes in the mounting ring (see illustration 5.11)

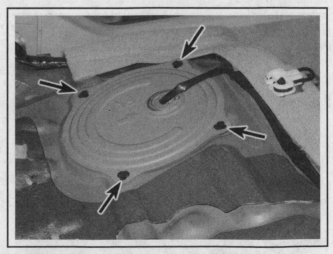

5.16 To remove the access cover for the fuel level sensor module, turn these four fasteners clockwise (see illustration 5.5b)

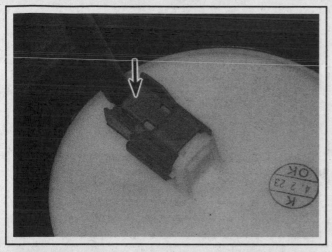

5.17 To disconnect the electrical connector from the fuel level sensor module, depress this release tab

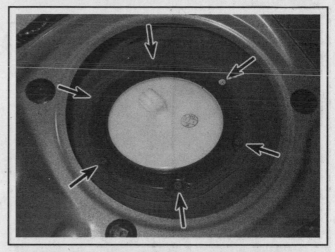

5.18 To detach the fuel level sensor retainer from the fuel tank, remove these bolts

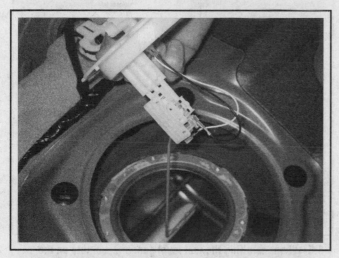

5.19 When removing the fuel level sensor module, tilt it as necessary to protect the sensor float arm from damage

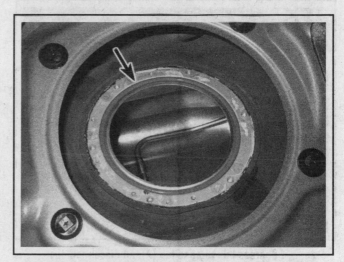

5.20 Remove and discard the old O-ring for the fuel level sensor mounting flange. Always use a new O-ring when installing the sensor

6   Fuel pump/fuel level sensor module - component replacement

2004 THROUGH 2006 G35 SEDANS AND 2004 G35 COUPES

➡Note: The procedure applies only to the fuel pump/fuel level sensor module used in 2004 through 2006 G35 Sedans and 2004 G35 Coupes. The pumps installed on all other models cannot be disassembled, except for the fuel level sensor (see below).

1   Remove the fuel pump/fuel level sensor module (see Section 5).

Fuel level sensor

▶ **Refer to illustrations 6.2a, 6.2b, 6.2c and 6.5**

2   Carefully disengage the catches. Separate the fuel level sensor assembly from the fuel filter/fuel pump assembly far enough to access the fuel pump electrical connector. Disconnect the connector and separate the two assemblies (see illustrations).

3   No further disassembly is possible. The fuel level sensor and the fuel temperature sensor are both integral components of the main fuel

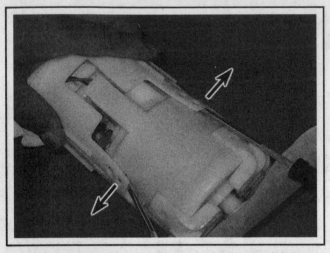

6.2a To separate the fuel level sensor assembly from the fuel filter/fuel pump assembly, pry the catches apart . . .

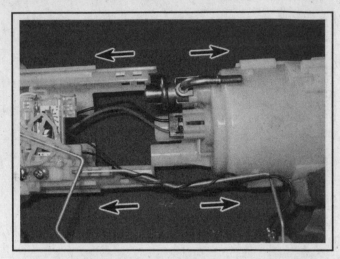

6.2b . . . pull the two assemblies apart . . .

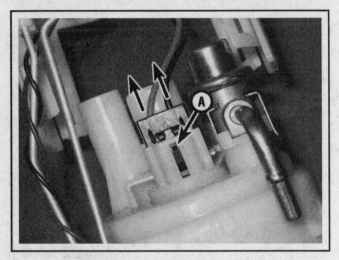

6.2c . . . depress this release tab (A) and disconnect the electrical connector

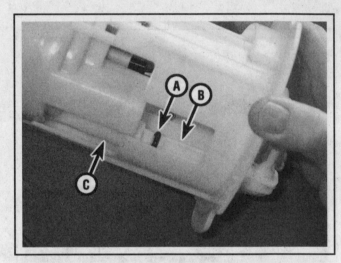

6.5 When installing the fuel level sensor assembly on the fuel filter housing, always replace the O-ring (A) on the fuel filter assembly outlet pipe (B), and make sure that the outlet pipe is aligned with, and fits into, the outlet pipe (C) on top of the fuel filter housing

level sensor unit. If either of them must be replaced, the unit must be replaced as a single assembly.

4   Whether you're planning to reuse the old fuel level sensor assembly or are installing a new unit, be sure to remove and discard the old outlet pipe O-ring.

5   Installation is otherwise the reverse of removal. When reassembling the fuel level sensor assembly and the fuel filter housing, make sure that the outlet pipe on the fuel level sensor is aligned with the outlet pipe on top of the fuel filter housing (see illustration).

Fuel pump/fuel inlet strainer

♦ **Refer to illustrations 6.7a, 6.7b, 6.8, 6.9, 6.11, 6.12 and 6.14**

6   Separate the fuel level sensor from the fuel filter/fuel pump assembly (see Step 2).

7   Disengage the fuel pump retainer cap from the lower end of the

fuel filter housing and pull the cap and fuel pump out of the filter housing (see illustrations).

8   Disengage the retainer cap from the fuel pump (see illustration). Remove the rubber grommet from the outlet end of the fuel pump and discard it. Always use a new rubber grommet whether you're installing the old pump or a new unit.

9   Remove the rubber insulator from the fuel pump (see illustration).

10 If you're replacing the fuel pump, no further disassembly is necessary. If you're replacing the fuel filter, you'll also need to remove the fuel pressure regulator (see below).

11 Install the rubber insulator on the pump. Make sure that the hole in the insulator is aligned with the mounting pin for the fuel inlet strainer (see illustration).

12 Install the retainer cap on the inlet end of the fuel pump. Make sure that the protrusion on the insulator is correctly aligned with the recess of the same shape in the retainer cap (see illustration).

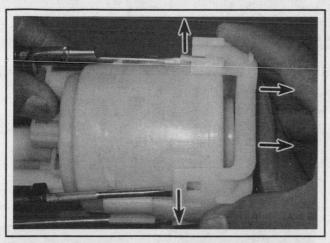

6.7a To disengage the fuel pump retainer cap from the lower end of the fuel filter housing pry the catches apart . . .

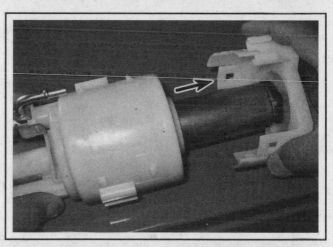

6.7b . . . and pull the retainer cap and the fuel pump out of the fuel filter housing

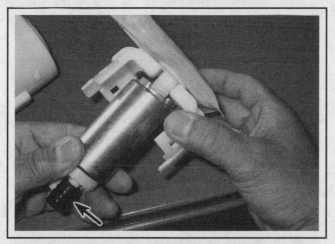

6.8 After removing the pump from the filter housing, remove the retainer cap from the pump. Also remove the rubber grommet from the outlet end of the pump and discard it. Always use a new grommet when installing the pump

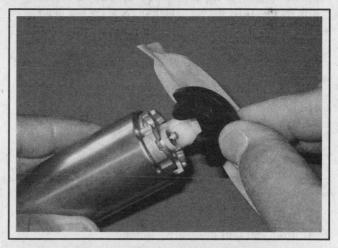

6.9 Disengage and remove the rubber insulator from between the fuel inlet strainer and the fuel pump

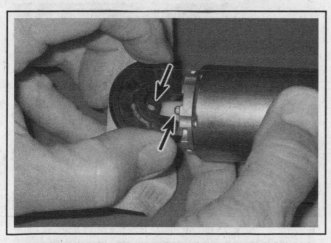

6.11 When installing the insulator, make sure that the hole in the insulator is aligned with the fuel inlet strainer mounting pin

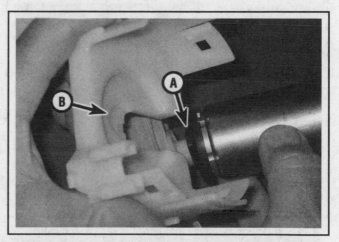

6.12 When installing the retainer cap, make sure that the protrusion (A) on the insulator is correctly aligned with the recess (B) in the retainer cap

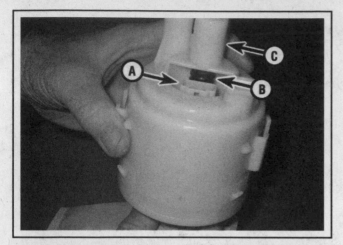

6.14 When installing the fuel pump in the fuel filter housing, make sure that the electrical terminal (A) on top of the pump is aligned with the hole in the top of the filter housing, and the grommet (B) on the outlet pipe of the pump is aligned with the recess for the outlet pipe on top of the fuel filter housing (C)

13 Install a new rubber grommet on the outlet pipe at the upper end of the fuel pump.

14 Insert the fuel pump into the fuel filter housing. Make sure that the electrical terminal is aligned with the hole in the upper end of the filter housing, and that the rubber grommet is inserted into the recess for the outlet pipe on top of the fuel filter housing (see illustration). If the grommet is difficult to push into this hole, put a little petroleum jelly on it.

15 Reconnect the fuel level sensor to the fuel filter/fuel pump assembly (see Steps 3 through 5).

16 Installation is otherwise the reverse of removal.

Fuel filter and fuel pressure regulator

♦ **Refer to illustrations 6.19, 6.22a and 6.22b**

17 Separate the fuel level sensor from the fuel filter/fuel pump assembly (see Step 2).

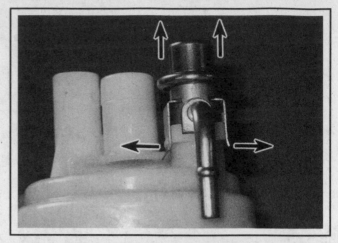

6.19 To disengage the fuel pressure regulator from the fuel filter housing, pry the two mounting tangs off the mounting lugs on the filter housing and pull out the regulator

18 Remove the fuel pump from the fuel filter housing (see Step 7).

19 Spread the fuel pressure regulator mounting tangs apart and pull the regulator out of the fuel filter housing (see illustration).

20 Remove and discard the old pressure regulator O-ring. Always use a new O-ring whether you're installing the old regulator or a new unit.

21 No further disassembly of the fuel filter housing is possible.

22 When installing the fuel pressure regulator, be sure to use a new O-ring and make sure that the regulator mounting tangs are aligned with, and snapped onto, the mounting lugs on the fuel filter housing (see illustrations).

23 Install the fuel pump in the fuel filter housing (see Steps 11 through 14).

24 Reattach the fuel filter/fuel pump assembly and the fuel level sensor assembly (see Steps 4 and 5).

25 Installation is otherwise the reverse of removal.

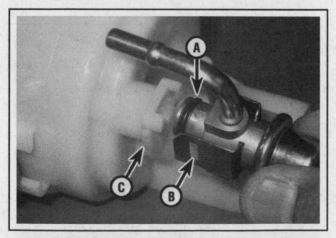

6.22a When installing the fuel pressure regulator into the fuel filter housing, make sure that you replace the O-ring (A), then align the slots (B) in the two regulator mounting tangs with the mounting lugs (C) on the filter housing . . .

6.22b . . . and push the regulator into the filter housing until the slots in the mounting tangs snap into place around the mounting lugs

7 Fuel tank - removal and installation

✷✷ WARNING 1:

See the Warning in Section 1.

✷✷ WARNING 2:

Removing and installing the fuel tank is difficult on these vehicles. You must lower the entire rear suspension assembly, which is potentially dangerous because you must devise a way to firmly support the entire rear suspension assembly, and lower it far enough to allow sufficient clearance to lower the rear part of the fuel tank. If you're working at home, you're likely going to be working under the vehicle while it's on jackstands, which means that you won't have a lot of room to work. We therefore don't recommend tackling this job at home. It's much easier to do when the vehicle is raised on a commercial vehicle hoist.

1   Relieve the fuel system pressure (see Section 2).
2   Disconnect the cable from the negative battery terminal (see Chapter 5, Section 1).
3   Remove the fuel pump/fuel level sensor module and the fuel level sensor module from the fuel tank (see Section 5).
4   Working through the access holes for the fuel pump/fuel level sensor and the fuel level sensor, siphon as much fuel out of the tank as you can.

✷✷ WARNING:

Never start the siphoning action by mouth! Use a siphoning kit (available at most auto parts stores).

5   Raise the vehicle and place it securely on jackstands.
6   Remove the entire rear part of the exhaust system from the flange in front of the pre-muffler to the muffler/tailpipe (see Section 14).

7   Remove the small heat shield mounting nuts and remove the small heat shield.
8   Remove the driveshaft (see Chapter 8).
9   Remove the parking brake cables (see Chapter 9).
10 Remove the fuel tank heat shield mounting nuts and remove the heat shield.
11 Disconnect the rear brake caliper hoses (see Chapter 9).
12 Remove the coil springs (see Chapter 10).
13 Disconnect the upper ends of both rear shock absorbers (see Chapter 10).
14 Remove the suspension assembly support brackets. There's one on each side, and each support bracket is attached by two bolts and two nuts.
15 Using a pair of floor jacks, support the rear suspension assembly below both ends of both crossmembers. Be sure to strap the suspension assembly to the jack head to ensure that it doesn't fall off.
16 Remove the four large nuts that attach the rear suspension assembly and carefully lower the rear suspension assembly.
17 Locate the connection between the fuel filler neck hose and the fuel filler pipe at the upper rear of the fuel tank, then loosen the hose clamp and disconnect the fuel filler neck hose. Also loosen the hose clamp and disconnect the fuel filler neck EVAP hose (the smaller hose right next to the filler neck hose).
18 Support the fuel tank.
19 Remove the fuel tank strap bolts and remove the fuel tank straps.
20 Lower the tank slightly and, using a flashlight, disconnect any remaining electrical harnesses and EVAP hoses.
21 Once everything is disconnected, lower and remove the fuel tank.
22 Installation is the reverse of removal, noting the following points:

a) *If you're replacing the fuel tank, remove all components from the old fuel tank and install them on the new tank. If you need help with the fuel pump/fuel level sensor module and the fuel filter/fuel pressure regulator/fuel level sensor module, refer to Sections 5 and 6. If you need help with the EVAP lines, refer to Chapter 6.*

b) *Tighten the fuel tank strap bolts securely.*

8 Fuel tank cleaning and repair - general information

1   The fuel tank installed in the vehicles covered by this manual is not repairable. If it becomes damaged, it must be replaced.
2   Cleaning the fuel tank (due to fuel contamination) should be performed by a professional with the proper training to carry out this critical and potentially dangerous work. Even after cleaning and flushing, explosive fumes may remain inside the fuel tank.
3   If the fuel tank is removed from the vehicle, it should not be placed in an area where sparks or open flames could ignite the fumes coming out of the tank. Be especially careful inside a garage where a gas-type appliance is located.

9 Air filter housing and air intake duct - removal and installation

2003 THROUGH 2006 G35 SEDANS AND 350Z MODELS AND ALL G35 COUPES

➡**Note: The photos accompanying this Section depict a typical air intake duct assembly on a G35 Sedan or Coupe. The air intake duct assembly used on 350Z models is similar, though not identical, to the one shown here.**

Air intake duct assembly

2003 through 2006 G35 Sedans and all G35 Coupes

▶ **Refer to illustrations 9.2 and 9.3**

1 Remove the engine cover.

2 Loosen the hose clamp screws (see illustration) and remove the first air intake duct, which connects the Mass Air Flow/Intake Air Temperature (MAF/IAT) sensor to the air intake duct resonator.

3 Disconnect the Positive Crankcase Ventilation (PCV) fresh air inlet hose from the resonator (see illustration), then loosen the hose clamp screw that secures the second air intake duct to the throttle body. Remove the air intake duct and resonator as a single assembly. If you're replacing the second air intake duct or the resonator, loosen the other hose clamp screw and pull the duct off the resonator.

4 Inspect the condition of the two air intake ducts and the resonator. Look for cracks, tears, deterioration and other damage. If either air intake duct is damaged in any way, replace it. A leaking air intake duct will allow the introduction of false (unmetered) air into the air intake manifold, which will cause the air/fuel mixture to become excessively lean. A lean air/fuel mixture can cause rough running at idle and, if the leak is big enough, a lean misfire condition.

5 Installation is the reverse of removal.

2003 through 2006 350Z models

6 Remove the engine cover.

7 Disconnect the Positive Crankcase Ventilation (PCV) fresh air inlet hose from the air intake duct.

8 Loosen the hose clamp screws and remove the air intake duct, which connects the Mass Air Flow/Intake Air Temperature (MAF/IAT) sensor to the throttle body.

9 Inspect the condition of the air intake duct. Look for cracks, tears, deterioration and other damage. If the air intake duct is damaged in any way, replace it. A leaking air intake duct will allow the introduction of false (unmetered) air into the air intake manifold, which will cause the air/fuel mixture to become excessively lean. A lean air/fuel mixture can cause rough running at idle and, if the leak is big enough, a lean misfire condition.

10 Installation is the reverse of removal.

Air filter housing

▶ **Refer to illustration 9.12**

➡**Note: The following procedure is for replacing the air filter housing, not for replacing the air filter element. If you want to replace the air filter element, refer to Chapter 1.**

11 Disconnect the air intake duct from the air filter housing (see illustration 9.2).

12 On G35 Sedans and Coupes, remove the fresh air inlet housing (see illustration).

13 Disconnect the electrical connector from the Mass Air Flow/Intake Air Temperature (MAF/IAT) sensor, then remove the air filter housing retaining bolt (see illustration 9.2) and remove the housing by lifting it straight up.

14 The air filter housing is positioned by a single locator pin, on the bottom of the housing, which is inserted into a large insulator grommet.

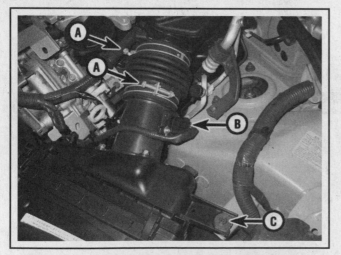

9.2 To remove the first air intake duct, loosen these two hose clamp screws (A) and pull off the duct (350Z models have a single longer air intake duct with no resonator between the two ducts). To remove the air filter housing, disconnect the electrical connector (B) and remove the air filter housing retaining bolt (C)

9.3 To remove the air intake resonator and the second air intake duct, disconnect the PCV fresh air inlet hose (A), then loosen the hose clamp screws (B)

9.12 To remove the fresh air inlet housing from the air filter housing, remove the two pop-up fasteners, then slide the housing to the right (passenger side) to disconnect it from the filter housing

Inspect the condition of the rubber insulator grommet. If it's cracked, torn, deteriorated or otherwise damaged, replace it.

15 When installing the air filter housing, make sure that the air filter housing locator pin is aligned with the insulator grommet, then install the filter housing retaining bolt. Installation is otherwise the reverse of removal.

2007 AND 2008 G35 SEDANS AND 350Z MODELS

➡**Note: On these models there are two air filter housings, two Mass Air Flow (MAF) sensors, two air intake ducts and two throttle bodies. But each assembly is quite similar to the single air intake duct and air filter housing assembly used on earlier models.**

Air intake duct

➡**Note: The following procedure applies to either air intake duct.**

16 Remove the engine cover.

17 Disconnect the Positive Crankcase Ventilation (PCV) fresh air inlet hose from the air intake duct.

18 Loosen the hose clamp screws at the Mass Air Flow/Intake Air Temperature (MAF/IAT) sensor and at the throttle body and remove the air intake duct.

19 Inspect the condition of the air intake duct. Look for cracks, tears, deterioration and other damage. If the air intake duct is damaged in any way, replace it. A leaking air intake duct will allow the introduction of false (unmetered) air into the air intake manifold, which will cause the air/fuel mixture to become excessively lean. A lean air/fuel mixture can cause rough running at idle, and even misfires if the leak is big enough.

20 Installation is the reverse of removal.

Air filter housing

➡**Note: The following procedure applies to either air filter housing.**

21 Disconnect the air intake duct from the air filter housing.

22 Disconnect the electrical connector from the Mass Air Flow/Intake Air Temperature (MAF/IAT) sensor.

23 Remove the air filter housing retaining bolt and remove the housing by lifting it straight up. The air filter housing is positioned by a pair of locator pins inserted into holes in the fender, and by a large inlet pipe on the bottom of the housing that fits over the outlet pipe of the air resonator box.

24 Inspect the condition of the rubber insulators covering the locator pins. If they're cracked, torn, deteriorated or otherwise damaged, replace them.

25 When installing the air filter housing, make sure that the air filter housing locator pin is aligned with the insulator grommet, then install the filter housing retaining bolt. Installation is otherwise the reverse of removal

10 Multiport Fuel Injection (MFI) system - general information

The Multiport Fuel Injection (MFI) system is the sequential type, which means that the fuel injectors inject fuel in cylinder firing order. The injectors are turned on and off by the Powertrain Control Module (PCM). When the engine is running, the PCM constantly monitors engine operating conditions with an array of information sensors, calculates the correct amount of fuel, then varies the pulse width, which is the interval of time during which the injectors are open. Sequential MFI systems provide good power, decent mileage and lower emissions.

The MFI system uses the PCM and information sensors to determine and deliver the correct air/fuel ratio under all operating conditions. The MFI system consists of three sub-systems: air induction, electronic control and fuel delivery. The MFI system is integrated with many PCM-controlled emission control systems. (For information about the PCM, information sensors and emission control systems, refer to Chapter 6.)

AIR INDUCTION SYSTEM

The air induction system consists of the air filter housing, the Mass Air Flow/Intake Air Temperature (MAF/IAT) sensor, the air intake duct, the intake resonator (on G35 models only), the throttle body and the intake manifold. The throttle body contains a throttle plate that regulates the amount of air entering the intake manifold. There is no accelerator cable. The throttle plate is opened and closed in response to input from the Accelerator Pedal Position (APP) sensor. When you depress the accelerator pedal, the APP sensor measures the angle of the pedal and sends a voltage signal to the Powertrain Control Module (PCM) that's proportional to the pedal angle. The PCM processes this input, then commands a solenoid motor inside the throttle body to open or close the throttle plate accordingly.

On 2007 and 2008 G35 Sedans and 350Z models, there are two air filter housings, two Mass Air Flow/Intake Air Temperature (MAF/IAT) sensors, two air intake ducts, two throttle bodies and the intake manifold. Each air induction system serves one cylinder bank. But each induction system is similar to the earlier single induction system. On these models, the air intake manifold is different in design from earlier manifolds (see Chapter 2A).

The Mass Air Flow/Intake Air Temperature (MAF/IAT) sensor is located between the air filter housing and the air intake duct. The MAF sensor measures the mass of air entering the engine. The Intake Air Temperature (IAT) sensor, which is an integral component of the MAF sensor, relays a voltage signal to the PCM that varies in accordance with the temperature of the incoming air. The PCM uses this data from the MAF and IAT sensors to calculate how rich or lean the air/fuel mixture should be.

All of the air induction components are covered in this Chapter, except for the intake manifold, which is covered in Chapter 2, and the information sensors, which are covered in Chapter 6.

The idle speed is controlled by the PCM in response to the running conditions of the engine (cold or warm running, power steering pressure high or low, air conditioning system on or off, etc.). As the PCM receives data from the information sensors (vehicle speed, coolant temperature, air conditioning and/or power steering load, etc.) it adjusts the idle according to the demands of the engine and driver. The idle control system consists of the PCM, the throttle plate solenoid motor inside the throttle body, and several information sensors, including the Engine Coolant Temperature (ECT) sensor, the Intake Air Temperature (IAT) sensor and the Mass Air Flow (MAF) sensor.

ELECTRONIC CONTROL SYSTEM

For more information about the electronic control system, including the PCM, its information sensors and output actuators, refer to Chapter 6.

FUEL DELIVERY SYSTEM

The fuel delivery system consists of the fuel pump/fuel level sensor module, the fuel rail and fuel injectors, and the hoses, lines and pipes that carry fuel between all of these components. This is a returnless system; there is no fuel return line from the fuel rail back to the fuel tank. For more information about the fuel lines and the various types of fittings used on different models, refer to Section 4.

Because of the tunnel in the fuel tank for the driveshaft and the exhaust system, the tank is essentially divided into two tanks, although it's a one-piece assembly. The two halves of the fuel tank are connected by a crossover tube which utilizes a siphon effect produced by the fuel pressure regulator to ensure that the two sides of the fuel tank contain an equal amount of fuel.

There are two fuel level sensors, one for each side of the tank. The fuel level sensor for the left half of the tank is a stand-alone unit. If it must be replaced, simply remove the seat cushion and the left-side access plate in the floor, then remove the fuel level sensor and install a new unit. The fuel level sensor for the right half of the tank is an integral component of the fuel pump/fuel level sensor module. To access it, remove the rear seat cushion and the right-side access plate in the floor. To replace the right fuel level sensor, remove the fuel pump/fuel level sensor module (see Section 5), then separate the fuel level sensor from the fuel filter housing (see Section 6).

The fuel pump/fuel level sensor module also includes the fuel inlet strainer, the fuel filter and the fuel pressure regulator. The fuel pump/fuel level sensor module consists of two main assemblies. The upper part includes the fuel level sensor and Fuel Tank Temperature (FTT) sensor. The lower part consists of the fuel inlet strainer, the fuel pump, the fuel filter housing and the fuel pressure regulator. Fuel is drawn through the strainer at the pump inlet, then pumped out the upper end of the pump and into the fuel filter housing. There, it's filtered before exiting out the top of the fuel filter housing, through a pipe in the fuel level sensor assembly, and out a pipe on the module mounting flange. From there, it's pumped up to the fuel rail via a system of under-vehicle fuel lines and pipes.

The fuel pressure regulator maintains the fuel pressure within the specified operating range. When the fuel pressure inside the fuel filter housing exceeds the design threshold, the fuel pressure regulator opens and dumps the excess fuel back into the fuel tank (there is no fuel return line from the fuel rail back to the tank). The pressure regulator is mounted on the upper part of the fuel filter housing. When the fuel pressure regulator is open. it also produces the siphoning effect that pulls fuel from the left half of the fuel tank to the right half, which keeps the two halves of the tank equalized.

The fuel rail - which is bolted to the intake manifold - functions as a reservoir for pressurized fuel so that there's always enough fuel available for acceleration and high speed operation. The upper end of each injector is inserted into the fuel rail and the lower end of each injector is inserted into the intake manifold. The upper and lower ends of each injector are sealed by O-rings.

Each fuel injector is a solenoid-actuated, pintle-type design consisting of a solenoid, plunger, ball or needle valve, and housing. When the engine is running, there is always voltage on the hot side of each injector terminal. Injector drivers inside the PCM turn the injectors on and off by switching their ground paths on and off. When the ground path for an injector is closed by the PCM, current flows through the solenoid coil, a valve inside the injector opens and pressurized fuel squirts out the nozzle into the intake port above the intake valves. The quantity of fuel injected each time an injector opens is determined by its pulse width, which is the interval of time during which the valve is open.

11 Fuel injection system - check

➡**Note: The following procedure is based on the assumption that the fuel pressure is adequate (see Section 3).**

1   Inspect all electrical connectors that are related to the system. Check the ground wire connections on the intake manifold for tightness. Loose connectors and poor grounds can cause many problems that resemble more serious malfunctions.

2   Verify that the battery is fully charged, as the control unit and sensors depend on an accurate supply of voltage in order to properly meter the fuel.

3   Inspect the air filter element (see Chapter 1). A dirty or partially blocked filter will severely impede performance and economy.

4   Check the related fuses. If a blown fuse is found, replace it and see if it blows again. If it does, search for a grounded wire in the harness.

5   Inspect the condition of all vacuum hoses connected to the intake manifold.

6   Remove the air intake duct and air resonator box (if equipped) and inspect the mouth of the throttle body for dirt, carbon or other residue build-up. If it's dirty, wipe it clean with a shop towel.

7   For more information about the engine control system, refer to Chapter 6 (a problem with the fuel injection system will most likely set a trouble code).

12 Throttle body - removal and installation

2003 THROUGH 2006 G35 SEDANS AND 350Z MODELS AND ALL G35 COUPES

♦ **Refer to illustrations 12.3 and 12.4**

➡**Note: The accompanying photos depict a typical throttle body on a G35 Sedan, but the throttle bodies used on all models are virtually identical.**

1   Remove the engine cover.

2   Remove the air intake duct (see Section 9).

3   Disconnect the electrical connector from the throttle body (see illustration).

4   Remove the four throttle body mounting bolts (see illustration) and remove the throttle body.

5   Remove the throttle body gasket and discard it. Always use a new gasket when installing the throttle body.

6   Wipe off the gasket mating surfaces of the throttle body and the intake manifold.

❋❋ **CAUTION:**

Never soak the throttle body in solvent or in any type of carburetor cleaner. Do not even spray carburetor cleaners or silicone lubricants to wipe off any part of the throttle body.

7   Installation is the reverse of removal. Be sure to tighten the throttle body mounting bolts to the torque listed in this Chapter's Specifications.

2007 AND 2008 G35 SEDANS AND 350Z MODELS

8   Remove the engine cover.

9   Drain the engine coolant (see Chapter 1).

10   Remove the air intake duct (see Section 9).

11   Disconnect the electrical connector from the throttle body.

12   Disconnect both coolant hoses from the throttle body.

13   Remove the four throttle body mounting bolts and remove the throttle body.

14   Remove the throttle body gasket and discard it. Always use a new gasket when installing the throttle body.

15   Wipe off the gasket mating surfaces of the throttle body and the intake manifold.

❋❋ **CAUTION:**

Never soak the throttle body in solvent or in any type of carburetor cleaner. Do not even use spray carburetor cleaners or silicone lubricants on any part of the throttle body.

16   Installation is the reverse of removal. Be sure to tighten the throttle body mounting bolts to the torque listed in this Chapter's Specifications.

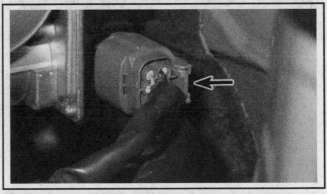

12.3 To disconnect the electrical connector from the throttle body, depress this release tab

12.4 To detach the throttle body from the intake manifold plenum, remove the four bolts

13 Fuel rail and injectors - removal and installation

♦ Refer to illustrations 13.9, 13.10a, 13.10b, 13.12, 13.13, 13.14, 13.16a, 13.16b, 13.16c, 13.17a, 13.17b, 13.17c, 13.18a and 13.18b

❋❋ WARNING 1:

See the Warning in Section 1.

❋❋ WARNING 2:

The engine must be completely cool before beginning this procedure.

13.9 To detach the fuel supply line and pulsation damper from its mounting flange, remove these two bolts. Have a rag handy to catch any spilled fuel. Remove and discard the old pulsation damper O-ring. Always use a new O-ring here when reconnecting the pulsation damper to its mounting flange

➥Note: The photos accompanying this Section depict the fuel rail and injector assembly used on 2003 through 2006 G35 Sedans and 350Z models and on all G35 Coupes. 2007 and 2008 G35 Sedans and 350Z models use a slightly different fuel rail assembly, but it's similar enough that you will have no problem using this procedure to remove, disassemble, reassemble and install it.

1 Remove the engine cover.

2 Remove the fuel tank filler neck cap to relieve any pressure inside the fuel tank.

3 Relieve the fuel system pressure (see Section 2).

4 On G35 Coupes and on 350Z models, roll down the windows.

5 Disconnect the cable from the negative terminal of the battery (see Chapter 5, Section 1).

6 Drain the engine coolant (see Chapter 1).

7 Remove the air intake duct (see Section 9).

8 Remove the intake manifold plenum (see Chapter 2A).

9 Detach the fuel supply line and pulsation damper from the mounting flange on the end of the fuel supply tube (see illustration). Remove and discard the old O-ring for the pulsation damper mounting flange. Always use a new O-ring here when installing the fuel rail assembly.

10 Clearly label the electrical connectors for the fuel injectors, then disconnect them from the injectors, detach all injector harness clips and set the injector harness aside (see illustrations).

11 Clean any debris from around the injectors so that it doesn't fall into the injector holes when you remove the fuel rail and injector assembly.

12 Remove the fuel rail mounting bolts (see illustration).

13 Gently rock the fuel rail and injectors side-to-side to loosen the injectors and remove the fuel rail and injectors as a single assembly (see illustration).

14 Remove the fuel rail mounting bolt spacers (see illustration). Inspect the condition of the spacers. If they're damaged, replace them.

13.10a To disconnect the electrical connector from each fuel injector, depress this release tab and pull up on the connector

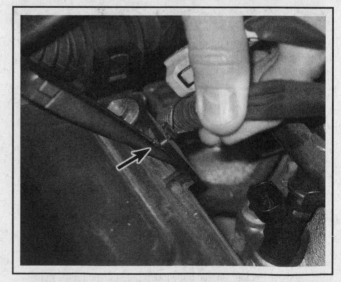

13.10b The fuel injector harness is secured to small support brackets by push clips. To disengage each push clip from its support bracket, carefully lever the push clip out of the hole in the bracket with a suitable tool

15 Place the fuel rail and injector assembly upside down on a clean work bench surface.

16 Remove the injectors from the fuel rail, then remove and discard the O-rings (see illustrations).

➡**Note: Whether you're replacing an injector or a leaking O-ring, it's a good idea to remove all the injectors from the fuel rail and replace all the O-rings.**

17 There is no reason to remove the pulsation damper for the left fuel rail or the fuel sub-tube (the hard line between the remote damper for the right fuel rail and the mounting flange where it's connected to the rear end of the right fuel rail) unless one of them has a leaking O-ring or you are replacing the fuel rail - in which case you will have to swap the pulsation damper and the fuel sub-tube over to the new fuel rail. In either event, remove the pulsation damper mounting bolts and the fuel sub-tube mounting bolts, then remove, discard and replace the old O-rings (see illustrations). Install both pieces on the new fuel rail assembly. Be sure to tighten the mounting bolts for both components to the torque listed in this Chapter's Specifications.

18 Coat the new O-rings with clean engine oil and install them on the injectors, then install each injector retaining clip and insert each injector into its corresponding bore in the fuel rail until the retainer clip snaps into place (see illustrations).

19 Clean the injector bores in the intake manifold.

20 Install the fuel rail mounting bolt spacers (see illustration 13.14).

13.12 To detach the fuel rail assembly from the intake manifold, remove these four bolts

13.13 Carefully wiggle the fuel rail assembly side-to-side to work the injectors free of their bores in the intake manifold, then remove the fuel rail and injectors as a single assembly

13.14 Remove the four fuel rail mounting bolt spacers and store them in a plastic bag. If any of the spacers are damaged, replace them

13.16a To free each injector from the fuel rail, pull off the retainer with a pair of pliers . . .

13.16b . . . then pull the injector straight out of its bore in the fuel rail

13.16c Whether you're installing new injectors or reusing the old ones, always remove the old upper and lower O-rings and discard them. Install new O-rings and coat them with clean engine oil to facilitate injector installation in the fuel rail and the intake manifold

13.17a To detach the fuel sub-tube flange and the pulsation damper for the left fuel rail, remove these bolts . . .

13.17b . . . then remove and discard the O-ring for the pulsation damper for the left fuel rail . . .

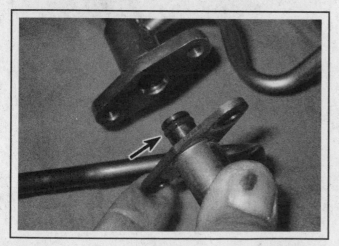

13.17c . . . and the old O-ring for the fuel sub-tube flange. Install new O-rings at both of these locations before bolting the pulsation damper and the sub-tube flange onto the fuel rail

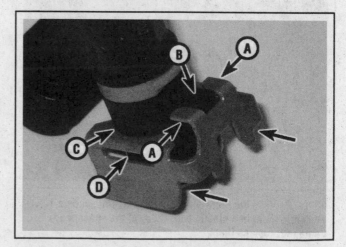

13.18a Align the tangs (A) on each injector retainer clip with the lug (B) on the injector body, then push the retainer onto the injector until the curved sides (C) snap into the groove on the injector body ([D] is the retainer slot)

13.18b To install each injector, align this slot (A) with the tab (B) on the fuel rail, then push the injector firmly into its mounting bore until the retainer slots (D in the previous illustration) snap onto the ridge around the circumference of the injector bore

21 Work the injectors into the injector bores on the intake manifold. Make sure the injectors are fully seated, then tighten the fuel rail mounting bolts securely.

22 Reconnect the fuel supply line/pulsation damper to its mounting flange on the end of the fuel sub-tube. Be sure to use a new O-ring and tighten the pulsation damper bolts to the torque listed in this Chapter's Specifications.

23 The remainder of installation is the reverse of removal.

24 After installation is completed, turn the ignition switch to ON, but don't operate the starter. This activates the fuel pump for about two seconds, which builds up fuel pressure in the fuel lines and the fuel rail. Repeat this step two or three times, then check the fuel lines, fuel rail and injectors for fuel leakage.

14 Exhaust system servicing - general information

▶ **Refer to illustrations 14.1a, 14.1b, 14.4a and 14.4b**

❖❖ **WARNING:**

The vehicle's exhaust system generates very high temperatures and must be allowed to cool down completely before touching any of the components. Be especially careful around the catalytic converter, which stays hot longer than other exhaust components.

1 The exhaust system consists of the exhaust manifolds, the exhaust pipes, the catalytic converters, the resonator (or pre-muffler), the muffler/tailpipe assembly, various exhaust heat shields and the exhaust pipes and flanges that connect these components together.

The exhaust system is isolated from the vehicle body and from chassis components by a series of rubber hangers (see illustrations). Inspect these hangers periodically for cracks or other signs of deterioration, and replace them as necessary. Some exhaust components are also supported by brackets bolted to the underside of the vehicle. Make sure that these brackets are tightly fastened to the exhaust system and to the vehicle and that they're neither cracked nor corroded.

2 Conduct regular inspections of the exhaust system to keep it safe and quiet. Look for any damaged or bent parts, open seams, holes, loose connections, excessive corrosion or other defects which could allow exhaust fumes to enter the vehicle. Do not repair deteriorated exhaust system components; replace them with new parts.

3 If the exhaust system components are extremely corroded, or rusted together, you'll need welding equipment and a cutting torch to remove them. The convenient strategy at this point is to have a muffler

14.1a Two typical rubber exhaust hangers at the rear end of the exhaust system resonator (pre-muffler)

14.1b Another typical rubber exhaust hanger at the rear end of the muffler

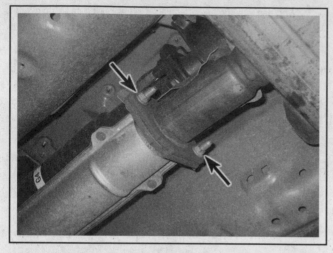

14.4a Typical exhaust pipe flange and fasteners at the front end of the exhaust system resonator (pre-muffler)

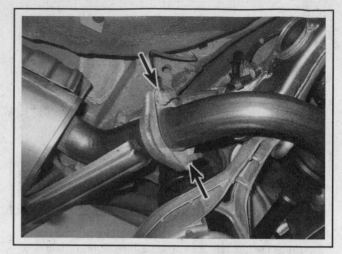

14.4b Typical exhaust pipe flange and fasteners at the front end of the muffler (for other exhaust pipe flanges and fasteners, see "Catalytic converter - description, check and replacement" in Chapter 6)

repair shop remove the corroded sections with a cutting torch. If you want to save money by doing it yourself, but you don't have a welding outfit and cutting torch, simply cut off the old components with a hacksaw. If you have compressed air, there are special pneumatic cutting chisels (available from specialty tool manufacturers) that can also be used. If you decide to tackle the job at home, be sure to wear safety goggles to protect your eyes from metal chips and wear work gloves to protect your hands.

4   Replacement of exhaust system components is basically a matter of removing the heat shields, disconnecting the component and installing a new one. The heat shields and exhaust system hangers must be reinstalled in the original locations or damage could result. Due to the high temperatures and exposed locations of the exhaust system components, rust and corrosion can seize parts together. Penetrating oils are available to help loosen frozen fasteners. However, in some cases it may be necessary to cut the pieces apart with a hacksaw or cutting torch. (Only persons experienced in this work should employ the latter method.) Here are some simple guidelines to follow when repairing the exhaust system:

a) Work from the back to the front when removing exhaust system components.
b) Apply penetrating oil to the exhaust system component fasteners (see illustrations) to make them easier to remove.
c) While you're waiting for the penetrant to loosen up the exhaust system fasteners, always disconnect the electrical connectors for the downstream oxygen sensors and remove the sensors before removing the exhaust pipe section that includes the catalytic converter (see "Catalytic converter - description, check and replacement" in Chapter 6).
d) Use new gaskets, fasteners and rubber hangers when installing exhaust systems components.
e) Apply anti-seize compound to the threads of all exhaust system fasteners during reassembly.
f) Be sure to allow sufficient clearance between newly installed parts and all points on the underbody to avoid overheating the floor pan and possibly damaging the interior carpet and insulation. Pay particularly close attention to the catalytic converter and heat shield.

Specifications

General

Fuel pressure	53 to 63 psi
Fuel injector resistance*	
2003 and 2004	13.5 to 17.5 ohms
2005 on	11.1 to 14.5 ohms

Approximate values, depending on temperature

Torque specifications	Ft-lbs (unless otherwise indicated)	Nm

➡Note: One foot-pound (ft-lb) of torque is equivalent to 12 inch-pounds (in-lbs) of torque. Torque values below approximately 15 ft-lbs are expressed in inch-pounds, since most foot-pound torque wrenches are not accurate at these smaller values.

Throttle body mounting bolts (all engines, all models)	75 in-lbs	8.5
Fuel rail/fuel injector assembly		
Fuel supply line/pulsation damper flange bolts	75 in-lbs	8.5
Fuel sub-tube flange bolts (right fuel rail)	85 in-lbs	9.6
Pulsation damper flange bolts (left fuel rail)	85 in-lbs	9.6

Notes

Section

Reference to other Chapters

5

ENGINE ELECTRICAL SYSTEMS

1   The engine electrical systems include all ignition, charging and starting components. Because of their engine-related functions, these components are discussed separately from chassis electrical devices such as the lights, the instruments, etc. (which are included in Chapter 12).

2   Always observe the following precautions when working on the electrical systems:

a) *Be extremely careful when servicing engine electrical components. They are easily damaged if checked, connected or handled improperly.*

b) *Never leave the ignition switch on for long periods of time with the engine off.*

c) *Don't disconnect the battery cables while the engine is running.*

d) *Maintain correct polarity when connecting a battery cable from another vehicle during jump starting.*

e) *Always disconnect the negative cable first and hook it up last, or the battery may be shorted by the tool being used to loosen the cable clamps.*

3   It's also a good idea to review the safety-related information regarding the engine electrical systems - located in the *Safety First!* Section near the front of this manual - before beginning any operation included in this Chapter.

4   Anytime that you disconnect the battery, you must carry out the following procedures before disconnecting and after reconnecting the battery.

BEFORE DISCONNECTING THE BATTERY, ROLL DOWN THE WINDOWS ON G35 COUPES AND 350ZS

5   ALWAYS roll down the windows on a G35 Coupe or on a 350Z BEFORE disconnecting the battery. These models have a feature that automatically lowers the windows slightly when you open the door, then closes the window after you close the door. If you fail to lower the windows before disconnecting the battery, then open and close either door while this feature is disabled, you might damage the window or the vehicle body or weatherstrip along the top of the window. After you have done this, you'll find the correct procedure for disconnecting the battery in Section 3.

AFTER RECONNECTING THE BATTERY, PERFORM THE FOLLOWING RE-LEARN PROCEDURES:

Accelerator Pedal Released Position Learning procedure

➡**Note: You must perform the Accelerator Pedal Released Position Learning procedure after reconnecting the battery, the electrical connector to the Accelerator Pedal Position (APP) sensor, the electrical connector(s) to the Powertrain Control Module (PCM) or any connector in the harness between the PCM and the APP sensor.**

6   The Accelerator Pedal Released Position Learning procedure monitors the Accelerator Pedal Position (APP) sensor output signal and recalibrates it so that it's accurately synchronized with the actual released position of the accelerator pedal. To begine, make sure the accelerator pedal is fully released.

7   Turn the ignition switch to ON and wait at least two seconds.

8   Turn the ignition switch to OFF and wait at least 10 seconds.

9   Turn the ignition switch to ON and wait at least two seconds.

10 Turn the ignition switch to OFF and wait at least 10 seconds.

Throttle Valve Closed Position Learning

➡**Note: You must perform the Throttle Valve Closed Position Learning procedure after reconnecting the battery, the electrical connector to the throttle body or the electrical connector(s) to the Powertrain Control Module (PCM).**

11 The Throttle Valve Closed Position Learning procedure monitors the Throttle Position (TP) sensor output signal to enable the PCM to relearn the fully closed position of the throttle plate inside the throttle body. You'll need an assistant to perform Steps 13 and 14 so that you can listen to the solenoid motor inside the throttle body.

12 Make sure that the accelerator pedal is fully released.

13 Turn the ignition switch to ON.

14 Turn the ignition switch to OFF and wait at least 10 seconds.

15 During that 10 seconds, listen carefully, with your ear close to the throttle body, and verify that the throttle plate is moving by confirming that the electric motor in the throttle body is operating.

Idle Air Volume Learning

➡**Note: You must perform the Idle Air Volume Learning procedure after reconnecting the battery, and after replacing either the throttle body or the Powertrain Control Module (PCM).**

16 Before performing the Idle Air Volume Learning procedure, the following conditions must be met:

Battery voltage is more than 12.9 volts
Engine coolant temperature is 158 to 212-degrees F (70 to 100-degrees C)
Park Neutral Position (PNP) switch is on
Electric loads (air conditioning, headlights, rear window defogger, etc.) are off
Steering wheel is in the straight-ahead position
Vehicle is not moving
Transmission is warmed up

17 Drive the vehicle for 10 minutes.

18 Perform the Accelerator Pedal Released Position Learning procedure (see Steps 6 through 10).

19 Perform the Throttle Valve Closed Position Learning procedure (see Steps 11 through 15).

20 Start the engine and allow it to warm up to its normal operating temperature.

21 Verify that all the conditions in Step 16 are met.

22 Turn the ignition switch to OFF and wait at least 10 seconds.

23 Verify that the accelerator pedal is fully released, then turn the ignition switch to ON for at least three seconds.

24 Repeat the following procedure quickly five times within five seconds:

Fully depress the accelerator pedal
Fully release the accelerator pedal

25 Wait seven seconds, fully depress the accelerator pedal and keep it depressed for about 20 seconds until the SERVICE ENGINE SOON light stops blinking and turns on steadily.

26 Fully release the accelerator pedal within three seconds after the SERVICE ENGINE SOON light turns on steadily.

27 Start the engine and allow it to idle.

28 Wait 20 seconds.

29 Rev up the engine two or three times and verify that idle speed and ignition timing are within the specifications.

Idle speed: 600 to 700 rpm (in Park or Neutral)

Ignition timing: 10 to 20 degrees BTDC (in Park or Neutral)

If the idle speed and ignition timing are within specification, then the Idle Air Volume Learning procedure is successful.

30 If the idle speed and ignition timing are not within specification, then the Idle Air Volume Learning procedure will not be successful. Proceed with the following steps.

31 Verify that the throttle valve is fully closed.

32 Verify that the PCV valve is operating correctly (see Chapter 6).

33 Verify that there is no air leak downstream from the throttle plate.

34 If the above three conditions are okay, some engine component is installed incorrectly.

35 If the engine stalls or idles incorrectly, find the cause of this condition, correct it, then repeat the Idle Air Volume Learning procedure.

2 Battery - emergency jump starting

Refer to the *Booster battery (jump) starting* procedure at the front of this manual

3 Battery - check, removal and installation

✳✳ WARNING:

Hydrogen gas is produced by the battery, so keep open flames and lighted cigarettes away from it at all times. Always wear eye protection when working around a battery. Rinse off spilled electrolyte immediately with large amounts of water.

✳✳ CAUTION:

Always disconnect the negative cable first and hook it up last or you might accidentally short the battery with the tool that you're using to loosen the cable clamps.

CHECK

1 A battery cannot be accurately tested until it is at or near a fully charged state. Disconnect the negative battery cable from the battery and perform the following tests:

Battery state of charge test

▶ **Refer to illustration 3.2**

2 Visually inspect the indicator eye (if equipped) on the top of the battery. If the indicator eye is dark in color, charge the battery as described in Chapter 1. If the battery is equipped with removable caps, check the battery electrolyte. The electrolyte level should be above the upper edge of the plates. If the level is low, add distilled water. DO

NOT OVERFILL. The excess electrolyte may spill over during periods of heavy charging. Test the specific gravity of the electrolyte using a hydrometer (see illustration). Remove the caps and extract a sample of the electrolyte and observe the float inside the barrel of the hydrometer. Follow the instructions from the tool manufacturer and determine the specific gravity of the electrolyte for each cell. A fully charged battery will indicate approximately 1.260 (green zone) at 68-degrees F (20-degrees C). If the specific gravity of the electrolyte is low (red zone), charge the battery as described in Chapter 1.

3.2 Test the specific gravity of the battery electrolyte with a hydrometer. This hydrometer is equipped with a thermometer to make temperature corrections

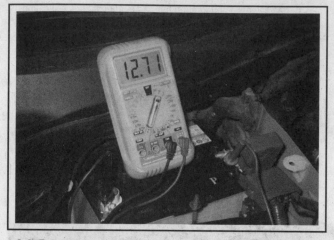

3.3 To test the open circuit voltage of the battery, connect the negative (black) probe of the voltmeter to the negative battery terminal and the positive (red) probe to the positive terminal. A fully charged battery should have at least 12.6 volts

3.4 Some battery load testers are equipped with an ammeter, which enables the battery load to be precisely dialed in. Less expensive testers like this one only have a load switch and a voltmeter

Open circuit voltage test

▶ **Refer to illustration 3.3**

3   Using a digital voltmeter, perform an open circuit voltage test (see illustration). Connect the negative probe of the voltmeter to the negative battery post and the positive probe to the positive battery post. The battery voltage should be greater than 12.5 volts. If the battery is less than the specified voltage, charge the battery before proceeding to the next test. Do not proceed with the battery load test until the battery is fully charged.

Battery load test

▶ **Refer to illustration 3.4**

4   An accurate check of the battery condition can only be performed with a load tester (available at most auto parts stores). This test evaluates the ability of the battery to operate the starter and other accessories during periods of heavy amperage draw (load). Connect a battery load-testing tool to the battery terminals (see illustration). Load test the battery according to the tool manufacturer's instructions. This tool increases the load demand (amperage draw) on the battery. Maintain the load on the battery for 15 seconds and observe that the battery voltage does not drop below 9.6 volts. If the battery condition is weak or defective, the tool will indicate this condition immediately.

➡**Note: Cold temperatures will cause the minimum voltage reading to drop slightly. Follow the chart given in the tool manufacturer's instructions to compensate for cold climates. Minimum load voltage for freezing temperatures (32-degrees F/0-degrees C) should be approximately 9.1 volts.**

Battery drain test

5   This test will indicate whether there's a constant drain on the vehicle's electrical system that can cause the battery to discharge. Make sure all accessories are turned off. If the vehicle has an underhood light, verify that it's working properly, then disconnect it. Connect one lead of a digital ammeter to the disconnected negative battery cable clamp and the other lead to the negative battery post. A drain of approximately 100 milliamps or less is considered normal (due to the engine control computers, clocks, digital radios and other components that normally cause

a key-off battery drain). An excessive drain (approximately 500 milliamps or more) will cause the battery to discharge. The problem circuit or component can be located by removing the fuses, one at a time, until the excessive drain stops and normal drain is indicated on the meter.

REPLACEMENT

▶ **Refer to illustrations 3.6, 3.7, 3.8 and 3.9**

❖❖ **CAUTION:**

Before you disconnect the battery cable on a G35 Coupe or a 350Z, be sure to roll down the windows (see Section 1 for more information.)

6   Remove the battery cover (see illustration).

7   Disconnect the cable from the negative battery terminal, then disconnect the cable from the positive terminal (see illustration).

8   Remove the two nuts that retain the battery hold-down strap (see illustration) and remove the hold-down strap. To access the rear hold-down strap nut on 350Z models, you'll have to remove the two clips that secure the cowl cover, then raise up the cowl cover.

9   Release the fuse and relay box (see illustration), then lift it up and out of the way.

10 Lift out the battery. Be careful - it's heavy.

➡**Note: Battery straps and handlers are available at most auto parts stores for a reasonable price. They make it easier to remove and carry the battery.**

11 While the battery is out, inspect the tray for corrosion deposits. Clean the battery tray, then use a baking soda/water solution to neutralize any deposits to prevent further oxidation. If the metal around the tray is corroded, too, clean it as well and spray the area with a rust-inhibiting paint. If any corrosion has leaked down past the battery tray, use baking soda and water to neutralize the deposits.

12 If you're replacing the battery, make sure you get an identical unit, with the same dimensions, amperage rating, cold cranking rating, etc.

13 Installation is the reverse of removal.

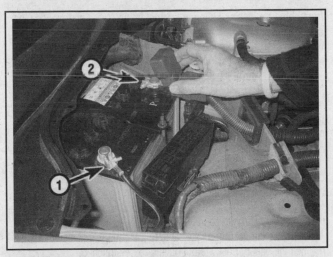

3.6 To remove the battery cover, use a small screwdriver to pry up these pop fasteners, then lift off the cover (G35 Sedan shown, other covers similar)

3.7 When disconnecting the battery cables, always disconnect the cable from the negative terminal (1) first, then flip open the red plastic terminal cover and disconnect the cable from the positive terminal (2)

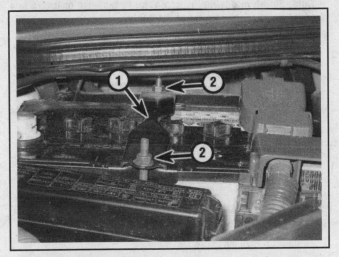

3.8 To remove the battery hold-down strap (1), remove the hold-down nuts (2)

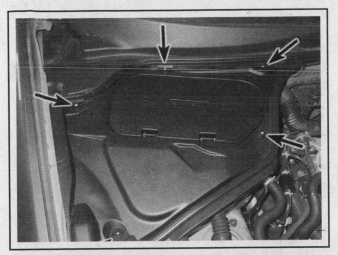

3.9 To remove the fuse and relay box, depress this lock tab and pull the box up

---

4   Battery cables - check, general information and replacement

CHECK

1 Periodically inspect the entire length of each battery cable for damage, cracked or burned insulation and corrosion. Poor battery cable connections can cause starting problems and decreased engine performance.

2 Check the cable-to-terminal connections at the ends of the cables for cracks, loose wire strands and corrosion. The presence of white, fluffy deposits under the insulation at the cable terminal connection is a sign that the cable is corroded and should be replaced. Check the terminals for distortion, missing mounting bolts and corrosion.

GENERAL INFORMATION

3 When removing the cables, always disconnect the cable from the negative battery terminal first and hook it up last to prevent the battery

from being accidentally shorted by the tool you're using to loosen the cable clamps. Even if you're only replacing the cable for the positive terminal, be sure to disconnect the cable from the negative battery terminal first.

4 When buying new battery cables, take the old cables with you. It is critical that you replace the old cables with identical replacement cables. Battery cables have characteristics that make them easy to identify: positive cables are usually red and larger in cross-section; ground cables are usually black and smaller in cross-section.

5 Clean the threads of the solenoid terminals and/or ground terminals with a wire brush to remove rust and corrosion. Apply a light coat of battery terminal corrosion inhibitor or petroleum jelly to the threads to prevent future corrosion.

6 Attach the cable to the solenoid or ground connection and tighten the mounting nut/bolt securely.

7 Before connecting a new cable to the battery, make sure that it reaches the battery post without having to be stretched.

8 Connect the positive cable first, followed by the negative cable.

4.10 To remove the battery ground cable, disconnect it from the negative battery terminal, then disconnect it from the vehicle body

REPLACEMENT

> **✳✳ CAUTION:**
>
> **If you're replacing the battery cable(s) on a G35 Coupe or a 350Z, be sure to roll down the windows before disconnecting the battery (see Section 1 for more information).**

Ground cable

◆ **Refer to illustrations 4.10**

9 Remove the battery cover (see illustration 3.6).
10 Disconnect the ground cable from the negative battery terminal and from the vehicle body (see illustration).
11 Installation is the reverse of removal.

Positive battery cable

◆ **Refer to illustrations 4.13, 4.15a, 4.15b and 4.16**

➡**Note: Before removing the cable, make a sketch or take a few digital photos of the routing of the cable.**

12 Disconnect the cable from the negative battery terminal, then disconnect the battery cable from the positive terminal (see illustration 3.7).
13 Disengage the cable grommet from the sheetmetal between the battery and the engine compartment (see illustration), then disengage the cable from the harness clip that secures it to the right side of the engine compartment. (You might find it easier to disengage the harness from this clip from underneath after you raise the vehicle in the next step.)
14 Raise the front of the vehicle and place it securely on jackstands.
15 Remove the battery cable from the B+ terminal on the alternator (see illustrations).
16 Trace the cable harness back to the starter motor and disconnect the cable from the terminal on the starter motor solenoid (see illustration).
17 Installation is the reverse of removal.

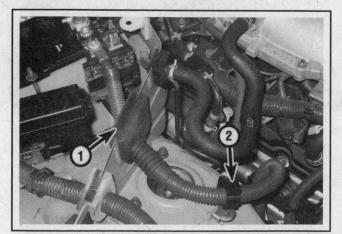

4.13 To remove the battery positive cable, pull the cable grommet (1) straight up, then disengage the cable from the upper clip (2) by prying it open at the split (there are two more clips down below)

4.15a To disconnect the battery cable from the battery terminal on the alternator, peel back this rubber cover . . .

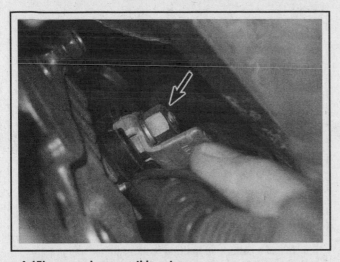

4.15b . . . and remove this nut

4.16 To disconnect the battery cable from the terminal on the starter motor solenoid, remove this nut

5 Electronic Ignition (EI) system - general information

All engines are equipped with a distributorless Electronic Ignition (EI) system. The ignition system consists of the following components:

Accelerator Pedal Position (APP) sensor
Battery
Camshaft Position (CMP) sensor
Crankshaft Position (CKP) sensor
Engine Coolant Temperature (ECT)sensor
Ignition coils (six coils)
Ignition switch
Knock sensor
Mass Air Flow (MAF) sensor
Park/Neutral Position (PNP) switch
Powertrain Control Module (PCM).
Spark plugs
Throttle Position (TP) sensor
Wheel sensors

The PCM uses input voltage signals from the information sensors listed above to calculate and control ignition timing under all operating conditions. The PCM calculates the optimum timing in response to engine speed, coolant temperature, throttle position and other parameters, each of which varies in accordance with the operating conditions such as cranking, warm-up, idle, acceleration, deceleration, etc. The PCM and the CKP sensor are the key components of the EI system. If the PCM or the CKP sensor is defective, the EI system will not operate and the engine will not start. For more information about the information sensors, refer to Chapter 6.

All engines use a coil-over-plug system, which consists of an individual coil above, and connected directly to, each spark plug. The PCM fires the coils in firing order sequence by turning the ground paths for their primary circuits on and off.

6 Ignition system - check

▶ **Refer to illustration 6.5**

✳✳ **WARNING 1:**

Because of the high voltage generated by the ignition system, extreme care should be taken whenever an operation is performed involving ignition components. This not only includes the ignition coil, but also related components and test equipment.

✳✳ **WARNING 2:**

The following procedure requires the engine to be cranked during testing. When cranking the engine, make sure that no meter leads, loose clothing, long hair, etc. come in contact with any moving parts (drivebelt, cooling fan, etc.).

1   Before proceeding with the ignition system checks, check the following items:
   a) *Make sure the battery cable clamps, where they connect to the battery, are clean and tight.*
   b) *Test the condition of the battery (see Section 3). If it does not pass all the tests, replace it with a new battery.*
   c) *Check the ignition system wiring and connections for tightness, damage, corrosion or any other signs of a bad connection.*
   d) *Check the related fuses inside the engine compartment fuse and relay box (see Chapter 12). If they're burned, determine the cause and repair the circuit.*

2   If the engine turns over but won't start or has a severe misfire, perform the following steps using a calibrated ignition tester to make sure there is sufficient secondary ignition voltage to fire the spark plugs.

3   Disable the fuel system by removing the fuel pump relay, which is located in the fuse and relay box in the engine compartment (see illustration 2.1 in Chapter 4).

4   Remove the ignition coil (see Section 7) to test for spark to the plug that it fires.

➡**Note: Disregard Step 2 in that Section, which says to disconnect the negative battery cable; you'll have to leave the battery connected to conduct the following test.**

5   Hook up a calibrated ignition system tester (available at most auto parts stores) between the boot underneath the coil and the spark plug (see illustration).

6   Crank the engine and see if the tester body flashes.

7   If the tester flashes during cranking, sufficient voltage is reaching the plug to fire it. Repeat this test for each spark plug to verify that all the coils are OK.

8   If no flashes occur during cranking at any one cylinder, inspect the primary wire connection at the coil that isn't functioning. Make sure that it's clean and tight.

9   If the coil is operating but a cylinder still has a misfire condition, a spark plug might be fouled. So remove and inspect the suspect plug (see Chapter 1), then retest.

10 If no sparks or intermittent sparks occur during cranking at all cylinders, the Powertrain Control Module (PCM) might be defective. Have the PCM checked out by a dealer service department or other

6.5 To use a calibrated ignition tester, remove an ignition coil, then connect the tester between the coil and the spark plug. Crank over the engine; if there's enough power to fire the plug, the tester will flash

qualified repair shop (testing the PCM is beyond the scope of the do-it-yourselfer because it requires expensive special tools). Any additional testing of the ignition system must be done by a dealer service department or by an independent repair shop with the right tools.

---

7   Ignition coil - check and replacement

CHECK

1   If a coil seems to be misfiring or not firing at all, or is causing the Powertrain Control Module (PCM) to set a Diagnostic Trouble Code (DTC) that indicates a misfire, try swapping it with an adjacent coil. If the suspect coil was causing a DTC for one cylinder, it will likely set another DTC when it's installed above another cylinder. If this is the case, the coil is probably defective because it's unlikely that the harnesses for two adjacent ignition coils would both be defective. At any rate, no further testing is possible at home. If you're not sure whether you should replace the coil at this point, consult a dealer service department or other qualified repair shop.

REPLACEMENT

▸ **Refer to illustrations 7.4, 7.5 and 7.6**

✳✳ **CAUTION:**

Before you disconnect the battery cable on a G35 Coupe or a 350Z, be sure to roll down the windows (see Section 1 for more information.)

2   Disconnect the cable from the negative battery terminal (see Section 1).

3   Remove the engine cover.

4   If you're removing an ignition coil from the left cylinder bank, remove the air filter housing and the air intake duct (see Chapter 4),

then detach the engine harness (see illustration) and push the harness aside as necessary. Also move aside any hoses routed over the ignition coil.

5   If you're removing an ignition coil from the right cylinder bank, detach the engine harness (see illustration) and push the harness aside as necessary. Also move aside any hoses routed over the ignition coil.

6   Disconnect the electrical connector from the coil (see illustration).

7   Remove the ignition coil mounting bolt and remove the coil.

8   Installation is the reverse of removal.

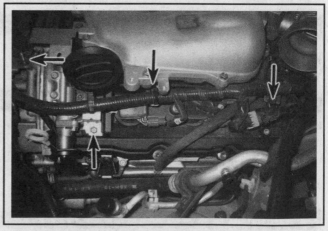

7.4 If you're removing an ignition coil from the left cylinder head, remove the air filter housing and the air intake duct, then remove these bolts to detach the engine harness brackets, and push the harness aside

7.5 If you're removing an ignition coil from the right cylinder head, remove these bolts to detach the engine harness brackets, and push the harness aside

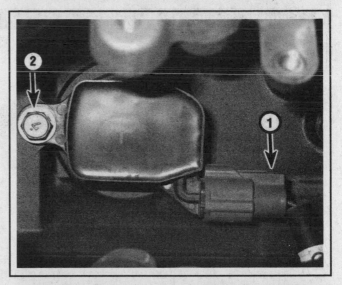

7.6 To remove an ignition coil, depress the release tab (1) and disconnect the electrical connector, remove the coil mounting bolt (2), then grasp the coil firmly and pull it off the spark plug

8 Charging system - general information and precautions

The charging system supplies electrical power for the ignition system, all lighting and audio-visual components, etc. The charging system consists of the alternator and an integral IC voltage regulator, the ignition switch, the battery, the charge warning light, the voltage gauge (350Z models) and the wiring between all the components. The alternator is driven by a serpentine drivebelt at the front of the engine.

When the engine is started on G35 models, the charge warning light should come on briefly, indicating that the charge warning light circuit is operating correctly, then go off after a few seconds. If it stays on, or comes on and stays on during normal driving, inspect the charging system (see Section 9).

When the engine is running on 350Z models, the voltage gauge on the instrument cluster indicates electrical system voltage. The indicator needle should be within the normal range if the battery is charged. If the needle moves outside the normal range and stays there during normal driving, inspect the charging system (see Section 9). If the voltage gauge is defective, replace the instrument cluster (see Chapter 12). The voltage gauge cannot be serviced separately from the cluster.

The charging system doesn't ordinarily require periodic maintenance. However, you should inspect the drivebelt and the battery at the intervals outlined in Chapter 1, as well as the charging system wiring harness and all connections. Be very careful when making electrical circuit connections to the alternator or the charging system circuit and note the following:

a) *When reconnecting wires to the alternator from the battery, be sure to note the polarity.*

b) *Before using arc-welding equipment to repair any part of the vehicle, disconnect the wires from the alternator and the battery terminals.*

c) *Never start the engine with a battery charger connected.*

d) *Always disconnect both battery cables before using a battery charger.*

e) *The alternator is turned by an engine drivebelt, which could cause serious injury if your hands, hair or clothes become entangled in it with the engine running.*

f) *Because the alternator is connected directly to the battery, it could arc or cause a fire if overloaded or shorted out.*

g) *Before steam-cleaning the engine, wrap a plastic bag over the alternator and secure it with rubber bands.*

9   Charging system - check

◆ **Refer to illustration 9.3**

1   If a malfunction occurs in the charging circuit, do not immediately assume that the alternator is causing the problem. First check the following items:

   a) *The battery cables where they connect to the battery. Make sure the connections are clean and tight.*
   b) *The battery electrolyte specific gravity (by observing the charge indicator on the battery [maintenance-free type battery] or by checking it with a hydrometer [serviceable-type battery]). If it is low, charge the battery.*
   c) *Inspect the external alternator wiring and connections.*
   d) *Check the drivebelt condition and tension (see Chapter 1).*
   e) *Check the alternator mounting bolts for tightness.*
   f) *Run the engine and check the alternator for abnormal noise.*

2   Using a voltmeter, check the battery voltage with the engine off. It should be at least 12.6 volts with a fully charged battery.

3   Start the engine and check the battery voltage again (see illustration). It should now be at least 13.0 volts, but should not read more than 15.0 volts.

4   If the indicated voltage reading is less or more than the specified charging voltage, have the charging system checked at a dealer service department or other properly equipped repair facility. The voltage regulator is contained within the alternator.

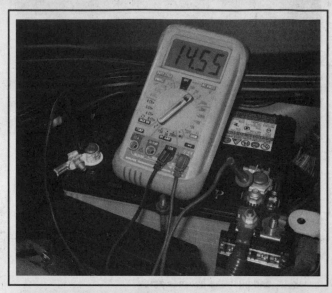

9.3 To test the charging voltage of the battery, connect a voltmeter to the battery terminals. A healthy charging system should put out at least 13 volts, but not more than 15 volts

10   Alternator - removal and installation

◆ **Refer to illustrations 10.8, 10.9, 10.11 and 10.12**

➡**Note 1: If you are replacing the alternator, take the old one with you when purchasing a replacement unit. Make sure the new/rebuilt unit looks identical to the old alternator. Look at the terminals - they should be the same in number, size and location as the terminals on the old alternator. Finally, look at the identification numbers - they will be stamped into the housing or printed on a tag attached to the housing. Make sure the numbers are the same on both alternators.**

➡**Note 2: Many new and remanufactured alternators do not have a pulley installed, so you may have to switch the pulley from the old unit to the new/rebuilt one. When buying an alternator, find out the shop's policy regarding pulleys; some shops will perform this service free of charge.**

✳✳ CAUTION:

Before you disconnect the battery cable on a G35 Coupe or a 350Z, be sure to roll down the windows (see Section 1 for more information.)

1   Disconnect the cable from the negative terminal of the battery (see Section 1).

2   Raise the front of the vehicle and place it securely on jackstands.

3   On G35 Coupes, remove the front air spoiler (see Chapter 11).

4   Remove the engine undercover (see Chapter 2A). On G35 Coupes, remove the right engine undercover as well.

5   On G35 Sedans, remove the stabilizer bar bushing retainers and allow the stabilizer bar to swing down, out of the way (see Chapter 10).

6   On G35 Coupes and 350Z models, remove the radiator fan assembly (see Chapter 3).

7   Remove the alternator/power steering pump/fan drivebelt (see Chapter 1).

8   Disconnect the electrical connector from the alternator (see illustration).

9   Disconnect the electrical connector from the oil pressure switch and detach the switch harness clip from the lower alternator mounting bracket (see illustration).

10   Detach the battery cable harness clip from the alternator battery terminal, remove the nut that secures the battery cable to the battery terminal (see illustrations 4.15a and 4.15b) and disconnect the battery cable from the B terminal.

11   Remove the upper alternator mounting bolt (see illustration).

12   Remove the lower alternator mounting bolt and the mounting bracket bolt (see illustration), remove the mounting bracket and remove the alternator.

13   Installation is the reverse of removal.

10.8 To disconnect the electrical connector from the alternator, depress this release tab and pull up on the connector

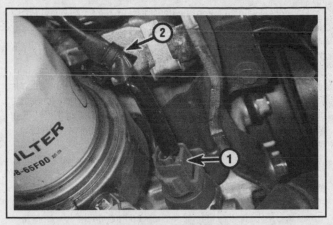

10.9 To disconnect the oil pressure switch harness connector, depress the release tab (1) and pull off the connector. Then, pry the harness clip (2) loose from the lower alternator mounting bracket

10.11 Remove the upper alternator mounting bolt

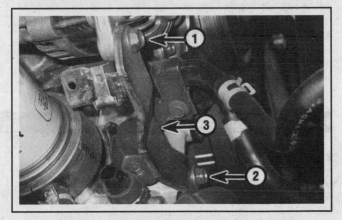

10.12 To remove the alternator, remove the lower alternator mounting bolt (1), the alternator mounting bracket bolt (2) and the alternator mounting bracket (3), then remove the alternator

11 Starting system - general description and precautions

GENERAL DESCRIPTION

The starter motors on the vehicles covered by this manual are all located on the lower part of the engine, near the transmission bellhousing, where they can engage the ring gear on the flywheel/driveplate.

The starting system consists of the following components:
Battery and battery cables
40-amp fusible link (inside the fusible link box at the battery positive terminal)
Ignition switch
Starter relay (inside the engine compartment fuse and relay box)
Starter solenoid and starter motor assembly
Clutch interlock switch (manual transmission models)
Park-Neutral Position (PNP) switch function, inside the Transmission Control Module (TCM) (automatic models)
The wiring harnesses connecting these components

The starting system has two separate circuits: A low-amperage control circuit and a high-amperage supply circuit between the battery and the starter motor. The low-amp control circuit includes the:
Battery
40-amp fusible link (inside the fusible link box at the battery positive terminal)
Ignition switch
Starter relay (inside the engine compartment fuse and relay box)
Clutch interlock switch (manual transmission models)
Transmission Control Module (TCM) (automatics)
Coil winding inside the starter solenoid
Wire harnesses connecting these components
The high-amperage supply circuit consists of the:
Battery
Battery starter cable
Contact disc inside the starter solenoid
Starter motor

On models with an automatic transmission, the Park/Neutral Position (PNP) switch - which is not an external component, but rather an integral circuit inside the TCM - energizes the starter relay only when the shift lever is in PARK or NEUTRAL. The PNP switch is normally open to prevent the starter relay from being energized unless the shift lever is in the PARK or NEUTRAL position. When the ignition switch is turned to START, battery voltage is supplied through the low-amperage control circuit to the starter relay coil if the shift lever is in the PARK or NEUTRAL position. If it isn't, the starter circuit remains open and the engine won't start.

On models with a manual transmission, the clutch interlock switch (at the clutch pedal) energizes the starter relay only when the clutch pedal is depressed. The clutch interlock switch is normally open to prevent the starter relay from being energized. When the ignition switch is turned to START, battery voltage is supplied through the low-amperage control circuit to the starter relay coil if the clutch pedal is depressed. If it isn't, the starter circuit remains open and the engine won't start.

When the starter relay coil is energized, the normally-open relay contacts close, which energize the windings of the starter solenoid pull-in coil, which pulls in the solenoid plunger, which pulls the shift lever in the starter motor, which engages the starter's overrunning clutch and pinion gear with the starter's ring gear. As the solenoid plunger reaches the end of its travel, the solenoid contact disc completes the high-current starter supply circuit and energizes the solenoid plunger hold-in coil. Current flows from the solenoid battery terminal to the starter motor and energizes the starter.

The starter motors used on the vehicles covered in this manual are not rebuildable. They're available only as new or remanufactured units. If any part of the starter motor fails, including the starter solenoid, replace the entire starter assembly.

PRECAUTIONS

Always observe the following precautions when working on the starting system:

a) *Excessive cranking of the starter motor can overheat it and cause serious damage. Never operate the starter motor for more than 15 seconds at a time without pausing to allow it to cool for at least two minutes.*

b) *The starter is connected directly to the battery and could arc or cause a fire if mishandled, overloaded or shorted.*

c) *Always detach the cable(s) from the negative terminal of the battery before working on the starting system.*

---

12 Starter motor and circuit - check

◆ **Refer to illustrations 12.3 and 12.4**

1 If a malfunction occurs in the starting circuit, do not immediately assume that the starter is causing the problem. First, check the following items:

a) *Make sure the battery cable clamps, where they connect to the battery, are clean and tight.*

b) *Check the condition of the battery cables (see Section 4). Replace any defective battery cables with new ones.*

c) *Test the condition of the battery (see Section 3). If it does not pass all the tests, replace it with a new battery.*

d) *Check the starter motor wiring and connections.*

e) *Check the starter motor mounting bolts for tightness.*

f) *Check the related fuses in the engine compartment fuse box (see Chapter 12). If they're blown, determine the cause and repair the circuit.*

g) *Check the ignition switch circuit for correct operation (see the Wiring Diagrams at the end of Chapter 12).*

h) *Check the starter relay (see the Wiring Diagrams at the end of Chapter 12).*

2 If the starter does not activate when the ignition switch is turned to the start position, check for battery voltage to the starter solenoid. This will determine if the solenoid is receiving the correct voltage from the ignition switch. Connect a 12-volt test light or a voltmeter to the starter solenoid positive terminal. While an assistant turns the ignition switch to the start position, observe the test light or voltmeter. The test light should shine brightly or battery voltage should be indicated on the voltmeter. If voltage is not available to the starter solenoid, refer to the wiring diagrams in Chapter 12 and check the fuses and starter relay in series with the starting system. If voltage is available but there is no movement from the starter motor, remove the starter from the engine (see Section 13) and bench test the starter (see Step 4).

3 If the starter turns over slowly, check the starter cranking voltage and the current draw from the battery. This test must be performed with the starter assembly on the engine. Crank the engine over (for 10 seconds or less) and observe the battery voltage. It should not drop below 9.6 volts. Also, observe the current draw with an ammeter (see illustration). Typically a starter should not exceed 160 amps. If the starter motor amperage draw is excessive, have it tested by a dealer service department or other qualified repair shop. There are several conditions that may affect the starter cranking potential. The battery must be in good condition and the battery cold-cranking rating must not be underrated for the particular application. Be sure to check the battery specifications carefully. The battery terminals and cables must be clean and not corroded. Also, in cases of extreme cold temperatures, make sure the battery and/or engine block is warmed before performing the tests.

12.3 Use an inductive ammeter to measure starter current draw

4   If the starter is receiving voltage but does not activate, remove and check the starter motor assembly on the bench (see illustration). Most likely the solenoid is defective. In some rare cases, the engine may be seized, so be sure to try and rotate the crankshaft pulley (see Chapter 2) before proceeding. With the starter assembly mounted in a vise on the bench, install one jumper cable from the positive terminal of a test battery to the B+ terminal on the starter. Install another jumper cable from the negative terminal of the battery to the body of the starter. Install a starter switch and apply battery voltage to the solenoid S terminal (for 10 seconds or less) and observe the solenoid plunger, shift lever and overrunning clutch extend and rotate the pinion drive. If the pinion drive extends but does not rotate, the solenoid is operating, but the starter motor is defective. If there is no movement but the solenoid clicks, the solenoid and/or the starter motor is defective. If the solenoid plunger extends and rotates the pinion drive, the starter assembly is operating properly.

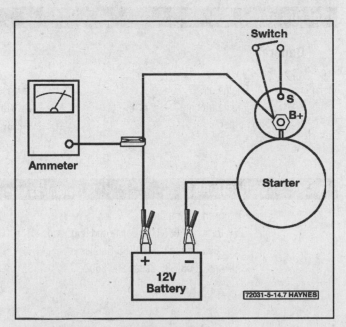

12.4 Starter motor bench-testing details

13   Starter motor - removal and installation

▶ **Refer to illustrations 13.6 and 13.7**

❈❈ CAUTION:

Before you disconnect the battery cable on a G35 Coupe or a 350Z, be sure to roll down the windows (see Section 1 for more information.)

1   Disconnect the cable from the negative terminal of the battery (see Section 1).
2   Raise the vehicle and support it securely on jackstands.
3   Remove the engine undercover (see Chapter 2A).
4   On 2007 and 2008 G35 Sedans, remove the exhaust mounting bracket.
5   On 2007 and 2008 G35 Sedans and 350Z models, disconnect the intermediate steering shaft U-joint from the steering gear and from the intermediate shaft and remove the U-joint.
6   Remove the nut that secures the battery starter cable to the B terminal stud on the starter solenoid (see illustration) and disconnect the cable from the terminal.
7   Disconnect the starter (S) connector from its terminal on the starter motor solenoid (see illustration).
8   Remove the two starter motor mounting bolts (see illustration 13.7) and remove the starter motor.
9   Installation is the reverse of removal. Be sure to tighten the starter motor mounting bolts to the torque listed in this Chapter's Specifications.

13.6 Remove the nut that secures the battery cable to the terminal on the starter motor solenoid and disconnect the battery cable from the terminal

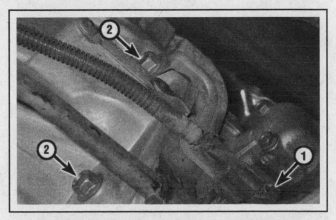

13.7 Depress this release tab (1) and disconnect the starter motor electrical connector from the solenoid. To remove the starter motor, remove these two bolts (2)

Specifications

General

Battery voltage
    Engine off   At least 12.0 volts
    Engine running   14.1 to 14.7 volts
Firing order   1-2-3-4-5-6

Torque specifications	Ft-lbs (unless otherwise indicated)	Nm
Starter motor mounting bolts		
2003 through 2006 G35 Sedan and 350Z and		
2003 through 2007 G35 Coupes	41	55.4
2007 and 2008 G35 Sedan and 350Z	35	48

Section

6

EMISSIONS AND ENGINE CONTROL SYSTEMS

1 General information

▶ **Refer to illustrations 1.5 and 1.7**

To prevent pollution of the atmosphere from incompletely burned and evaporating gases, and to maintain good driveability and fuel economy, a number of emission control systems are incorporated on the vehicles covered in this manual. These emission control systems and their components are an integral part of the engine management system. The engine management system also includes all the government mandated diagnostic features of the second generation of on-board diagnostics, which is known as On-Board Diagnostics II (OBD-II).

At the center of the engine management and OBD-II systems is the on-board computer, which is known as the Powertrain Control Module (PCM). Using a variety of information sensors, the PCM monitors all of the important engine operating parameters (temperature, speed, load, etc.). It also uses an array of output actuators - such as the ignition coils, the fuel injectors, the electronic throttle control and Idle Speed Control (ISC) system, the Torque Converter Clutch (TCC) and various solenoids and relays - to respond to and alter these parameters as necessary to maintain optimal performance, economy and emissions. The principal emission control systems used on the vehicles covered in this manual include the:

Catalytic converters
Evaporative Emission Control (EVAP) system
Intake Valve Timing (IVT) control system
Positive Crankcase Ventilation (PCV) system
Torque Converter Clutch (TCC) system

The Sections in this Chapter include general descriptions and component replacement procedures for most of the information sensors and output actuators, as well as the important components that are part of the systems listed above. Refer to Chapter 4 for more information on the air induction, fuel delivery and injection systems and exhaust systems, and to Chapter 5 for information on the ignition system. Refer to Chapter 1 for any scheduled maintenance for emission-related systems and components.

The procedures in this Chapter are intended to be practical, affordable and within the capabilities of the home mechanic. The diagnosis of most engine and emission control functions and driveability problems requires specialized tools, equipment and training. When servicing emission devices or systems becomes too difficult or requires special test equipment, consult a dealer service department.

Although engine and emission control systems are very sophisticated on late-model vehicles, you can do most of the regular maintenance and some servicing at home with common tune-up and hand tools and relatively inexpensive digital multimeters. Because of the Federally mandated extended warranty that covers the emission control system, check with a dealer about warranty coverage before working on any emission-related systems. After the warranty has expired, you might want to perform some of the component replacement procedures in this Chapter to save money. Remember that the most frequent cause of emission and driveability problems is a loose electrical connector or a broken wire or vacuum hose, so before jumping to conclusions, the first thing you should always do is to inspect all electrical connections, electrical wiring and vacuum hoses related to a system. The wiring diagrams are at the end of Chapter 12. You'll find a vacuum hose routing diagram label (see illustration) under the hood.

Pay close attention to any special precautions given in this Chapter. Remember that illustrations of various system components might not exactly match the component installed on the vehicle on which you're working because of changes made by the manufacturer during production or from year to year.

A Vehicle Emission Control Information (VECI) label (see illustration) is also located under the hood. This label contains emission-control and engine tune-up specifications and adjustment information. It also includes a vacuum hose routing diagram for emission-control components. When servicing the engine or emission systems, always check the VECI label in your vehicle. If any information in this manual contradicts what you read on the VECI label on your vehicle, always defer to the information on the VECI label.

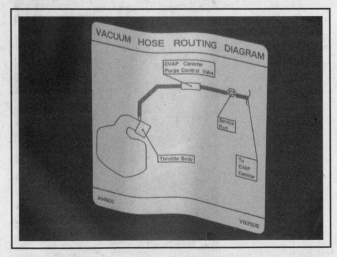

1.5 The vacuum hose routing diagram label is located under the hood

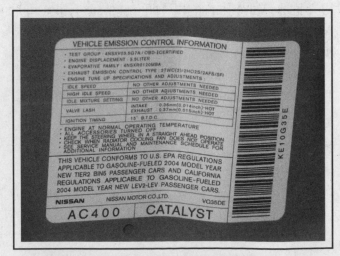

1.7 The Vehicle Emission Control Information (VECI) label, which is located under the hood, contains information on the emission devices installed on your vehicle

SCAN TOOL INFORMATION

▶ **Refer to illustrations 2.1 and 2.2**

1   Hand-held scanners are handy for analyzing the engine management systems used on late-model vehicles. Because extracting the Diagnostic Trouble Codes (DTCs) from an engine management system is now the first step in troubleshooting many computer-controlled systems and components, even the most basic generic code readers are capable of accessing a computer's DTCs (see illustration). More powerful scan tools can also perform many of the diagnostics once associated with expensive factory scan tools. If you're planning to obtain a generic scan tool for your vehicle, make sure that it's compatible with OBD-II systems. If you don't plan to purchase a code reader or scan tool and don't have access to one, you can have the codes extracted by a dealer service department or by an independent repair shop. Some auto parts stores even provide this service for free.

2   With the advent of the Federally mandated emission control system known as On-Board Diagnostics-II (OBD-II), specially designed scanners were developed. Several tool manufacturers have released OBD-II scan tools for the home mechanic (see illustration).

➡**Note: An aftermarket generic scanner should work with any model covered by this manual. Before purchasing a generic scan tool, verify that it will work properly with the OBD-II system you want to scan. If necessary, of course, you can always have the codes extracted by a dealer service department or an independent repair shop with a professional scan tool. Some auto parts stores even provide this service.**

OBD-II SYSTEM

3   All vehicles covered by this manual are equipped with the OBD-II system. This system consists of the on-board computer, known as the Powertrain Control Module (PCM) and information sensors that monitor various functions of the engine and send a constant stream of data to the PCM during engine operation. Unlike earlier on-board diagnostics systems, the OBD-II system doesn't just monitor everything, store Diagnostic Trouble Codes (DTCs) and illuminate a Service Engine Soon light, also called the Malfunction Indicator Light (MIL), when there's a problem.

4   The PCM is the brain of the electronically controlled OBD-II system. It receives data from a number of information sensors and switches. Based on the data that it receives from the sensors, the PCM constantly alters engine operating conditions to optimize driveability, performance, emissions and fuel economy. It does so by turning on and off and by controlling various output actuators such as relays, solenoids, valves and other devices. The PCM can only be accessed with an OBD-II scan tool plugged into the 16-pin Data Link Connector (DLC), which is located underneath the driver's end of the dashboard, near the steering column.

5   If your vehicle is still under warranty, virtually every fuel, ignition and emission control component in the OBD-II system is covered by a Federally mandated emissions warranty that is longer than the warranty covering the rest of the vehicle. Vehicles sold in California and in some other states have even longer emissions warranties than other states. Read your owner's manual for the terms of the warranty protecting the emission-control systems on your vehicle. It isn't a good idea to do-it-yourself at home while the vehicle emission systems are still under warranty because owner-induced damage to the PCM, the sensors and/or the control devices might VOID this warranty. So as long as the emission systems are still under warranty, take the vehicle to a dealer service department if there's a problem.

INFORMATION SENSORS

6   **Accelerator Pedal Position (APP) sensor** - The APP sensor is located at the upper end of and is an integral component of the accelerator pedal assembly. The APP sensor provides the PCM with a variable voltage signal that's proportional to the position (angle) of the accelerator pedal. The PCM uses this data to control the position of the throttle plate inside the throttle body.

7   **Camshaft Position (CMP) sensor** - The CMP sensor pro-

2.1 Simple code readers are an economical way to extract trouble codes when the SERVICE ENGINE SOON light comes on

2.2 Scanners like these from Actron and AutoXray are powerful diagnostic aids - they can tell you just about anything that you want to know about your engine management system

duces a signal which the PCM uses to monitor the position of the camshaft, which in turn enables the Powertrain Control Module (PCM) to determine the identification and position of each piston. The CMP sensor is positioned adjacent to the circumference of a tone wheel machined into the rear end of the intake camshaft. The tone wheel has notches machined into it. When the engine is operating, the CMP sensor receives a 5-volt signal from the Powertrain Control Module (PCM), then produces a fluctuating voltage signal every time one of the notches in the tone wheel passes by it. This data enables the PCM to determine the position of the camshaft (and therefore the valve train and the pistons) so that it can time the firing sequence of the fuel injectors. The PCM also uses the signal from the CMP sensor and the signal from the Crankshaft Position (CKP) sensor to distinguish between fuel injection and spark timing. In the event that the CKP sensor fails, the PCM uses the CMP sensor to provide the cylinder identification necessary for controlling spark timing as well. The two CMP sensors are located on the rear ends of the cylinder heads. (Infiniti and Nissan also refer to the CMP sensor as a PHASE sensor.)

8 **Crankshaft Position (CKP) sensor** - Like the CMP sensor, the CKP sensor uses a tone wheel with notches machined into it to produce a fluctuating voltage signal every time a notch passes by it. The PCM uses data from the CKP sensor to calculate engine speed and crankshaft position, which enables it to synchronize ignition timing with fuel injector timing, to control spark knock and to detect misfires. The CKP sensor is located on the oil pan, below the starter motor. The tone wheel is on the flywheel.

9 **Engine Coolant Temperature (ECT) sensor** - The ECT sensor is a Negative Temperature Coefficient (NTC) thermistor (temperature-sensitive variable resistor). In an NTC-type thermistor, the resistance of the thermistor decreases as the coolant temperature increases, so the voltage output of the ECT sensor increases. Conversely, the resistance of the thermistor increases as the coolant temperature decreases, so the voltage of the ECT sensor decreases. The PCM uses this variable voltage signal to calculate the temperature of the engine coolant. The ECT sensor tells the PCM when the engine is sufficiently warmed up to go into closed-loop operation and helps the PCM control the air/fuel mixture ratio and ignition timing. The ECT sensor is located on the coolant crossover pipe at the rear of the engine.

10 **EVAP control system pressure sensor** - The pressure sensor monitors the pressure of evaporative gases inside the purge line to the intake manifold, which is determined by the vapor pressure inside the fuel tank, the EVAP hoses between the fuel tank and the EVAP canister and the canister itself. The pressure sensor sends a voltage signal to the PCM that increases as the pressure increases. When the signal reaches a specified threshold, the PCM energizes the EVAP canister purge solenoid, which allows the evaporative emissions to be drawn into the intake manifold. The EVAP system pressure sensor is located on the purge line at the EVAP canister.

11 **Exhaust Valve Timing (EVT) control position sensors** - The EVT control position sensors are components of the EVT system (see Section 20). Each EVT sensor monitors the position of the concave groove in the rear end of the exhaust camshaft. The EVT sensors send signals to the Powertrain Control Module (PCM), which uses these signals to determine the position of the exhaust camshafts. The PCM then uses this information to control the position of the EVT magnet retarders on the exhaust camshaft timing chain sprockets to alter the position of the exhaust camshafts to improve the power and torque during high-speed operating conditions.

12 **Fuel Tank Temperature (FTT) sensor** - The FTT sensor monitors the temperature of the fuel inside the fuel tank. The FTT sensor receives a voltage signal from the Powertrain Control Module (PCM) and modifies it in proportion to the changing fuel temperature. The FTT sensor is a Negative Temperature Coefficient (NTC) type thermistor, which means that its electrical resistance decreases as the temperature increases. So the voltage signal that the FTT sensor receives from the PCM is returned to the PCM as a fuel temperature input signal whose voltage increases as the fuel temperature increases. The FTT sensor is an integral component of the fuel pump/fuel level sensor module, which is located inside the fuel tank.

13 Intake Air Temperature (IAT) sensor - The IAT sensor is a Negative Temperature Coefficient (NTC) thermistor (temperature-sensitive variable resistor) that monitors the temperature of the air entering the engine and sends a variable voltage signal to the PCM. (See the explanation for how an NTC-type thermistor works in the ECT sensor description above.) The voltage signal from the IAT sensor is one of the parameters used by the PCM to determine injector pulse-width (the duration of each injector's on-time) and to adjust spark timing (to prevent spark knock). The IAT sensor is an integral component of the Mass Air Flow (MAF) sensor, which is located on the air filter housing. See *Mass Air Flow/Intake Air Temperature (MAF/IAT) sensor* below.

14 **Knock sensor** - The knock sensor is a piezoelectric crystal that oscillates in proportion to engine vibration. (The term piezoelectric refers to the property of certain crystals that produce a voltage when subjected to a mechanical stress.) The oscillation of the piezoelectric crystal produces a voltage output that is monitored by the PCM, which retards the ignition timing when the oscillation exceeds a certain threshold. When the engine is operating normally, the knock sensor oscillates consistently and its voltage signal is steady. When detonation occurs, engine vibration increases, and the oscillation of the knock sensor exceeds a design threshold. (Detonation is an uncontrolled explosion, after the spark occurs at the spark plug, which spontaneously combusts the remaining air/fuel mixture, resulting in a pinging or slapping sound.) If allowed to continue, the engine could be damaged. The knock sensor is located on top of the block, in the valley between the cylinder heads, under the intake manifold.

➡**Note: On 2007 and 2008 G35 Sedans and 350Z models, there are two knock sensors, and both of them are in this same area.**

15 **Mass Air Flow/Intake Air Temperature (MAF/IAT) sensor** - The MAF/IAT sensor is used by the PCM to measure the amount of intake air drawn into the engine. It uses a hot-wire sensing element to measure the amount of air entering the engine. The wire is constantly maintained at a specified temperature above the ambient temperature of the incoming air by electrical current. As intake air passes through the MAF sensor and over the hot wire, it cools the wire, and the control system immediately corrects the temperature back to its constant value. The current required to maintain the constant value is used by the PCM to determine the amount of air flowing through the MAF sensor. The MAF sensor also includes an integral Intake Air Temperature (IAT) sensor. The two components cannot be serviced separately; if either sensor is defective, replace the MAF/IAT sensor. The MAF/IAT sensor is located at the air filter housing.

16 **Oxygen sensors** - An oxygen sensor is a galvanic battery that generates a small variable voltage signal in proportion to the difference between the oxygen content in the exhaust stream and the oxygen content in the ambient air. The PCM uses the voltage signal from the upstream oxygen sensor to maintain a stoichiometric air/fuel ratio of

14.7:1 by constantly adjusting the on-time of the fuel injectors. There are four oxygen sensors: two upstream (1/1 and 2/1) and two downstream (1/2 and 2/2). The left upstream (1/1) sensor is located on the left exhaust manifold, just above the manifold flange; the left downstream (1/2) sensor is located on the left catalytic converter. The right upstream (2/1) sensor is located on the right exhaust manifold, just above the manifold flange; the right downstream (2/2) sensor is located on the right catalytic converter.

17 **Park/Neutral Position (PNP) switch** - The PNP switch prevents the engine from starting in any gear position other than PARK or NEUTRAL. The PNP switch includes a Transmission Range (TR) switch, which monitors the selector lever position and sends a signal to the Transmission Control Module (TCM). The TCM uses this information to determine the correct pressure for the electronic pressure control system of the transaxle. Do not attempt to replace the PNP switch yourself; it's located on the transmission valve body and is difficult to access. Have the work performed by a dealer service department or a qualified automatic transmission shop.

18 **Power Steering Pressure (PSP) switch -** The PSP switch monitors the pressure of the power steering fluid inside the high-pressure side of the power steering system. Fluid pressure is proportional to the load on the power steering system. The PSP switch is a potentiometer. It receives an input voltage signal from the Powertrain Control Module (PCM) and converts this into an output voltage back to the PCM that's proportional to the fluid pressure inside the high-pressure side of the power steering system. The PCM uses this information to control idle speed, which is dragged down by extra loads on the engine at idle such as higher resistance in the power steering pump. When the PCM detects this higher load on the engine, it alters the air/fuel mixture ratio, throttle plate position, fuel injection timing and/or spark timing to maintain the correct idle speed. The PSP switch is located on the power steering high pressure tube right at the power steering pump, which is located at the right front corner of the engine.

19 **Throttle Position (TP) sensor** - The TP sensor is a potentiometer that receives constant voltage input from the PCM and sends back a voltage signal that varies in relation to the opening angle of the throttle plate inside the throttle body. This voltage signal tells the PCM when the throttle is closed, half-open, wide open or anywhere in between. The PCM uses the TP sensor inputs along with the input from the Accelerator Pedal Position (APP) sensor and other information to open and close the throttle plate in proportion to the position of the accelerator pedal. The PCM also uses this data, along with information from other sensors, to calculate injector pulse width (the interval of time during which an injector solenoid is energized by the PCM). All models are equipped with an Electronic Control Actuator (electronically-controlled throttle body). The throttle body actually has two TP sensors. One of them, TP sensor 1, is the primary sensor; the other, TP sensor 2, is used as a rationality check and, in the event that TP sensor 1 fails, as a back-up TP sensor. When the engine is warmed up and running, both TP sensors have an output voltage range between 0.36 and 4.75 volts. The output voltage of TP sensor 1 goes up as the throttle plate opens; the output signal from TP sensor 2 goes down as the throttle plate is opened. Both TP sensors are integral components of the throttle body assembly and cannot be serviced separately. On 2007 and 2008 G35 Sedans and 350Z models there are two throttle bodies, each of which is equipped with two TP sensors.

20 **Vehicle Speed Sensor (VSS)** - There is no actual physical VSS component on the transmission (the conventional setup). Instead, the Vehicle Dynamic Control/Traction Control System/Anti-Lock Brake System (VDC/TCS/ABS) control unit uses voltage signals from the wheel sensors in the Anti-Lock Brake System (ABS) to calculate vehicle speed and sends the VSS signal to the instrument cluster over the Controller Area Network (CAN), which sends the signal on to the Powertrain Control Module (PCM), also via the CAN. (The CAN is a high-speed multiplex cable system that allows multiple serial data transmissions on the same line.) If you see a DTC for a bad VSS, have the vehicle diagnosed by the dealer.

21 **Transmission speed sensors** - The turbine revolution sensors monitor input shaft rpm on automatic transmissions. The turbine revolution sensors provide the Transmission Control Module (TCM) with an output signal that's proportional to the rotational speed of the input shaft. The revolution sensor (or vehicle speed sensor) monitors the idler gear parking pawl lock gear. All three sensors provide output signals to the Transmission Control Module (TCM). The TCM uses the two turbine revolution sensors to monitor wear inside the transmission so that it can predict trouble and/or failure. The TCM uses the revolution sensor output signal to calculate vehicle speed, then sends this signal to the PCM. The PCM uses this information to control the torque converter, to calculate speed scheduling and to determine the correct operating pressure for the transaxle. It also uses the signals from the two sensors to determine the condition of the transmission and to predict its probable failure. Because the transmission speed sensors are located inside the transmission, we don't recommend trying to replace any of them yourself. Have the work performed by a dealer service department or a qualified automatic transmission shop.

POWERTRAIN CONTROL MODULE (PCM)

22 The **PCM** is a computer. Think of it as the brain of the engine management system. Like all computers, the PCM receives data inputs, processes the data and outputs commands. The PCM receives data from all of the information sensors described above (input), compares the data to its program and calculates the appropriate responses (processing), then turns the output actuators on or off, or changes their pulse width or duty cycle (output) to keep everything running smoothly, cleanly and efficiently. The PCM is located under the right part of the dash.

OUTPUT ACTUATORS

23 **Electric Throttle Control Actuator** - The Electric Throttle Control Actuator assembly includes the throttle body, the two Throttle Position (TP) sensors, the throttle control motor and the throttle plate. The Powertrain Control Module (PCM) operates the throttle control motor to open and close the throttle plate in accordance with the position of the accelerator pedal and driving conditions.

24 **EVAP canister purge solenoid** - The EVAP canister purge solenoid is a PCM-controlled solenoid that controls the purging of evaporative emissions from the EVAP canister to the intake manifold. The EVAP purge solenoid is never turned on during cold start warm-ups or during hot start time delays. But once the engine reaches a specified temperature and enters closed-loop operation, the PCM energizes the canister purge solenoid under certain open-throttle operating conditions (acceleration, high speed cruising, etc.). When the solenoid is energized by the PCM, it allows fuel vapors stored in the EVAP canister to be drawn into the intake manifold, where they're mixed with intake air, then burned along with the normal air/fuel mixture. The PCM regulates the

flow rate of the vapors by controlling the pulse-width of the solenoid (the length of time during which the solenoid is turned on) in accordance with operating conditions. The EVAP canister purge solenoid is located on the intake manifold.

25 **EVAP canister vent control valve** - The canister vent control valve, which is used only for diagnosis of the EVAP system, is normally open. Under normal conditions the canister vent is open. When energized by the PCM, the canister vent closes, which depressurizes the EVAP system and enables the PCM to diagnose other components in the EVAP system. The vent control solenoid is located on the EVAP canister.

26 **Fuel injectors** - The fuel injectors spray a fine mist of fuel into the intake ports, where it mixes with air being drawn into the combustion chambers, in the same firing order as the spark plugs. The injector valves are opened and closed by tiny PCM-controlled inductive coils built right into the injector bodies. The injectors are installed between the fuel rail and the intake ports that connect the intake manifold runners to the combustion chambers. For more information about the injectors, see Chapter 4.

27 **Ignition coils** - The ignition coils are controlled by the Powertrain Control Module (PCM). There is no separate ignition control module. This function is handled inside the PCM, which controls the ground path for the primary side of each coil. For more information about the ignition coils, refer to Chapter 5.

28 **Exhaust Valve Tuning (EVT) magnet retarders** - The EVT magnet retarders are part of the EVT system. The Powertrain Control Module (PCM) monitors crankshaft position, camshaft position, engine speed and engine coolant temperature and compares these inputs to its program. When commanded to do so by the PCM, the EVT magnet retarders alter the opening and closing phase of the exhaust valves, which improves engine torque and horsepower in the high-speed range. The EVT magnet retarders are integrated into the camshaft timing chain sprockets. The EVT system is used on 2005 and 2006 G35 models with manual transmissions and on all 2007 and 2008 G35 models. EVT is also used on 2005 35th Anniversary 350Z models, on 2006 350Z models with manual transmissions and on all 2007 and 2008 350Z models. For more information about the EVT system, see Section 20.

29 **Intake Valve Tuning (IVT) control solenoids** - The IVT control solenoids are part of the IVT system. The Powertrain Control Module (PCM) monitors crankshaft position, camshaft position, engine speed and engine coolant temperature and compares these inputs to its program. When commanded to do so by the PCM, the IVT control solenoids alter the opening and closing phase of the intake valves, which improves engine torque in the low and mid-speed range and engine power in the high-speed range. The IVT solenoids are located on the front end of the valve covers. The IVT system is used on all models. For more information about the IVT system, see Section 19.

OBTAINING AND CLEARING DIAGNOSTIC TROUBLE CODES (DTCS)

30 All models covered by this manual are equipped with on-board diagnostics. When the PCM recognizes a malfunction in a monitored emission control system, component or circuit, it turns on the Malfunction Indicator Light (MIL) on the dash. The PCM will continue to display the MIL until the problem is fixed and the Diagnostic Trouble Code (DTC) is cleared from the PCM's memory. You'll need a scan tool to access any DTCs stored in the PCM. Before outputting any DTCs stored in the PCM, thoroughly inspect ALL electrical connectors and hoses.

Make sure that all electrical connections are tight, clean and free of corrosion. And make sure that all hoses are correctly connected, fit tightly and are in good condition (no cracks or tears). Also, make sure that the engine is tuned up. A poorly running engine is probably one of the biggest causes of emission-related malfunctions. Often, simply giving the engine a good tune-up will correct the problem.

Accessing the DTCs

▶ Refer to illustration 2.31

31 On the vehicles covered in this manual, all of which are equipped with On-Board Diagnostic II (OBD-II) systems, the Diagnostic Trouble Codes (DTCs) can only be accessed with a scan tool. Simply plug the connector of the scan tool into the Data Link Connector (DLC) or diagnostic connector, which is located under the lower edge of the instrument panel, to the right of the hood release handle **(see illustration)**. Then follow the instructions included with the scan tool to extract the DTCs.

32 Once you have outputted all of the stored DTCs, look them up on the accompanying DTC chart.

33 After troubleshooting the source of each DTC, make any necessary repairs or replace the defective component(s).

Clearing the DTCs

34 Clear the DTCs with the scan tool in accordance with the instructions provided by the scan tool's manufacturer.

DIAGNOSTIC TROUBLE CODES

35 The accompanying tables are a list of the Diagnostic Trouble Codes (DTCs) that can be accessed by a do-it-yourselfer working at home (there are many more DTCs available to professional service technicians with proprietary scan tools and software, but those codes cannot be accessed by a generic scan tool). If, after you have checked and repaired the connectors, wire harness and vacuum hoses (if applicable) for an emission-related system, component or circuit, the problem persists, have the vehicle checked by a dealer service department.

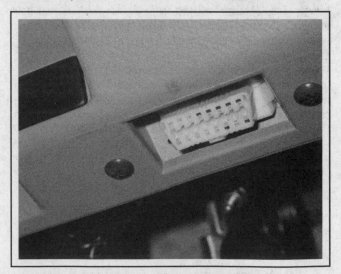

2.31 The Data Link Connector (DLC), or diagnostic connector, is located under the left end of the instrument panel, to the right of the hood release handle

OBD-II DIAGNOSTIC TROUBLE CODES (DTCS)

➡Note: Not all trouble codes apply to all models.

Code	Probable cause
P0011	Intake Valve Timing (IVT) control (Bank 1), gap between target angle and phase-control angle
P0014	Exhaust Valve Timing (EVT) control (Bank 1), gap between target angle and phase-control angle
P0021	Intake Valve Timing (IVT) control (Bank 2), gap between target angle and phase-control angle
P0024	Exhaust Valve Timing (EVT) control (Bank 2), gap between target angle and phase-control angle
P0031	Upstream oxygen sensor heater control circuit (Bank 1), excessively low voltage signal
P0032	Upstream oxygen sensor heater control circuit (Bank 1), excessively high voltage signal
P0037	Downstream oxygen sensor heater control circuit (Bank 1), excessively low voltage signal
P0038	Downstream oxygen sensor heater control circuit (Bank 1), excessively high voltage signal
P0051	Upstream oxygen sensor heater control circuit (Bank 2), excessively low voltage signal
P0052	Upstream oxygen sensor heater control circuit (Bank 2), excessively high voltage signal
P0057	Downstream oxygen sensor heater control circuit (Bank 2), excessively low voltage signal
P0058	Downstream oxygen sensor heater control circuit (Bank 2), excessively high voltage signal
P0075	Intake Valve Timing (IVT) control solenoid valve (Bank 1), incorrect voltage signal
P0078	Exhaust Valve Timing (EVT) control magnet retarder (Bank 1), incorrect voltage signal
P0081	Intake Valve Timing (IVT) control solenoid valve (Bank 2), incorrect voltage signal
P0084	Exhaust Valve Timing (EVT) control magnet retarder (Bank 2), incorrect voltage signal
P0101	Mass Air Flow (MAF) sensor circuit, high voltage signal with light load or low voltage signal with heavy load
P0102	Mass Air Flow (MAF) sensor circuit, excessively low voltage signal
P0103	Mass Air Flow (MAF) sensor circuit, excessively high voltage signal
P010A	Manifold Absolute Pressure (MAP) sensor circuit, excessively low or high voltage from sensor to PCM
P010B	Mass Air Flow (MAF) sensor circuit (Bank 2), range/performance problem, high voltage signal under light load condition or low voltage signal under heavy load condition
P010C	Mass Air Flow (MAF) sensor circuit (Bank 2), low input voltage from sensor

OBD-II DIAGNOSTIC TROUBLE CODES (DTCS) (CONTINUED)

➡ Note: Not all trouble codes apply to all models.

Code	Probable cause
P010D	Mass Air Flow (MAF) sensor circuit (Bank 2), high input voltage from sensor
P0112	Intake Air Temperature (IAT) sensor circuit, excessively low voltage signal
P0113	Intake Air Temperature (IAT) sensor circuit, excessively high voltage signal
P0117	Engine Coolant Temperature (ECT) sensor circuit, excessively low voltage signal
P0118	Engine Coolant Temperature (ECT) sensor circuit, excessively high voltage signal
P0121	Throttle Position (TP) sensor circuit, high voltage signal with light load or low voltage signal with heavy load
P0122	Throttle Position (TP) sensor circuit, displayed with P0121
P0123	Throttle Position (TP) sensor circuit, displayed with P0121
P0125	Engine Coolant Temperature (ECT) sensor circuit, voltage signal not rational or coolant temperature insufficient for closed loop fuel control
P0127	Intake Air Temperature (IAT) sensor circuit, voltage signal irrational compared to ECT sensor signal
P0128	Thermostat malfunction, engine coolant temperature doesn't reach specified temperature after warm-up
P0130	Upstream oxygen sensor circuit (Bank 1), voltage signal is constantly about 1.5 volts
P0131	Upstream oxygen sensor circuit (Bank 1), voltage signal is constantly zero
P0132	Upstream oxygen sensor circuit (Bank 1), excessively high voltage signal
P0133	Upstream oxygen sensor circuit (Bank 1), response of voltage signal takes more than specified time
P0134	Upstream oxygen sensor circuit (Bank 1), no activity detected, voltage signal is constantly about 0.3 volts
P0137	Downstream oxygen sensor circuit (Bank 1), sensor signal voltage doesn't reach specified voltage
P0138	Downstream oxygen sensor circuit (Bank 1), excessively high voltage signal
P0139	Downstream oxygen sensor circuit (Bank 1), excessive time for response interval between rich and lean
P0150	Upstream oxygen sensor circuit (Bank 2), voltage signal is constantly about 1.5 volts
P0151	Upstream oxygen sensor circuit (Bank 2), voltage signal is constantly zero
P0152	Upstream oxygen sensor circuit (Bank 2), excessively high voltage signal

Code	Probable cause
P0153	Upstream oxygen sensor circuit (Bank 2), response of voltage signal takes more than specified time
P0154	Upstream oxygen sensor circuit (Bank 2), no activity detected, voltage signal is constantly about 0.3 volts
P0157	Downstream oxygen sensor circuit (Bank 2), sensor signal voltage doesn't reach specified voltage
P0158	Downstream oxygen sensor circuit (Bank 2), excessively high voltage signal
P0159	Downstream oxygen sensor circuit (Bank 2), excessive time for response interval between rich and lean
P0171	Fuel system mixture ratio too lean or fuel injection system malfunction (Bank 1)
P0172	Fuel system mixture ratio too rich or fuel injection system malfunction (Bank 1)
P0174	Fuel system mixture ratio too lean or fuel injection system malfunction (Bank 2)
P0175	Fuel system mixture ratio too rich or fuel injection system malfunction (Bank 2)
P0181	Fuel Tank Temperature (FTT) sensor circuit range/performance problem, rationally incorrect voltage signal compared to signals from ECT and IAT sensors
P0182	Fuel Tank Temperature (FTT) sensor circuit, excessively low voltage signal
P0183	Fuel Tank Temperature (FTT) sensor circuit, excessively high voltage signal
P0196	Engine Oil Temperature (EOT) sensor range/performance problem, rationally incorrect voltage from sensor compared to voltage signals from ECT and IAT sensors
P0197	Engine Oil Temperature (EOT) sensor circuit, low input voltage
P0198	Engine Oil Temperature (EOT) sensor circuit, high input voltage
P0221	Throttle Position (TP) sensor circuit range/performance problem, rationally incorrect voltage signal compared to signals from TP sensor 2 and TP sensor 2
P0222	Throttle Position (TP) sensor 1 circuit, excessively low voltage signal
P0223	Throttle Position (TP) sensor 1 circuit, excessively high voltage signal
P0226	Accelerator Pedal Position (APP) sensor circuit range/performance problem, rationally incorrect voltage compared with signals from APP sensor 1 and APP sensor 2
P0227	Accelerator Pedal Position (APP) sensor 1 circuit, excessively low voltage signal (2003 G35 Sedan only)
P0227	Throttle Position (TP) sensor 2 circuit (Bank 2), low input voltage signal to PCM (2007 and 2008 G35 Sedan and 350Z)
P0228	Accelerator Pedal Position (APP) sensor 1 circuit, excessively high voltage signal (2003 G35 Sedan only)
P0228	Throttle Position (TP) sensor 2 circuit (Bank 2), high input voltage signal to PCM (2007 and 2008 G35 Sedan and 350Z)
P0300	Multiple cylinder misfire

OBD-II DIAGNOSTIC TROUBLE CODES (DTCS) (CONTINUED)

➡**Note: Not all trouble codes apply to all models.**

Code	Probable cause
P0301	Cylinder 1 misfire
P0302	Cylinder 2 misfire
P0303	Cylinder 3 misfire
P0304	Cylinder 4 misfire
P0305	Cylinder 5 misfire
P0306	Cylinder 6 misfire
P0327	Knock sensor circuit (Bank 1), excessively low voltage signal
P0328	Knock sensor circuit (Bank 1), excessively high voltage signal
P0332	Knock sensor circuit (Bank 2), low input voltage to PCM
P0333	Knock sensor circuit (Bank 2), high input voltage to PCM
P0335	Crankshaft Position (CKP) sensor circuit, no voltage signal, incorrect signal or signal with irregular pattern
P0340	Camshaft Position (CMP) sensor circuit (Bank 1), no voltage signal first few seconds during cranking, no signal while engine running or signal with irregular pattern
P0345	Camshaft Position (CMP) sensor circuit (Bank 2), no voltage signal first few seconds during cranking, no signal while engine running or signal with irregular pattern
P0420	Three-way catalyst function (Bank 1), catalyst doesn't operate correctly or has insufficient oxygen storage capacity
P0430	Three-way catalyst function (Bank 2), catalyst doesn't operate correctly or has insufficient oxygen storage capacity
P0441	Evaporative Emissions (EVAP) control system, incorrect purge flow
P0442	Evaporative Emissions (EVAP) control system, small leak detected
P0443	Evaporative Emissions (EVAP) control system, canister purge flow occurs when EVAP canister purge volume control solenoid valve is completely closed
P0444	Evaporative Emissions (EVAP) control system, purge volume control solenoid valve, low voltage signal
P0445	Evaporative Emissions (EVAP) control system, purge volume control solenoid valve, high voltage signal
P0447	Evaporative Emissions (EVAP) control system, vent control valve, incorrect voltage signal

Code	Probable cause
P0448	EVAP canister vent control valve, valve stays closed under conditions during which it's supposed to open
P0451	Evaporative Emissions (EVAP) control system, pressure sensor, incorrect voltage signal
P0452	Evaporative Emissions (EVAP) control system, pressure sensor, low voltage signal
P0453	Evaporative Emissions (EVAP) control system, pressure sensor, high voltage signal
P0455	Evaporative Emissions (EVAP) control system, large leak detected
P0456	Evaporative Emissions (EVAP) control system, very small leak detected
P0460	Fuel level sensor, sloshing voltage signal from sensor while vehicle is stationary
P0461	Fuel level sensor, no change in voltage signal
P0462	Fuel level sensor circuit, excessively low voltage signal
P0463	Fuel level sensor circuit, excessively high voltage signal
P0500	Vehicle Speed Sensor (VSS) circuit, 0 mph signal sent to PCM when vehicle is moving
P0506	Idle Speed Control (ISC) system, idle speed less than target idle speed by 100 rpm or more
P0507	Idle Speed Control (ISC) system, idle speed more than target idle speed by 200 rpm or more
P0524	Intake Valve Timing (IVT) system, engine oil pressure too low because of a gap between target angle and phase-control angle
P0550	Power steering pressure sensor circuit, excessively high or low voltage signal
P0555	Brake booster pressure sensor, excessively low or high voltage from sensor to PCM
P0603	Powertrain Control Module (PCM) back-up Random Access Memory (RAM) system not functioning correctly
P0605	Powertrain Control Module (PCM), calculation, EEPROM or self shut-off malfunction
P0643	Sensor power supply, PCM detects excessively high or low voltage to APP, EVAP control system pressure, PSP or refrigerant pressure sensor
P0650	Malfunction Indicator Lamp (MIL) circuit, excessively high or low voltage sent
P0700	Transmission Control Module (TCM), defective TCM
P0705	Park Neutral Position (PNP) switch circuit, incorrect or missing voltage signal
P0710	Automatic Transmission Fluid (ATF) temperature sensor circuit, excessively high or low voltage signal
P0717	Turbine revolution sensor circuit, turbine sensor circuit is open or shorted
P0720	Vehicle Speed Sensor (VSS) circuit, incorrect voltage signal

OBD-II DIAGNOSTIC TROUBLE CODES (DTCS) (CONTINUED)

➡Note: Not all trouble codes apply to all models.

Code	Probable cause
P0725	Engine speed signal, no voltage signal
P0731	Automatic transmission first gear function, TCM detects any inconsistency in actual gear ratio
P0732	Automatic transmission second gear function, TCM detects any inconsistency in actual gear ratio
P0733	Automatic transmission third gear function, TCM detects any inconsistency in actual gear ratio
P0734	Automatic transmission fourth gear function, TCM detects any inconsistency in actual gear ratio
P0735	Automatic transmission fifth gear function, TCM detects any inconsistency in actual gear ratio
P0740	Torque Converter Clutch (TCC) solenoid circuit, incorrect or irregular voltage signal
P0744	Torque Converter Clutch (TCC) solenoid valve, incorrect or irregular voltage signal
P0745	Line pressure solenoid circuit, incorrect or irregular voltage signal
P0850	Park Neutral Position (PNP) position switch circuit, PNP switch signal doesn't change when starting and driving

3 Accelerator Pedal Position (APP) sensor - replacement

♦ **Refer to illustrations 3.2a and 3.2b**

➡Note: The Accelerator Pedal Position (APP) sensor is located at the upper end of the accelerator pedal assembly. The APP sensor is an integral component of the accelerator pedal assembly; to replace the APP sensor, you must replace the pedal assembly.

1 Remove the knee bolster cover (see Chapter 11).
2 Disconnect the electrical connector from the APP sensor (see illustrations).
3 Remove the two APP sensor assembly mounting nuts (see illustration 3.2a).
4 Remove the APP sensor assembly.
5 Installation is the reverse of removal.

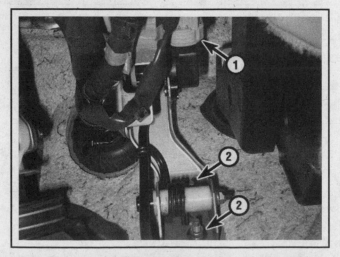

3.2a To remove the APP sensor/accelerator pedal assembly, disconnect the electrical connector (1) from the APP sensor, then remove the mounting nuts (2)

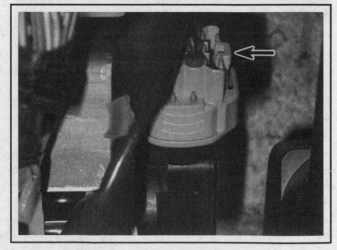

3.2b To disconnect the electrical connector from the APP sensor, depress this release tab

4   Camshaft Position (CMP) sensor - replacement

2003 THROUGH 2006 G35 SEDANS AND 350Z MODELS AND ALL G35 COUPES

▶ **Refer to illustrations 4.2a and 4.2b**

➡**Note:** The CMP sensors are located on the rear ends of the cylinder heads. On 2005 and 2006 G35 Sedans and 350Z models with manual transmissions and on 2005 and later G35 Coupes you will also find the Exhaust Valve Timing (EVT) control position sensors in this same spot. Do not confuse a CMP sensor with an EVT control position sensor. The CMP sensors are the inner sensors (nearer the intake manifold); the EVT control position sensors are the outer units (nearer the exhaust manifolds).

1   If you're replacing the CMP sensor for the left cylinder head on a 2003 through 2006 model, remove the upper half of the intake manifold plenum (see Chapter 2A). If you're replacing the CMP sensor for the left head on a 2007 or later model, remove the intake manifold plenum (see Chapter 2A). You should be able to access the CMP sensor on the right cylinder head without removing these components, but if you need more room then you'll have to remove the same parts.

2   Disconnect the electrical connector from the CMP sensor (see illustrations).

3   Remove the sensor mounting bolt and remove the CMP sensor.

❋❋ **CAUTION:**

If you're removing the CMP sensor for any reason other than replacement, and intend to reuse the same CMP sensor, be extremely careful how you handle the sensor. Do not drop it and don't allow metal particles to adhere to the magnetic tip of the sensor, or place the sensor near a source of magnetism.

4   Remove and replace the old CMP sensor O-ring. Whether you're installing the old CMP sensor or a new unit, be sure to use a new O-ring.

5   Installation is the reverse of removal.

2007 AND LATER G35 SEDANS AND 350Z MODELS

➡**Note:** The CMP sensors are located on top and at the rear of the valve covers. On 2007 and later G35 Sedans and 350Z models, you will also find the Exhaust Valve Timing (EVT) control position sensors in this same location. Do not confuse a CMP sensor with an EVT control position sensor, which looks virtually identical, and is located next to it. The CMP sensors are the inner sensors (nearer the intake manifold); the EVT control position sensors are the outer units (nearer the exhaust manifolds).

6   Remove the engine cover.

7   Remove the air intake duct (see *Air filter housing - removal and installation* in Chapter 4).

8   Remove the intake manifold plenum (see Chapter 2A).

9   Disconnect the electrical connector from the CMP sensor.

10 Remove the CMP sensor mounting bolt and remove the CMP sensor.

❋❋ **CAUTION:**

If you're removing the CMP sensor for any reason other than replacement, and intend to reuse the same CMP sensor, be extremely careful how you handle the sensor. Do not drop it and don't allow metal particles to adhere to the magnetic tip of the sensor, or place the sensor near a source of magnetism.

11 Remove and replace the old CMP sensor O-ring. Whether you're installing the old CMP sensor or a new unit, be sure to use a new O-ring.

12 Installation is the reverse of removal.

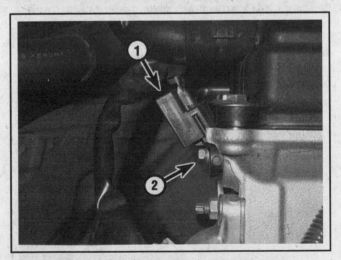

4.2a To remove the left CMP sensor, push the release tab (1) down, and simultaneously pull up on the electrical connector, then remove the sensor mounting bolt (2). Note: This view is from the right side of the engine (it's more easily accessible from the right)

4.2b To remove the right CMP sensor, push the release tab (1) in (it's on the underside of the connector), and simultaneously pull back on the electrical connector, then remove the sensor mounting bolt (2)

5 Crankshaft Position (CKP) sensor - replacement

▶ **Refer to illustration 5.2**

➡ **Note:** The CKP sensor is located on the lower left front edge of the transmission bellhousing.

1 Raise the front end of the vehicle and place it securely on jackstands.

2 Disconnect the electrical connector from the CKP sensor (see illustration).

3 Remove the CKP sensor mounting bolt and remove the sensor from the transmission bellhousing.

✳✳ CAUTION:

If you are simply removing (rather than replacing) the CKP sensor, and therefore intend to reuse the same CKP sensor, be extremely careful how you handle the sensor. Do not drop it and don't allow metal particles to adhere to the magnetic tip of the sensor or place the sensor near a source of magnetism.

4 Installation is the reverse of removal.

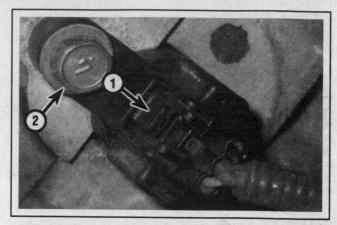

5.2 To disconnect the electrical connector from the CKP sensor, depress the release tab (1). To remove the CKP sensor from the transmission bellhousing, remove the sensor mounting bolt (2)

6 Engine Coolant Temperature (ECT) sensor - replacement

▶ **Refer to illustrations 6.2 and 6.4**

✳✳ WARNING:

Wait until the engine is completely cool before beginning this procedure.

➡ **Note:** The ECT sensor is located on the coolant crossover pipe, which is located at the rear of the engine and is bolted to the rear ends of the two cylinder heads. On 2003 through 2006 G35 Sedans and 350Z models and all G35 Coupes, the ECT sensor is located behind the right cylinder head, near the flange where the crossover pipe is bolted to the right cylinder head. On 2007 and later G35 Sedans and 350Z models, the coolant crossover pipe is slightly different in appearance than the pipe used on earlier models, and the ECT sensor is located at the left end of the crossover pipe, near the flange where the crossover pipe bolts to the left cylinder head.

1 Partially drain the cooling system, to a level that's slightly below the cylinder heads (see Chapter 1).

2 Disconnect the electrical connector from the ECT sensor (see illustration).

3 Using a deep socket, unscrew the ECT sensor from the coolant crossover pipe.

4 To prevent leakage and thread corrosion, wrap the threads of the ECT sensor with Teflon sealing tape (see illustration) before installing the sensor. (Seal the sensor threads whether you're installing the old sensor or a new unit.)

5 Installation is otherwise the reverse of removal. Be sure to tighten the ECT sensor to the torque listed in this Chapter's Specifications.

6 Refill the cooling system (see Chapter 1).

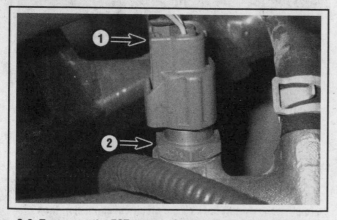

6.2 To remove the ECT sensor, depress the release tab (1) and disconnect the electrical connector, then unscrew the ECT sensor (2) from the coolant crossover pipe

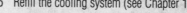
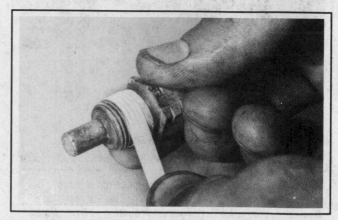

6.4 Before installing the ECT sensor, be sure to wrap the threads of the sensor with Teflon tape to prevent leaks and thread corrosion

7   Fuel Tank Temperature (FTT) sensor - replacement

The FTT sensor is an integral component of the fuel pump/fuel level sensor module. To replace it, you have to replace the fuel pump/fuel level sensor module (see Chapter 4).

8   Intake Air Temperature (IAT) sensor - replacement

The IAT sensor is an integral component of the Mass Air Flow (MAF) sensor. See Section 10.

9   Knock sensor - replacement

♦ **Refer to illustration 9.4**

➡ **Note:** The knock sensor is located on top of the block, in the valley between the cylinder heads, underneath the intake manifold. On 2007 and later G35 Sedans and 350Z models, there are two knock sensors, and both of them are in this same area.

1   Remove the intake manifold plenum assembly (see Chapter 2A).

2   Remove the fuel rail and fuel injector assembly (see Chapter 4).

3   Remove the intake manifold (see Chapter 2A).

4   Disconnect the electrical connector from the knock sensor (see illustration).

5   Remove the knock sensor mounting bolt and remove the knock sensor.

6   Installation is the reverse of removal. Be sure to tighten the knock sensor mounting bolt to the torque listed in this Chapter's Specifications.

✳✳ CAUTION:

Over- or under-tightening the knock sensor mounting bolt(s) will affect knock sensor performance, which might affect the PCM's spark control ability.

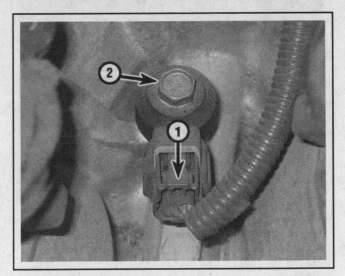

9.4 To remove the knock sensor, depress the release tab (1) and disconnect the electrical connector, then remove the knock sensor retaining bolt (2) and pull the sensor out of the block

10 Mass Air Flow/Intake Air Temperature (MAF/IAT) sensor - replacement

2003 THROUGH 2006 G35 SEDANS AND 350Z MODELS AND ALL G35 COUPES

▶ **Refer to illustrations 10.2 and 10.4**

➡ Note: The MAF/IAT sensor is located on the air filter housing.

1   Disconnect the air intake duct from the MAF/IAT sensor and from the air intake resonator, then remove it (see *Air filter housing - removal and installation* in Chapter 4).

2   Disconnect the electrical connector from the MAF/IAT sensor (see illustration).

3   Remove the air filter housing cover (see *Air filter replacement* in Chapter 1).

4   Remove the MAF/IAT sensor from the air filter housing cover (see illustration).

5   Installation is the reverse of removal.

2007 AND LATER G35 SEDANS AND 350Z MODELS

➡ Note: There are two MAF/IAT sensors. They're located on the air filter housings in the same spot as the single MAF/IAT sensor used on earlier models. And unlike the earlier MAF/IAT sensor, either sensor can be removed without removing the air filter housing cover.

6   Disconnect the electrical connector from the MAF/IAT sensor.

7   Remove the MAF/IAT sensor mounting bolt and pull the sensor out of the air filter housing cover.

8   Installation is the reverse of removal.

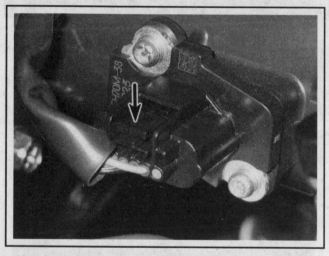

10.2 To disconnect the electrical connector from the MAF sensor, depress this release tab (2003 through 2006 G35 Sedans and 350Z models, and 2003 and later G35 Coupes)

10.4 To remove the MAF sensor from the air filter housing cover, remove these four bolts (2003 through 2006 G35 Sedans and 350Z models and all G35 Coupes)

11 Oxygen sensors - description and replacement

DESCRIPTION

1   An oxygen sensor is a galvanic battery. Unburned oxygen in the exhaust reacts with elements inside the oxygen sensor to produce a voltage output that varies from 0.1 volt (high oxygen, lean mixture) to 0.9 volt (low oxygen, rich mixture). The upstream oxygen sensors, which are located on the exhaust manifolds, ahead of the catalytic converters, provide feedback signals to the PCM that indicate the amount of leftover oxygen in the exhaust. The PCM monitors this variable voltage to determine the correct fuel injector pulse width (the duration of the

time interval during which each injector sprays fuel) required to support complete combustion. A mixture ratio of 14.7 parts air to 1 part fuel is the ideal ratio for complete combustion and minimum exhaust emissions, as well as the best combination for fuel economy and engine performance. Using the input signals from the oxygen sensors, the PCM tries to maintain this air/fuel ratio of 14.7:1 at all times.

2   The downstream sensors, which are mounted on the catalytic converters, are identical to the upstream sensors and operate in the same way. But the downstream oxygen sensors have no effect on PCM control of the air/fuel ratio. Instead, the PCM uses the downstream

oxygen sensor signals to monitor the efficiency of the catalytic converters. Downstream oxygen sensors produce an output voltage signal that fluctuates more slowly, which reflects the lower oxygen content of the catalyzed exhaust gases. As a catalyst ages, its efficiency diminishes and the signal produced by a downstream oxygen sensor starts to fall outside the expected range. The PCM uses this degraded signal to calculate and predict failure of the catalytic converter.

3   There are four oxygen sensors on all models covered by this manual. The two upstream sensors (1/1 and 2/1) are located on the exhaust manifolds and the downstream sensors (1/2 and 2/2) are located on the catalytic converters.

4   An oxygen sensor produces no voltage when it is below its normal operating temperature of about 600-degrees F. During this warm-up period, the PCM operates in an open-loop fuel control mode. It does not use the oxygen sensor signal as a feedback indication of residual oxygen in the exhaust. Instead, the PCM controls fuel metering based on the inputs of other sensors and its own programs.

5   An oxygen sensor depends on four conditions in order to operate correctly:

   a) *Electrical* - *The low voltage generated by the sensor requires good, clean connections. Always check the connectors whenever an oxygen sensor problem is suspected or indicated.*

   b) *Outside air supply* - *The sensor needs air circulation to the internal portion of the sensor. Whenever the sensor is installed, make sure that the air passages are not restricted.*

   c) *Correct operating temperature* - *The PCM will not react to the sensor signal until the sensor reaches approximately 600-degrees F. This factor must be considered when evaluating the performance of the sensor.*

   d) *Unleaded fuel* - *Unleaded fuel is essential for correct sensor operation.*

6   The PCM can detect several different oxygen sensor problems and set Diagnostic Trouble Codes (DTCs) to indicate the specific fault (see Section 2). When an oxygen sensor DTC occurs, the PCM disregards the oxygen sensor signal voltage and reverts to open-loop fuel control as described previously.

REPLACEMENT

✱✱ WARNING:

Be careful not to burn yourself during the following procedure.

➡**Note: Since the exhaust pipe contracts when cool, the oxygen sensor may be difficult to unscrew. To make sensor removal easier, start the engine and let it run for a minute or two, then turn it off.**

Upstream oxygen sensors

▸ **Refer to illustrations 11.7a, 11.7b, 11.7c, 11.7d and 11.9**

➡**Note: The upstream oxygen sensors are located on the exhaust manifolds, right above the flanges. The connectors for the upstream sensors are located in the engine compartment, but the upstream sensors are more easily accessed from underneath the vehicle.**

7   Using a flashlight, locate the upstream oxygen sensor that you want to replace, then trace the sensor's lead up to the electrical connector in the engine compartment, flip open the lock and disconnect it (see illustrations).

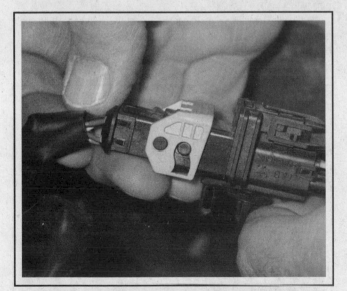

11.7a Trace the electrical lead from the left upstream oxygen sensor up to the connector in the engine compartment . . .

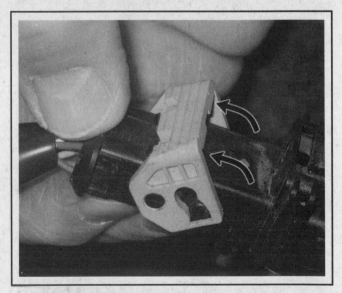

11.7b . . . flip open the lock . . .

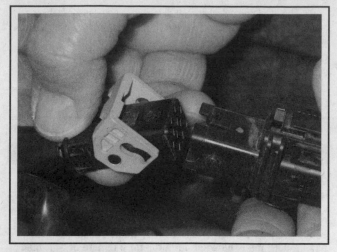

11.7c . . . and disconnect the two halves of the connector

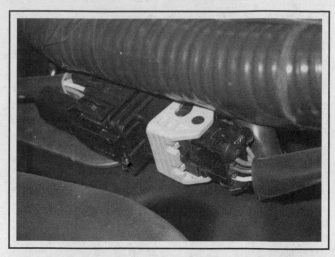

11.7d Trace the lead from the right upstream oxygen sensor up to its connector, then disconnect the two halves of the connector (see illustrations 11.7b and 11.7c)

8 Raise the front of the vehicle and place it securely on jackstands.

9 Locate the upstream oxygen sensor that you're going to remove or replace (see illustration). Ideally, if there's enough room, you should use an oxygen sensor socket to remove an oxygen sensor. On some models there isn't enough room to use a socket-style oxygen sensor socket, though you might be able to use the type that employs a shallower socket. The larger style oxygen sensor sockets are available at most auto parts stores; oxygen sensor sockets with a shallower socket are generally available only from specialty tool suppliers.

10 If you're installing the old sensor, clean off the threads, then apply a coat of anti-seize compound (such as Loctite® 771-64 or a suitable equivalent) to the threads before installing the sensor. If you're installing a new sensor, do NOT apply anti-seize compound; new sensors are already coated with anti-seize.

11 Installation is otherwise the reverse of removal. Be sure to tighten the oxygen sensor to the torque listed in this Chapter's Specifications.

Downstream oxygen sensors

▶ **Refer to illustrations 11.13 and 11.14**

➡ **Note: The downstream oxygen sensors are located on the catalytic converters.**

12 Raise the vehicle and place it securely on jackstands.

13 Locate the downstream sensor that you want to replace (see illustration), then trace the sensor's electrical lead to the sensor electrical connector and disconnect it.

14 Remove the downstream sensor with an oxygen sensor socket (see illustration), if you have one, or use a wrench, if you don't.

15 Clean the threads inside the sensor mounting hole in the exhaust pipe with a tap.

16 If you're installing the old sensor, clean off the threads, then apply a coat of anti-seize compound (such as Loctite® 771-64 or a suitable equivalent) to the threads before installing the sensor. If you're install-

11.9 The left upstream oxygen sensor (shown) is screwed into the left exhaust manifold; the right upstream oxygen sensor (not shown) is screwed into the right exhaust manifold at the same spot

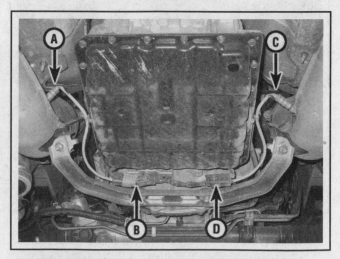

11.13 Left downstream oxygen sensor (A) and electrical connector (B); right downstream oxygen sensor (C) and electrical connector (D)

ing a new sensor, do NOT apply anti-seize compound; new sensors are already coated with anti-seize.

17 Installation is otherwise the reverse of removal. Be sure to tighten the oxygen sensor to the torque listed in this Chapter's Specifications.

All sensors

18 Disconnect the cable from the negative terminal of the battery and leave it disconnected for a couple of minutes (see Chapter 5, Section 1). This will erase the old operating values that the Powertrain Control Module (PCM) has learned, allowing it to learn the characteristics of the new sensor. (If this isn't done, the vehicle may exhibit driveability problems.)

➡Note: Whenever the battery is disconnected, operating parameters stored in the Powertrain Control Module (PCM) might be lost, which might cause the engine to run rough for a period of time while the PCM relearns the information.

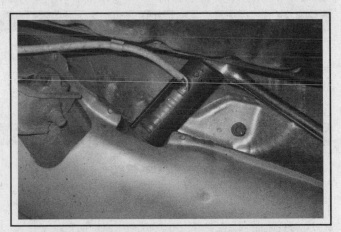

11.14 Use an oxygen sensor socket to remove a downstream oxygen sensor (left downstream sensor shown)

12 Park Neutral Position (PNP) switch - replacement

The PNP switch is an integral component of the valve body inside the automatic transmission. If the PNP switch must be replaced, have it done by a dealer service department or a qualified automatic transmission shop.

13 Power Steering Pressure (PSP) sensor - replacement

▶ **Refer to illustrations 13.3 and 13.4**

➡**Note: The PSP sensor is located on the high-pressure power steering fluid line at the power steering pump, which is located on the right side of the engine, directly above the alternator.**

1   Raise the front of the vehicle and place it securely on jackstands.

2   Locate the PSP sensor on the right upper side of the power steering pump

3   Disconnect the electrical connector from the PSP sensor (see illustration).

4   Unscrew the PSP sensor (see illustration). Be prepared for fluid spillage.

5   Installation is the reverse of removal. Check the power steering fluid level, adding as necessary to bring it to the appropriate level (see Chapter 1).

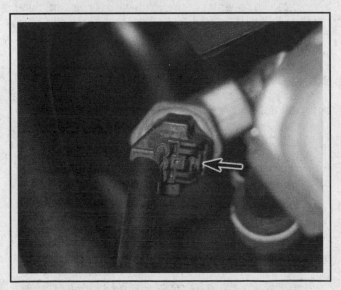

13.3 To disconnect the electrical connector from the PSP switch, depress this release tab and pull the connector off

13.4 Use a wrench or deep socket to unscrew the PSP switch

14 Transmission speed sensors - replacement

The speed sensors are located inside the transmission, on the valve body. Replacing a transmission speed sensor is a job for a dealer service department or a professional automatic transmission specialist.

15 Powertrain Control Module (PCM) - removal and installation

The PCM is located under the right part of the instrument panel, near the blower motor housing for the heating and air conditioning system. You can remove the blower motor and other components in this area, and even the entire instrument panel, without disturbing or even disconnecting the PCM. To avoid problems with the PCM, we recommend that you leave it alone. If you ever see a Diagnostic Trouble Code (DTC) that indicates a problem with the PCM, have it replaced by a dealer. A new PCM must be programmed with a factory scan tool by a dealership service department, so even if you were to replace the old PCM with a new unit, it wouldn't work until the vehicle was towed to a dealer for programming.

16 Catalytic converter - description, check and replacement

→ **Note: Because of a Federally mandated extended warranty which covers emission-related components such as the catalytic converter, check with a dealer service department before replacing the converter at your own expense.**

GENERAL DESCRIPTION

♦ **Refer to illustration 16.2**

1 A catalytic converter (or catalyst) is an emission control device in the exhaust system that reduces certain pollutants in the exhaust gas stream. There are two types of converters. An oxidation catalyst reduces hydrocarbons (HC) and carbon monoxide (CO). A reduction catalyst reduces oxides of nitrogen (NOx). A catalyst that can reduce all three pollutants is known as a "Three-Way Catalyst" (TWC).

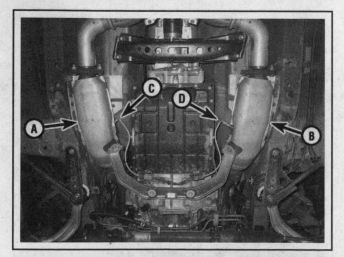

16.2 The catalytic converters (A and B) are located under the vehicle, between the exhaust manifolds and the Y-pipe that connects them to the rest of the exhaust system. Before removing the catalytic converters, be sure to remove the oxygen sensors (C and D)

2 All models covered by this manual are equipped with two catalysts (see illustration), one below each exhaust manifold flange. The upper end of each catalyst has a short inlet pipe with a mounting flange that bolts to the exhaust manifold flange. The lower end of each catalyst has a short outlet pipe with a flange that bolts to the Y-pipe that connects the two catalysts to the remainder of the exhaust system.

CHECK

3 The test equipment for a catalytic converter (a loaded-mode dynamometer and a 5-gas analyzer) is expensive. If you suspect that the converter on your vehicle is malfunctioning, take it to a dealer or authorized emission inspection facility for diagnosis and repair.

4 Whenever you raise the vehicle to service underbody components, inspect the converter for leaks, corrosion, dents and other damage. Carefully inspect the welds and/or flange bolts and nuts that attach the front and rear ends of the converter to the exhaust system. If you note any damage, replace the converter.

5 Although catalytic converters don't break too often, they can become restricted or even plugged up. The easiest way to check for a restricted converter is to use a vacuum gauge to diagnose the effect of a blocked exhaust on intake vacuum.

   a) Connect a vacuum gauge to an intake manifold vacuum source (see Chapter 2A).
   b) Warm the engine to operating temperature, place the transaxle in PARK (automatic transmission) or NEUTRAL (manual transmission) and apply the parking brake.
   c) Note the vacuum reading at idle and write it down.
   d) Quickly open the throttle to near its wide-open position, then quickly get off the throttle and allow it to close. Note the vacuum reading and write it down.
   e) Do this test three more times, recording your measurement after each test.
   f) If your fourth reading is more than one in-Hg lower than the reading that you noted at idle, the exhaust system might be restricted (the catalytic converter could be plugged, OR an exhaust pipe or muffler could be restricted).

16.7a To disconnect the upper end of either catalyst from the exhaust manifold, remove these three nuts. Before trying to remove the nuts, spray some penetrating oil onto the threads of the flange studs and give it some time to loosen things up

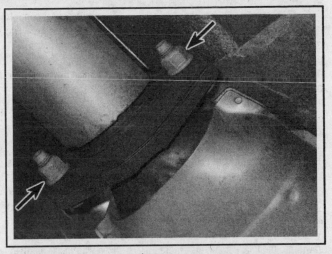

16.7b To disconnect the lower end of either catalyst from the Y-pipe flange, remove these three nuts. Again, if the nuts are tight, spray the threads of the flange studs with penetrant and wait awhile, then try again

REPLACEMENT

▶ **Refer to illustrations 16.7a and 16.7b.**

❊❊ WARNING:

Make sure that the exhaust system is completely cooled down before proceeding. If the vehicle has just been driven, the catalytic converter can be hot enough to cause serious burns.

6 Raise the vehicle and place it securely on jackstands.
7 Spray a liberal amount of penetrating oil onto the threads of the catalyst-to-exhaust manifold studs and on the threads of the clamp bolt nut that connects the catalyst outlet pipe to the rest of the exhaust system. Also spray some penetrant on the two bolts and nuts that secure the small bracket between the two catalyst outlet pipes (see illustrations). Wait awhile for the penetrant to loosen things up.

8 While you're waiting for the penetrant to do its work, disconnect the electrical connector for the downstream oxygen sensor and remove the downstream oxygen sensor (see Section 11).

9 Unscrew the upper and lower catalyst mounting nuts. Once the nuts are removed, remove the catalytic converter. Remove and discard the old flange gaskets.

10 Installation is the reverse of removal. Be sure to use new flange gaskets and replace any damaged fasteners. Tighten the nuts securely.

17 Evaporative emissions control (EVAP) system - description and component replacement

GENERAL DESCRIPTION

1 The Evaporative Emissions Control (EVAP) system prevents fuel system vapors (which contain unburned hydrocarbons) from escaping into the atmosphere. On warm days, vapors trapped inside the fuel tank expand. When the pressure reaches a certain threshold, these vapors are routed from the fuel tank through the fuel vapor vent valve and the fuel vapor control valve to the EVAP canister, where they're stored temporarily, until they can be consumed by the engine during normal operation. Under certain conditions (engine warmed up, vehicle up to speed, moderate or heavy loads, etc.) the Powertrain Control Module (PCM) opens the canister purge solenoid, which allows intake vacuum to pull fuel vapors from the EVAP canister into the intake manifold, where they mix with the air/fuel mixture before being consumed in the combustion chambers. This system is complex and virtually impossible to troubleshoot without the right tools and training. However, the following description should give you a good idea of how the system works and where the components are located:

2 **EVAP canister -** The canister, which contains activated charcoal, is the repository for storing fuel vapors produced by gasoline as it heats up inside the fuel tank. You'll have to raise the vehicle to inspect or replace the canister, but the canister is designed to be maintenance-free and should last the life of the vehicle. The EVAP canister is located in the right rear corner of the vehicle, above the right rear wheel. You'll have to raise the vehicle and remove the small splash shield behind the right rear wheel to access the EVAP canister.

3 **EVAP control system pressure sensor -** The pressure sensor monitors the pressure of evaporative gases inside the purge line to the intake manifold, which is determined by the vapor pressure inside the fuel tank, the EVAP hoses between the fuel tank and the EVAP canister and the canister itself. The pressure sensor sends a voltage signal to the PCM that increases as the pressure increases. When the signal reaches a specified threshold, the PCM energizes the EVAP canister purge solenoid, which allows the evaporative emissions to be drawn into the intake manifold. The EVAP system pressure sensor is located on the purge line at the EVAP canister.

4 **EVAP canister vent control valve** - The canister vent control valve, which is used only for diagnosis of the EVAP system, is normally open. Under normal conditions the canister vent is open. When energized by the PCM, the canister vent closes, which depressurizes the EVAP system and enables the PCM to diagnose other components in the EVAP system. The vent control solenoid is located on the EVAP canister.

5 **EVAP canister purge solenoid** - The EVAP canister purge solenoid is a PCM-controlled solenoid that controls the purging of evaporative emissions from the EVAP canister to the intake manifold. The EVAP purge solenoid is never turned on during cold start warm-ups or during hot start time delays. But once the engine reaches a specified temperature and enters closed-loop operation the PCM energizes the canister purge solenoid under certain open-throttle operating conditions (acceleration, high speed cruising, etc.). When the solenoid is energized by the PCM, it allows fuel vapors stored in the EVAP canister to be drawn into the intake manifold, where they're mixed with intake air, then burned along with the normal air/fuel mixture. The PCM regulates the flow rate of the vapors by controlling the pulse-width of the solenoid (the length of time during which the solenoid is turned on) in accordance with operating conditions. The EVAP canister purge solenoid is located on the intake manifold.

GENERAL SYSTEM CHECKS

.6 The most common symptom of a faulty EVAP system is a strong fuel odor (particularly during hot weather). If you smell fuel while driving or (more likely) right after you park the vehicle and turn off the engine, check the fuel filler cap first. Make sure that it's screwed onto the fuel filler neck all the way.

7 If the odor persists, inspect all EVAP hose connections, both in the engine compartment and under the vehicle. You'll have to raise the vehicle and place it securely on jackstands to inspect most of the EVAP system, since it's located under the vehicle. Be sure to inspect each hose attached to the canister for damage and leakage along its entire length. Repair or replace as necessary. Inspect the canister for damage and look for fuel leaking from the bottom. If fuel is leaking or the canister is otherwise damaged, replace it.

8 Poor idle, stalling, and poor driveability can be caused by a defective fuel vapor vent valve or canister purge solenoid, a damaged canister, cracked hoses, or hoses connected to the wrong tubes. Fuel loss or fuel odor can be caused by fuel leaking from fuel lines or hoses, a cracked or damaged canister, or a defective vapor valve.

COMPONENT REPLACEMENT

EVAP canister purge solenoid

▶ Refer to illustrations 17.9 and 17.11

➡Note: The EVAP canister purge solenoid is located in the right rear corner of the engine compartment, on a small bracket attached to the right strut tower.

9 Disconnect the electrical connector from the EVAP canister purge solenoid (see illustration).

10 Clearly label the EVAP hoses, then disconnect them from the EVAP canister purge solenoid.

11 To detach the EVAP canister purge solenoid from its mounting bracket, remove the mounting nut (see illustration).

12 Installation is the reverse of removal.

17.9 Depress the release tab (1) and disconnect the electrical connector from the EVAP canister purge solenoid, then clearly label and disconnect the two EVAP hoses (2) from the solenoid

17.11 To detach the EVAP canister purge solenoid from its mounting bracket, remove this nut

EVAP canister, EVAP canister vent control valve and EVAP control system pressure sensor assembly

▶ Refer to illustrations 17.14, 17.15, 17.18 and 17.19

➡Note: The EVAP canister/EVAP canister vent control valve/ EVAP control system pressure sensor assembly is located behind the right rear wheel well, above a small splash shield, on 2003 through 2006 G35 Sedans, on 2003 through 2006 G35 Coupes and on all 350Z models. On 2007 and later G35 Sedans, the canister is still located under the back of the vehicle, but is in the center instead of behind the right rear wheel. The photos accompanying this Section depict the EVAP canister assembly on a 2004 G35 Sedan, but the components and replacement procedures are essentially the same on all models.

13 Loosen the right rear wheel lug nuts, raise the vehicle and place it securely on jackstands.

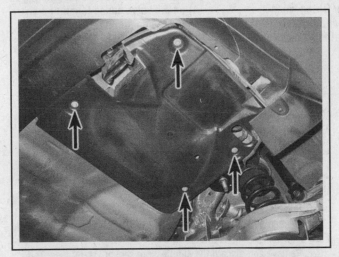

17.14 To detach the EVAP canister splash shield, remove these bolts

17.18 To remove the EVAP canister, remove this bolt . . .

14 Remove the small splash shield that protects the EVAP canister (see illustration).

15 Disconnect the EVAP canister vent hose and electrical connector from the EVAP canister vent control valve (see illustration).

16 Disconnect the fuel tank evaporative emissions hose and the canister purge hose from the EVAP canister.

17 Disconnect the electrical connector from the EVAP control system pressure sensor.

18 Remove the EVAP canister mounting bolt (see illustration).

19 Disengage the EVAP canister mounting tab from its slot (see illustration) and remove the EVAP canister.

20 Installation is the reverse of removal.

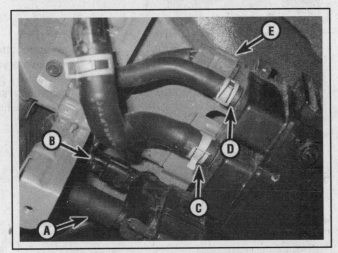

17.15 Disconnect the following parts from the EVAP canister:

A *Disconnect the EVAP canister vent hose from the canister vent control valve*
B *Disconnect the electrical connector from the vent control valve (easier to disconnect after lowering canister)*
C *Disconnect the fuel tank evaporative emissions hose from the EVAP canister*
D *Disconnect the EVAP canister purge hose from the EVAP canister*
E *Disconnect the electrical connector from the EVAP control system pressure sensor (easier to disconnect after lowering canister)*

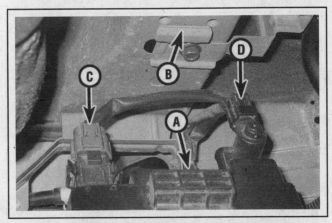

17.19 . . . lower the rear end of the canister and disengage the tab (A) from its mounting slot (B). Depress the tab (C) to detach the connector from the vent control valve, then depress tab (D) to disconnect the connector from the control system pressure sensor

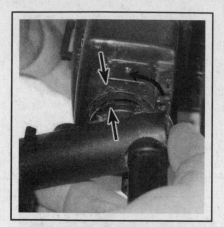

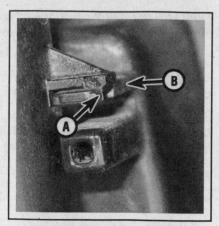

17.22 To remove the vent control valve from the EVAP canister, rotate it counterclockwise and align the boss on the control valve with the boss on the canister, then pull out the valve

17.23 Remove the old O-ring from the vent control valve and discard it. Always use a new O-ring when installing the vent control valve whether you're installing a new valve or the old unit

17.24 When installing the vent control valve, make sure that the lug (A) on the valve snaps together with the lug (B) on the EVAP canister

EVAP canister vent control valve

♦ Refer to illustrations 17.22, 17.23 and 17.24

➡Note: The EVAP canister vent control valve is located on the EVAP canister.

21 Remove the EVAP canister (see Steps 13 through 19).

22 Rotate the vent control valve counterclockwise, align the boss on the valve with the boss on the EVAP canister (see illustration) and remove the valve from the canister.

23 Remove the vent control valve O-ring (see illustration) and discard it. Do NOT reuse the old O-ring.

24 Install a new O-ring on the vent control valve, insert the valve into the EVAP canister, align the lugs on the valve and the canister (see illustration 17.22) and turn it clockwise until the locking lugs on the valve and the canister snap together (see illustration).

25 Installation is otherwise the reverse of removal.

EVAP control system pressure sensor

♦ Refer to illustration 17.27a and 17.27b

➡Note: The EVAP control system pressure sensor is located on the EVAP canister.

26 Remove the EVAP canister (see Steps 13 through 19).

27 Unsnap and remove the control system pressure sensor from the EVAP canister (see illustrations).

28 Remove and discard the old pressure sensor O-ring (see illustration 7.27b).

29 Install a new O-ring on the pressure sensor and insert the pressure sensor into its mounting hole in the EVAP canister.

30 Installation is otherwise the reverse of removal

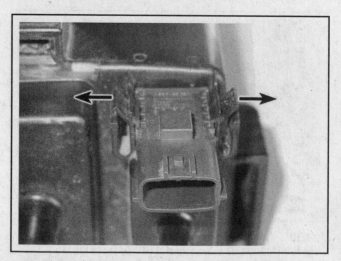

17.27a To disengage the control system pressure sensor from the EVAP canister, spread these two locking tangs apart . . .

17.27b . . . then pull the sensor straight up. Be sure to remove and discard the old sensor O-ring

18 Positive Crankcase Ventilation (PCV) system - description and check

DESCRIPTION

▶ **Refer to illustrations 18.2a, 18.2b, 18.2c, 18.3a, 18.3b, 18.4a and 18.4b**

1   The Positive Crankcase Ventilation (PCV) system reduces hydrocarbon emissions by scavenging crankcase vapors, which are rich in unburned hydrocarbons. A PCV valve regulates the flow of gases into the intake manifold in proportion to the amount of intake vacuum available. At idle, when intake vacuum is very high, the PCV valve restricts the flow of vapors so that the engine doesn't run poorly. As the throttle plate opens and intake vacuum begins to diminish, the PCV valve opens more to allow vapors to flow more freely.

2   The PCV system consists of the fresh air inlet hose, the PCV valve and the crankcase ventilation hose (or PCV hose). The fresh air inlet hose connects the air intake duct to a pipe on the back end of the left valve cover (see illustrations). The crankcase ventilation hose (or PCV hose) connects the PCV valve in the right valve cover to the intake manifold (see illustration).

3   The PCV valve (see illustration) is screwed into the top of right valve cover. To remove it, simply unscrew it. Anytime you remove the PCV valve, check the O-ring (see illustration), replacing it if necessary.

4   There is also a PCV breather hose (see illustration) that connects the two valve covers. This hose is routed between a pair of pipes on the valve covers (see illustration).

18.2a The PCV fresh air inlet hose connects this pipe on the air intake duct . . .

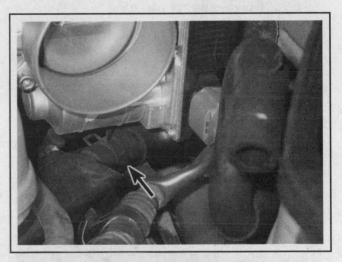

18.2b . . . to a pipe on the back end of the left valve cover, below the throttle body

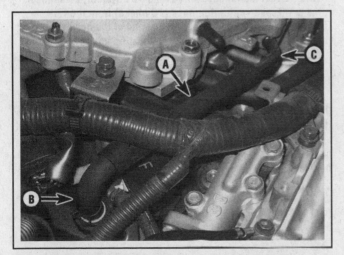

18.2c The crankcase ventilation hose (or PCV hose) (A) connects the PCV valve (A) on the right valve cover to a pipe (C) on the intake manifold

18.3a The PCV valve is screwed into the top of the right valve cover. To remove it, simply unscrew it . . .

18.3b . . . then check the PCV valve O-ring

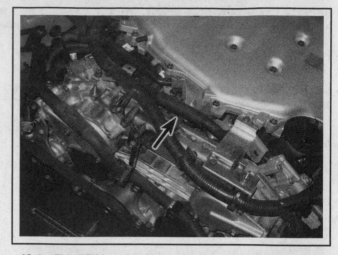

18.4a This PCV breather hose, which connects the two valve covers . . .

18.4b . . . is routed between these two pipes on the valve covers (intake manifold plenum removed for clarity)

18.8 To test the functionality of the PCV system, disconnect the crankcase ventilation hose (PCV hose) from the PCV valve, start the engine and plug the end of the hose with your thumb. You should feel suction, indicating intake manifold vacuum

INSPECTION

▶ **Refer to illustration 18.8**

5   An engine that is operated without a properly functioning crankcase ventilation system can be damaged. So anytime you're servicing the engine, be sure to inspect the PCV system hose(s) for cracks, tears, deterioration and other damage. Disconnect the hose(s) and inspect it/them for damage and obstructions. If a hose is clogged, clean it out. If you're unable to clean it satisfactorily, replace it.

6   A plugged PCV hose might cause any or all of the following conditions: A rough idle, stalling or a slow idle speed, oil leaks or sludge in the engine. So if the engine is running roughly, stalling and idling at a lower than normal speed, is losing oil, has oil in the throttle body or air intake manifold plenum, or has a build-up of sludge, a PCV system hose might be clogged. Repair or replace the hose(s) as necessary.

7   A leaking PCV hose might cause any or all of the following conditions: a rough idle, stalling or a high idle speed. So if the engine is running roughly, stalling and/or idling at a higher-than-normal speed, a PCV system hose might be leaking. Repair or replace the hose(s) as necessary.

8   Here's an easy functional check of the PCV system on a vehicle with a fresh air inlet hose and a crankcase ventilation hose with a PCV valve in it:

a) *Start the engine and let it warm up to its normal idle.*

b) *Disconnect the crankcase ventilation hose (PCV hose) from the PCV valve.*

c) *Plug the end of the PCV hose with your thumb (see illustration) and verify that there is vacuum. If there is no vacuum, look for a plugged hose or a clogged port or pipe on the intake manifold. Also look for a hose that collapses when it's blocked (that is, when vacuum is applied). Replace clogged or deteriorated hoses.*

d) *Remove the engine oil dipstick and install a vacuum gauge in the dipstick hole.*

e) *Pinch off or plug the PCV system's fresh air inlet hose.*

f) *Run the engine at 1500 rpm for 30 seconds, then read the vacuum gauge while the engine is running at 1500 rpm.*

g) *If there's vacuum present, the crankcase ventilation system is operating correctly.*

h) *If there's NO vacuum present, the engine might be drawing in outside air. The PCV system won't function correctly unless the engine is a sealed system. Inspect the valve cover(s), oil pan gasket or other sealing areas for leaks.*

i) *If the vacuum gauge indicates positive pressure, look for a plugged hose or suspect engine blow-by.*

9   If the PCV system is functioning correctly, but there's evidence of engine oil in the throttle body or air filter housing, it could be caused by excessive crankcase pressure. Have the crankcase pressure tested by a dealer service department.

10   In the PCV system, excessive blow-by (caused by worn rings, pistons and/or cylinders, or by constant heavy loads) is discharged into the intake manifold and consumed. If you discover heavy sludge deposits or a dilution of the engine oil, even though the PCV system is functioning correctly, look for other causes (see *Troubleshooting* and Chapter 2B) and correct them as soon as possible.

19 Intake Valve Timing (IVT) control system - description and component replacement

DESCRIPTION

▶ **Refer to illustration 19.4**

1   The Intake Valve Timing (IVT) control system improves engine torque in the low-to-mid-speed range and increases horsepower at higher speeds. PCM-controlled Intake Valve Timing (IVT) control solenoid valves (one for each intake camshaft) adjust the opening and closing time of the intake valves to advance or retard the valve angle by redirecting the path and the pressure of oil through the intake camshafts.

2   The PCM uses information sensor inputs - crankshaft position, camshaft position, engine speed and engine coolant temperature - to determine the optimal intake valve angle, then responds with ON/OFF pulse duty signals to the intake valve timing control solenoid valves.

3   The IVT control solenoid valves respond to these pulse duty signals by altering the amount of oil and the direction of flow through the solenoid valves and through the camshafts, or they halt oil flow. A longer pulse width signal from the PCM advances the valve angle; a shorter pulse width retards the valve angle. When the ON and OFF pulse widths are equal, the IVT solenoid valves halt oil pressure flow and the intake valve angle is fixed.

4   On 2003 through 2006 models, the IVT control solenoid valves are mounted on top of the rear timing chain cover (see illustration).

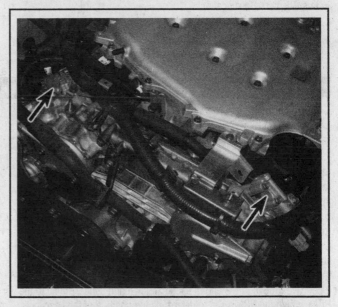

19.4 On 2003 through 2006 models, the Intake Valve Timing (IVT) control solenoid valves are located at the front of the valve covers

5   On 2007 and 2008 models, the IVT control solenoid valves are integral components of the valve timing control covers, which are the small access covers on the front of the timing chain cover (see Chapter 2A).

COMPONENT REPLACEMENT

Intake Valve Timing (IVT) control solenoid valve

♦ Refer to illustration 19.7

➡Note: The intake valve timing control solenoid valves are located on top of the timing chain cover. This procedure applies to either solenoid valve.

6   If there is an engine harness routed over the top of the IVT control solenoid valve, detach the wiring harness clips and set the harness aside to provide enough room to remove the solenoid valve.

7   Disconnect the electrical connector from the IVT control solenoid valve (see illustration).

8   Remove the IVT control solenoid valve mounting bolts and remove the IVT control solenoid valve.

9   Remove the old IVT control solenoid valve gasket and discard it.

10 Installation is the reverse of removal. Be sure to use a NEW gasket whether you're installing the old IVT control solenoid valve or a new unit. Tighten the IVT control solenoid valve mounting bolts to the torque listed in this Chapter's Specifications.

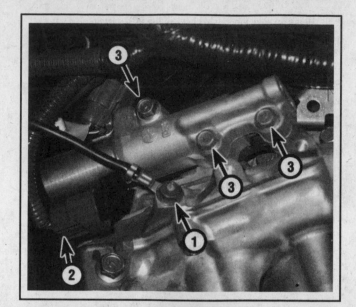

19.7 To remove an Intake Valve Timing (IVT) control solenoid valve:

1   *Disconnect the ground bolt (right IVT control solenoid valve only)*
2   *Depress the release tab and disconnect the electrical connector*
3   *Remove the IVT control solenoid valve mounting bolts*

---

20 Exhaust Valve Timing (EVT) control system - description and component replacement

DESCRIPTION

1   The Exhaust Valve Timing (EVT) control system improves engine torque and horsepower at higher engine speeds. The EVT control system consists of the PCM, a pair of EVT control position sensors and several other information sensors, and a pair of PCM-controlled magnet retarders (one retarder for each exhaust camshaft) to control the opening and closing timing of the exhaust valves.

2   The EVT control position sensors, which are located next to the Camshaft Position (CMP) sensors, are used by the PCM to monitor the position of the camshafts. The EVT control position sensors detect a concave groove in the end of each camshaft and send a signal to the PCM, which the PCM uses to determine the position of the camshafts.

3   The PCM also monitors signals from the Crankshaft Position (CKP) sensor, the Camshaft Position (CMP) sensors, the Engine Coolant Temperature (ECT) sensor and responds by sending ON and OFF pulse duty signals to the EVT control magnet retarders on the front ends of the exhaust camshafts to optimize the position of the camshafts.

COMPONENT REPLACEMENT

EVT control position sensors

2005 and 2006 G35 Sedans and 350Z models with manual transmissions and 2005 and later G35 Coupes with manual transmissions

➡Note: The EVT control position sensors are located on the backs of the cylinder heads, next to the Camshaft Position (CMP) sensors. Do not confuse the two sensors. The CMP sensors are the inner sensors (nearer the intake manifold); the EVT control position sensors are the outer units (nearer the exhaust manifolds).

4   Remove the four engine cover nuts and remove the engine cover.

5   If you're replacing the EVT control position sensor for the left cylinder head, remove the upper half of the intake manifold plenum (see Chapter 2A). You should be able to access the EVT control position sensor on the right cylinder head without removing these components, but if you need more room, you'll have to remove the same parts.

6   Disconnect the electrical connector from the EVT control position sensor.

7   Remove the EVT control position sensor mounting bolt and remove the sensor.

> **✳✳ CAUTION:**
>
> **If you're removing the EVT control position sensor for any reason other than replacement, and intend to reuse the same sensor, be extremely careful how you handle the sensor. Do not drop it and don't allow metal particles to adhere to the magnetic tip of the sensor or place the sensor near a source of magnetism.**

8   Remove and replace the old EVT control position sensor O-ring. Whether you're installing the old sensor or a new unit, be sure to use a new O-ring.

9   Installation is the reverse of removal.

2007 and later G35 Sedans and 350Z models

➡**Note: The EVT control position sensors are located on top and at the rear of the valve covers. Do not confuse an Exhaust Valve Timing (EVT) control position sensor with a CMP sensor, which looks virtually identical, and is located next to it. The CMP sensors are the inner sensors (nearer the intake manifold); the EVT control position sensors are the outer units (nearer the exhaust manifolds).**

10   Remove the engine cover.

11   Remove the air intake duct (see *Air filter housing - removal and installation* in Chapter 4).

12   Remove the intake manifold plenum (see Chapter 2A).

13   Disconnect the electrical connector from the EVT control position sensor.

14   Remove the EVT control position sensor mounting bolt and remove the control position sensor.

> **✳✳ CAUTION:**
>
> **If you're removing the EVT control position sensor for any reason other than replacement, and intend to reuse the same sensor, be extremely careful how you handle the sensor. Do not drop it and don't allow metal particles to adhere to the magnetic tip of the sensor, or place the sensor near a source of magnetism.**

15   Remove and replace the old EVT control position sensor O-ring. Whether you're installing the old sensor or a new unit, be sure to use a new O-ring.

16   Installation is the reverse of removal.

Magnet retarders

17   The magnet retarders are located inside the valve timing control covers. Removing and installing the valve timing control covers is part of the timing chain cover removal procedure (see Chapter 2A).

21   Electric throttle control and Idle Speed Control (ISC) systems - description

1   The electric throttle control and Idle Speed Control (ISC) system consists of the Powertrain Control Module (PCM), the Accelerator Pedal Position (APP) sensor, the electronic throttle body, the Throttle Position (TP) sensors and a number of other engine sensors.

2   The PCM controls the electric throttle control actuator (the throttle body). A motor in the actuator controls the throttle plate in response to commands from the PCM.

3   The PCM also controls the Idle Speed Control (ISC) system, which dispenses with the conventional idle speed control valve or idle speed control motor. Instead, the PCM controls the electric throttle control actuator to maintain the lowest possible idle speed at which the engine can operate smoothly and steadily. This speed varies somewhat in accordance with engine operating conditions such as warm-up, deceleration and engine load, which varies with air conditioning, power steering, cooling fan operation, etc.

4   The electric throttle control actuator (throttle body) is covered in Chapter 4. The Throttle Position (TP) sensors are integrated into the throttle body and cannot be replaced separately.

Torque specifications	Ft-lbs (unless otherwise indicated)	Nm

➡ **Note:** One foot-pound (ft-lb) of torque is equivalent to 12 inch-pounds (in-lbs) of torque. Torque values below approximately 15 ft-lbs are expressed in inch-pounds, since most foot-pound torque wrenches are not accurate at these smaller values.

Engine coolant temperature sensor	18	24.5
Intake Valve Timing (IVT) control solenoid		
valve mounting bolts	96 in-lbs	11.3
Knock sensor mounting bolt	17	23.6
Oxygen sensors		
2003 to 2006 G35 Sedan and 350Z	33	45
2003 to 2007 G35 Coupe	33	45
2007 and 2008 G35 Sedan	36	50

Section

Reference to other Chapters

7A

MANUAL
TRANSAXLE

1 General information

Vehicles covered by this manual are equipped with either a six-speed manual or a five-speed automatic transmission. The TR3650 is a fully-synchronized, six-speed manual transmission with an overdrive sixth gear. Information on the manual transmission is included in this Part of Chapter 7. Information on the automatic transmission can be found in Part B of this Chapter. You'll also find certain procedures common to both transmissions - such as oil seal replacement - in Part A.

Depending on the expense involved in having a transmission overhauled, it might be a better idea to consider replacing it with either a used or rebuilt unit. Your local dealer or transmission shop should be able to supply information concerning cost, availability and exchange policy. Regardless of how you decide to remedy a transmission problem, you can still save a lot of money by removing and installing the unit yourself.

2 Shift lever - removal and installation

1 Position the shift lever into Neutral. Refer to Chapter 11 for removal of the trim panel surrounding the shifter upper boot.

2 If the shift knob and upper boot are being replaced, push the upper boot down away from the shift knob. Apply masking tape around the base of the knob, then use a crescent wrench or water pump pliers to rotate the knob from shifter shaft. With the knob removed, the upper boot can be removed.

3 Raise the vehicle and suitably support it on jackstands.

4 From below, pull down the linkage boot around the shift mechanism and remove the through-bolt securing the shift lever to the linkage.

5 From above, remove the four bolts securing the lower boot to the floor and remove the boot.

6 Remove the three bolts securing the shifter lever-to-base plate.

7 Pull up to remove the shift lever.

8 During installation, install the lever-to-base plate with the bolts just finger-tight.

9 Move the shift into the Sixth-gear position and apply slight pressure towards Reverse, then tighten the bolt at the right-rear of the guide plate.

10 Move the shift into the Fifth-gear position and apply slight pressure towards Reverse, then tighten the bolt at the front of the guide plate.

11 Tighten the left-rear bolt by hand, then tighten all three bolts to the torque listed in this Chapter's Specifications. The remainder of installation is the reverse of the removal procedure. If the shift knob was removed, apply a small amount of adhesive sealant to the threads before installation of the knob. Allow the adhesive to set for at least an hour before driving the vehicle.

3 Oil seal - replacement

EXTENSION HOUSING SEAL

▶ **Refer to illustrations 3.4 and 3.5**

➡**Note: This procedure applies to both manual and automatic transmissions.**

1 Oil leaks frequently occur due to wear of the extension housing oil seal or the transmission speed sensor seal. Replacement of these seals is relatively easy, since the repairs can usually be performed without removing the transmission from the vehicle.

2 If you suspect a leak at the extension housing seal, raise the vehicle and support it securely on jackstands. The extension housing seal is located at the rear end of the transmission, where the driveshaft yoke enters the transmission. If the extension housing seal is leaking,

transmission lubricant will be dripping from the rear of the transmission.

3 Remove the driveshaft (see Chapter 8).

4 Using a seal removal tool, carefully pry out the extension housing seal (see illustration). Do not damage the splines on the transmission output shaft.

➡**Note: On manual transmissions, the shifter extension on the back of the transmission may necessitate using a deep-reach, two-jaw or three-jaw puller.**

5 Using a seal driver or a large deep socket, install the new extension housing seal (see illustration). Drive it into the bore squarely and make sure it's completely seated.

6 Lubricate the lip of the seal with clean oil and install the driveshaft (see Chapter 8).

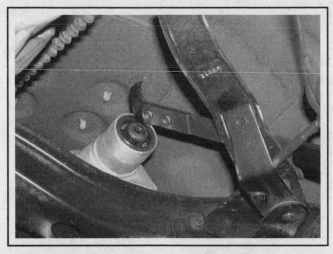

3.4 Pry out the extension housing seal with a seal removal tool

3.5 Install the new extension housing seal with a seal driver or a large deep socket

4 Transmission mount - check and replacement

CHECK

1   Insert a large screwdriver or prybar into the space between the transmission and the crossmember and try to pry the transmission up. If there is any separation of the rubber, the mount is worn out.

REPLACEMENT

2   Remove the transmission crossmember mounting bolts (see Section 5).

3   Remove the through-bolt attaching the mount to the crossmember (see illustration 6.17 in Chapter 7B). Remove the two bolts securing the mount to the transmission.

4   Installation is the reverse of the removal procedure. Be sure to tighten the nuts/bolts to the torque listed in this Chapter's Specifications.

5 Manual transmission - removal and installation

REMOVAL

♦ **Refer to illustrations 5.17a, 5.17b, 5.17c and 5.17d**

1   Disconnect the cable from the negative battery terminal (see Chapter 5, Section 1).

2   Place the transmission in NEUTRAL.

3   Raise the vehicle and support it securely on jackstands.

4   Disconnect the shift linkage from the transmission (see Section 2).

5   Remove the driveshaft (see Chapter 8).

6   Disconnect the clutch hydraulic line (see Chapter 8).

7   Remove the starter motor (see Chapter 5).

8   Disconnect the electrical connectors from the two upstream oxygen sensors and the two downstream oxygen sensors (see Chapter 6).

9   Refer to Chapter 4 and disconnect the left and right catalytic converters from the exhaust manifolds and remove the catalytic converter Y-pipe (the forward section of the exhaust system). You must remove the crossmember-like brace on the chassis that the converters are bolted to.

10 Disconnect the connectors from the back-up light switch and PNP switch.

11 Remove the crankshaft position sensor (see Chapter 6).

12 Support the engine with a floor jack. Put a block of wood between the jack head and the engine oil pan to protect the pan.

13 Support the transmission with a transmission jack (available at most auto parts stores and at equipment rental yards) or with a large, heavy duty floor jack. Safety chains should be used to secure the transmission to the jack.

14 Raise the transmission slightly to take the weight off the crossmember.

15 Remove the transmission crossmember bolts.

16 Remove the transmission mount-to-transmission bolts (see illustration 6.17 in Chapter 7B).

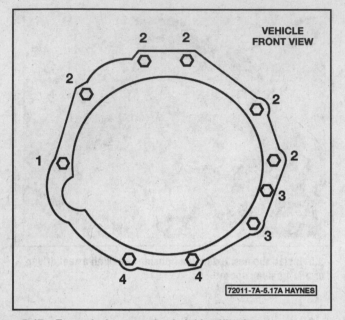

5.17a Transmission mounting bolt identification - 2003 models

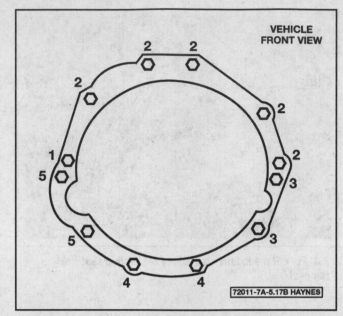

5.17b Transmission mounting bolt identification - 2004 models

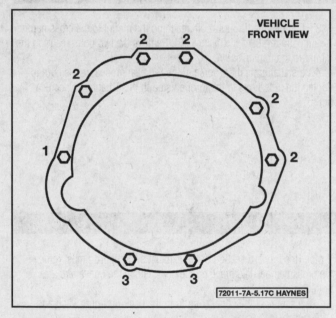

5.17c Transmission mounting bolt identification - 2005 and 2006 models

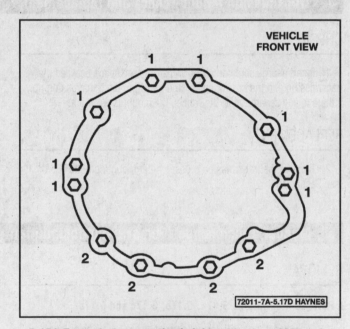

5.17d Transmission mounting bolt identification - 2007 and later G35 Sedan and 350Z models

17 Remove the engine-to-transmission and transmission-to-engine bolts (see illustrations). Lowering the jack will make access to the upper transmission bolts easier.

18 Make a final check that all wires have been disconnected from the transmission, then move the transmission and jack toward the rear of the vehicle until the transmission input shaft is clear of the clutch or clutch housing. If the transmission input shaft is difficult to disengage from the clutch hub, use a prybar to separate the transmission from the engine. Keep the transmission level as you pull it to the rear.

19 Once the input shaft is clear, lower the transmission and remove it from under the vehicle.

⁂ **CAUTION:**

Do not depress the clutch pedal while the transmission is out of the vehicle.

20 Inspect the clutch components. Generally speaking, new clutch components should always be installed whenever the transmission is removed (see Chapter 8).

INSTALLATION

21 Install the clutch components, if they were removed (see Chapter 8). Apply a thin film of high-temperature grease to the splines of the transmission input shaft and to the inner surface of the pilot bearing.

22 With the transmission secured to the jack, raise it into position behind the engine and carefully slide it forward, engaging the input shaft with the clutch plate hub. Do not use excessive force to install the transmission - if the input shaft won't slide into place, readjust the angle of the transmission or turn the input shaft so the splines engage properly with the clutch.

23 Once the transmission is flush with the engine, install the transmission-to-engine bolts. Tighten the bolts to the torque listed in this Chapter's Specifications.

✳✳ CAUTION:

Don't use the bolts to force the transmission and engine together. If the transmission doesn't slide up to the engine easily, find out what's wrong before proceeding.

24 Install the transmission mount and crossmember. Tighten all nuts and bolts to the torque listed in this Chapter's Specifications.

25 Remove the jacks supporting the transmission and the engine.

26 Install the various components removed previously. To connect the clutch hydraulic line and bleed the clutch hydraulic system, refer to Chapter 8.

27 Make a final check to verify all wires and hoses have been reconnected and the transmission has been filled with lubricant to the proper level (see Chapter 1). Lower the vehicle.

28 Reconnect the shift linkage.

29 Connect the negative battery cable. Road test the vehicle and check for leaks. Make sure the shifter operates smoothly in all gears.

6   Manual transmission overhaul - general information

Overhauling a manual transmission is a difficult job for the do-it-yourselfer. It involves the disassembly and reassembly of many small parts. Numerous clearances must be precisely measured and, if necessary, changed with select fit spacers and snap-rings. As a result, if transmission problems arise, it can be removed and installed by a competent do-it-yourselfer, but overhaul should be left to a transmission repair shop. Rebuilt transmissions may be available - check with your dealer parts department and auto parts stores. At any rate, the time and money involved in an overhaul is almost sure to exceed the cost of a rebuilt unit.

Nevertheless, it's not impossible for an inexperienced mechanic to rebuild a transmission if the special tools are available and the job is done in a deliberate step-by-step manner so nothing is overlooked.

The tools necessary for an overhaul include internal and external snap-ring pliers, a bearing puller, a slide hammer, a set of pin punches, a dial indicator and possibly a hydraulic press. In addition, a large, sturdy workbench and a vise or transmission stand will be required.

During disassembly of the transmission, make careful notes of how each piece comes off, where it fits in relation to other pieces and what holds it in place.

Before taking the transmission apart for repair, it will help if you have some idea what area of the transmission is malfunctioning. Certain problems can be closely tied to specific areas in the transmission, which can make component examination and replacement easier. Refer to the *Troubleshooting* Section at the front of this manual for information regarding possible sources of trouble.

Torque specifications	Ft-lbs (unless otherwise indicated)	Nm

➡ **Note: One foot-pound of torque is equivalent to 12 inch-pounds of torque. Torque values below approximately 15 foot-pounds are expressed in inch-pounds, because most foot-pound torque wrenches are not accurate at these smaller values.**

Drain plug	25	34
PNP and backup-light switches	21	27
Shift lever-to-guide plate bolts	75 to 88 in-lbs	8.4 to 10
Transmission crossmember-to-chassis bolts	32 to 40	43 to 55
Transmission-to-engine bolts (see illustrations 5.17a through 5.17d)		
2003 models		
Bolts designated 1 and 2	52 to 59	70 to 80
Bolts designated 3	37 to 44	49 to 61
Bolts designated 4	31 to 38	42 to 51
2004 models		
Bolts designated 1 and 2	55	75
Bolts designated 3	41	55
Bolts designated 4	34	46
Bolts designated 5	41	55
2005 and 2006 models		
Bolts designated 1 and 2	55	75
Bolts designated 3	34	46
2007 and later G35 Sedan and 350Z models		
Bolts designated A	55	75
Bolts designated B	34	46
Transmission mount-to-crossmember through-bolt	32 to 40	43 to 54
Transmission mount-to-transmission bolts	32 to 40	43 to 54

Section

Reference to other Chapters

7B

AUTOMATIC TRANSMISSION

1 General information

The automatic transmission used in these models is known as the RE5R05A. It is an electronic-shift five-speed transmission with three planetary gears and three one-way clutches. The shifting is controlled by the Transmission Control Module (TCM) using information from various engine and transmission sensors and output actuators through communication with the vehicle's PCM and BCM (see Chapter 6). The TCM is mounted inside the valve body of the transmission.

Because of the complexity of the clutches and the electronic and hydraulic control systems, and because of the special tools and expertise needed to overhaul an automatic transmission, diagnosis and repair of this transmission should be handled by a dealer service department or a transmission repair shop. But if the transmission must be rebuilt or replaced, you can save money by removing and installing it yourself, so instructions for that procedure are included as well.

2 Diagnosis - general

➡**Note: Automatic transmission malfunctions may be caused by five general conditions: poor engine performance, improper adjustments, hydraulic malfunctions, mechanical malfunctions or malfunctions in the TCM or its signal network. Diagnosis of these problems should always begin with a check of the easily repaired items: fluid level and condition (see Chapter 1), and shift cable adjustment. Next, perform a road test to determine if the problem has been corrected or if more diagnosis is necessary. If the problem persists after the preliminary tests and corrections are completed, additional diagnosis should be done by a dealer service department or transmission repair shop. Refer to the Troubleshooting section at the front of this manual for information on symptoms of transmission problems. Problems with the electronic transmission controls can be diagnosed with a scan tool to retrieve DTC's (Diagnostic Trouble Codes).**

PRELIMINARY CHECKS

1   Drive the vehicle to warm the transmission to normal operating temperature.

2   Check the fluid level as described in Chapter 1:

a) *If the fluid level is unusually low, add enough fluid to bring the level within the designated area of the dipstick, then check for external leaks (see below).*

b) *If the fluid level is abnormally high, drain off the excess, then check the drained fluid for contamination by coolant. The presence of engine coolant in the automatic transmission fluid indicates that a failure has occurred in the internal radiator walls that separate the coolant from the transmission fluid (see Chapter 3).*

c) *If the fluid is foaming, drain it and refill the transmission, then check for coolant in the fluid or a high fluid level.*

3   Check for any stored trouble codes (see Chapter 6).

➡**Note: If the engine is malfunctioning, do not proceed with the preliminary checks until it has been repaired and runs normally.**

4   Inspect the shift linkage (see Section 4). Make sure it's properly adjusted and operates smoothly.

FLUID LEAK DIAGNOSIS

5   Most fluid leaks are easy to locate visually. Repair usually consists of replacing a seal or gasket. If a leak is difficult to find, the following procedure may help.

6   Identify the fluid. Make sure it's transmission fluid and not engine oil or brake fluid (automatic transmission fluid is a deep red color).

7   Try to pinpoint the source of the leak. Drive the vehicle several miles, then park it over a large sheet of cardboard. After a minute or two, you should be able to locate the leak by determining the source of the fluid dripping onto the cardboard.

8   Make a careful visual inspection of the suspected component and the area immediately around it. Pay particular attention to gasket mating surfaces. A mirror is often helpful for finding leaks in areas that are hard to see.

9   If the leak still cannot be found, clean the suspected area thoroughly with a degreaser or solvent, then dry it.

10 Drive the vehicle for several miles at normal operating temperature and varying speeds. After driving the vehicle, visually inspect the suspected component again.

11 Once the leak has been located, the cause must be determined before it can be properly repaired. If a gasket is replaced but the sealing flange is bent, the new gasket will not stop the leak. The bent flange must be straightened.

12 Before attempting to repair a leak, check to make sure the following conditions are corrected or they may cause another leak.

➡**Note: Some of the following conditions cannot be fixed without highly specialized tools and expertise. Such problems must be referred to a transmission repair shop or a dealer service department.**

Gasket leaks

13 Check the pan periodically. Make sure the bolts are tight, no bolts are missing, the gasket is in good condition and the pan is flat (dents in the pan may indicate damage to the valve body inside).

14 If the pan gasket is leaking, the fluid level or the fluid pressure may be too high, the vent may be plugged, the pan bolts may be too tight, the pan sealing flange may be warped, the sealing surface of the transmission housing may be damaged, the gasket may be damaged or the transmission casting may be cracked or porous. If sealant instead of gasket material has been used to form a seal between the pan and the transmission housing, it may be the wrong sealant.

Seal leaks

15 If a transmission seal is leaking, the fluid level or pressure may be too high, the vent may be plugged, the seal bore may be damaged, the seal itself may be damaged or improperly installed, the surface of the shaft protruding through the seal may be damaged or a loose bearing may be causing excessive shaft movement.

16 Make sure the dipstick tube seal is in good condition and the tube is properly seated. Periodically check for leakage in the area around the rear seal or the transmission control electrical harness where it enters the case. If transmission fluid is evident, replace the rear seal (see Chapter 7A) or the O-ring around the control harness sealing nut for damage.

Case leaks

17 If the case itself appears to be leaking, the casting is porous and will have to be repaired or replaced.

18 Make sure the oil cooler hose fittings are tight and in good condition.

Fluid comes out vent pipe or fill tube

19 If this condition occurs, the transmission is overfilled, there is coolant in the fluid, the case is porous, the dipstick is incorrect, the vent is plugged or the drain-back holes are plugged.

---

3 Shift lever - removal and installation

▶ **Refer to illustrations 3.2 and 3.8**

1 Set the parking brake, then place the shift lever in the Neutral position. Move the front seats to the rear as far as they go.

2 Push down the small plastic cover just below the shift knob, then pull off the retaining clip with pliers and remove the shift knob from the shift handle (see illustration).

3 Remove the center console shifter bezel and the center console (see Chapter 11).

4 Raise the vehicle and secure it on jackstands.

5 Separate the shift control rod end from the shift lever on the transmission (see Section 4).

6 Disconnect the shift control rod from the shift assembly lever (see Section 4).

7 Disconnect the shift lock solenoid electrical connector, and release the shift/lock cable (see Section 5).

8 Remove the shift assembly-to-floor mounting bolts and remove the shift lever assembly from the floor (see illustration).

9 Installation is the reverse of the removal procedure. Adjust the shift rod if necessary (see Section 4).

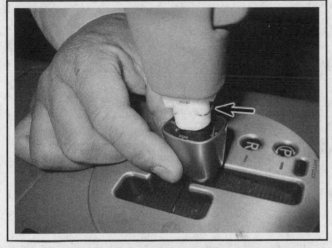

3.2 Pull off the retaining clip securing the shift knob

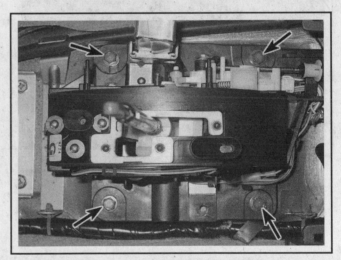

3.8 Location of the shift lever assembly mounting bolts

---

4 Shift control rod - check, replacement and adjustment

※ WARNING:

The models covered by this manual are equipped with a Supplemental Restraint System (SRS), more commonly known as airbags. Always disable the airbag system before working in the vicinity of any airbag system component to avoid the possibility of accidental deployment of the airbag(s), which could cause personal injury (see Chapter 12). Do not use a memory saving device to preserve the PCM or radio memory when working on or near airbag system components.

CHECK

1 Firmly apply the parking brake, depress the brake pedal and try to momentarily operate the starter in each shift lever position. The starter should only operate when the manual shift lever is in the PARK or NEUTRAL positions. If the starter operates in any position other than PARK or NEUTRAL, adjust the shift control rod (see below). If, after adjustment, the starter still operates in positions other than PARK or NEUTRAL, the transmission range (TR) sensor is defective (see Chapter 6). If there are problems with the automatic transmission, the "Automatic

Transmission Check" light on the instrument panel will illuminate and a DTC will be stored that can be read with a scan tool.

REPLACEMENT

▶ **Refer to illustrations 4.5 and 4.6**

2   Place the shift lever in the NEUTRAL position.

3   Raise the vehicle and support it on jackstands.

4   Remove the center console shifter bezel and the center console (see Chapter 11).

5   Pull the clip securing the control rod end at the top of the shift lever on the transmission (see illustration).

6   From below, remove the clip securing the control rod end to the adjuster at the shift lever (see illustration). Do not loosen the nut on the adjuster.

7   Installation is the reverse or removal.

ADJUSTMENT

8   If adjustment is necessary, place the floor shift lever in the Park position.

9   From below, loosen the nut where the adjuster goes through the slot in the end of the shift arm on the transmission (see illustration 4.6).

10   With the arm on the transmission in the Park position, pull the arm toward the rear of the vehicle (without moving it out of the Park position) and tighten the nut on the adjuster.

11   Verify that the engine will start only in PARK and NEUTRAL, and that the back-up lights come on when the shifter is placed in REVERSE. If necessary, readjust the control rod until these conditions are met.

➡**Note: On AWD models, make sure that when the shift selector is moved to the Manual Shift mode that the shift actions correctly correspond to the "+" and "-" positions. Meaning, when the shifter is moved forward (the "+" position), the transmission upshifts, and when the lever is moved rearward (the "-" position), the transmission downshifts.**

4.5 Pull the clip securing the control rod at the transmission shift arm

4.6 Pull the clip (A) securing the control rod to the adjuster on the shift lever - do not loosen the adjuster nut (B) at the lever itself

5   Brake Transmission Shift Interlock (BTSI) system - description, check and solenoid replacement

✳✳ WARNING:

The models covered by this manual are equipped with a Supplemental Restraint System (SRS), more commonly known as airbags. Always disable the airbag system before working in the vicinity of any airbag system component to avoid the possibility of accidental deployment of the airbag(s), which could cause personal injury (see Chapter 12). Do not use a memory saving device to preserve the PCM or radio memory when working on or near airbag system components.

DESCRIPTION

1   The Brake Transmission Shift Interlock (BTSI) system is a solenoid-operated device located under the shift lever in the center console. The solenoid locks the shift lever in the PARK position when the ignition key is in the LOCK or ACCESSORY position. When the ignition key is in the RUN position, a magnetic holding device is energized. When the system is functioning correctly, the only way to unlock the shift lever and move it out of PARK is to depress the brake pedal. The BTSI

system also prevents the ignition key from being turned to the LOCK or ACCESSORY position unless the shift lever is fully locked into the PARK position. In addition to the interlock solenoid in the shift console, other key components of the system include the brake light switch and the interlock cable that connects the ignition switch to the transmission shifter assembly.

CHECK

2 Verify that the ignition key can be removed only in the PARK position.

3 When the shift lever is in the PARK position, you should be able to rotate the ignition key from OFF to LOCK. But when the shift lever is in any gear position other than PARK (including NEUTRAL), you should not be able to rotate the ignition key to the LOCK position.

4 You should not be able to move the shift lever out of the PARK position when the ignition key is turned to the OFF position.

5 You should not be able to move the shift lever out of the PARK position when the ignition key is turned to the RUN or START position until you depress the brake pedal.

6 You should not be able to move the shift lever out of the PARK position when the ignition key is turned to the ACC or LOCK position.

7 Once in gear, with the ignition key in the RUN position, you should be able to move the shift lever between gears, or put it into NEUTRAL or PARK, without depressing the brake pedal.

8 If the BTSI system doesn't operate as described, try adjusting it as follows.

SOLENOID REPLACEMENT

◆ **Refer to illustration 5.13**

9 The shift/lock solenoid is mounted on the left side of the shifter assembly. The shift/lock solenoid relay is located in the shift control assembly, next to the solenoid, on models through 2005, and in the underhood fuse/relay box on later models.

10 Disconnect the cable from the negative terminal of the battery (see Chapter 5, Section 1). The key should be OFF and the shifter positioned in Park.

11 Disconnect the shift/lock adjustment rod from the solenoid.

12 Remove the mounting screw(s) and the solenoid.

13 Installation is the reverse of the removal procedure, with the following Steps to adjust the interlock rod:

   a) *Release the clip at the Shift/Lock cable on the shifter and pull the adjuster, away from the rod to unlock, and toward it to Lock. Lock the rod at the correct distance (no slack) by slightly pushing the adjuster toward the rod to lock it.*

   b) *If the interlock cable is broken, remove it at the shifter end, then remove the ignition switch end (see illustration). Remove the steering column covers to access the ignition end of the cable (see Chapter 11).*

SHIFT LOCK OVERRIDE FEATURE

◆ **Refer to illustration 5.15**

➡**Note: If the shift lever is non-operational and the shift override feature must be activated to move the shift lever, be sure to check the brake light fuse and the brake light system for a possible short that could have deactivated the BTSI system.**

14 In the event the Brake Transmission Shift Interlock (BTSI) system fails and the shift lever cannot be moved out of gear, the system is equipped with an override feature. The BTSI system can be bypassed and the shift lever can be used in manual operation.

15 Apply the parking brake and remove the access cover using a small screwdriver (see illustration). Locate the button for the BTSI solenoid, push the button down, depress the brake pedal and shift the console select lever into NEUTRAL.

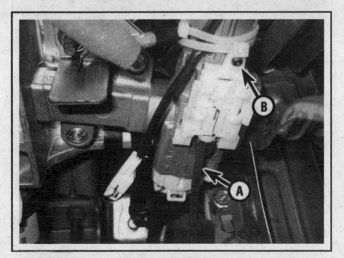

5.13 At the ignition switch end of the interlock cable (A), remove the screw (B) and separate the cable end from the ignition switch

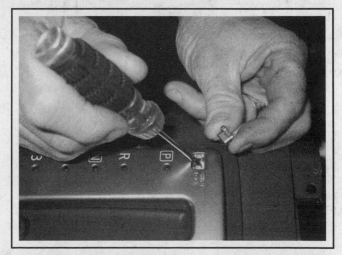

5.15 Remove the small cover, then depress the shift override button with a small tool

6 Automatic transmission - removal and installation

✳✳ CAUTION:

The transmission and torque converter must be removed as a single assembly. If you try to leave the torque converter attached to the driveplate, the converter driveplate, pump bushing and oil seal will be damaged. The driveplate is not designed to support the load, so none of the weight of the transmission should be allowed to rest on the plate during removal.

➡Note: On AWD models, the manufacturer suggests that the transmission and transfer case be removed as a unit from below the vehicle, which involves dropping the front suspension assembly, then separating the transmission from the engine while out of the vehicle (see Chapter 2A).

REMOVAL

▶ Refer to illustrations 6.5, 6.13, 6.15 and 6.17

1   Place the shift lever in the NEUTRAL position. Apply the parking brake and block the rear wheels.
2   Disconnect the cable from the negative terminal of the battery (see Chapter 5, Section 1).
3   Raise the vehicle and support it securely on jackstands.
4   Drain the transmission fluid (see Chapter 1), then reinstall the fluid pan's drain plug.
5   Disconnect the transmission fluid cooler lines from the side of the transmission (see illustration). On 350Z models, remove the brace between the shock towers, and the front crossbar (see Chapter 10), so that the engine/transmission can be raised enough to remove the fluid cooler lines. Use an overhead crane to support and raise the engine, and remove the left-side engine mount before raising the engine/transmission (see Chapter 2A).
6   Disconnect the catalytic converters from the exhaust manifolds and the Y-pipe, then remove the converters and Y-pipe (see Chapter 4). On most models, a brace on the body that supports the catalytic converters must be removed.
7   Disconnect the main wiring plug on the right side of the transmission. Unbolt the clips securing the wiring harness to the transmission case and set the wiring aside with plastic ties or tape.
8   Disconnect and remove the crankshaft position sensor from the bellhousing (see Chapter 6).
9   Remove the transmission fluid dipstick. Unbolt and remove the dipstick tube from the transmission.

➡Note: On some models, the transmission has a breather hose coming from the case. It is secured to a bracket on the dipstick tube, so unplug the hose before removing both the tube and the hose.

10 Disconnect the shift control rod from the lever on the transmission (see Section 4).
11 Remove the driveshaft (see Chapter 8).
12 Support the transmission with a transmission jack (available at most equipment rental facilities) and secure the transmission to the jack with safety chains.
13 Remove the access cover at the bottom of the bellhousing (see illustration) and mark the relationship of the torque converter to the driveplate so they can be installed in the same position.
14 Remove the starter motor and the metal plate behind it (see Chapter 5).

6.5 Disconnect the transmission fluid cooler lines from the transmission by removing the banjo bolts

6.13 Remove the access cover on the bellhousing (retaining bolt indicated)

15 Remove the driveplate-to-torque converter bolts (see illustration). Rotate the engine by using a socket on the crankshaft pulley bolt until all four of the converter mounting bolts have been removed.

16 Support the engine with a floor jack. Place a wood block between the jack head and the engine oil pan.

17 Raise the transmission slightly to take the weight off the crossmember, then remove the crossmember (see illustration).

18 Remove the transmission-to-engine bolts. Be sure to note the length and the location of each bolt for correct reassembly.

19 Make a final check that all wires have been disconnected from the transmission, then move the transmission and jack toward the rear of the vehicle until the torque converter is separated from the driveplate. Clamp a pair of locking pliers to the bellhousing so the torque converter won't fall out during removal.

INSTALLATION

20 Prior to installation, make sure the torque converter is securely engaged in the pump. If you've removed the converter, apply a small amount of transmission fluid on the torque converter rear hub, where the transmission front seal rides. Install the torque converter onto the input shaft of the transmission while rotating the converter back and forth. It should engage with the transmission front pump and input shaft in stages. Make sure it's completely engaged and rotates freely.

21 With the transmission secured to the jack, raise it into position. Be sure to keep it level so the torque converter doesn't fall out and disengage itself from the pump gear.

22 Turn the torque converter to line up the studs with the holes in the driveplate. The marks on the torque converter and driveplate must line up.

23 Move the transmission forward carefully until the dowel pins on the engine are engaged with the holes on the transmission. Make sure the transmission mates with the engine with no gap. If there's a gap, make sure there are no wires or other objects pinched between the engine and transmission.

24 Install the transmission-to-engine bolts and tighten them to the torque listed in this Chapter's Specifications. As you're tightening the bolts, make sure that the engine and transmission mate completely at all points. If not, find out why. Never try to force the engine and transmission together with the bolts or you'll break the transmission case!

25 Attach the shift control rod to the lever on the transmission (see Section 4).

26 Install the transmission mount and crossmember and tighten the bolts/nuts to the torque listed in this Chapter's Specifications.

27 Install the torque converter bolts and tighten them to the torque listed in this Chapter's Specifications.

28 The remainder of installation is the reverse of removal.

29 Fill the transmission with the specified fluid (see Chapter 1), run the engine and check for fluid leaks.

6.15 Remove the converter bolts by rotating the engine until each appears in the opening

6.17 Location of the transmission crossmember mounting bolts (A), the transmission mount-to-transmission bolts (B), and the mount-to-crossmember throughbolt (C)

7 Automatic transmission overhaul - general information

In the event of a fault occurring, it will be necessary to establish whether the fault is electrical, mechanical or hydraulic in nature, before repair work can be contemplated. Diagnosis requires detailed knowledge of the transmission's operation and construction, as well as access to specialized test equipment, and so is deemed to be beyond the scope of this manual. It is therefore essential that problems with the automatic transmission are referred to a dealer service department or other qualified repair facility for assessment.

Note that a faulty transmission should not be removed before the vehicle has been assessed by a knowledgeable technician equipped with the proper tools, as troubleshooting must be performed with the transmission installed in the vehicle.

Specifications

General

Transmission fluid type   See Chapter 1

Torque specifications	Ft-lbs (unless otherwise indicated)	Nm

Note: One foot-pound of torque is equivalent to 12 inch-pounds of torque. Torque values below approximately 15 foot-pounds are expressed in inch-pounds, because most foot-pound torque wrenches are not accurate at these smaller values.

Drain plug	25	34
Shift lever assembly-to-floor bolts	43 in-lbs	4.9
Torque converter bolts	38	51
Transmission fluid dipstick tube mounting bolts	45 in-lbs	5.1
Transmission crossmember-to-chassis bolts		
2003 350Z models	32 to 40	43 to 55
All other models	36	49
Transmission-to-engine bolts (see illustrations 5.17a through 5.17d in Chapter 7, Part A)		
2003 models		
Bolts designated 1 and 2	52 to 59	70 to 80
Bolts designated 3	37 to 44	49 to 61
Bolts designated 4	31 to 38	42 to 51
2004 models		
Bolts designated 1 and 2	55	75
Bolts designated 3	41	55
Bolts designated 4	34	46
Bolts designated 5	41	55
2005 and 2006 models		
Bolts designated 1 and 2	55	75
Bolts designated 3	34	46
2007 and 2008 models		
Bolts designated A	55	75
Bolts designated B	34	46
Transmission mount-to-crossmember throughbolt	32 to 40	43 to 54
Transmission mount-to-transmission bolts	32 to 40	43 to 54

Section

8

CLUTCH AND DRIVELINE

1 General information

The information in this Chapter deals with the components from the rear of the engine to the front wheels, except for the transmission, which is dealt with in Chapter 7. For the purposes of this Chapter, these components are grouped into three categories - clutch, driveshaft and axle(s).

Since nearly all the procedures covered in this Chapter involve working under the vehicle, make sure it's securely supported on sturdy jackstands or on a hoist where the vehicle can be easily raised and lowered.

2 Clutch - description and check

1   All vehicles with a manual transmission have a single dry plate, diaphragm spring-type clutch. The clutch disc has a splined hub which allows it to slide along the splines of the transmission input shaft. The clutch and pressure plate are held in contact by spring pressure exerted by the diaphragm in the pressure plate.

2   The clutch release system is operated by hydraulic pressure. The hydraulic release system consists of the clutch pedal, a master cylinder, fluid reservoir, a release (or slave) cylinder and the hydraulic line connecting the two components.

3   When the clutch pedal is depressed, a pushrod pushes against brake fluid inside the master cylinder, applying hydraulic pressure to the release cylinder, which pushes the release bearing against the diaphragm fingers of the clutch pressure plate.

4   Terminology can be a problem when discussing the clutch components because common names are in some cases different from those used by the manufacturer. For example, the driven plate is also called the clutch plate or disc, the clutch release bearing is sometimes called a throwout bearing, the release cylinder is sometimes called the slave cylinder.

5   Unless you're replacing components with obvious damage, do these preliminary checks to diagnose clutch problems:

a) *The first check should be of the fluid level in the master cylinder reservoir. If the fluid level is low, add fluid as necessary and inspect the hydraulic system for leaks. If the master cylinder reservoir is dry, bleed the system as described in Section 5 and recheck the clutch operation.*

b) *To check clutch spin-down time, run the engine at normal idle speed with the transmission in Neutral (clutch pedal up - engaged). Disengage the clutch (pedal down), wait several seconds and shift the transmission into Reverse. No grinding noise should be heard. A grinding noise would most likely indicate a bad pressure plate or clutch disc.*

c) *To check for complete clutch release, run the engine (with the parking brake applied to prevent vehicle movement) and hold the clutch pedal approximately 1/2-inch from the floor. Shift the transmission between 1st gear and Reverse several times. If the shift is rough, component failure is indicated.*

d) *Visually inspect the pivot bushing at the top of the clutch pedal to make sure there's no binding or excessive play.*

3 Clutch master cylinder - removal and installation

REMOVAL

1   Clamp a pair of locking pliers onto the clutch fluid feed hose, a couple of inches downstream of the clutch fluid reservoir (the clutch master cylinder is supplied with fluid from the clutch fluid reservoir). The pliers should be just tight enough to prevent fluid flow when the hose is disconnected. Disconnect the reservoir hose from the clutch master cylinder.

2   Working under the dashboard, remove the driver's side knee bolster (see Chapter 11), disconnect the clutch master cylinder pushrod from the pedal by removing the clip from the clutch pedal pin.

3   Separate the hydraulic line from the cylinder. Have rags handy, as some fluid will be lost as the line is removed. Cap or plug the end of the line to prevent fluid leakage and the entry of contaminants.

✳✳ CAUTION:

Don't allow brake fluid to come into contact with the paint, as it will damage the finish.

4   Working under the dash, remove the master cylinder mounting nuts and detach the master cylinder.

INSTALLATION

5   Connect the hydraulic line fitting to the clutch master cylinder.

6   Attach the fluid feed hose from the reservoir to the clutch master cylinder and tighten the hose clamp. Remove the locking pliers.

7   Place the master cylinder in position on the clutch pedal bracket and install the mounting nuts finger tight. Install the clutch pedal pin and clip.

8   Tighten the mounting bolts to the torque listed in this Chapter's Specifications.

9   Fill the reservoir with brake fluid conforming to DOT 3 specifications and bleed the clutch system as outlined in Section 5.

4   Clutch release cylinder - removal and installation

✳✳ WARNING:

Dust produced by clutch wear is hazardous to your health. DO NOT blow it out with compressed air and DO NOT inhale it. DO NOT use gasoline or petroleum-based solvents to remove the dust. Brake system cleaner should be used to flush the dust into a drain pan. After the clutch components are wiped clean with a rag, dispose of the contaminated rags and cleaner in a covered, marked container.

2006 AND EARLIER 350Z, 2007 AND EARLIER G35 COUPE AND 2006 AND EARLIER G35 SEDAN MODELS

1   Raise the vehicle and support it securely on jackstands.

2   Unscrew the fluid hose fitting bolt.

➡Note: There is a sealing washer on either side of the brake hose inlet fitting; be sure to replace these with new ones when reconnecting the hose.

Have rags handy, as some fluid will be lost as the line is removed.

✳✳ CAUTION:

Don't allow fluid to come into contact with the paint - it will damage the finish. Also have a plug ready and immediately plug the line to prevent leakage and fluid contamination.

3   Unscrew the two release cylinder mounting bolts and detach the release cylinder.

4   Installation is the reverse of removal. Make sure the pushrod dust boot is in good condition and the pushrod is seated correctly in its pocket in the release lever. Tighten the release cylinder mounting bolts to the torque listed in this Chapter's Specifications.

5   Fill the clutch fluid reservoir with the recommended fluid (see Chapter 1).

6   Bleed the clutch hydraulic system (see Section 5).

7   Lower the vehicle and check for proper operation.

ALL OTHER MODELS

Removal

8   Raise the vehicle and support it securely on jackstands.

9   Remove the clip and disconnect the hydraulic line at the transmission. Have a small can and rags handy, as some fluid will be spilled as the line is removed. Plug the line to prevent excessive fluid loss and contamination.

10   Remove the transmission (see Chapter 7, Part A).

11   On the outside of the transmission, remove the bolt securing the release cylinder hydraulic line.

12   Remove the clip and disconnect the hydraulic line at the release cylinder.

13   Remove the release cylinder mounting bolts. Remove the release cylinder.

Installation

14   Install the release cylinder into the transmission. Tighten the bolts to the torque listed in this Chapter's Specifications.

15   Connect the hydraulic line at the release cylinder and install the clip. On the outside of the transmission, install the bolt securing the release cylinder hydraulic line.

16   Install the transmission (see Chapter 7, Part A).

17   Connect the hydraulic line fitting to the transmission and install the clip.

18   Check the fluid level in the clutch fluid reservoir, adding brake fluid conforming to DOT 3 specifications until the level is correct.

19   Bleed the system as described in Section 5, then recheck the brake fluid level.

5   Clutch hydraulic system - bleeding

1   Bleed the hydraulic system whenever any part of the system has been removed or the fluid level has fallen so low that air has been drawn into the master cylinder. The bleeding procedure is very similar to bleeding a brake system.

2   Fill the clutch master cylinder reservoir with new brake fluid conforming to DOT 3 specifications.

✳✳ CAUTION:

Do not re-use any of the fluid coming from the system during the bleeding operation or use fluid which has been inside an open container for an extended period of time.

3   Working at the transmission, remove the cap from the bleeder valve and attach a length of clear hose to the valve. Place the other end of the hose into a container partially filled with clean brake fluid.

4   Have an assistant depress the clutch pedal and hold it. Open the bleeder valve on the hydraulic line, allowing fluid and any air to escape. Close the bleeder valve when the flow of fluid (and bubbles) ceases. Once closed, have your assistant release the pedal.

5   Continue this process until all air is evacuated from the system, indicated by a solid stream of fluid being ejected from the bleeder valve each time with no air bubbles. Keep a close watch on the fluid level inside the brake master cylinder reservoir - if the level drops too far, air will get into the system and you'll have to start all over again.

➡Note: Wash the area with water to remove any spilled brake fluid.

6   Check the clutch fluid level again, and add some, if necessary, to bring it to the appropriate level. Check carefully for proper operation before placing the vehicle into normal service.

6 Clutch release bearing - removal, inspection and installation

※※ WARNING:

Dust produced by clutch wear is hazardous to your health. DO NOT blow it out with compressed air and DO NOT inhale it. DO NOT use gasoline or petroleum-based solvents to remove the dust. Brake system cleaner should be used to flush the dust into a drain pan. After the clutch components are wiped clean with a rag, dispose of the contaminated rags and cleaner in a covered, marked container.

2006 AND EARLIER 350Z, 2007 AND EARLIER G35 COUPE AND 2006 AND EARLIER G35 SEDAN MODELS

Removal

▶ **Refer to illustration 6.3**

1 Remove the release cylinder (see Section 4).
2 Remove the transmission (see Chapter 7, Part A).
3 Remove the boot from the side of the transmission and disengage the release lever retainer from the ballstud (see illustration).

Inspection

▶ **Refer to illustration 6.5**

4 Hold the outer portion of the bearing and rotate the center while applying pressure. If the bearing doesn't turn smoothly or if it's noisy, replace it with a new one. Wipe the bearing with a clean rag and inspect it for damage, wear and cracks. Don't immerse the bearing in solvent - it's sealed for life and to do so would ruin it.

5 If the bearing needs to be replaced, remove it from the hub with a puller (see illustration). The new bearing will have to be pressed onto the hub (if you don't have a press, take the hub and bearing to an automotive machine shop).

Installation

▶ **Refer to illustration 6.7**

6 Lightly lubricate the clutch release lever where it contacts the release bearing hub and the ballstud.
7 Attach the release bearing to the release lever. Make sure the bearing is properly engaged by the retainer clip (see illustration).

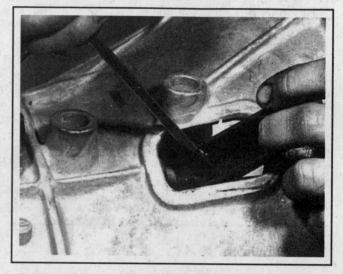

6.3 A screwdriver can be used to disengage the release lever retainer spring from the ballstud

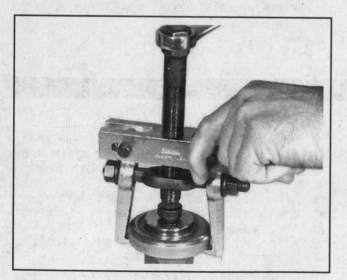

6.5 A puller is needed to separate the release bearing from the hub

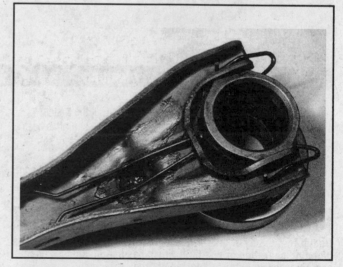

6.7 The release bearing retainer must engage the lever like this

8   Lubricate the clutch release lever ballstud or pivot pin with high-temperature grease, insert the release lever through the boot, slide the release bearing onto the input shaft bearing retainer and push the lever onto the ballstud until the lever retainer pops onto the stud. Make sure that the release lever pivots freely and the release bearing slides freely on the input shaft bearing retainer.

9   Apply a light coat of high-temperature grease to the face of the release bearing, where it contacts the pressure plate diaphragm fingers.

10 The remainder of installation is the reverse of the removal proce-dure. Tighten all transmission-to-engine bolts to the torque listed in the Chapter 7A Specifications.

ALL OTHER MODELS

11 The clutch release bearing and bearing hub are integral compo-nents of the clutch release cylinder. Replace the release cylinder as a single assembly (see Section 4).

---

7   Clutch components - removal, inspection and installation

✳✳ WARNING:

Dust produced by clutch wear is hazardous to your health. DO NOT blow it out with compressed air and DO NOT inhale it. DO NOT use gasoline or petroleum-based solvents to remove the dust. Brake system cleaner should be used to flush the dust into a drain pan. After the clutch components are wiped clean with a rag, dispose of the contaminated rags and cleaner in a covered, marked container.

REMOVAL

♦ **Refer to illustration 7.5**

1   Access to the clutch components is normally accomplished by removing the transmission, leaving the engine in the vehicle. If the engine is being removed for major overhaul, check the clutch for wear and replace worn components as necessary. However, the relatively low cost of the clutch components compared to the time and trouble spent gaining access to them warrants their replacement anytime the engine or transmission is removed, unless they are new or in near-perfect condition. The following procedures are based on the assumption the engine will stay in place.

2   Remove the transmission from the vehicle (see Chapter 7, Part A). Support the engine while the transmission is out. Preferably, an engine support fixture or a hoist should be used to support it from above.

3   The release bearing can remain attached to the transmission housing for the time being.

4   To support the clutch disc during removal, install a clutch align-ment tool through the clutch disc hub.

5   Carefully inspect the flywheel and pressure plate for indexing marks. The marks are usually an X, an O or a black mark. If they cannot be found, scribe or paint marks yourself so the pressure plate and the flywheel will be in the same alignment during installation (see illustration).

6   Turning each bolt a little at a time, loosen the pressure plate-to-flywheel bolts. Work in a criss-cross pattern until all spring pressure is relieved. Then hold the pressure plate securely and completely remove the bolts, followed by the pressure plate and clutch disc.

INSPECTION

♦ **Refer to illustrations 7.9, 7.11a, 7.11b and 7.13**

7   Ordinarily, when a problem occurs in the clutch, it can be attrib-uted to wear of the clutch driven plate assembly (clutch disc). However, all components should be inspected at this time.

8   Inspect the flywheel for cracks, heat checking, grooves and other obvious defects. If the imperfections are slight, a machine shop can machine the surface flat and smooth, which is highly recommended regardless of the surface appearance. Refer to Chapter 2 for the flywheel removal and installation procedure.

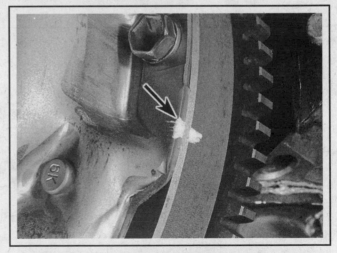

7.5 Mark the relationship of the pressure plate to the flywheel (if you're planning to re-use the old pressure plate)

9   Inspect the lining on the clutch disc. There should be at least 1/16-inch of lining above the rivet heads. Check for loose rivets, distortion, cracks, broken springs and other obvious damage (see illustration). As mentioned above, ordinarily the clutch disc is routinely replaced, so if in doubt about the condition, replace it with a new one.

10   The release bearing and release cylinder should also be replaced along with the clutch disc (see Sections 4 and 6).

11   Check the machined surfaces and the diaphragm spring fingers of the pressure plate (see illustrations). If the surface is grooved or otherwise damaged, replace the pressure plate. Also check for obvious damage, distortion, cracking, etc. Light glazing can be removed with emery cloth or sandpaper. If a new pressure plate is required, new and re-manufactured units are available.

12   Check the pilot bearing in the end of the crankshaft for excessive wear, scoring, dryness, roughness and any other obvious damage. If any of these conditions are noted, replace the bearing.

13   Removal can be accomplished with a slide hammer and puller attachment (see illustration), which are available at most auto parts stores or tool rental yards.

INSTALLATION

▶ **Refer to illustrations 7.14 and 7.16**

14   To install a new pilot bearing, lightly lubricate the outside surface with grease, then drive it into the recess with a bearing driver or a socket (see illustration).

➡**Note: The seal end of the bearing must be facing toward the transmission.**

15   Before installation, clean the flywheel and pressure plate machined surfaces with brake cleaner. It's important that no oil or grease is on these surfaces or the lining of the clutch disc. Handle the parts only with clean hands.

16   Position the clutch disc and pressure plate against the flywheel, with the clutch held in place with an alignment tool (see illustration). Make sure the disc is installed properly (most replacement clutch discs will be marked "flywheel side" or something similar - if not marked, install the clutch disc with the damper springs toward the transmission).

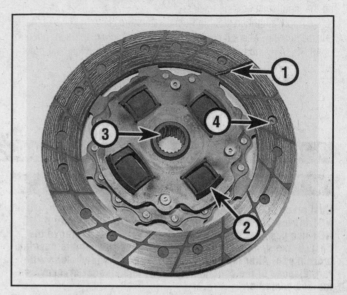

7.9   The clutch disc

1   *Lining* - this will wear down in use
2   *Springs or dampers* - check for cracking and deformation
3   *Splined hub* - the splines must not be worn and should slide smoothly on the transmission input shaft splines
4   *Rivets* - these secure the lining and will damage the flywheel or pressure plate if allowed to contact the surfaces

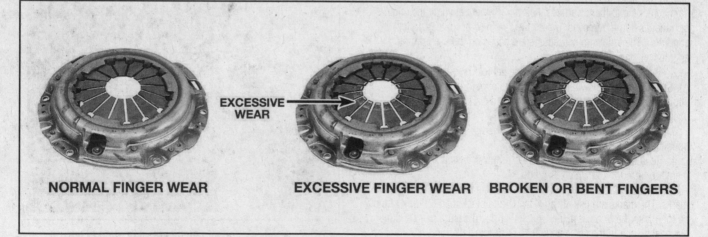

NORMAL FINGER WEAR   EXCESSIVE WEAR   **EXCESSIVE FINGER WEAR**   **BROKEN OR BENT FINGERS**

7.11a   Replace the pressure plate if excessive wear or damage are noted

17 Install the new pressure plate-to-flywheel bolts only finger tight, working around the pressure plate.

18 Center the clutch disc by ensuring the alignment tool extends through the splined hub and into the pilot bearing in the crankshaft. Wiggle the tool up, down or side-to-side as needed to center the disc. Tighten the pressure plate-to-flywheel bolts a little at a time, working in a criss-cross pattern to prevent distorting the cover. After all of the bolts are snug, tighten them to the torque listed in this Chapter's Specifications. Remove the alignment tool.

19 Install the clutch release bearing and release cylinder (see Sections 4 and 6).

20 Install the transmission and all components removed previously.

7.11b Inspect the pressure plate surface for excessive score marks, cracks and signs of overheating

7.13 A small slide hammer is handy for removing a pilot bearing

7.14 Tap the bearing into place with a bearing driver or a socket that is slightly smaller than the outside diameter of the bearing

7.16 Center the clutch disc in the pressure plate with a clutch alignment tool

8 Clutch start switch - check and replacement

♦ **Refer to illustration 8.1**

1   The clutch start switch is located near the top of the clutch pedal, facing the opposite direction of the cruise control switch (or pedal stopper) (see illustration).

2   Verify that the engine will not start when the clutch pedal is released.

3   Verify that the engine will start when the clutch pedal is depressed all the way.

4   If the clutch start switch doesn't perform as described above, loosen the locknut, depress the clutch pedal all the way and turn the switch in its bracket until the gap between the switch body and the pedal is adjusted to the clearance listed in this Chapter's Specifications. Check the operation of the switch again; if it still doesn't work properly, check switch continuity.

5   Verify that there is continuity between the clutch start switch terminals when the pedal is depressed.

6   Verify that no continuity exists between the switch terminals when the pedal is released.

7   If the switch fails either of these continuity tests, replace it: Loosen the nut near the body of the switch, then unscrew the switch from the bracket. Unplug the electrical connector. Installation is the reverse of removal.

8   Adjust the switch as described in Step 4.

9   Verify that the engine doesn't start when the clutch pedal is released.

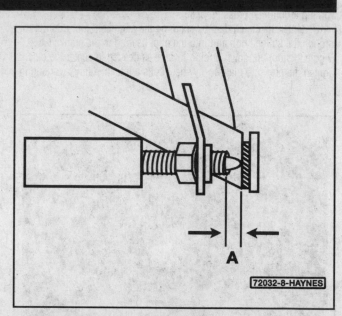

72032-8-HAYNES

8.1 Depress the pedal, then loosen the locknut and turn the clutch start switch in its bracket until the gap between the switch thread and the pedal stopper (A) is as listed in this Chapter's Specifications

9 Driveshaft - inspection

1   Raise the vehicle and support it securely on jackstands.

2   Crawl under the vehicle and visually inspect the driveshaft. Look for any dents or cracks in the tubing. If any are found, the driveshaft must be replaced.

3   Check for any oil leakage at the front and rear of the driveshaft. Leakage where the driveshaft enters the transmission indicates a defective transmission rear seal. Leakage where the driveshaft connects to the differential indicates a defective pinion seal. Leakage where the driveshaft enters the transfer case (AWD models) indicates a defective transfer case seal.

4   While under the vehicle, have an assistant turn the rear wheel so the driveshaft will rotate. As it does, make sure the universal joints are operating properly without binding, noise or looseness.

5   The universal joints can also be checked with the driveshaft motionless, by gripping your hands on either side of the joint and attempting to twist the joint. Any movement at all in the joint is a sign of considerable wear. Lifting up on the shaft will also indicate movement in the universal joints.

6   Finally, check the driveshaft mounting bolts at the ends to make sure they are tight.

10 Driveshaft - removal and installation

REAR DRIVESHAFT

♦ **Refer to illustration 10.3**

1   Raise the vehicle an support it securely on jackstands. Block the front wheels.

2   Remove the rear section of the exhaust system to gain access to the driveshaft (see Chapter 4).

3   Mark the relationship of the driveshaft to the differential companion flange, then remove the bolts and separate the driveshaft from the differential companion flange (see illustration).

4   If the vehicle is equipped with a two-piece driveshaft, remove the center support bearing mounting bolts.

5   Lower the rear of the driveshaft, then slide the front yoke out of the transmission.

6   Wrap a plastic bag over the transmission housing and hold it

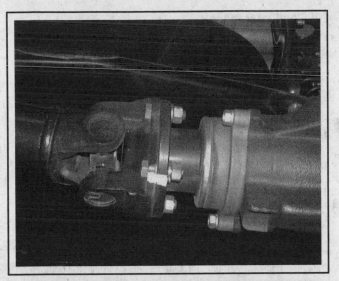

10.3 After marking the relationship of the driveshaft to the differential companion flange, remove the bolts and separate the driveshaft from the differential companion flange

in place with a rubber band. This will prevent loss of fluid and protect against contamination while the driveshaft is out.

7   Installation is the reverse of removal. If the shaft cannot be lined up due to the components of the differential or transmission having been rotated, put the vehicle in Neutral or rotate one wheel to allow the original alignment to be achieved. Tighten the fasteners to the torque listed in this Chapter's Specifications.

FRONT DRIVESHAFT

8   Apply the parking brake, then raise the front of the vehicle and support it securely on jackstands.

9   Mark the relationship of the driveshaft to the differential companion flange (see illustration 10.3), then remove the bolts.

10 Support the transfer case with a floor jack. Remove the mount bolts, then slowly lower the transfer case approximately two inches (50 mm).

11 Separate the front of the driveshaft from the front differential and pull the splined yoke from the transfer case.

12 Installation is the reverse of removal. Be sure to replace the O-ring on the splined yoke with a new one, and tighten the driveshaft-to-front differential companion flange bolts to the torque listed in this Chapter's Specifications.

11 Universal joints - replacement

The universal joints on the driveshaft cannot be repaired or replaced. If any of the joints are worn or damaged, replace the driveshaft assembly (see Section 10).

12 Differential pinion oil seal - replacement

1   Raise the vehicle and place it securely on jackstands.
2   Drain the differential (see Chapter 1).

REAR DIFFERENTIAL

2005 and earlier models

▶ Refer to illustrations 12.3, 12.5 and 12.7

3   A flange holding tool will be required to keep the companion flange from moving while the self-locking pinion nut is loosened. A chain wrench will also work (see illustration).

4   Remove the pinion nut. Obtain a new nut for installation. Apply matchmarks on the flange and the differential pinion shaft.

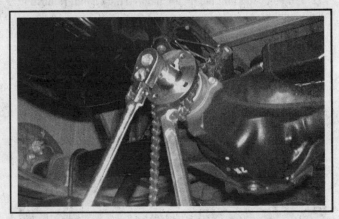

12.3 A chain wrench is being used here to prevent the pinion flange from turning while the nut is loosened

5   Withdraw the flange. It may be necessary to use a two-jaw puller engaged behind the flange to draw it off (see illustration). Do not attempt to pry or hammer behind the flange or hammer on the end of the pinion shaft.

6   Pry out the old seal and discard it.

7   Lubricate the lips of the new seal with clean differential lubricant, then tap it evenly into position with a seal installation tool or a large socket (see illustration). Make sure it enters the housing squarely and is tapped in to its full depth.

8   Install the pinion flange. If necessary, tighten the pinion nut to draw the flange into place. Do not try to hammer the flange into position.

9   Apply a bead of RTV sealant to the ends of the splines visible in the center of the flange so oil will be sealed in.

10 Install a new pinion nut. Tighten the nut to the torque listed in this Chapter's Specifications.

11 Reconnect the driveshaft to the pinion flange (see Section 10). Fill the differential with the specified fluid (see Chapter 1).

2006 and later models

▶ **Refer to illustrations 12.12, 12.14 and 12.23**

12 Disconnect the rear driveaxles from the differential flanges (see illustration 13.3). Suspend the driveaxle with a wire (see illustration).

13 Remove the ABS rear wheel speed sensors (see Chapter 9).

14 Using a slide hammer, remove the side flanges (see illustration).

15 Mark the driveshaft and companion flange to ensure realignment during reassembly, then remove the driveshaft (see Section 10).

16 Using an inch-pound torque wrench, measure and record the torque required to turn the pinion nut through several revolutions. This value, known as pinion bearing preload, will be used when the pinion flange is reinstalled.

17 A flange holding tool will be required to keep the companion flange from moving while the self-locking pinion nut is loosened. A chain wrench will also work (see illustration 12.3). Obtain a new nut for installation. Mark the relationship of the companion flange to the drive pinion shaft, then, using a suitable puller, remove the companion flange.

12.5 If you can't pull the pinion flange off by hand, remove it with a puller

12.7 Lubricate the lips of the new seal and seat it squarely in the bore, then drive it into the carrier with a seal driver or a large socket

12.12 Suspend the end of the driveaxle with a wire

12.14 Use a slide hammer with an angle attachment

18 Pry out the old seal with a seal removal tool.

19 Lubricate the lips of the new seal with clean differential lubricant. Clean the oil seal mounting surface, then tap the new seal into place, taking care to insert it squarely in the bore, tapped in to its full depth.

20 Inspect the splines on the pinion shaft for burrs and nicks. Remove any rough areas with a crocus cloth. Wipe the splines clean.

21 Install the companion flange, aligning it with the marks made during removal. Gently tap the flange on with a soft-faced hammer until you can start the new pinion nut on the pinion shaft.

22 Using a suitable tool, hold the companion flange while tightening the pinion nut, stopping frequently to take rotational torque measurements, using the inch-pound torque wrench, until the measurement recorded in Step 7 is reached.

✳✳ CAUTION:

If the measurement recorded in Step 7 was less than the pinion bearing preload torque listed in this Chapter's Specifications, continue tightening until the specified torque is reached. If it was more than specified, continue tightening until the recorded measurement is reached. Under no circumstances should the pinion nut be backed off to reduce pinion bearing preload. Increase the nut torque in small increments and check the preload after each increase.

23 Reinstall the side flanges, starting with the right-side flange first (see illustration).

24 Reinstall the driveaxles (see Section 13).

25 Fill the differential with the specified fluid (see Chapter 1).

FRONT DIFFERENTIAL

26 The procedure for replacing the pinion oil seal on the front differential is similar to the 2005 and earlier rear differential pinion oil seal replacement procedure. Follow Steps 1 through 11 of this Section.

12.23 Using a drift at the center of the flange, drive the flange in until it's seated

13 Driveaxles - removal and installation

REAR DRIVEAXLES

Removal

▶ **Refer to illustration 13.3**

1 Loosen the wheel lug nuts, remove the cotter pin from the driveaxle/hub nut, then use a breaker-bar and a socket to loosen the driveaxle/hub nut. Raise the rear of the vehicle and support it securely on jackstands. Remove the rear wheel(s).

2 Remove the driveaxle/hub nut.

3 Make reference marks on the driveaxle flange and the differential side gear flange, then remove the fasteners (see illustration).

4 Detach the axle from the differential side gear flange, then remove the outer end of the driveaxle from the hub.

Installation

5 Installation is the reverse of removal. tighten the side gear flange fasteners to the torque listed in this Chapter's Specifications.

6 Install a new driveaxle/hub nut. Tighten the hub nut securely, but don't tighten it to the actual torque specification until you've lowered the vehicle.

13.3 Make reference marks on the driveaxle flange and the differential side gear flange (A), then remove the fasteners

7   Install the wheel and lug nuts. Lower the vehicle and tighten the lug nuts to the torque listed in the Chapter 1 Specifications.

8   Tighten the driveaxle/hub nut to the torque listed in this Chapter's Specifications, then install a new cotter pin.

FRONT DRIVEAXLES (AWD MODELS)

Removal

9   Loosen the wheel lug nuts, remove the cotter pin from the driveaxle/hub nut, then use a breaker-bar and a socket to loosen the driveaxle/hub nut. Raise the front of the vehicle and support it securely on jackstands. Remove the front wheel(s).

10   Remove the screws and the engine undercover.

11   Remove the ABS wheel speed sensor harness at the knuckle and wire it out of the way.

12   Remove the brake caliper and disc (see Chapter 9).

➡**Note: Don't disconnect the brake hose; hang the caliper out of the way with a length of wire (see Chapter 9).**

13   Remove the driveaxle/hub nut.

14   Separate the upper control arm and tie-rod end from the steering knuckle (see Chapter 10).

15   Pull the steering knuckle outward enough for the splines of the driveaxle to clear the knuckle.

16   If you're working on the right side driveaxle, use a large flat prybar to release the inner end of the driveaxle from the front differential assembly.

17   If you're working on the left side driveaxle, make reference marks on the driveaxle flange and the differential side gear flange, then remove the fasteners and detach the axle from the differential side gear flange (see illustration 13.3).

18   Installation is the reverse of the removal procedure, noting the following points:

a)   *When installing the right side driveaxle, hold the driveaxle straight out, then push it in sharply to seat the set-ring on the splines of the inner CV joint. To make sure the set-ring is properly seated, attempt to pull the inner CV joint housing out of the differential by hand. If the set-ring is properly seated, the inner joint will not move out.*

b)   *Tighten the suspension fasteners to the torque listed in the Chapter 10 Specifications.*

c)   *Tighten the driveaxle/hub nut to the torque listed in this Chapter's Specifications, then install a new cotter pin.*

d)   *Install the wheel and lug nuts, lower the vehicle and tighten the lug nuts to the torque listed in the Chapter 1 Specifications.*

14   Driveaxle boot - replacement

➡**Note 1: If the CV joints are worn, indicating the need for an overhaul (usually due to torn boots), explore all options before beginning the job. Complete rebuilt driveaxles are available on an exchange basis, which eliminates much time and work.**

➡**Note 2: Some auto parts stores carry split type replacement boots, which can be installed without removing the driveaxle from the vehicle. This is a convenient alternative; however, the driveaxle should be removed and the CV joint disassembled and cleaned to ensure the joint is free from contaminants such as moisture and dirt which will accelerate CV joint wear.**

1   Remove the driveaxle from the vehicle (see Section 13).

2   Mount the driveaxle in a vise. The jaws of the vise should be lined with wood or rags to prevent damage to the driveaxle.

REAR DRIVEAXLE

Disassembly

⬧ **Refer to illustrations 14.3, 14.4, 14.5, 14.7, 14.9, 14.10 and 14.11**

3   Pry open the locking tabs on the boot clamps, remove the clamps from the boot and discard them (see illustration).

4   Slide the boot back on the axleshaft and pry the wire ring ball retainer from the outer race (see illustration).

5   Pull the outer race off the inner bearing assembly (see illustration).

6   Wipe as much grease as possible off the inner bearing.

7   Remove the snap-ring from the end of the axleshaft (see illustration).

8   Slide the inner bearing assembly off the axleshaft.

9   Mark the inner race and cage to ensure that they are reassembled with the correct sides facing out (see illustration).

10   Using a screwdriver or piece of wood, pry the balls from the cage (see illustration). Be careful not to scratch the inner race, the balls or the cage.

11   Rotate the inner race 90-degrees, align the inner race lands with the cage windows and rotate the race out of the cage (see illustration).

14.3 To remove the boot clamps, pry open the locking tabs

14.4 Pry the wire retainer ring from the CV joint housing with a small screwdriver

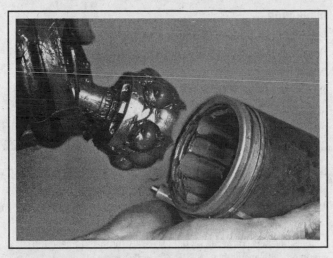

14.5 With the retainer removed, the outer race can be pulled off the bearing assembly

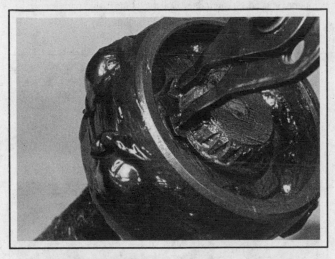

14.7 Remove the snap-ring from the end of the axleshaft

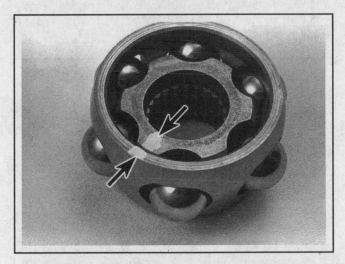

14.9 Make index marks on the inner race and cage so they'll both be facing the same direction when reassembled

14.10 Pry the balls from the cage with a screwdriver (be careful not to nick or scratch them)

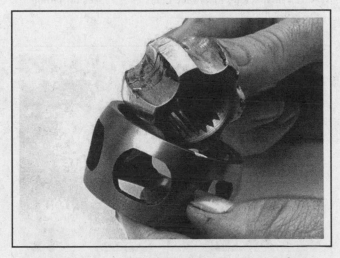

14.11 Tilt the inner race 90-degrees and rotate it out of the cage

Inspection

♦ **Refer to illustrations 14.12a and 14.12b**

12 Clean the components with solvent to remove all traces of grease. Inspect the cage and races for pitting, score marks, cracks and other signs of wear and damage. Shiny, polished spots are normal and will not adversely affect CV joint performance (see illustrations). If the outer CV joint boot is torn or damaged, now is the time to set aside the inner CV joint parts, remove the outer boot, and clean and inspect the outer CV joint.

Reassembly

♦ **Refer to illustrations 14.14, 14.16, 14.17, 14.20, 14.23, 14.24a, 14.24b and 14.24c**

13 Insert the inner race into the cage. Verify that the matchmarks are on the same side. However, it's not necessary for them to be in direct alignment with each other.

14 Press the balls into the cage windows with your thumbs (see illustration).

15 Wrap the axleshaft splines with tape to avoid damaging the boot.

16 Slide the small boot clamp and boot onto the axleshaft, then remove the tape (see illustration).

17 Install the inner race and cage assembly on the axleshaft with the larger diameter side, or bulge, of the cage facing the axleshaft end (see illustration).

18 Install the snap-ring (see illustration 14.7).

19 Fill the boot with CV joint grease (normally included with the new boot kit).

20 Pack the inner race and cage assembly with grease, by hand, until grease is worked completely into the assembly (see illustration).

21 Slide the outer race down onto the inner race and install the wire ring retainer.

22 Wipe any excess grease from the axle boot groove on the outer race. Seat the small diameter of the boot in the recessed area on the axleshaft and install the clamp. Push the other end of the boot onto the outer CV joint housing and seat it into the recessed area on the housing.

23 Position the CV joint mid-way through its travel, then equalize the pressure in the boot by inserting a dull screwdriver between the boot and the outer race (see illustration). Don't damage the boot with the tool.

24 Install the boot clamps (see illustrations). A special clamp installation tool is needed. The tool is available at most auto parts stores.

25 Install the driveaxle assembly (see Section 1).

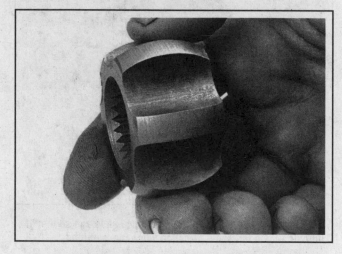

14.12a Inspect the inner race lands and grooves for pitting and score marks

14.12b Inspect the cage for cracks, pitting and score marks (shiny spots are normal and don't affect operation)

14.14 Press the balls into the cage through the windows

14.16 Wrap the splined area of the axleshaft with tape to prevent damage to the boot(s) when installing it

14.17 Install the inner race and cage assembly with the large diameter end toward the splined end of the axleshaft

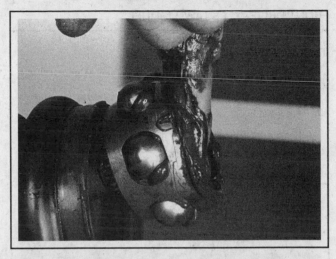

14.20 Pack grease into the bearing until it's completely full

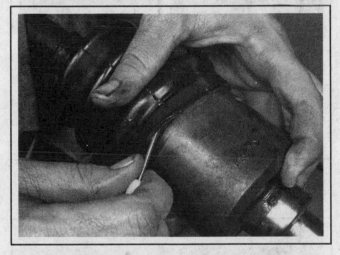

14.23 With the CV joint positioned mid-way through its travel, equalize the pressure inside the boot by inserting a small, dull screwdriver between the boot and the outer race

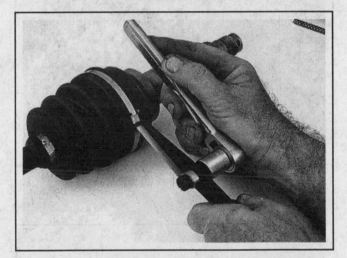

14.24a Secure the boot clamps with a special banding tool such as the one shown here (available at most auto parts stores); install the clamp, thread it onto the tool, pull the clamp tight . . .

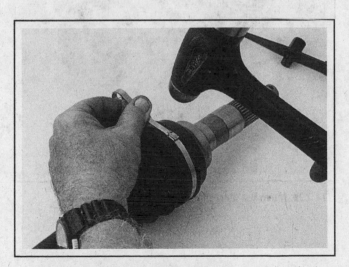

14.24b . . . peen over the locking tabs . . .

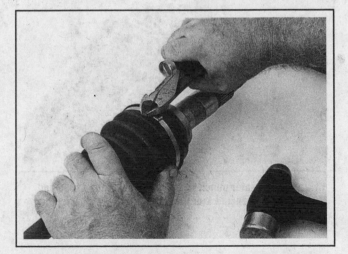

14.24c . . . and cut off the excess

FRONT DRIVEAXLES (AWD MODELS)

Inner CV joint and boot

Removal

▶ **Refer to illustrations 14.26, 14.27, 14.28, 14.29a, 14.29b and 14.30**

26 Remove the boot clamps (see illustration).

27 Pull the boot back from the inner CV joint and slide the joint housing off. Be sure to mark the relationship of the tripod to the outer race (see illustration).

28 Use a center punch to mark the tripod and axleshaft to ensure that they are reassembled properly (see illustration).

29 Remove the bearing retainer clip from the end of the axleshaft (see illustrations).

30 Use a hammer and a brass punch to drive the tripod joint from the driveaxle (see illustration).

31 Remove the ring from the axleshaft. Discard it if it isn't a tight fit.

14.26 Cut off the boot clamps and discard them

14.27 Mark the relationship of the tripod assembly to the outer race

14.28 Use a center punch to place marks on the tripod and the driveaxle to ensure that they are properly reassembled

14.29a Move the stop-ring down the axleshaft

Inspection

32 Clean the old grease from the outer race and the tripod bearing assembly. Carefully disassemble each section of the tripod assembly, one at a time so as not to mix up the parts, and clean the needle bearings with solvent.

33 Inspect the rollers, tripod, bearings and outer race for scoring, pitting or other signs of abnormal wear, which will warrant the replacement of the inner CV joint.

Reassembly

♦ **Refer to illustrations 14.37, 14.40a, 14.40b, 14.40c, 14.40d and 14.40e**

34 Slide the clamps and boot onto the axleshaft. It's a good idea to wrap the axleshaft splines with tape to prevent damaging the boot (see illustration 14.16).

35 Install a new stop-ring.

36 Place the tripod on the shaft (making sure the marks are aligned) and install a new circlip. Slide the tripod out to the end of the shaft, then install the stop ring into its groove.

37 Apply grease to the tripod assembly, the inside of the joint housing and the inside of the boot (see illustration).

38 Slide the boot into place.

39 Position the CV joint mid-way through its travel, then equalize the pressure in the boot by inserting a dull screwdriver between the boot and the outer race (see illustration 14.23). Don't damage the boot with the tool.

40 Tighten the boot clamps (see illustrations).

41 Install the driveaxle assembly (see Section 13).

14.29b . . . slide the tripod back and remove the circlip

14.30 Drive the tripod joint from the axleshaft with a brass punch and hammer - make sure you don't damage the bearing surfaces or the splines on the shaft

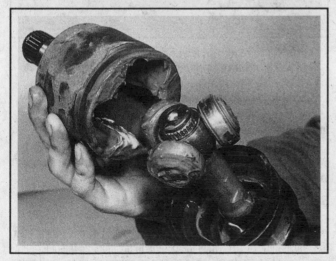

14.37 Pack the outer race with grease and slide it over the tripod assembly - make sure the match marks on the CV joint housing and tripod line up

14.40a To install new fold-over type clamps, bend the tang down . . .

14.40b . . . and flatten the tabs to hold it in place

14.40c To install band-type clamps you'll need a special tool; install the band with its end pointing in the direction of axle rotation and tighten it securely, then pivot the tool up 90-degrees and tap the center of the clip with a center punch . . .

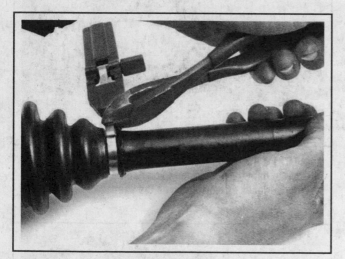

14.40d . . . then bend the end of the clamp back over the clip and cut off the excess

14.40e If you're installing crimp-type boot clamps, you'll need a pair of special crimping pliers (available at most auto parts stores)

Outer CV joint

Disassembly

42 Remove the driveaxle (see Section 13).

43 Mount the driveaxle in a vise with wood lined jaws to prevent damage to the axleshaft. Check the outer CV joint for excessive play in the radial direction, which indicates worn parts. Check for smooth operation throughout the full range of motion for each CV joint. If a boot is torn, the recommended procedure is to disassemble the joint, clean the components and inspect for damage due to loss of lubrication and possible contamination by foreign matter. If the CV joint is in good condition, lubricate it with CV joint grease and install a new boot.

44 Remove the inner CV joint and boot as described previously.

45 Cut the outer CV joint boot clamps with side-cutters, then remove and discard them.

46 Slide the outer boot off the shaft.

Inspection

47 Rotate the outer CV joint housing at an angle to the driveaxle to expose the bearings, inner race and cage. Inspect the bearing surfaces for signs of wear. If the CV joint is worn, replace the driveaxle.

Reassembly

48 Slide the new outer boot onto the axleshaft. It's a good idea to wrap tape around the splines of the shaft to prevent damage to the boot (see illustration 14.16). When the boot is in position, fill the outer joint with CV joint grease (pack the joint with as much grease as it will hold and put the rest into the boot). Slide the boot on the rest of the way and install the new clamps (see illustrations 14.40a through 14.40e).

➡**Note: The length of the outer joint isn't adjustable; just make sure that each end of the boot is seated properly and that there are no dimples in the folds in the boot.**

15 Differential assembly - removal and installation

REAR DIFFERENTIAL

♦ **Refer to Illustrations 15.7 and 15.8**

1   Raise the rear of the vehicle and support it securely on jackstands. Block the front wheels to prevent the vehicle from rolling. Place the transmission in Neutral with the parking brake off.

2   Drain the differential lubricant (see Chapter 1).

3   Remove the ABS sensors from the differential (see Chapter 9).

4   Remove the rear stabilizer bar (see Chapter 10).

5   Detach the driveaxles from the side gear flanges (see Section 13). Support the driveaxles with wire or rope - don't let them hang by the other CV joints.

6   Mark the relationship of the driveshaft to the pinion flange, then unbolt the driveshaft from the flange (see Section 10). Suspend the driveshaft with a piece of wire (don't let it hang by the center support bearing).

7   Support the differential with a floor jack. Remove the mounting bracket nut at the rear of the differential (see illustration).

8   Remove the two differential front mounting bolts (see illustration). Slowly lower the jack and remove the differential out from under the vehicle.

9   Installation is the reverse of the removal procedure. Tighten all fasteners to the torque values listed in this Chapter's Specifications. Fill the differential with the proper lubricant (see Chapter 1).

FRONT DIFFERENTIAL

10 Apply the parking brake, then raise the front of the vehicle and support it securely on jackstands.

11 Drain the differential lubricant (see Chapter 1).

12 Remove the three upper bolts from the engine mounting bracket.

13 Remove the right-bank catalytic converter (see Chapter 6).

14 Remove the front stabilizer bar (see Chapter 10).

15 Remove the steering gear mounting bolts (see Chapter 10).

16 Remove the front driveaxles (see Section 13).

17 Remove the left-front side shaft.

18 Remove the front driveshaft (see Section 10).

19 Remove the suspension crossmember (see Chapter 10).

20 Detach the breather tube from the top of the differential.

21 Support the differential with a floor jack. Remove the mounting bolts and slowly lower the differential.

22 Installation is the reverse of the removal procedure. Tighten all fasteners to the torque values listed in this Chapter's Specifications and the Chapter 10 Specifications. Fill the differential with the proper lubricant (see Chapter 1).

15.7 Remove the mounting nut at the rear of the differential

15.8 Remove the mounting bolts at the front of the differential

16 Transfer case (AWD models) - removal and installation

1   Apply the parking brake, then raise the front of the vehicle and support it securely on jackstands.

2   Remove the front section of the exhaust system (see Chapter 4).

3   Drain the transfer case lubricant (see Chapter 1).

4   Remove the driveshafts (see Section 10).

5   Disconnect the electrical connector from the transfer case, and free any harness clips.

6   Detach the breather hose from the transfer case.

7   Support the transmission with a floor jack, then remove the rear engine mount. Lower the transmission and transfer case far enough to access the transfer case upper mounting bolts.

8   Support the transfer case with another floor jack. Remove the mounting bolts, pull the transfer case to the rear and carefully lower it to the ground.

9   Installation is the reverse of removal. Tighten the mounting bolts to the torque listed in this Chapter's Specifications.

10 Fill the transfer case with the proper lubricant.

17 Transfer case (AWD models) - oil seal replacement

1   Apply the parking brake, then raise the front of the vehicle and support it securely on jackstands.

2   Drain the transfer case lubricant (see Chapter 1).

FRONT OIL SEAL

3   Remove the front driveshaft (see Section 10).

4   Carefully pry the seal out of the transfer case.

5   Lubricate the new seal with clean transfer case lubricant, then install the seal using a seal driver or a large socket with an outer circumference slightly smaller than that of the seal.

6   Install the driveshaft (see Section 10).

7   Fill the transfer case with the proper lubricant (see Chapter 1).

REAR OIL SEAL

8   Detach the front of the rear driveshaft from the transfer case flange (see Section 10).

9   A flange holding tool will be required to keep the transfer case flange from moving while the self-locking flange nut is loosened. A chain wrench will also work (see illustration 12.3).

10 Remove the flange nut. Obtain a new nut for installation.

11 Apply matchmarks on the flange and the transfer case output shaft. Withdraw the flange. It may be necessary to use a two-jaw puller engaged behind the flange to draw it off (see illustration 12.5). Do not attempt to pry or hammer behind the flange or hammer on the end of the pinion shaft.

12 Pry out the old seal and discard it.

13 Lubricate the lips of the new seal with clean transfer case lubricant, then install the seal using a seal driver or a large socket with an outer circumference slightly smaller than that of the seal. Install the seal to a depth of 17/64 to 9/32-inch (6.7 to 7.3 mm).

14 Install the flange, aligning the marks made in Step 5. If necessary, tighten the nut to draw the flange into place. Do not try to hammer the flange into position.

15 Apply a bead of RTV sealant to the ends of the splines visible in the center of the flange so oil will be sealed in.

16 Install a new flange nut. Tighten the nut to the torque listed in this Chapter's Specifications.

17 Reconnect the driveshaft to the transfer case flange (see Section 10). Fill the differential with the specified fluid (see Chapter 1).

Specifications

General

Differential lubricant	See Chapter 1
Differential drive pinion bearing preload	
Front	7 to 13 in-lbs (0.78 to 1.57 Nm)
Rear	24 to 28 in-lbs (2.65 to 3.23 Nm)

Torque specifications

→Note: One foot-pound (ft-lb) of torque is equivalent to 12 inch-pounds (in-lbs) of torque. Torque values below approximately 15 ft-lbs are expressed in inch-pounds, since most foot-pound torque wrenches are not accurate at these smaller values.

	Ft-lbs (unless otherwise indicated)	Nm
Clutch master cylinder mounting bolts	82 in-lbs	9.3
Clutch pressure plate-to-flywheel bolts	29	39
Clutch release cylinder mounting bolts		
2006 and earlier 350Z, 2007 and earlier G35 Coupe and 2006 and earlier G35 Sedan models	17	23.4
All other models	80 in-lbs	9
Differential pinion nut		
Front	94 to 181	128 to 245
Rear	109 to 238	147 to 323
Driveaxle/hub nuts		
Rear driveaxle	177	240
Front driveaxle (AWD models)	174 to 230	236 to 313
Driveaxle-to-differential side gear flange		
Front (left side)	36	49
Rear	52	71
Driveshaft-to-differential flange		
Front (AWD models)	29	39
Rear	54	73.5
Center support bearing mounting bolts	33	45
Front differential mounting fasteners	26	35.8
Engine mounting bracket-to-front differential bolts	36	49
Rear differential mounting fasteners		
Bolts	74	100
Nut	81	110
Transfer case mounting bolts	27	37
Transfer case companion flange	275	372
Wheel lug nuts	See Chapter 1	

Notes

Section

Reference to other Chapters

9

BRAKES

1 General information

The vehicles covered by this manual are equipped with hydraulically operated front and rear disc brake systems. These brakes are self-adjusting and automatically compensate for pad wear.

HYDRAULIC SYSTEM

The hydraulic system consists of two separate circuits. In the event of a leak or failure in one hydraulic circuit, the other circuit will remain operative.

POWER BRAKE BOOSTER

The power brake booster is mounted on the firewall in the engine compartment. It uses engine manifold vacuum and atmospheric pressure to provide assistance to the hydraulically operated brakes.

PARKING BRAKE

The parking brake actuates a pair of parking brake shoes mounted inside a drum (hub) portion of each rear brake disc. The parking brake cables and shoes are adjustable.

SERVICE

After completing any operation involving disassembly of any part of the brake system, always test-drive the vehicle to check for proper braking performance before resuming normal driving. When testing the brakes, perform the tests on a clean, dry, flat surface. Conditions other than these can lead to inaccurate test results.

Test the brakes at various speeds with both light and heavy pedal pressure. The vehicle should stop evenly without pulling to one side or the other. Avoid locking the brakes, because this slides the tires and diminishes braking efficiency and control of the vehicle.

Tires, vehicle load and wheel alignment are other factors that affect braking performance as well.

PRECAUTIONS

There are some general cautions and warnings involving the brake system on this vehicle:

a) *Use only brake fluid conforming to DOT 3 specifications.*

b) *The brake pads and linings contain fibers which are hazardous to your health if inhaled. Whenever you work on brake system components, clean all parts with brake system cleaner. Do not allow the fine dust to become airborne. Also, wear an approved filtering mask.*

c) *Safety should be paramount whenever any servicing of the brake components is performed. Do not use parts or fasteners which are not in perfect condition, and be sure that all clearances and torque specifications are adhered to. If you are at all unsure about a certain procedure, seek professional advice. Upon completion of any brake system work, test the brakes carefully in a controlled area before putting the vehicle into normal service. If a problem is suspected in the brake system, don't drive the vehicle until it's fixed.*

d) *Clean up any spilled brake fluid immediately and then wash the area with large amounts of water. This is especially true for any finished or painted surfaces.*

2 Anti-lock Brake System (ABS) - general information

1   The Anti-lock Brake System (ABS) is designed to help maintain vehicle steerability, directional stability and optimum deceleration under severe braking conditions on most road surfaces. The ABS system is primarily designed to prevent wheel lockup during heavy or panic braking situations. It works by monitoring the rotational speed of each wheel and controlling the brake line pressure to each wheel when engaged. The data provided by the ABS wheel speed sensors is shared with other systems that aid in vehicle control and handling. These systems help with traction control, over/under-steering and acceleration control. These systems work along with the ABS system to maximize braking performance and vehicle control in panic braking situations.

COMPONENTS

Actuator assembly

▶ Refer to illustration 2.2

2   The actuator assembly is mounted in the engine compartment and consists of an electric hydraulic pump and solenoid valves (see illustration).

a) *The electric pump provides hydraulic pressure to charge the reservoirs in the actuator, which supplies pressure to the braking system. The pump and reservoirs are housed in the actuator assembly.*

b) *The solenoid valves modulate brake line pressure during ABS operation.*

2.2 The location of an ABS actuator assembly on a 2004 G35 Sedan - other models are similar

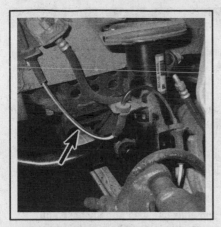

2.11 Follow the wheel speed sensor wire harness away from the wheel to the connector (front shown)

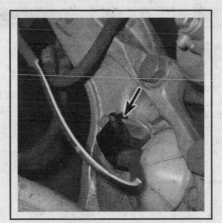

2.12a The front wheel speed sensors are mounted on the back sides of the steering knuckles

2.12b The rear wheel speed sensors are mounted at the rear differential cover

Wheel speed sensors

3   There is a wheel speed sensor for each wheel. When the wheels are turning, they send a signal to the electronic controller indicating wheel rotational speed.

4   The front speed sensors are mounted to the front steering knuckles in close relationship to toothed sensor rings, which are pressed onto the back of the hub and bearing assemblies.

5   The rear wheel sensors are bolted to the rear differential. The rear sensor rings are pressed onto the differential side gear flanges that bolt up to the rear driveaxles.

ABS control unit

6   The ABS control unit (or computer) is mounted in the interior of the vehicle by the steering column (Infiniti models) or under the hood (Nissan models) and is the brain for the ABS system. The unit accepts and processes information received from various sources and the wheel speed sensors to control the hydraulic line pressure and avoid wheel lock up. The computer also constantly monitors the system, even under normal driving conditions, to find faults within the system. The ABS control unit also controls the Vehicle Dynamic Control (VDC), the Traction Control System (TCS) and the Electronic Brake Force Distribution (EBD) (if equipped).

DIAGNOSIS AND REPAIR

7   If a dashboard warning light comes on and stays on while the vehicle is in operation, the ABS system requires attention. Although special electronic ABS diagnostic testing tools are necessary to properly diagnose the ABS system, you can perform a few preliminary checks before taking the vehicle to a dealer service department.

   a) *Check the brake fluid level in the reservoir.*
   b) *Verify that the computer electrical connectors are securely connected.*
   c) *Check the electrical connectors at the hydraulic control unit.*
   d) *Check the fuses.*
   e) *Follow the wiring harness to each wheel speed sensor and verify that all connections are secure and that the wiring is undamaged.*

8   If the above preliminary checks do not rectify the problem, the

vehicle should be diagnosed by a dealer service department or other qualified repair shop. Due to the complexity of this system, all actual repair work must be done by a qualified automotive technician.

⁂ **WARNING:**

Do NOT try to repair an ABS wiring harness. The ABS system is sensitive to even the smallest changes in resistance. Repairing the harness could alter resistance values and cause the system to malfunction. If the ABS wiring harness is damaged in any way, it must be replaced.

⁂ **CAUTION:**

Make sure the negative battery terminal is disconnected before unplugging or reattaching any electrical connections.

WHEEL SPEED SENSOR - REMOVAL AND INSTALLATION

◆ **Refer to Illustrations 2.11, 2.12a and 2.12b**

9   Disconnect the cable from the negative battery terminal (see Chapter 5, Section 1).

10 If you're removing a front wheel speed sensor, loosen the wheel lug nuts, raise the vehicle and support it securely on jackstands. Remove the wheel.

11 Trace the wiring back from the sensor, detaching all brackets and clips while noting its correct routing, then disconnect the electrical connector (see illustration).

12 Remove the mounting bolt and carefully pull the sensor out from the steering knuckle or the rear differential (see illustrations).

13 Installation is the reverse of the removal procedure. Tighten the mounting fastener securely.

14 Install the wheel and lug nuts, tightening them securely. Lower the vehicle and tighten the lug nuts to the torque listed in the Chapter 1 Specifications.

3 Disc brake pads - replacement

❈ WARNING:

Disc brake pads must be replaced on both front or on both rear wheels at the same time - never replace the pads for only one wheel. Also, the dust created by the brake system is harmful to your health. Never blow it out with compressed air and don't inhale any of it. An approved filtering mask should be worn when working on the brakes. Do not, under any circumstances, use petroleum-based solvents to clean brake parts. Use brake system cleaner only!

1 Loosen the wheel lug nuts, raise the front or rear of the vehicle and support it securely on jackstands. Block the wheels at the opposite end.

2 Remove the cap from the brake fluid reservoir.

3 Remove the wheels. Work on one brake assembly at a time, using the assembled brake for reference if necessary.

4 Inspect the brake disc carefully as outlined in Section 5. If machining is necessary, follow the information in that Section to remove the disc.

FLOATING (NON-BREMBO) CALIPERS

◗ **Refer to illustrations 3.5, 3.6, 3.7a through 3.7o and 3.8a through 3.8n**

➡**Note: This procedure applies to both the front and rear disc brakes.**

5 Push the piston completely back into its bore to provide room for the new brake pads. A C-clamp can be used to accomplish this (see illustration). As the piston is depressed to the bottom of the caliper bore, the fluid in the master cylinder reservoir will rise. Remove enough brake fluid so that the reservoir is about half full. Continue to make sure that it doesn't overflow while pushing on the caliper pistons with the C-clamp.

6 Wash the brake caliper with brake cleaner (see illustration).

7 For front calipers, follow the accompanying photos (illustrations 3.7a through 3.7o) for the actual pad replacement procedure. Be sure to stay in order and read the caption under each illustration.

➡**Note: Brake springs and clips can vary slightly based on design. It is a good practice to note how the springs and clips are configured for your specific brake calipers before removing the brake pads. Also, work on one side at a time so that you can use the assembled side for reference.**

❈ CAUTION:

2007 and later G35 Sedan models may be equipped with brake pads that are directional. Match the arrows on the back of the pad with the rotation of the brake rotor for installation on these types of brakes.

3.5 Before removing the caliper, slowly depress the piston into the caliper bore by using a large C-clamp between the outer brake pad and the back of the caliper

3.6 Wash down the brake caliper assembly and the disc with brake cleaner to remove brake dust; DO NOT blow off brake dust with compressed air

3.7a Remove the lower caliper mounting bolt

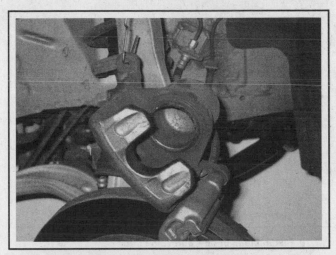

3.7b Pivot the caliper up and secure it with a piece of wire; do not allow the caliper to hang by the flexible brake hose. Be careful not to damage the upper guide-pin boot while rotating the caliper

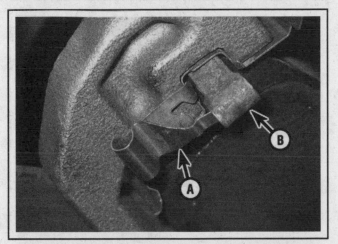

3.7c Note how the return spring (A) (integrated with the upper anti-rattle clip on this design) engages with the pad's wear sensor (B)

3.7d Remove the inner pad . . .

3.7e . . . and the outer pad

3.7f Remove the upper and lower anti-rattle clips; make sure they fit tightly and aren't worn. Replace them if necessary

3.7g Install clean or new anti-rattle clips

3.7h Pull out the lower guide-pin - be careful not to damage the boot. Clean the guide-pin, apply a coat of disc brake grease to it, then reinstall it. Seat the guide-pin boot securely around the guide-pin. Replace any boots that are worn or damaged

3.7i Unhook the caliper from the wire, securing it upwards. Slide the caliper and upper guide-pin away from the mounting bracket as an assembly - be careful not to tear the guide-pin boot in the process. Clean and lubricate the upper guide-pin while holding on to the caliper, then place the caliper back in position (with the upper guide-pin installed into the caliper mounting bracket) and secure it. Seat the guide-pin boot securely around the guide-pin

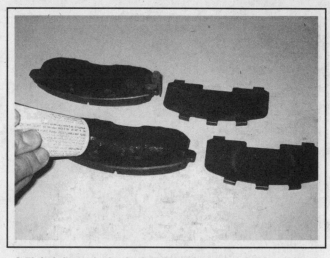

3.7j Lubricate the back of each pad and related shims with a thin coat of disc brake grease . . .

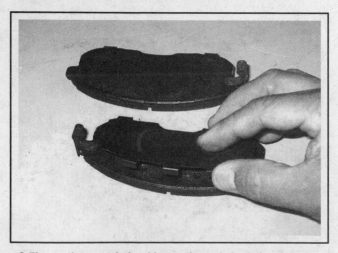

3.7k . . . then match the shims to the pads in their original positions - some models may have more than one shim for each pad and they may differ on each side

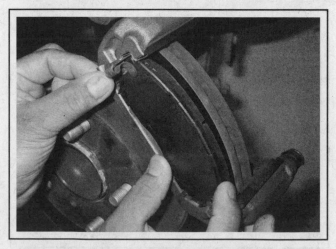

3.7l Install the outer pad, making sure that the ends are seated correctly into the anti-rattle clips and springs . . .

3.7m . . . then install the inner pad in the same way

3.7n Place the caliper back into position over the brake pads and onto the caliper mounting bracket

3.7o Install the caliper mounting bolt into the lower guide-pin and tighten it to the torque listed in this Chapter's Specifications

8 For rear calipers, follow the accompanying photos (illustrations 3.8a through 3.8n) for the actual pad replacement procedure. Be sure to stay in order and read the caption under each illustration.

➡Note: Brake springs and clips can vary slightly based on design. It is a good practice to note how the springs and clips are configured for your specific brake calipers before removing the brake pads. Also, work on one side at a time so that you can use the assembled side for reference.

9 When reinstalling the caliper, be sure to tighten the mounting bolts and mounting bolt/guide-pins to the torque listed in this Chapter's Specifications.

FIXED (BREMBO) CALIPERS

10 From the large opening on the caliper, locate the two horizontal pad pins that go through the caliper and the brake pad backing plates. Look closely at the end of each pad pin and find the small lock-pins

that go through the pad pins. Carefully remove the small lock-pins.

11 Locate the cross-spring in the center of the caliper opening that contacts both pad pins. Push the lower end of the cross-spring away from the bottom pad pin, then remove the pad pin out the same side that the small lock-pin was installed. Remove the top pad pin and the cross-spring.

✳✦ CAUTION:

The pad pins will only come out in one direction; they are removed towards the inboard side on front calipers or the out-board side on rear calipers.

➡Note the direction for installation.

12 Using needle-nose pliers, pull the inboard (inner) brake pad from the caliper.

➡Note: Remove only one pad during this step.

3.8a Remove the upper caliper mounting bolt/guide-pin and pivot the caliper down and secure it with a piece of wire; do not allow the caliper to hang by the flexible brake hose. Be careful not to damage the lower guide-pin boot while rotating the caliper

3.8b Remove the inner pad . . .

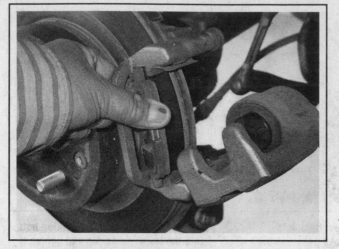

3.8c . . . and the outer pad

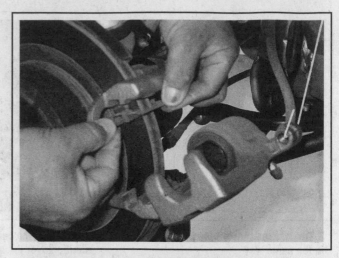

3.8d Remove the upper and lower anti-rattle clips; make sure they fit tightly and aren't worn. Replace them if necessary

3.8e Loosen the mounting bracket bolts (A) and move the bracket so that the lower caliper mounting bolt/guide pin (B) can be removed, cleaned and lubricated

3.8f Install clean or new anti-rattle clips

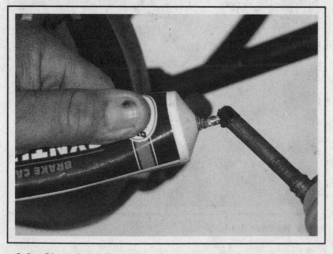

3.8g Clean the caliper mounting bolt/guide-pins and coat them with disc brake grease

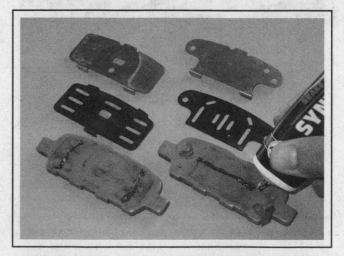

3.8h Lubricate the back of each pad and related shims with disc brake grease - note that they differ on each side. . .

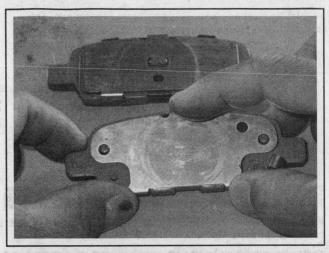

3.8i . . . then match the shims to the pads in their original positions

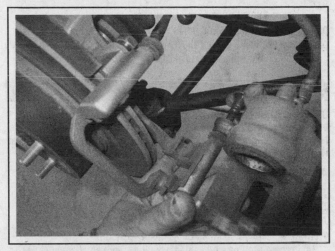

3.8j Pivot the caliper mounting bracket to install the lower caliper mounting bolts/guide-pin (tighten the fasteners later)

3.8k Install the inner pad, making sure that the correct pad is used and the ends are properly seated into the anti-rattle clips and springs . . .

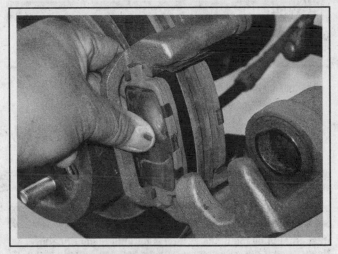

3.8l . . . then install the outer pad in the same way

3.8m Place the caliper back into position over the brake pads and onto the caliper mounting bracket and install the upper caliper mounting bolt/guide-pin

3.8n Tighten the caliper mounting bracket fasteners, then the upper and lower caliper mounting bolts to the torque values listed in this Chapter's Specifications

13 Using a small pry tool or screwdriver, slowly push the caliper piston(s) into the bore(s) on the inboard side. Front calipers have two pistons on each side of the caliper for a total of four. Rear calipers have one piston on each side for a total of two.

✳✳ CAUTION:

On front calipers, one piston can be forced out of the caliper bore while the other is being pushed in on the same side. Use two pry tools to keep one piston from coming out while the other is being pushed in.

As a piston is depressed to the bottom of the caliper bore, the fluid in the master cylinder reservoir will rise. Remove enough brake fluid so the reservoir is about half full. Continue to make sure that it doesn't overflow while pushing on all of the caliper pistons.

14 Prepare each new brake pad by using a very small amount of silicone-based grease on the side edges (not top and bottom) of the pad's metal back plate, and also between the plate and shims (if equipped).

✳✳ WARNING:

Do not get grease on the pad material or any surfaces that are not designated here.

15 Position the new inboard brake pad into the caliper.

➡Note: **No wear sensor should be attached to this pad. The wear sensor is for the outboard brake pad.**

16 Using needle-nose pliers, pull the outboard (outer) brake pad from the caliper.

17 Repeat Step 13 on the outboard side of the caliper.

18 Position the new outboard brake pad (with wear sensor forward) into the caliper.

19 Install the top pad pin and place the cross-spring in position.

20 Press the bottom end of the cross-spring and install the bottom pad pin.

21 Carefully install the small lock-pins to the ends of the pad pins.

✳✳ WARNING:

If the lock-pins are not installed correctly, the pad pins and pads could fall out while the vehicle is moving.

ALL CALIPERS

22 Install the wheels, then lower the vehicle to the ground. Tighten the wheel lug nuts to the torque listed in the Chapter 1 Specifications. Depress the brake pedal a few times to bring the brake pads into contact with the disc. Check the level of the brake fluid, adding some if necessary. Check the operation of the brakes carefully before placing the vehicle into normal service.

---

4   Disc brake caliper - removal and installation

✳✳ WARNING:

Dust created by the brake system is harmful to your health. Never blow it out with compressed air and don't inhale any of it. An approved filtering mask should be worn when working on the brakes. Do not, under any circumstances, use petroleum-based solvents to clean brake parts. Use brake system cleaner only!

➡Note: **Always replace the calipers in pairs - never replace just one of them.**

REMOVAL

1   Loosen the wheel lug nuts, raise the vehicle and support it securely on jackstands. Remove the wheels.

Non-Brembo (floating) calipers

▶ **Refer to illustrations 4.2a, 4.2b and 4.4**

2   Remove the brake hose banjo bolt and disconnect the hose from the caliper. Plug the hose to keep contaminants out of the brake system and to prevent losing any more brake fluid than is necessary (see illustrations).

➡Note: **If you're just removing the caliper for access to other components, don't detach the hose.**

3   Remove the caliper mounting bolts/guide-pins, lift the caliper from the bracket and, if the hose is still attached, support it with a length of wire.

4   On rear calipers, remove the caliper mounting bracket in order to remove the caliper (see illustration).

Brembo (fixed) calipers

5   Remove the brake pads (see Section 3).

➡Note: **Mark the brake pads so that they can be placed in the same position if they are going to be reused.**

6   Detach the brake line from the fitting at the caliper using a flare nut wrench. Plug all openings to minimize brake fluid loss.

✳✳ CAUTION:

Brake fluid will damage paint or finished surfaces. Cover all body parts and be careful not to spill fluid during this procedure. Clean up any spilled brake fluid immediately and wash the area with large amounts of water.

7   Remove the two caliper mounting bolts and the caliper.

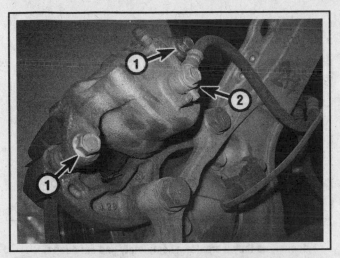

4.2a Brake caliper mounting details (front caliper shown - rear caliper similar)

1. *Caliper mounting bolts (rear calipers have integrated mounting bolts and guide-pins)*
2. *Brake hose fitting and banjo bolt*

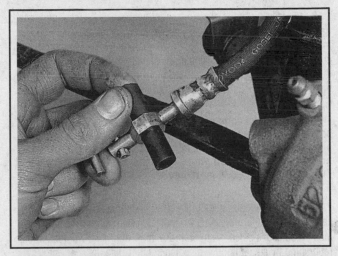

4.2b Using a piece of rubber hose of the appropriate size, plug the brake line banjo fitting to prevent brake fluid from leaking out, and to prevent dirt and moisture from contaminating the fluid in the hose

INSTALLATION

8 Install the caliper by reversing the removal procedure. Tighten the caliper mounting bolts to the torque listed in this Chapter's Specifications. For non-Brembo type calipers, install new sealing washers, one on each side of the brake hose fitting, then tighten the banjo bolt to the torque listed in this Chapter's Specifications. For Brembo type calipers, carefully install the brake line to the caliper using a flare nut wrench and tighten it securely.

9 Bleed the brake system (see Section 8).

10 Install the wheels and lug nuts. Lower the vehicle and tighten the lug nuts to the torque listed in the Chapter 1 Specifications. Check the operation of the brakes carefully before placing the vehicle into normal service.

4.4 Loosen the rear caliper mounting bracket bolts (A) and move the bracket so that the lower caliper mounting bolt (B) can be removed

5 Brake disc - inspection, removal and installation

INSPECTION

▶ **Refer to illustrations 5.4, 5.5a, 5.5b, 5.6a and 5.6b**

➡**Note: The manufacturer suggests using a specialized (on-vehicle) brake lathe that can cut the disc for disc refinishing (machining) while it is still installed on the vehicle, although it is not essential. Moreover, this service requires a repair facility with the specialized tool to have the vehicle, as opposed to your taking just the brake discs to a machine shop for refinishing.**

1 Loosen the wheel lug nuts, raise the vehicle and support it securely on jackstands. Remove the wheel.

2 Remove the brake caliper as outlined in Section 4. On models with floating calipers, it's not necessary to disconnect the brake hose for this procedure. On models with Brembo (fixed) calipers, unscrew the brake line fitting and plug the line. After removing the caliper bolts, suspend the caliper out of the way with a piece of wire. Don't let the caliper hang by the hose and don't stretch or twist the hose.

3 Reinstall two lug nuts with washers (for spacing) to hold the disc securely against the hub.

4   Visually check the disc surface for score marks, cracks and other damage. Light scratches and shallow grooves are normal after use and may not always be detrimental to brake operation. Deep score marks or cracks may require disc refinishing by an automotive machine shop, or disc replacement (see illustration). Be sure to check both sides of the disc. If the brake pedal pulsates during brake application, suspect disc runout.

→ **Note: The most common symptoms of damaged or worn brake discs are pulsation in the brake pedal when the brakes are applied or loud grinding noises caused from severely worn brake pads. If these symptoms are extreme, it is very likely that the disc(s) will need to be replaced.**

5   To check disc runout, place a dial indicator at a point about 1/2-inch from the outer edge of the disc (see illustration). Set the indicator to zero and turn the disc. An indicator reading that exceeds 0.003 inch could cause pulsation upon brake application and will require disc refinishing by an automotive machine shop or disc replacement.

→ **Note: If disc refinishing or replacement is not necessary, you can deglaze the brake pad surface on the disc with emery cloth or sandpaper (use a swirling motion to ensure a non-directional finish) (see illustration).**

6   The disc must not be machined to a thickness less than the specified minimum refinish thickness. The minimum wear (or discard)

5.4 The brake pads on this vehicle were obviously neglected, as they wore down completely and cut deep grooves into the disc - wear this severe means the disc must be replaced

thickness is cast into either the front or backside of the disc (see illustration). The disc thickness can be checked with a micrometer (see illustration).

5.5a Use a dial indicator to check disc runout; if the reading exceeds the maximum allowable runout limit, the disc will have to be machined or replaced

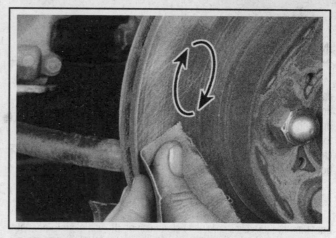

5.5b Using a swirling motion, remove the glaze from the disc surface with sandpaper or emery cloth

5.6a The minimum wear dimension is usually cast into the back side of the disc (typical shown)

5.6b Use a micrometer to measure disc thickness

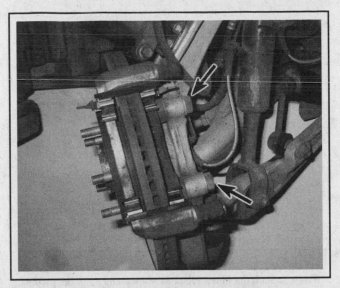

5.7 The caliper mounting bracket is retained by these two bolts (front caliper shown - rear caliper similar)

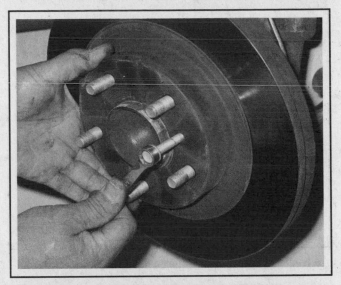

5.8 This disc has a threaded hole where a bolt can be used to push a stuck disc off of the hub flange

REMOVAL AND INSTALLATION

▶ **Refer to illustrations 5.7 and 5.8**

7   Remove the caliper mounting bracket (see illustration).

➡**Note: This step does not apply to Brembo brakes.**

8   Mark the disc in relation to the hub so that it can be installed in its original position on the hub, then remove the disc. If it's stuck, make sure you have removed any lug nuts installed during inspection. You can use a mallet to free a stuck disc from the hub. Or, on some discs, install a bolt into the threaded hole to free the disc (see illustration).

➡**Note: On rear discs, make sure the parking brake is released. If the disc still cannot be removed, retract the parking brake shoes using the adjuster (see Section 11).**

9   Clean the hub flange and the inside of the brake disc thoroughly,

removing any rust or corrosion, then install the disc onto the hub assembly.

10   Install the caliper mounting bracket (non-Brembo calipers) and tighten the bolts to the torque listed in this Chapter's Specifications.

11   Install the brake pads and caliper, tightening the bolts to the torque listed in this Chapter's Specifications. Bleeding of the system will not be necessary unless the brake hose was disconnected from the caliper.

12   On models with Brembo brakes, bleed the brake system (see Section 8).

13   Install the wheel, then lower the vehicle to the ground. Tighten the wheel lug nuts to the torque listed in the Chapter 1 Specifications. Depress the brake pedal a few times to bring the brake pads into contact with the disc. Check the operation of the brakes carefully before placing the vehicle into normal service.

6   Master cylinder - removal and installation

▶ **Refer to illustration 6.5**

❊❊ CAUTION:

Brake fluid will damage paint or finished surfaces. Cover all body parts and be careful not to spill fluid during this procedure. Clean up any spilled brake fluid immediately and wash the area with large amounts of water.

1   Disconnect the cable(s) from the negative battery terminal(s) (see Chapter 5, Section 1).

2   Firmly depress the brake pedal several times to remove all vacuum from the power brake booster.

3   Clean the master cylinder and reservoir thoroughly with brake cleaner.

4   Remove as much fluid as possible from the reservoir with a large syringe.

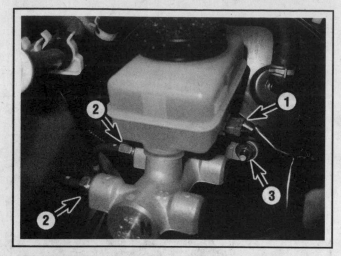

6.5 Master cylinder installation details

1   *Electrical connector*
2   *Brake line fittings*
3   *Mounting nut (one hidden - located on the other
     side of the mounting flange)*

5   Unplug the electrical connector for the brake fluid level warning switch (see illustration).

6   Place rags under the fittings and prepare caps or plastic bags to cover the ends of the lines once they're disconnected.

7   Loosen the fittings at the ends of the brake lines where they enter the master cylinder. To prevent rounding off the corners on the tube-nuts, use a flare-nut wrench (see illustration 6.5).

8   Carefully move the brake lines away from the master cylinder and plug the ends to prevent contamination.

9   Remove the master cylinder mounting nuts. Pull the master cylinder off the studs to remove it. Again, be careful not to spill fluid or bend the brake lines as this is done.

✳✳ CAUTION:

The primary piston of the master cylinder is exposed when the master cylinder is withdrawn. Be careful not to damage, strain or pull on the piston while the master cylinder is removed.

INSTALLATION

▶ **Refer to illustrations 6.11 and 6.21**

10   Bench bleed the new master cylinder before installing it. Because it will be necessary to depress the master cylinder piston and, at the same time, control flow from the brake line outlets, it is recommended that the master cylinder be mounted in a vise.

➡ **Note: If the replacement master cylinder is not equipped with a reservoir, remove the reservoir from the old master cylinder and place it on the new one using new seals.**

11   Attach a pair of master cylinder bleeder tubes to the outlet ports of the master cylinder (see illustration).

6.11 Place the master cylinder in a vise by its mounting flange, attach the bleed tubes as shown and push the piston with a blunt tool several times to bench bleed the master cylinder

12   Fill the reservoir with brake fluid of the recommended type (see Chapter 1).

13   Slowly push the pistons into the master cylinder (a large Phillips screwdriver can be used for this) - air will be expelled from the pressure chambers and into the reservoir. Because the tubes are submerged in fluid, air can't be drawn back into the master cylinder when you release the pistons (see illustration 6.11).

14   Repeat the procedure until no more air bubbles are present.

15   Remove the bleed tubes, one at a time, and install plugs in the open ports to prevent fluid leakage and air from entering the system.

16   Install a new O-ring seal in the groove on the end of the master cylinder and coat it with silicone grease. Continue to grease the entire area from the O-ring to the end of the master cylinder that is inserted into the power brake booster. Also, coat the bore of the booster itself.

✳✳ WARNING:

Do not reuse the old O-ring.

17   Install the reservoir cover and remove the master cylinder from the vise.

18   Using a new gasket on the master cylinder (if equipped), install the master cylinder over the studs on the power brake booster and tighten the attaching nuts only finger tight at this time.

19   Thread the brake line fittings into the master cylinder until they are finger tight. Since the master cylinder is still a bit loose, it can be moved slightly in order for the fittings to thread in easily. Do not force the tube nuts with a tool; they should turn easily when screwed in straight.

20   Tighten the mounting nuts to the torque listed in this Chapter's Specifications, then tighten the brake line fittings securely.

21   Fill the master cylinder reservoir with the correct fluid (see Chapter 1), then bleed the brake system as described in Section 8. To bleed

the master cylinder on the vehicle, have an assistant pump the brake pedal several times slowly, then hold the pedal to the floor. Loosen the line fittings one at a time to allow air and fluid to escape. Repeat this procedure on both fittings until the fluid is clear of air bubbles (see illustration).

✳✳ CAUTION:

Have plenty of rags on hand to catch the fluid - brake fluid will ruin painted surfaces. Wash off spilled fluid with plenty of water.

22 The remainder of installation is the reverse of removal. Test the operation of the brake system carefully before placing the vehicle into normal service.

✳✳ WARNING:

Do not operate the vehicle if you are in doubt about the effectiveness of the brake system. On models equipped with ABS, it is possible for air to become trapped in the anti-lock brake system hydraulic control unit. If the pedal continues to feel spongy after repeated bleedings, or the BRAKE or ANTI-LOCK light stays on, have the vehicle towed to a dealer service department or other qualified repair shop to be bled with the aid of a scan tool.

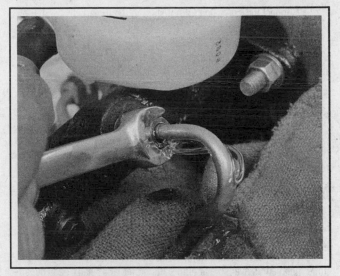

6.21 Have an assistant depress the brake pedal and hold it down, then loosen the fitting nut, allowing the air and fluid to escape; repeat this procedure on both fittings until the fluid is clear of air bubbles

7   Brake hoses and lines - inspection and replacement

INSPECTION

1   About every six months, with the vehicle raised and supported securely on jackstands, the rubber hoses which connect the steel brake lines with the front and rear brake assemblies should be inspected for cracks, chafing of the outer cover, leaks, blisters and other damage. These are important and vulnerable parts of the brake system and inspection should be complete. A light and mirror will be helpful for a thorough check. If a hose exhibits any of the above conditions, replace it with a new one.

REPLACEMENT

Front brake hose

▶ **Refer to illustration 7.3**

2   Loosen the wheel lug nuts, raise the vehicle and support it securely on jackstands. Remove the wheel.

3   At the frame bracket, unscrew the brake line fitting from the hose (see illustration). Use a flare-nut wrench to prevent rounding off the corners.

4   Remove the U-clip from the female fitting at the frame bracket with a pair of pliers, then pass the hose through the bracket.

5   At the caliper end of the hose, remove the banjo fitting bolt, then separate the hose from the caliper. Note that there are two copper sealing washers, one on each side of the fitting - they should be replaced with new ones during installation.

6   Remove the fasteners from the hose blocks at the steering knuckle and shock absorber, then detach the hose.

➡**Note 1: The replacement hose(s) should be identical to the original one(s).**

➡**Note 2: Some later models will have an additional metal brake line connected between two rubber hoses. Use a flare nut wrench to loosen the line fittings at the hose mounting blocks before removing the fasteners for the hoses at the steering knuckle and shock absorber.**

7   To install the hose, attach the hose to the steering knuckle and shock absorber, then connect the fitting to the caliper with the banjo bolt and new sealing washers. Tighten the bolt to the torque listed in this Chapter's Specifications.

8   Push the metal support into the frame bracket and install the U-clip. Make sure the hose isn't twisted between the caliper and the steering knuckle bracket.

7.3 Using a flare-nut wrench, unscrew the threaded fitting on the brake line (A), then pry the U-clip (B) off the end of the hose and separate the hose from the bracket

9 Connect the brake line fitting, starting the threads by hand, then tighten the fitting securely.

10 Bleed the caliper (see Section 8).

11 Install the wheel and lug nuts, lower the vehicle and tighten the lug nuts to the torque listed in the Chapter 1 Specifications.

Rear brake hose

♦ **Refer to illustration 7.12**

12 The rear brake hose has a fitting and a bracket that is fastened to the rear frame. Otherwise, refer to the previous steps for rear brake hose replacement (see illustration).

Metal brake lines

13 When replacing brake lines, be sure to use the correct parts. Don't use copper tubing for any brake system components. Purchase genuine steel brake lines from a dealer or auto parts store.

14 Prefabricated brake line, with the tube ends already flared and fittings installed, is available at auto parts stores and dealer parts departments.

15 When installing the new line, make sure it's securely supported in the brackets and has plenty of clearance between moving or hot components.

16 After installation, check the master cylinder fluid level and add fluid as necessary. Bleed the brake system (see Section 8) and test the brakes carefully before driving the vehicle in traffic.

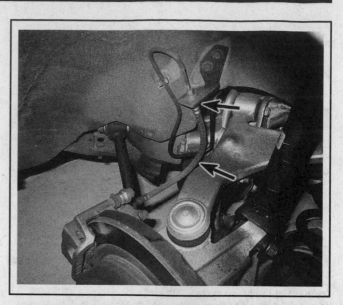

7.12 The rear brake hose and line fitting bracket

8   Brake hydraulic system - bleeding

♦ **Refer to illustration 8.8**

❋❋ WARNING:

Wear eye protection when bleeding the brake system. If the fluid comes in contact with your eyes, immediately rinse them with water and seek medical attention.

➡**Note: Bleeding the hydraulic system is necessary to remove any air that manages to find its way into the system when it's been opened during removal and installation of a hose, line, caliper or master cylinder.**

1   You'll probably have to bleed the system at all four brakes if air has entered it due to low fluid level, or if the brake lines have been disconnected at the master cylinder.

2   If a brake line was disconnected only at a wheel, then only that caliper must be bled. If a brake line is disconnected at a fitting located between the master cylinder and any of the brakes, that part of the system served by the disconnected line must be bled.

3   Disconnect the cable from the negative battery terminal (see Chapter 5, Section 1).

4   Remove any residual vacuum from the brake power booster by applying the brake several times with the engine off.

5   Remove the master cylinder reservoir cover and fill the reservoir with brake fluid. Reinstall the cover.

➡**Note: Check the fluid level often during the bleeding operation and add fluid as necessary to prevent the fluid level from falling low enough to allow air bubbles into the master cylinder.**

6   Have an assistant on hand, as well as a supply of new brake fluid, a clear container partially filled with clean brake fluid, a length of tubing to fit over the bleeder valve and a wrench to open and close the bleeder valve.

7   Beginning at the right rear wheel, loosen the bleeder valve slightly, then tighten it to a point where it's snug but can still be loosened quickly and easily.

➡**Note: Vehicle models with Brembo (or fixed) type calipers will have two bleeder valves - there is one for each side of the caliper. Both sides of the caliper will need to be bled.**

8   Place one end of the tubing over the bleeder valve and submerge the other end in brake fluid in the container (see illustration).

9   Have the assistant depress the brake pedal slowly, then hold the pedal down firmly.

10 While the pedal is held down, open the bleeder valve just enough to allow a flow of fluid to leave the valve. Watch for air bubbles to exit the submerged end of the tube. When the fluid flow slows after a couple of seconds, close the valve and have your assistant release the pedal.

8.8 When bleeding the brakes, a hose is connected to the bleeder valve at the caliper and the other end is submerged in brake fluid. Air will be seen as bubbles in the tube and container. All air must be expelled before moving to the next wheel (typical shown)

11 Repeat Steps 9 and 10 until no more air is seen leaving the tube, then tighten the bleeder valve and proceed to the left front wheel, the left rear wheel and the right front wheel, in that order, and perform the same procedure. Be sure to check the fluid in the master cylinder reservoir frequently.

12 Never use old brake fluid. It contains moisture that will deteriorate the brake system components.

13 Refill the master cylinder with fluid at the end of the operation.

14 Check the operation of the brakes. The pedal should feel solid when depressed, with no sponginess. If necessary, repeat the entire process.

✹✹ WARNING:

Do not operate the vehicle if you are in doubt about the effectiveness of the brake system. It's possible for air to become trapped in the ABS hydraulic control unit, so, if the pedal continues to feel spongy after repeated bleedings or the BRAKE or ANTI-LOCK (ABS) light stays on, have the vehicle towed to a dealer service department or other qualified repair shop to be bled with the aid of a scan tool.

---

9 Power brake booster - check, removal and installation

OPERATING CHECK

1 Depress the brake pedal several times with the engine off and make sure there's no change in the pedal reserve distance (the distance from the depressed pedal to the floor).

2 Depress the pedal and start the engine. If the pedal goes down slightly, operation is normal.

AIRTIGHTNESS CHECK

3 Start the engine and turn it off after one or two minutes. Depress the brake pedal slowly three to four times. If the pedal depresses less each time, the booster is airtight.

4 Depress the brake pedal while the engine is running, then stop the engine with the pedal depressed. If there's no change in the pedal reserve travel after holding the pedal for 30 seconds, the booster is airtight.

REMOVAL

♦ Refer to illustrations 9.10 and 9.11

➡Note: The power brake booster is not serviceable and must be replaced with a new or rebuilt unit.

5 With the engine off, press the brake pedal several times to remove any stored vacuum in the power brake booster.

6 Disconnect the cable(s) from the negative battery terminal(s) (see Chapter 5, Section 1).

7 Remove the brake master cylinder (see Section 6).

8 On 2007 and later G35 Sedan models and 2008 G35 Coupe models, remove the cowl cover (see Chapter 11).

9 Carefully disconnect the vacuum hose(s) from the brake booster.

10 Remove the lock pin and clevis pin that attach the booster pushrod clevis to the brake pedal and disconnect them (see illustration).

➡Note: Be careful not to damage the small plastic keeper on the end of the clevis pin. Squeeze the tabs on it while removing the clevis pin.

9.10 Power brake booster mounting details (2004 G35 Sedan shown - other models similar)

1	Booster pushrod clevis	3	Clevis lock pin
2	Clevis pin		

11 Remove the booster mounting fasteners. Angle the booster up from the firewall until the studs and pushrod clear the holes and remove it from the engine compartment (see illustration).

✳✳ WARNING:

Be careful not to damage any of the brake lines running above the brake booster during removal.

INSTALLATION

▶ **Refer to illustrations 9.12a, 9.12b and 9.12c**

12 Installation procedures are basically the reverse of removal while noting the following points:

   a) *Replace the gasket that goes between the power booster and the firewall.*

   b) *Set the pushrod length at the clevis (see illustration).*

➡**Note: This step is only necessary if the previous setting was changed or the booster is being replaced.**

   c) *Using a hand-held vacuum pump, apply 20 in-Hg of vacuum to the booster and measure the distance from the end of the pushrod to the surface of the booster (see illustration). Compare your measurement to the one in this Chapter's Specifications and adjust the pushrod length if necessary (see illustration).*

➡**Note: The pushrod may be recessed into the booster or it may protrude out depending on your particular design.**

   d) *Tighten the booster mounting nuts to the torque listed in this Chapter's Specifications.*

   e) *Install the booster pushrod clevis to the brake pedal. Replace the clevis pin and lock pin if they show any sign of wear. Apply multi-purpose grease to the pivoting areas of the assembly.*

   f) *Adjust the brake pedal height (see Section 13).*

   g) *Bleed the brake system (see Section 8) and test the operation of the brakes before putting the vehicle into normal service.*

9.11 Power brake booster mounting fasteners (one fastener not seen in photo)

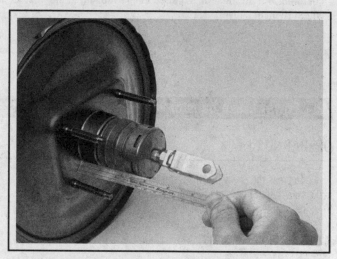

9.12a Set the clevis at about five inches from the center of the clevis pin hole to the mounting face of the booster

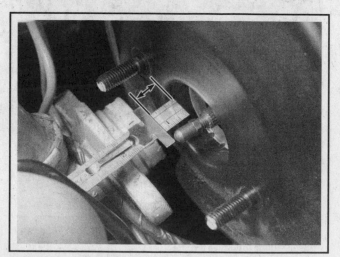

9.12b Measure the distance that the booster pushrod protrudes from the face of the power booster (typical shown)

9.12c To adjust the length of the booster pushrod, hold the serrated portion of the rod with a pair of pliers and turn the adjusting screw

10 Parking brake shoes - replacement

♦ Refer to illustrations 10.5a through 10.5m

1   Remove the rear brake discs (see Section 5).

2   Measure the thickness of the lining material on the shoes. If the lining has worn down to 1.5 mm or less, replace the shoes.

3   Inspect the drum portion of the disc for scoring, grooves or cracks due to heat. If any of these conditions exist or there is significant wear to the drum, the disc must be replaced.

4   Wash off the brake parts with brake system cleaner.

5   Follow the accompanying illustrations for the brake shoe replacement procedure (see illustrations 10.5a through 10.5m). Be sure to stay in order and read the caption under each illustration.

➡ **Note: Work on one side at a time using the opposite side for reference as necessary.**

6   Install the brake disc and use two lug nuts with washers (for spacing) to hold the disc securely against the hub.

7   Adjust the rear parking brake shoes (see Section 11).

10.5a Turn the adjuster until it's at its shortest setting (the threads disappear into the adjuster)

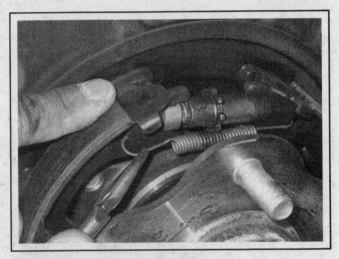

10.5b Remove the adjuster spring

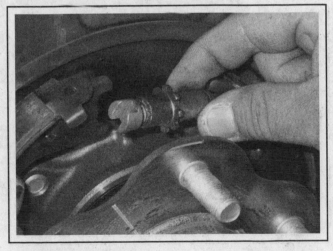

10.5c Remove the adjuster

10.5d Remove the return spring

10.5e Remove the rear shoe hold-down retainer, spring, pin and shoe

10.5f Remove the forward shoe hold-down retainer, spring, pin and shoe

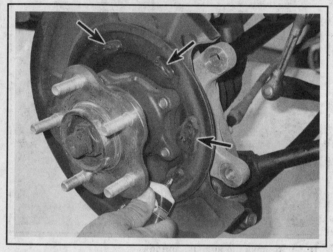

10.5g Clean the backing plate thoroughly, then lubricate the brake shoe contact areas on the plate with high-temperature grease (some contact areas not seen in photo)

10.5h Clean and lubricate the adjuster

10.5i Place the forward shoe in position and install the hold-down retainer, spring and pin

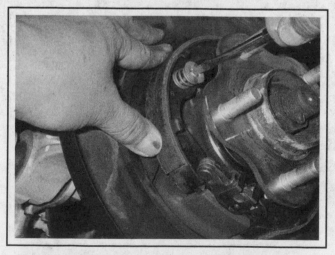

10.5j Place the rear shoe in position and install the hold-down retainer, spring and pin

10.5k Install the return spring

10.5l Install the adjuster

10.5m Install the adjuster spring

8 Install the caliper bracket (see Section 5) and brake caliper (see Section 4). Be sure to tighten the bolts to the torque values listed in this Chapter's Specifications.

9 Install the wheel and lug nuts. Lower the vehicle and tighten the lug nuts to the torque listed in the Chapter 1 Specifications.

10 Check the parking brake for proper operation. If they are not fully operational, perform a break-in procedure.

11 Break-in the new shoes by performing the following procedure.

 a) *Set and release the parking brake a few times.*
 b) *Set the parking brake.*

 c) *Drive the vehicle to 20 miles per hour.*
 d) *Stop the vehicle and RELEASE THE PARKING BRAKE. Allow the parking brake shoes and disc/drum to cool for 5 minutes, then drive the vehicle normally for another two minutes.*
 e) *Repeat these break-in steps again if necessary, but no more than three cycles. Do not shorten the cooling period between driving cycles.*

12 Check the parking brake adjustment and adjust it again if necessary (see Section 11).

11 Parking brake - adjustment

▶ Refer to illustrations 11.4, 11.6 and 11.7

➡**Note: If the parking brake shoe clearance or cable adjusting nut require a significant amount of adjustment, it is advisable to inspect the brake shoe lining thickness (see Section 10).**

1 Models equipped with a parking brake pedal should fully engage in three to four clicks. Models equipped with a hand lever should fully engage in six to seven clicks. If the number of clicks is less than specified, there's a chance the parking brake might not be releasing completely, and might be dragging on the drum portion of the disc. If the number of clicks is greater than specified, the parking brake may not hold the vehicle adequately on an incline, allowing the car to roll.

2 There are two areas of adjustment for the parking brake: the star-wheel adjuster at the top of the shoes for each wheel and the adjusting nut on the brake cable at the parking brake pedal or lever assembly. Adjustment at the shoes is performed first.

3 Block the front wheels, raise the rear of the vehicle and support it securely on jackstands. Remove the rear wheels.

4 Use the access hole in the disc to adjust the parking brake shoe clearance (see illustration). Turn the star-wheel adjuster until the disc cannot be rotated, then reverse the adjuster five notches. Adjust both wheels, then reinstall the rubber plugs that cover the access holes.

5 Set the parking brake fully and compare the number of clicks to those specified in Step 1. If more adjustment is necessary, move on to the next adjustment at the parking brake pedal or lever assembly.

11.4 Turn the star adjuster until the brake disc cannot be moved, then back off the adjustment five notches

11.6 The adjuster nut location on a pedal type parking brake assembly

11.7 An adjuster nut location on a hand lever type parking brake assembly (typical shown)

6   For vehicles equipped with a parking brake pedal, locate the adjusting nut at the pedal assembly and either tighten or loosen it to achieve the proper number of clicks when the parking brake is set (see illustration). Tightening the nut (turning it clockwise) decreases the number of clicks, while the opposite is achieved by loosening the nut (turning it counterclockwise).

7   Locate the adjusting nut at the base of the hand lever assembly and either tighten or loosen it to achieve the proper number of clicks when the parking brake is set (see illustration). Tightening the nut (turning it clockwise) decreases the number of clicks, while the opposite is

achieved by loosening the nut (turning it counterclockwise).

➡Note: In order to get to the adjustment nut on the cable end, you'll need to remove a small cover or coin tray from the center console. Any cover that is near the base of the hand lever and towards the center should be adequate. Lift the hand lever a few clicks and the adjustment nut should be visible.

8   Confirm that the parking brake is fully engaged within the number of clicks stated in Step 1.

9   Release the parking brake and confirm that the brakes don't drag when the rear wheels are turned.

12   Brake light switch - removal and installation

▶ Refer to illustration 12.2

➡Note: There is an additional switch mounted next to the brake light switch that is used for the speed control feature. This switch is very similar to the brake light switch and can be removed in the same manner on most vehicle models. One difference between the two switches is that the brake light switch has four terminals (wires) at the connector and the speed control switch only has two.

1   Remove the lower instrument panel insulator below the driver's side knee bolster for access, if equipped (see Chapter 11).

2   The brake light switch is mounted to a bracket attached near the top of the brake pedal assembly (see illustration).

3   Depress and hold the brake pedal.

4   Rotate the switch about 45 degrees counterclockwise and remove it from its bracket.

➡Note: If you are removing the switch for the speed control also, use the same procedure unless it is equipped with a locknut setup. If that's the case, loosen the locknut and unscrew the switch to remove it.

5   Disconnect the electrical connector for the brake light switch and remove it.

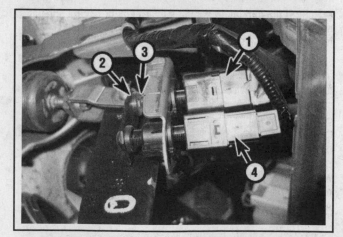

12.2 Brake light switch details (2004 G35 Sedan shown - other models similar)

1   *Brake light switch (four terminals)*
2   *Rubber stopper*
3   *Small gap between the stopper and the threaded portion of the switch*
4   *Cruise control brake pedal switch (two terminals)*

6   To install the switch, pull up on the brake pedal (it will move slightly upward). Place the switch into the bracket fitting until it touches the rubber stop on the brake pedal bracket, then turn the switch 45-degrees clockwise to lock it in place (see illustration 12.2).

7   Press and release the brake pedal and make sure that there is a small gap between the threaded portion of the switch and the rubber stop of about 1 to 2 mm.

8   Inspect the mounting bracket for the switch(s) and confirm that any welds or rivets are fully intact.

9   Test the brake lights for proper operation.

13 Brake pedal - adjustment

BRAKE PEDAL RELEASED HEIGHT

♦ **Refer to illustrations 13.2 and 13.4**

1   Remove the brake light and speed control switches (see Section 12).

2   Peel back the carpet and insulator pad. With the brake pedal fully released, measure the distance from the top of the pad to the floor (see illustration).

3   If the height is not as listed in the Specifications Section at the end of this Chapter, it must be adjusted.

4   Loosen the pushrod locknut just in front of the power brake booster clevis (see illustration).

5   Turn the booster pushrod until the pedal height is correct.

6   Tighten the locknut.

7   After adjusting the pedal height, check the freeplay.

BRAKE PEDAL FREEPLAY

8   Press down lightly on the brake pedal and measure the distance that it moves freely before resistance is felt. The freeplay should be within the measurements listed in this Chapter's Specifications. If it isn't, check and adjust the pedal height.

BRAKE PEDAL DEPRESSED HEIGHT

9   Check the pedal depressed height only after the brake pedal released height and freeplay are within specification.

10 With the engine running, press the brake pedal fully and measure the pedal pad-to-floor distance.

11 If the height is less than specified in this Chapter's Specifications, check the brake system for fluid leaks or other damage.

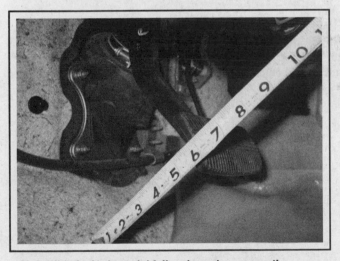

13.2 With the brake pedal fully released, measure the distance from the top of the pedal pad to the floor

13.4 Brake pedal adjustment details (2004 G35 Sedan shown - other models similar)

Specifications

General

Brake fluid type	See Chapter 1
Brake pedal freeplay	0.12 to 0.43 inch (3 to 11 mm)
Brake pedal depressed height	
M/T model	More than 3.54 inches (90 mm)
A/T model	More than 3.74 inches (95 mm)
Brake pedal released height	
M/T model	6.06 to 6.46 inches (154 to 164 mm)
A/T model	6.38 to 6.77 inches (162 to 172 mm)
Power brake booster pushrod length	
350Z models with TCS	
Protruding	0.409 inch (10.4 mm)
All other models	
Protruding or recessed	0.244 inch (6.2 mm)
Recessed	1.20 inches (30.5 mm)

Disc brakes

Minimum brake pad thickness	See Chapter 1
Disc minimum thickness	Cast into disc
Disc runout limit	
Front	0.0014 inch (0.035 mm)
Rear	0.0039 inch (0.10 mm)

Torque specifications

	Ft-lbs (unless otherwise indicated)	Nm

➡**Note: One foot-pound (ft-lb) of torque is equivalent to 12 inch-pounds (in-lbs) of torque. Torque values below approximately 15 ft-lbs are expressed in inch-pounds, since most foot-pound torque wrenches are not accurate at these smaller values.**

	Ft-lbs	Nm
Floating non-Brembo calipers (typical)		
Caliper mounting bolts		
Front	20	26
Rear	32	43
Caliper mounting bracket bolts		
Front		
G35 Coupe	113	153
G35 Sedan		
2006 and earlier models	113	153
2007 and later models	98	132
350Z models	113	153
Rear		
G35 Coupe and G35 Sedan		
2005 and earlier models	53 to 71	71 to 97
2006 and later models	62	84

Torque specifications (continued)	Ft-lbs (unless otherwise indicated)	Nm

➡️**Note:** One foot-pound (ft-lb) of torque is equivalent to 12 inch-pounds (in-lbs) of torque. Torque values below approximately 15 ft-lbs are expressed in inch-pounds, since most foot-pound torque wrenches are not accurate at these smaller values.

Fixed Brembo calipers		
Caliper mounting bolts		
Front	112	152
Rear	62	84
Brake hose-to-caliper banjo bolt	156 in-lbs	18
Master cylinder-to-brake booster nuts	132 in-lbs	15
Power brake booster mounting nuts	120 in-lbs	14
Wheel lug nuts	See Chapter 1	

Notes

10

SUSPENSION AND STEERING SYSTEMS

1   General information

FRONT SUSPENSION

▶ Refer to illustration 1.1

All models are equipped with an independent, multi-link, front suspension system with upper and lower control arms and shock absorber/coil spring assemblies. A stabilizer bar controls body roll. Each steering knuckle is positioned by balljoints at the ends of the control arms and links (see illustration).

REAR SUSPENSION

▶ Refer to illustration 1.2

All models are equipped with an independent multi-link suspension consisting of shock absorbers, coil springs and several specialized links. Additionally, all models incorporate a stabilizer bar to control body roll (see illustration).

STEERING

The steering system consists of a rack-and-pinion steering gear and two adjustable tie-rods. Power assist is achieved through a hydraulic fluid pump and related components.

PRECAUTIONS

Frequently, when working on the suspension or steering system components, you may come across fasteners which seem impossible to loosen. These fasteners on the underside of the vehicle are continually subjected to water, road grime, mud, etc., and can become rusted or frozen, making them extremely difficult to remove. In order to unscrew these stubborn fasteners without damaging them (or other components), be sure to use lots of penetrating oil and allow it to soak in for a while. Using a wire brush to clean exposed threads will also ease removal of the nut or bolt and prevent damage to the threads. Sometimes a

1.1 Front suspension and steering components (2004 G35 Sedan model shown)

1   Stabilizer bar
2   Lower control arm
3   Shock absorber/coil spring assembly
4   Steering knuckle
5   Tie-rod end
6   Compression rod (350Z and 2006 and earlier G35 Sedans only)
7   Steering gear

sharp blow with a hammer and punch is effective in breaking the bond between a nut and bolt threads, but care must be taken to prevent the punch from slipping off the fastener and ruining the threads. Heating the stuck fastener and surrounding area with a torch sometimes helps too, but isn't recommended because of the obvious dangers associated with fire. Long breaker bars and extension, or cheater, pipes will increase leverage, but never use an extension pipe on a ratchet - the ratcheting mechanism could be damaged. Sometimes, turning the nut or bolt in the tightening (clockwise) direction first will help to break it loose. Fasteners that require drastic measures to unscrew should always be replaced with new ones.

Since most of the procedures that are dealt with in this Chapter involve jacking up the vehicle and working underneath it, a good pair of jackstands will be needed. A hydraulic floor jack is the preferred type of jack to lift the vehicle, and it can also be used to support certain components during various operations.

❊❊ WARNING:

Never, under any circumstances, rely on a jack to support the vehicle while working on it. Also, whenever any of the suspension or steering fasteners are loosened or removed they must be inspected and, if necessary, be replaced with new ones of the same part number or of original equipment quality and design. Torque specifications must be followed for proper reassembly and component retention. Never attempt to heat or straighten any suspension or steering components. Instead, replace any bent or damaged part with a new one.

1.2 Rear suspension components (2004 G35 Sedan model shown)

1	Stabilizer bar	3	Radius rod	5	Lower spring link
2	Front lower link	4	Knuckle	6	Coil spring

2 Shock absorber/coil spring assembly (front) - removal and installation

※※ **WARNING:**

Always replace shock absorbers or shock absorber/coil spring assemblies in pairs - never replace just one of them.

➡ Note: These vehicles are equipped with shock absorber/coil spring assemblies. It is possible to replace the shocks or springs individually but the unit will have to be disassembled by a qualified repair shop with the proper equipment. This will add considerable cost to the project. You can compare the cost of replacing the complete assemblies yourself to the cost of replacing individual components (with the help of a shop).

REMOVAL

▶ **Refer to illustrations 2.3 and 2.7**

1 Loosen the front wheel lug nuts. If you're working on an AWD model, also loosen the driveaxle/hub nut. Raise the front of the vehicle and support it securely on jackstands. Remove the front wheels.

2 Remove the lower engine splash shield (see Chapter 2A, illustration 12.4).

3 Remove the ABS wheel speed sensor harness and brake hose bracket from the shock absorber (see illustration).

4 On 2007 and later G35 Sedan models, detach the stabilizer bar link from the control arm (see Section 3).

5 On 2007 and later G35 Sedan models with AWD, remove the front driveaxle (see Chapter 8) and separate the upper control arm from the steering knuckle (see Section 5).

6 Remove the lower mounting fasteners attaching the shock absorber to the lower control arm (see illustration 2.3).

7 Mark the relationship of the shock absorber to the shock tower, remove the upper mounting fasteners, then remove the shock absorber assembly (see illustration). On 350Z models, remove the shock tower bar (above the shock absorbers in the engine compartment) in order to remove the shock absorber upper mounting fasteners.

8 Inspect the shock absorber for leaking fluid, dents, cracks and other damage. Inspect the coil spring for chips and cracks which could cause premature failure. Inspect the spring seats for hardness and general deterioration. If any of the components of the assembly are worn or damaged, have the unit serviced by a qualified repair shop or replace it.

INSTALLATION

9 Installation is the reverse of removal. Tighten the mounting fasteners to the torque listed in this Chapter's Specifications.

➡ Note: **Raise the lower control arm with a floor jack to simulate normal ride height before tightening the shock absorber lower mounting fasteners.**

10 Tighten the wheel lug nuts to the torque listed in the Chapter 1 Specifications.

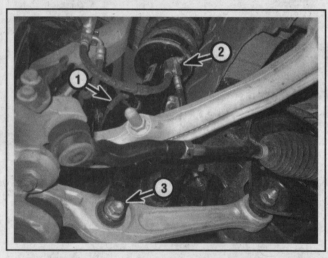

2.3 Shock absorber lower mounting details (2004 G35 Sedan model shown):

1 *ABS wire harness*
2 *Brake hose mounting block and fastener*
3 *Shock absorber lower mounting bolt*

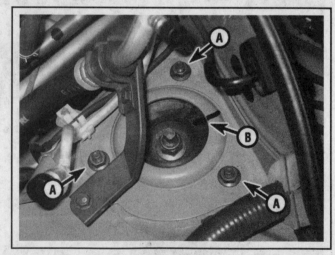

2.7 Shock absorber upper mounting fasteners (A) and index mark (B) (2004 G35 Sedan model shown)

3 Stabilizer bar, bushings and links (front) - removal and installation

▶ **Refer to illustrations 3.2, 3.3 and 3.4**

1   Raise the front of the vehicle and support it securely on jackstands. Remove the front wheels.

2   Remove the lower engine splash shield (see Chapter 2A, illustration 12.4) and the small shield around the stabilizer bar, if equipped (see illustration).

3   Remove the nuts from the stabilizer bar links and separate them from the bar (see illustration).

4   Remove the stabilizer bar bracket fasteners and remove the brackets (see illustration).

➡**Note: On stabilizer bar designs with two-piece brackets (most models), there is no need to remove the base bracket unless it requires replacement.**

5   Remove the stabilizer bar. Remove the rubber bushings from the stabilizer bar.

6   Clean the stabilizer bar where the bushings contact it. Inspect all rubber bushings for wear and damage. If any of the rubber parts are cracked, torn or generally deteriorated, replace them.

7   Lubricate the inside and outside of the new bushings with vegetable oil (used in cooking) to simplify reassembly.

✳✳ CAUTION:

Don't use petroleum or mineral-based lubricants or brake fluid - they will lead to deterioration of the bushings.

8   Check each stabilizer link for signs of excessive wear and replace them as necessary.

9   Installation is the reverse of removal. Be sure to tighten all the fasteners to the torque listed in this Chapter's Specifications.

3.2 Remove the fasteners for the small splash shield

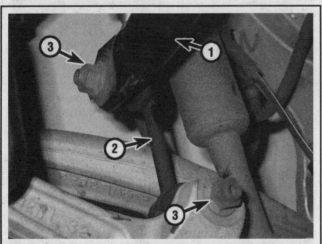

3.3 Stabilizer bar link mounting details:

1	Stabilizer bar	3	Link nuts
2	Stabilizer bar link		

3.4 Stabilizer bar bracket fasteners

4 Compression rod - removal and installation

▶ Refer to illustrations 4.3a, 4.3b, 4.3c and 4.4

➡**Note 1: This component is installed on 350Zs and 2006 and earlier G35 Sedans only.**

➡**Note 2: A special tool, available at most auto parts stores, is necessary to separate the balljoint from the steering knuckle.**

1 Loosen the front wheel lug nuts. Raise the front of the vehicle and support it securely on jackstands. Remove the front wheel.

2 Remove any lower engine splash shields as necessary (see Chapter 2).

3 Separate the balljoint on the compression rod from the steering knuckle (see illustrations).

➡**Note: Be careful not to damage the balljoint seal during this Step.**

4 Remove the compression rod reinforcement mounting fasteners (see illustration).

➡**Note: On Coupe models, there is a front reinforcement bracket that reaches to both sides of the suspension that is under the compression rods. This component will have to be removed when removing the compression rod on either side.**

5 Remove the compression rod-to-chassis mounting nut, then slide the rod off the mounting stud.

6 Check the balljoint for excessive play or looseness (see Section 7). If the balljoint is bad, the compression arm must be replaced.

7 Check the condition of the rubber bushing, if it is deteriorated or damaged, the compression rod must be replaced.

8 Installation is the reverse of removal. Use a new cotter pin on the ballstud. Tighten all fasteners to the torque listed in this Chapter's Specifications.

9 Install the wheel, remove the jackstands and lower the vehicle.

10 Tighten the wheel lug nuts to the torque listed in the Chapter 1 Specifications.

11 Have the front end alignment checked and, if necessary, adjusted.

4.3a Compression rod mounting details:

1 *Balljoint stud nut*	3 *Compression rod-to-chassis*
2 *Compression rod*	*mounting stud and nut*

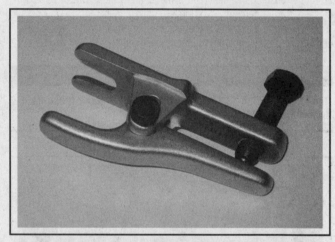

4.3b A balljoint separator tool like this one is available at most automotive parts stores and will not damage the balljoint boot when used correctly

4.3c To separate the compression rod balljoint from the steering knuckle, loosen the balljoint stud nut, then install the tool as shown

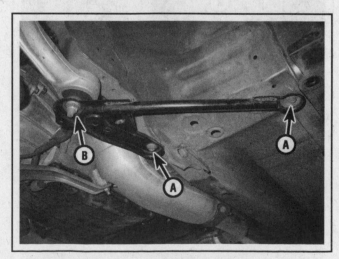

4.4 Compression rod reinforcement mounting bolts (A) and compression rod-to-chassis nut (B)

5   Upper control arm - removal and installation

REMOVAL

▶ **Refer to illustrations 5.4 and 5.6**

➡**Note: A special tool, available at most auto parts stores, is necessary to separate the balljoint from the steering knuckle.**

1   Remove the upper fasteners for the shock absorber so that it can be moved outward in order to remove the control arm fasteners (see Section 2).

2   Loosen the wheel lug nuts, raise the front of the vehicle and support it securely on jackstands placed under the frame rails. Remove the wheel.

3   Remove the ABS wheel speed sensor harness and brake hose from the shock absorber assembly (see illustration 2.3).

4   Loosen (but don't remove) the nut on the upper balljoint stud, then disconnect the balljoint from the steering knuckle with a balljoint removal tool (see illustration).

➡**Note: Other balljoint separator tools can be used as long as the balljoint boot is not damaged (see illustration 4.3b).**

5   Carefully secure the steering knuckle aside, then move the shock absorber outward.

✳✳ CAUTION:

Be careful not to damage the ABS wire harness or the brake hose while moving the steering knuckle outward. Remove the ABS wheel speed sensor if necessary (see Chapter 9).

6   Remove the control arm mounting bolts and pull the upper arm from its frame brackets (see illustration).

7   Check the balljoint for excessive play or looseness (see Section 7). If the balljoint is bad, the control arm must be replaced.

8   Check the condition of the rubber bushings; if they are deteriorated or damaged, the control arm must be replaced.

INSTALLATION

9   Installation is the reverse of removal. Use a new cotter pin on the ballstud after installing the nut. Tighten all fasteners to the torque values listed in this Chapter's Specifications.

➡**Note: Raise the lower control arm with a floor jack to simulate normal ride height before tightening the upper control arm mounting bolts at the shock tower.**

10   Install the wheel and lug nuts. Lower the vehicle and tighten the lug nuts to the torque listed in the Chapter 1 Specifications.

11   Have the front end alignment checked and, if necessary, adjusted.

5.4   To separate the balljoint from the steering knuckle, loosen the balljoint stud nut a few turns and install a puller tool like this one, or a balljoint separator (leaving the nut on the ballstud will prevent the balljoint from separating violently)

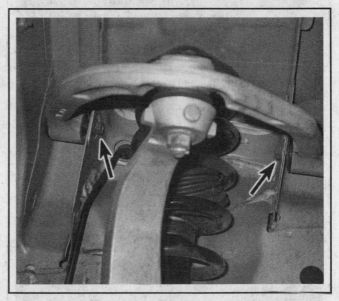

5.6   Upper control arm mounting bolts

6   Lower control arm - removal and installation

REMOVAL

➡Note: A special tool, available at most auto parts stores, is necessary to separate the balljoint from the lower control arm.

1   Loosen the wheel lug nuts, raise the front of the vehicle and support it securely on jackstands placed under the frame rails. Remove the wheel.

2   Remove any lower engine splash shields as necessary (see Chapter 2).

3   Detach the stabilizer bar link from the control arm (see Section 3).

6.6 To separate the balljoint from the lower control arm, loosen the balljoint stud nut and install the tool as shown (leaving the nut on the ballstud will prevent the balljoint from separating violently)

2006 and earlier G35 Sedans, all 350Z Coupes and 2007 and earlier G35 Coupes

▶ Refer to illustrations 6.6 and 6.8

4   On Coupe models, remove the suspension reinforcement brace.

➡Note: The reinforcement brace is recognized by a series of tubes and plates formed into a single wing-like shaped unit that reaches across the suspension and is held by eight bolts and the mounting nuts for the compression rod.

5   Remove the shock absorber lower mounting fasteners (see Section 2).

6   Loosen (but don't remove) the nut on the balljoint stud, then disconnect the balljoint from the steering knuckle with a balljoint removal tool (see illustration 4.3b and the accompanying illustration).

7   Remove the balljoint tool and the nut on the balljoint stud.

8   Remove the mounting fasteners holding the control arm to the front suspension crossmember, then remove the control arm (see illustration).

2007 and later G35 Sedans

▶ Refer to illustration 6.14

9   Remove the shock absorber (see Section 2).

10 Remove the suspension reinforcement brace.

➡Note: On AWD models, the reinforcement brace is recognized by a series of tubes and plates formed into a single wing-like shaped unit that reaches across the suspension and is held by eight bolts. On 2WD models, it is a smaller plate.

11 Detach the tie-rod end from the steering knuckle (see Section 18).

12 Loosen (but don't remove) the nut on the balljoint stud, then disconnect the balljoint from the steering knuckle with a balljoint removal tool (see illustration 4.3b).

13 Remove the balljoint tool and nut on the balljoint stud.

14 Remove the control arm front pivot and rear mounting bracket fasteners, then remove the control arm (see illustration).

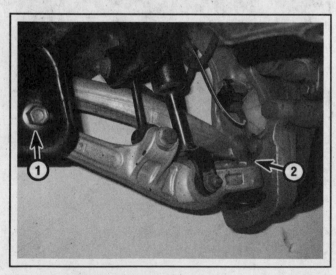

6.8 Lower control arm mounting details:

1   *Lower control arm mounting bolt*
2   *Balljoint stud nut*

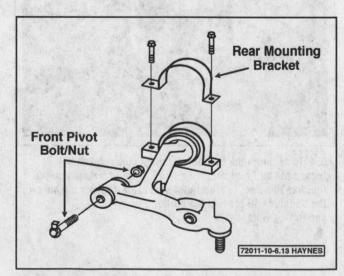

6.14 Lower control arm mounting details on 2007 and later G35 Sedans (AWD models are similar)

INSTALLATION

15 Check the balljoint for excessive play or looseness (see Section 7). If the balljoint is bad, the control arm must be replaced.

16 Check the condition of the rubber bushings; if they are deteriorated or damaged, the control arm must be replaced.

17 Installation is the reverse of removal. Transfer the steering lock stud to the replacement control arm if necessary. Install a new cotter pin on the balljoint stud after tightening the nut. Be sure to tighten all fasteners to the torque values listed in this Chapter's Specifications.

➡**Note: Raise the lower control arm with a floor jack to simulate normal ride height before tightening the lower control arm and lower shock absorber mounting fasteners.**

18 Install the wheel and lug nuts. Lower the vehicle and tighten the lug nuts to the torque listed in the Chapter 1 Specifications.

19 Have the front end alignment checked and, if necessary, adjusted.

---

7 Balljoints - check and replacement

1 Inspect the balljoints for looseness anytime any of them is separated from the steering knuckle. See if you can turn the ballstud in its socket with your fingers. If the balljoint is loose, or if the ballstud can be turned, replace the component. You can also check the balljoints with the suspension assembled as follows:

2 Park the vehicle with the wheels pointing straight-ahead.

UPPER CONTROL ARM BALLJOINT

▶ **Refer to illustration 7.3**

3 Using a large prybar inserted between the upper control arm and the steering knuckle, pry upwards on the upper control arm (see illustration). The manufacturer specifies that no movement should occur; a dial indicator can be used to check for play. If you are unable to accurately measure balljoint play, have the balljoint checked at an automotive repair shop.

4 If replacement is indicated, replace the upper control arm (see Section 5); the balljoint cannot be replaced separately.

LOWER CONTROL ARM BALLJOINT

▶ **Refer to illustration 7.5**

5 Using a large prybar inserted between the wheel and the lower control arm, pry upwards on the steering knuckle (see illustration). The manufacturer specifies that no movement should occur; a dial indicator can be used to check for play. If you are unable to accurately measure balljoint play, have the balljoint checked at an automotive repair shop.

6 If replacement is indicated, replace the lower control arm (see Section 6); the balljoint cannot be replaced separately.

7.3 Pry upwards on the upper control arm from the steering knuckle to check for balljoint wear

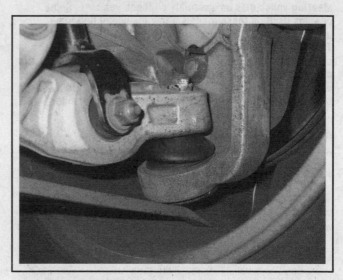

7.5 Pry upward on the steering knuckle from the wheel to check for balljoint wear

COMPRESSION ROD BALLJOINT

♦ **Refer to illustration 7.7**

7 Using a large prybar inserted between the lower control arm and the compression rod, pry upwards on the compression rod (see illustration). The manufacturer specifies that no movement should occur; a dial indicator can be used to check for play. If you are unable to accurately measure balljoint play, have the balljoint checked at an automotive repair shop.

8 If replacement is indicated, replace the compression rod (see Section 4); the balljoint cannot be replaced separately.

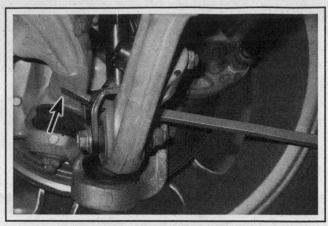

7.7 Pry upwards on the compression rod from the lower control arm to check for balljoint wear

8 Hub and wheel bearing (front) - removal and installation

✳ WARNING:

The dust created by the brake system is harmful to your health. Never blow it out with compressed air and don't inhale any of it. Do not, under any circumstances, use petroleum-based solvents to clean brake parts. Use brake system cleaner only.

➡**Note: All wheel bearings and hubs are removed from the steering knuckle as an assembly on these vehicles. Some designs used on these models allow the wheel hub to be pressed out of the wheel bearing and used with a new bearing. This operation requires a professional mechanic due to the special tools and expertise necessary. However, other designs simply are replaced as a single unit. The best way to know which design you have is to see what replacement parts are available from a dealership parts department or an auto parts store.**

REMOVAL

♦ **Refer to illustration 8.4**

1 Loosen the wheel lug nuts, raise the front of the vehicle and support it securely on jackstands placed under the frame rails. Remove the wheel.

2 Remove the brake disc and the ABS wheel speed sensor (see Chapter 9).

3 On AWD models, remove the driveaxle/hub nut and loosen the driveaxle from the hub splines.

4 Remove the hub and wheel bearing mounting fasteners (see illustration).

5 Remove the hub from the steering knuckle. Be careful not to damage the small plastic cover in the rear of the hub, if equipped.

INSTALLATION

6 Installation is the reverse of removal, noting the following points:
   a) Tighten the brake caliper mounting bracket and brake caliper mounting bolts to the torque listed in the Chapter 9 Specifications.
   b) Tighten the hub mounting fasteners to the torque listed in this Chapter's Specifications.
   c) Install the wheel, lower the vehicle and tighten the lug nuts to the torque listed in the Chapter 1 Specifications.
   d) On AWD models, tighten the driveaxle/hub nut to the torque listed in the Chapter 8 Specifications.

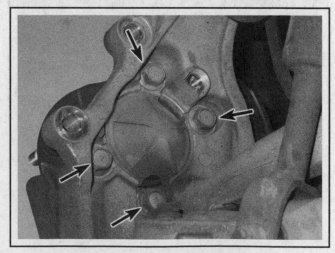

8.4 Hub and wheel bearing mounting bolts

9 Steering knuckle - removal and installation

⋇⋇ WARNING:

The dust created by the brake system is harmful to your health. Never blow it out with compressed air and don't inhale any of it. Do not, under any circumstances, use petroleum-based solvents to clean brake parts. Use brake system cleaner only.

1 If you're working on an AWD model, loosen the driveaxle/hub nut.

2 Loosen the wheel lug nuts, raise the front of the vehicle and support it securely on jackstands. Remove the wheel.

3 Remove the brake disc, the wheel speed sensor and the bracket that holds the brake hose to the knuckle (see Chapter 9).

4 Disconnect the tie-rod end from the steering knuckle (see Section 18).

5 Separate the upper control arm from the steering knuckle (see Section 5).

6 Separate the compression rod from the steering knuckle (see Section 4).

7 Separate the lower control arm from the steering knuckle (see Section 6). If you're working on an AWD model, remove the driveaxle from the hub splines as the knuckle is removed.

8 Carefully inspect the steering knuckle for cracks, especially around the steering arm and hub and bearing mounting area. Inspect the balljoint (see Section 7). If the balljoint is bad, replace the steering knuckle. Also, inspect the balljoint stud holes. If they're elongated, or if you find any cracks in the knuckle, replace the steering knuckle.

9 Remove the hub and wheel bearing, the steering stop bracket and brake dust shield as necessary for replacement.

10 Installation is the reverse of removal. Be sure to tighten all suspension fasteners to the torque listed in this Chapter's Specifications. Refer to the torque values listed in the Chapter 9 Specifications for brake-related fasteners.

11 Tighten the wheel lug nuts to the torque listed in the Chapter 1 Specifications. If you're working on an AWD model, tighten the driveaxle/hub nut to the torque listed in the Chapter 8 Specifications.

10 Shock absorber (rear) - removal and installation

▶ **Refer to illustrations 10.3 and 10.4**

⋇⋇ WARNING:

Always replace shock absorbers in pairs - never replace just one of them.

1 Loosen the wheel lug nuts, raise the rear of the vehicle and support it securely on jackstands placed under the frame rails. Remove the wheel.

2 Raise the lower spring link with a floor jack to relieve the coil spring tension (see illustration 12.26).

3 Remove the nuts that attach the upper end of the shock absorber to the chassis (see illustration). If the nuts won't loosen because of rust, apply some penetrating oil and allow it to soak in for awhile.

4 Remove the bolt that attaches the lower end of the shock to the spring link (see illustration). Again, if the bolt is frozen, apply some penetrating oil, wait awhile and try again.

5 Installation is the reverse of removal. Tighten the mounting fasteners to the torque listed in the Chapter's Specifications.

➡**Note: Raise the lower spring link with a floor jack to simulate normal ride height before tightening the lower shock absorber mounting fastener.**

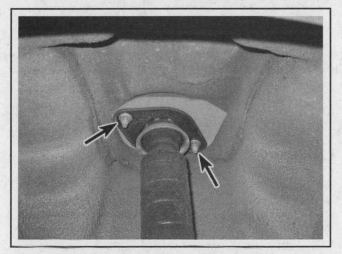

10.3 Rear shock absorber upper mounting nuts

10.4 Rear shock absorber lower mounting bolt

11 Stabilizer bar, bushings and links (rear) - removal and installation

◆ **Refer to illustrations 11.2 and 11.3**

1   Raise the rear of the vehicle and support it securely on jackstands.

2   Remove the nuts from the stabilizer bar links and separate them from the bar (see illustration).

➡**Note: The stabilizer bar links can be removed completely by removing the both nuts on each link.**

3   Remove the stabilizer bar bracket nuts and remove the brackets (see illustration).

4   Remove the stabilizer bar. Remove the rubber bushings from the stabilizer bar.

5   Clean the stabilizer bar where the bushings contact it. Inspect all rubber bushings for wear and damage. If any of the rubber parts are cracked, torn or generally deteriorated, replace them.

6   Lubricate the inside and outside of the new bushings with vegetable oil (used in cooking) to simplify reassembly.

✳✳ CAUTION:

Don't use petroleum or mineral-based lubricants or brake fluid - they will lead to deterioration of the bushings.

7   Check each stabilizer link for signs of excessive wear and replace them as necessary.

8   Installation is the reverse of removal. Be sure to tighten all the fasteners to the torque values listed in this Chapter's Specifications.

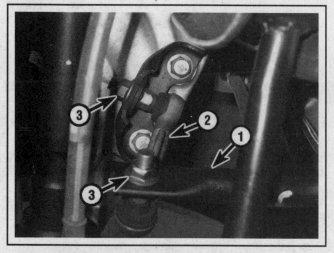

11.2 Rear stabilizer bar link details:

1   Stabilizer bar   3   Stabilizer bar link nuts
2   Stabilizer bar link

11.3 Rear stabilizer bar bracket (A) and mounting nuts (B)

12 Suspension links (rear) - removal and installation

✳✳ WARNING:

Whenever a suspension link is removed, the manufacturer states to discard the old mounting fasteners and use NEW fasteners for installation.

1   Loosen the wheel lug nuts, raise the rear of the vehicle and support it securely on jackstands placed under the frame rails. Remove the wheel.

RADIUS ROD

◆ **Refer to illustration 12.3**

2   Support the lower spring link and coil spring tension with a floor jack (see illustration 12.26).

3   Remove the radius rod mounting fasteners from the rear knuckle (see illustration).

4   Remove the radius rod mounting fasteners from the rear subframe, then remove the link.

5   Inspect all rubber bushings for wear and damage. If any of the rubber parts are cracked, torn or generally deteriorated, the manufacturer states to replace the rod.

➡**Note: It may be possible for the rod's bushing to be replaced by an automotive repair shop that specializes in suspension repair.**

6   Installation is the reverse of removal. Tighten the mounting fasteners to the torque listed in this Chapter's Specifications. Proceed to Step 31.

➡**Note: Raise the lower spring link with a floor jack to simulate normal ride height before tightening the radius rod mounting fasteners (see illustration 12.26).**

UPPER ARM

7   Support the lower spring link and coil spring tension with a floor jack (see illustration 12.26).

8   Detach the stabilizer bar link from the upper arm and move it aside (see Section 11).

2007 and later G35 Sedans

9   Remove the brake caliper and mounting bracket (see Chapter 9).

10 Remove the height sensor, if equipped. The height sensor is recognized by a small electrical component attached to the subframe with a bracket having movable linkage. Mark the sensor's mounted position precisely in relation to the components it's mounted to.

➡**Note: According to the manufacturer, a special calibration procedure must be performed after installing this sensor. This procedure can only by performed by a dealership service department. If the sensor can be installed exactly where it was before removal, it may be possible to avoid the need for calibration.**

All models

▶ **Refer to illustrations 12.11 and 12.12**

11 Remove the upper arm mounting fasteners at the subframe (see illustration).

12 Detach the upper arm balljoint from the knuckle. Loosen (but don't remove) the nut on the balljoint stud, then disconnect the balljoint from the knuckle with a balljoint removal tool (see illustration 4.3b and the accompanying illustration).

13 Remove the balljoint tool and nut on the balljoint stud, then carefully remove the upper arm.

14 Inspect all rubber bushings for wear and damage. If any of the rubber parts are cracked, torn or generally deteriorated, the manufacturer states to replace the arm.

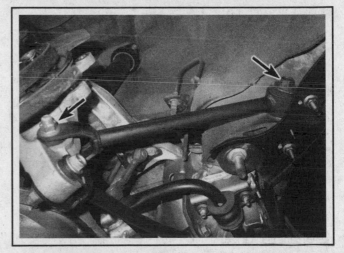

12.3 Radius rod mounting fasteners

➡**Note: It may be possible for the arm's bushing to be replaced by an automotive repair shop that specializes in suspension repair.**

15 Installation is the reverse of removal. Tighten the mounting fasteners to the torque listed in this Chapter's Specifications. Refer to the torque values listed in the Chapter 9 Specifications for brake-related fasteners. Proceed to Step 31.

➡**Note: Raise the lower spring link with a floor jack to simulate normal ride height before tightening the upper arm mounting fasteners (see illustration 12.26).**

12.11 Upper arm mounting fasteners at the rear subframe

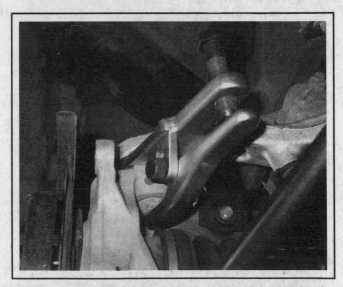

12.12 A balljoint separator tool can be used to separate the upper arm balljoint from the rear knuckle

FRONT LOWER LINK

▶ **Refer to illustrations 12.17a and 12.17b**

16 Support the lower spring link and coil spring tension with a floor jack (see illustration 12.26).

17 Mark the relationship of the adjusting cam bolt for the front lower link to the subframe bracket on both sides (see illustrations).

18 Remove the link mounting fasteners from the rear knuckle.

➡**Note: It may be necessary to remove the stabilizer bar from its brackets in order to remove the lower link mounting fasteners at the subframe.**

19 Hold the cam bolt while loosening the mounting nut at the rear subframe, then remove them and the link.

20 Inspect all rubber bushings for wear and damage. If any of the rubber parts are cracked, torn or generally deteriorated, the manufacturer states to replace the link.

➡**Note: It may be possible for the link's bushing to be replaced by an automotive repair shop that specializes in suspension repair.**

21 Installation is the reverse of removal. Place the adjusting cam bolt back in the same position to restore the rear alignment to its original setting. Tighten the mounting fasteners to the torque listed in this Chapter's Specifications. Proceed to Step 31.

➡**Note: Raise the lower spring link with a floor jack to simulate normal ride height before tightening the front lower link mounting fasteners (see illustration 12.26).**

LOWER SPRING LINK (AND COIL SPRING)

▶ **Refer to illustrations 12.22, 12.24a, 12.24b and 12.26**

22 Mark the coil spring and upper spring seat so that they can be placed in their original positions during installation (see illustration).

23 Support the lower spring link and coil spring tension with a floor jack (see illustration 12.26).

24 Mark the relationship of the adjusting cam bolt for the lower link

to the subframe bracket on both sides. Hold the cam bolt, then loosen (but don't remove) the nut (see illustrations).

✳✳ WARNING:

Do not attempt to remove the cam bolt and nut at this time, as the link is still under tension from the coil spring.

25 Remove the link mounting fasteners from the rear knuckle.

26 Slowly lower the lower spring link with the floor jack until the spring tension is relieved (see illustration).

27 Note the position of the coil spring in the lower spring link as well as the position of the seats (or insulators), then remove all of them (see illustration 12.22).

28 Remove the adjusting cam bolt and nut, then remove the link.

29 Inspect all rubber bushings for wear and damage. Inspect the coil spring seats (insulators) as well. If any of the rubber parts are cracked, torn or generally deteriorated, the manufacturer states to replace the link or seats.

➡**Note: It may be possible for the link's bushing to be replaced by an automotive repair shop that specializes in suspension repair.**

30 Installation is the reverse of removal. Be sure to return the coil spring and seats to their original positions. Place the adjusting cam bolt back in the same position to restore the rear alignment to its original setting. Tighten the mounting fasteners to the torque listed in this Chapter's Specifications. Refer to the torque values listed in the Chapter 9 Specifications for brake related fasteners.

➡**Note: Raise the lower spring link with a floor jack to simulate normal ride height before tightening the lower link mounting fasteners (see illustration 12.26).**

ALL LINKS

31 Tighten the wheel lug nuts to the torque listed in the Chapter 1 Specifications.

32 Have the wheel alignment checked and, if necessary, adjusted.

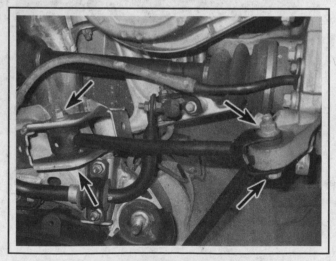

12.17a Front lower link mounting fasteners

12.17b Mark both adjuster cams (one on each side of the subframe bracket) of the front lower link mounting fasteners at the subframe

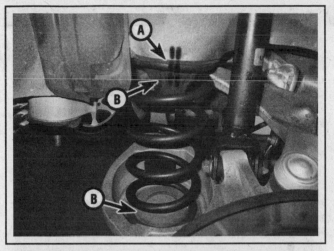

12.22 Mark the spring (A) to index its position (the top and bottom of the spring are different) and note the position of the upper and lower seats (B) (insulators)

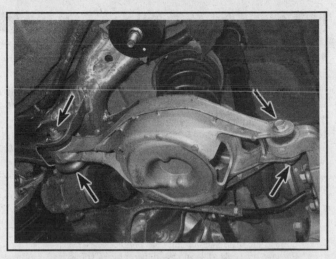

12.24a Lower spring link mounting fasteners

12.24b Mark both adjuster cams (one on each side of the subframe bracket) of the lower spring link mounting fasteners at the subframe

12.26 Using a floor jack, the lower spring link can be raised or lowered as necessary. To remove the lower spring link or coil spring, the link is supported until the fasteners are removed and then it is lowered until the coil spring tension is relieved

13 Coil spring (rear) - removal and installation

✳ WARNING:

Always replace coil springs in pairs - never replace just one of them.

Refer to Section 12, beginning with Step 22, for coil spring removal and installation.

14 Knuckle (rear) - removal and installation

◆ **Refir to illustration 14.4**

✳✳ WARNING:

The dust created by the brake system is harmful to your health. Never blow it out with compressed air and don't inhale any of it. Do not, under any circumstances, use petroleum-based solvents to clean brake parts. Use brake system cleaner only.

1   Loosen the wheel lug nuts, raise the rear of the vehicle and support it securely on jackstands placed under the frame rails. Remove the wheel.

2   Loosen the driveaxle/hub nut (see Chapter 8).

3   Remove the brake disc and the parking brake shoes (see Chapter 9).

4   Remove the parking brake anchor and cable from the knuckle (see illustration).

5   Remove the hub and wheel bearing (see Section 15) and the brake backing plate.

✳✳ CAUTION:

Support the driveaxle and do not allow extreme angles on the CV joints or over-extend the inner sliding joint (see Chapter 8).

➡**Note: Use a puller or suitable tool if the driveaxle splines are stuck in the wheel hub (see Chapter 8).**

6   Remove the lower spring link and coil spring from the rear knuckle (see Section 12).

7   Remove the front lower link and radius rod from the rear knuckle (see Section 12).

8   Remove the lower shock absorber mounting fastener from the rear knuckle (see Section 10).

9   Detach the upper arm link balljoint from the rear knuckle (see Section 12), then remove the rear knuckle.

10   Inspect all rubber bushings for wear and damage. If they are cracked, torn or generally deteriorated, replace them. If the metal seat where the upper arm balljoint mounts is worn, it can be replaced also.

➡**Note: A dealership service department or an automotive shop that specializes in suspension repair can replace the rear knuckle bushings and balljoint seat.**

11   Installation is the reverse of removal. Tighten the mounting fasteners to the torque listed in this Chapter's Specifications. Refer to the torque values listed in the Chapter 9 Specifications for brake related fasteners.

➡**Note: Raise the lower spring link with a floor jack to simulate normal ride height before tightening the mounting fasteners for the rear suspension components (see illustration 12.26).**

14.4 Remove the parking brake cable (A) and the parking brake anchor fasteners (B) from the knuckle

15 Hub and wheel bearing (rear) - removal and installation

✳✳ WARNING:

The dust created by the brake system is harmful to your health. Never blow it out with compressed air and don't inhale any of it. Do not, under any circumstances, use petroleum-based solvents to clean brake parts. Use brake system cleaner only.

➡**Note: All wheel bearings and hubs are removed from the rear knuckle as an assembly on these vehicles. Some designs used on these models allow the wheel hub to be pressed out of the wheel bearing and used with a new bearing. This operation requires a professional mechanic due to the special tools and expertise necessary. However, other designs simply are**

replaced as a single unit. The best way to know which design you have is to see what replacement parts are available for your year and model.

REMOVAL

◆ **Refer to illustration 15.5**

1   Loosen the driveaxle/hub nut (see Chapter 8).

2   Loosen the wheel lug nuts, raise the rear of the vehicle and support it securely on jackstands placed under the frame rails. Remove the wheel.

3   Remove the brake caliper and disc (see Chapter 9).

4   Remove the driveaxle/hub nut and push the driveaxle through the hub splines far enough to get access to the hub and wheel bearing mounting bolts on the back of the knuckle. If the driveaxle sticks in the hub, it's best to push it out with a puller (see Chapter 8).

5   Remove the hub mounting bolts from the back of the rear knuckle enough to release the hub assembly (see illustration).

INSTALLATION

6   Installation is the reverse of removal, noting the following points:

a)   *Tighten the hub mounting bolts to the torque listed in this Chapter's Specifications.*

b)   *Tighten the brake caliper mounting bracket bolts, caliper mounting bolts to the torque values listed in the Chapter 9 Specifications.*

c)   *Tighten the driveaxle/hub nut to the torque listed in the Chapter 8 Specifications.*

d)   *Tighten the wheel lug nuts to the torque listed in the Chapter 1 Specifications.*

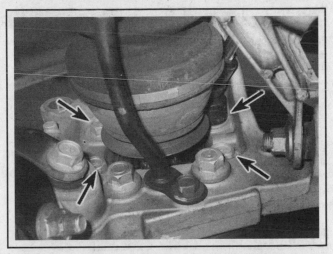

15.5   Locations of the rear hub and wheel bearing mounting bolts. Use a flex socket (upper right arrow) to unscrew the bolts

16   Steering wheel - removal and installation

✳✳ WARNING 1:

These models are equipped with a Supplemental Restraint System (SRS), more commonly known as airbags. Always disable the airbag system before working in the vicinity of any airbag system component to avoid the possibility of accidental deployment of the airbag(s), which could cause personal injury (see Chapter 12).

✳✳ WARNING 2:

Do not use a memory saving device to preserve the PCM or radio memory when working on or near airbag system components.

REMOVAL

▶ **Refer to illustrations 16.3, 16.4, 16.5, 16.6, 16.7, 16.8a and 16.8b**

1   Park the vehicle with the front wheels in the straight-ahead position.

2   Disconnect the cable from the negative battery terminal (see Chapter 5, Section 1). Wait at least two minutes before proceeding (to allow the backup power supply for the airbag system to become depleted).

3   Remove the two airbag module retaining screws (see illustration).

4   Carefully lift off the airbag module and expose the connectors beneath. Unplug the electrical connectors for the airbag module, then remove it (see illustration).

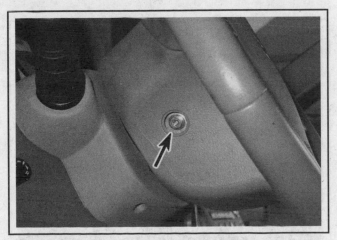

16.3   Remove the airbag module retaining screws

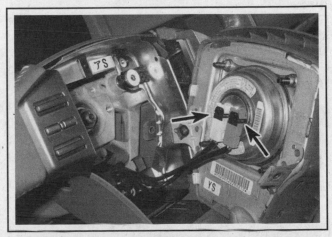

16.4   Lift the airbag module off the steering wheel and unplug the electrical connectors (lift the small locking tabs on the connectors up first, then pull the connectors straight out from the back of the module)

✳✳ WARNING:

Carry the airbag module with the trim cover (upholstered side) facing away from you, and set the airbag module in a safe location with the trim cover facing up.

5 Disconnect the electrical connector for the horn and other steering wheel control switches from the clockspring (see illustration).

6 Remove the steering wheel nut from the steering shaft. Note the index marks on the steering wheel hub and the steering shaft and confirm that they are in the 12 o'clock position (see illustration).

7 Install a steering wheel puller, then remove the steering wheel while detaching and guiding the various wire harnesses through the steering wheel hub (see illustration).

✳✳ CAUTION 1:

Don't thread the bolts of the puller into the steering wheel hub more than five turns as they could contact the airbag clockspring and damage it.

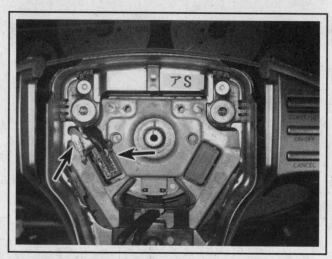

16.5 Disconnect the electrical connectors for the horn and other switches and detach them from the steering wheel hub

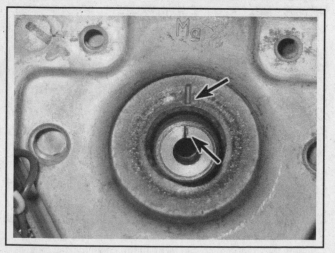

16.6 Steering wheel hub and steering shaft index marks

✳✳ CAUTION 2:

While the steering wheel is removed, DO NOT turn the steering shaft (or the front wheels). Damage to the clockspring will occur if the steering wheel is installed and the steering shaft and clockspring are not centered.

8 If it is necessary to remove the clockspring, remove the steering column upper and lower covers (see Chapter 11). Remove the mounting screws and disconnect the electrical connectors, then lift the clockspring off of the steering column while keeping it centered (see illustrations).

➡Note: Use tape to keep the clockspring in the centered position until it is installed.

INSTALLATION

9 When installing the clockspring, make absolutely sure that the airbag clockspring is centered with the arrows on the clockspring rotor and case lined up (see illustration 16.8a). This shouldn't be a problem as long as you have not turned the steering shaft while the wheel was removed, or if it was removed and became uncentered. If for some reason the shaft was turned or the clockspring became uncentered, center the clockspring as follows:

a) Rotate the clockspring clockwise until it stops (don't apply too much force, though).

b) Rotate the clockspring counterclockwise about 2-1/2 turns until the arrows on the clockspring rotor and case line up.

10 Installation is the reverse of removal, noting the following points:

a) Make sure the airbag clockspring is centered before installing the steering wheel (see Step 9).

b) When installing the steering wheel, align the locating pin on the clockspring with the steering wheel hub.

c) Tighten the steering wheel nut to the torque listed in this Chapter's Specifications.

d) Install the airbag module on the steering wheel and tighten the mounting screws to the torque listed in this Chapter's Specifications.

e) Enable the airbag system (see Chapter 12).

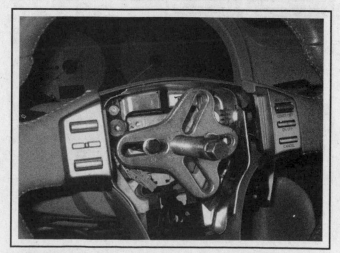

16.7 Install a steering wheel puller to remove the steering wheel from the steering shaft

16.8a Clockspring details:

1   Mounting screws
2   Alignment arrows
3   Steering wheel locating pin

16.8b The clockspring electrical connectors are located at the bottom

17 Steering column - removal and installation

✳✳ WARNING:

These models are equipped with airbags. Always disable the airbag system whenever working in the vicinity of any airbag system component to avoid the possibility of accidental airbag deployment, which could cause personal injury (see Chapter 12).

➡Note: On models with four wheel active steering or with steering angle sensors, the vehicle will have to have its sensors calibrated before and after the procedure at a dealership service department.

REMOVAL

▸ **Refer to illustrations 17.10, 17.11, 17.12, 17.14 and 17.15**

1   Park the vehicle with the wheels pointing straight ahead. Extend the column all the way out and up. Disconnect the cable(s) from the negative battery terminal(s) (see Chapter 5, Section 1). Wait at least two minutes before proceeding (to allow the backup power supply for the airbag system to become depleted).

2   Remove the steering wheel (see Section 16).

✳✳ CAUTION:

Turn the ignition key to the LOCK position to prevent the steering shaft from turning. If this is not done, the airbag clockspring could be damaged.

3   Remove the clockspring (see Section 16).

4   Remove the knee bolster (see Chapter 11) and reinforcement brace underneath it.

5   Detach the interlock system cable from beneath the ignition key cylinder (see Chapter 7B).

6   Remove the instrument cluster (see Chapter 12).

7   On vehicles equipped with four-wheel active steering, remove the control module. It is located near the bottom of the column on the right side. It is a flat and square module mounted by a bracket with two mounting bolts. Disconnect the electrical connectors at the rear of the module.

✳✳ CAUTION:

The ignition key must be off 10 minutes before disconnecting this module.

8   Remove the steering column switches (see Chapter 12).

➡Note: If the steering column is being replaced, you will need to remove the base for the switches (also known as the combination switch) and install it on the replacement column.

9   Remove the instrument cluster (see Chapter 12).

10 Remove the ABS control module that is mounted to the steering column, on models that have it mounted in this location (see illustration).

17.10 Remove the ABS module mounting fasteners and place the module aside

11 Detach the electrical wiring harness for the column (see illustration).

12 Mark the relationship of the steering column shaft to the intermediate shaft coupler, then remove the pinch-bolt by removing the nut first (see illustration).

13 Check for any remaining electrical connectors or wiring harnesses that would interfere with removal.

14 Remove the lower steering column mounting fasteners (see illustration).

15 Remove the upper steering column mounting bolts and remove the column while separating the steering shaft coupler from the intermediate shaft (see illustration).

✳✳ CAUTION:

Handle the steering column with care to avoid damaging it.

INSTALLATION

16 Guide the steering column into position and install the mounting fasteners. Tighten them to the torque listed in this Chapter's Specifications.

17 The remainder of installation is the reverse of removal. Be sure to center the clockspring as described in Section 16.

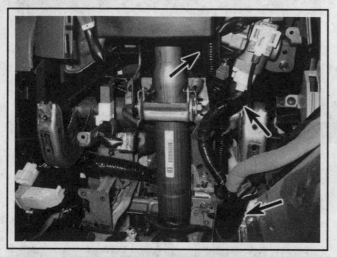

17.11 Disconnect the electrical connectors for the wiring harness and detach the harness from the column (2004 G35 Sedan model shown - other models are similar)

17.12 Mark the relationship of the steering shaft coupler to the intermediate shaft (A) and remove the coupler fasteners (B) (2004 G35 Sedan model shown - other models are similar)

17.14 Lower steering column mounting nut (A) and bolt (B) (2004 G35 Sedan model shown - other models are similar)

17.15 Steering column upper mounting bolts (2004 G35 Sedan model shown - other models are similar)

18 Tie-rod ends - removal and installation

REMOVAL

▶ **Refer to illustrations 18.2, 18.3, and 18.4**

1   Loosen the wheel lug nuts, raise the front of the vehicle and support it securely on jackstands. Apply the parking brake. Remove the wheel.

2   Loosen the tie-rod end jam nut (see illustration).

3   Mark the relationship of the tie-rod end to the threaded portion of the tie-rod. This will ensure the toe-in setting is restored when reassembled (see illustration).

4   Loosen (but don't remove) the nut on the tie-rod end ballstud and disconnect the tie-rod end from the steering knuckle with a balljoint removal tool or puller (see illustration 4.3b and the accompanying illustration).

5   If you're replacing the tie-rod end, unscrew it from the tie-rod, then thread the new one onto the tie-rod to the marked position.

INSTALLATION

6   Connect the tie-rod end to the steering knuckle. Install the nut on the ballstud and tighten it to the torque listed in this Chapter's Specifications. Tighten the jam nut securely. Install the wheel. Lower the vehicle and tighten the lug nuts to the torque listed in the Chapter 1 Specifications.

7   Have the front end alignment checked and, if necessary, adjusted.

18.2 Hold the tie-rod with a wrench while loosening the jam nut

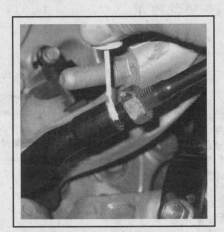

18.3 Mark the position of the tie-rod end in relation to the threads

18.4 Back-off the ballstud nut a few turns, then separate the tie-rod end from the steering knuckle with a balljoint tool or puller (leaving the nut on the ballstud will prevent the tie-rod end from separating violently)

19 Steering gear boots - replacement

▶ **Refer to illustration 19.3**

1   Loosen the wheel lug nuts, raise the front of the vehicle and support it securely on jackstands. Remove the wheel.

2   Remove the tie-rod end and jam nut (see Section 18).

3   Remove the steering gear boot clamps and slide the boot off (see illustration).

➡**Note: Check for the presence of power steering fluid in the boot. If there is a substantial amount, it means the steering gear seals are leaking and the power steering gear should be replaced with a new or rebuilt unit.**

4   Before installing the new boot, wrap the threads and serrations on the end of the steering rod with a layer of tape so the small end of the new boot isn't damaged.

5   Slide the new boot into position on the steering gear until it seats in the grooves, then install new clamps.

6   Remove the tape and install the tie-rod end (see Section 18).

7   Install the wheel and lug nuts. Lower the vehicle and tighten the lug nuts to the torque listed in the Chapter 1 Specifications.

8   Have the front end alignment checked and, if necessary, adjusted.

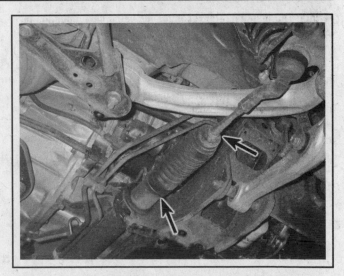

19.3 Remove both clamps to remove the steering gear boot

20 Steering gear - removal and installation

> ✳✳✳ **WARNING:**
>
> **Make sure the steering column shaft is not turned while the steering gear is removed or you could damage the airbag system clockspring. To prevent the shaft from turning, turn the ignition key to the lock position before beginning work, and run the seat belt through the steering wheel and clip it into its latch.**

➡ **Note 1:** On 2007 and later G35 Sedans, the front subframe must be lowered for clearance to remove the steering gear. A suitable floor jack will be necessary.

➡ **Note 2:** On models with four wheel active steering or with steering angle sensors, the vehicle will have to have its sensors calibrated before and after the procedure at a dealership service department.

REMOVAL

♦ **Refer to illustration 20.4**

1   Park the vehicle with the wheels pointing straight ahead. Loosen the front wheel lug nuts, raise the front of the vehicle and support it securely on jackstands. Apply the parking brake. Remove the wheels.

2   Remove the lower engine splash shield (see Chapter 2).

3   Detach the tie-rod ends from the steering knuckles (see Section 18).

4   Mark the relationship of the intermediate shaft coupler to the steering gear input shaft, remove the pinch bolt and separate the coupler from the input shaft (see illustration).

➡ **Note:** Do not disturb the plastic cap on the input shaft of the steering gear. The small key on the cap aligns the steering shaft with the steering gear input shaft. If a new steering gear is used, simply match the key on the cap with the opening on the coupler. Make sure that the front wheels are pointing straight ahead and that the key is pointing directly to the tube and hose fittings when installing the steering gear.

2007 and later G35 Sedans

➡ **Note:** The manufacturer recommends using new mounting fasteners for the subframe.

5   On 2WD models, remove the brace under the rear portion of the subframe.

6   On AWD models, remove the suspension reinforcement brace installed on the front of the suspension.

➡ **Note:** The reinforcement brace is recognized by a series of tubes and plates formed into a single wing-like shaped unit that reaches across the suspension and is held by eight bolts.

7   Remove the ABS wheel speed sensors from the steering knuckles (see Chapter 9).

8   On AWD models, remove the shock absorbers (see Section 2).

9   Remove the lower control arm (see Section 6).

10   On 2WD models, remove the stabilizer bar (see Section 3).

11   Install an engine support fixture to the top of the engine or install an engine hoist to support the engine and transaxle (see Chapter 2).

12   Detach the steering gear line and hose bracket from the subframe.

13   Detach the engine mounts from the subframe (see Chapter 2).

14   Support the rear part of the subframe with a floor jack, then remove the two rear subframe mounting bolts.

> ✳✳✳ **CAUTION:**
>
> **Do not position any part of your body beneath the subframe.**

15   Slowly and carefully lower the subframe with the floor jack just enough to get access to the steering gear mounting fasteners. At the same time, make sure the steering gear input shaft and intermediate shaft coupler separate without binding. Also, check for any wiring harnesses or hoses that may come under tension as the subframe is lowered, and detach them if necessary.

> ✳✳✳ **WARNING:**
>
> **Lowering the subframe more than necessary could damage other components, so be careful not to lower it too much.**

16   On models with four wheel active steering, remove any electrical connectors attached to the steering gear.

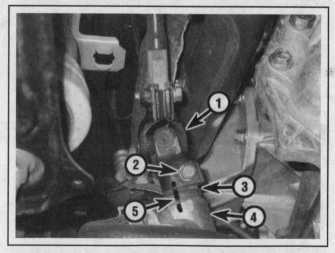

20.4 Intermediate shaft coupler and steering gear input shaft details:

1	Intermediate shaft coupler	4	Steering gear
2	Coupler pinch bolt	5	Index mark
3	Steering gear input shaft cap (with key) and key opening in coupler		

All models

◆ **Refer to illustrations 20.17 and 20.18**

17 Position a drain pan under the steering gear. Using a flare-nut wrench, disconnect the power steering pressure line from the steering gear. Detach the return hose from the steering gear by releasing the hose clamp (see illustration). Cap all openings to prevent excessive fluid loss and contamination.

18 Remove the mounting fasteners and remove the steering gear (see illustration).

➡**Note: On most models, remove the hose and line bracket attached to the steering gear mounting bracket, if equipped.**

19 Inspect all rubber bushings for wear and damage. If any of the rubber parts are cracked, torn or generally deteriorated, replace them.

INSTALLATION

20 Installation is the reverse of removal, noting the following points:

a) Tighten the steering gear mounting bolts and the lower intermediate shaft coupler pinch bolt to the torque values listed in this Chapter's Specifications.

b) Slowly and carefully raise the subframe with the floor jack while guiding the steering gear input shaft into the Intermediate shaft coupler, if applicable.

c) Install the rear subframe mounting bolts and tighten them to the torque listed in this Chapter's Specifications, if applicable.

d) Make sure that any wire harnesses or brackets that were removed to lower the subframe are reattached, if applicable.

e) Fill the power steering pump with the recommended fluid (see Chapter 1), bleed the system (see Section 22) and recheck the fluid level, if applicable.

f) Run the engine and check for proper operation and leaks. Shut off the engine and recheck fluid levels, if applicable.

g) Install the wheel and lug nuts. Lower the vehicle and tighten the lug nuts to the torque listed in the Chapter 1 Specifications.

h) Have the front end alignment checked and, if necessary, adjusted.

i) On models with four wheel active steering or steering angle sensors, have the system calibrated at a dealership service department.

20.17 Remove the high-pressure line fitting (A) with a flare-nut wrench and remove the return hose (B) from the steering gear by removing the hose clamp

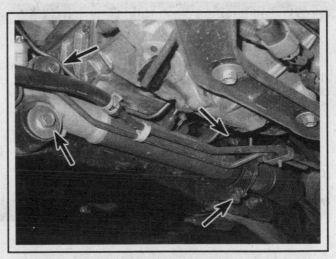

20.18 Steering gear mounting fasteners (2004 G35 Sedan model shown - other models are similar)

21 Power steering pump - removal and installation

◆ **Refer to illustrations 21.6 and 21.7**

1 Disconnect the cable from the negative battery terminal, (see Chapter 5, Section 1).

2 Using a large syringe or suction gun, suck as much fluid out of the power steering fluid reservoir as possible (see Chapter 1).

3 Remove the air filter housing (see Chapter 4).

4 Remove the drivebelt (see Chapter 1).

5 Remove the cooling fans (see Chapter 3).

➡**Note: This Step is not necessary on 2007 and later G35 models.**

6 Position a drain pan under the power steering pump, then disconnect the pressure line and the supply hose (see illustration). Plug the openings to prevent excessive fluid loss and the entry of contaminants.

7 Remove the pump mounting bolts. The bolts can be accessed through the holes in the power steering pump pulley (see illustration).

8 Lift the pump from the engine compartment, being careful not to let any power steering fluid drip on the vehicle's paint.

9 Installation is the reverse of removal. Be sure to tighten all fasteners securely. Use new copper gaskets on the pressure line fitting. Fill the power steering reservoir with the recommended fluid (see Chapter 1) and bleed the system following the procedure described in Section 22. Re-check the power steering fluid level.

21.6 Detach the supply hose (A) and the pressure line fitting (B)

21.7 Remove the power steering pump mounting bolts

22 Power steering system - bleeding

1 The power steering system must be bled whenever a line is disconnected. Bubbles can be seen in power steering fluid that has air in it and the fluid will often have a milky appearance. Low fluid level can cause air to mix with the fluid, resulting in a noisy pump as well as foaming of the fluid.

2 Open the hood and check the fluid level in the reservoir, add-ing the specified fluid necessary to bring it up to the proper level (see Chapter 1).

3 Start the engine and slowly turn the steering wheel several times from left-to-right and back again. Do not turn the wheel completely from lock-to-lock. Check the fluid level, topping it up as necessary until it remains steady and no more bubbles are visible.

23 Wheels and tires - general information

♦ Refer to illustration 23.1

All models covered by this manual are equipped with radial tires (see illustration). Use of other size or type of tires may affect the ride and handling of the vehicle. Don't mix different types of tires, such as radials and bias belted tires, on the same vehicle - handling may be seriously affected. It's recommended that tires be replaced in pairs on the same axle, but if only one tire is being replaced, be sure it's the same size, structure and tread design as the other tire on the same axle.

Because tire pressure has a substantial effect on handling and wear, the pressure of all tires should be checked at least once a month or before any extended trips are taken (see Chapter 1).

Wheels must be replaced if they are bent, dented, leak air, have elongated bolt holes, are heavily rusted, out of vertical symmetry or if the lug nuts won't stay tight. Wheel repairs that use welding or peening are not recommended.

Tire and wheel balance are important to the overall handling, brak-ing and performance of the vehicle. Unbalanced wheels can adversely affect handling and ride characteristics as well as tire life. Whenever a tire is installed on a wheel, the tire and wheel should be balanced by a shop with the proper equipment and expertise.

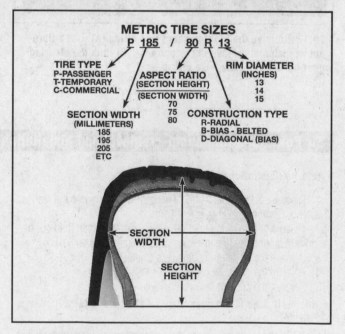

23.1 Metric tire size code

24 Wheel alignment - general information

▶ **Refer to illustration 24.1**

➡**Note: Since wheel alignment requires special equipment and techniques, it is beyond the scope of this manual. This Section is intended only to familiarize the reader with the basic terms used and procedures followed during a typical wheel alignment.**

The three basic checks made when aligning a vehicle's front wheels are camber and caster angles and toe-in. These settings are commonly adjustable, but not in every suspension (see illustration). The rear wheel alignment is also checked and often has some adjustability as well.

Camber and caster are the angles at which the wheels and suspension are inclined in relation to a vertical centerline. Camber is the angle of the wheel in the lateral, or side-to-side plane, while caster is the tilt between the steering axis and the vertical plane, as viewed from the side. Camber angle affects the amount of tire tread which contacts the road and compensates for changes in suspension geometry as the vehicle travels around curves and over bumps. Caster angle affects the self-centering action of the steering, which governs straight-line stability.

Toe-in is the amount the front wheels are angled in relationship to the center line of the vehicle. For example, in a vehicle with zero toe-in, the distance measured between the front edges of the wheels and the distance measured between the rear edges of the wheels are the same. In other words, the wheels are running parallel with the centerline of the vehicle. Toe-in is adjusted by lengthening or shortening the tie-rods. Incorrect toe-in will cause the tires to wear improperly by allowing them to scrub against the road surface.

Proper wheel alignment is essential for safe steering and even tire wear. Symptoms of alignment problems are pulling of the steering to one side or the other and uneven tire wear. If these symptoms are present, check for the following before having the alignment adjusted:

a) Loose steering gear mounting bolts
b) Damaged or worn steering gear mounts
c) Worn or damaged wheel bearings
d) Bent tie-rods
e) Worn balljoints
f) Improper tire pressures
g) Mixing tires of different construction

Front wheel alignment should be left to an alignment shop with the proper equipment and experienced personnel.

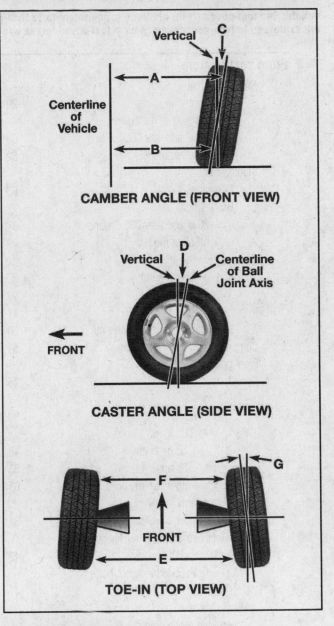

24.1 Wheel alignment details

A minus B = C (degrees camber)
D = degrees caster
E minus F = toe-in (measured in inches)
G = toe-in (expressed in degrees)

Torque specifications	Ft-lbs (unless otherwise indicated)	Nm

→Note: One foot-pound (ft-lb) of torque is equivalent to 12 inch-pounds (in-lbs) of torque. Torque values below approximately 15 ft-lbs are expressed in inch-pounds, since most foot-pound torque wrenches are not accurate at these smaller values.

Front suspension

	Ft-lbs	Nm
Shock absorber		
Upper mounting nuts	28	38
Lower mounting nut/bolt		
2007 and later G35 Sedans	68	92
All other models	62	85
Stabilizer bar		
Link nuts	62	85
Bracket bolts		
2007 and later G35 Sedans	37	50
All other models	49	67
Compression rod		
Rod-to-subframe nut		
Sedans	93	127
Coupes	114	155
Balljoint-to-steering knuckle nut	68	92
Compression rod reinforcement	51	70
Front brace		
Coupes	46	63
Sedans		
2WD	30	40
AWD		
Large bolts	46	63
Small bolts	33	45
Hub/wheel bearing mounting bolts	65	88
Upper control arm		
Arm-to-shock tower bolts	51	70
Balljoint-to-steering knuckle nut (most models)	43	58
Steering knuckle pinch nut/bolt (some models)	41	55
Lower control arm		
Mounted at two points		
Arm-to-subframe nut/bolt	93	127
Balljoint-to-steering knuckle nut	59	75
Mounted at three points		
Front pivot nut/bolt	93	127
Rear bracket mounting bolt(s)		
2WD models	53	72
AWD models	93	127
Balljoint-to-steering knuckle nut	100	136
Compression rod (350Z and 2006 and earlier G35 Sedans)		
To steering knuckle	59	75
To chassis	80	108

Torque specifications (continued)	Ft-lbs (unless otherwise indicated)	Nm

Note: One foot-pound (ft-lb) of torque is equivalent to 12 inch-pounds (in-lbs) of torque. Torque values below approximately 15 ft-lbs are expressed in inch-pounds, since most foot-pound torque wrenches are not accurate at these smaller values.

Rear suspension

Front lower link		
Link-to-subframe nut/bolt	53	72
Link-to-knuckle nut/bolt	65	87
Hub/wheel bearing mounting bolts	65	88
Shock absorber		
Upper mounting nuts	21	28
Lower mounting nut/bolt	53	72
Lower spring link		
Link-to-subframe nut/bolt	53	72
Link-to-knuckle nut/bolt	53	72
Parking brake anchor	72	98
Parking brake cable fitting	18	24
Radius rod link		
To subframe bolt	53	72
To knuckle nut/bolt	65	87
Stabilizer bar		
Link nuts/bolts	41	55
Bracket bolts	25	33
Upper arm link		
To subframe nut/bolt	53	72
Balljoint-to-rear knuckle nut	74	100

Steering

Airbag module-to-steering wheel screws	106 in-lbs	12
Steering wheel nut	25	34
Steering column mounting fasteners	144 in-lbs	17
Steering shaft pinch bolts		
Steering shaft-to-lower coupling shaft	33	44
Lower coupler-to-steering gear input shaft	20	27
Steering gear mounting bolts		
2007 and later G35 Sedans		
2WD		
Right	76	103
Left	68	92
AWD	76	103
All other models		
Mounting bolts (left)	103	140
Mounting bracket bolts (right)	56	76
Tie-rod-to-steering knuckle (ballstud) nut	25	35
Wheel lug nuts	See Chapter 1	

Notes

Section

11

BODY

1   General information

These models feature a unibody construction, using a floor pan with front and rear frame side rails which support the body components, front and rear suspension systems and other mechanical components. Certain components are particularly vulnerable to accident damage and can be unbolted and repaired or replaced. Among these parts are the body moldings, bumpers, hood and trunk lids and all glass.

Only general body maintenance practices and body panel repair procedures within the scope of the do-it-yourselfer are included in this Chapter.

2   Body - maintenance

1   The condition of your vehicle's body is very important, because the resale value depends a great deal on it. It's much more difficult to repair a neglected or damaged body than it is to repair mechanical components. The hidden areas of the body, such as the wheel wells, the frame and the engine compartment, are equally important, although they don't require as frequent attention as the rest of the body.

2   Once a year, or every 12,000 miles, it's a good idea to have the underside of the body steam cleaned. All traces of dirt and oil will be removed and the area can then be inspected carefully for rust, damaged brake lines, frayed electrical wires, damaged cables and other problems. The front suspension components should be greased after completion of this job.

3   At the same time, clean the engine and the engine compartment with a steam cleaner or water soluble degreaser.

4   The wheel wells should be given close attention, since undercoating can peel away and stones and dirt thrown up by the tires can cause the paint to chip and flake, allowing rust to set in. If rust is found, clean down to the bare metal and apply an anti-rust paint.

5   The body should be washed about once a week. Wet the vehicle thoroughly to soften the dirt, then wash it down with a soft sponge and plenty of clean soapy water. If the surplus dirt is not washed off very carefully, it can wear down the paint.

6   Spots of tar or asphalt thrown up from the road should be removed with a cloth soaked in solvent.

7   Once every six months, wax the body and chrome trim. If a chrome cleaner is used to remove rust from any of the vehicle's plated parts, remember that the cleaner also removes part of the chrome, so use it sparingly.

3   Vinyl trim - maintenance

Don't clean vinyl trim with detergents, caustic soap or petroleum-based cleaners. Plain soap and water works just fine, with a soft brush to clean dirt that may be ingrained. Wash the vinyl as frequently as the rest of the vehicle.

After cleaning, application of a high quality rubber and vinyl protectant will help prevent oxidation and cracks. The protectant can also be applied to weatherstripping, vacuum lines and rubber hoses (which often fail as a result of chemical degradation) and to the tires.

4   Upholstery and carpets - maintenance

1   Every three months remove the carpets or mats and clean the interior of the vehicle (more frequently if necessary). Vacuum the upholstery and carpets to remove loose dirt and dust.

2   Leather upholstery requires special care. Stains should be removed with warm water and a very mild soap solution. Use a clean, damp cloth to remove the soap, then wipe again with a dry cloth. Never use alcohol, gasoline, nail polish remover or thinner to clean leather upholstery.

3   After cleaning, regularly treat leather upholstery with a leather wax. Never use car wax on leather upholstery.

4   In areas where the interior of the vehicle is subject to bright sunlight, cover leather seats with a sheet if the vehicle is to be left out for any length of time.

♦ **See photo sequence**

REPAIR OF MINOR SCRATCHES

1   If the scratch is superficial and does not penetrate to the metal of the body, repair is very simple. Lightly rub the scratched area with a fine rubbing compound to remove loose paint and built-up wax. Rinse the area with clean water.

2   Apply touch-up paint to the scratch, using a small brush. Continue to apply thin layers of paint until the surface of the paint in the scratch is level with the surrounding paint. Allow the new paint at least two weeks to harden, then blend it into the surrounding paint by rubbing with a very fine rubbing compound. Finally, apply a coat of wax to the scratch area.

3   If the scratch has penetrated the paint and exposed the metal of the body, causing the metal to rust, a different repair technique is required. Remove all loose rust from the bottom of the scratch with a pocket knife, then apply rust inhibiting paint to prevent the formation of rust in the future. Using a rubber or nylon applicator, coat the scratched area with glaze-type filler. If required, the filler can be mixed with thinner to provide a very thin paste, which is ideal for filling narrow scratches. Before the glaze filler in the scratch hardens, wrap a piece of smooth cotton cloth around the tip of a finger. Dip the cloth in thinner and then quickly wipe it along the surface of the scratch. This will ensure that the surface of the filler is slightly hollow. The scratch can now be painted over as described earlier in this Section.

REPAIR OF DENTS

4   When repairing dents, the first job is to pull the dent out until the affected area is as close as possible to its original shape. There is no point in trying to restore the original shape completely as the metal in the damaged area will have stretched on impact and cannot be restored to its original contours. It is better to bring the level of the dent up to a point which is about 1/8-inch below the level of the surrounding metal. In cases where the dent is very shallow, it is not worth trying to pull it out at all.

5   If the back side of the dent is accessible, it can be hammered out gently from behind using a soft-face hammer. While doing this, hold a block of wood firmly against the opposite side of the metal to absorb the hammer blows and prevent the metal from being stretched.

6   If the dent is in a section of the body which has double layers, or some other factor makes it inaccessible from behind, a different technique is required. Drill several small holes through the metal inside the damaged area, particularly in the deeper sections. Screw long, self-tapping screws into the holes just enough for them to get a good grip in the metal. Now the dent can be pulled out by pulling on the protruding heads of the screws with locking pliers.

7   The next stage of repair is the removal of paint from the damaged area and from an inch or so of the surrounding metal. This is done with a wire brush or sanding disk in a drill motor, although it can be done just as effectively by hand with sandpaper. To complete the preparation for filling, score the surface of the bare metal with a screwdriver or the tang of a file, or drill small holes in the affected area. This will provide a good grip for the filler material. To complete the repair, see the subsection on filling and painting later in this Section.

REPAIR OF RUST HOLES OR GASHES

8   Remove all paint from the affected area and from an inch or so of the surrounding metal using a sanding disk or wire brush mounted in a drill motor. If these are not available, a few sheets of sandpaper will do the job just as effectively.

9   With the paint removed, you will be able to determine the severity of the corrosion and decide whether to replace the whole panel, if possible, or repair the affected area. New body panels are not as expensive as most people think and it is often quicker to install a new panel than to repair large areas of rust.

10   Remove all trim pieces from the affected area except those which will act as a guide to the original shape of the damaged body, such as headlight shells, etc. Using metal snips or a hacksaw blade, remove all loose metal and any other metal that is badly affected by rust. Hammer the edges of the hole in to create a slight depression for the filler material.

11   Wire brush the affected area to remove the powdery rust from the surface of the metal. If the back of the rusted area is accessible, treat it with rust inhibiting paint.

12   Before filling is done, block the hole in some way. This can be done with sheet metal riveted or screwed into place, or by stuffing the hole with wire mesh.

13   Once the hole is blocked off, the affected area can be filled and painted. See the following subsection on filling and painting.

FILLING AND PAINTING

14   Many types of body fillers are available, but generally speaking, body repair kits which contain filler paste and a tube of resin hardener are best for this type of repair work. A wide, flexible plastic or nylon applicator will be necessary for imparting a smooth and contoured finish to the surface of the filler material. Mix up a small amount of filler on a clean piece of wood or cardboard (use the hardener sparingly). Follow the manufacturer's instructions on the package, otherwise the filler will set incorrectly.

15   Using the applicator, apply the filler paste to the prepared area. Draw the applicator across the surface of the filler to achieve the desired contour and to level the filler surface. As soon as a contour that approximates the original one is achieved, stop working the paste. If you continue, the paste will begin to stick to the applicator. Continue to add thin layers of paste at 20-minute intervals until the level of the filler is just above the surrounding metal.

16   Once the filler has hardened, the excess can be removed with a body file. From then on, progressively finer grades of sandpaper should be used, starting with a 180-grit paper and finishing with 600-grit wet-or-dry paper. Always wrap the sandpaper around a flat rubber or wooden block, otherwise the surface of the filler will not be completely flat. During the sanding of the filler surface, the wet-or-dry paper should be periodically rinsed in water. This will ensure that a very smooth finish is produced in the final stage.

17   At this point, the repair area should be surrounded by a ring of bare metal, which in turn should be encircled by the finely feathered edge of good paint. Rinse the repair area with clean water until all of the dust produced by the sanding operation is gone.

18   Spray the entire area with a light coat of primer. This will reveal any imperfections in the surface of the filler. Repair the imperfections

These photos illustrate a method of repairing simple dents. They are intended to supplement Body repair - minor damage in this Chapter and should not be used as the sole instructions for body repair on these vehicles.

1 If you can't access the backside of the body panel to hammer out the dent, pull it out with a slide-hammer-type dent puller. In the deepest portion of the dent or along the crease line, drill or punch hole(s) at least one inch apart . . .

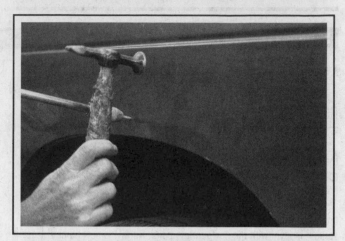

2 . . . then screw the slide-hammer into the hole and operate it. Tap with a hammer near the edge of the dent to help 'pop' the metal back to its original shape. When you're finished, the dent area should be close to its original contour and about 1/8-inch below the surface of the surrounding metal

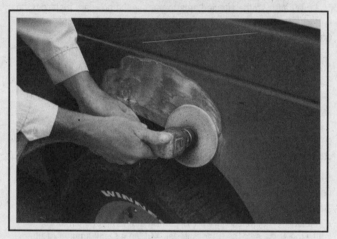

3 Using coarse-grit sandpaper, remove the paint down to the bare metal. Hand sanding works fine, but the disc sander shown here makes the job faster. Use finer (about 320-grit) sandpaper to feather-edge the paint at least one inch around the dent area

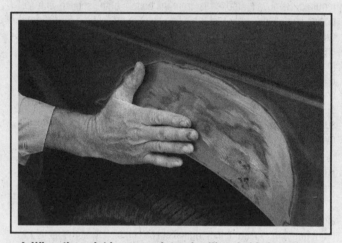

4 When the paint is removed, touch will probably be more helpful than sight for telling if the metal is straight. Hammer down the high spots or raise the low spots as necessary. Clean the repair area with wax/silicone remover

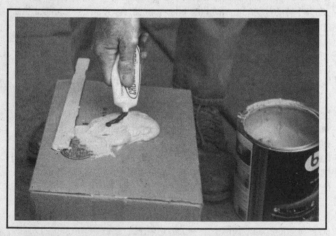

5 Following label instructions, mix up a batch of plastic filler and hardener. The ratio of filler to hardener is critical, and, if you mix it incorrectly, it will either not cure properly or cure too quickly (you won't have time to file and sand it into shape)

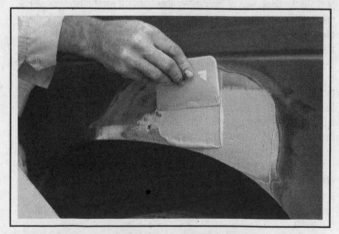

6 Working quickly so the filler doesn't harden, use a plastic applicator to press the body filler firmly into the metal, assuring it bonds completely. Work the filler until it matches the original contour and is slightly above the surrounding metal

7 Let the filler harden until you can just dent it with your fingernail. Use a body file or Surform tool (shown here) to rough-shape the filler

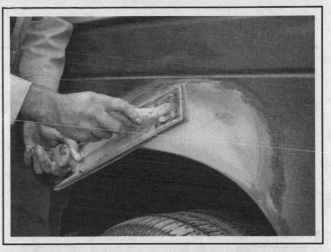

8 Use coarse-grit sandpaper and a sanding board or block to work the filler down until it's smooth and even. Work down to finer grits of sandpaper - always using a board or block - ending up with 360 or 400 grit

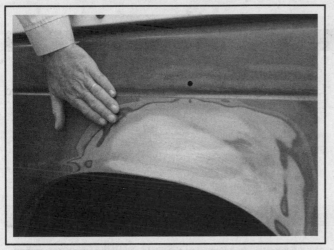

9 You shouldn't be able to feel any ridge at the transition from the filler to the bare metal or from the bare metal to the old paint. As soon as the repair is flat and uniform, remove the dust and mask off the adjacent panels or trim pieces

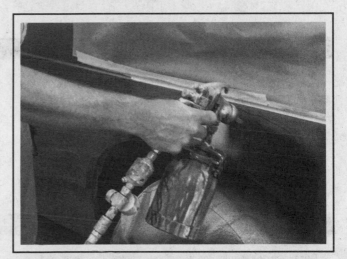

10 Apply several layers of primer to the area. Don't spray the primer on too heavy, so it sags or runs, and make sure each coat is dry before you spray on the next one. A professional-type spray gun is being used here, but aerosol spray primer is available inexpensively from auto parts stores

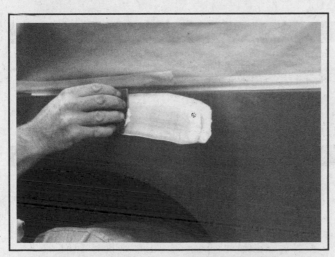

11 The primer will help reveal imperfections or scratches. Fill these with glazing compound. Follow the label instructions and sand it with 360 or 400-grit sandpaper until it's smooth. Repeat the glazing, sanding and respraying until the primer reveals a perfectly smooth surface

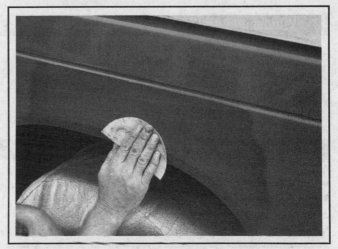

12 Finish sand the primer with very fine sandpaper (400 or 600-grit) to remove the primer overspray. Clean the area with water and allow it to dry. Use a tack rag to remove any dust, then apply the finish coat. Don't attempt to rub out or wax the repair area until the paint has dried completely (at least two weeks)

with fresh filler paste or glaze filler and once more smooth the surface with sandpaper. Repeat this spray-and-repair procedure until you are satisfied that the surface of the filler and the feathered edge of the paint are perfect. Rinse the area with clean water and allow it to dry completely.

19 The repair area is now ready for painting. Spray painting must be carried out in a warm, dry, windless and dust free atmosphere. These conditions can be created if you have access to a large indoor work area, but if you are forced to work in the open, you will have to pick the day very carefully. If you are working indoors, dousing the floor in the work area with water will help settle the dust which would otherwise be in the air. If the repair area is confined to one body panel, mask off the surrounding panels. This will help minimize the effects of a slight mismatch in paint color. Trim pieces such as chrome strips, door handles, etc., will also need to be masked off or removed. Use masking tape and several thickness of newspaper for the masking operations.

20 Before spraying, shake the paint can thoroughly, then spray a test area until the spray painting technique is mastered. Cover the repair area with a thick coat of primer. The thickness should be built up using several thin layers of primer rather than one thick one. Using 600-grit wet-or-dry sandpaper, rub down the surface of the primer until it is very smooth. While doing this, the work area should be thoroughly rinsed with water and the wet-or-dry sandpaper periodically rinsed as well. Allow the primer to dry before spraying additional coats.

21 Spray on the top coat, again building up the thickness by using several thin layers of paint. Begin spraying in the center of the repair area and then, using a circular motion, work out until the whole repair area and about two inches of the surrounding original paint is covered. Remove all masking material 10 to 15 minutes after spraying on the final coat of paint. Allow the new paint at least two weeks to harden, then use a very fine rubbing compound to blend the edges of the new paint into the existing paint. Finally, apply a coat of wax.

Body repair - major damage

1 Major damage must be repaired by an auto body shop specifically equipped to perform these repairs. Most shops have the specialized equipment required to do the job properly.

2 If the damage is extensive, the body must be checked for proper alignment or the vehicle's handling characteristics may be adversely affected and other components may wear at an accelerated rate.

3 Due to the fact that all of the major body components (hood, fenders, etc.) are separate and replaceable units, any seriously damaged components should be replaced rather than repaired. Sometimes the components can be found in a wrecking yard that specializes in used vehicle components, often at considerable savings over the cost of new parts.

Hinges and locks - maintenance

Once every 3000 miles, or every three months, the hinges and latch assemblies on the doors, hood and trunk should be given a few drops of light oil or lock lubricant. The door latch strikers should also be lubricated with a thin coat of grease to reduce wear and ensure free movement. Lubricate the door and trunk locks with spray-on graphite lubricant.

Windshield and fixed glass - replacement

Replacement of the windshield and fixed glass requires the use of special fast-setting adhesive/caulk materials and some specialized tools. It is recommended that these operations be left to a dealer or a shop specializing in glass work.

Hood - removal, installation and adjustment

➡Note: The hood is heavy and somewhat awkward to remove and install - at least two people should perform this procedure.

REMOVAL AND INSTALLATION

♦ Refer to illustration 9.4

1 Use blankets or pads to cover the cowl area of the body and fenders. This will protect the body and paint as the hood is lifted off.

2 Disconnect any cables or wires that will interfere with removal.

3 Make marks or scribe a line around the hood hinges to ensure proper alignment during installation.

4 Have an assistant support one side of the hood. Take turns removing the hinge-to-hood bolts and lift off the hood (see illustration).

5 Lift off the hood.

6 Installation is the reverse of removal.

9.4 Support the hood with your shoulder while removing the hood bolts

ADJUSTMENT

♦ **Refer to illustrations 9.10 and 9.11**

7   Fore-and-aft and side-to-side adjustment of the hood is done by moving the hinge plate slot after loosening the bolts or nuts.

8   Scribe a line around the entire hinge plate so you can determine the amount of movement.

9   Loosen the bolts or nuts and move the hood into correct alignment. Move it only a little at a time. Tighten the hinge bolts and carefully lower the hood to check the position.

10 If necessary after installation, the entire hood latch assembly can be adjusted up-and-down as well as from side-to-side on the radiator support, so the hood closes securely and flush with the fenders. To make the adjustment, scribe a line or mark around the hood latch mounting bolts to provide a reference point, then loosen them and reposition the latch assembly, as necessary (see illustration). Following adjustment, retighten the mounting bolts.

11 Finally, adjust the hood bumpers on the hood so the hood, when closed, is flush with the fenders (see illustration).

12 The hood latch assembly, as well as the hinges, should be periodically lubricated with white, lithium-base grease to prevent binding and wear.

9.10 Scribe a line around the latch to use as a reference point. To adjust the hood latch, loosen the retaining bolts, move the latch and retighten the bolts, then close the hood to check the fit

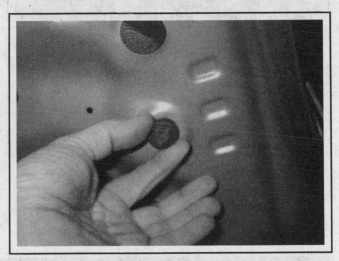

9.11 Adjust the hood closing height by turning the hood bumpers in or out

10 Hood release latch and cable - removal and installation

LATCH

1   Scribe a line around the latch to aid alignment when installing, then detach the latch retaining bolts to the radiator support (see illustration 9.10) and remove the latch.

2   Disconnect the hood release cable by disengaging the cable from the latch assembly.

3   Installation is the reverse of the removal procedure.

➡**Note: Adjust the latch so the hood engages securely when closed and the hood bumpers are slightly compressed.**

CABLE

♦ **Refer to illustrations 10.4, 10.6 and 10.8**

4   Remove the radiator grille (see illustration).

5   Disconnect the hood release cable from the latch.

6 Remove the inner fender splash shield (see illustration).

7 Attach a piece of stiff wire to the end of the cable, then follow the cable back to the firewall and detach all the cable retaining clips.

8 Working in the passenger compartment, remove the driver's side knee bolster (see Section 24). Then detach the cable from the hood release lever (see illustration).

9 Pull the cable and grommet rearward into the passenger compartment until you can see the wire. Ensure that the new cable has a grommet attached, then remove the old cable from the wire and replace it with the new cable.

10 Working from the fenderwell, pull the wire back through the firewall.

11 Installation is the reverse of removal.

➥Note: Push on the grommet with your fingers from the passenger compartment to seat the grommet in the firewall correctly.

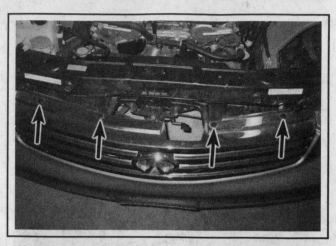

10.4 Remove the fasteners securing the radiator grille

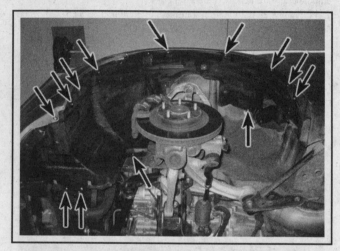

10.6 Inner fenderwell splash shield mounting fasteners

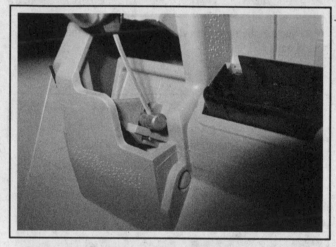

10.8 Detach the cable from the release lever

11 Bumper covers - removal and installation

FRONT BUMPER COVER

♦ **Refer to illustrations 11.2, 11.4 and 11.5**

1 Apply the parking brake, raise the vehicle and support it securely on jackstands.

2 Working under the vehicle, remove the fasteners securing the lower edges of the bumper cover (see illustration).

3 Working in the front wheel opening, detach the retaining screws securing the bumper cover to the inner fenderwell splash shield (see illustration 10.6).

4 Pry out the lower edge of the splash shield, then reach up behind the bumper cover and remove the bumper cover-to-fender retaining fastener (see illustration).

5 Remove the fasteners securing the upper portion of the bumper cover and pull the bumper cover out and away from the vehicle (see illustration).

6 Disconnect any electrical connections which would interfere with removal.

REAR BUMPER COVER

♦ **Refer to illustrations 11.8, 11.9a and 11.9b**

7 Apply the parking brake, raise the vehicle and support it securely on jackstands.

8 Working under the vehicle, detach the fasteners securing the lower edges of the bumper cover (see illustration).

9 Working in the trunk, pry out the fasteners securing the rear inside trunk finishing panel to allow access to the bumper cover retaining fasteners (see illustrations).

10 Detach the fasteners securing the bumper cover to the right and left quarter panels, then pull the bumper cover out and away from the vehicle.

11 Installation is the reverse of removal.

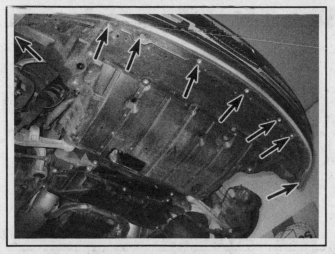

11.2 Bumper cover lower mounting fasteners

11.4 Peel back the splash shield and remove the bumper cover-to-fender retaining fastener

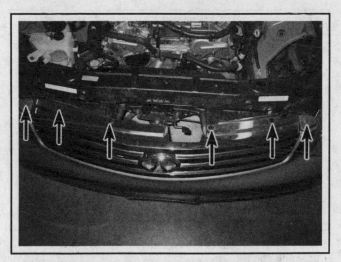

11.5 Remove the upper mounting fasteners from the bumper cover

11.8 Remove the bumper cover lower mounting fasteners (left side shown, right side similar)

11.9a Remove the fasteners securing the trunk finishing panel . . .

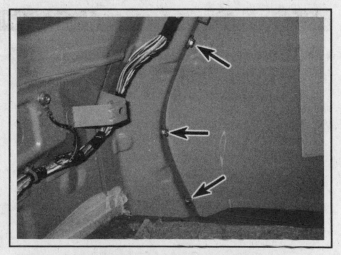

11.9b . . . to allow access to the bumper cover retaining bolts

12 Front fender - removal and installation

▶ **Refer to illustrations 12.3a, 12.3b and 12.3c**

1   Raise the vehicle, support it securely on jackstands and remove the front wheel.

2   Remove the inner fenderwell splash shield (see illustration 10.6).

3   Remove the fender mounting bolts (see illustrations).

4   Detach the fender. It's a good idea to have an assistant support the fender while it's being moved away from the vehicle to prevent damage to the surrounding body panels.

5   Installation is the reverse of removal.

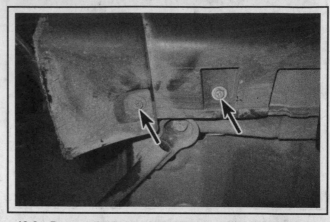

12.3a Remove the fasteners securing the bottom of the rocker panel . . .

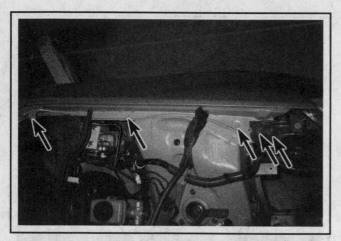

12.3b . . . and the fender-to-body upper mounting bolts

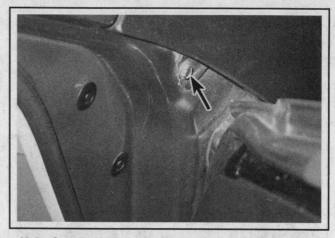

12.3c Open the door to access and remove the fender-to-door pillar bolt

13 Trunk lid support struts - removal and installation

▶ **Refer to illustration 13.2**

1   Open the trunk lid and support it securely.

2   Using a small screwdriver, detach the retaining clips at both ends of the support strut. Then pry or pull sharply to detach it from the vehicle (see illustration).

3   Installation is the reverse of removal.

13.2 Use a small screwdriver to pry the clip out of its locking groove, then detach the end of the strut from the locating stud

14 Trunk lid - removal, installation and adjustment

➡Note: The trunk lid is heavy and somewhat awkward to remove and install - at least two people should perform this procedure.

REMOVAL AND INSTALLATION

▶ **Refer to illustration 14.4**

1   Open the trunk lid and cover the edges of the trunk compartment with pads or cloths to protect the painted surfaces when the lid is removed.

2   Disconnect any cables or wire harness connectors attached to the trunk lid that would interfere with removal. Make marks or scribe a line around the trunk lid hinges to ensure proper alignment during installation.

3   Detach the trunk lid support struts from the trunk lid (see Section 13).

4   Have an assistant support one side of the trunk lid. Take turns removing the hinge-to-trunk lid bolts and lift off the trunk lid (see illustration).

5   Installation is the reverse of removal.

➡Note: When reinstalling the trunk lid, align the marks made during removal.

ADJUSTMENT

6   Fore-and-aft and side-to-side adjustment of the trunk lid is accomplished by moving the lid in relation to the hinge after loosening the bolts or nuts.

7   Scribe a line around the entire hinge plate so you can determine the amount of movement.

8   Loosen the nuts and move the trunk lid into correct alignment. Move it only a little at a time. Tighten the hinge nuts and carefully lower the trunk lid to check the alignment.

9   If necessary after installation, the entire trunk lid striker assembly can be adjusted up and down as well as from side to side on the trunk lid, so the lid closes securely and is flush with the rear quarter panels. To do this, scribe a line around the trunk lid striker assembly to provide a reference point. Then loosen the nuts and reposition the striker as necessary. Following adjustment, retighten the mounting nuts.

10   The trunk lid latch assembly, as well as the hinges, should be periodically lubricated with white lithium-base grease to prevent sticking and wear.

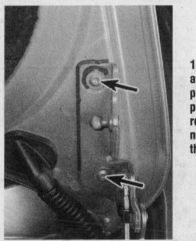

14.4 Scribe a mark around the hinge plate for realignment purposes, then remove the retaining nuts on each side of the trunk lid

15 Trunk lid latch - removal and installation

▶ **Refer to illustrations 15.1 and 15.3**

1   Open the trunk and remove the latch trim cover (see illustration).

2   Make a mark or scribe a line around the trunk lid latch for a reference point to aid the installation procedure.

3   Disconnect the electrical connectors and the emergency opener cable lock cylinder, then detach the retaining bolts and remove the latch (see illustration).

4   Installation is the reverse of removal.

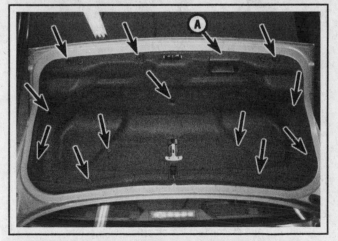

15.1 Pry off the plastic pull handle (A), then remove the fasteners securing the cover

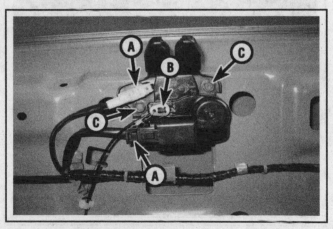

15.3 Trunk lid latch details

A   Electrical connectors
B   Emergency opener cable
C   Latch mounting nuts

16 Door trim panel - removal and installation

♦ Refer to illustrations 16.1, 16.2, 16.3, 16.4a, 16.4b, 16.5a and 16.5b

1   Remove the inside door handle cover (see illustration).
2   Remove the door pull handle cover (see illustration).
3   Detach the retaining screws securing the door panel (see illustration).
4   Pry out the switch control plate and disconnect the electrical connectors (see illustrations).
5   Once all of the fasteners are removed, detach the trim panel (see illustration). Disconnect the door handle actuating cable (see illustration). Disconnect any electrical connectors and remove the trim panel from the door.
6   Installation is the reverse of removal.

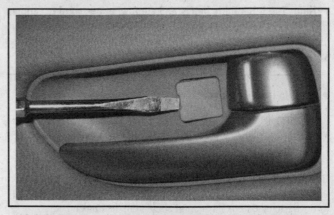

16.1 Using a small screwdriver, pry open the cover, then remove the inside door handle mounting fastener

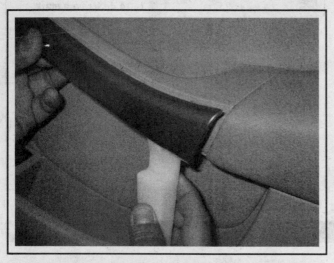

16.2 Using a trim stick, remove the pull handle trim cover . . .

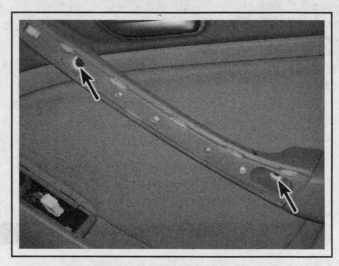

16.3 . . . then remove these screws

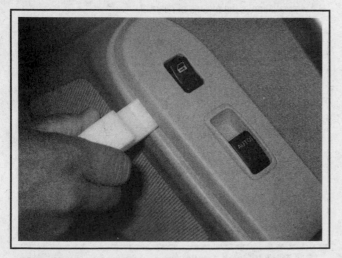

16.4a Using a trim stick, pry out the armrest switch control plate . . .

16.4b . . . and disconnect the electrical connectors

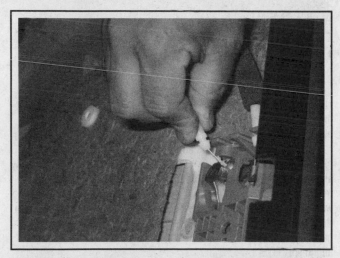

16.5a Carefully pry around the door panel to release the clips, then remove the panel . . .

16.5b . . . and disconnect the door handle actuating cable

17 Door - removal, installation and adjustment

➡**Note: The door is heavy and somewhat awkward to remove and install - at least two people should perform this procedure.**

REMOVAL AND INSTALLATION

Refer to illustrations 17.4, 17.5 and 17.7

1   Lower the window completely in the door, then disconnect the negative cable from the battery (see Chapter 5, Section 1).
2   Open the door all the way and support it on jacks or blocks cov-ered with rags to prevent damaging the paint.

3   Remove the door trim panel and water shield as described in Section 16.
4   Unplug the door electrical harness from the A-pillar (see illustration).
5   Remove the door check strap mounting bolt (see illustration).
6   Mark around the door hinges with a pen or a scribe to facilitate realignment during reassembly.
7   Have an assistant hold the door, then remove the hinge-to-door fasteners (see illustration) and lift the door off.
8   Installation is the reverse of the removal.

17.4 Pull the release handle and unplug the electrical harness

17.5 Remove the door check strap retaining bolt

17.7 Remove the hinge-to-door fasteners

ADJUSTMENT

▸ **Refer to illustration 17.12**

9 Having proper door-to-body alignment is a critical part of a well functioning door assembly. First check the door hinge pins for excessive play. Fully open the door and lift up and down on the door without lifting the body. If a door has 1/16-inch or more excessive play, the hinges should be replaced.

10 Door-to-body alignment adjustments are made by loosening the hinge-to-body or hinge-to-door bolts and moving the door. Proper body alignment is achieved when the top of door is aligned with the top of front fender and rear quarter panel and the bottom of the door is aligned with the lower rocker panel. If these goals can't be reached by adjusting the hinge-to-body or hinge-to-door bolts, body alignment shims may have to be purchased and inserted behind the hinges to achieve correct alignment.

11 To adjust the door closed position, first check that the door latch is contacting the center of the latch striker. If not, remove the striker and add or subtract shims to achieve correct alignment.

12 Finally adjust the latch striker as necessary (up-and-down or sideways) to provide positive engagement with the latch mechanism (see illustration) and so the door panel is flush with the rear quarter panel.

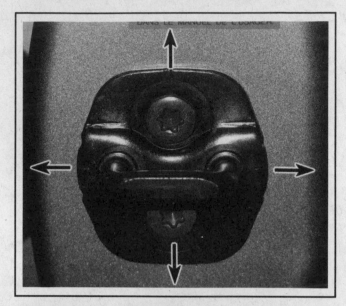

17.12 Adjust the door latch striker by loosening the mounting screws and gently tapping the striker in the desired direction

18 Door latch, lock cylinder and handle - removal and installation

DOOR LATCH

▸ **Refer to illustrations 18.4 and 18.5**

1 Remove the door trim panel as described in Section 16.

2 Remove the door window glass as described in Section 19.

3 Remove the window glass module assembly as described in Section 20, Step 3.

4 Disconnect the door latch actuator rod from the handle (see illustration).

5 Remove the screws securing the latch to the door (see illustration), then remove the latch assembly from the door.

6 Installation is the reverse of removal.

DOOR LOCK CYLINDER AND OUTSIDE HANDLE

7 Remove the door trim panel as described in Section 16.

8 Remove the door window glass as described in Section 19.

9 Remove the window glass module assembly as described in Section 20, Step 3.

10 Disconnect the door latch actuator rod from the handle, then remove the outside handle retaining fasteners and pull the handle from the door (see illustration 18.4).

11 Installation is the reverse of removal.

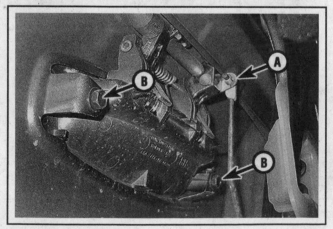

18.4 Door handle details

A *Door latch actuator rod*
B *Door handle mounting fasteners*

18.5 Remove the latch retaining screws from the end of the door

19 Door window glass - removal and installation

FRONT WINDOW

▶ **Refer to illustration 19.3**

1   Remove the door trim panel (see Section 16).
2   Remove the door speaker (see Chapter 12).
3   Raise the window just enough to access the window retaining bolts through the hole in the door frame (see illustration), then remove the bolts.
4   Remove the glass by pulling it up and out.
5   Installation is the reverse of removal.

REAR WINDOW (SEDAN MODELS)

▶ **Refer to illustrations 19.8 and 19.10**

6   Lower the window, then remove the door trim panel (see Section 16).
7   Remove the door speaker (see Chapter 12).
8   Remove the water shield (see illustration).
9   Raise the window just enough to access the window retaining bolts through the hole in the door frame.

10 Remove the window sash (see illustration).
11 Remove the window retaining bolts.
12 Remove the glass by pulling it up and out.
13 Installation is the reverse of removal.

19.3 Window glass retaining bolts

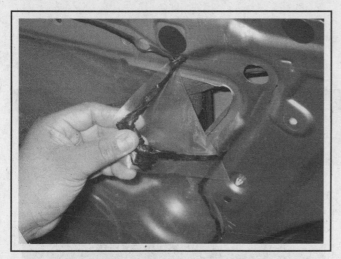

19.8 Carefully peel back the plastic water shield

19.10 Remove the fasteners securing the window sash

20 Door window glass regulator - removal and installation

FRONT WINDOW

▶ **Refer to illustration 20.3**

1   Remove the door trim panel (see Section 16).
2   Remove the window glass (see Section 19).
3   Disconnect the electrical connector, then remove the window

glass module assembly (see illustration).
4   Remove the fasteners securing the regulator and motor assembly to the glass module assembly.
5   Pull the regulator and motor assembly off the glass module assembly to remove it.
6   Installation is the reverse of removal.

REAR WINDOW (SEDAN MODELS)

▶ **Refer to illustration 20.10**

7   Lower the window, then remove the door trim panel (see Section 16).

8   Remove the watershield (see illustration 19.8).
9   Remove the window glass (see Section 19).
10 Remove the fasteners securing the regulator and motor assembly, then disconnect the electrical connector for the motor and remove the assembly (see illustration).
11 Installation is the reverse of removal.

20.3 Disconnect the electrical connector (A), then remove the window glass module mounting fasteners

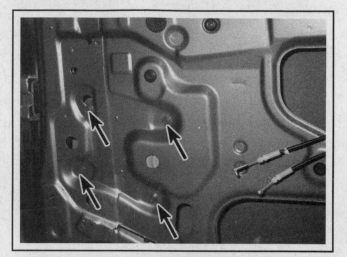

20.10 Window regulator mounting bolts

21 Side view mirrors - removal and installation

▶ **Refer to illustrations 21.2 and 21.3**

1   Remove the door trim panel (see Section 16).
2   Disconnect the mirror electrical connector, then remove the mirror

trim cover from the door panel (see illustration).

3   Remove the three mirror retaining nuts and detach the mirror from the vehicle (see illustration).

4   Installation is the reverse of removal.

21.2 Detach the side view mirror trim cover by removing the push-pin fasteners

21.3 Side view mirror mounting fasteners

22 Center console - removal and installation

▶ **Refer to illustrations 22.2, 22.3a and 22.3b**

1   Remove the front seats (see Section 27). Remove the shifter knob (see Chapter 7).

2   Pry out the gear selector trim bezel (see illustration).

3   Remove the center console mounting screws, then remove the trim panel (see illustrations).

4   Lift the console up and over the shift lever. Disconnect any electrical connections and remove the console from the vehicle.

5   Installation is the reverse of removal.

22.2 Carefully pry off the gear selector trim bezel

22.3a Remove the retaining screws securing the front half of the console . . .

22.3b . . . and the retaining screws securing the rear half of the console

23 Steering column cover - removal and installation

▶ **Refer to illustration 23.1**

1   Remove the screws from the lower steering column cover (see illustration).

2   Separate the cover halves and detach them from the steering column.

3   Installation is the reverse of removal.

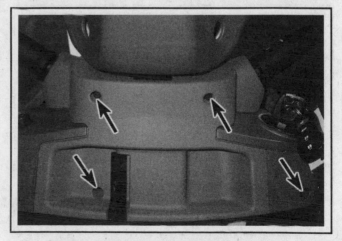

23.1 Steering column cover mounting fasteners

24 Dashboard trim panels - removal and installation

✳✳ WARNING:

The models covered by this manual are equipped with Supplemental Restraint Systems (SRS), more commonly known as airbags. Always disable the airbag system before working in the vicinity of any airbag system components to avoid the possibility of accidental deployment of the airbags, which could cause personal injury (see Chapter 12).

1   Disconnect the cable from the negative battery terminal (see Chapter 5, Section 1).

KNEE BOLSTER

▶ **Refer to illustrations 24.2 and 24.3**

2   Working in the driver's side passenger compartment, detach the retaining screw at the lower edge of the knee bolster (see illustration).

3   Using a trim stick, pry loose the panel (see illustration), then pull outward on the lower edge of the knee bolster and detach it from the vehicle.

4   Disconnect the hood release cable (see illustration 10.8).

5   Installation is the reverse of removal.

CENTER TRIM PANEL

▶ **Refer to illustrations 24.8, 24.9, 24.10a and 24.10b**

6   Remove the gear selector trim bezel (see illustration 22.2).

7   Remove the lower glove box (see Step 12).

8   Remove the screws from the side of the center trim panel (see illustration).

9   Remove the clock trim panel (see illustration).

10 Detach the retaining screws from the center trim panel, disconnect any electrical connections and remove the unit from the vehicle (see illustrations).

11 Installation is the reverse of removal.

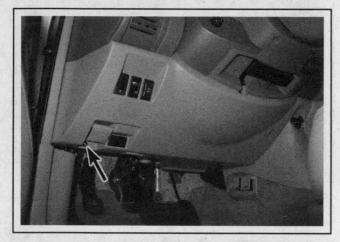

24.2 Remove the retaining screw at the lower edge of the knee bolster

24.3 Using a trim stick, carefully pry around the panel and release the clips

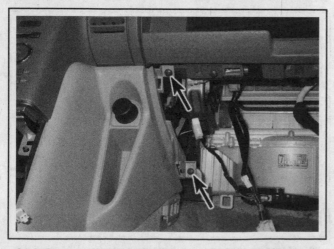

24.8 Remove the fasteners, then carefully detach the side trim panels

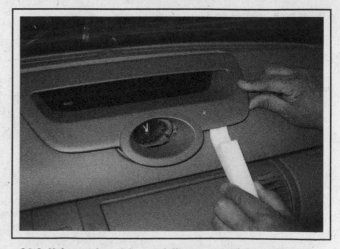

24.9 Using a trim stick, carefully pry around the panel and release the clips

24.10a Remove the fasteners securing the center trim panel . . .

24.10b . . . then disconnect any electrical connections and remove the unit from the vehicle

GLOVE BOX

Lower box

▶ **Refer to illustration 24.12**

12 Open the glove box door and remove the glove box retaining screws (see illustration), then pull straight out to remove the glove box assembly. Disconnect any electrical connectors.

13 Installation is the reverse of removal.

Upper box

▶ **Refer to illustrations 24.15a and 24.15b**

14 Remove the lower glove box (see Step 12).

15 Remove the glove box retaining screws (see illustration), then pull straight out to remove the glove box assembly (see illustration).

16 Installation is the reverse of removal.

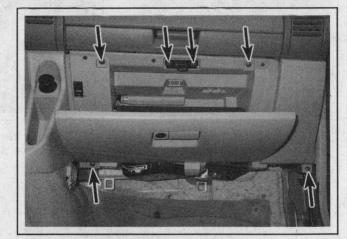

24.12 Remove the glove box retaining screws

24.15a Remove the upper glove box fasteners . . .

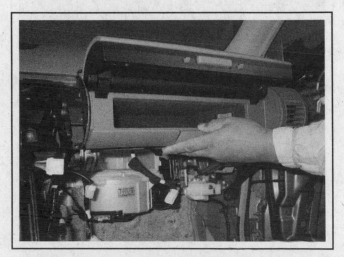

24.15b . . . then pull straight out to remove the glove box assembly

INSTRUMENT PANEL TOP COVER

▶ **Refer to illustrations 24.17, 24.18, 24.19a, 24.19b and 24.19c**

17 Using a trim stick, carefully pry around the defrost vents and release the clips, then detach them from the dashboard (see illustration).

18 Remove the A-pillar trim (see illustration).

19 Remove the fasteners securing the instrument panel top cover (see illustrations), then detach the cover from the instrument panel support beam.

20 Installation is the reverse of removal.

KICK PANELS

▶ **Refer to illustrations 24.21, 24.22 and 24.23**

21 Pry up the front end of the door sill plates with a trim tool (see illustration).

22 If you're removing the left side kick panel, remove the foot rest (see illustration).

23 Remove the fastener securing the kick panel (see illustration), then carefully pry off the panel to release the clips.

24 Installation is the reverse of removal.

24.17 Using a trim stick, carefully pry around the defrost vents to release the clips

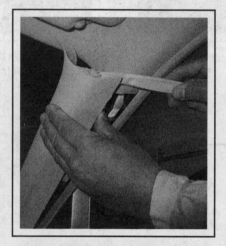

24.18 Using a trim stick, carefully pry around the A-pillar trim to release the clips

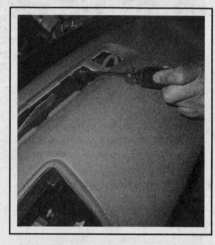

24.19a Remove the fasteners inside the defrost vents . . .

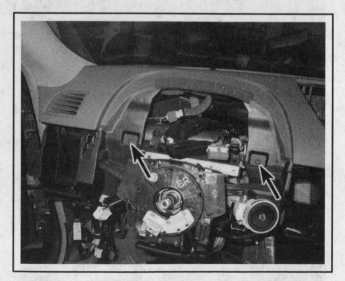

24.19b . . . at the cluster area . . .

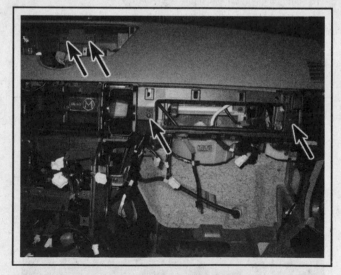

24.19c . . . and at the passenger side of the instrument panel

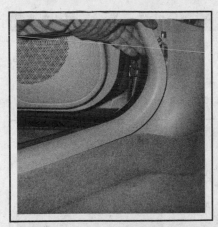

24.21 Pry up the front end of the door sill plates with a trim tool

24.22 Remove the fastener securing the foot rest

24.23 Remove the fastener securing the kick panel, then carefully pry off the panel to release the clips

25 Rear parcel shelf - removal and installation

◊ Refer to illustrations 25.2, 25.3a and 25.3b

1 Remove the rear seat (see Section 27).
2 Remove the rear window trim panels (see illustration).
3 Remove the fasteners securing the parcel shelf (see illustrations).
4 Remove the seat belt anchor bolts, then remove the parcel shelf.
5 Installation is the reverse of removal.

25.2 Carefully pry around the panel and release the clips

25.3a Carefully pry off the trim from the child seat anchor . . .

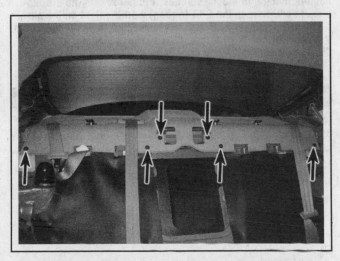

25.3b . . . then remove the push-pin fasteners securing the parcel shelf

26 Cowl cover - removal and installation

▶ **Refer to illustrations 26.2 and 26.3**

1 Remove the windshield wiper arms (see Chapter 12).
2 Carefully peal off the cowl cover seal (see illustration).

3 Remove the retaining fasteners securing the cowl cover (see illustration).
4 Remove the right side cowl cover, then the left side.
5 Installation is the reverse of removal.

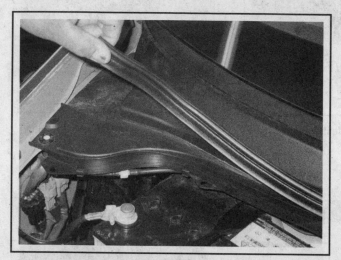

26.2 Carefully peal off the cowl cover seal

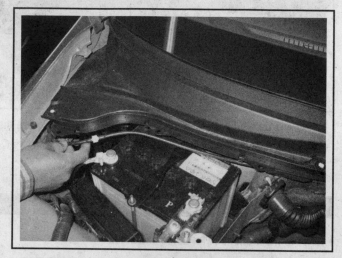

26.3 Remove the fasteners securing the cowl cover

27 Seats - removal and installation

⁂ **WARNING 1:**

The front seat belts on some models are equipped with pre-tensioners, which are pyrotechnic (explosive) devices designed to retract the seat belts in the event of a collision. On models equipped with pre-tensioners, do not remove the front seat belt retractor assemblies, and do not disconnect the electrical connectors leading to the assemblies. Problems with the pre-tensioners will turn on the SRS (airbag) warning light on the dash. If any pre-tensioner problems are suspected, take the vehicle to a dealer service department. Also on these models, be sure to disable the airbag system (see Chapter 12).

⁂ **WARNING 2:**

On models with side-impact airbags, be sure to disarm the airbag system before beginning this procedure (see Chapter 12).

FRONT SEAT

▶ **Refer to illustrations 27.2a and 27.2b**

1 Position the seat all the way forward or all the way to the rear to access the front seat retaining bolts.
2 Detach any bolt trim covers and remove the retaining bolts (see illustrations).
3 Tilt the seat upward to access the underneath, then disconnect any electrical connectors and lift the seat from the vehicle.
4 Installation is the reverse of removal.

REAR SEAT

▶ **Refer to illustrations 27.5 and 27.6**

5 Working at the front of each seat cushion, pull the retaining tabs, then lift up on the front edge of the cushion and release the seat cushion retaining tabs (see illustration). Remove the cushion from the vehicle.
6 Remove the retaining bolts at the lower edge of the seat back (see illustration).
7 Lift up on the lower edge of the seat back and remove it from the vehicle.
8 Installation is the reverse of removal.

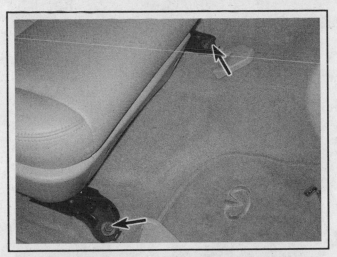

27.2a Detach the trim covers, then remove the bolts at the front . . .

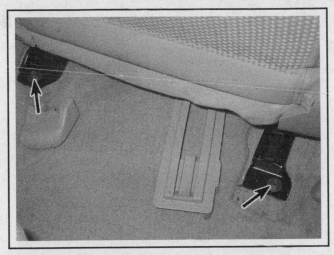

27.2b . . . and rear of the seat

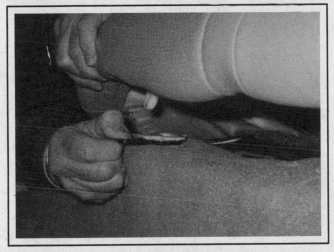

27.5 Pull the retaining tabs, then lift up on the front edge of the cushion

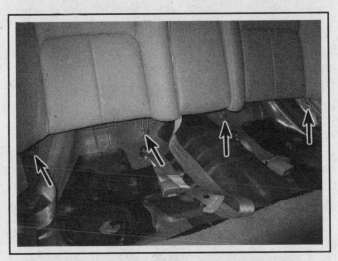

27.6 Remove the retaining bolts at the lower edge of the seat back

Notes

Section

12

CHASSIS ELECTRICAL SYSTEM

1   General information

The electrical system is a 12-volt, negative ground type. A lead/acid-type battery that is charged by the alternator supplies power for the lights and all electrical accessories.

This Chapter covers repair and service procedures for the various electrical components not associated with the engine. Information on the battery, alternator, ignition system and starter motor can be found in Chapter 5. Warning: When working on the electrical system, disconnect the cable from the negative battery terminal to prevent electrical shorts and/or fires (see Chapter 5, Section 1).

2   Electrical troubleshooting - general information

▶ **Refer to illustrations 2.5a, 2.5b, 2.6, 2.9 and 2.15**

A typical electrical circuit consists of an electrical component, any switches, relays, motors, fuses, fusible links or circuit breakers related to that component and the wiring and connectors that link the component to both the battery and the chassis. To help you pinpoint an electrical circuit problem, wiring diagrams are included at the end of this Chapter.

Before tackling any troublesome electrical circuit, first study the appropriate wiring diagrams to get a complete understanding of what makes up that individual circuit. You can often narrow down trouble spots, for instance, by noting whether other components related to the circuit are operating correctly. If several components or circuits fail at one time, chances are that the problem is in a fuse or ground connection, because several circuits are often routed through the same fuse and ground connections.

Electrical problems usually stem from simple causes, such as loose or corroded connections, a blown fuse, a melted fusible link or a failed relay. Visually inspect the condition of all fuses, wires and connections in a problem circuit before troubleshooting the circuit.

If test equipment and instruments are going to be utilized, use the diagrams to plan ahead of time where you will make the necessary connections in order to accurately pinpoint the trouble spot.

For electrical troubleshooting you'll need a circuit tester or voltmeter, a continuity tester, which includes a bulb, battery and set of test leads, and a jumper wire, preferably with a circuit breaker incorporated, which can be used to bypass electrical components (see illustrations). Before attempting to locate a problem with test instruments, use the wiring diagram(s) to decide where to make the connections.

VOLTAGE CHECKS

Voltage checks should be performed if a circuit is not functioning properly. Connect one lead of a circuit tester to either the negative battery terminal or a known good ground. Connect the other lead to a connector in the circuit being tested, preferably nearest to the battery or fuse (see illustration). If the bulb of the tester lights, voltage is present, which means that the part of the circuit between the connector and the battery is problem free. Continue checking the rest of the circuit in the same fashion. When you reach a point at which no voltage is present, the problem lies between that point and the last test point with voltage. Most of the time the problem can be traced to a loose connection.

➡**Note: Keep in mind that some circuits receive voltage only when the ignition key is in the ACC or RUN position.**

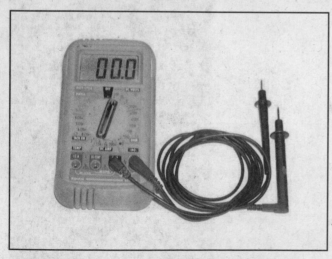

2.5a The most useful tool for electrical troubleshooting is a digital multimeter that can check volts, amps, and test continuity

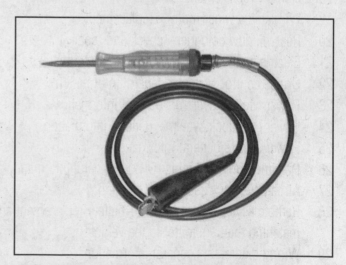

2.5b A simple test light is a very handy tool for testing voltage

2.6 Clip the ground lead of a test light to a known good ground, then use the pointed probe to test connectors, wires or electrical sockets. If the bulb lights, battery voltage is present at the test point

2.9 To measure resistance across two terminals, set a multimeter to the ohm scale. When checking for continuity, a low reading indicates continuity, a very high or infinite reading indicates lack of continuity

FINDING A SHORT

One method of finding shorts in a circuit is to remove the fuse and connect a test light or voltmeter to the fuse terminals. There should be no voltage present in the circuit when it is turned off. Move the wiring harness from side-to-side while watching the test light. If the bulb goes on, there is a short to ground somewhere in that area, probably where the insulation has rubbed through. The same test can be performed on each component in the circuit, even a switch.

GROUND CHECK

Perform a ground test to check whether a component is properly grounded. Disconnect the battery and connect one lead of a continuity tester or multimeter (set to the ohm scale), to a known good ground. Connect the other lead to the wire or ground connection being tested. If the resistance is low (less than 5 ohms), the ground is good. If the bulb on a self-powered test light does not go on, the ground is not good.

CONTINUITY CHECK

A continuity check determines whether there are any breaks in a circuit (whether it's conducting electricity correctly). With the circuit off (no power in the circuit), use a self-powered continuity tester or multimeter to check the circuit. Connect the test leads to both ends of the circuit (or to the power end and a good ground). If the test light comes on, the circuit is conducting current correctly (see illustration). If the resistance is low (less than 5 ohms), there is continuity; if the reading is 10,000 ohms or higher, there is a break somewhere in the circuit. The same procedure can be used to test a switch, by connecting the continuity tester to the switch terminals. With the switch turned on, the test light should come on (or low resistance should be indicated on a meter).

FINDING AN OPEN CIRCUIT

When diagnosing for possible open circuits, it is often difficult to locate them by sight because the connectors hide oxidation or terminal misalignment. Merely wiggling a connector on a sensor or in the wiring harness may correct the open circuit condition. Remember this when an open circuit is indicated when troubleshooting a circuit. Intermittent problems may also be caused by oxidized or loose connections.

Electrical troubleshooting is simple if you keep in mind that all electrical circuits are basically electricity running from the battery, through the wires, switches, relays, fuses and fusible links to each electrical component (light bulb, motor, etc.) and to ground, from which it is passed back to the battery. Any electrical problem is an interruption in the flow of electricity to and from the battery.

CONNECTORS

Most electrical connections on these vehicles are made with multi-wire plastic connectors. The mating halves of many connectors are secured with locking clips molded into the plastic connector shells. The mating halves of large connectors, such as some of those under the instrument panel, are held together by a bolt through the center of the connector.

To separate a connector with locking clips, use a small screwdriver to pry the clips apart carefully, then separate the connector halves. Pull only on the shell; never pull on the wiring harness as you may damage the individual wires and terminals inside the connectors. Look at the connector closely before trying to separate the halves. Often the locking clips are engaged in a way that is not immediately clear. Additionally, many connectors have more than one set of clips.

Each pair of connector terminals has a male half and a female half. When you look at the end view of a connector in a diagram, be sure to understand whether the view shows the harness side or the component side of the connector. Connector halves are mirror images of each other, and a terminal shown on the right side end-view of one half will be on the left side end view of the other half.

It is often necessary to take circuit voltage measurements with a connector connected. Whenever possible, carefully insert a small straight pin (not your meter probe) into the rear of the connector shell to contact the terminal inside, then clip your meter lead to the pin. This kind of connection is called "backprobing" (see illustration). When inserting a test probe into a male terminal, be careful not to distort the terminal opening. Doing so can lead to a poor connection and corrosion at that terminal later. Using the small straight pin instead of a meter probe results in less chance of deforming the terminal connector.

2.15 To backprobe a connector, insert a small, sharp probe (such as a straight-pin) into the back of the connector alongside the desired wire until it contacts the metal terminal inside; connect your meter leads to the probes - this allows you to test a functioning circuit

3   Fuses and fusible links - general information

FUSES

♦ **Refer to illustrations 3.1a, 3.1b, 3.1c, 3.1d, 3.1e and 3.3**

1   The electrical circuits of the vehicle are protected by a combination of fuses and relays. The engine compartment fuse and relay boxes are located at the right rear corner of the engine compartment, in the same void as the battery (see illustrations). You can access the smaller fuse and relay box by simply opening the battery cover. To access the larger fuse and relay box back in the corner, you'll have to remove the cowl trim panel (see Chapter 11). There's a third fuse box inside the vehicle, behind a small access door on the left kick panel (see illustrations). On this fuse box, as well as the ones in the engine compartment, you'll find a handy fuse and (if equipped, relay) guide either inside or on top of the cover (see illustration).

2   At a dealer parts department you might hear the phrase "Intelligent Power Distribution Module" or "IPDM." These are Nissan/Infiniti terms for the engine compartment fuse and relay box (see illustration 3.1b). In this manual, we use the simpler term "fuse and relay box." However, you should know the factory terminology so that you can

3.1a There are two engine compartment fuse and relay boxes located at the right rear corner of the engine compartment, in the same void as the battery. This is the smaller of the two boxes, with the lid removed

3.1b This is the larger fuse and relay box (cover removed) which is also located in the battery void. To access this box you must remove the cowl trim panel (see Chapter 11)

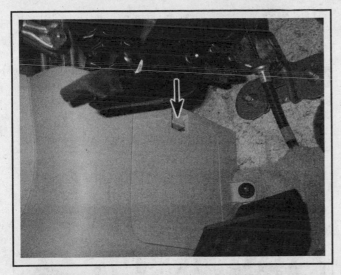

3.1c The interior fuse box is located behind this access panel in the left kick panel. To remove the access cover, push down on the tab at the top

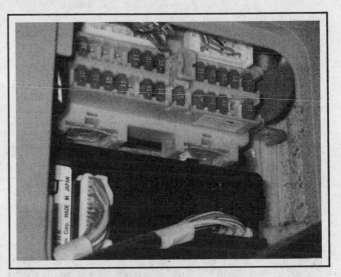

3.1d Interior fuse box, access cover removed

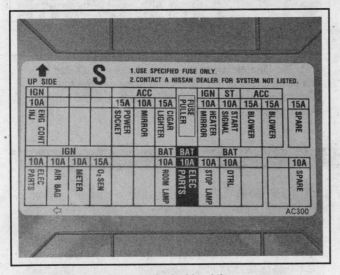

3.1e This fuse guide is on the inside of the access cover. There's also a handy fuse guide on the covers for the two engine compartment fuse and relay boxes

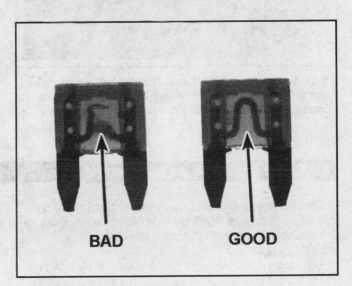

3.3 When a fuse blows, the element between the terminals melts

communicate with a dealer parts department if you have to buy fuses or relays. The Intelligent Power Distribution Module (IPDM), or what we call the fuse and relay box, is the larger of the two fuse and relay boxes located at the right rear corner of the engine compartment, in the same void as the battery.

3   Each fuse is designed to protect a specific circuit, and the various circuits are identified (in a highly abbreviated way) on the fuse panel itself. Different sizes of fuses are employed. There are mini and maxi sizes, with the larger located in the fuse and relay box. You'll need to use electronics needle-nose pliers or a small plastic fuse-puller tool to remove most fuses. There should be one of these fuse-puller tools in the fuse and relay box. If an electrical component fails, always check the fuse first. The best way to check the fuses is with a test light. Check

for power at the exposed terminal tips of each fuse. If power is present at one side of the fuse but not the other, the fuse is blown. A blown fuse can also be identified by visually inspecting it (see illustration).

4   Be sure to replace blown fuses with the correct type. Fuses of different ratings are physically interchangeable, but only fuses of the proper rating should be used. Replacing a fuse with one of a higher or lower value than specified is not recommended. Each electrical circuit needs a specific amount of protection. The amperage rating of each fuse is molded into the fuse body.

5   If the replacement fuse immediately fails, don't replace it again until the cause of the problem is isolated and corrected. In most cases, the cause will be a short circuit In the wiring caused by a broken or deteriorated wire.

FUSIBLE LINKS

▶ **Refer to illustrations 3.6a and 3.6b**

6 The wiring between the battery and the alternator, between the ignition switch and the battery and in other high-load circuits is protected by fusible links (see illustrations). These links look and function like a fuse, but they're rated for higher amperage. To replace a fusible

link, first disconnect the negative cable from the battery (see Chapter 5, Section 1). Remove the burned-out fusible link and replace it with a new one (available from your dealer or auto parts store).

✳✳ CAUTION:

Before installing a new fusible link, be sure to determine the cause of the circuit overload that melted the fusible link.

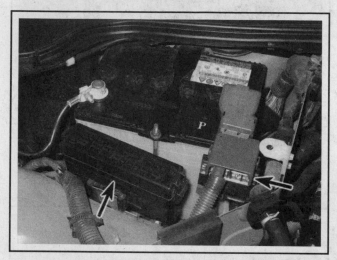

3.6a Some of the fusible links are located inside a special box at the positive battery terminal. Other fusible links are located inside the fuse and relay box in front of the battery

3.6b The ignition switch-to-battery circuit is protected by this 40 amp fusible link (A) located at the positive battery terminal. Other fusible links are located inside the small plastic housing (B)

4 Circuit breakers - general information

Circuit breakers protect certain heavy-load circuits. Depending on the vehicle's accessories, there might be circuit breakers located in the engine compartment fuse and relay boxes (see illustrations 3.1a and 3.1b).

Because the circuit breakers reset automatically, an electrical overload in a circuit-breaker-protected system will cause the circuit to fail momentarily, then come back on. If the circuit does not come back on, check it immediately.

For a basic check, pull the circuit breaker up out of its socket on the fuse panel, but just far enough to probe with a voltmeter. The breaker should still contact the sockets.

With the voltmeter negative lead on a good chassis ground, touch each end prong of the circuit breaker with the positive meter probe. There should be battery voltage at each end. If there is battery voltage only at one end, the circuit breaker must be replaced.

5 Relays - general information and testing

1 Many electrical accessories in the vehicle utilize relays to transmit current to the component. If the relay is defective, the component won't operate properly.

2 Most relays are located in the engine compartment fuse and relay box (see illustration 3.1a or 3.1b).

3 Some relays are located in other parts of the vehicle or in various wiring harnesses underneath the instrument panel.

4 If a faulty relay is suspected, it can be removed and tested using the procedure below, or by a dealer service department or a repair shop. Defective relays must be replaced as a unit.

TESTING

▶ **Refer to illustrations 5.5a and 5.5b**

5 Most of the relays used in these vehicles are of a type often called "ISO" relays, which refers to the International Standards Organization. The terminals of ISO relays are numbered to indicate their usual circuit connections and functions. There are two basic layouts of terminals on the relays used in the vehicles covered by this manual (see illustrations).

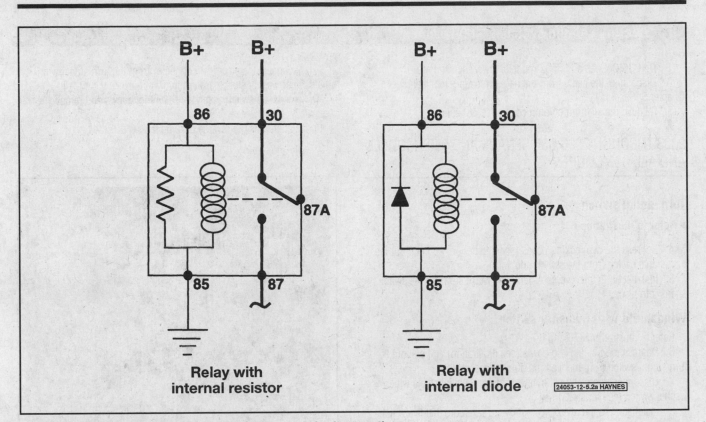

Relay with internal resistor

Relay with internal diode

24053-12-5.2a HAYNES

5.5a Typical ISO relay designs, terminal numbering and circuit connections

6   Refer to the wiring diagram for the circuit to determine the proper connections for the relay you're testing. If you can't determine the correct connection from the wiring diagrams, however, you may be able to determine the test connections from the information that follows.

7   Two of the terminals are the relay control circuit and connect to the relay coil. The other relay terminals are the power circuit. When the relay is energized, the coil creates a magnetic field that closes the larger contacts of the power circuit to provide power to the circuit loads.

8   Terminals 85 and 86 are normally the control circuit. If the relay contains a diode, terminal 86 must be connected to battery positive (B+) voltage and terminal 85 to ground. If the relay contains a resistor, terminals 85 and 86 can be connected in either direction with respect to B+ and ground.

9   Terminal 30 is normally connected to the battery voltage (B+) source for the circuit loads. Terminal 87 is connected to the ground side of the circuit, either directly or through a load. If the relay has several alternate terminals for load or ground connections, they usually are numbered 87A, 87B, 87C, and so on.

10 Use an ohmmeter to check continuity through the relay control coil.

a) *Connect the meter according to the polarity shown in illustration 5.5a for one check, then reverse the ohmmeter leads and check continuity in the other direction.*

b) *If the relay contains a resistor, resistance will be indicated on the meter, and should be the same value with the ohmmeter in either direction.*

c) *If the relay contains a diode, resistance should be higher with the ohmmeter in the forward polarity direction than with the meter leads reversed.*

d) *If the ohmmeter shows infinite resistance in both directions, replace the relay.*

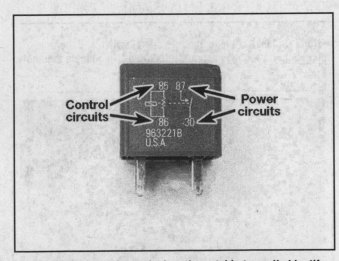

5.5b Most relays are marked on the outside to easily identify the control circuit and power circuits - this one is of the four-terminal type

11 Remove the relay from the vehicle and use the ohmmeter to check for continuity between the relay power circuit terminals. There should be no continuity between terminal 30 and 87 with the relay de-energized.

12 Connect a fused jumper wire to terminal 86 and the positive battery terminal. Connect another jumper wire between terminal 85 and ground. When the connections are made, the relay should click.

13 With the jumper wires connected, check for continuity between the power circuit terminals. Now there should be continuity between terminals 30 and 87.

14 If the relay fails any of the above tests, replace it.

6   Steering column switches - replacement

1 On G35 Coupes and 350Z models, lower the windows.
2 Disconnect the cable from the negative battery terminal (see Chapter 5, Section 1).
3 Remove the steering column covers (see Chapter 11).

2003 THROUGH 2006 G35 SEDANS AND 350Z MODELS AND ALL G35 COUPES

Turn signal switch

◆ **Refer to illustration 6.4**

4 Depress the two locking pawls (see illustration) and pull out the turn signal switch from the switch housing.
5 Installation is the reverse of removal. Make sure that the switch snaps into place.

Windshield wiper/washer switch

Refer to illustrations 6.6 and 6.7
6 Depress the two locking pawls (see illustration) and pull out the turn signal switch from the steering column assembly.
7 Disconnect the electrical connector from the windshield wiper/washer switch (see illustration).
8 Installation is the reverse of removal. Make sure that the switch snaps into place.

2007 AND LATER G35 SEDANS AND 350Z MODELS

➡**Note: On these vehicles the turn signal switch and the windshield wiper/washer switch are integrated into a single assembly.**

9 Disconnect the electrical connector from the turn signal/windshield wiper/washer switch assembly.
10 Remove the switch assembly retaining screws and remove the switch.
11 Installation is the reverse of removal.

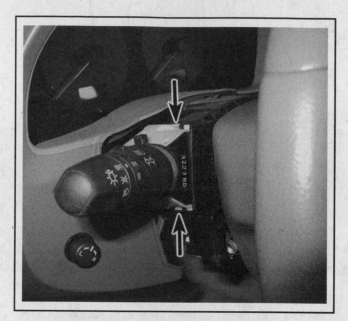

6.4 To remove the turn signal switch from the switch housing, depress these two locking pawls and pull out the switch

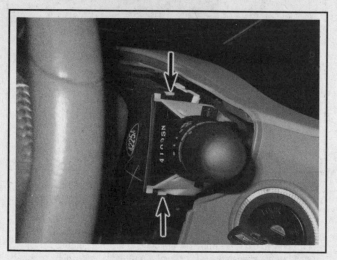

6.6 To remove the windshield wiper/washer switch from the steering column assembly, depress these two locking pawls and pull out the switch . . .

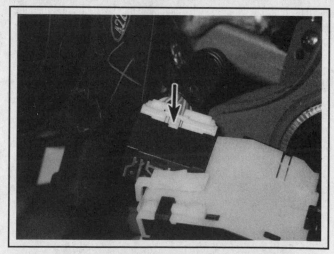

6.7 . . . then depress this release tab and disconnect the electrical connector from the switch

7   Instrument cluster - removal and installation

1   On G35 Coupes and 350Z models, roll down the windows.
2   Disconnect the cable from the negative battery terminal (see Chapter 5, Section 1).

G35 SEDANS AND COUPES

▶ **Refer to illustrations 7.4a, 7.4b, 7.4c, 7.4d, 7.4e and 7.5**

3   Remove the steering column covers and the knee bolster (see Chapter 11).
4   Remove the instrument cluster trim bezel (see illustrations).
5   Remove the two instrument cluster mounting screws, disengage the two spring clips at the bottom of the cluster and remove the cluster from the cluster trim bezel (see illustration).
6   Installation is the reverse of removal.

350Z MODELS

7   Remove the knee bolster and the steering column covers (see Chapter 11).
8   Remove the six instrument cluster mounting screws that secure the cluster to the steering column assembly.
9   Remove the instrument cluster from the instrument panel and disconnect the electrical connectors from the backside of the cluster.
10   Installation is the reverse of removal.

7.4a To detach the instrument cluster trim bezel, remove these two screws . . .

7.4b . . . and these four bolts . . .

7.4c . . . then work the cluster trim bezel loose, remove the trim ring from the ignition key lock cylinder and lift off the cluster trim and cluster as a single assembly

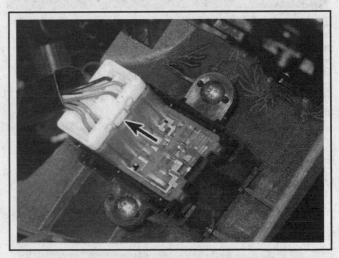

7.4d To disconnect the electrical connector from the mirror adjustment switch, depress this release tab and pull off the connector

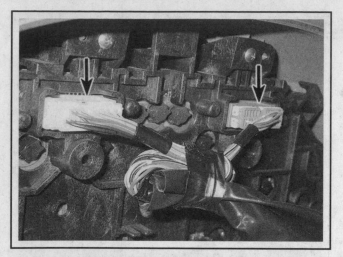

7.4e To disconnect the electrical connectors from the instrument cluster, depress these release tabs and pull off the connectors

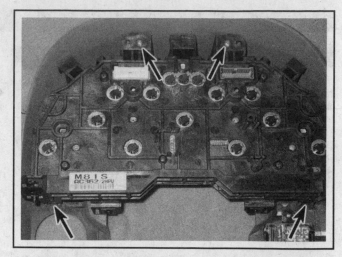

7.5 To detach the instrument cluster from the cluster trim bezel, remove these two screws at the top, then work these two spring clips loose at the bottom and pull off the cluster

8 Key lock cylinder and ignition switch - replacement

IGNITION KEY LOCK CYLINDER

1 Because a new ignition key lock cylinder comes with new ignition keys, which must be programmed with a factory scan tool, we don't recommend that you attempt to replace the ignition key lock cylinder assembly at home.

IGNITION SWITCH

▶ **Refer to illustrations 8.5, 8.6 and 8.7**

❊❊ **WARNING:**

The models covered by this manual are equipped with a Supplemental Restraint System (SRS), more commonly known as airbags. Always disarm the airbag system before working in the vicinity of any airbag system component to avoid the possibility of accidental deployment of the airbag, which could cause personal injury (see Section 27). Do not use a memory-saving device to preserve the PCM's memory when working on or near airbag system components.

2 Disconnect the cable from the negative battery terminal (see Chapter 5, Section 1).

3 Remove the steering column covers (see Chapter 11).

4 Remove the instrument cluster/trim panel assembly (see Section 9).

5 Disconnect the electrical connector from the ignition switch (see illustration).

6 Remove the ignition switch mounting screws (see illustration) and remove the switch from the key lock cylinder housing.

7 When installing the new ignition switch, make sure that the T-shaped hole in the switch is aligned with the T-shaped protrusion on the ignition key lock cylinder assembly (see illustration).

8 Rotate the ignition switch as necessary to align the mounting screw holes in the switch with the screw holes in the ignition key lock cylinder housing, then install the mounting screws and tighten them securely.

9 Installation is otherwise the reverse of removal.

10 Rotate the ignition key through all of its positions and make sure it operates smoothly. Verify that the engine starts when the key is turned to START.

8.5 To disconnect the electrical connector from the ignition switch, depress this release tab and pull off the connector

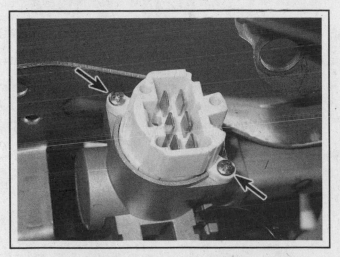

8.6 To remove the ignition switch assembly from the key lock cylinder housing, remove these two screws

8.7 When installing the ignition switch, make sure that the T-shaped receptacle in the switch is aligned with the T-shaped protrusion on the key lock cylinder

9   Instrument panel and center console switches - replacement

❊❊ WARNING:

The models covered by this manual are equipped with a Supplemental Restraint System (SRS), more commonly known as airbags. Always disarm the airbag system before working in the vicinity of any airbag system component to avoid the possibility of accidental deployment of the airbag, which could cause personal injury (see Section 27). Do not use a memory-saving device to preserve the PCM's memory when working on or near airbag system components.

1   On G35 Coupes and 350Z models, roll down the windows.
2   Disconnect the cable from the negative battery terminal (see Chapter 5, Section 1).

SWITCHES AT THE LEFT END OF THE INSTRUMENT PANEL

▶ Refer to illustrations 9.4 and 9.5

➡ Note: All vehicles have an array of switches at the left end of the instrument panel on the knee bolster trim panel. They include the instrument panel brightness control rheostat (G35 models only); the trunk lid release switch; the Vehicle Dynamics Control (VDC) OFF switch; the fuel filler neck lid opener switch (350Z models only); and the soft top operating switch (350Z Roadsters only).

3   Remove the knee bolster trim panel (see Chapter 11).
4   Disconnect the electrical connectors from the switches (see illustration).
5   Depress the release tabs (see illustration) and push out the headlight switch through the front side of the knee bolster.

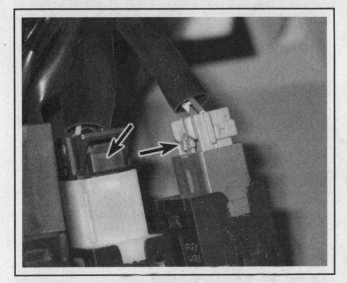

9.4 Typical electrical connector release tabs

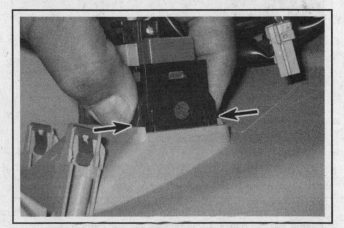

9.5 To remove one of the switches from the knee bolster trim panel, depress the two release tabs as shown and push the switch through from the backside of the panel

6   When installing a switch, make sure that it snaps into place. Installation is otherwise the reverse of removal.

MIRROR ADJUSTMENT SWITCH

♦ **Refer to illustration 9.8**

➡**Note: The mirror adjustment switch is located to the left of the steering column, on the instrument cluster trim bezel.**

7   Remove the instrument cluster trim bezel (see Section 7) and disconnect the electrical connector for the mirror adjustment switch (see illustration 7.4d).

8   Remove the mirror adjustment retaining screws (see illustration) and remove the mirror adjustment switch.

9   Installation is the reverse of removal.

HAZARD FLASHER SWITCH

♦ **Refer to illustrations 9.11 and 9.12**

➡**Note: The hazard flasher switch is located on the center console.**

10   Remove the center console (see Chapter 11).

11   Disconnect the electrical connector from the hazard flasher switch (see illustration).

12   Remove the hazard flasher switch mounting screws (see illustration) and remove the switch.

13   Installation is the reverse of removal.

HEATED SEAT SWITCHES

♦ **Refer to illustrations 9.15 and 9.16**

➡**Note: There are two heated seat switches, one for each front seat, in the center console. The following procedure applies to either switch.**

14   Remove the center console (see Chapter 11).

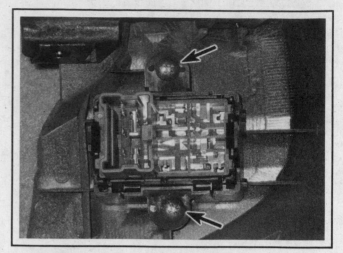

9.8   To detach the mirror adjustment switch from the instrument cluster trim bezel, remove these two retaining screws

15   Disconnect the electrical connector from the hazard flasher switch (see illustration).

16   Remove the hazard flasher switch mounting screws (see illustration) and remove the switch.

17   Installation is the reverse of removal.

TRUNK LID OPENER SWITCH

♦ **Refer to illustrations 9.18 and 9.19**

➡**Note: The trunk lid opener switch is located inside the glove box.**

18   Open the glove box, then carefully pry out the trunk lid opener switch (see illustration).

19   Disconnect the electrical connector from the trunk lid opener switch (see illustration).

20   Installation is the reverse of removal.

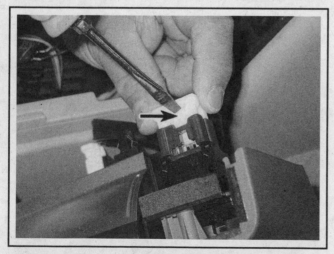

9.11   To disconnect the electrical connector from the hazard flasher switch, depress this release tab and pull off the connector

9.12   To remove the hazard flasher switch from the center console, remove these two retaining screws

9.15 To disconnect the electrical connector for either heated seat switch, depress this release tab and pull apart the two halves of the connector

9.16 To remove either heated seat switch from the center console, carefully pry the mounting brackets at each end away from the switch and pull off the switch

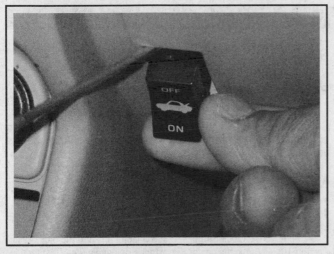

9.18 To replace the trunk lid opener switch, carefully pry it out . . .

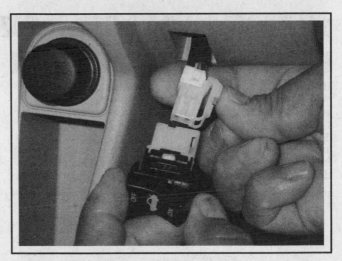

9.19 . . . then depress the release tab on the electrical connector and disconnect the connector

10 Clock - replacement

▶ **Refer to illustrations 10.2 and 10.3**

➡**Note: This procedure applies to the analog clock used in G35 models. 350Z models use a digital clock that is an integral function of the audio unit.**

1   Remove the clock trim panel (see Chapter 11).
2   Remove the clock mounting screws (see illustration).
3   Pull out the clock and disconnect the electrical connector from the clock (see illustration).
4   Installation is the reverse of removal.

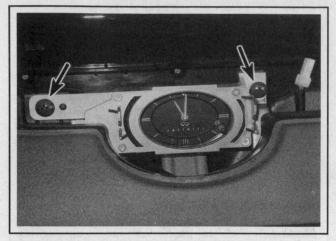

10.2 To remove the clock, remove these two screws

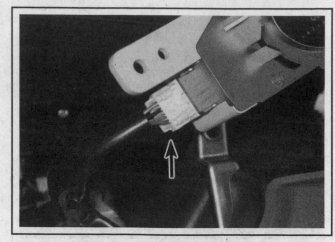

10.3 Pull out the clock and disconnect the electrical connector

11 Radio and speakers - removal and installation

☀☀ WARNING:

The models covered by this manual are equipped with a Supplemental Restraint System (SRS), more commonly known as airbags. Always disarm the airbag system before working in the vicinity of any airbag system component to avoid the possibility of accidental deployment of the airbag, which could cause personal injury (see Section 27). Do not use a memory-saving device to preserve the PCM's memory when working on or near airbag system components.

1   On G35 Coupes and 350Z models, roll down the windows.
2   Disconnect the cable from the negative battery terminal (see Chapter 5, Section 1).

G35 SEDANS AND COUPES

Radio

➡Note: The photos accompanying this Section depict a typical G35 Sedan or Coupe audio unit on a vehicle without a navigation system. The procedure for removing the radio on 350Z models is very similar.

Audio unit

▶ Refer to illustrations 11.4a, 11.4b, 11.5a, 11.5b, 11.5c, 11.6, 11.7a, 11.7b and 11.9

3   Remove the clock trim panel (see Chapter 11) and the clock (see Section 10). Remove the center trim panel side panels (see Chapter 11).
4   Remove the instrument panel center trim bezel mounting bolts, then remove the center trim bezel, the audio unit and, if equipped, the display unit as a single assembly (see illustrations).

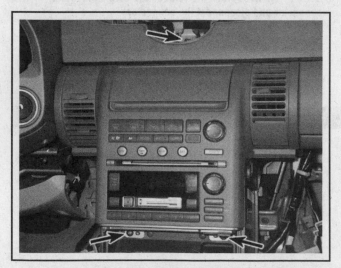

11.4a To detach the center trim bezel from the instrument panel, remove these three screws . . .

11.4b . . . then pull the center trim bezel out of the instrument panel. This assembly is fairly heavy because it includes the heater and air conditioning controller, the audio unit and, if equipped, the display unit for the navigation system

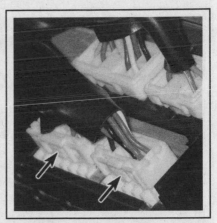

11.5a To disconnect this electrical connector for the air conditioning and audio controller, depress the release tab and pull the two halves of the connector apart

11.5b To disconnect the antenna connector from the audio unit, pull out on the locking tab and pull off the connector

11.5c To disconnect these four electrical connectors from the audio unit, depress the release tabs and pull the connectors out of the module

5   Disconnect the electrical connectors for the air conditioning and audio controller and the audio unit (and, if equipped, the display unit), and disconnect the radio antenna (see illustrations).

6   Disconnect the ribbon connector that connects the audio unit to the air conditioning/audio controller (see illustration).

7   Remove the screws (see illustrations) for the audio unit (and if equipped, the display unit) mounting bracket, then remove the mounting bracket and audio unit (and, if equipped, the display unit) as a single assembly from the center trim bezel.

8   On vehicles equipped with navigation, remove the screws that secure the display unit to the audio unit and to the audio unit mounting bracket, then separate the display unit from the audio unit.

9   Remove the screws (see illustration) that secure the audio unit (and, if equipped, the display unit) to the mounting bracket and separate the audio unit and display unit as a single assembly from the mounting bracket.

10 Installation is the reverse of removal.

11.6 To disconnect the ribbon connector, carefully pry it apart where shown with a small screwdriver

11.7a To detach the lower end of the audio (or audio/display) unit mounting bracket, remove the two screws from each side

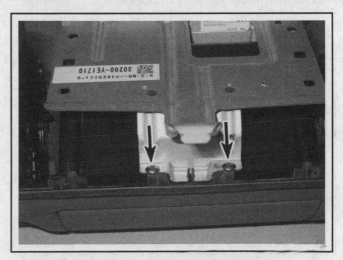

11.7b To detach the upper end of the audio (or audio/display) unit mounting bracket, remove these two screws

11.9 To detach the audio (or audio/display) unit from the mounting bracket, remove these four screws from each side

11.12 On vehicles without navigation, remove these two screws and remove the storage receptacle

11.13 To remove the air conditioning and audio controller, remove these three screws

Air conditioning and audio controller

◆ Refer to illustrations 11.12 and 11.13

➡Note: The air conditioning and audio controller is the thin circuit board mounted between the audio unit/navigation unit mounting bracket and the inside face of the center trim panel.

11 Remove the audio unit and, if equipped, the navigation unit (see Steps 1 through 9).

12 On vehicles without navigation, remove the center storage receptacle (see illustration) from the center trim bezel.

13 Remove the air conditioning/audio controller mounting screws (see illustration) and remove the air conditioning and audio controller from the center trim bezel.

14 When installing the air conditioning and audio controller, make sure that all the locator pins are aligned with their corresponding holes in the mounting brackets.

15 Installation is otherwise the reverse of removal.

Speakers

Door speakers

◆ Refer to illustration 11.17

➡Note: The photo accompanying this Section depicts a typical front-door speaker, but rear-door speakers are virtually identical.

16 Remove the door trim panel (see Chapter 11).

17 Disconnect the electrical connector (see illustration).

18 Remove the three speaker mounting screws (see illustration 11.17).

➡Note: Some models are equipped with Bose speakers, which use four bolts.

19 Installation is the reverse of removal.

Tweeters

◆ Refer to illustrations 11.21 and 11.22

➡Note: The tweeters are located in the front doors, behind the mirror covers, the small triangular-shaped plastic trim panels that cover up the power mirror wiring.

20 Remove the door trim panel and the mirror cover (see Chapter 11).

21 Locate the tweeter, trace the electrical lead down to the electrical connector and disconnect the connector (see illustration).

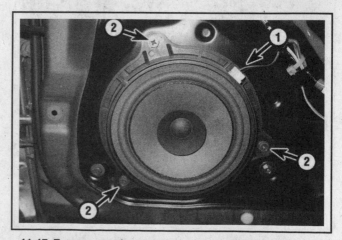

11.17 To remove a door speaker, disconnect the electrical connector (1) and remove the speaker mounting bolts (2) (front door speaker shown; rear door speaker similar)

22 Remove the tweeter mounting screws (see illustration) and remove the tweeter.

23 Installation is the reverse of removal.

Woofer or rear speaker

➡Note: The woofer, if equipped, is located under the middle of the rear parcel shelf on 2003 through 2006 G35 Sedans and all G35 Coupes. The rear speaker on 2007 and later G35 Sedans is located in the same spot.

24 Remove the rear parcel shelf (see Chapter 11).

25 Remove the woofer or rear speaker mounting screws.

26 Pull out the speaker and disconnect the electrical connector.

27 Installation is the reverse of removal.

350Z MODELS

Audio unit

28 Remove the center trim panel (see Chapter 11).

29 On 2003 through 2005 models, remove the four radio mounting screws. On 2006 and later models, there are eight mounting screws.

11.21 To disconnect the electrical connector for the tweeter, depress this release tab and pull apart the two halves of the connector

30 Pull out the audio unit and disconnect the electrical connectors and antenna cable from the backside of the unit.

31 Remove the four screws from each side mounting bracket and remove the brackets.

32 Installation is the reverse of removal.

Door speakers

33 The procedure for replacing door speakers is identical to the procedure above for G35 Sedans and Coupes.

Tweeters

34 The procedure for replacing tweeters is identical to the procedure above for G35 Sedans and Coupes.

Rear speakers

➡Note: The rear speaker is located inside the upper luggage floor trim panel.

35 Remove the upper luggage floor trim panel (see Chapter 11).

36 Remove the speaker mounting screws, pull out the speaker and disconnect the electrical connector.

37 Installation is the reverse of removal.

11.22 To detach the tweeter from the door, remove these two mounting screws

12 Antenna and antenna cables - replacement

ANTENNA

G35 Sedans and Coupes

1 The grid-type antenna is bonded to, and is an integral component of, the rear window glass. If the antenna is faulty, the rear glass must be replaced. This is a job best left to a professional. However, you can repair a break in the antenna grid the same way that you would repair the rear window defogger grid (see Section 20).

350Z models

➡Note: The antenna mast is located on the left rear quarter-panel.

2 Unscrew the antenna mast retaining nut and remove the antenna mast.

3 Installation is the reverse of removal.

ANTENNA CABLES

G35 Sedans and Coupes

4 The antenna cables connect the rear window grid-type antenna to the audio system in the instrument panel. They're routed along the underside of the roof, above the headliner.

350Z models

5 The antenna cables connect the antenna on the rear quarter panel with the audio system in the instrument panel. They're routed underneath the carpeting. To replace an antenna cable, you'll need to remove the seats, all necessary interior trim and the carpeting.

13 Navigation system - component replacement

2003 THROUGH 2006 G35 SEDANS AND ALL G35 COUPES

Navigation control unit

➡**Note: The navigation control unit is located in the same spot as the upper glove box on vehicles without a navigation system, directly above the main glove box and is covered by the center box assembly.**

1 Remove the center box assembly retaining screw, then pull the center box away from the instrument panel, toward the rear of the vehicle. It's retained along its front edge by three metal clips that will pop loose when you apply sufficient force.

2 Remove the four navigation control unit mounting screws (two in front, two underneath).

3 Pull out the navigation control unit and disconnect the electrical connector and the GPS antenna.

4 Remove the four mounting bracket screws (two on each bracket) and detach the two mounting brackets from the navigation control unit.

5 Installation is the reverse of removal.

GPS antenna

➡**Note: The GPS antenna is routed between the navigation control unit and the recess for the clock in the center of the instrument panel. You have to remove the instrument panel to replace it.**

6 Remove the navigation control unit (see Steps 1 through 4).

7 Remove the instrument panel (see Chapter 11).

8 On the backside of the instrument panel, trace the routing of the GPS antenna cable and remove the three screws that secure the antenna cable clips to the instrument panel.

9 Remove the screw that secures the upper end of the GPS antenna to the recess in the instrument panel for the clock.

10 Installation is the reverse of removal.

Navigation switch module

➡**Note: The navigation switch module is located on the backside of the center trim panel, directly above the air conditioning and audio controller.**

11 Remove the center trim panel, then remove the audio unit and display unit as a single assembly from the backside of the center trim panel (see Section 11).

12 Remove the two navigation switch module mounting screws and remove the navigation switch module.

13 Installation is the reverse of removal.

Display unit

➡**Note: The display unit is located directly above the audio unit and is supported by the same mounting bracket.**

14 Remove the center trim panel, then remove the audio unit and display unit as a single assembly from the backside of the center trim panel (see Section 11).

15 Remove the four screws that secure the display unit to the audio unit mounting bracket and remove the display unit.

16 Installation is the reverse of removal.

2007 AND LATER G35 SEDANS

Multi-function switch

17 Using a trim stick or panel removal tool, carefully pry off the center trim panel, pull it free of the instrument panel, then disconnect the multi-function switch ribbon connector.

18 Remove the multi-function switch mounting screws and remove the multi-function switch from the center trim panel.

19 Installation is the reverse of removal.

Display unit

20 Using a trim stick or panel removal tool, carefully pry off the center trim panel, pull it free of the instrument panel, then disconnect the multi-function switch ribbon connector.

21 Remove the display unit mounting bracket screws and remove the display unit and mounting bracket as a single assembly.

22 Remove the mounting bracket screws and remove the mounting bracket from the display unit.

23 Installation is the reverse of removal.

Audio-visual control unit

24 Using a trim stick or panel removal tool, carefully pry off the center trim panel, pull it free of the instrument panel, then disconnect the multi-function switch ribbon connector.

25 Remove the display unit (see Steps 21 and 22).

26 Remove the audio-visual unit mounting bracket screws and remove the audio-visual unit, air conditioning controller and mounting brackets as a single assembly.

27 Remove the unified meter and air conditioning amplifier mounting screws and remove the unified meter and air conditioning amplifier.

28 Remove the mounting bracket screws and remove the mounting brackets from the audio-visual unit.

29 Installation is the reverse of removal.

350Z MODELS

Navigation control unit

30 Carefully pry off the upper luggage floor trim panel.

31 Remove the four navigation control unit mounting bracket screws.

32 Pull out the navigation control unit and mounting bracket as a single assembly and disconnect the electrical connector.

33 Remove the four mounting bracket screws and remove the mounting brackets from the navigation control unit.

34 Installation is the reverse of removal.

GPS antenna

➡**Note: The GPS antenna is located in the left end of the instrument panel, under the upper instrument panel trim (the semi-circular piece just ahead of the instrument cluster).**

35 Remove the two upper instrument panel trim panel screws.

36 Using a trim stick or panel removal tool, carefully pry off the upper instrument panel trim panel.

37 Remove the screw that secures the GPS antenna to the instrument panel.

38 Installation is the reverse of removal.

Navigation switch module

39 On 2003 through 2005 models, cover a screwdriver tip with a clean shop rag to prevent scratching the plastic, then carefully insert the covered screwdriver tip into the gap between the navigation switch module and the center trim panel. Gently pry out the switch module and disconnect the electrical connector.

40 On 2006 and later models, there's a thin trim piece between the display unit and the center trim panel. Cover a small screwdriver tip with a clean shop rag to prevent scratching the plastic, then very carefully insert the covered screwdriver tip into the gap between the thin trim piece and the center trim panel and gently pry out the trim piece.

Then remove the two navigation switch module mounting screws, pull out the module and disconnect the electrical connector.

41 Installation is the reverse of removal.

Display unit

42 Remove the center trim panel (see Chapter 11).

43 Remove the two display unit mounting bracket screws, remove the display unit and mounting bracket as a single assembly and disconnect the electrical connector from the display unit.

44 Remove the four display unit mounting bracket screws and remove the mounting bracket from the display unit.

45 Installation is the reverse of removal

---

14 Headlight housing - removal and installation

▶ **Refer to illustrations 14.2 and 14.3**

❄ **WARNING:**

This procedure involves disconnecting an electrical connector for a High Intensity Discharge (HID) bulb; to avoid the possibility of accidental electrocution, it is imperative that you verify that the headlight switch is turned to OFF, and that you disconnect the battery.

1 Remove the bumper cover (see Chapter 11).

2 Remove the upper headlight housing bolt (see illustration).

3 Remove the three lower headlight mounting bolts (see illustration).

4 Pull out the headlight housing far enough to disconnect the electrical connectors, then remove the headlight housing.

➡ **Note: To disconnect the electrical connector from a High Intensity Discharge (HID) bulb, rotate it 1/4-turn counterclockwise and pull it off.**

5 Installation is the reverse of removal.

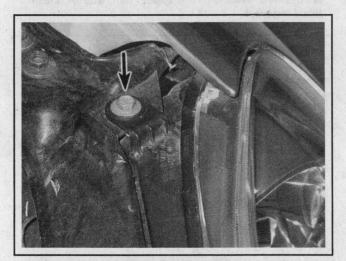

14.2 To detach the upper part of the headlight housing, remove this bolt

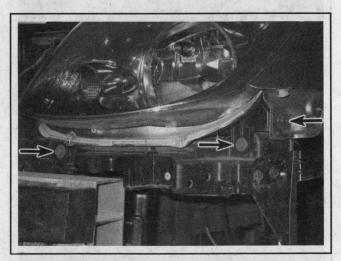

14.3 To detach the lower part of the headlight housing, remove these three bolts

15 Headlights - adjustment

◆ Refer to illustrations 15.1a, 15.1b, 15.1c and 15.2

✳ WARNING:

The headlights must be aimed correctly. If adjusted incorrectly, they could temporarily blind the driver of an oncoming vehicle and cause an accident or seriously reduce your ability to see the road. The headlights should be checked for proper aim every 12 months and any time a new headlight is installed or front-end bodywork is performed. The following procedure is only intended to provide temporary adjustment until you can have the headlights professionally adjusted by a dealer service department.

1   Open the hood and locate the headlight vertical adjusting screw (see illustrations) for each headlight in the upper radiator crossmember. Each headlight has a vertical adjustment screw; there are no horizontal adjustment screws.

2   There are several ways to adjust the headlights. The simplest method requires an open area with a blank wall and a level floor (see illustration).

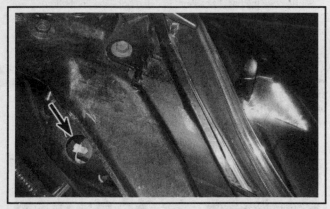

15.1a To adjust the headlight aim, find the adjuster access hole above the rear part of the headlight housing, in the radiator core support . . .

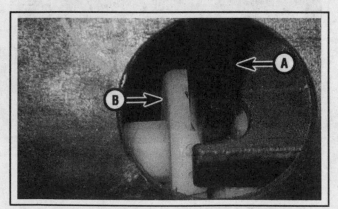

15.1c When engaged with the adjuster wheel, the Phillips screwdriver tip functions as a bevel drive. Simply turn the screwdriver clockwise or counterclockwise to move the headlight aim up or down

A   Phillips screwdriver   *B   Adjuster wheel*

3   Position masking tape vertically on the wall in reference to the vehicle centerline and the centerlines of both headlights.

4   Position a horizontal tape line in reference to the centerline of the headlights.

➡**Note: It might be easier to position the tape on the wall with the vehicle parked only a few inches away.**

5   Adjustment should be made with the vehicle parked 25 feet from the wall, sitting level, the gas tank full and no unusually heavy load in the vehicle.

6   The high intensity zone should be vertically centered with the exact center, about three inches below the horizontal line.

7   Have the headlights adjusted by a qualified technician at the earliest opportunity.

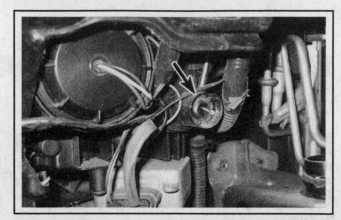

15.1b . . . then insert a Phillips screwdriver into the hole and engage it with the adjuster wheel (you won't be able to see this view, which is from the wheel well, with the splash shield removed)

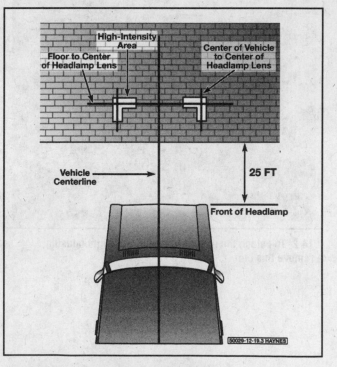

15.2 Headlight adjustment screen details

16 Headlight bulb - replacement

HEADLIGHT BULB GUIDE

1   The base model 2003 Infiniti G35 Sedan uses halogen low-beam bulbs and halogen high-beam/fog bulbs. Other 2003 and all 2004 through 2006 Sedans use Xenon low-beam bulbs and halogen high-beam/fog bulbs.

2   2007 and later G35 Sedans use a single Xenon low-beam/high-beam bulb.

3   2003 through 2005 G35 Coupes use a Xenon low-beam bulb and a halogen high-beam/fog light bulb.

4   2006 and 2007 G35 Coupes use a single Xenon low-beam/high-beam bulb.

5   Base 2003 through 2005 Nissan 350Z models use two halogen bulbs, one for low-beam bulb and one for high-beam. All other 2003 through 2005 Nissan 350Z models use a Xenon low-beam bulb and a halogen high-beam bulb. All bulbs are accessed through a single protective cover.

6   2006 and later 350Z models use a single Xenon low-beam/high-beam bulb.

7   High Intensity Discharge (HID) headlight bulbs put out three times as much light of a standard halogen bulb, use less energy doing so, and last 10 times longer. HID bulbs use an alternating current (AC) electrical charge to ignite xenon gas inside the sealed bulb. They're similar in operation to vapor-filled streetlights, except that the Xenon gas enables them to warm up much more quickly. Instead of a filament, the Xenon gas inside the bulb is ignited by creating an arc between two electrodes. A ballast module converts battery voltage to alternating current, stepping it up from 12 volts DC to about 800 volts AC. The HID bulb takes about 10-15 seconds to warm up before it operates normally. The igniter (part of the HID bulb) controls the voltage applied to the electrodes. The igniter steps up the 800 volt AC input to about 25,000 volts to start up the light, then once ignited, it reduces voltage to about 85 volts.

HEADLIGHT BULB REPLACEMENT

All bulbs

8   Loosen the wheel lug nuts on the left or right wheel, depending on which bulb you're replacing. Raise the front of the vehicle and support it securely on jackstands. Remove the front wheel. Remove the front part of the wheel well splash shield (see Chapter 11).

9   Make sure that the headlight switch is turned to OFF, then disconnect the cable from the negative battery terminal (see Chapter 5, Section 1).

❊❊ **CAUTION:**

On G35 Coupes and 350Z models, lower the windows before disconnecting the battery.

Halogen bulbs

▶ **Refer to illustrations 16.10, 16.12a and 16.12b**

❊❊ **WARNING:**

Halogen bulbs are gas-filled and under pressure and they can shatter if the surface is scratched or the bulb is dropped. Wear eye protection and handle the bulbs carefully, grasping only the base whenever possible. Don't touch the surface of the bulb with your fingers because the oil from your skin could cause it to overheat and fail prematurely. If you do touch the bulb surface, clean it with rubbing alcohol.

➡**Note: On 2003 through 2005 350Z base models there are two halogen bulbs, one for high beam and one for low beam. Both of them are located under a single protective cover, but the procedure for replacing either bulb is similar to what you see here.**

10   Remove the protective cover (see illustration). Inspect the cover O-ring seal for cracks, tears and deterioration. If the seal is damaged, replace it.

11   Pull off the electrical connector from the headlight bulb that you want to replace.

12   Remove the headlight bulb from the headlight housing (see illustrations).

13   When installing a new bulb, make sure that the three locator tabs on the bulb base are aligned with their corresponding slots in the headlight housing.

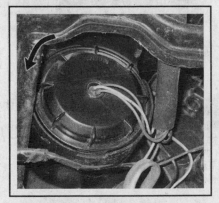

16.10 To remove the protective cover, turn it counterclockwise and pull it off

16.12a To remove a halogen bulb, squeeze the upper ends of the retainer wire together and swing the retainer wire down out of the way . . .

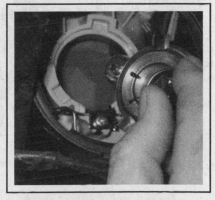

16.12b . . . then remove the bulb from the headlight housing

14 Swing the retainer wire back up and make sure that the retainer snaps into place.

15 Installation is otherwise the reverse of removal.

High Intensity Discharge (HID) bulbs (Xenon bulbs)

▶ Refer to illustrations 16.16, 16.17, 16.18a and 16.18b

❄ WARNING:

An HID circuit can retain a charge from which you might receive an accidental shock. We therefore strongly recommend that, before proceeding, you verify that the headlight switch is turned to OFF and disconnect the battery (see Chapter 5, Section 1).

16 Remove the cover (see illustration). Inspect the cover O-ring seal for cracks, tears and deterioration. If the seal is damaged, replace it.

17 Disconnect the electrical connector (see illustration).

18 Remove the bulb from the headlight housing (see illustrations).

19 When installing the bulb, align the notch in the bulb mounting flange with the lug on the headlight housing.

20 Swing the retainer wire back down and make sure that the retainer snaps into place.

21 Installation is the reverse of removal.

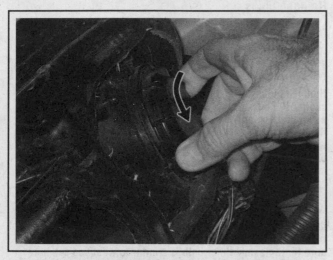

16.16 To remove the protective cover for access to a Xenon bulb, turn it counterclockwise and pull it off

16.17 To disconnect the electrical connector from a Xenon bulb, rotate it 1/4-turn counterclockwise and pull it off

16.18a To remove an HID bulb, squeeze the ends of the retainer wire together and swing the wire retainer up and out of the way . . .

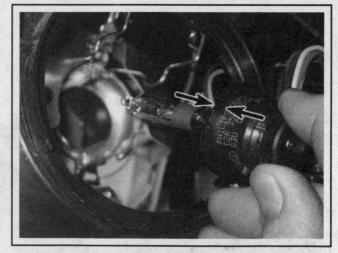

16.18b . . . then pull out the bulb. Note the alignment notch in the bulb mounting flange. When you install a bulb, this notch must be aligned with the lug on the headlight housing

17 Bulb replacement

EXTERIOR LIGHTS

Light bulbs in headlight housing

➡Note: The front turn signal bulbs, parking light bulbs, side-marker light bulbs (2003 through 2005 350Z models), and fog light bulbs (2007 and later G35 Sedans) are all located inside the headlight housing, and you'll find the replacement procedures for those bulbs here. If you want to replace an actual headlight bulb, refer to Section 16.

Front turn signal light bulbs

▶ **Refer to illustration 17.3**

➡**Note:** The photos accompanying this Section depict a typical front turn signal bulb replacement. The turn signal bulbs are located in the headlight housings on all models, although the location of the bulbs in the headlight housings varies slightly. But the replacement procedures for these bulbs are very similar regardless of model.

1   Loosen the wheel lug nuts on the left or right wheel, depending on which bulb you're replacing. Raise the front of the vehicle and support it securely on jackstands. Remove the front wheel.

2   Remove the front part of the wheel well splash shield (see Chapter 11), then locate the front turn signal bulb socket.

3   Rotate the front turn signal bulb socket counterclockwise and pull it out of the headlight housing (see illustration).

4   Remove the bulb from the turn signal socket by pulling it straight out. To install a new bulb into the socket, push it straight into the socket until it's fully seated.

5   Installation is the reverse of removal.

Parking light bulbs

▶ **Refer to Illustrations 17.8a and 17.8b**

➡Note: The photos accompanying this Section depict a typical parking light bulb replacement. The parking light bulbs are located in the headlight housings on all models, although the location of the bulbs in the headlight housings varies slightly. But the replacement procedures for these bulbs are very similar regardless of model.

6   Loosen the wheel lug nuts on the left or right wheel, depending on which bulb you're replacing. Raise the front of the vehicle and support it securely on jackstands. Remove the front wheel.

7   Remove the front part of the wheel well splash shield (see Chapter 11), then locate the parking light bulb socket.

8   Rotate the parking light bulb socket counterclockwise and pull it out of the headlight housing (see illustrations).

9   Remove the parking light bulb from its socket by pulling it straight out. To install a new bulb into the socket, push it straight into the socket until it's fully seated.

10 Installation is the reverse of removal.

Front sidemarker lights

➡**Note:** The front sidemarker lights are located in the outer end of the headlight housing on 2003 through 2005 G35 Coupes and 350Z models. They're similar in appearance to the front turn signal bulbs and sockets described above.

11 Loosen the wheel lug nuts on the left or right wheel, depending on which bulb you're replacing. Raise the front of the vehicle and support it securely on jackstands. Remove the front wheel. Remove the front part of the wheel well splash shield (see Chapter 11).

17.3 To unlock the front turn signal bulb socket, turn it counterclockwise, then pull it out of the headlight housing

17.8a To remove a parking light bulb socket, rotate it counterclockwise . . .

17.8b . . . and pull it out of the headlight housing

12 Disconnect the electrical connector from the sidemarker light bulb socket.

13 To remove the front sidemarker light bulb socket, turn it counterclockwise and pull it out.

14 To remove a front sidemarker light bulb from its socket, pull it straight out of the socket. To install a new bulb, push it straight into the socket until it's fully seated.

15 Installation is the reverse of removal.

Fog light bulbs (2007 G35 Sedans)

→**Note: The fog light bulbs are located in the headlight housing, near the inner end of the housing. The fog light is a halogen type bulb. It's not removable from its socket; the replacement bulb includes a new socket.**

16 Loosen the wheel lug nuts on the left or right wheel, depending on which bulb you're replacing. Raise the front of the vehicle and support it securely on jackstands. Remove the front wheel. Remove the front part of the wheel well splash shield (see Chapter 11).

17 Disconnect the electrical connector from the fog light bulb socket.

18 To remove the fog light bulb socket, turn it counterclockwise and pull it out of the headlight housing.

19 To install a new bulb, insert the bulb into the headlight housing, then turn the socket clockwise until it stops.

20 Installation is otherwise the reverse of removal.

Fog light bulbs (2008 G35 Sedans)

→**Note: The fog lights are located in the headlight housing, near the inner end of the housing. The fog light bulb is a halogen-type bulb.**

21 Loosen the wheel lug nuts on the left or right wheel, depending on which bulb you're replacing. Raise the front of the vehicle and support it securely on jackstands. Remove the front wheel. Remove the front part of the wheel well splash shield (see Chapter 11).

22 To remove the bulb socket, turn it counterclockwise and pull it out of the housing.

23 Remove and inspect the socket O-ring. If it's cracked, torn or deteriorated, replace it.

24 To remove the fog light bulb from its socket, pull it straight out. To install a new bulb, push it straight into the socket until it stops.

25 Installation is the reverse of removal.

FRONT SIDEMARKER LIGHT BULBS

▸ **Refer to illustrations 17.26 and 17.27**

→**Note: These bulbs are located between the front fender and the front bumper cover, just ahead of the front wheel well, on 2003 through 2006 G35 Sedans and 2003 through 2007 G35 Coupes.**

26 Pop out the trailing end of the front sidemarker light lens/housing assembly (see illustration), then pull it to the rear and remove it.

27 To remove the bulb socket from the sidemarker lens/housing assembly, turn it counterclockwise (see illustration) and pull it out. (It's not necessary to disconnect the electrical connector.)

28 To remove the sidemarker bulb from the socket, simply pull it straight out of the socket. To install a new bulb, push it into the socket

until it stops.

29 To install the socket in the lens/housing assembly, insert it into the housing and turn it clockwise until it stops.

30 When installing the sidemarker lens/housing assembly, make sure that the lug on the front end of the backside of the housing is aligned with, and inserted into, the square hole in the front fender bracket, then pop the rear end of the lens assembly back into place.

REAR EXTERIOR LIGHTS

License plate light bulbs

▸ **Refer to illustrations 17.31, 17.32, 17.35a and 17.35b**

→**Note: The license plate light is located in the rear bumper cover on all models and all license plate light assemblies are essentially the same.**

31 To remove the license plate light lens/housing assembly (see illustration), insert a small screwdriver between the retaining clip and the bumper cover mounting bracket and pry the right end of the assembly down and out of the bumper cover.

32 Remove the license plate light bulb socket from the housing (see illustration).

33 To remove the license plate light bulb from its socket, pull it straight out of the socket. To install a new bulb, insert it into the socket and push it in until it's fully seated.

34 To install the bulb socket, insert it into the lens/housing assembly and turn it clockwise until it stops.

35 When installing the license plate light lens/housing assembly, make sure that the locator tab on the left end of the assembly is aligned with the slot in the bumper cover bracket (see illustration), then swing the assembly up into position and push the right end of the assembly up into the rear bumper cover until it snaps into place (see illustration).

G35 taillight bulbs

Main taillight assembly (rear brake light, rear turn signal and parking light bulbs)

▸ **Refer to illustrations 17.37a, 17.37b, 17.38 and 17.40**

→**Note: On G35 Sedans it's not absolutely necessary to remove the taillight assembly in order to replace the taillight (rear brake/turn signal) bulb, but we show you how to remove it anyway because someday you might have to replace the taillight assembly. But you do have to remove the taillight assembly in order to replace a taillight bulb on G35 Coupes and 350Z models, so refer to the accompanying photos showing how to remove the taillight assembly on G35 Sedans. The taillight removal procedure is virtually identical on all models. Bulb replacement is similar too, except that on G35 Coupes and 350Z models, the taillight assembly houses not just the rear brake light and rear turn signal light bulbs but also houses the back-up light bulb. On G35 Sedans, the back-up light bulb is in a smaller, separate housing located on the trunk lid (see below).**

36 Open the trunk and remove the carpeting trim that lines the left or right corner of the trunk (see Chapter 11). Pull back the carpeting far enough to expose the taillight assembly mounting nuts and electrical connector.

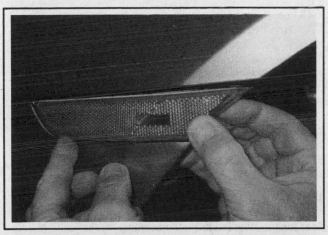

17.26 To remove the sidemarker lens assembly, pop out the rear end of the lens assembly, then pull the lens assembly to the rear to disengage the lug on the backside of the lens from the slot in the fender bracket

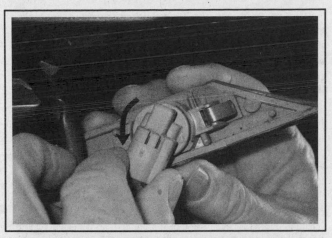

17.27 To remove the sidemarker light bulb socket from the lens assembly, turn it counterclockwise and pull it out

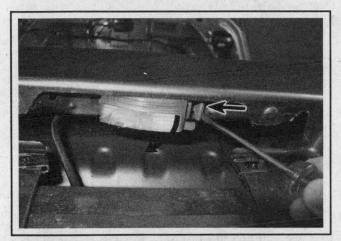

17.31 To remove the license plate light lens/housing assembly from the bumper cover, insert a small screwdriver between the retaining clip and the bumper cover and pry out the right end of the housing, then swing it down

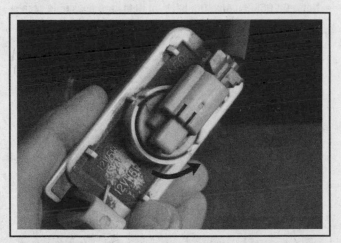

17.32 To remove the license plate light bulb socket from the lens/housing assembly, rotate it counterclockwise and pull it out

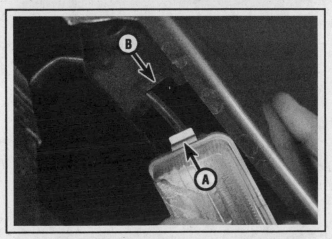

17.35a When installing the license plate light lens/housing assembly, make sure that this tab is aligned with the slot in the rear bumper cover bracket . . .

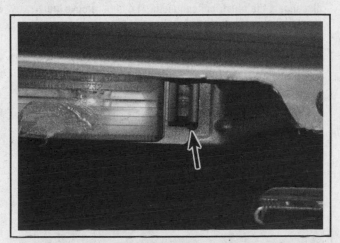

17.35b . . . then swing up the right end of the lens/housing assembly until it snaps into place. Make sure that the retainer clip is fully seated when you're done - and looks like this - or the lens/housing assembly will fall out

37 Disconnect the electrical connector from the taillight assembly and remove the taillight assembly retaining nuts (see illustration), then pull off the taillight housing (see illustration).

➡Note: This illustration depicts the taillight housing mounting nuts on a typical 2003 through 2006 G35 Sedan, but it's very similar to the setup used on all other models.

38 Remove the taillight bulb socket from the taillight assembly (see illustration), then remove the bulb from the socket. To install a new bulb in the socket, push it straight into the socket until it stops.

39 When installing the bulb socket in the taillight assembly, make sure that the lugs on the socket are aligned with the cutouts in the housing, then insert the socket into the housing and turn the socket clockwise until it stops.

40 Before installing the taillight assembly, inspect the gasket (see illustration) for cracks, tears and deterioration. If it's damaged, replace it. Installation is otherwise the reverse of removal.

Trunk lid taillight housing (G35 Sedans)

◆ Refer to illustrations 17.42 and 17.43

➡Note: On G35 Sedans, the back-up lights are housed in separate, smaller taillight assemblies, which are located in the trunk lid.

41 Open the trunk lid and remove the trunk trim panel (see Chapter 11).

42 Disconnect the electrical connector (see illustration) from the back-up light bulb socket.

43 Rotate the back-up light bulb socket counterclockwise (see illustration) and remove it from the housing.

44 Remove the back-up light bulb from the socket and install a new bulb.

45 When installing the bulb socket into the trunk lid taillight housing, make sure that the lugs on the socket are aligned with the cutouts in the housing, then insert the socket into the housing and turn it clockwise until it locks into place. Installation is otherwise the reverse of removal.

350Z taillight bulbs

Rear fender-mounted taillight assembly (brake/taillight bulb and rear sidemarker bulb)

➡Note: These taillight bulbs are located in the taillight assembly mounted in the rear quarter-panel.

46 Remove the trim plugs for the taillight mounting bolts.

47 Remove the taillight mounting bolts, pull out the taillight assembly to the side and disconnect the taillight electrical connector.

48 Rotate the taillight bulb socket counterclockwise to unlock it, then

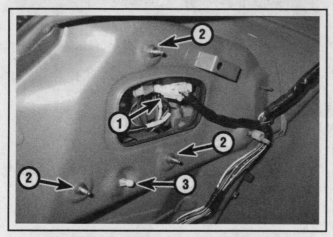

17.37a To detach the taillight assembly on a G35 Sedan, disconnect the electrical connector (1), then remove the mounting nuts (2), push out the locator pin (3) . . .

17.37b . . . and remove the taillight assembly

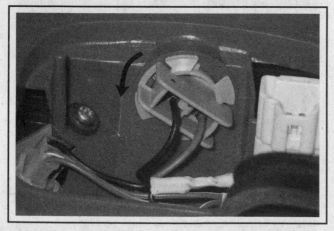

17.38 To remove the bulb socket from the taillight assembly, turn it counterclockwise and pull it out

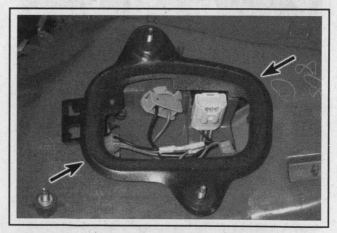

17.40 Before installing the taillight assembly, make sure that the gasket is in good shape and properly installed

pull it out of the taillight housing.

49 Remove the old bulb from the socket and install a new bulb.

50 Installation is the reverse of removal.

Rear bumper cover-mounted taillight assembly (back-up light bulb and rear sidemarker bulb)

➡Note: These taillight bulbs are located in the taillight assembly mounted in the rear bumper cover.

51 Remove the rear bumper cover (see Chapter 11).

52 Remove the taillight assembly mounting screws and remove the taillight assembly from the rear bumper cover.

53 Rotate the bulb socket counterclockwise to unlock it, then pull it out of the taillight housing.

54 Remove the old bulb from the socket and install a new bulb.

55 Installation is the reverse of removal.

Center high-mounted brake lights

➡Note: The center high-mounted brake light assembly uses LEDs (light emitting diodes). You cannot replace individual bulbs. If a bulb burns out, replace the center high-mounted brake light assembly.

G35 Sedans and Coupes (without spoiler)

◆ Refer to illustrations 17.56, 17.57a and 17.57b

➡Note: The center high-mounted brake light assembly is located under the rear parcel shelf.

56 Open the trunk and disconnect the electrical connector from the center high-mounted brake light housing (see illustration).

57 On some models you might be able to remove the center high-mounted brake light mounting screws through the access hole in the roof of the trunk (see illustrations). But the right screw is difficult to remove from below because it's a Phillips screw, so without some suitable extension such as a flexible shaft or a U-coupling, you probably won't be able to break it loose. Even if you're able to remove it, installing it will also be difficult. However, if you're able to replace the center high-mounted brake light assembly this way, it will save you the effort of removing and installing the rear parcel shelf.

58 If you're unable to remove the right mounting screw from the trunk side, remove the rear parcel shelf (see Chapter 11).

59 Remove the center high-mounted brake light housing mounting screws and remove the center high-mounted brake light housing.

60 Installation is the reverse of removal.

17.42 To disconnect the electrical connector from the trunk lid taillight bulb socket, depress this release tab and pull off the connector

17.43 To remove the bulb socket from the trunk lid taillight housing, turn it counterclockwise

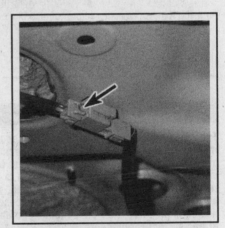

17.56 To disconnect the center high-mounted brake light electrical connector, depress this release tab and pull apart the two halves of the connector

17.57a To detach the center high-mounted brake light assembly from the underside of the rear parcel shelf from the trunk side, remove the sound deadening material . . .

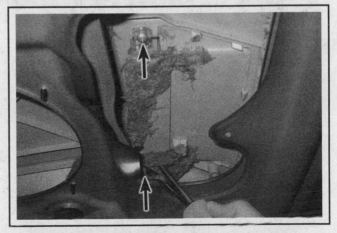

17.57b . . . then remove the two mounting screws (three screws on 2007 and later models) (right screw not visible)

G35 Sedans and Coupes (with spoiler)

➡**Note: On these models the center high-mounted brake light assembly is located in the rear spoiler.**

61 On all models except 2003 G35 Sedans, remove the rear spoiler (see Chapter 11). (You can remove the center high-mounted brake light on 2003 G35 Sedans without removing the spoiler.)

62 On 2003 G35 Sedans, disconnect the center high-mounted brake light electrical connector.

63 Remove the center high-mounted brake light assembly mounting screws and remove the light assembly from the spoiler.

64 Remove the center high-mounted brake light housing.

65 Installation is the reverse of removal.

350Z models

➡**Note: On these models the center high-mounted brake light assembly is located in the trailing edge of the rear hatch.**

66 Remove the five mounting screws from the rear hatch upper trim panel and remove the trim panel.

67 Disconnect the center high-mounted brake light assembly electrical connector.

68 Remove the center high-mounted brake light assembly mounting nuts and remove the center high-mounted brake light assembly.

69 Installation is the reverse of removal.

INTERIOR LIGHTS

✳✳ WARNING:

The models covered by this manual are equipped with a Supplemental Restraint System (SRS), more commonly known as airbags. Always disarm the airbag system before working in the vicinity of any airbag system component to avoid the possibility of accidental deployment of the airbag, which could cause personal injury (see Section 27). Do not use a memory-saving device to preserve the PCM's memory when working on or near airbag system components.

Trunk light

◆ **Refer to illustration 17.70**

➡**Note: This procedure applies to sedan models.**

70 Open the trunk lid and locate the trunk light on the ceiling of the trunk space, ahead of the trunk lid. Carefully pry loose the lens with a small screwdriver and swing it down (see illustration).

71 To remove the trunk light bulb from its socket, pull it straight down. To install a new bulb, push it straight into the socket until it's fully seated.

72 Installation is the reverse of removal.

Map light bulbs

◆ **Refer to illustrations 17.73 and 17.74**

✳✳ CAUTION:

Removing the lens from one of the map lights can be tricky. If you try to force the lens out, it will break, so proceed carefully.

73 Using a small, thin-blade screwdriver or a trim stick, carefully pry out the map light lens (see illustration).

74 Carefully pry out the old map light bulb with a small screwdriver (see illustration). To install a new bulb, push it into the two conductors until it pops into place.

75 Installation of the lens is the reverse of removal, but do not use any tools to install the lens. Carefully work it into place and push firmly until it snaps back into place. Don't force it or it will break.

Rear lights

◆ **Refer to illustrations 17.76, 17.77 and 17.78**

➡**Note: The rear lights are located above the rear doors on G35 Sedans.**

76 Insert a small flat-bladed screwdriver between the rear light and the headliner and carefully pry out the rear light housing (see illustration).

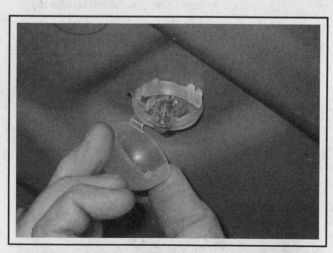

17.70 To open the trunk light lens, carefully pry open the locking tab and swing down the lens

17.73 To remove a map light lens, carefully pry it out with a small screwdriver. The lens mounting tabs are fragile, so don't try to force the lens off. Just keep moving the screwdriver around the periphery of the lens gently but firmly until it comes loose

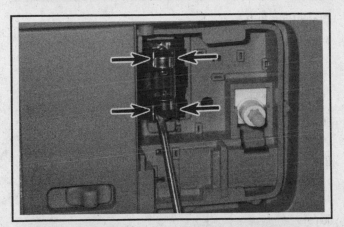

17.74 To remove the light bulb from these spring-type metal conductors, carefully pry it down and out with a small screwdriver. Warning: Pry only on the metal terminal ends, not the glass! When installing the new bulb, push it up and between the conductors until it pops into place

77 Disconnect the electrical connector from the rear light assembly (see illustration).

78 Remove the old bulb from the rear light housing (see illustration).

79 To install a new bulb, insert the bulb straight into the conductors until it pops into place.

80 When installing the rear light housing, don't forget to reconnect the electrical connector and make sure that the housing pops into place so that the lens is fully seated against the headliner.

Glove box light bulb

▶ **Refer to illustration 17.82**

➡**Note: The glove box light bulb is located on top of the glove box.**

81 Detach the glove box from the instrument panel (see Chapter 11). (It's not necessary to disconnect all the electrical harnesses; just swing down the glove box so that you can access the bulb housing on top of the box.)

82 Turn the glove box light bulb socket counterclockwise and pull it out of the bulb housing (see illustration).

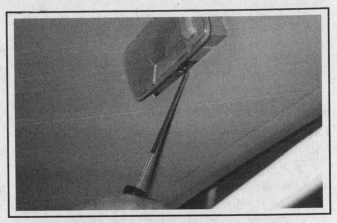

17.76 To remove a rear light housing from the headliner, carefully pry it out with a small screwdriver as shown

17.77 To disconnect the electrical connector from the rear light housing, depress this release tab and pull off the connector

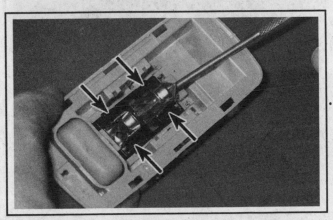

17.78 Use a small screwdriver to pry the old bulb from the rear light housing conductors. Warning: Pry only on the metal terminal ends, not the glass! When installing the new bulb, push it into place between the conductors until it pops into place

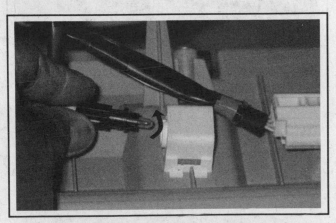

17.82 To remove the glove box light bulb socket, turn it counterclockwise and pull it out of the housing

83 To remove the glove box light bulb from its socket, simply pull it straight out of the socket. To install a new bulb in the socket, push it straight into the socket until it's fully seated.

84 To install the glove box light bulb socket into its housing, insert it into the housing and turn it clockwise until it stops.

85 Installation is otherwise the reverse of removal.

Instrument cluster light bulbs

▶ **Refer to illustrations 17.87 and 17.88**

86 Remove the instrument cluster (see Section 7).

87 The instrument cluster uses a number of removable and replaceable bulbs (see illustration).

88 To remove a bulb from the instrument cluster, simply turn it counterclockwise and pull it out (see illustration).

89 To install a new bulb, insert it into the cluster and turn it clockwise until it locks into position.

90 Install the instrument cluster (see Section 7).

Clock light bulbs

▶ **Refer to illustration 17.92**

91 Remove the clock (see Section 10).

92 To remove a clock light bulb, turn it counterclockwise and pull it out (see illustration).

93 To install a new bulb, insert it into the clock and turn it clockwise until it locks into position.

94 Install the clock (see Section 10).

Instrument panel switch light bulbs

▶ **Refer to illustration 17.96**

95 Remove the instrument panel switch with the bad bulb (see Section 9).

96 To remove an instrument panel switch light bulb (see illustration), turn it counterclockwise and pull it out.

97 To install a new bulb, insert it into the switch and turn it clockwise until it locks into position.

98 Install the instrument panel switch (see Section 9).

17.87 Instrument cluster light bulbs

17.88 To remove an instrument cluster light bulb, turn it counterclockwise and pull it out. To install a new bulb, insert it into the cluster and turn it clockwise until it stops

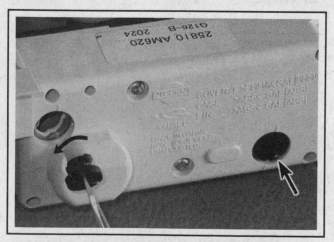

17.92 To remove a light bulb from the clock, turn it counterclockwise and pull it out. To install a new bulb in the clock, insert it into the clock and turn it clockwise until it locks into place

17.96 To remove a light bulb from an instrument panel switch, turn it counterclockwise and pull it out. To install a new bulb in the clock, insert it into the clock and turn it clockwise until it locks into place (VDC switch shown, other switches similar)

Key lock cylinder illumination ring bulb

▶ **Refer to illustration 17.100**

99 Remove the instrument cluster trim bezel (see Section 7).

100 Pull the illumination ring off the key lock cylinder and disconnect the electrical connector (see illustration).

101 To remove the bulb socket from the key lock cylinder illumination ring, turn it counterclockwise and pull it out.

102 To remove the old bulb from the bulb socket, pull it straight out. To install a new bulb in the socket, push it straight into the socket until it stops.

103 To install the bulb socket in the key lock cylinder illumination ring, align the lugs on the socket with the cutouts in the mounting hole, insert the socket into the hole and turn it clockwise until it locks into place.

104 Connect the electrical connector and push the illumination ring onto the key lock cylinder until it snaps into place.

105 Install the instrument cluster trim bezel (see Section 7).

Gear position indicator light bulb

▶ **Refer to illustration 17.107**

106 Remove the center console (see Chapter 11).

107 Turn the gear position indicator light bulb socket counterclockwise and pull it out (see illustration).

108 To remove the old bulb from the socket, pull it straight out of the socket. To install a new bulb, push it into the socket until it stops.

109 To install the bulb socket into its mounting hole, align the lugs on the socket with the cutouts in the mounting hole, then insert the socket into the hole and turn it clockwise until it locks into place.

110 Install the center console (see Chapter 11).

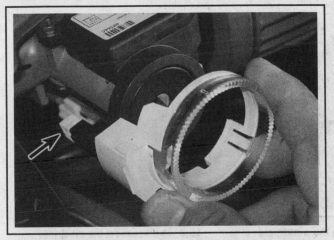

17.100 To remove the key lock cylinder illumination ring, pull the ring off the key lock cylinder, then depress the release tab on the electrical connector and disconnect the connector

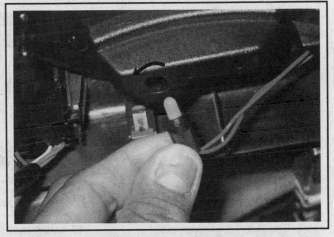

17.107 To remove the gear position indicator light bulb, turn the socket counterclockwise and pull it out.

18 Horns - replacement

▶ **Refer to illustration 18.3**

➡ **Note: The horns are located behind the grille, in front of the air conditioning condenser. The easiest way to access them is from underneath the vehicle, with the lower engine splash shield removed.**

1 Raise the vehicle and place it securely on jackstands.

2 Remove the lower engine splash shield (see Chapter 2A).

3 Disconnect the electrical connector from the horn that you want to replace (see illustration).

4 Remove the horn mounting bracket bolt and remove the horn. Separate the bracket from the horn.

5 Installation is the reverse of removal.

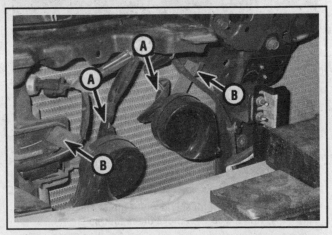

18.3 To remove either horn, simply disconnect the electrical connector (A), then remove the horn mounting bracket bolt (B) (the horns are seen here with the grille removed)

19 Windshield wiper motor - replacement

▶ **Refer to illustrations 19.2, 19.3, 19.5, 19.6a, 19.6b, 19.7 and 19.8**

1 Disconnect the cable from the negative battery terminal (see Chapter 5, Section 1).

2 Disconnect the windshield washer hoses and remove the wiper arm retaining nuts (see illustration).

3 Mark the relationship of the wiper arms to their shafts (see illustration), then remove the wiper arms.

4 Remove the cowl cover (see Chapter 11).

5 Disconnect the electrical connector from the windshield wiper motor (see illustration).

6 Remove the windshield wiper motor and bell crank assembly mounting bolts (see illustration), lift it up and detach the wire harness clip (see illustration) and remove the assembly.

7 Using a panel removal tool or a similar tool, disconnect the link rod from the bell crank arm (see illustration).

8 Remove the nut that secures the bell crank to the motor shaft (see illustration), then remove the crank arm from the wiper motor shaft. If the crank arm is stuck, use a small puller to remove it from the wiper motor shaft.

9 Remove the windshield wiper motor mounting bolts (see illustration 19.8) and remove the wiper motor from its mounting bracket.

10 Installation is the reverse of removal.

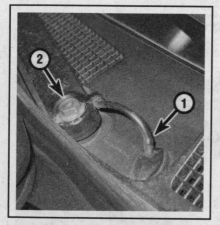

19.2 Disconnect the windshield washer hose (1) from the pipe on the cowl (don't disconnect it from the wiper arm), then remove the wiper arm retaining nut

19.3 After removing the windshield wiper arm retaining nut, mark the relationship of the wiper arm to the shaft to ensure that the wiper arm goes back on in the same position

19.5 To disconnect the electrical connector from the windshield wiper motor, depress this release tab and pull off the connector

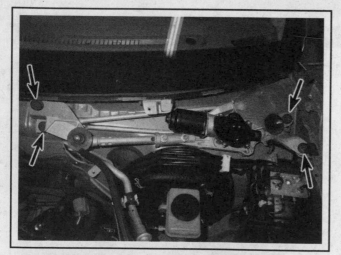

19.6a To detach the windshield wiper motor and link assembly from the cowl, remove these four bolts

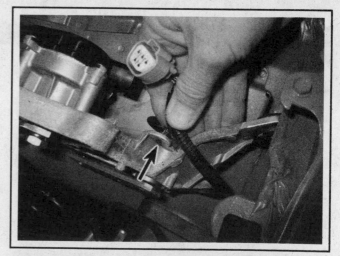

19.6b Lift out the windshield wiper motor and link as a single assembly and detach the wiring harness clip from the motor mounting bracket

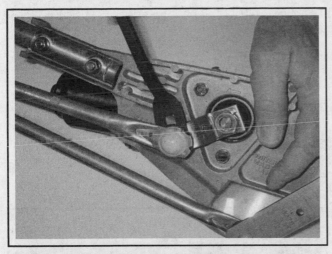

19.7 Using a trim removal tool or a similar tool, carefully pry the link arm loose from the wiper motor crank arm

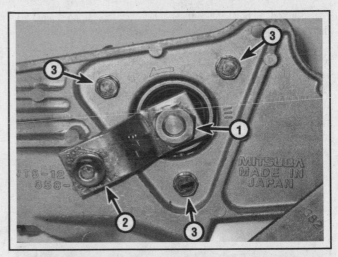

19.8 Remove the crank arm retaining nut (1) and remove the crank arm (2), then remove the three wiper motor mounting bolts (3) and remove the motor from its mounting bracket

20 Rear window defogger - check and repair

1   The rear window defogger consists of a number of horizontal heating elements baked onto the inside surface of the glass. Power is supplied through a relay and fuse from the interior fuse/relay box. A defogger switch on the instrument panel controls the defogger grid.

2   Small breaks in the element can be repaired without removing the rear window.

CHECK

◆ **Refer to illustrations 20.5, 20.6 and 20.8**

3   Turn the ignition and defogger switches to the ON position.

4   Using a voltmeter, place the positive probe against the defogger grid positive side and the negative probe against the ground side. If battery voltage is not indicated, check that the ignition switch is On and that the feed and ground wires are properly connected. Check the two fuses, defogger switch, defogger relay and related wiring. The dealer

can scan the body control module if necessary. If voltage is indicated, but all or part of the defogger doesn't heat, proceed with the following tests.

5   When measuring voltage during the next two tests, wrap a piece of aluminum foil around the tip of the voltmeter positive probe and press the foil against the heating element with your finger (see illustration). Place the negative probe on the defogger grid ground terminal.

6   Check the voltage at the center of each heating element (see illustration). If the voltage is 5 to 6 volts, the element is okay (there is no break). If the voltage is 0 volts, the element is broken between the center of the element and the positive end. If the voltage is 10 to 12 volts, the element is broken between the center of the element and the ground side. Check each heating element.

7   If none of the elements are broken, connect the negative probe to a good chassis ground. The voltage reading should stay the same, if it doesn't the ground connection is bad.

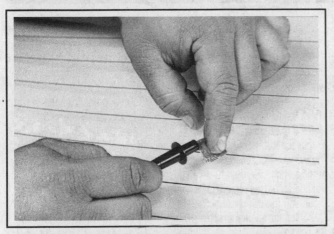

20.5 When measuring voltage at the rear window defogger grid, wrap a piece of aluminum foil around the positive probe of the voltmeter and press the foil against the wire with your finger

20.6 To determine if a heating element has broken, check the voltage at the center of each element - if the voltage is 6-volts, the element is unbroken

8 To find the break, place the voltmeter negative probe against the defogger ground terminal. Place the voltmeter positive probe with the foil strip against the heating element at the positive side and slide it toward the negative side. The point at which the voltmeter deflects from several volts to zero is the point where the heating element is broken (see illustration).

REPAIR

▶ **Refer to illustration 20.14**

9 Repair the break in the element using a repair kit specifically for

this purpose, available at most auto parts stores. The kit includes conductive plastic epoxy.

10 Before repairing a break, turn off the system and allow it to cool for a few minutes.

11 Lightly buff the element area with fine steel wool; then clean it thoroughly with rubbing alcohol.

12 Use masking tape to mask off the area being repaired.

13 Thoroughly mix the epoxy, following the kit instructions.

14 Apply the epoxy material to the slit in the masking tape, overlapping the undamaged area about 3/4-inch on either end (see illustration).

15 Allow the repair to cure for 24 hours before removing the tape and using the system.

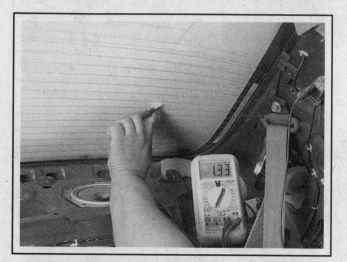

20.8 To find the break, place the voltmeter negative lead against the defogger ground terminal, place the voltmeter positive lead with the foil strip against the heat wire at the positive terminal end and slide it toward the negative terminal end. The point at which the voltmeter deflects from several volts to zero volts is the point at which the wire is broken

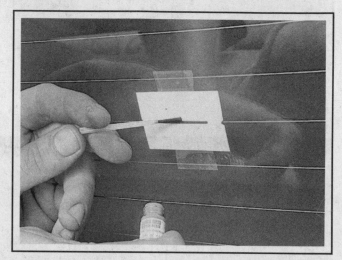

20.14 To use a defogger repair kit, apply masking to the inside of the window at the damaged area, then brush on the special conductive coating

21 Electric side-view mirrors - general information

1 The electric side-view mirrors can be adjusted up-and-down and left-to-right by a driver's side switch located on the left door trim panel. On models with factory-installed dual power mirrors, each mirror is also equipped with a heater grid behind the mirror glass to clear the mirror surface of fog, ice or snow. On these models, the mirror heater grid is an integral component of each mirror. If a heater grid fails, replace the mirror (see Chapter 11). The heater grid switches and the heated mirror system indicator light are integral components of the heater/air conditioning control panel on the dash. If one of these components fails, replace the heater/air conditioning control assembly (see Chapter 3). The heated mirror relay is located in one of the fuse and relay boxes.

2 The power mirror control switch has a LEFT-RIGHT selector switch that allows you to send voltage to the side-view mirror that you want to adjust. With the ignition switch in the ACC position, roll down the windows and operate the mirror control switch through all functions (left-right and up-down) for both the left and right side-view mirrors.

3 Listen carefully for the sound of the electric motors running in the mirrors.

4 If you can hear the motors but the mirror glass doesn't move, the problem is probably a defective drive mechanism inside the mirror, which will necessitate replacement of the mirror.

5 If the mirrors don't operate and no sound comes from the mirrors, check the fuse in one of the fuse and relay boxes (see Section 3).

6 If the fuse is OK, refer to Chapter 11 and remove the door panel for access to the back of the mirror control switch, without disconnecting the wires attached to it. Turn the ignition ON and check for voltage at the switch. There should be voltage at one terminal. If there's no voltage at the switch, check for an open in the wiring between the fuse panel and the switch.

7 If there's voltage at the switch, disconnect it. Check the switch for continuity in all its operating positions. If the switch does not have continuity, replace it.

8   Reconnect the switch. Locate the wire going from the switch to ground. Leaving the switch connected, connect a jumper wire between this wire and ground. If the mirror works normally with this wire in place, repair the faulty ground connection.

9   If the mirror still doesn't work, remove the mirror and check the wires at the mirror for voltage. Check with the ignition key turned to ON and the mirror selector switch on the appropriate side. Operate the mirror switch in all its positions. There should be voltage at one of the switch-to-mirror wires in each switch position, except the neutral (off) position.

10 If voltage is not present in each switch position, check the wiring between the mirror and control switch for opens and shorts.

11 If there's voltage, remove the mirror and test it off the vehicle with jumper wires. Replace the mirror if it fails this test.

22 Cruise control system - general information

The Powertrain Control Module (PCM) controls the cruise control system electronically via the electronic throttle control system. If you have problems with the cruise control system, check for the presence of trouble codes stored in the PCM (see Chapter 6). If that doesn't turn up any problems, have it checked by a dealer service department or other qualified repair shop.

23 Power window system - general information

1   The power window system controls the electric motors, mounted inside the doors, that lower and raise the windows. The power window system consists of the control switches, the fuse, the circuit breaker, the motors, the window regulators (the scissor-like mechanisms that raise and lower the window glass) and the wiring connecting the switches to the motors. When the ignition switch is turned to ON, current flows through the power window fuse in the engine compartment fuse and relay box to a circuit breaker located in the instrument panel wiring harness (located near the parking brake pedal). From there, current flows to the power window switches.

2   The power windows are wired so that they can be lowered and raised from the master control switch by the driver or by passengers using remote switches located at each passenger window. Each window has a separate motor that is reversible. The position of the control switch determines the polarity and therefore the direction of operation.

3   The power window system will only operate when the ignition switch is turned to ON. In addition, a window lockout switch at the master control switch can, when activated, disable the power window switches on the other doors. Always check these items before trouble-shooting a window problem.

4   These procedures are general in nature, so if you can't find the problem using them, take the vehicle to a dealer service department.

5   If the power windows don't work at all, check the fuse or circuit breaker.

6   If only the rear windows are inoperative, or if the windows only operate from the master control switch, check the window lockout switch for continuity in the unlocked position. If it doesn't have continuity, replace it.

7   Check the wiring between the switches and the fuse for continuity. Repair the wiring, if necessary.

8   If only one window is inoperative from the master control switch, try the control switch at the window that doesn't work.

➡**Note: This doesn't apply to the driver's door window.**

9   If the same window works from one switch, but not the other, check the switch for continuity.

10 If the switch tests OK, check for a short or open in the wiring between the affected switch and the window motor.

11 If one window is inoperative from both switches, remove the trim panel from the affected door (see Chapter 11), then check for voltage at the switch and at the motor while operating the switch. First check for voltage at the electrical connectors for the circuit. With the ignition key turned to ON and the connectors all connected, backprobe at the designated wire (see the wiring diagrams at the end of this Chapter) with a grounded test light. Pushing the driver's window switch to the DOWN position, there should be voltage at one terminal. Pushing the same switch to the UP position, there should be voltage at another terminal. If these voltage checks are OK, disconnect the electrical connector at the driver's motor, and check it for voltage when the switch is operated.

12 If voltage is reaching the motor and the switch is OK, disconnect the door glass from its regulator (see Chapter 11). Move the window up and down by hand while checking for binding and damage. Also check for binding and damage to the regulator. If the regulator is not damaged and the window moves up and down smoothly, replace the motor. If there's binding or damage, lubricate, repair or replace parts, as necessary.

13 If voltage isn't reaching the motor, check the wiring in the circuit for continuity between the switches and motors (see the wiring diagram at the end of this Chapter).

14 If you have to replace the main power window switch, pry it out of the door trim panel, then disconnect the electrical connector(s) from the switch.

15 When you're done, test the windows to confirm that the window system is functioning correctly.

24 Power door lock system - general information

1   The power door lock system operates the power door motors, which are integral components of the door latch units in each door. The system consists of a fuse (in the engine compartment fuse and relay box), the instrument cluster, the control switches (in each of the front doors), the power door motors and the electrical wiring harnesses connecting all of these components.

2   The lock mechanisms in the door latch units are actuated by a reversible electric motor in each door. When you push the door lock switch to LOCK, the motor operates one way and locks the latch mechanism. When you push the door lock switch the other way, to the UNLOCK position, the motor operates in the other direction, unlocking the latch mechanism. Because the motors and lock mechanisms are an integral part of the door latch units, they cannot be repaired. If a door lock motor or lock mechanism fails, replace the door latch unit (see Chapter 11).

3   Even if you don't manually lock the doors or press the door lock switch to the LOCK position before driving, the instrument cluster automatically locks the doors when the vehicle speed exceeds 15 mph, as long as all the doors are closed and the accelerator pedal is depressed. (You can turn off this feature if you don't want the doors to lock automatically. Refer to your owner's manual.)

4   Some vehicles have an optional Remote Keyless Entry (RKE) system that allows you to lock and unlock the doors from outside the vehicle. The RKE system consists of the transmitter (the electronic push-button key) and a receiver located on the instrument cluster. The RKE receiver, which operates all the time, is protected by a fuse in the engine compartment fuse and relay box. Vehicles are shipped from the factory with two RKE transmitters but, if you want to purchase extra units, the RKE receiver can actually handle up to four vehicle access codes.

5   Some features of the door lock system on these vehicles rely on resources that they share with other electronic modules through the data bus network. Professional diagnosis of these modules and the data bus network requires the use of a proprietary factory scan tool and factory diagnostic information. At-home repairs are therefore limited to inspecting the wiring for bad connections and for minor faults that can be easily repaired. If you are unable to locate the trouble using the following general steps, consult your dealer service department.

6   Always check the circuit fuses (in the engine compartment fuse and relay box) first.

7   When depressed, each power door lock switch locks or unlocks all of the doors. The easiest way to verify that each door lock switch is operating correctly is to watch the door lock button in each door as you operate the switch. The door lock buttons should all go down when you push the door lock switch to the LOCK position, and go up when you push the door lock switch to the UNLOCK position. Also, with the engine turned off so that you can hear better, operate the door lock switches in both directions and listen for the faint click of the motors locking and unlocking the latch mechanisms.

8   If there's no click, check for voltage at the switches. If no voltage is present, check the wiring between the fuse and the switches for shorts and opens (see the wiring diagrams at the end of this Chapter).

9   If voltage is present, but no clicking sound is apparent, remove the switch from the door trim panel (see Chapter 11) and test it for continuity. If there is no continuity in either direction, replace the switch.

10 If the switch has continuity but the latch mechanism doesn't click, check the wiring between the switch and the motor in the latch mechanism for continuity. If the circuit is open between the switch and the motor, repair the wiring.

11 If all but one motor is operating, remove the trim panel from the affected door (see Chapter 11) and check for voltage at the motor while operating the lock switch. One of the wires should have voltage in the LOCK position; the other should have voltage in the UNLOCK position.

12 If the inoperative motor is receiving voltage, replace the latch mechanism.

13 If the inoperative motor isn't receiving voltage, check for an open or short in the circuit between the switch and the motor.

→**Note: It's common for wires to break in the harness between the body and the door because repeatedly opening and closing the door fatigues and eventually breaks the wires.**

25 Power seats - general information

⁘ WARNING:

The models covered by this manual are equipped with a Supplemental Restraint System (SRS), more commonly known as airbags. Additionally, some models are equipped with seat belt pre-tensioners, which are explosive devices. Always disarm the airbag/restraint system before working in the vicinity of any airbag/restraint system component to avoid the possibility of accidental deployment of the airbag/seat belt pre-tensioners, which could cause personal injury (see Section 27). Do not use a memory-saving device to preserve the PCM's memory when working on or near airbag system components.

1   Some models feature an optional eight-way power seat system that allows the driver and passenger to adjust the front seats up, down, front up, front down, rear up, rear down, forward and rearward. The system consists of the driver's power seat switch, the passenger power seat switch, the driver's power seat track, the passenger power seat track and, on some models, the optional power lumbar adjusters.

2   The power seat switches are located on the outboard side of the seat cushions, on the seat cushion side panels. If the vehicle is equipped with the optional power lumbar adjusters, the lumbar switches are located on the power seat switch assemblies. Each switch assembly is attached to the seat side panel by two Torx screws. Refer to your owner's manual for instructions regarding switch functions. Individual switches in the power seat switch assemblies cannot be repaired or replaced separately. If one of the switches in a power seat switch assembly fails, replace the entire switch assembly.

3   The seats are powered by three reversible motors that are attached to the upper half of the power seat track assembly. These motors are controlled by the power seat switches on the sides of the

seats. Each switch changes the direction of seat travel by reversing polarity to the drive motor. The motors are an integral part of the power seat track assembly and cannot be repaired or replaced separately. If a motor fails, replace the power seat track assembly.

4   The optional power lumbar adjuster and motor are located on the back of the seat, under the seat trim cover and padding, where they're attached to a molded plastic back panel and to the seat back frame. The power lumbar adjuster and motor cannot be repaired or replaced separately from the seat back frame. If either the adjuster or the motor fails, replace the entire seat back frame unit.

5   Diagnosis is usually a simple matter, using the following procedures.

6   Look under the seat for any object which may be preventing the seat from moving.

7   If the seat won't work at all, check the fuse, which is located in the engine compartment fuse and relay box.

8   With the engine off to reduce the noise level, operate the seat controls in all directions and listen for sound coming from the seat motors.

9   If the motor doesn't work or make noise, check for voltage at the motor while an assistant operates the switch.

10 If the motor is getting voltage but doesn't run, test it off the vehicle with jumper wires. If it still doesn't work, replace it. The individual components are not available separately. The whole power-seat track must be purchased as an assembly.

11 If the motor isn't getting voltage, remove the seat side panel to access the switch and check for voltage. If there's no voltage at the switch, check the wiring between the fuse and the switch. If there's voltage at the switch, check for a short or open in the wiring between the switch and the motor. If that circuit is okay, replace the switch. No further testing is recommended. If the power seat system is still malfunctioning at this point, have the system checked out by a dealer service department.

26 Daytime Running Lights (DRL) - general information

Canadian models are equipped with Daytime Running Lights (DRL). The DRL system illuminates the headlights whenever the engine is running and the parking brake is disengaged. The DRL system provides reduced power to the headlights so that they won't be too bright for daytime use and it prolongs the headlight bulbs' service life. It does this by modulating the pulse-width of the power to the headlights. The duration and interval of these power pulses is programmed into the Front Control Module (FCM), which is located on the instrument cluster. If you want to alter the pulse-width, you must have it done by a dealer service department.

27 Airbag system - general information

These models are equipped with a Supplemental Restraint System (SRS), more commonly called an airbag system. There are at least two airbags, one for the driver and one for the front seat passenger, on all models. The SRS system is designed to protect the driver and passenger from serious injury in the event of a head-on or frontal collision. The airbag control module is located on the transmission tunnel, directly below the center of the instrument panel. Some models are also equipped with optional side curtain airbags. Vehicles with this option can be identified by the "SRS - AIRBAG" logo printed on the headliner above the B-pillar.

AIRBAG MODULES

The airbag module houses the airbag and the inflater unit. The inflater unit is mounted on the back of the housing over a hole through which gas is expelled, inflating the bag almost instantaneously when an electrical signal is received from the airbag control module. On the driver's airbag, the specially wound wire that carries this signal to the module is called a clockspring. The clockspring is a flat, ribbon-like electrically conductive tape that winds and unwinds as the steering wheel is turned so it can transmit an electrical signal regardless of wheel position. The procedure for removing the driver's airbag is part of *Steering wheel - removal and installation* in Chapter 10.

The passenger airbag is located in the top of the dashboard, above the glove box. There's also a passenger airbag ON/OFF switch located at the lower right corner of the center instrument panel bezel. This switch allows you to deactivate the passenger airbag if you're transporting an infant or a young child in a child safety seat. We don't recommend removing the passenger airbag because there is no reason to do so unless it has been activated during an accident and needs to be replaced afterward.

Optional side-curtain airbags, if equipped, are located on each roof side rail, above the headliner, and they extend from the A-pillar to the C-pillar. Again, we don't recommend trying to remove the side-curtain airbags because there is no reason to do so unless they've been deployed in an accident and must be replaced.

IMPACT SEAT BELT RETRACTORS

Some models are equipped with pyrotechnic (explosive) units in the front seat belt retracting mechanisms for both the lap and shoulder belts. During an impact that would trigger the airbag system, the airbag control unit also triggers the seat belt retractors. When the pyrotechnic charges go off, they accelerate the retractors to instantly take up any slack in the seat belt system to more fully prepare the driver and front seat passenger for impact.

The airbag system should be disabled any time work is done to or around the seats.

⁑ WARNING:

Never strike the pillars or floorpan with a hammer or use an impact-driver tool in these areas unless the system is disabled.

SERVICING COMPONENTS NEAR THE SRS SYSTEM

There are times when you need to remove the steering wheel, the instrument cluster, the radio, the heater/air conditioning control assembly or other components on or near the dashboard. At these times you'll be working around components and wire harnesses for the SRS system. Do not use electrical test equipment on airbag system wires; it could cause the airbag(s) to deploy. ALWAYS DISABLE THE SRS SYSTEM BEFORE WORKING NEAR THE SRS SYSTEM COMPONENTS OR RELATED WIRING.

DISABLING THE SYSTEM

Whenever working in the vicinity of the steering wheel, steering column, floor console or other airbag system components, the system should be disarmed. To do this, perform the following steps:

a) *Turn the ignition switch to the OFF position.*
b) *Disconnect the cable from the negative battery terminal (see Chapter 5, Section 1).*
c) *WAIT FOR AT LEAST TWO MINUTES before beginning work (during this two-minute interval the capacitor that provides emergency back-up power to the system loses its charge).*

ENABLING THE SYSTEM

To enable the airbag system, perform the following steps:

a) *Turn the ignition switch to the OFF position.*
b) *Connect the cable to the negative battery terminal.*
c) *Without putting your body in front of either airbag, turn the ignition switch to the ON position. Note whether the airbag indicator light glows for six seconds, then goes out. If it does, this indicates that the system is functioning properly.*

---

28 Remote keyless entry system - battery replacement and matching the transmitter to the vehicle

1 Here's how the transmitter inside the remote keyless entry fob should work:

a) *When you press the UNLOCK button, the driver's door unlocks. If you press the UNLOCK button a second time within five seconds, all the doors unlock.*
b) *If the doors aren't opened within a period of one minute, they should automatically lock again.*
c) *Pressing the lock button sets the alarm and locks all of the doors.*

BATTERY REPLACEMENT

♦ **Refer to illustration 28.3**

2 When the transmitter becomes weak, operation will become intermittent and require you to be closer to the vehicle for it to work. Eventually it won't work at all.

3 To replace the transmitter battery, carefully pry open the keyless entry fob by inserting a coin into the notch in the body of the transmitter (see illustration) and separate the upper and lower halves of the fob.

➡ **Note: On some transmitters the slot is in the end, where the key ring attaches. On other models, the slot is on the side.**

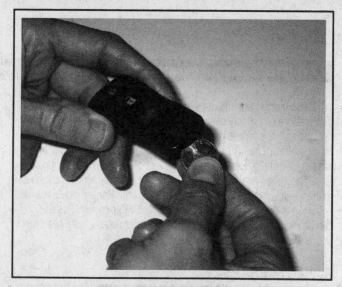

28.3 Using a coin, carefully pry the halves of the transmitter apart (a screwdriver could damage the plastic)

4   Carefully pry out the old battery with a small screwdriver.

5   Installation is the reverse of removal. Make sure that the new battery is a CR2025 or equivalent. Also make sure that the two halves of the cover snap together tightly to keep out dirt, dust, humidity and rain.

MATCHING THE TRANSMITTER TO THE VEHICLE

6   Have the transmitters with you (up to five can be programmed), and sit in the driver's seat. Make sure all of the vehicle's doors are shut.

7   Place the ignition key into the ignition lock cylinder and pull it back out. Do this at least seven times within a ten second period. The hazard flasher lights should blink twice.

➡**Note: The key must be inserted and removed completely each time. Also, if this is done too fast, it won't work.**

8   Install the key again and turn it to the Accessory position. Push one of the buttons on the remote; the hazard flasher lights will blink twice again. The old code is now erased and the new one programmed in. If another remote is going to be programmed, proceed to the next Step.

9   Have ready the next remote transmitter to be programmed. Push the driver's door Unlock button, then press the Lock button. Now push any button on the remote; the hazard flasher lights will blink twice. The old code is now erased from this remote, and the new one is programmed in.

10 If another remote is going to be programmed, repeat Step 9. You can match up to five transmitters to the vehicle.

11 To exit the programming mode, open the driver's door.

29 Wiring diagrams - general information

Since it isn't possible to include all wiring diagrams for every year covered by this manual, the following diagrams are those that are typical and most commonly needed.

Prior to troubleshooting any circuits, check the fuse and circuit breakers (if equipped) to make sure they are in good condition. Make sure the battery is properly charged and has clean, tight cable connections (see Chapter 1).

When checking the wiring system, make sure that all electrical connectors are clean, with no broken or loose pins. When disconnecting an electrical connector, do not pull on the wires, only on the connector housings.

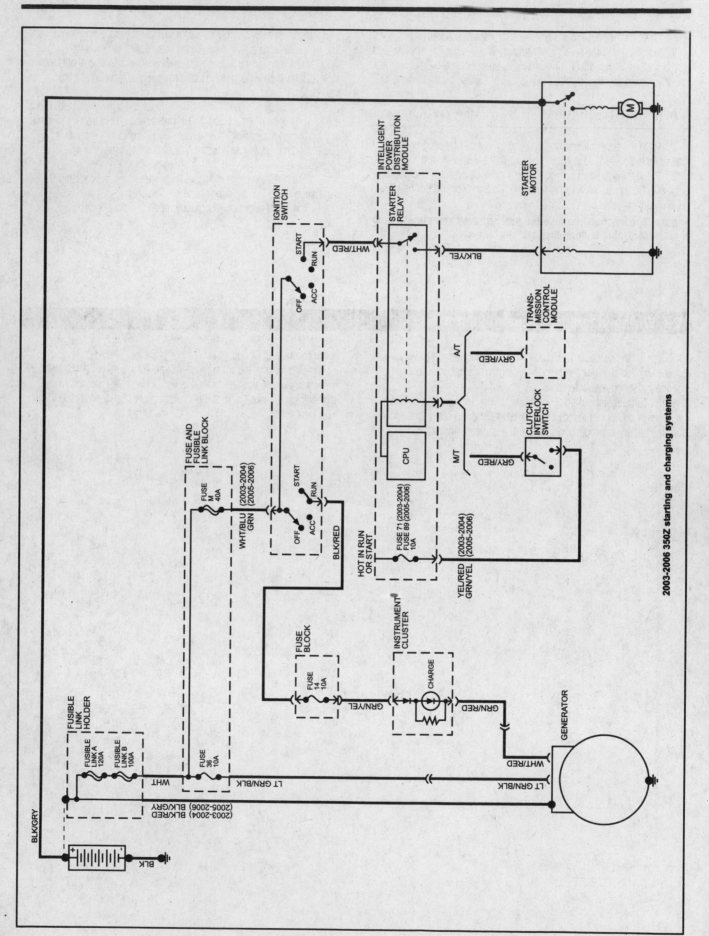

2003-2006 350Z starting and charging systems

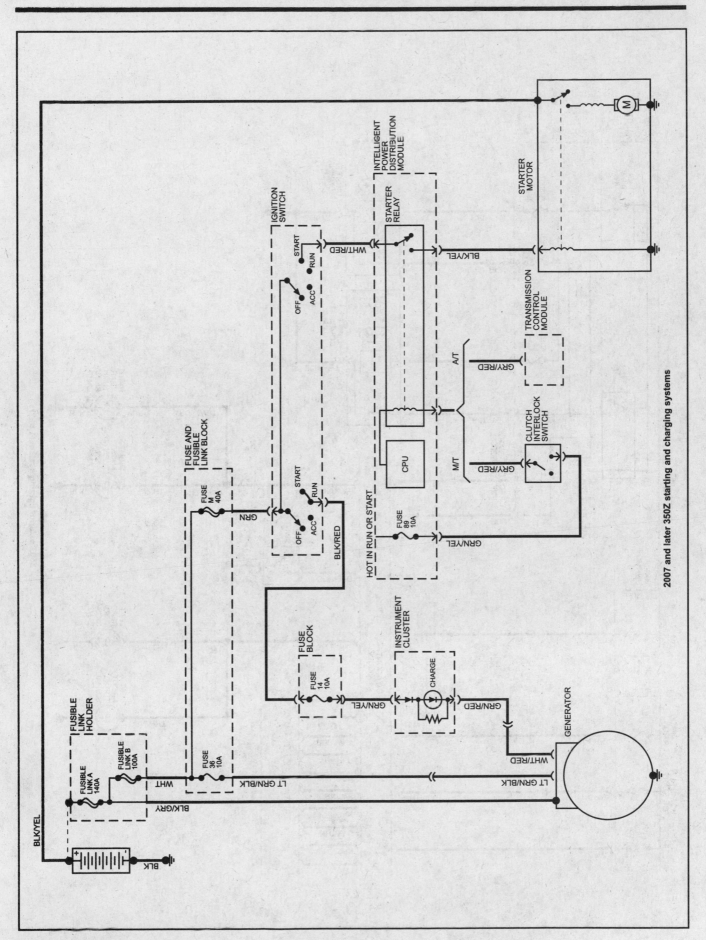

2007 and later 350Z starting and charging systems

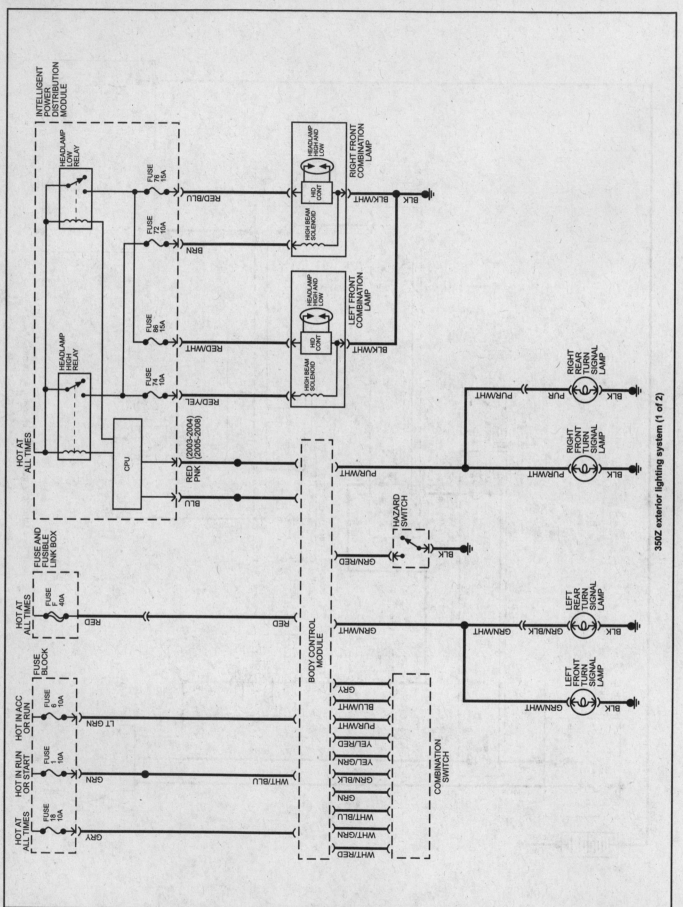

350Z exterior lighting system (1 of 2)

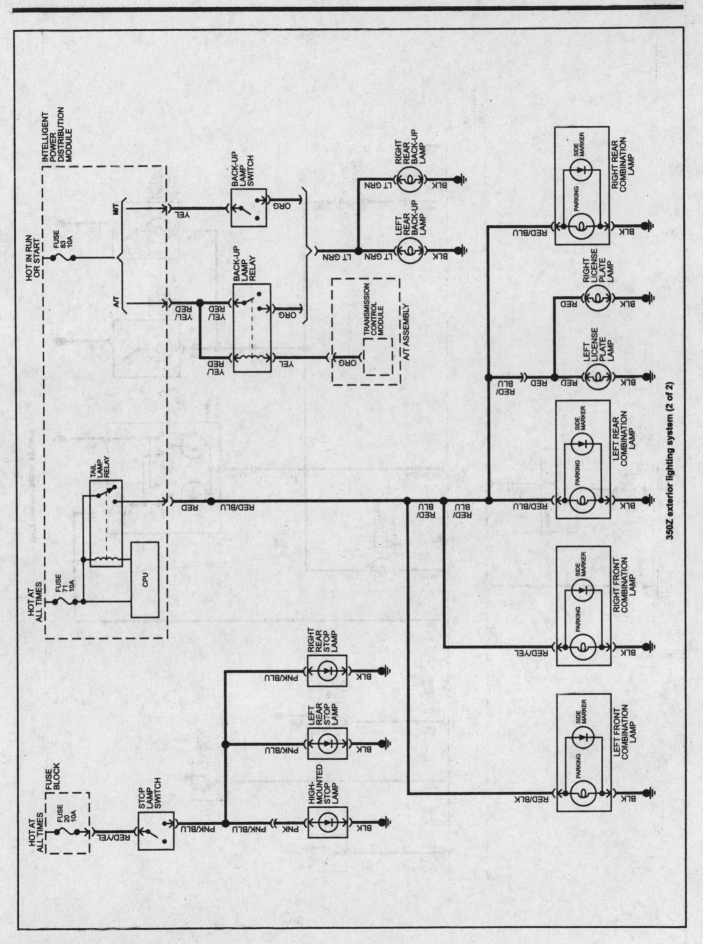

350Z exterior lighting system (2 of 2)

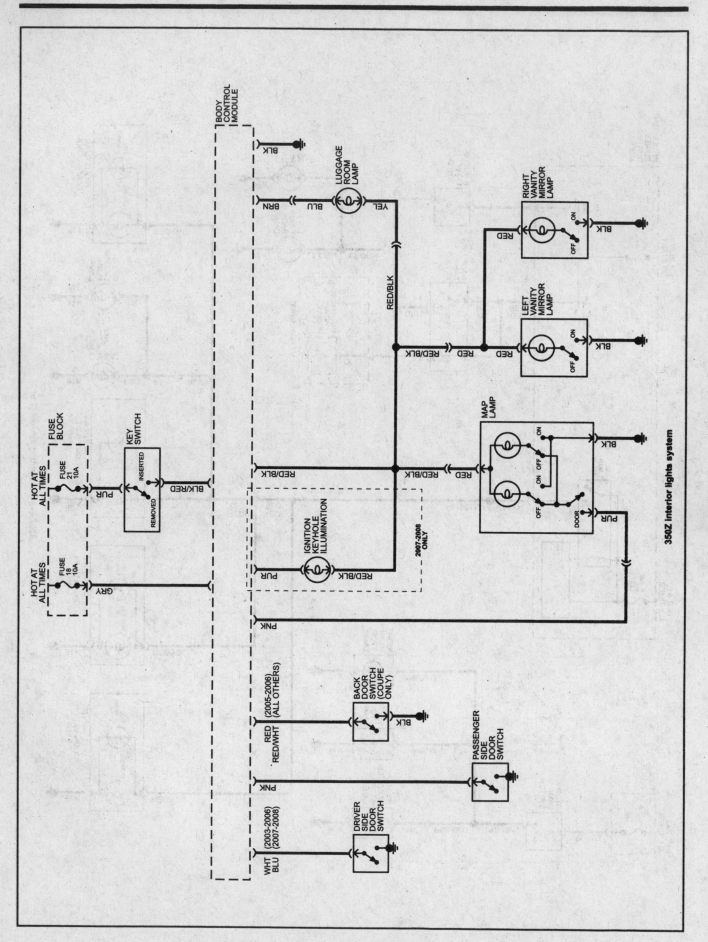

350Z interior lights system

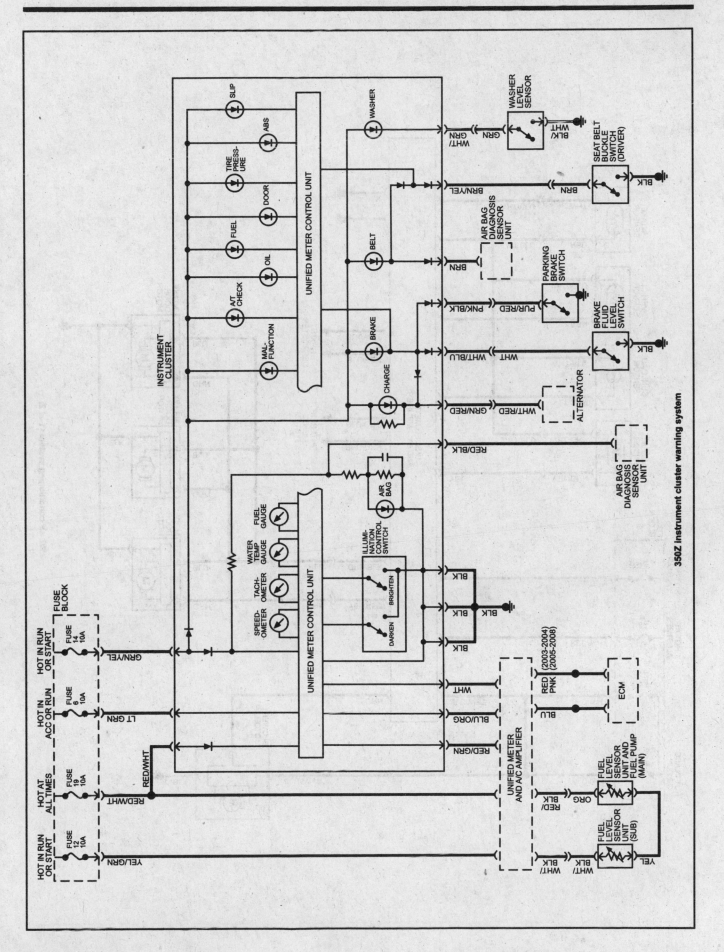

350Z instrument cluster warning system

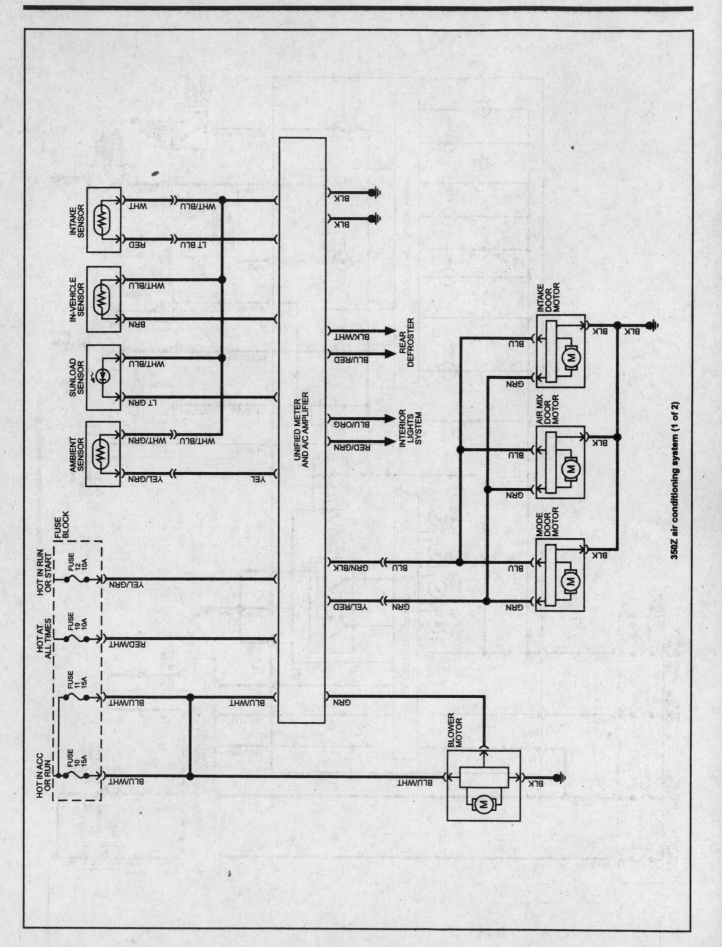

350Z air conditioning system (1 of 2)

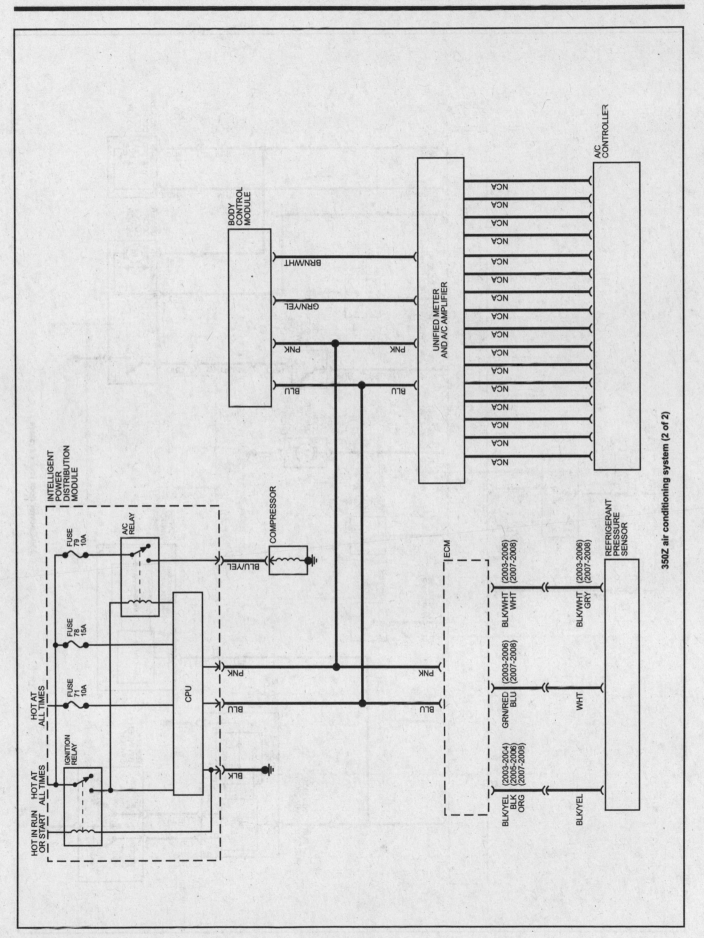

350Z air conditioning system (2 of 2)

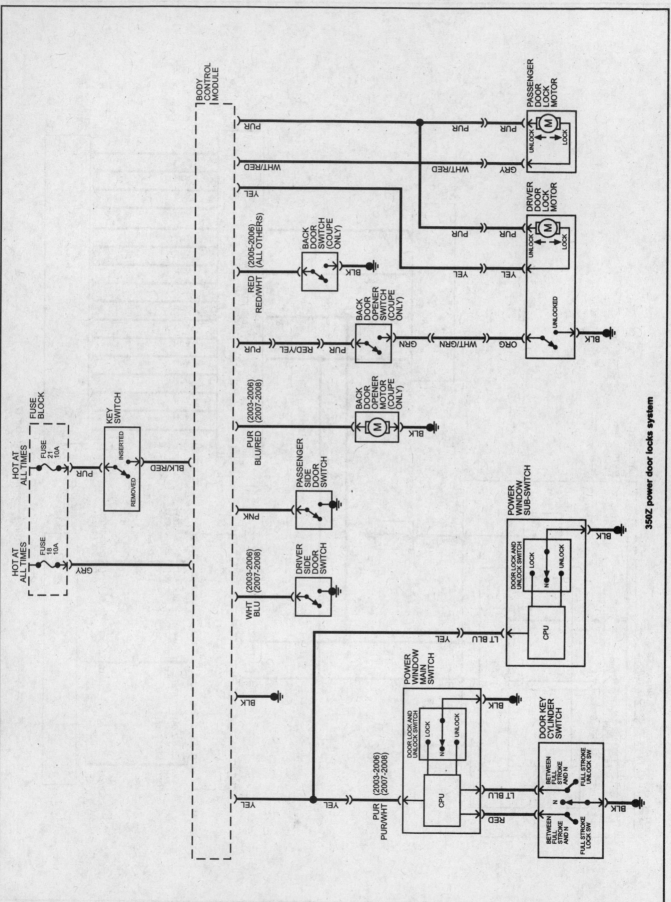

350Z power door locks system

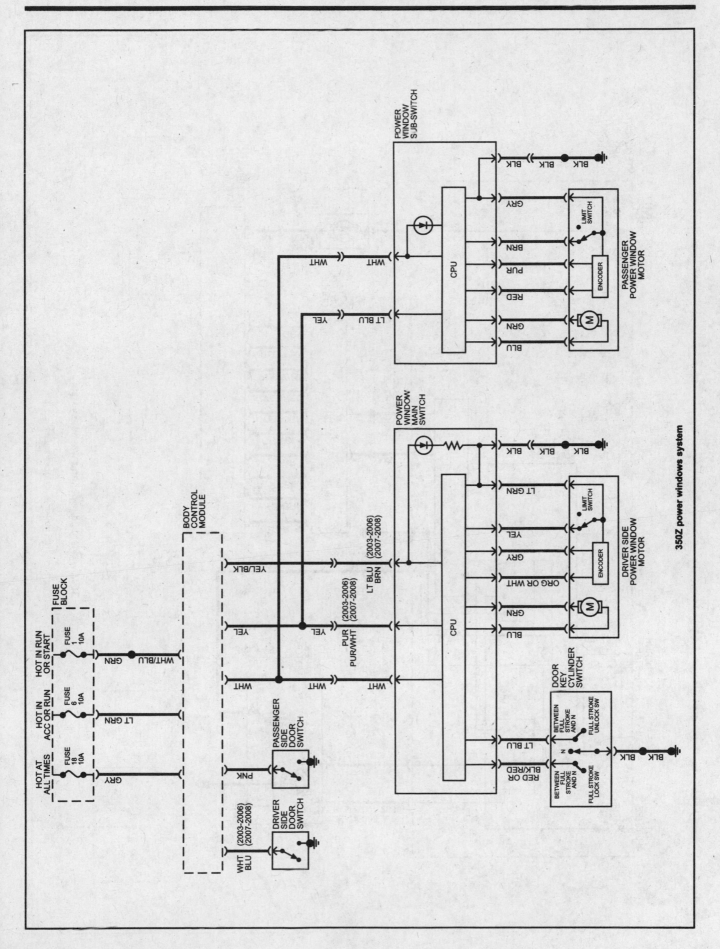

350Z power windows system

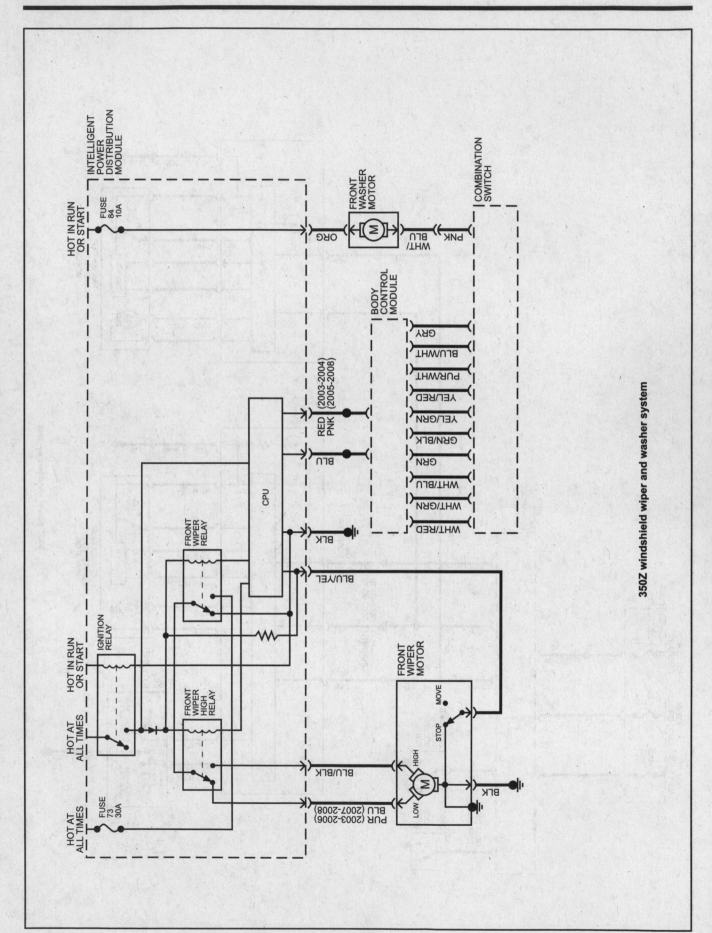

350Z windshield wiper and washer system

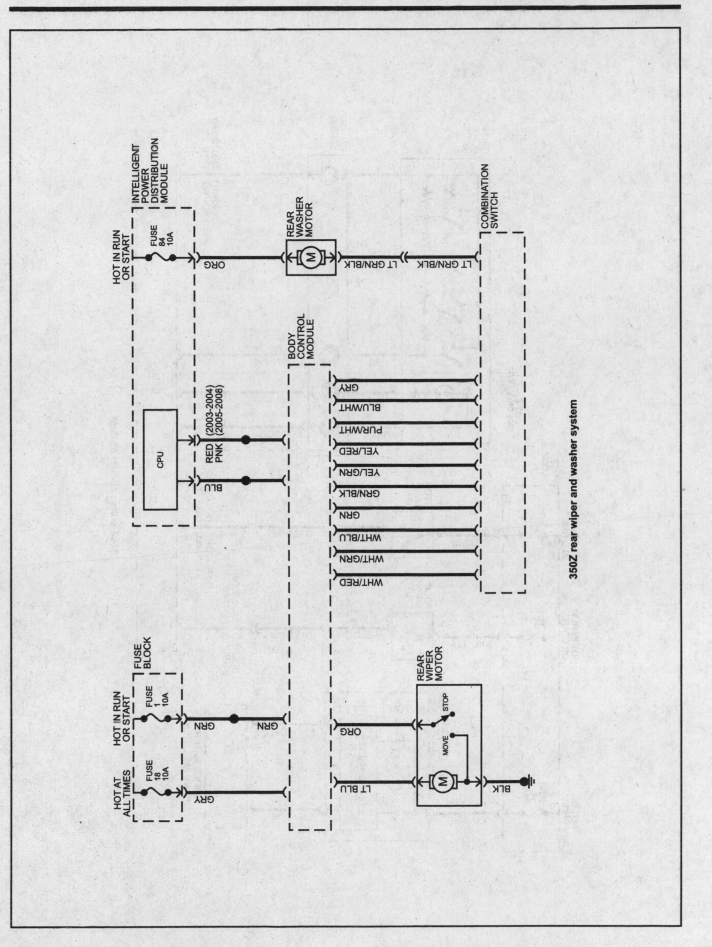

350Z rear wiper and washer system

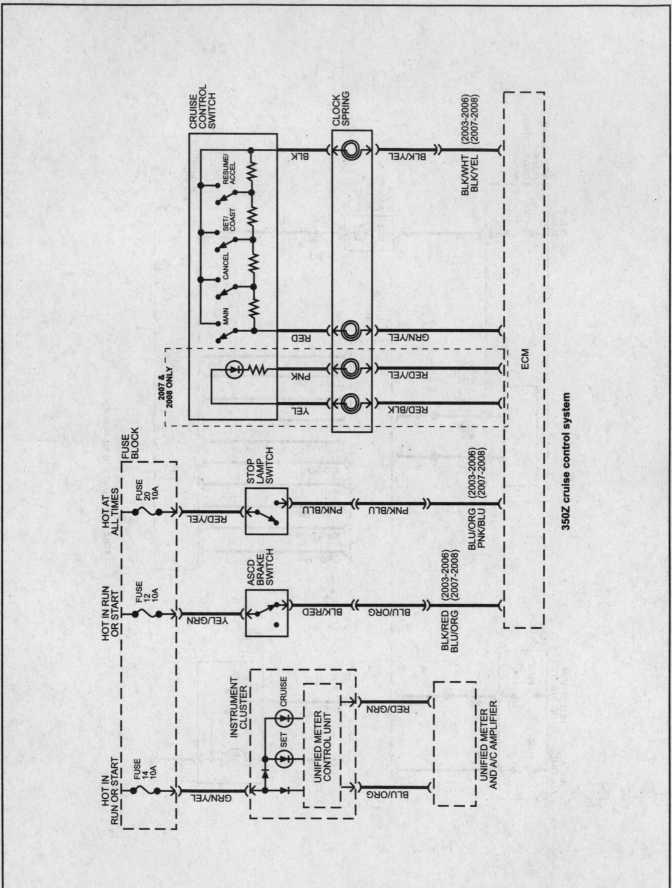

350Z cruise control system

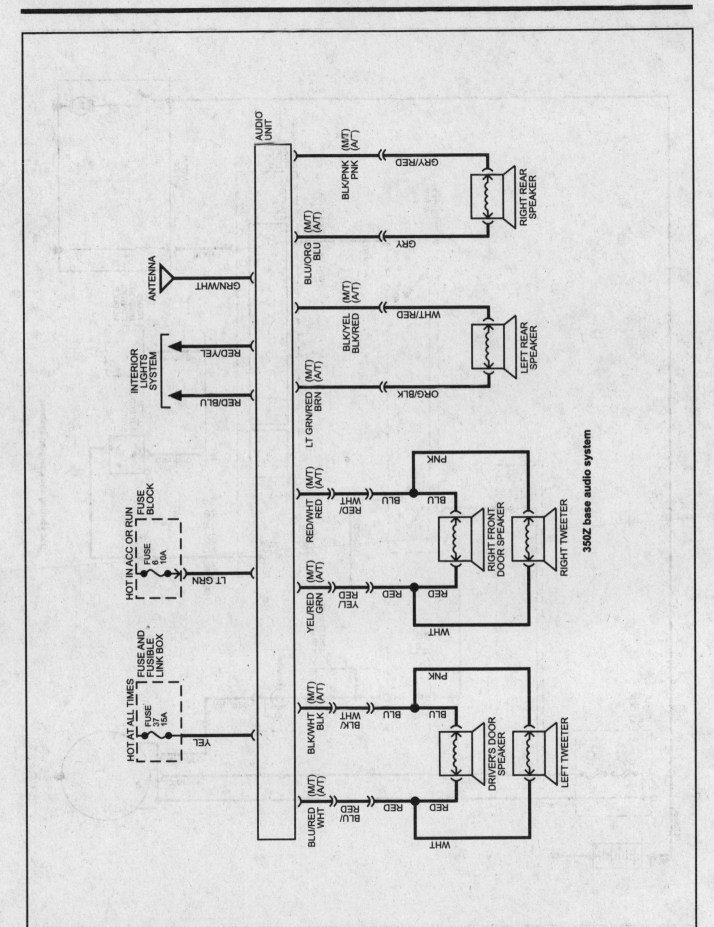

350Z base audio system

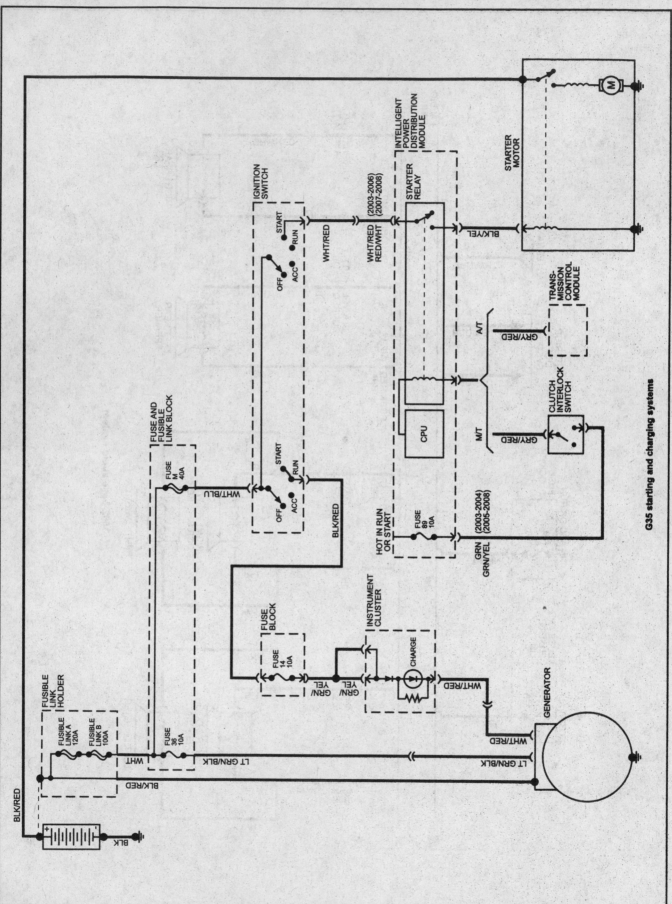

G35 starting and charging systems

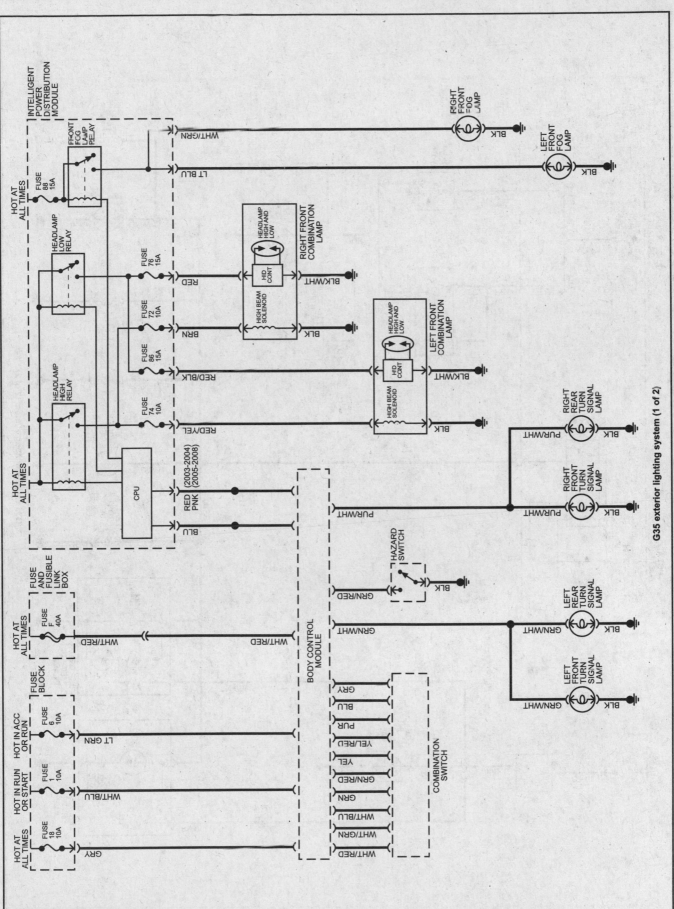

G35 exterior lighting system (1 of 2)

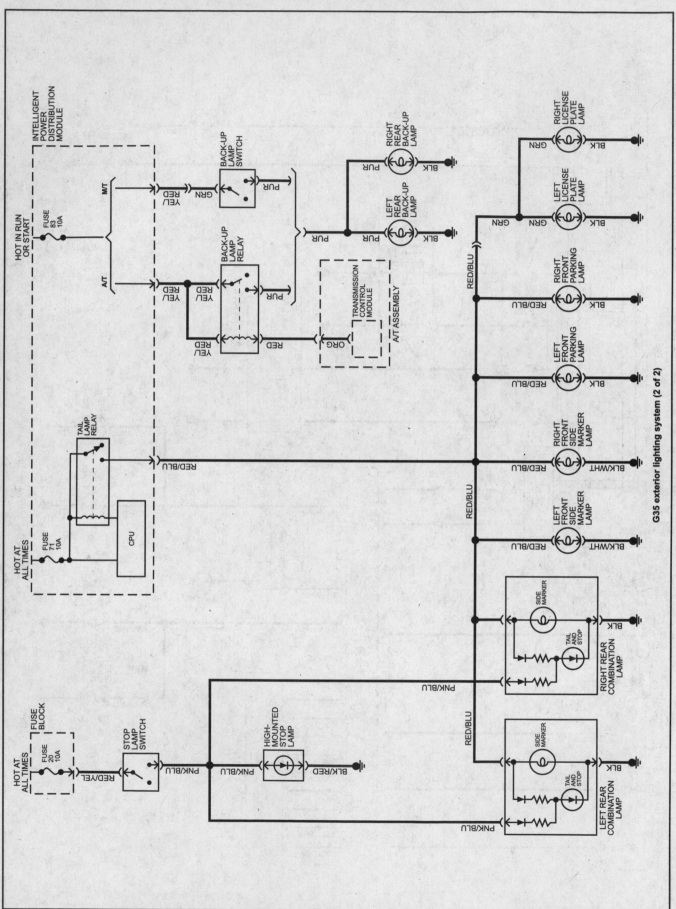

G35 exterior lighting system (2 of 2)

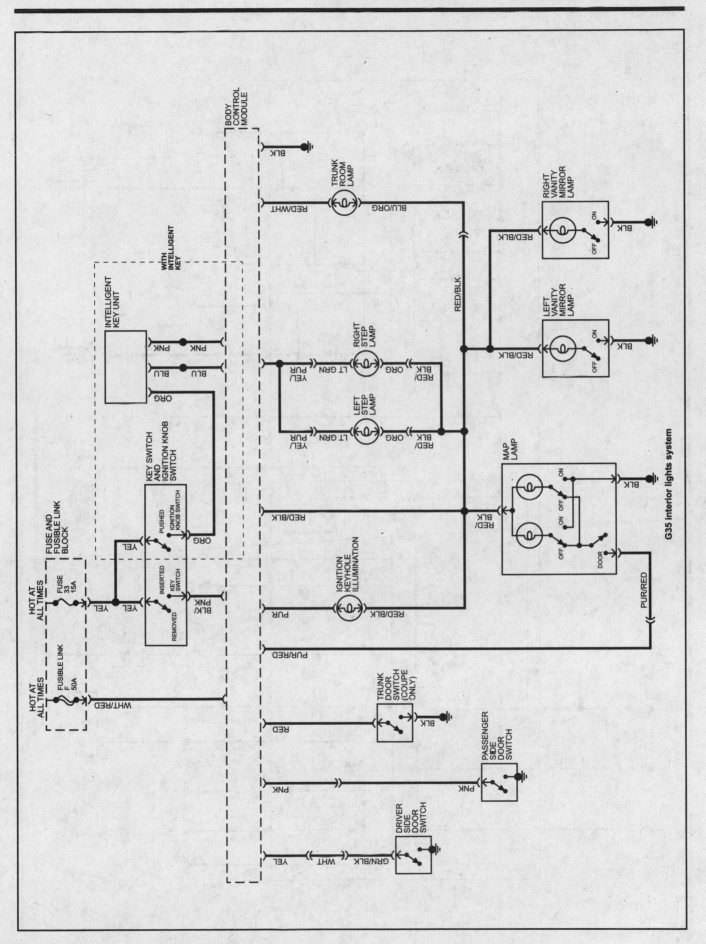

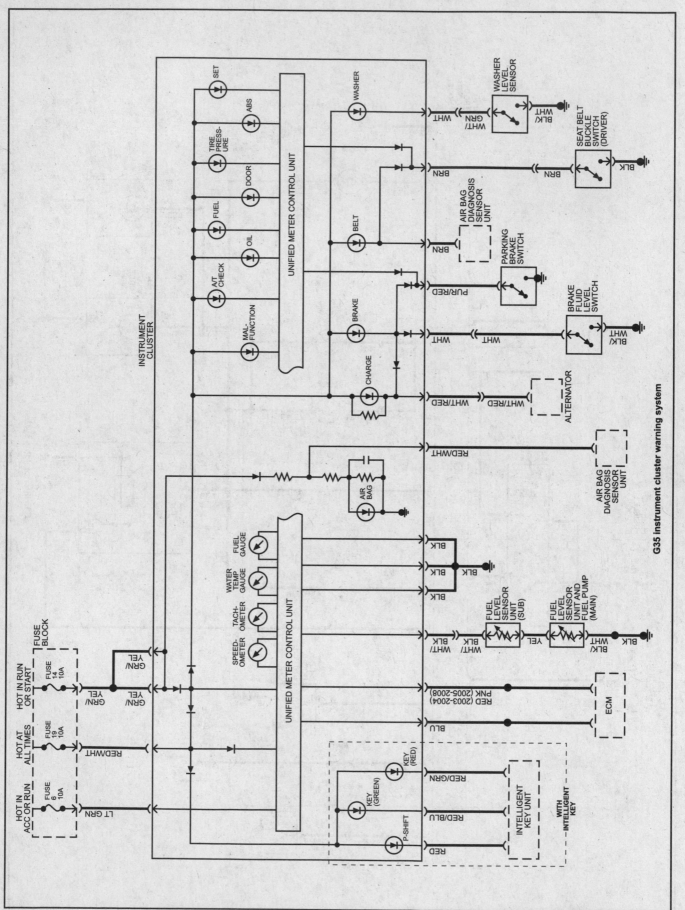

G35 instrument cluster warning system

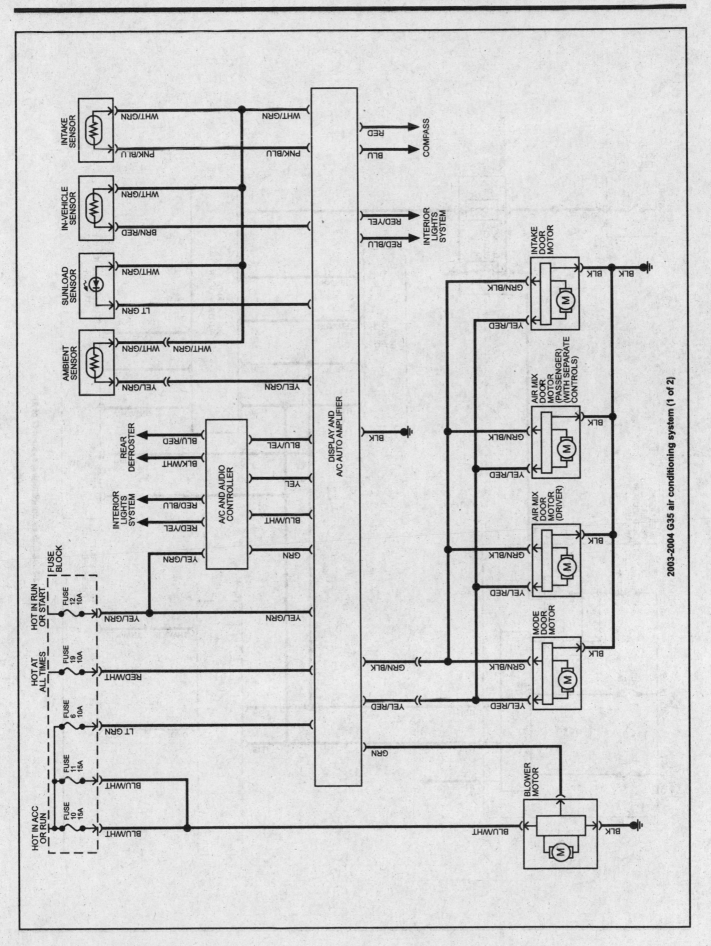

2003-2004 G35 air conditioning system (1 of 2)

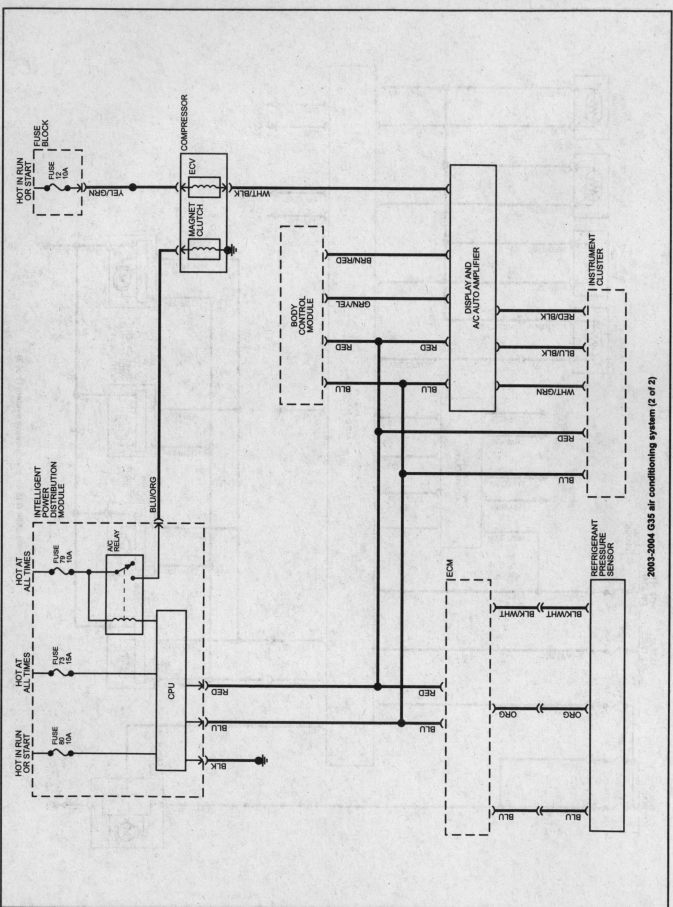

2003-2004 G35 air conditioning system (2 of 2)

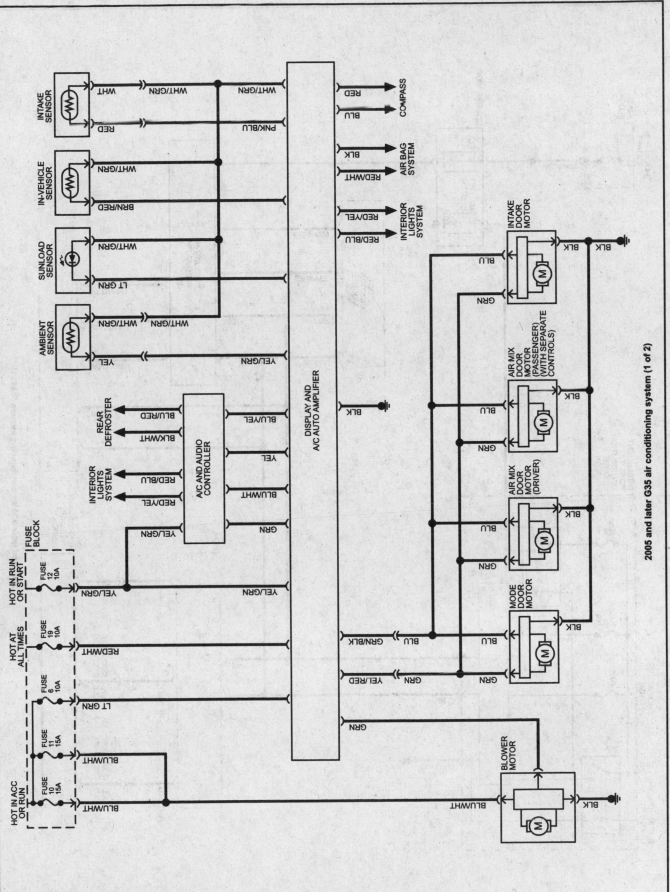

2005 and later G35 air conditioning system (1 of 2)

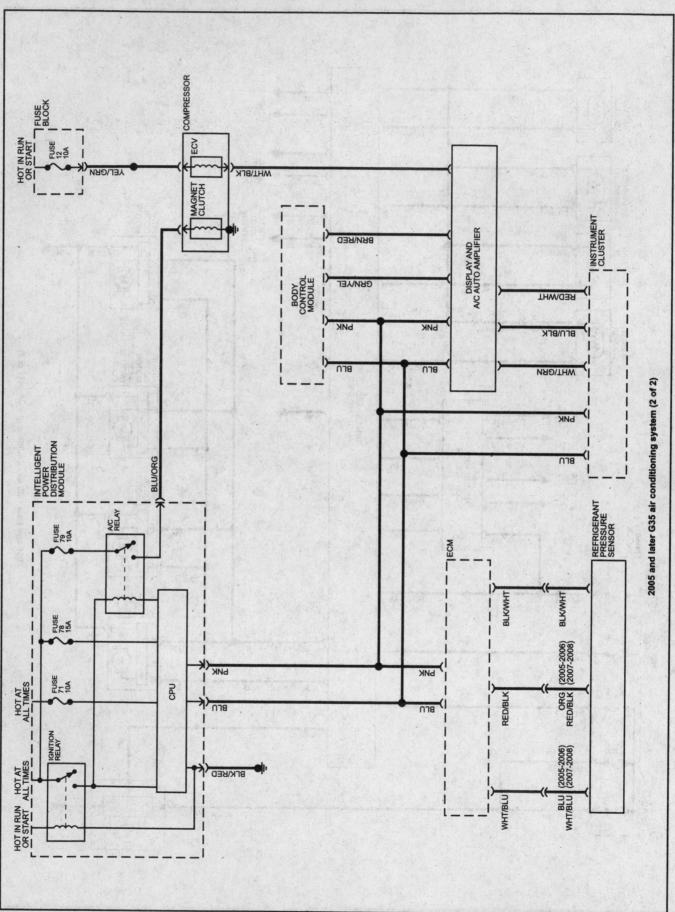

2005 and later G35 air conditioning system (2 of 2)

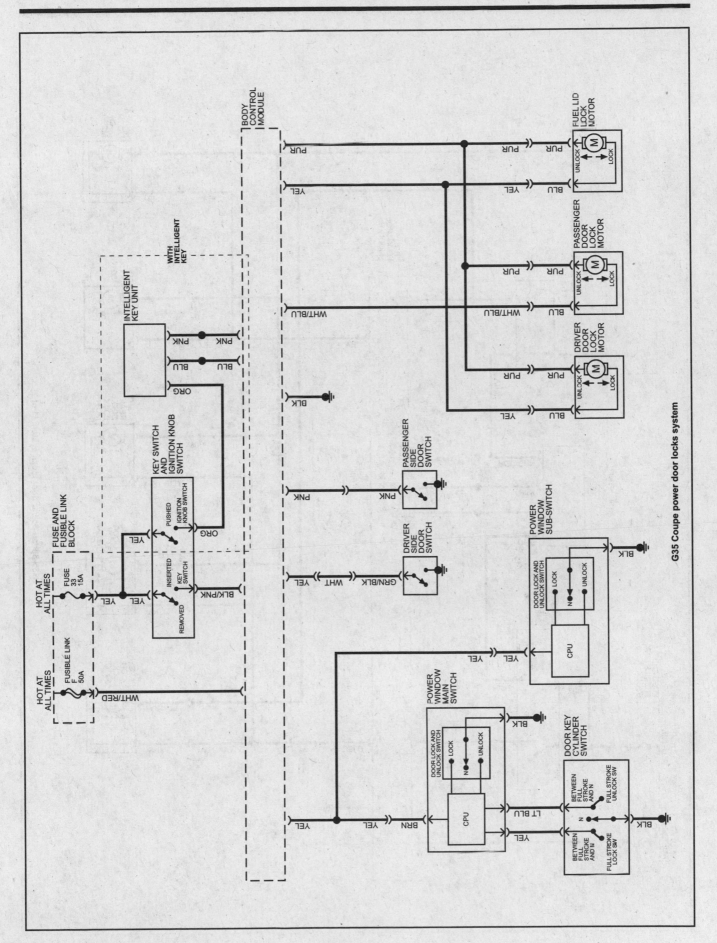

G35 Coupe power door locks system

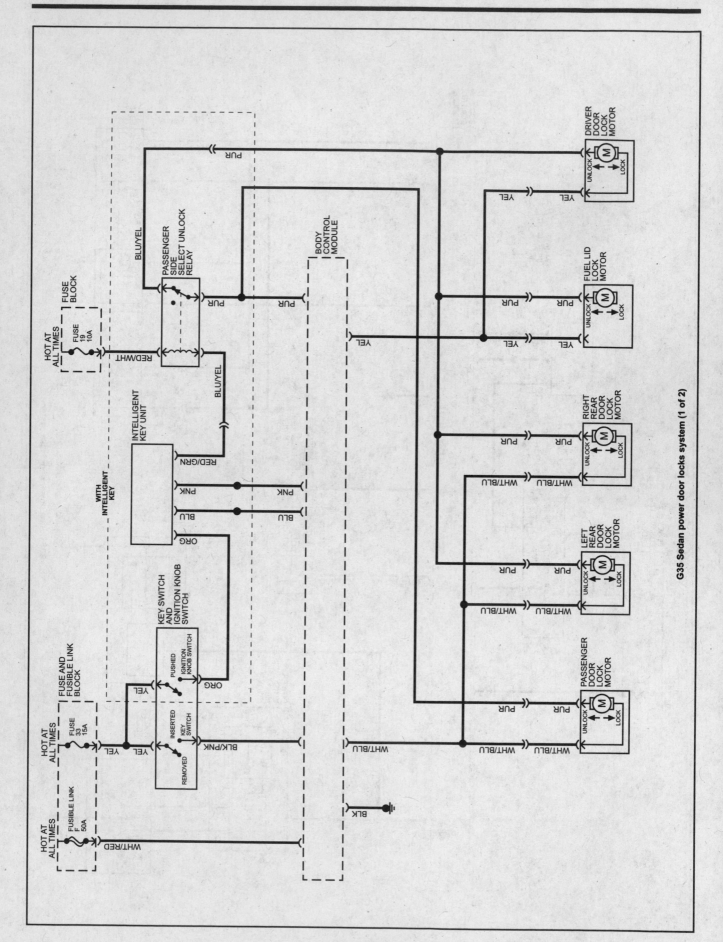

G35 Sedan power door locks system (1 of 2)

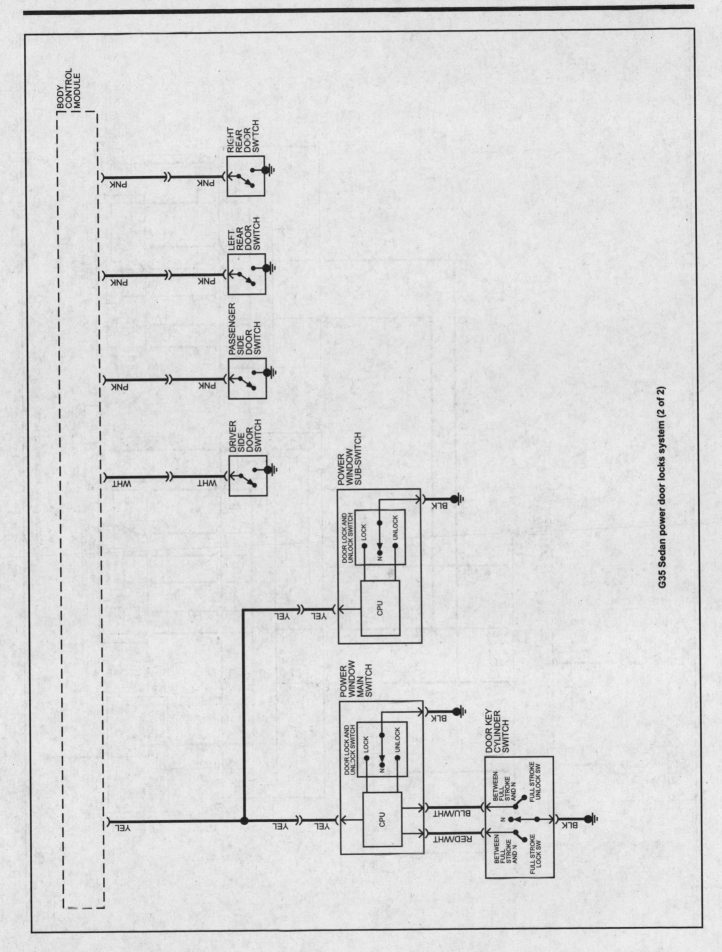

G35 Sedan power door locks system (2 of 2)

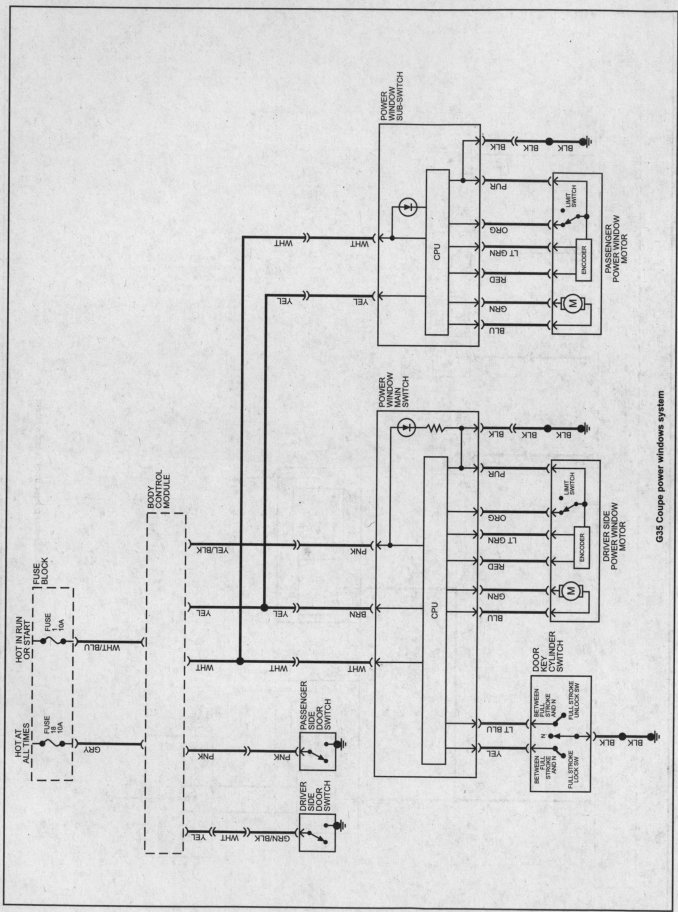

G35 Coupe power windows system

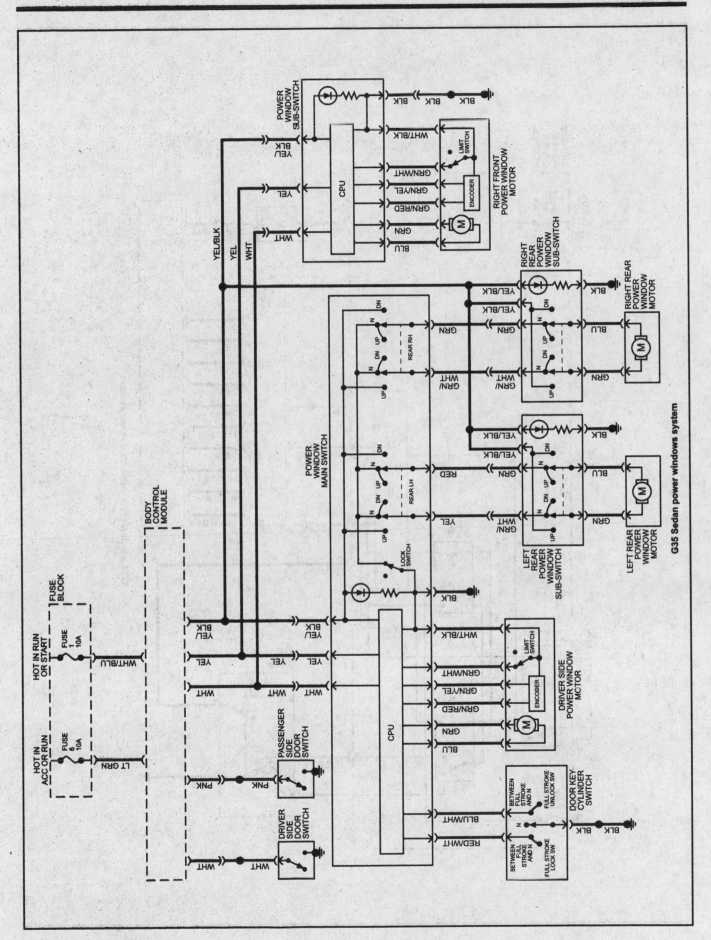

G35 Sedan power windows system

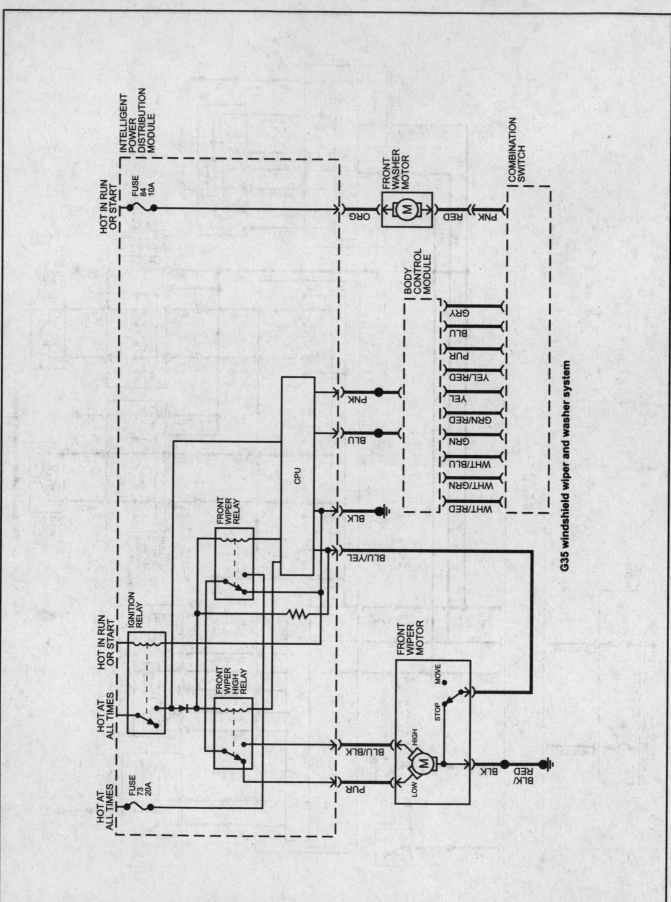

G35 windshield wiper and washer system

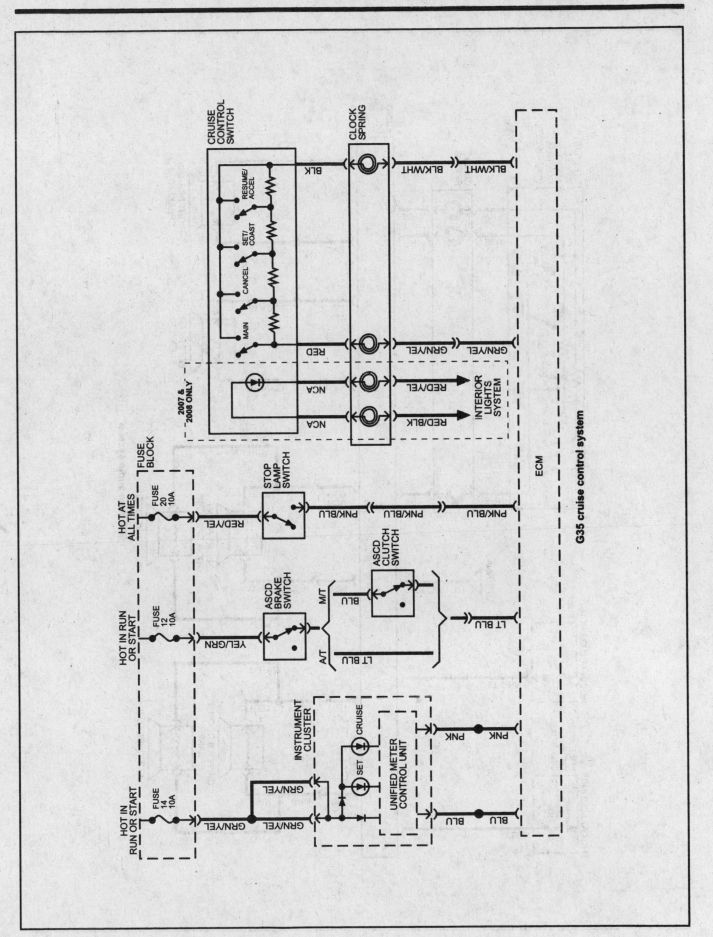

CRUISE CONTROL SWITCH

RESUME/ACCEL

SET/COAST

CANCEL

MAIN

CLOCK SPRING

BLK

BLK/WHT

BLK/WHT

RED

GRN/YEL

GRN/YEL

2007 & 2008 ONLY

NCA

RED/YEL

NCA

RED/BLK

INTERIOR LIGHTS SYSTEM

FUSE BLOCK

HOT AT ALL TIMES

FUSE 20 10A

RED/YEL

STOP LAMP SWITCH

PNK/BLU

PNK/BLU

PNK/BLU

ECM

HOT IN RUN OR START

FUSE 12 10A

YEL/GRN

ASCD BRAKE SWITCH

M/T

BLU

ASCD CLUTCH SWITCH

A/T

LT BLU

LT BLU

INSTRUMENT CLUSTER

CRUISE

SET

HOT IN RUN OR START

FUSE 14 10A

GRN/YEL

GRN/YEL

GRN/YEL

UNIFIED METER CONTROL UNIT

PNK

PNK

BLU

BLU

G35 cruise control system

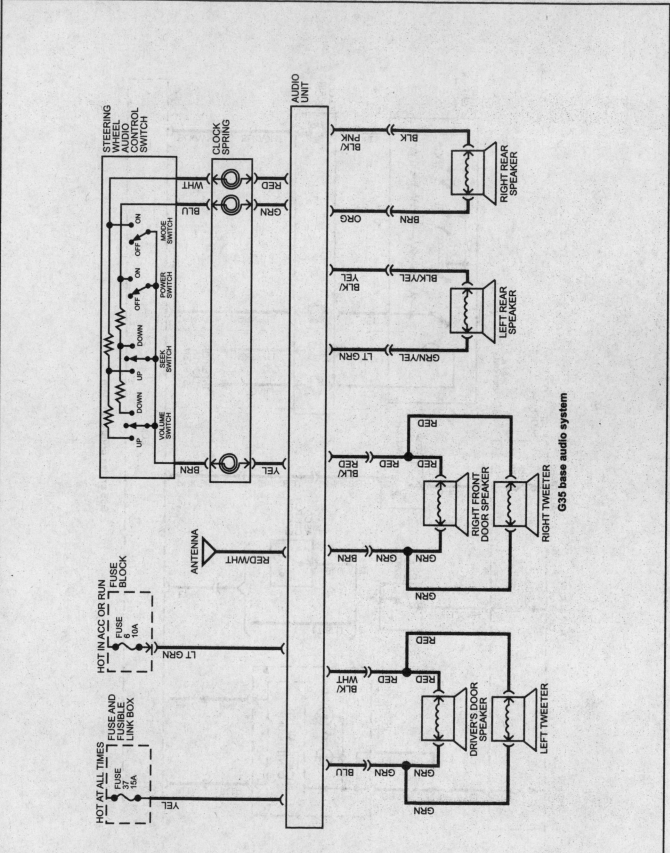

G35 base audio system

GLOSSARY

AIR/FUEL RATIO: The ratio of air-to-gasoline by weight in the fuel mixture drawn into the engine.

AIR INJECTION: One method of reducing harmful exhaust emissions by injecting air into each of the exhaust ports of an engine. The fresh air entering the hot exhaust manifold causes any remaining fuel to be burned before it can exit the tailpipe.

ALTERNATOR: A device used for converting mechanical energy into electrical energy.

AMMETER: An instrument, calibrated in amperes, used to measure the flow of an electrical current in a circuit. Ammeters are always connected in series with the circuit being tested.

AMPERE: The rate of flow of electrical current present when one volt of electrical pressure is applied against one ohm of electrical resistance.

ANALOG COMPUTER: Any microprocessor that uses similar (analogous) electrical signals to make its calculations.

ARMATURE: A laminated, soft iron core wrapped by a wire that converts electrical energy to mechanical energy as in a motor or relay. When rotated in a magnetic field, it changes mechanical energy into electrical energy as in a generator.

ATMOSPHERIC PRESSURE: The pressure on the Earth's surface caused by the weight of the air in the atmosphere. At sea level, this pressure is 14.7 psi at 32°F (101 kPa at 0°C).

ATOMIZATION: The breaking down of a liquid into a fine mist that can be suspended in air.

AXIAL PLAY: Movement parallel to a shaft or bearing bore.

BACKFIRE: The sudden combustion of gases in the intake or exhaust system that results in a loud explosion.

BACKLASH: The clearance or play between two parts, such as meshed gears.

BACKPRESSURE: Restrictions in the exhaust system that slow the exit of exhaust gases from the combustion chamber.

BAKELITE: A heat resistant, plastic insulator material commonly used in printed circuit boards and transistorized components.

BALL BEARING: A bearing made up of hardened inner and outer races between which hardened steel balls roll.

BALLAST RESISTOR: A resistor in the primary ignition circuit that lowers voltage after the engine is started to reduce wear on ignition components.

BEARING: A friction reducing, supportive device usually located between a stationary part and a moving part.

BIMETAL TEMPERATURE SENSOR: Any sensor or switch made of two dissimilar types of metal that bend when heated or cooled due to the different expansion rates of the alloys. These types of sensors usually function as an on/off switch.

BLOWBY: Combustion gases, composed of water vapor and unburned fuel, that leak past the piston rings into the crankcase during normal engine operation. These gases are removed by the PCV system to prevent the buildup of harmful acids in the crankcase.

BRAKE PAD: A brake shoe and lining assembly used with disc brakes.

BRAKE SHOE: The backing for the brake lining. The term is, however, usually applied to the assembly of the brake backing and lining.

BUSHING: A liner, usually removable, for a bearing; an anti-friction liner used in place of a bearing.

CALIPER: A hydraulically activated device in a disc brake system, which is mounted straddling the brake rotor (disc). The caliper contains at least one piston and two brake pads. Hydraulic pressure on the piston(s) forces the pads against the rotor.

CAMSHAFT: A shaft in the engine on which are the lobes (cams) which operate the valves. The camshaft is driven by the crankshaft, via a belt, chain or gears, at one half the crankshaft speed.

CAPACITOR: A device which stores an electrical charge.

CARBON MONOXIDE (CO): A colorless, odorless gas given off as a normal byproduct of combustion. It is poisonous and extremely dangerous in confined areas, building up slowly to toxic levels without warning if adequate ventilation is not available.

CARBURETOR: A device, usually mounted on the intake manifold of an engine, which mixes the air and fuel in the proper proportion to allow even combustion.

CATALYTIC CONVERTER: A device installed in the exhaust system, like a muffler, that converts harmful byproducts of combustion into carbon dioxide and water vapor by means of a heat-producing chemical reaction.

CENTRIFUGAL ADVANCE: A mechanical method of advancing the spark timing by using flyweights in the distributor that react to centrifugal force generated by the distributor shaft rotation.

CHECK VALVE: Any one-way valve installed to permit the flow of air, fuel or vacuum in one direction only.

CHOKE: A device, usually a moveable valve, placed in the intake path of a carburetor to restrict the flow of air.

CIRCUIT: Any unbroken path through which an electrical current can flow. Also used to describe fuel flow in some instances.

CIRCUIT BREAKER: A switch which protects an electrical circuit from overload by opening the circuit when the current flow exceeds a predetermined level. Some circuit breakers must be reset manually, while most reset automatically.

COIL (IGNITION): A transformer in the ignition circuit which steps up the voltage provided to the spark plugs.

COMBINATION MANIFOLD: An assembly which includes both the intake and exhaust manifolds in one casting.

COMBINATION VALVE: A device used in some fuel systems that routes fuel vapors to a charcoal storage canister instead of venting them into the atmosphere. The valve relieves fuel tank pressure and allows fresh air into the tank as the fuel level drops to prevent a vapor lock situation.

COMPRESSION RATIO: The comparison of the total volume of the cylinder and combustion chamber with the piston at BDC and the piston at TDC.

CONDENSER: 1. An electrical device which acts to store an electrical charge, preventing voltage surges. 2. A radiator-like device in the air conditioning system in which refrigerant gas condenses into a liquid, giving off heat.

CONDUCTOR: Any material through which an electrical current can be transmitted easily.

CONTINUITY: Continuous or complete circuit. Can be checked with an ohmmeter.

COUNTERSHAFT: An intermediate shaft which is rotated by a mainshaft and transmits, in turn, that rotation to a working part.

CRANKCASE: The lower part of an engine in which the crankshaft and related parts operate.

CRANKSHAFT: The main driving shaft of an engine which receives reciprocating motion from the pistons and converts it to rotary motion.

CYLINDER: In an engine, the round hole in the engine block in which the piston(s) ride.

CYLINDER BLOCK: The main structural member of an engine in which is found the cylinders, crankshaft and other principal parts.

CYLINDER HEAD: The detachable portion of the engine, usually fastened to the top of the cylinder block and containing all or most of the combustion chambers. On overhead valve engines, it contains the valves and their operating parts. On overhead cam engines, it contains the camshaft as well.

DEAD CENTER: The extreme top or bottom of the piston stroke.

DETONATION: An unwanted explosion of the air/fuel mixture in the combustion chamber caused by excess heat and compression, advanced timing, or an overly lean mixture. Also referred to as "ping".

DIAPHRAGM: A thin, flexible wall separating two cavities, such as in a vacuum advance unit.

DIESELING: A condition in which hot spots in the combustion chamber cause the engine to run on after the key is turned off.

DIFFERENTIAL: A geared assembly which allows the transmission of motion between drive axles, giving one axle the ability to turn faster than the other.

DIODE: An electrical device that will allow current to flow in one direction only.

DISC BRAKE: A hydraulic braking assembly consisting of a brake disc, or rotor, mounted on an axle, and a caliper assembly containing, usually two brake pads which are activated by hydraulic pressure. The pads are forced against the sides of the disc, creating friction which slows the vehicle.

DISTRIBUTOR: A mechanically driven device on an engine which is responsible for electrically firing the spark plug at a predetermined point of the piston stroke.

DOWEL PIN: A pin, inserted in mating holes in two different parts allowing those parts to maintain a fixed relationship.

DRUM BRAKE: A braking system which consists of two brake shoes and one or two wheel cylinders, mounted on a fixed backing plate, and a brake drum, mounted on an axle, which revolves around the assembly.

DWELL: The rate, measured in degrees of shaft rotation, at which an electrical circuit cycles on and off.

ELECTRONIC CONTROL UNIT (ECU): Ignition module, module, amplifier or igniter. See Module for definition.

ELECTRONIC IGNITION: A system in which the timing and firing of the spark plugs is controlled by an electronic control unit, usually called a module. These systems have no points or condenser.

END-PLAY: The measured amount of axial movement in a shaft.

ENGINE: A device that converts heat into mechanical energy.

EXHAUST MANIFOLD: A set of cast passages or pipes which conduct exhaust gases from the engine.

FEELER GAUGE: A blade, usually metal, or precisely predetermined thickness, used to measure the clearance between two parts.

FIRING ORDER: The order in which combustion occurs in the cylinders of an engine. Also the order in which spark is distributed to the plugs by the distributor.

FLOODING: The presence of too much fuel in the intake manifold and combustion chamber which prevents the air/fuel mixture from firing, thereby causing a no-start situation.

FLYWHEEL: A disc shaped part bolted to the rear end of the crankshaft. Around the outer perimeter is affixed the ring gear. The starter drive engages the ring gear, turning the flywheel, which rotates the crankshaft, imparting the initial starting motion to the engine.

FOOT POUND (ft. lbs. or sometimes, ft.lb.): The amount of energy or work needed to raise an item weighing one pound, a distance of one foot.

FUSE: A protective device in a circuit which prevents circuit overload by breaking the circuit when a specific amperage is present. The device is constructed around a strip or wire of a lower amperage rating than the circuit it is designed to protect. When an amperage higher than that stamped on the fuse is present in the circuit, the strip or wire melts, opening the circuit.

GEAR RATIO: The ratio between the number of teeth on meshing gears.

GENERATOR: A device which converts mechanical energy into electrical energy.

HEAT RANGE: The measure of a spark plug's ability to dissipate heat from its firing end. The higher the heat range, the hotter the plug fires.

HUB: The center part of a wheel or gear.

HYDROCARBON (HC): Any chemical compound made up of hydrogen and carbon. A major pollutant formed by the engine as a byproduct of combustion.

HYDROMETER: An instrument used to measure the specific gravity of a solution.

INCH POUND (inch lbs.; sometimes in.lb. or in. lbs.): One twelfth of a foot pound.

INDUCTION: A means of transferring electrical energy in the form of a magnetic field. Principle used in the ignition coil to increase voltage.

INJECTOR: A device which receives metered fuel under relatively low pressure and is activated to inject the fuel into the engine under relatively high pressure at a predetermined time.

INPUT SHAFT: The shaft to which torque is applied, usually carrying the driving gear or gears.

INTAKE MANIFOLD: A casting of passages or pipes used to conduct air or a fuel/air mixture to the cylinders.

JOURNAL: The bearing surface within which a shaft operates.

KEY: A small block usually fitted in a notch between a shaft and a hub to prevent slippage of the two parts.

MANIFOLD: A casting of passages or set of pipes which connect the cylinders to an inlet or outlet source.

MANIFOLD VACUUM: Low pressure in an engine intake manifold formed just below the throttle plates. Manifold vacuum is highest at idle and drops under acceleration.

MASTER CYLINDER: The primary fluid pressurizing device in a hydraulic system. In automotive use, it is found in brake and hydraulic clutch systems and is pedal activated, either directly or, in a power brake system, through the power booster.

MODULE: Electronic control unit, amplifier or igniter of solid state or integrated design which controls the current flow in the ignition primary circuit based on input from the pick-up coil. When the module opens the primary circuit, high secondary voltage is induced in the coil.

NEEDLE BEARING: A bearing which consists of a number (usually a large number) of long, thin rollers.

OHM: (Ω) The unit used to measure the resistance of conductor-to-electrical flow. One ohm is the amount of resistance that limits current flow to one ampere in a circuit with one volt of pressure.

OHMMETER: An instrument used for measuring the resistance, in ohms, in an electrical circuit.

OUTPUT SHAFT: The shaft which transmits torque from a device, such as a transmission.

OVERDRIVE: A gear assembly which produces more shaft revolutions than that transmitted to it.

OVERHEAD CAMSHAFT (OHC): An engine configuration in which the camshaft is mounted on top of the cylinder head and operates the valve either directly or by means of rocker arms.

OVERHEAD VALVE (OHV): An engine configuration in which all of the valves are located in the cylinder head and the camshaft is located in the cylinder block. The camshaft operates the valves via lifters and pushrods.

OXIDES OF NITROGEN (NOx): Chemical compounds of nitrogen produced as a byproduct of combustion. They combine with hydrocarbons to produce smog.

OXYGEN SENSOR: Use with the feedback system to sense the presence of oxygen in the exhaust gas and signal the computer which can reference the voltage signal to an air/fuel ratio.

PINION: The smaller of two meshing gears.

PISTON RING: An open-ended ring with fits into a groove on the outer diameter of the piston. Its chief function is to form a seal between the piston and cylinder wall. Most automotive pistons have three rings: two for compression sealing; one for oil sealing.

PRELOAD: A predetermined load placed on a bearing during assembly or by adjustment.

PRIMARY CIRCUIT: the low voltage side of the ignition system which consists of the ignition switch, ballast resistor or resistance wire, bypass, coil, electronic control unit and pick-up coil as well as the connecting wires and harnesses.

PRESS FIT: The mating of two parts under pressure, due to the inner diameter of one being smaller than the outer diameter of the other, or vice versa; an interference fit.

RACE: The surface on the inner or outer ring of a bearing on which the balls, needles or rollers move.

REGULATOR: A device which maintains the amperage and/or voltage levels of a circuit at predetermined values.

RELAY: A switch which automatically opens and/or closes a circuit.

RESISTANCE: The opposition to the flow of current through a circuit or electrical device, and is measured in ohms. Resistance is equal to the voltage divided by the amperage.

RESISTOR: A device, usually made of wire, which offers a preset amount of resistance in an electrical circuit.

RING GEAR: The name given to a ring-shaped gear attached to a differential case, or affixed to a flywheel or as part of a planetary gear set.

ROLLER BEARING: A bearing made up of hardened inner and outer races between which hardened steel rollers move.

ROTOR: 1. The disc-shaped part of a disc brake assembly, upon which the brake pads bear; also called, brake disc. 2. The device

mounted atop the distributor shaft, which passes current to the distributor cap tower contacts.

SECONDARY CIRCUIT: The high voltage side of the ignition system, usually above 20,000 volts. The secondary includes the ignition coil, coil wire, distributor cap and rotor, spark plug wires and spark plugs.

SENDING UNIT: A mechanical, electrical, hydraulic or electromagnetic device which transmits information to a gauge.

SENSOR: Any device designed to measure engine operating conditions or ambient pressures and temperatures. Usually electronic in nature and designed to send a voltage signal to an on-board computer, some sensors may operate as a simple on/off switch or they may provide a variable voltage signal (like a potentiometer) as conditions or measured parameters change.

SHIM: Spacers of precise, predetermined thickness used between parts to establish a proper working relationship,

SLAVE CYLINDER: In automotive use, a device in the hydraulic clutch system which is activated by hydraulic force, disengaging the clutch.

SOLENOID: A coil used to produce a magnetic field, the effect of which is to produce work.

SPARK PLUG: A device screwed into the combustion chamber of a spark ignition engine. The basic construction is a conductive core inside of a ceramic insulator, mounted in an outer conductive base. An electrical charge from the spark plug wire travels along the conductive core and jumps a preset air gap to a grounding point or points at the end of the conductive base. The resultant spark ignites the fuel/air mixture in the combustion chamber.

SPLINES: Ridges machined or cast onto the outer diameter of a shaft or inner diameter of a bore to enable parts to mate without rotation.

TACHOMETER: A device used to measure the rotary speed of an engine, shaft, gear, etc., usually in rotations per minute.

THERMOSTAT: A valve, located in the cooling system of an engine, which is closed when cold and opens gradually in response to engine heating, controlling the temperature of the coolant and rate of coolant flow.

TOP DEAD CENTER (TDC): The point at which the piston reaches the top of its travel on the compression stroke.

TORQUE: The twisting force applied to an object.

TORQUE CONVERTER: A turbine used to transmit power from a driving member to a driven member via hydraulic action, providing changes in drive ratio and torque. In automotive use, it links the driveplate at the rear of the engine to the automatic transmission.

TRANSDUCER: A device used to change a force into an electrical signal.

TRANSISTOR: A semi-conductor component which can be actuated by a small voltage to perform an electrical switching function.

TUNE-UP: A regular maintenance function, usually associated with the replacement and adjustment of parts and components in the electrical and fuel systems of a vehicle for the purpose of attaining optimum performance.

TURBOCHARGER: An exhaust driven pump which compresses intake air and forces it into the combustion chambers at higher than atmospheric pressures. The increased air pressure allows more fuel to be burned and results in increased horsepower being produced.

VACUUM ADVANCE: A device which advances the ignition timing in response to increased engine vacuum.

VACUUM GAUGE: An instrument used to measure the presence of vacuum in a chamber.

VALVE: A device which control the pressure, direction of flow or rate of flow of a liquid or gas.

VALVE CLEARANCE: The measured gap between the end of the valve stem and the rocker arm, cam lobe or follower that activates the valve.

VISCOSITY: The rating of a liquid's internal resistance to flow.

VOLTMETER: An instrument used for measuring electrical force in units called volts. Voltmeters are always connected parallel with the circuit being tested.

WHEEL CYLINDER: Found in the automotive drum brake assembly, it is a device, actuated by hydraulic pressure, which, through internal pistons, pushes the brake shoes outward against the drums.

Notes

MASTER INDEX

A

Notes